Handbook of Advanced
Business Valuation

Handbook of Advanced Business Valuation

Robert F. Reilly, CFA, ASA, CPA, CBA
Managing Director
Willamette Management Associates

Robert P. Schweihs, ASA
Managing Director
Willamette Management Associates

McGraw-Hill
New York • San Francisco • Washington, D.C. • Auckland
Bogotá • Caracas • Lisbon • London • Madrid • Mexico City
Milan • Montreal • New Delhi • San Juan • Singapore
Sydney • Tokyo • Toronto

Library of Congress Cataloging-in-Publication Data

Reilly, Robert F.
    Handbook of advanced business valuation / Robert F. Reilly and
  Robert P. Schweihs.
        p.   cm.
    Includes index.
    ISBN 0-07-134769-0
    1. Business enterprises--Valuation Handbooks, manuals, etc.
  I. Schweihs, Robert P.   II. Title.
  HG4028.V3R433   1999
  658.15—dc21   99-21968
                                                 CIP

McGraw-Hill

A Division of The McGraw·Hill Companies

ISBN 0-07-134769-0

The sponsoring editor for this book was Roger Marsh, the editing supervisor was John M. Morriss, and the production supervisor was Elizabeth J. Strange. It was set in Times Roman by Douglas & Gayle Limited.

Printed and bound by R. R. Donnelley & Sons Company.

McGraw-Hill books are available at special quantity discounts to use as
premiums and sales promotions, or for use in corporate training programs.
For more information, please write to Director of Special Sales, McGraw-Hill,
11 West 19th Street, New York, NY 10011. Or contact your local bookstore.

This publication is designed to provide accurate and authoritative information in regard to the subject matter covered. It is sold with the understanding that neither the author nor the publisher is engaged in rendering legal, accounting, or other professional service. If legal advice or other expert assistance is required, the services of a competent professional person should be sought.
—*From a Declaration of Principles jointly adopted by a Committee of the American Bar Association and a Committee of Publishers.*

Dedication

The editors dedicate this book to their colleague Shannon P. Pratt.

We dedicate this book to Shannon in recognition of his contribution to the literature that is advanced in this text. More important, we dedicate the book to Shannon because of his pioneering contribution to the business valuation profession during the last 30 years. Many have contributed to the field in many ways, but none have carried the business valuation flag the way he has. As much as any one individual, Shannon Pratt has helped convert the business valuation industry into a recognized profession and the business valuation art into a recognized science. As practitioner, author, educator, and entrepreneur, he has contributed more than anyone to the professional literature, the professional standards, and the professional societies and institutes of the business valuation discipline. We are grateful.

Robert F. Reilly
Robert P. Schweihs

Preface

Intent of the Book

The business of business valuation has been changing at a pace that is even more accelerated than the pace of change in the world's economy. At the start of the new millenium, we are experiencing a global transformation of financial markets and business procedures. The number of situations in which business valuation techniques apply is expanding exponentially. In this unsettled climate, conventional business valuation principles and procedures are proving to be robust and remarkably versatile. To keep abreast, this anthology of advanced business valuation wisdom provides a new benchmark of contemporary discussions of topics of interest to experienced business valuation practitioners.

As a profession, business valuation is the most rapidly growing of the major appraisal disciplines. There are many new entrants into the field. What they may not know is that there has been an entire generation of professional business analysts who have spent their careers in the field. Many of the new entrants consider complicated business valuation situations to be too infrequently encountered or too esoteric to be of interest.

On the contrary, we have found that the advanced business valuation matters are instructive because they shine a bright light on what many of the less experienced consider to be "gray areas." Studying the advanced business valuation situations like those covered in this book demystifies issues that the uninitiated might consider controversial. This book includes some of the leading ideas on advanced business valuation topics, contributed by prominent members of the business valuation community—ideas that will be instructive to both the beginner and the experienced business valuation practitioner.

There are several well-regarded books that provide a solid foundation for the general theory and application of business valuation. We have coauthored three: *Valuing a Business*, *Valuing Small Businesses and Professional Practices*, and *Valuing Intangible Assets*. *Handbook of Advanced Business Valuation* is intended to be the in-depth complement to these three popular valuation texts.

In fact, these four texts may be considered as a complementary collection that covers the spectrum of financial valuation. These texts present different levels of discussion of current financial valuation conceptual development and practical application. We have found that when common terminology and notations are used, even complex financial valuation concepts become easy to absorb.

In addition to presenting advanced discussions of technical financial valuation applications, this book is intended to be—and to remain—contemporary. Accordingly, each chapter shares with the reader the current state of conceptual thinking, methodological applications, judicial precedent, and empirical data sources. It is the intention of the editors to update this book periodically with new topics and fresh ideas on these topics. Such periodic updates will allow the *Handbook of Advanced Business Valuation* to be a current and timely reference source to all valuation analysts.

Content of the Book

We explore and debunk controversial topics unlike any other book. *Handbook of Advanced Business Valuation* sheds light on critical issues such as:

- What is the best way to estimate the required return on an investment and how is that estimate different if the investment is not in the United States?
- How is the value of securities that are not traded on organized stock markets affected by their lack of liquidity?
- What business valuation opportunities exist for wealthy individuals?
- How are business valuation techniques used and abused in litigation over economic damages or the fair value of a minority shareholder's interest?
- What are the essential factors that drive the value of sports franchises?
- How can business valuation techniques be used to reduce property taxes?
- What are ESOPs and why are they valued differently from other business interests?
- Will my company be worth more if I make the S election?

This book is presented in four parts. The earlier parts include more general topics. The later chapters present more specific topics.

Part I presents general technical topics that may be applicable to most complex business valuations. These topics include estimating the appropriate cost of capital (for both domestic and international valuation analyses), estimating equity risk premiums, and quantifying various valuation discounts.

Part II presents examples of special applications of valuation methods. These special applications include S corporation valuations, family limited partnership valuations, and in-process research and development valuations.

Part III discusses the conceptualization and the conduct of business valuations for specific purposes. These specific purposes include estate planning and intergenerational wealth transfer, ESOP formation and financing, ad valorem taxation assessment, estimation of economic damages, fair value analyses in oppressed shareholder litigation, fairness and solvency analyses, and transaction planning and structuring.

Part IV presents special valuation issues related to specific industries. These chapters discuss advanced valuation issues in such diverse industries as sports franchises, automobile dealerships, radio broadcasting companies, health care, emerging and technology companies, and government contractors.

Audience for the Book

This book should be useful to a variety of constituencies who are interested in specialized business valuation topics, including:

1. Experienced business valuation analysts who want to remain current with the most up-to-date professional developments.
2. Less experienced valuation analysts who want to prepare for a specialized valuation assignment.
3. Investment bankers, business brokers, accountants, and other transactional intermediaries who participate in the valuations and sales of businesses and business interests.
4. Commercial bankers and merchant bankers who finance the purchases of businesses and business interests.
5. Lawyers, judges, regulators, and other members of the legal community who have to interpret business valuations.
6. Business owners, stockbrokers, chief financial officers, tax managers, and investors who rely upon business valuations for transactional, taxation, financing, and strategic planning purposes.

Each audience may have a different level of interest in the theoretical concepts, practical applications, and empirical data presented in this book. One word of caution is in order, however. Casual readers of a book like this may read only a few chapters and convince themselves that they have a rigorous comprehension of this complex subject. The valuation and economic analysis of businesses and business interests is an evolving discipline. Even the serious reader of the entire book will begin—but not complete—an exploration of this complex topic.

Robert F. Reilly
Robert P. Schweihs

Acknowledgments

First and foremost, we would like to thank each of the chapter authors. We were able to assemble a remarkable group of nationally recognized valuation practitioners and legal experts to contribute to this book. Each of the chapter authors is a leading valuation or legal practitioner. And each of the chapter authors enjoys individual prominence and eminence in the professional community.

Readers should appreciate that the chapter authors can look forward to virtually no compensation for their efforts. In fact, they received only a complimentary copy of the book. Therefore, these authors did not expend their valuable time and considerable effort for personal gain. Rather, each wanted to make a significant contribution to the professional literature of the financial valuation profession. The editors are extremely appreciative of each author's significant contribution.

As is often the case with leading authorities in any profession, the positions espoused by the chapter authors are not necessarily those that have been adopted by the profession's societies and institutes. In fact, sometimes the chapter authors may not agree with one another. However, in each case, the chapter authors have presented the most advanced and the most contemporary discussions of their respective topics.

In particular, we would like to thank Charlene M. Blalock, a research associate in our Portland (Oregon) office, who served as the project manager for this undertaking. Charlene coordinated all aspects of the writing, editing, and publication of this book. She was responsible for obtaining permission to use material reprinted in this book from other sources. Charlene also prepared the index and edited and proofread the manuscript. As with all our recent publications, this book would simply not have been completed without Charlene's dedication and project management. Sally Martin also provided proofreading assistance.

We also with to thank Roger Marsh, acquisitions editor of McGraw-Hill, for his guidance and assistance with this book.

For permission to use material, we especially wish to thank:

Appraisal Institute	John Wiley & Sons, Inc.
Brueggeman & Johnson	Merrill Lynch & Co., Inc.
Forbes Inc.	Robert W. Baird & Co.
Houlihan Lokay Howard & Zukin	University of Chicago
Howard Frazier Barker Elliott, Inc.	Value Line
Ibbotson Associates	

Robert F. Reilly
Robert P. Schweihs
Chicago, Illinois

About the Editors

Robert F. Reilly

Robert F. Reilly is a managing director of Willamette Management Associates. He is a certified public accountant, a certified management accountant, a chartered financial analyst, an accredited senior appraiser of the American Society of Appraisers (designated in business valuation), and a certified business appraiser of the Institute of Business Appraisers. He is an accredited tax adviser and an enrolled agent. He is also a certified real estate appraiser, a certified review appraiser, a state-certified general appraiser, and a state-certified affiliate of the Appraisal Institute. He serves as an issues resource panel member of the Appraisal Foundation.

Mr. Reilly provides consulting services relating to business valuation, intangible asset appraisal, security analysis, and damages analysis. He has testified as an expert witness in federal, state, and international courts on numerous occasions, and he regularly provides clients with litigation support and dispute resolution services. Mr. Reilly has also served as a court-appointed arbitrator.

He is the coauthor of *Valuing a Business: The Analysis and Appraisal of Closely Held Companies*, 3d ed. (McGraw-Hill, 1996), *Valuing Small Businesses and Professional Practices*, 3d ed. (McGraw-Hill, 1998), *Valuing Intangible Assets* (McGraw-Hill, 1999), and *Valuing Accounting Practices* (John Wiley & Sons, 1997).

He has authored chapters in numerous books related to specialized topics, such as ad valorem property taxation, matrimonial law and marital dissolution, and employee-owned corporations. He has also written over 200 articles on valuation-related topics that have been published in various professional journals.

Mr. Reilly is often called upon to speak at seminars and conferences of professional groups. He has also taught courses in business valuation both in the United States and abroad.

Prior to joining Willamette Management Associates, Mr. Reilly was a partner and national director of the Deloitte & Touche Valuation Group. Before that, he was vice president of Arthur D. Little Valuation, Inc., a national appraisal firm.

He received an MBA in finance from the Columbia University Graduate School of Business and a B.A. in economics from Columbia University.

Robert P. Schweihs

Robert P. Schweihs is a managing director of Willamette Management Associates. He is an accredited senior appraiser of the American Society of Appraisers (designated in business valuation). He is also a member of the ESOP Association, the Institute of Property Taxation, and the Association for Corporate Growth. He serves as a trustee of the Appraisal Foundation.

Mr. Schweihs provides consulting services relating to business valuation, intangible asset appraisal, security analysis, and damages analysis. He has testified as an expert witness in federal and state courts and regularly provides clients with transactional fairness opinions, solvency analyses, economic analyses, financial advisory services, and litigation support services.

He is the coauthor of *Valuing a Business: The Analysis and Appraisal of Closely Held Companies*, 3d ed. (McGraw-Hill, 1996), *Valuing Small Businesses and Professional Practices*, 3d ed. (McGraw-Hill, 1998), *Valuing Intangible Assets* (McGraw-Hill, 1999), and *Valuing Accounting Practices*, (John Wiley & Sons, 1997). He has also written numerous articles on valuation-related topics that have been published in various professional journals.

Mr. Schweihs is often called upon to speak at seminars and conferences of various professional groups. He has taught courses in business valuation both in the United States and abroad.

Prior to joining Willamette Management Associates, Mr. Schweihs was a partner and national director of Deloitte & Touche Valuation Group. Before that, he was a manager of Arthur D. Little Valuation, Inc., a national appraisal firm.

He received an MBA in economics and finance from the University of Chicago Graduate School of Business, and a B.S. in mechanical engineering from the University of Notre Dame.

Willamette Management Associates

Founded in the 1960s, Willamette Management Associates is one of the oldest and largest independent valuation consulting, economic analysis, and financial advisory services firms in the country. In addition to valuation consulting services, Willamette Management Associates provides specialized capital market and investment banking services.

Both Robert Reilly and Bob Schweihs can be reached at the Chicago office of Willamette Management Associates, 8600 West Bryn Mawr Avenue, Suite 950-N, Chicago, IL 60631-3505; phone 773-399-4300; fax 773-399-4310.

List of Contributors

Gregory K. Brown is a partner in the Chicago, Illinois, law firm of Seyfarth, Shaw, Fairweather & Geraldson, and a member of their Employee Benefits and Executive Compensation Group. Mr. Brown's practice is concentrated in employee benefits, executive compensation law, Employee Retirement Income Security Act (ERISA), and employee stock ownership plans (ESOPs). He is an active member of the American and Illinois Bar Associations and The ESOP Association. He has authored numerous articles and frequently speaks on retirement plan and ESOP matters. Mr. Brown received his B.S. from the University of Kentucky and his J.D. from the University of Illinois.

James T. Budyak is vice president and principal for American Appraisal Associates and is active in valuation and due diligence for businesses, equity and debt investments, intangible assets, and solvency and fairness opinions. He is an active public speaker and has taught several college courses. He is a member of the American Society of Appraisers Publications Committee and Editorial Review Board and a board member for the Milwaukee Investment Analysts Society. His publications include: "New IRS Position on Valuation May Result in Reduced Marital and Charitable Deductions," *Journal of Taxation*, September 1993; "Estate Freeze Rules Affect Partnership Valuation Discounts," *Taxation for Lawyers*, January 1997; and "Developing Discount Rates for Foreign Investments," *Valuation Strategies*, July 1998 (on which Chapter 2 of this book is partially based).

Claire H. Donias is a principal in the Los Angeles office of Arthur Andersen LLP, specializing in the valuation of business interests and intangible assets, and property tax valuations where functional and economic obsolescence are major issues. He has testified extensively in a career of more than 35 years. His formal education includes business administration and mechanical engineering, and he is a registered professional engineer. Past president of the American Society of Appraisers and a member of its College of Fellows, he is on the faculty of the National Judicial College, teaching business valuation to state and federal judges.

Drew S. Dorweiler, graduate of Dartmouth College, is senior manager of Wise, Blackman in Montreal. He has testified as an expert witness, is Eastern Canadian Director of the American Society of Appraisers, serves on committees of the Illinois CPA Society and Foundation, is a director of the Association of Certified Fraud Examiners (Montreal Chapter), and is a member of Mensa. He has contributed to *Forbes, Financial World, Guide to Canadian Business Valuations*, and publications of the AICPA and Canadian Institute of Chartered Accountants.

S. Stacy Eastland is a partner in the Business and Estate Planning department of the Houston office of Baker & Botts, L.L.P. He has developed innovative estate planning techniques and is a regular lecturer on diverse business and estate planning issues. Mr. Eastland is a member of the State Bar of Texas, the American Bar Association (Supervisory Council Member, Section of Real Property and Trust Law, 1990–present), a fellow of the Texas Bar Foundation, a regent of the American College of Trust and Estate Counsel, and a member of the International Academy of Estate and Trust Law. He is listed in *The Best Lawyers in America, Who's Who in America,* and was recently interviewed concerning estate planning by *Fortune* magazine.

Charles Elliott is a principal and senior managing director of Howard Frazier Barker Elliott, Inc., a valuation and financial consulting firm in Houston, Texas. He began his career as a financial analyst with a New York Stock Exchange firm and then advanced into investment management. In 1977, he began the corporate valuation department at Underwood, Neuhaus. Mr. Elliott is an accredited senior appraiser and a chartered financial analyst. He attained his undergraduate degree from Princeton University and his M.B.A. from the Wharton Graduate Division of the University of Pennsylvania.

Joseph S. Estabrook is a manager in the Business Valuation and Litigation Services Group of Ellin & Tucker, Chartered. He is a certified public accountant and has been accredited in business valuation by the AICPA. He is a member of the Institute of Business Appraisers and the American Society of Appraisers where he is a candidate member in its business valuation section. Mr. Estabrook is the past chairman of the Business Valuation and Litigation Services Committee of the Maryland Association of Certified Public Accountants. He has often testified as an expert witness on business valuation issues and is a frequent speaker to professional societies and various business groups.

Jay E. Fishman, ASA, CBA is president of Financial Research, Inc. in Fort Washington, Pennsylvania. He is co-author with Shannon Pratt of *Guide to Business Valuations* and co-author of *Guide to Canadian Business Valuations*. Mr. Fishman is the former chair of the Business Valuation Committee of the American Society of Appraisers and a trustee of The Appraisal Foundation. He has an M.B.A. from LaSalle University.

Steven D. Garber, CFA, ASA, is a partner of Willamette Management Associates and director of the firm's San Francisco office. His primary areas of expertise include the appraisal of closely held businesses and business interests for the purposes of litigation support, taxation, transaction analysis, and employee stock ownership plans (ESOPs). Steve has an M.B.A. from Carnegie-Mellon University and an undergraduate degree in bioengineering from The Johns Hopkins University.

Lawrence B. (Larry) Gooch has 28 years of corporate valuation experience with American Valuation Consultants, Arthur D. Little Valuation, and Price Waterhouse (now PricewaterhouseCoopers). During his career, Mr. Gooch has been involved in valuations of tangible and intangible property for over 100 of the top 1,000 companies. Mr. Gooch is an accredited senior appraiser (ASA) of the American Society of Appraisers and holds an MBA and engineering degree from Stanford University.

Chester A. Gougis, president and chief executive officer of Duff & Phelps, LLC, joined the firm in 1979 from the corporate finance group of Harris Trust and Savings Bank. Mr. Gougis graduated *magna cum laude* from Harvard University in 1974 with a B.A. in economics. He received his MBA in finance and accounting, with honors, in 1976 from the University of Chicago. He is a member of the Economists Club of Chicago and the Business Valuation Association. He also sits on the Board of Trustees of the Chicago Symphony Orchestra and the Greater Chicago Chapter of the National Multiple Sclerosis Society.

Roger J. Grabowski, partner in the Corporate Value Consulting practice of PricewaterhouseCoopers LLP, founded the Valuation Services practice of Price Waterhouse LLP. Roger has a broad valuation background in business interest and underlying asset (inventory, intangible assets, real property, and industrial equipment) valuation. Roger has testified in numerous cases. For example, his testimony on behalf of the taxpayers in District Court was quoted by Justice Blackmun in the landmark *Newark Morning Ledger* opinion (*Newark Morning Ledger* v. *U.S.*, No. 91–1135 S. Ct. (June 4, 1992)).

Lee P. Hackett is executive vice president of American Appraisal Associates, Inc., and a board member of AA Management Group. He coordinates American Appraisal's global operations and provides advisory services to American Appraisal's key clients worldwide. He is chair of the Affiliate Firm Committee of the American Society of Appraisers, member and past chair of the Industry Advisory Council of The Appraisal Foundation, and a member of the Counselors of Real Estate. He also serves as trustee, treasurer, and chair of the Investment Committee for St. Johnsbury Academy, board member of the Wisconsin Conservatory of Music, and corporation member for Milwaukee School of Engineering.

Jeffrey A. Herbst is a partner at the law firm of Wilson Sonsini Goodrich & Rosati in Palo Alto, California, where he represents high technology and other emerging growth companies in general business and securities matters. His areas of expertise include public offerings, venture capital financings, joint ventures, and mergers and acquisitions. Mr. Herbst also has extensive experience in strategic partnering, technology licensing, and other technology-driven transactions. His clients range from start-ups to large, public companies.

John E. (Jack) Kane is a principal in Kane Reece Associates, Inc., a valuation, management, and technical consultancy firm based in Westfield, New Jersey. Mr. Kane has over 25 years of experience as an executive at major media/communications corporations and in providing valuation and financial advisory services to entertainment, media, and communications firms. He is a chartered financial analyst, an accredited senior appraiser (certified in business valuation) of the American Society of Appraisers, and a member of the New York Society of Security Analysts.

David W. King is a director of the Corporate Value Consulting practice in the Chicago Office of PricewaterhouseCoopers LLP, where he has conducted extensive research into the theory and practical application of discount rates for domestic and international companies. His previous publications include articles reporting original empirical research on the relationship between company size and rates of return on corporate equity. He is a chartered financial analyst.

Dr. Robert Lawrence Kuhn is president of The Geneva Companies, the largest merger and acquisition company for private, middle-market businesses in the United States. Dr. Kuhn is a special advisor to various ministries in the People's Republic of China and the author or editor of over 25 books in business and finance. He is editor-in-chief of Irwin's seven-volume *The Library of Investment Banking* and McGraw-Hill's *Handbook for Creative and Innovative Managers*.

M. Mark Lee is KPMG LLP's national product partner for Fairness Opinions. Previously, he was KPMG's principal-in-charge of Valuation Advisory Services in the Northeastern Region of the United States. Prior to joining KPMG in December 1995, he was a managing director of Bear, Stearns & Co. Inc. and a member of its Valuation Committee. Mr. Lee has written many articles on business valuations and fairness opinions and has testified as an expert in court. He holds an M.B.A. from the New York University Graduate School of Business (Stern) and a Bachelor of Science in economics from the Wharton School of Finance and Commerce of the University of Pennsylvania. He is also a chartered financial analyst.

Tracy Lefteroff, partner-in-charge of PricewaterhouseCoopers Global Life Sciences Industry Services, is in charge of services to publicly traded, privately owned, and venture capital–funded life sciences companies worldwide. Mr. Lefteroff has been with PricewaterhouseCoopers for approximately 12 years and currently serves on the board of directors of the Stanford Venture Laboratory. He has served as treasurer of the Washington State Biotechnology Association and also as chairman of the MIT Enterprise Forum of the Northwest.

David C. Light is a senior associate in the Chicago office of Valuemetrics, Inc. He holds his undergraduate degree in economics from Princeton University and his master's degree from the University of Chicago.

Gilbert E. Matthews is chairman of the board and senior managing director of Sutter Securities Incorporated in San Francisco. From 1960 through 1995 he was with Bear, Stearns & Co. Inc. in New York where he had been senior managing director and a general partner of its predecessor partnership. From 1970 through 1995, he was chairman of Bear Stearns' Valuation Committee, which was responsible for all opinions and valuations issued by the firm. Mr. Matthews received an A.B. from Harvard in 1951 and an M.B.A. from Columbia in 1953. He is a member of the New York Society of Security Analysts and a chartered financial analyst (CFA).

Richard C. May is the president and founder of Valuemetrics, Inc., a corporate financial advisory firm. He has worked with owners of publicly and privately held corporations for more than 20 years and is regarded as a leading expert in the area of business valuation. Mr. May received his undergraduate degree in management from Purdue University and his master's degree from MIT's Sloan School of Management.

Michael Mendelevitz is managing director of ESOP Advisors, Inc., an investment banking firm that serves as financial advisor to middle-market companies worldwide. Mr. Mendelevitz is a graduate of Miami University (Ohio). He has successfully implemented ESOP LBOs in middle-market corporate transactions, providing analysis, financing, and structuring expertise. In recognition of his "groundbreaking" work in the area of applications of ESOPs to government privatization, he was named a fellow of Syracuse University's Maxwell School for Public Administration.

Roy H. Meyers, CFA, ASA, is a senior vice president of Management Planning, Inc., a leading national business valuation firm. He holds an M.B.A. from the Rutgers University Graduate School of Management and a bachelor degree from Rutgers College. He is a member of the New York Society of Security Analysts and the Construction Financial Management Association.

Thomas J. Millon Jr. is a principal of Willamette Management Associates and director of its McLean, Virginia, office. Mr. Millon has substantial experience in the appraisal of business entities and business interests, in the appraisal of fractional business interests , and in the valuation and remaining life analysis of intangible assets. He is an accredited senior appraiser (ASA) of the American Society of Appraisers, certified in business valuation. He is also a chartered financial analyst (CFA) of the Association for Investment Management and Research.

John L. Miscione is the managing director of the New York office of Valuemetrics, Inc. He received his undergraduate degree in psychology from Johns Hopkins University, an M.A. in psychology from the University of Virginia, where he was a Deans Fellow, and an M.B.A. in finance and business strategy from New York University.

John C. O'Brien is an associate in the Chicago office of Valuemetrics, Inc. Mr. O'Brien holds an undergraduate degree in business administration from Loyola University, where he graduated cum laude. He received a Master's of Science in finance degree from DePaul University where he graduated with distinction.

Robert P. Oliver, ASA, is the president of Management Planning, Inc., a leading national business valuation firm. A published author and frequent speaker on valuation topics, he is a recognized valuation expert. Mr. Oliver holds an M.B.A. from the New York University Graduate School of Business and an undergraduate degree from Rutgers College. He has participated as a speaker in business valuation educational programs.

John R. Phillips is a principal at PHB Hagler Bailly in Los Angeles, California. Mr. Phillips is a CFA and a CPA holding the accredited in business valuation (ABV) designation of the AICPA. He has co-authored a chapter in the *Litigation Services Handbook*, 2d ed., and has co-authored a course sponsored by the California CPA Education Foundation. He has written articles for the *ABA Journal*, the *Los Angeles Lawyer*, the *Commercial Damages Reporter*, and *Business Valuation Review*.

John W. Porter is a partner in the Houston office of the law firm Baker & Botts, L.L.P. He received his B.B.A. from Texas A&M University and his law degree from the Baylor University School of Law. A board-certified specialist in the area of probate, trust and estate law and a fellow of the American College of Trust and Estate counsel, Mr. Porter is the current co-chair of the Tax Litigation and Controversy Committee of the Real Property, Probate and Trust Law Section of the American Bar Association. Mr. Porter is also a certified public accountant (Texas). Mr. Porter specializes in fiduciary litigation, and gift, estate and income tax litigation and controversy work.

Shannon P. Pratt is a managing director of Willamette Management Associates. He is also editor-in-chief of *Shannon Pratt's Business Valuation Update* and *Business Valuation Update for Judges and Lawyers*. Dr. Pratt is co-author of *Valuing a Business: The Analysis and Appraisal of Closely Held Companies*, 3d ed. (McGraw-Hill, 1996); *Valuing Small Businesses and Professional Practices*, 3d ed. (McGraw-Hill, 1998); and *Guide to Business Valuations*, 9th ed. (Practitioners Publishing Company, 1999). He is also author of *Cost of Capital: Estimation and Applications* and *Business Valuation Body of Knowledge: Exam Review and Professional Reference* (John Wiley & Sons, 1998). Dr. Pratt currently serves as a trustee of The Appraisal Foundation.

James G. Rabe is co-director of the Portland, Oregon, office of Willamette Management Associates, where he has appraised numerous emerging growth companies for a variety of different purposes. He is an accredited senior appraiser (ASA) of the American Society of Appraisers (certified in business valuation), a chartered financial analyst (CFA), and holds an M.B.A. from Washington University in St. Louis and a B.S.B.A. in finance from the University of Missouri at Columbia.

Anne C. Singer is a shareholder in the Westmont, New Jersey, law firm, Earp Cohn P.C., where her practice focuses on commercial civil litigation, including shareholder disputes. Before entering private practice, she served for 12 years as an Assistant United States Attorney for the District of New Jersey. Ms. Singer holds a J.D. from the University of Cincinnati (1973), an M.S. from the University of Alabama (1969), and a B.S. from the University of Chicago (1966).

Robert S. Socol is a principal of Willamette Management Associates and national director of the firm's employee benefits practice. Mr. Socol has significant experience ina variety of valuation and financial advisory services, including ESOP opinions, transaction opinions, mergers and acquisitions, financing leveraged buyouts, corporate planning, business valuations, litigation support, and financial restructuring. In providing the foregoing services, he has extensive experience in equity allocation issues, complex deal structuring, deal negotiation, and design of innovated securities.

Gary R. Trugman is a certified public accountant as well as an accredited appraiser in business valuation by the American Institute of Certified Public Accountants, the Institute of Business Appraisers Inc., and the American Society of Appraisers. Gary has authored a text entitled *Understanding Business Valuation: A Practical Guide to Valuing Small and Medium Sized Businesses*. He regularly appears in court as an expert witness testifying on business valuation matters.

Michael J. Wagner is a managing director at Putnam, Hayes & Bartlett, Inc., in Palo Alto, California. He has a B.S. in engineering from the University of Santa Clara, an M.B.A. from U.C.L.A., and his J.D. degree from Loyola University at Los Angeles. Mr. Wagner is a licensed attorney and CPA in California. Mr. Wagner is the author of many articles on the topics of computation of damages. He is coeditor of the *Litigation Services Handbook*, 2d ed.

Charles A. Wilhoite is a principal of Willamette Management Associates and co-director of the firm's Portland, Oregon, office. Mr. Wilhoite's practice focuses on business valuations and intangible asset appraisal for mergers and acquisitions, ESOPs, gift and estate tax planning, damages estimation, and dispute resolution. Mr. Wilhoite received his B.S. degrees from Arizona State University in accounting and finance. He is an ASA (accredited senior appraiser in business valuation), an ABV (accredited in business valuation), and is certified as a public accountant (CPA), a management accountant (CMA), and in financial management.

James L. (Butch) Williams is managing shareholder of Williams, Taylor & Associates, P.C., a Birmingham, Alabama, accounting and consulting firm. He is the current chairman of the AICPA Consulting Services Business Valuations Subcommittee, and he is a former chairman of the NACVA Executive Advisory Board. His firm is a member of the Financial Consulting Group and CPA Associates International, Inc. He has extensive experience in automobile dealership and family limited partnership valuation matters.

Richard M. Wise of Wise, Blackman, one of Canada's leading valuation firms, is a graduate of McGill University, past president of The Canadian Institute of Chartered Business Valuators, fellow of the Institute of Chartered Accountants, and former regional governor of the American Society of Appraisers. Author of *Financial Litigation—Quantifying Business Damages and Values* (Canadian Institute of Chartered Accountants), Mr. Wise contributes extensively to professional publications; is a frequent speaker at conferences of lawyers, accountants, and business appraisers across North America; and is consultant to the Canadian Government.

Richard D. Wolfe, a financial analyst with Kane Reece Associates, Inc., provided research assistance on Chapter 19. He is a 1994 graduate of the Wharton School of Business of the University of Pennsylvania, a candidate for the chartered financial analyst and accredited senior appraiser designations, and a member of the New York Society of Security Analysts.

Contents

Handbook of Advanced
Business Valuation

Part I

Technical Topics

Chapter 1

The Income Approach—Estimating the Cost of Capital

Shannon P. Pratt, CFA, FASA, CBA

Introduction

This chapter provides an overview of the prevailing practices and procedures used by financial theorists and valuation practitioners to estimate the cost of capital in order to apply it as a present value discount rate in a classic present value model. Cost of capital is at the very heart of business valuation. "Value today always equals future cash flow discounted at the opportunity cost of capital."[1]

Definition of the Cost of Capital

The cost of capital is the expected rate of return that the market requires to attract funds to a particular investment. In economic terms, it is an *opportunity cost*—that is, the cost of foregoing the next best alternative investment (i.e., an investment of either (1) equivalent risk with a higher expected return or (2) lower risk with the same expected return).

The cost of capital is based on the *principle of substitution*—an investor will prefer an investment in the more attractive alternative (as defined above). The cost of capital is market-driven—it is the competitive rate of return available in the market on a comparable (from an economic perspective) investment. The most important component of comparability is *risk*.

Risk is the degree of certainty (or lack of it) that the investor will realize the expected economic income at the times specified. Risk cannot be observed directly. Therefore, analysts have developed several ways to estimate risk using available market data (generally based on some historical period of time).

Each component of a company's capital structure (i.e., various layers of debt and equity) has an associated cost of capital. The blended average of the costs of these capital components is the company's weighted average cost of capital (WACC).

Components of the Cost of Capital

There are three basic components of the cost of capital:

1. The "real" rate of return that investors expect in exchange for letting someone else use their money on a riskless basis.
2. Expected inflation—the expected depreciation in purchasing power while the money is tied up.
3. Risk—the uncertainty about when and how much cash flow (or some other measure of economic income) will be received.

---

[1] Paul Samuelson and William Nordhaus, *Economics*, 14th ed. (New York: McGraw-Hill, 1992), p. 738.

The combination of the first two of the above components is sometimes referred to as the *time value of money*. The time value of money is the same for all investments of the same expected duration. Although these component cost expectations may be different for different investors, the market tends to form a consensus. For the third component, the consensus analysis of the many factors causing uncertainty of returns determines the cost of capital for investments of varying levels of risk.

Cost of Capital Equals Discount Rate

The present value discount rate is also referred to as the *required rate of return*. A discount rate is an annually compounded percentage rate of return by which each increment of expected future economic income is discounted back to a present value. The essence of the cost of capital (i.e., the discount rate) is that it is the percentage rate of return that equates expected future increments of income with present value. The present value discount rate (i.e., the cost of capital) equals the total expected rate of return—that is, dividends or withdrawals plus expected annually compounded change in the value of the investment over the life of the investment.

Discount Rate versus Capitalization Rate

The present value discount rate is applied to each future increment of expected economic income. It differs from a direct capitalization rate in that the direct capitalization rate is applied only to a single-period expected economic income, usually the period immediately following the effective valuation date.

In the direct capitalization method, some base amount of economic income, usually the next period's expected amount, is divided by a rate called a *capitalization rate*. In the direct capitalization method, all changes in expected future increments of economic income are captured in the capitalization rate (the denominator) rather than in the specific projected economic income (the numerator), as in the discounting method. The changes in future elements of economic income are captured in the direct capitalization method by starting with a present value discount rate and subtracting the projected sustainable average annual rate of growth in the income variable being capitalized (see the discussion of the Gordon Growth Model in a later section). Therefore:

$$c = k - g$$

where:

c = direct capitalization rate
k = present value discount rate (cost of capital)
g = expected growth rate (expected long-term sustainable rate of growth, theoretically in perpetuity, in the net cash flow or other economic income variable being capitalized)

Mathematically, in a perfect world, if the expected growth rate is estimated accurately, the direct capitalization method will produce an indicated value exactly the same as that produced by the discounting method. The relationship between the present value discount rate and the direct capitalization rate is the same whether the analyst is capitalizing return on investment in equity or return on investment in total invested capital.

Characteristics of Cost of Capital

The cost of capital is forward-looking. It represents investors' *expectations*. Actual historical performance is relevant to an estimate of the cost of capital only to the extent that there is reason to believe that historical performance is representative of future expectations.

The cost of capital is a function of the investment, *not* the investor—that is, it depends on how the capital is used. The cost of capital for a given investment (e.g., acquisition or expansion) may be at, above, or below a company's overall cost of capital, depending on relative riskiness of the given investment.

If a present value discount rate other than that appropriate for the investment on a stand-alone basis is used to discount expected economic income, the resulting indication of value can be considered to be investment value rather than fair market value. It is considered investment value because the resulting indication of value depends on the circumstances or perspective of a particular investor rather than the hypothetical willing investor contemplated in the standard definition of fair market value. This investment value phenomenon often is reflected in acquisition prices, in which a buyer uses its own company's cost of capital to discount expected cash flows from the acquiree. It follows that, when the value of subsidiary business units of a conglomerate is estimated, each subsidiary may have a different cost of capital on a stand-alone basis depending on its relative risk.

The cost of capital is based on market value, not book value. It is based on expected financial performance relative to market prices. For example, the yield to maturity shown in the bond quotations in the financial press is based on the market price of the bond, not on its face value. Similarly, the implied cost of capital for a publicly traded stock is based on the market price of that stock, *not* on the company's book value per share of stock.

The cost of capital is usually stated in nominal terms. As noted earlier, one of the components of the cost of capital is expected inflation. This assumes, of course, that the expected economic income to be discounted includes the effect of expected inflation (normally the case in developed economies with predictable inflation rates).

For countries with hyperinflation, it is usually more reliable to state both (1) the economic income projections and (2) the present value discount rates in real rather than nominal terms.

Cost of Capital by Capital Structure Component

Cost of Debt

If a company is borrowing at prevailing market rates, the interest rate that the company is paying is usually the pretax cost of debt. If the company has various layers of long-term debt at rates different from the prevailing market, depending on the purpose and objective of the valuation assignment, it may be appropriate to substitute market-derived rates. The market-derived rates may be estimated by analyzing the yields on the debt of publicly traded companies of comparative risk. Since interest on debt is tax-deductible, the after-tax cost of debt (i.e., the market-derived rate multiplied by 1 minus the company's income tax rate) is the relevant cost to the company.[2]

Sometimes there are hidden costs that should be considered in the cost of debt analysis, such as:

- Points up front (a percentage of the loan paid as part of the loan fee).
- Compensating bank balance requirements.
- Personal guarantees (to date, there is no generally accepted method to measure their cost).

Cost of Preferred Equity

If the dividend rate for the company's preferred equity is at the market rate for preferred stocks of equivalent risk, the yield usually represents the cost of preferred equity. If the yield on the company's preferred equity is different from the prevailing market-derived rate, depending on the purpose and objective of the valuation assignment, it may be appropriate to substitute market-derived rates. The market-derived rate may be estimated by analyzing the yields of preferred equity of publicly traded companies of comparative risk. In considering yield rates for preferred stocks of comparative risk, the analyst should also consider the characteristics of the publicly traded companies' preferred equity, because the characteristics of preferred stocks can vary greatly.[3]

Cost of Common Equity

Unlike costs of debt and preferred equity, the cost of common equity is not directly observable in the market. This is because the amount of economic

---

[2] For more information on the cost of debt, see Chapter 20 of Shannon P. Pratt, Robert F. Reilly, and Robert P. Schweihs, *Valuing a Business: The Analysis and Appraisal of Closely Held Companies*, 3d ed. (New York: McGraw-Hill, 1996), pp. 479–491.

[3] For further discussion of cost of preferred equity, see Chapter 21 of Pratt, Reilly, and Schweihs, *Valuing a Business*, pp. 492–513.

income expected to flow to the common equity to which a market price can be related is not as predictable. The cost of equity covers a wide band of required rates of return because of the wide range of risk associated with its economic income stream. Consider, for example, the range of expected economic income for these publicly traded companies:

- Large, stable company with consistently predictable and significant dividends.
- Cyclical or erratic company whose expected return on investment depends more on stock price appreciation than on dividends.
- Small company with no dividends.
- Start-up company with no track record or venture capital.

The cost of equity for these companies could conceivably span a range from under 10 percent to more than 50 percent. The analysis of the subject company's risk in order to estimate the company's cost of equity within this wide band is arguably the most challenging exercise in business valuation.

Weighted Average Cost of Capital

Definition

The definition of the weighted average cost of capital (WACC) is the blended costs of the company's capital structure components, each weighted by the *market value* of that capital component.

The formula for the WACC is:

$$\text{WACC} = (k_e \times W_e) + (k_p \times W_p) + (k_{d(pt)}[1 - t] \times W_d)$$

where:

WACC	=	weighted average cost of capital
k_e	=	cost of common equity capital
W_e	=	percentage of common equity capital in the capital structure, at market value
k_p	=	cost of preferred equity capital
W_p	=	percentage of preferred equity capital in the capital structure, at market value
$k_{d(pt)}$	=	cost of debt capital, pretax
t	=	income tax rate
W_d	=	percentage of debt capital in the capital structure, at market value

Exhibit 1–1 presents the preceding computation example in tabular form.

In the typical business valuation, the value, and therefore the weight, of the subject company's equity is unknown. Therefore, the analyst often has to estimate the percentage of equity capital to be used in

Exhibit 1–1

WACC Example

Capital Component	Percentage of Capital Component in Capital Structure[a]	Cost of Capital Component		Weighted Cost of Capital Component
Debt	30%	$(10\% - 3\%)$[b]	=	2.1%
Preferred equity	10%	12%	=	1.2%
Common equity	60%	20%	=	12.0%
	100%			
	Weighted average cost of capital		=	15.3%

[a] At market value.
[b] Assuming a 30% income tax rate.

the WACC by just estimating the value of the subject company's equity. This percentage of equity capital estimation is often an iterative process. Since the cost of each capital component is supposed to be at market value, a reasonable test of the equity value indication is to test it in the WACC. In other words, the analyst may start by estimating the value of the subject company's equity capital, then compare that weighting in the WACC to test its reasonableness.

Company Actual versus Hypothetical Capital Structure

Minority Ownership Interest Basis.   If the subject business valuation is on minority ownership interest basis, the company's actual capital structure is usually used. This is because a minority stockholder cannot change the capital structure.

Ownership Control Basis.   If the subject business valuation is on a controlling ownership interest basis, a case can be made for using a hypothetical capital structure. If a hypothetical capital structure is used, industry average capital costs and weightings are most typical. If the analyst elects to use the industry average capital costs and weightings, they should be at relative market values of components, not at book values:

- Sources based on balance sheet numbers usually are not satisfactory because they are at book values (e.g., Robert Morris Associates *Annual Statement Studies, Financial Studies of the Small Business, Almanac of Business and Industrial Financial Ratios*).
- If available, it is better to use sources that compute capital structure percentages on the basis of market values (e.g., Ibbotson's *Cost of Capital Quarterly*).
- An analyst could also independently develop a set of guideline publicly traded companies or guideline merged and acquired companies in order to estimate industry average capital structures.

Estimation of Cost of Equity Capital

Elements Reflected in Cost of Equity

The risk-free rate is the rate of return available on a security considered free of default risk, usually a U.S. Treasury security (Ibbotson Associates recommends using the 20-year maturity Treasury instrument). The risk-free rate actually includes some degree of *maturity risk* (also called *horizon risk* or *interest rate risk*), the risk that the market value of the security will fluctuate with changes in the general level of interest rates.

The equity risk premium (ERP) is the return over and above the risk-free rate that investors require in order to incur the risk of investing in an equity security instead of a risk-free security. The ERP may include any or all of the following elements:

- **General market equity risk premium.** The expected return above the risk-free rate available by investing in common stocks of companies such as those included in the Standard & Poor's 500 composite or some other broad market index.
- **Size risk premium (small stock premium).** The additional expected return for incurring additional risk by investing in companies smaller than the market index (which, for Ibbotson Associates data, is the Standard & Poor's 500 composite).
- **Company-specific risk premium.** The additional expected return required if risks of the subject company are greater than those reflected in companies on which earlier risk premium elements are based; it is noteworthy that the company-specific component, in rather rare circumstances, could be a negative risk premium adjustment.

All the various models for estimating cost of equity include the previously mentioned cost component elements, either explicitly or implicitly.

Capital Asset Pricing Model (CAPM)

Description of the CAPM. The concept of the CAPM is that the cost of equity capital is equal to (1) the risk-free rate plus (2) a linear function of a measure of systematic risk times (3) the general equity risk premium. *Systematic risk* is the sensitivity (measured by covariance) of returns above the risk-free rate for the subject security to returns above the risk-free rate for a market average (such as the Standard & Poor's 500). *Beta,* the measure of systematic risk, is computed by regressing returns on a specific security or portfolio against returns for the market index.

The reason that the CAPM includes only systematic risk as a factor in determining the required rate of return is that, theoretically, *unsystematic risk* (risk unique to a company or industry) can be eliminated by holding a fully diversified portfolio of securities.

Since a private company does not have a track record of regular price changes, the equity appreciation part of the return included in the calculation of beta is not measurable. Therefore, in order to use the CAPM for estimating the cost of a private company's capital, betas are usually derived from publicly traded company average betas for a relevant industry group.

Computing a CAPM Estimate of Cost of Equity Capital.
The basic CAPM formula is:

$$E(R_i) = R_f + B(RP_m)$$

where:
$E(R_i)$ = expected return (cost of capital) for an individual security
R_f = rate of return available on a risk-free security (as of the valuation date)
B = beta (for the subject security or company)
RP_m = equity risk premium for the market as a whole (or, by definition, the equity risk premium for a security with a beta of 1.0)

It is noteworthy that the RP_m above is an *estimated* market risk premium. The market risk premium may be estimated in several different ways, as described in subsequent sections of this chapter.

The preceding formula is illustrated by an example in tabular form in Exhibit 1–2.

Modified (Expanded) CAPM Cost of Equity.
Empirical tests of the CAPM have found that CAPM does not fully explain the returns exhibited in the market, particularly for small companies. Therefore, modified CAPM models have been developed. The CAPM formula is often expanded to include (1) a size effect risk factor and (2) a company-specific risk factor:

$$E(R_i) = R_f + B(RP_m) + RP_s + RP_u$$

where:
$E(R_i)$ = expected return (cost of capital) for an individual security
R_f = rate of return available on a risk-free security (as of the valuation date)
B = beta (for the subject security or company)
RP_m = equity risk premium for the market as a whole (or, by definition, the equity risk premium for a security with a beta of 1.0)
RP_s = risk premium for small stock size effect
RP_u = risk premium attributable to the specific company (u stands for unsystematic risk)

Exhibit 1–2

CAPM Example

CAPM Component	CAPM Variable	
Risk-free rate of return		6.0%
General market equity risk premium	7.5%	
Times: subject security beta	1.2	
Equity risk premium for the subject security		9.0
Cost of equity capital for the subject security		15.0%

Selection of the Risk-Free Rate. The risk-free rate is usually based on short-term (30-day), intermediate-term (5-year), or long-term (20-year) U.S. Treasury security yields to maturity. The general preference is for the 20-year rate. This is because the 20-year Treasury security:

• Matches the typical long-term horizon of equity investment
• Is subject to less volatility than shorter-term rates

Selection of Equity Risk Premium. The ERP may be based on either of the following:

• Ibbotson Associates historical risk premium data from *Stocks, Bonds, Bills, and Inflation* yearbooks.
• The discounted cash flow (DCF) method (see the subsequent section on the DCF method of estimating the cost of equity capital).

If using Ibbotson Associates data to estimate the equity risk premium, the analyst should match the risk-free rate selection with short-, intermediate-, or long-term equity risk premium. The risk-free rate should be the rate existing in the market as of the effective valuation date. Also, if using Ibbotson Associates historical data, the analyst should select between:

• The arithmetic average historical equity risk premium (recommended by Ibbotson Associates). The primary reason that Ibbotson Associates recommends the arithmetic average as the best estimate of the expected risk premium is because there is no autocorrelation—that is, the returns are random (independent of each other; the next year's return is unrelated to the prior year's).[4]
• Geometric average historical equity risk premium.

[4] For a more complete explanation, see *Stocks, Bonds, Bills and Inflation, 1998 Yearbook* (Chicago: Ibbotson Associates, 1998) pp. 157–159.

Selection of Size Effect Risk Premium. Ibbotson Associates data show that small companies generate—and therefore investors require—returns over and above those that would be reflected by their specific betas. If using the CAPM, the analyst should use only size premium data in excess of CAPM return. Or, if not using beta, the analyst should use total return in excess of the risk-free rate for the relevant size decile. The size risk premium is not multiplied by beta; rather, beta is applied only to the general equity risk premium. It is noteworthy that all Ibbotson Associates return data are *after* entity-level income taxes.

Company-Specific Risk Premium. The estimation of the company-specific risk premium is subjective, based on analysis of the characteristics of the subject company—relative to companies from which other risk premium data are drawn (i.e., company-specific factors not captured in either beta or size premium). A company-specific risk premium may be appropriate if the subject company is affected by any of the following factors:

- Smaller than the smallest company in the size premium group from which the size premium was derived.
- Industry risk not fully reflected in beta.
- Relatively higher or lower volatility of economic income.
- Greater or less leverage (this factor may be adjusted using levered and unlevered betas).
- Concentration of customer base.
- Key person dependence or small management base.
- Key supplier dependence.
- Abnormal present or pending competition.
- Pending regulatory changes.
- Pending lawsuits.
- Relatively undiversified operations:
  - Products
  - Geographically
- Special environmental problems.

Levered and Unlevered Betas. Betas that are published by the various financial reporting services reflect whatever leverage the respective publicly traded companies have. The estimated effect of leverage can be removed by *unlevering* the betas. Then, the unlevered beta can be *relevered* to reflect any desired degree of leverage.

The published betas can be used for valuing either invested capital or equity. However, they are used primarily for valuing invested capital. The formula for unlevering beta (i.e., for deriving a beta implicitly assuming 100 percent equity in capital structure, known as the *Hamada formula*) is:

$$B_u = \frac{B_L}{1 + (1 - t)(W_d/W_e)}$$

where:
B_u = beta unlevered
B_L = beta levered

t = income tax rate for the company
W_d = percentage of debt capital in the capital structure
W_e = percentage of equity capital in the capital structure (at market value)

Presented below is an example illustrating the unlevering of betas. Assume the following for guideline company A:

Levered (published) beta: 1.2
Income tax rate: 40%
Market value capital structure: 20% debt, 80% equity

$$B_u = \frac{1.2}{1 + (1 - 0.40)(0.20/0.80)}$$

$$= \frac{1.2}{1 + 0.60(0.25)}$$

$$= \frac{1.2}{1.15}$$

$$= 1.04$$

The formula for relevering beta is:

$$B_L = B_u[1 + (1 - t)(W_d/W_e)]$$

where the definitions of the variables are the same as in the formula for computing unlevered betas.

An example of relevering beta is presented below. Assume the following variables for the subject company:

Unlevered beta: 1.1
Income tax rate: 25%
Subject company capital structure: 40% debt, 60% equity

$$B_L = 1.1[1 + (1 - 0.25)(0.40/0.60)]$$

$$= 1.1[1 + 0.75(0.67)]$$

$$= 1.1(1.50)$$

$$= 1.65$$

Assumptions Underlying the CAPM

Several of the key assumptions underlying the CAPM are as follows:

- Investors are risk-averse (i.e., for each increment of risk, an increment of expected return is required to induce the investor to choose the higher risk investment).

- Rational investors seek to hold efficient portfolios (i.e., portfolios that are fully diversified).
- All investors have identical investment time horizons (i.e., expected holding periods, generally speaking, indefinitely long term).
- All investors have identical and reasonable expectations about such variables as rates of return and how capitalization rates are generated.
- There are no transaction costs (i.e., transaction costs are ignored in the model).
- There are no investment-related taxes at the investor level; that is, all such individual taxation consequences are ignored, but there may be corporate income taxes.
- The rate received from lending money is the same as the cost of borrowing money.
- The market has perfect divisibility and liquidity (i.e., investors can readily buy or sell any desired fractional interest).

Obviously, the extent to which these assumptions are met in the real world affects the applicability of the CAPM for the valuation of closely held businesses, business interests, or investment projects. For example, although the perfect divisibility and liquidity assumption approximates reality for publicly traded stocks, it does not hold for privately held companies. Consequently, the company-specific, nonsystematic risk factor may be required in expected returns for closely held companies.

Build-Up Model

The build-up model is identical in form to the extended version of CAPM, except that the beta factor is not incorporated. Rather, the build-up model implicitly assumes that beta equals 1.0. The effect of not having a specific beta factor has important implications for other elements of the cost of capital:

- **Size risk premium.** Since betas incorporate some part of the size risk premium, a larger size risk premium is usually required in the build-up model than in the CAPM, including the portion of the size premium that would have been reflected in beta. It is noteworthy that some analysts think that the size premium has disappeared in recent years. However, Ibbotson Associates studies refute that position. While it is true that large stocks have generated higher returns than small stocks during the last several years, recent Ibbotson Associates data show that small stocks still have outperformed large stocks. This observation holds true when betas are adjusted for (1) their tendency to revert to industry means and (2) their tendency to lag, in their covariance, with the market. Betas adjusted to reflect these factors are called "shrunk" and "lagged" betas.
- **Company-specific risk premium.** Since at least some portion of industry risk normally would be reflected in beta, that should be considered in estimating the company-specific risk factor.

Discounted Cash Flow Method

Theory of the Discounted Cash Flow Method.   The discounted cash flow (DCF) method can be used to estimate the cost of capital by using the present value formula in reverse. That is, since stock prices are assumed to reflect the present value of expected economic income, the rate of return that the market requires can be computed by implication. The analyst can use the DCF method to estimate the cost of equity for publicly traded companies in the same industry in order to use it as a proxy for the private company cost of capital.

Single-Stage DCF Model.   The single-stage DCF model is based on an algebraic manipulation of the constant growth capitalization model. The formula is:

$$PV = \frac{NCF_0(1 + g)}{k - g}$$

where:

PV	=	present value
NCF_0	=	net cash flow in period 0, the period immediately preceding the valuation date
k	=	present value discount rate (cost of capital)
g	=	expected long-term sustainable growth rate in net cash flow to the investor

When the present value (i.e., the market price) is known, but the present value discount rate (i.e., the cost of capital) is unknown, the preceding formula can be rearranged to solve for the cost of capital:

$$k = \frac{NCF_0(1 + g)}{PV} + g$$

An example of the application of this formula is presented below. Substituting in the above formula to estimate the cost of equity capital for Morton's Restaurant Group as of December 31, 1996:

NCF_0	=	net cash flow $0.522 per share (from Compustat PC Plus version 6.01, a product of Standard & Poor's)
g	=	analysts' consensus expected long-term growth rate of 8.4% (reported by Morningstar Stock Tools, supplied by Zack's)
PV	=	stock price of $16.875 per share (as of December 31, 1996)

$$
\begin{aligned}
k &= \frac{0.552(1 + 0.084)}{16.875} + 0.084 \\[2mm]
&= \frac{0.522(1.084)}{16.875} + 0.084 \\[2mm]
&= \frac{0.566}{16.875} + 0.084 \\[2mm]
&= 0.034 + 0.084 \\[2mm]
&= 0.118
\end{aligned}
$$

It is noteworthy that the above example uses net cash flow as calculated by Compustat. Other financial services that project public company income use dividends plus some estimate of long-term dividend growth.

Multistage DCF Model. Multistage DCF models may have two stages of growth plus a terminal stage. A three-stage model would be as follows:[5]

$$V_s = \sum_{t=1}^{n1} \frac{CF_0(1 + g_1)^t}{(1 + k_s)^t} + \sum_{t=n1+1}^{n2} \frac{CF_{n1}(1 + g_2)^t}{(1 + k_s)^t} + \frac{\dfrac{CF_{n2}(1 + g_3)}{(k_s - g_3)}}{(1 + k_s)^t}$$

where:
V_s = the current market value of the stock
k_s = the cost of equity for company s
t = a measure of time; in this example the unit of measure is a year
$n1$ = the number of years in the first stage of growth
$n2$ = the number of years in the second stage of growth
CF_0 = the dividend, earnings, or cash flow amount (in \$) in year 0
CF_{n1} = the dividend, earnings, or cash flow amount (in \$) in year $n1$
CF_{n2} = the dividend, earnings, or cash flow amount (in \$) in year $n2$
g_1 = the dividend, earnings, or cash flow growth rate from year 1 to year $n1$
g_2 = the dividend, earnings, or cash flow growth rate from year $(n1 +1)$ to year $n2$
g_3 = the perpetual dividend, earnings, or cash flow growth rate starting in year $(n2+1)$

Since the present value of the stock (its market price) is known, the equation can be solved for k, the implied cost of capital, by an iterative process.

Multistage models generally are much more reliable than single-stage models. This is because single-stage models reflect only short-term growth expectations. The given DCF model formulation estimates the entire cost of equity capital without identifying how much of it is attributable to which elements (i.e., risk-free rate, general equity risk premium, size premium, and/or company-specific risk factors). To estimate the company's total equity risk premium, subtract the risk-free rate as of the same date as that for which the total DCF method cost of equity capital was estimated.

---

[5] This model is from *Stocks, Bonds, Bills, and Inflation, 1999 Yearbook*, special valuation edition (Chicago: Ibbotson Associates, 1999).

Arbitrage Pricing Model

Arbitrage Pricing Model Theory.   The arbitrage pricing model can be thought of as a multivariate extension of the CAPM, incorporating several systematic risk factors, one of which *may* be sensitivity to market returns as defined in the CAPM.

Arbitrage Pricing Model Formula.   The econometric estimation of the cost of capital by the arbitrage pricing model takes the following form:

$$E(R_i) = R_f + (B_{i1}K_1) + (B_{i2}K_2) + \ldots + (B_{in}K_n)$$

where:

$E(R_i)$	= expected rate of return on the subject security
R_f	= rate of return on a risk-free security
$K_i \ldots K_n$	= risk premium associated with factor K for the average asset in the market (general macroeconomic factors such as changes in investor confidence, inflation, and so on)
$B_{i1} \ldots B_{in}$	= sensitivity of the security to each risk factor relative to the market average condition to that factor

The variables used are generally based on measures of macroeconomic risk factors expected to have different impacts on different companies. The arbitrage pricing model is not widely used today; to the extent that the arbitrage pricing model is used, it is usually applied to the valuation of very large companies.

Common Errors in Estimation and Use of Cost of Capital[6]

Confusing Discount Rates with Capitalization Rates

The *discount rate* is the cost of capital, and it applies to *all* prospective economic income. This includes all distributions and realized or readily realizable capital appreciation. The *capitalization rate* is a divisor applied to some particular economic income (e.g., earnings or cash flow for the latest 12 months, coming 12 months, or some other period). Only when the expected level of economic income is constant in perpetuity are these two rates equal, other than by sheer coincidence.

Nevertheless, some analysts fall into the trap of using the present value discount rate (i.e., cost of capital) as a direct capitalization rate. Sometimes, the opposite mistake is made: the use of a direct capitalization rate to discount prospective cash flow or other expected economic income to a present value.

---

[6] This section is taken from Shannon P. Pratt, *Cost of Capital: Estimation and Applications* (New York: John Wiley & Sons, 1998).

Using the Firm's Cost of Capital to Evaluate a More or Less Risky Acquisition or Project

The cost of capital is market-driven. Also, it is a function of the investment, not the investor.

If an acquirer uses its own cost of capital to set an acquisition price by discounting the expected cash flows of a more risky acquiree, then the result will be some increase in the risk of the acquiring company after the acquisition. The further result will be an increase in the company's overall risk and cost of capital, and the market will be expected to respond by reducing the acquirer's stock price. A decrease in the acquirer's stock price as a result of an acquisition is a very common phenomenon. However, it is not possible to sort out the extent to which this is a result of perceived overestimation of future cash flows or a market adjustment to the company's cost of capital.

The same principle applies to internal capital budgeting and project selection as to acquisitions. If the project under consideration is more or less risky than the activities of the company as a whole, then the expected cash flows from the project should be evaluated by a correspondingly higher or lower discount rate. In deciding among competing potential projects, an analyst should be careful to appropriately reflect the risk of each project in the present value discount rate applied to the respective project.

Mistaking Historical Rates of Return for Expected Rates of Return

The analyst should keep in mind that cost of capital is a forward-looking concept. The cost of capital is the *expected* rate of return that the market requires to induce investment in a subject security.

One of the most common errors is to take the recent average historical rates of return that have been achieved for an industry, often from a source of industry composite statistics such as Robert Morris Associates' *Annual Statement Studies*, and to assume that this average is the expected return required to attract investment in that industry. The returns actually achieved for a particular industry in recent past years may be well above or below the level of expected return required to attract capital to the industry in the future. Returns shown in sources such as *Annual Statement Studies* are based on book values, whereas the relevant measure is return on market values. (This is not intended to totally eliminate *all* consideration of historical returns, such as long-term average equity risk premiums.)

Mismatching the Discount Rate with the Economic Income Measure

The most common type of error in application of the income approach to valuation is to use a discount rate or capitalization rate that is not appropriate for the definition of economic income being discounted or capitalized. This general category of error has almost infinite variations. Those discussed in the following paragraphs are only a few.

Using a Safe Rate to Discount or Capitalize a Risky Return.
Although not the most common version of the mismatching error, the use
of a safe rate to discount or capitalize a risky return certainly is one of
the most serious. For example, it is a serious error for analysts to discount a highly risky stream of projected economic income by the U.S.
Treasury bill rate.

**Applying a Discount Rate in Real Terms to an Economic
Income Projection in Nominal (Current) Terms.**   Some analysts erroneously subtract the anticipated inflation rate from the present value discount rate and then apply the adjusted discount rate to an
economic income projection that includes inflation (and vice versa). It is
noteworthy that all the Ibbotson Associates data are presented in nominal terms—that is, they include inflation. The most common way of performing the income approach to valuation in the United States—and in
other mature economies—is to express the economic income measure in
nominal terms (including the effect of inflation) and use a nominal discount rate. In countries with hyperinflation, it is more common to express expected economic income in real terms, and to use a discount rate
that does not include expected inflation.

**Applying Cost of Capital Derived from After-Tax Returns
to Pretax Returns.**   Whether costs of capital are estimated by the
build-up method, the CAPM, or the DCF method, in all cases they are
returns realized *after* the payment of corporate-level income taxes. If the
entity being valued is subject to entity-level income taxes, then it is inappropriate to apply the cost of capital estimated by those methods to
pretax economic income.

**Subtracting a Short-Term Supergrowth Rate from the
Discount Rate to Estimate a Capitalization Rate.**   Converting
a present value discount rate to a direct capitalization rate involves subtracting an estimate of the *long-term sustainable growth rate*. Many companies expect high short-term growth that will tend to decrease over
time. If the high short-term growth rate is subtracted from the present
value discount rate, the proper direct capitalization rate will be understated, resulting in overvaluation. In such circumstances, a two-stage or
three-stage DCF valuation model will usually produce a more valid valuation than a straight direct capitalization model.

Performing an Excess Earnings Method
of Valuation That Results in an Unrealistic
Cost of Capital

One very useful application of the cost of capital analysis is to perform
a reasonableness check on the valuation indication generated by the excess earnings method. In the excess earnings method, two capitalization
rates are estimated:

1. A capitalization rate (or rate of return) for tangible assets.
2. A direct capitalization rate for the excess earnings (an amount of return over and above the amount of economic income required to support the company's tangible assets).

The excess earnings method derives its capitalization rates by very different methods from those discussed earlier in this chapter. The excess earnings method is based on returns on assets, rather than returns on capital. Nevertheless, the value as estimated by the excess earnings method should reflect a direct capitalization rate very similar to that which would be derived if we developed a present value discount rate by any of the cost of capital estimation methods and subtracted a reasonable estimate of long-term sustainable growth. Exhibit 1–3 presents an example of such a reasonableness check.

According to the reasonableness check, the results of the excess earnings method make sense. If we capitalize the $270 net cash flow to equity at 23.8 percent, we would have an indicated value of $1,134, as compared with $1,205 achieved by the excess earnings method. These value indications fall within a reasonable range of one another, even though the required rates of return on assets and capital are different. If the value indications were significantly different, we would reexamine all our calculations and assumptions.

In the above example, we dealt only with a direct capitalization rate for equity. This is because most of the data sources used by analysts

Exhibit 1-3

Sanity Check

Is the overall equity capitalization rate approximately equal to what one would expect using a build-up capitalization rate?

1. Analysis of overall equity direct capitalization rate using the excess earnings method:

Net cash flow to equity	$270
Divided by: indicated equity value	$1,205
Equals: implied direct capitalization rate on equity ($270 ÷ $1,205 = 22.4%)	22.4%

2. Build-up method direct capitalization rate to equity:

20-year government bond rate	7.0%
Small stock equity risk premium (combined general equity premium and small stock premium)	15.8%
Company-specific risk premium for subject	5.0%
Total required rate of return (present value discount rate)	27.8%
Less: expected sustainable long-term growth rate	4.0%
Equals: direct capitalization rate applicable to net cash flow to equity	23.8%

making this error show only returns to equity rather than returns to total capital. However, the excess earnings method is used more often to value controlling ownership interests than minority ownership interests. Therefore, the return to total invested capital, as measured by the WACC, is relevant. Thus, the direct capitalization rate for total invested capital should also be considered in the reasonableness test.

Projecting Growth beyond That Which the Capital Being Valued Will Support

As businesses expand, they typically need additional working capital and capital expenditures to support the increased level of operations. One of the many advantages of using net cash flow as the prospective economic income measure is that it forces the analyst to explicitly consider such needs. Nevertheless, these investment requirements are often underestimated.

When the cost of capital is used for valuation, it values only the investment capital as of the valuation date. The calculation of net cash flow allows for necessary reinvestment in capital equipment and additions to working capital in order to support projected operations. However, if the projections being discounted will *not* be totally supported by the capital expenditure and working capital allowances in the net cash flow projections, then additional investment will be required to achieve those projected results. In this case, the indicated value of the *existing* investment will be overstated by the present value of the required capital infusion.

Internally Inconsistent Capital Structure Projection

Methods using weighted average cost of capital and betas adjusted for leverage require a projection of the subject company's capital structure. This projected capital structure is based on market value. Analysts often assume a capital structure in the process of estimating a market value of equity, and the resulting estimated market value of equity indicates a capital structure, at the estimated market value, different from that which was assumed.

In such cases, the projected capital structure has to be adjusted and the process iterated until the estimated market value of equity results in a capital structure consistent with that projected in estimating the cost of capital.

What is even worse, of course, is not even to estimate a market value capital structure, but to simply use book value. If the company is generating above-average economic earnings, then the market value of equity is likely to exceed book value. This is true not only for the subject company but also for the guideline companies that are being used to estimate an industry-average capital structure. If the market value of equity is understated, then the assumed proportion of low-cost debt in the capital structure will be too high. This will result in an understatement of the WACC and an overstatement of value.

Assumptions That Produce a Standard of Value Other Than That Called For in the Valuation Engagement

A common error is to project a capital structure other than the company's actual capital structure (thereby deriving a WACC different from the company's actual WACC) when the standard of value is fair market value on a minority ownership interest basis. If an acquirer were to use its own WACC, then the implied result would be investment value to that acquirer instead of fair market value. Moreover, if the equity ownership interest is a minority ownership interest, the holder could not force a change in capital structure.

Summary

Estimating the cost of capital is one of the most challenging aspects of closely held business valuation. Many business valuation methods rely on an accurate estimate of the cost of capital. In this chapter, the components of the cost of capital were described and the typical methods used to estimate the value were presented.

The concepts of the weighted average cost of capital were explored, as were several commonly used methods to estimate the cost of equity capital: the capital asset pricing method, the build-up method, and the discounted cash flow method.

Finally, some of the most important factors involved in estimating the cost of capital were highlighted by discussing the most common errors made when estimating the cost of capital.

Chapter 2

International Cost of Capital

James T. Budyak, MBA, CPA, CFA, ASA, and Lee. P. Hackett, MBA, ASA, CRE

Introduction[1]

As discussed in the previous chapter, the appropriate income capitalization rate to use in the income approach to business valuation is the cost of capital appropriate for that specific investment. The cost of capital is sometimes referred to as the *discount rate*. The cost of capital will be a function of the perceived risk of the investment. This chapter addresses the most important considerations in the development of an international cost of capital, which is the present value discount rate to be applied for foreign projects.

The minimum risk-adjusted return required by the firm undertaking a given investment (the acquirer) is the cost of capital for that investment. The focus here is on the cost of capital for the specific project (the target) rather than the firm as a whole (the acquirer). This emphasis becomes more important when the target investment is in a different country than the acquiring firm. The evaluation of prospective foreign investments that are expected to change the risk complexion of the acquiring firm warrants careful consideration of the cost of capital.

Multiple-Step Process

There is nowhere like the United States for finding data on equity risk premiums, guideline companies, and other relevant market factors for estimating the cost of capital. This convenience leads many analysts to estimate foreign discount rates by (1) first considering U.S.-based discount rates for the same industry and then (2) making relevant adjustments. In the unlikely event that an analyst can obtain the necessary financial data on guideline companies whose shares trade on foreign markets, the base discount rate can be a meaningful starting point in the development of a foreign discount rate.

This chapter assumes that a thorough and reasonable U.S. base discount rate has been developed, applying the concepts of the weighted average cost of capital (WACC) and the capital asset pricing model (CAPM) for the cost of equity capital component. Inherent in the development of the U.S. WACC is a review of guideline companies, capital structures, risk-free rates, costs of debt, income tax rates, and equity risk premiums. Typical sources for some of these ingredients include the client, One Source database, *ValueLine*, Ibbotson Associates, and the *Wall Street Journal*. With this assumption as a starting point, the second step is to adjust for country-specific factors—namely, political risk, interest rate differential, and tax rate differences. This chapter addresses the second step: the theory behind adjusting the U.S. base discount rate for a foreign project and key sources of data to develop the adjustment factors. We conclude with a narrative report example.

---

[1]This chapter is based on James T. Budyak, "Developing Discount Rates for Foreign Investments," *Valuation Strategies*, August 1998, pp. 30–38.

Political Risk Analysis

"Political risk measures may include the frequency of changes of government, the level of violence in the country, number of armed insurrections, conflicts with other states, and so on. Other popular indicators of political risk include various economic factors such as inflation, balance of payments deficits or surpluses, and the level and growth rate of per capita GNP. The intention behind these measures is to determine whether the economy is in good shape or requires a quick fix such as expropriation, to increase government revenues, or currency inconvertibility to improve the balance of payments."[2] Thus, an analysis of political risk includes an analysis not only of violence and expropriation but also of currency devaluation and inflation.

"The way a country effectively defaults on its own currency debt is by running a high rate of inflation. If inflation is high, one would also anticipate the exchange rate would depreciate. So, effectively the default takes the form of exchange rate depreciation precipitated by high inflation. Country risk becomes exchange rate risk."[3] Thus, political risk —or country risk, as it is sometimes called—can be comprised of both (1) an exchange rate risk and (2) a default risk. Whether an investment evaporates because the business is expropriated or whether the economics of the investment are diminished because of high inflation and resulting currency devaluation, each is an element of political risk. This notion is supported by the publication *Country Forecasts,*[4] which defines political risk forecast factors to include turmoil, financial transfer, direct investment, and export market.

Turmoil includes large-scale protests, general strikes, demonstrations, riots, terrorism, guerrilla warfare, civil war, and cross-border war. It also includes turmoil caused by a government's reaction to unrest. *Financial transfer* includes the risk of being unable to convert from local currency to the desired foreign currency and to transfer foreign currency out of the country. The transfer could be for the payment of exports, repatriation of profits or capital, or any other business purpose. *Direct investment* refers to the risks to foreign investment in wholly owned subsidiaries, joint ventures, and other forms of direct ownership of assets in a foreign country. *Export market* refers to the risks faced by exporters to the country, especially risks related to the market conditions, barriers to imports, and delays or difficulties in receiving payments for goods.

"No risk factor has a greater impact on sovereign creditworthiness than the stance of the ruling government and the political forces in power. History has shown that wherever domestic instability rises, the

---

[2] Alan C. Shapiro, *International Corporate Finance*, 2d ed. (Cambridge, MA: Ballinger Publishing Company, 1988), p. 112.

[3] Lee R. Thomas III, "Country Risk Analysis: Traditional and Modern Perspectives," *Global Bond Management* (Charlottesville, VA: Association for Investment Management and Research, 1997), p. 24.

[4] William D. Coplin and Michael K. O'Leary, *Country Forecasts* (Syracuse, NY: The PRS Group, July 1997).

tides of war often follow. Economic and social problems at home are often dealt with, consciously or fortuitously, by war away from home."[5]

A country, or political, risk analysis goes beyond the traditional physical war or turmoil element to include economic turmoil that could diminish the value of the investment or the returns that it could produce to the foreign investor. After a thorough political risk analysis, an analyst typically finds that the political risk differences between developed countries are often immaterial. It is in the developing or emerging market countries that a political risk analysis becomes more worthwhile and helps to demonstrate that the interest rate analysis discussed below runs parallel to a political risk analysis. Thus, adding the risks assessed in a political risk analysis to an interest rate analysis could result in double-counting certain risks.

Interest Rate Analysis

Just as comparative political risk analysis provides insight as to extra risk inherent in certain countries versus the United States, a comparative interest rate analysis also provides insight about country-specific risk issues. Interest rates are a function of the general economic health of a country and are directly related to inflation. The following discussion on economic considerations, yield differentials, and high-yield debt provides a background for analysis of interest rates.

Economic Considerations

In general, developed countries have inflation rates that are in the low to middle single digits. However, developing or emerging market countries have inflation rates that are greater, from the high single digits to the double digits or higher (hyperinflation). The analyst should not ignore interest rate differentials or income tax rates within developed countries when performing a foreign discount rate analysis. In a discount rate analysis for a developing country, the analyst has less empirical data to rely on and has more judgments and more qualitative considerations to make. However, the analyst should also view a developing country not as static, but as developing or maturing toward a developed stage.

Take Chile or Argentina, for instance. These countries have relatively low expected future inflation rates. For the period 1998 through 2002 according to *Country Forecasts*,[6] Argentina's inflation rate is estimated at 1.8 percent per annum while Chile's is estimated at 6 percent per annum. Contrast these inflation rates to Brazil with 8 percent,

---

[5] "Effective Sovereign Credit Analysis," *Credit Analysis Around the World* (Charlottesville, VA: Association for Investment Management and Research, February 10, 1998).

[6] Coplin and O'Leary, *Country Forecasts*, pp. xix–xxi.

Venezuela with 30 percent, Russia with 12 percent, and Mexico with 8 percent. Mexico's historical inflation rate for the period 1992 through 1996 was 20.3 percent per annum. Mexico is a good example of a country still in the developing stage but making progress toward stability. Argentina, which has an attractive outlook for inflation of only 1.8 percent, had an average annual inflation rate of 8.6 percent during the period 1992 through 1996.

However, low inflation is not always indicative of low turmoil. Argentina has a high probability of turmoil even though inflation is low. The grades given by *Country Forecasts* to Argentina for transfer, investment, and export factors average approximately the grade of *B*, whereas the United States and essentially every recognized, developed country typically is given a grade of *A*. Argentina has made great progress in the past six years. And, clearly, it is an upper-tier emerging market country. However, the analyst would not want to mistake its low inflation outlook as membership in the developed country club!

The economic health of a specific country is a central theme. For example, if an economy has positive inflation performance, stable real economic activity, and a strong interest rate differential versus the rest of the world, then that economy's currency, other things being equal, is more likely to appreciate than a currency that is on a negative side of these indicators.

Countries with low levels of corruption are successful in that they are efficient administrators. On the other hand, countries that are noted for cronyism—with economic decisions based on loyalty, friendship, and politics—tend to be the corrupt countries that are likely to run into financial problems, such as seen in the late 1990s in Thailand. But the political risk analysis by *Country Forecasts* graded Thailand as having a low turmoil and gave it an average *B* score on transfer, investment, and export risks and a projected 1998 to 2002 inflation rate of only 6 percent. This demonstrates the need to look beyond available empirical data and stay in touch with current market trends, such as topical articles in the *Wall Street Journal* and other periodicals that discuss the latest events. Professional judgment needs to be applied. In addition, the analyst should look for surrogates in the global marketplace of other countries that have gone through turmoil to see how they have worked themselves out of it. This emphasizes the need to view any country not as static but as dynamic, improving in some areas and deteriorating in others.

Yield Differentials

A yield differential or interest rate differential between the United States and another foreign country is typically measured with emphasis on government securities. Interest rates can change suddenly for developing countries, and a review of recent interest rates and yield differentials can provide important updated news about a certain country's economic situation.

Let's consider Mexico as an example. The January 1995 *Country Forecasts* analysis of Mexico indicated an investment risk of grade *A*. However, by March 1995, a currency crisis had forced a major devaluation of the peso and caused the yield differential to the United States for long-term government bonds from Mexico to jump to over 1,000 basis points. If an analyst had used the January *Country Forecasts* data naively, he or she would have ignored more recent market events. By early 1997, Mexico was issuing government bonds at a premium of only 550 basis points over comparative U.S. Treasury bonds. But if an investment were being made in March 1995, what would be the appropriate interest rate differential to apply: the 1,000 basis points, the 550 basis points, or some other amount?

The answer may be found in how U.S. discount rates are developed. Bear in mind that when an analyst develops a discount rate and a cost of equity for a U.S.-based firm, he or she often uses 70+ years' worth of Ibbotson Associates data[7] for a normalized risk premium. Why wouldn't the analyst take a similar long-term view when developing a cost of equity for a foreign country that is in an emerging market stage or recovering from recent economic turmoil? Paying attention to market evidence of yield spreads over U.S. Treasury bonds for various emerging markets is one important aspect of making a sound decision for a foreign discount rate. High-flying emerging market bonds periodically run into serious downdrafts. The yield spread over comparable U.S. Treasuries in the late 1990s ranged from 3.3 to 15.5 percent.[8] This range demonstrates the boom and bust of the emerging market for bonds. It represents the extreme ends of the pendulum and also parallels the extremes observed in the U.S. high-yield bond market.

High-Yield Debt

The high-yield debt market in the United States provides evidence that investors want added compensation for added default risk. Default risk in a U.S. high-yield bond is somewhat similar to the added risk associated with investing in developing countries. Emerging market debt returns are so volatile that many investors are wondering whether emerging market debt is truly debt or rather equity in disguise.[9]

Rising junk bond prices dropped the interest yield on Merrill Lynch's high yield master index to only 2.74 percent over the yield offered by 10-year U.S. Treasury notes.[10] "In normal times, investors would demand about 4 percentage points of extra yield for the default risk of investing in junk," according to Martin Fridson, Merrill's chief junk bond market strategist.[11] "In 1990, when the junk bond market crashed and

---

[7] *Stocks, Bonds, Bills, and Inflation, 1998 Yearbook* (Chicago: Ibbotson Associates, 1998). Contains historical analysis for the period January 1926 to December 1997 on various market returns.

[8] According to J. P. Morgan Emerging Market Bonds Index.

[9] Jonathon M. Kelly, "The Relationship Between Bonds and Stocks in Emerging Countries," *Global Bond Management* (Charlottesville, VA: Association for Investment Management and Research, 1997), p. 93.

[10] *USA Today,* Money Section, March 11, 1997, p. 3B.

[11] Ibid.

more than 10% of issues defaulted, junk bonds went begging even as they offered investors an extra nine percentage points over treasuries. In early 1997, the junk bond default rate was incredibly low, around 1.5%, half its normal rate." According to Fridson, one reason defaults are rare is that banks are giving leeway to borrowers slipping into financial jeopardy. According to Joseph Rizzi of the Dutch bank ABN AMRO, "The market is in the stage of the cycle where credit is given to riskier borrowers. The next 12 to 24 months will likely bring heavy losses to lenders. Next comes the stage when bankers turn down one borrower after another. That's the stage that gave the economy such trouble in 1990 that Greenspan and the Fed had to cut short-term interest rates more than half to 3%."[12]

The parallels between the U.S. high-yield market and the emerging market bonds are obvious, involving a classic bull to bear and back to bull cycle phenomenon. Late in the economic cycle investors forget the lessons they learned in the last bear market and accept an insufficient risk premium on the riskier investments. The "easy money" mentality that characterizes every market froth ultimately results in a crisis in which credit is given to practically no one. The implication for *valuation theory* is not to use either the peak or the valley but rather to use the midpoint or long-term rates as a representative proxy for risk. This is particularly important if the valuation is conducted at a time when the local market is especially bullish or bearish.

The consideration of a normalized interest rate (yield) differential is appealing. This is because it recognizes that the default risk in a developing country should be viewed as incremental. Investors require added basis points to invest in high-yield bonds in order to be compensated for the added default risk.

When the yield differential of high-yield bonds narrows because of demand for the bonds (as when investors get overly speculative in a late bull market), the yield differential is inadequate to compensate for the risk of default. And when the reverse happens (such as when the yield differential over Treasuries hits an all-time high), investors are being overly compensated for the default risk. Investors in developing countries would be wise to recognize that speculation in foreign government bonds also can drive risk premiums to inadequate levels, such that compensation for political risks is not adequate.

The key reason emerging markets still have a higher return than the high-yield market in the United States is that in the event of a default, investors do not know what a workout scenario would look like in an emerging market country.[13] The untested workout scenario is enough to justify emerging market debt trading at a higher spread than the debt of the U.S. high-yield market.

[12] Ibid.

[13] Joyce Chang, "Investing in Exotic Emerging Market Debt," *Global Bond Management* (Charlottesville, VA: Association for Investment Management and Research, 1997), p. 116.

The incremental default risk associated with investments in developing countries is consistent with finance texts that discuss the risks inherent in fixed income investments. The risks for bondholders include (1) interest rate, (2) purchasing power, (3) liquidity or marketability, and (4) business.[14] Interest rates are a function of inflation and inflation is linked to purchasing power. Marketability deals with the potentially nonpublic nature of an obligation. Business risk is the risk of default because of the financial or operating risks of the issuer. The default risk inherent in high-yield bonds drives an incremental risk premium over and above investment grade debt securities.

Similarly, for debt securities issued by developing countries, the additional basis points demanded by investors address the added risk of default present in the developing country's bonds. The default risk associated with the developing country deals with loss of value from the collection of political risks. Political risk, as discussed above, not only includes loss due to violence or expropriation of assets, but also includes loss of value due to a series of economic factors such as currency erosion and inflation.

In a sense, the default risk of investments in foreign developing countries represents a semipermanent level of risk that should be compensated for regardless of a market's swing from bullish to bearish. This can be thought of as a new level of risk or added layer of risk over and above that found in developed countries' securities. Similarly, equity risk premiums in the U.S. financial markets are viewed as an added return covering the risk in equity investments that is greater than the risk in fixed income securities.

Income Tax Rate Analysis

A third ingredient, along with political risk and interest rates, in making a country-specific adjustment to a U.S.-based discount rate is country-specific income taxes. Taxes are an economic issue and may be relevant to the subject valuation. When income taxes are relevant, specific income tax differences between the United States and the foreign countries analyzed need to be considered. At minimum, to a taxpaying corporation, income taxes affect the discount rate. This impact is the result of a recognition of the income tax savings on the cost of debt that a firm includes in its cost of capital calculation for a specific investment. Income taxes will also likely impact the cash flows that are discounted to their present value in the valuation formula.

As discussed above, one can argue that political risk analysis and interest rate analysis cover many—if not all—of the same issues. Differences in income taxes are incorporated into both the political risk

---

[14] Frank K. Reilly, *Investment Analysis and Portfolio Management*, 2d ed. (Philadelphia: The Dryden Press, 1985), p. 513–514.

and interest rate differential methods. Income taxes are a matter of government policy. For example, in Germany there are special regional taxes and surcharges; the income tax aspect of a discount rate is not that complex. An issue regarded as more complex, and often with less empirical data available, is estimating the appropriate equity risk premium to apply in each of the political risk and interest rate differential methods.

Applying Risk Premiums

The typical U.S.-based WACC incorporates a cost of debt and a cost of equity. When dealing in foreign countries, the analyst may add an incremental risk premium to address the results of his or her political risk and interest rate differential analysis. The risk premium to apply is not typically available from a text or a published equity risk premium source. Rather, it can be estimated on the basis of the comparative analysis of political risk and interest rates of the subject foreign country versus the United States.

Stated alternatively, the use of U.S.-based risk premium data requires some adjustment to acknowledge different risks in other countries. A typical business valuation assignment presumes that it is a long-term investment, and long-term normalized returns may be the most appropriate for use as the benchmark. This is why analysts typically use a 70+ year cycle for Ibbotson Associates data rather than picking the most recent year's equity return in the market and considering that to be a proxy to extrapolate over all future years. It is noteworthy that the objective of estimating a return threshold is to consider what we know about investor behavior in the United States as well as globally. Also consider that equity risk premium data from the United States are a good starting point, since they are readily available. However, the dynamics of foreign countries and their own struggle to move from emerging markets to developed countries cannot be ignored. Neither can one ignore that many emerging countries are going from survival to revival.

In addition, the observed risk premium from the study of a developing country's securities yield versus that of the United States will include the survival and revival phases of that individual country. To ignore the swings in risk premiums—from the skimpy risk premiums offered in easy-money periods to the fat risk premiums offered in times of financial crisis—may distort what a reasonable normal cost of capital should be for a long-term hold strategy. Furthermore, to ignore the swings in apparent equity risk premiums in developing countries' securities can result in a discount rate that inadequately compensates for the special default risk associated with developing countries.

This theory borrows from the accepted methods of developing present value discount rates in the United States. In the United States, normalized equity risk premiums are applied rather than using the latest year or the forecasted years' total return from some broad market index. This theory also recognizes that equity returns for developed countries, such as the United States, provide compensation to investors for risks inherent in the subject developed country. The challenge is to compensate investors adequately for the added risks inherent in developing countries where there is a new level of risk to account for: political risk. This political risk generally coincides with observed interest rate differentials.

The results of a political risk analysis and interest rate differential analysis may reveal that there are significant risks above that of a U.S. entity. Simply stated, an incremental adjustment should be considered to recognize the observed incremental country risk. The adjustment process is discussed further below.

Stage of Development

If the valuation objective relates to a foreign investment in a developed country, the discussion above concerning emerging markets and high-yield bonds has less relevance. The analyst can use the 70+-year Ibbotson Associates data and adjust the discount rate for the mere yield spread difference between the developed countries' government bonds and that of the United States. Taking this simple yield differential methodology and combining it with a recognition of country-specific income tax rates in the development of the WACC completes the analysis of a base discount rate for a foreign investment in a developed country.

The due diligence investigation for a developed country still includes a political risk analysis to confirm that there is no significant political risk issue. Next, the analysis focuses on the interest rate differential and the income tax rate. For a developing country or an emerging market country, the analysis includes due diligence for political risk as well as for interest rate differential. The analyst should recognize that political risk analysis and interest rate analysis are not additive but are parallel processes. In addition, both of these analyses should be performed in conjunction with the income tax rate analysis.

For an emerging market, the analyst typically uses a two-pronged approach: (1) a political risk and income tax rate analysis and (2) an interest rate differential and income tax rate analysis. The analyst correlates the indicated discount rates from both of these methodologies and can select an appropriate weighting to apply to both the political risk and the interest rate driven methods. Facts and circumstances will indicate what weight to use and considerations will include what country is being analyzed and more specifically what quality of data is available for analysis. In the end, the analyst should step back, look over the numbers, and decide if it all makes sense.

To expand on the concept of different strata being present in the arena of country analysis, a review of several thoughts from the publication *Eastern Europe—Credit Analysis Around the World* is provided.[15]

---

[15] "Eastern Europe," *Credit Analysis Around the World* (Charlottesville, VA: Association for Investment Management and Research, February 10, 1998).

According to the publication, Eastern European sovereign credits can be divided into two tiers: (1) the high-quality Tier 1 and (2) the low-quality Tier 2. The Tier 1 countries' sovereign debt is investment grade. Spreads are as tight as 125 to 150 basis points above U.S. Treasury securities for the Czech Republic and Hungary, but as wide as 375 basis points for Croatia. The Croatian yield spread reflects continued uncertainty regarding political issues and the Dayton Peace Accords.

Tier 1 countries have some checks and balances in place on government abuse of power and possess relatively advanced government institutions. Both Poland and Hungary have voted communists back into power, and the market-oriented economic policy has improved under the new regimes. Tier 1 countries generally have instituted privatization programs. The success of these privatization programs has been correlated with whether the country employed voucher privatization or a cash mechanism. Most of the problems have occurred or are occurring in countries that used the voucher route, since ownership was too widely distributed, discouraging reforms or efficiencies in companies from taking place.

Tier 2 countries possess credit ratings in the *B* range with spread differentials that are much more significant, such as presented in Exhibit 2–1.

Tier 2 countries have government institutions that are not well developed. Checks and balances on government power are virtually nonexistent, and creditors are reliant on powerful core groups in central banks or finance ministries to solve problems. The Russian democracy has been described as crony capitalism. Political forces in Tier 2 countries can easily threaten an economic reform, and the fact that armed forces play a major role in politics has a dramatic impact on credit markets. Finally, the use of fixed or near-fixed exchange rates to lower inflation, which is prevalent in Tier 2 countries, has the impact of stressing the economic system to make radical internal changes to justify the peg.

Exhibit 2–1

Tier 2 Counties

Country	Yield Spread[a]
Bulgaria	+670
Moldavia	+650
Romania	+400
Russia[b]	+780
Turkey	+400

[a] Spread over U.S. Treasury securities (basis points).
[b] Before 1997–1998's Asian crisis and carryover to other emerging markets.
SOURCE: *Eastern Europe—Credit Analysis around the World* (Charlottesville, VA: Association for Investment Management and Research, February 10, 1998), p. 21.

Economic Dependencies

Another dimension to consider in terms of developing countries—or economies that are more prone to volatility—is their reliance on commodities (such as oil, aluminum, and forest products) for a significant portion of their gross domestic product. Developing economies can face a double whammy from (1) the effects of lower market prices on their exports and (2) the flight away from their currency as investors shun emerging markets. Some governments may face increased pressure for reforms, as a result of commodity-related weakness in their economies. Continued price weakness in oil prices, for example, could have produced enormous destabilization in the oil exporting countries, such as Saudi Arabia, Indonesia, and Venezuela.

Mexico is also vulnerable to petroleum-related products. According to the *Economist*,[16] although Mexican oil exports account for only one-tenth of all exports, the government still relies heavily on Petroleos Mexicanos (Pemex), the inefficient state-owned oil monopoly. Petroleum provides nearly 40 percent of the Mexican government's revenues. Changes in world oil prices combined with regional weather and economic conditions can disrupt the flow of cash and derail the Mexican economy because of its heavy reliance on oil.

Besides their dependency on commodity-related industries, developing countries are also characterized by their relatively smaller market size. "If something turns negative in a relatively small market, you won't be able to get out," observed Jaideep Khanna, manager of the Morgan Stanley Africa Investment Fund.[17] Khanna was referring to currency risk in small economies, where no derivatives markets exist and where traditional hedging strategies are impossible. A market's illiquidity can translate into it taking a long time for that particular market to reach a critical mass. As in the case of a thinly traded stock on U.S. markets, lack of liquidity may make it impossible to make a quick exit in a downturn. In Africa, for example, as in most emerging markets, the economic and political climate can change suddenly and drastically. The terrorist attack by Islamic militants on tourists visiting Queen Hatshepsut's temple in Egypt in the fall of 1997 triggered an 11 percent decline on the Cairo Stock Exchange for the fourth quarter of 1997.

The economies of Africa and the Middle East (including Turkey and Pakistan) tend to be based on resources and reliant on exports of primary goods to the developed world.[18] The Saudi Arabian situation is a good illustration of reliance on a key commodity—oil—indicative of the six Arab Gulf countries (Saudi Arabia, Kuwait, United Arab Emirates, Bahrain, Qatar, and Oman) that make up the Gulf Cooperation Council (GCC). No GCC citizen pays income tax or sales tax, and typically only foreign businesses pay a corporate income tax. Further, these governments display a reluctance to impose any income taxes on their citizens, even as oil prices sink to severe lows.

[16] "Mexico's Economy—Miracle or Mirage?"*Economist*, April 11, 1998.
[17] Deepak Gopinath, "Taking the Road Less Traveled," *Institutional Investor*, March 1998, p. 174.
[18] "Africa and the Middle East," *Credit Analysis Around the World* (Charlottesville, VA: Association for Investment Management and Research, February 10, 1998).

GCC government behavior is a result of an implicit social arrangement whereby the ruling family is granted broad authority politically. However, the ruling family is expected to provide a standard of living for the population. When oil prices were high, this role was no problem. In addition, citizens developed an expectation of well-being, which provided rulers comfort in the longevity of their position. But in less prosperous times, the inability of the government to maintain the status quo may lead to perceptions of government mismanagement and create uncertainty in the political situation. This occurs as citizens begin to voice discontent and ask for a greater role and voice in government.

Another country that is regarded as pivotal to continued world stability is China. Although China has experienced a balance of payments surplus and would appear to have no reason to devalue its currency, China may devalue its currency to maintain competitiveness with other Asian countries. China may not be known for traditional capitalism. Rather, China is known for a government run by a core group of leaders who may be interested in maintaining their political position. In addition, the government may have a dilemma on its hands with potential increasing unemployment, exacerbated by the Asian crisis and past fiscal mismanagement.

In summary, risk analysis should be performed with awareness of the world in which we live and the potential uncertainties that exist for a downside scenario that could translate into an economic loss in value for an investor.

Summary of International Cost of Capital Theory

The general steps associated with the discount rate development for a foreign investment entail (1) the creation of a base WACC using U.S. parameters and (2) adjusting the base WACC for the subject-specific factors:

* Country-specific income tax rate
* Interest rate yield structure
* Political risk adjustment factor

Once a U.S.-based WACC is developed, the following two methods are used to estimate a base WACC for the subject:

1. Method A—adjust U.S. WACC for country income tax rate and add political risk factor, if applicable.
2. Method B—adjust U.S. WACC for country income tax rate and interest rate differential to the United States.

If the political risk analysis indicates that there is no significant difference, then only Method B, the country income tax rate and yield differential method, may be applied.

Forecast Considerations

A related topic includes acknowledging (1) whether the present value calculation will be in U.S. or local currency and (2) whether the currency will be stated on a nominal or real (constant dollar) basis. In the most simplistic sense, depending upon the purpose of and audience for the appraisal, the currency selected might appropriately be addressed to the audience, given the availability of data. For example, if it's a French investment and it's for French income tax authorities, and if the data are available in French francs, then a valuation performed in French francs seems most appropriate. On the other hand, if it's a French investment for U.S. income tax purposes and if the data are available in French francs and U.S. dollars, the analyst may prepare the forecast in U.S. dollars as the basis for the analysis.

Nominal or Real?

One simple but very important distinction should be made in developing a discount rate: Is the forecast prepared with (nominal) or without (real or constant) inflation? Nominal rates reflect future expectations of inflation. Forecasts developed without inflation warrant a discount rate adjustment to eliminate the anticipated inflation rate from the discount rate. Therefore, with respect to nominal versus real discount rates, if the forecast is nominal, then development of the discount rate as discussed above is applicable.

On the other hand, if the forecast is on a real basis, then the developed discount rate needs a further refinement to adjust it to a real basis using the traditional conversion formula—that is, where the nominal rate equals $[(1 + \text{real rate}) \times (1 + \text{inflation rate})] - 1$. As an example, if the real rate is 3 percent and the expected inflation rate is 8 percent, then the required nominal rate would approximate 11 percent. This result is calculated as follows: $[(1 + 0.03) \times (1 + 0.08)] - 1 = 1.1124 - 1 = 0.1124$, or approximately 11 percent. The analyst may also apply this mathematical formula to estimate a real rate using an assumed inflation rate and a nominal rate.

Currency Exchange Risk

It is noteworthy that in the above discussion we did not make a specific adjustment for foreign exchange risk. The reason is relatively simple: Interest rates taken from the marketplace are forward-looking and include the expectation of inflation. Other things constant, inflation will cause a currency to depreciate on the exchange market. "Purchasing power parity, which has been shown in modern times to have exerted a negative impact on the German mark, the Swiss franc, and the Japanese yen, states the changes in exchange rates over time should reflect differences in national inflation rates ... Countries with relatively high inflation rates see their currencies weaken and vice versa."[19]

---

[19]Michael R. Rosenberg, "Fundamental and Technical Analysis in Currency Forecasting," *Global Bond Management* (Charlottesville, VA: Association for Investment Management and Research, 1997), p.17.

Purchasing power parity borrows from a general theme of regression to the mean. For example, Japan has experienced periods with an extremely strong yen and periods with a much weaker yen. An overvalued currency leads to a significant decline in domestic economic activity brought about by a loss in competitiveness and a deterioration in trade. An overvalued currency makes a country's exports expensive, and it permits cheap imports to flood the market, causing a trade deficit. An overvalued currency effectively prices a country out of the global marketplace, making its goods too expensive to outsiders. Overvalued currency also makes the country a victim for rampant lower-priced imports. Since the country's productive capacities are underutilized, the economy falls into a recession, forcing monetary policy to be extremely easy. This in turn leads to a decline in the overvalued currency.

An easy monetary policy generates an excess supply of the country's currency in the world marketplace. When supply exceeds demand, the price of the country's currency in relation to other currencies goes down. So the typical boom and bust cycle occurs in the currency marketplace and follows the traditional "regression to the mean" theme.

As a country experiences a trade deficit, more and more of its currency goes out into the marketplace, creating an oversupply and hence a weakening currency. Investors react to the weaker currency negatively. In addition, governments in such a situation typically compensate by raising internal interest rates to attract investors back to the currency and back to investments in the country. Higher interest rates restrain domestic demand and eventually lead to reduced trade deficits.

Because of the rapidly deteriorating situation in Asia, the International Monetary Fund (IMF) updated its October 1997 "World Economic Outlook." A rebound in Asia starting in late 1998 was predicted, based on the pattern of the 1995 currency crisis in Mexico, where, after a deep but brief recession, growth resumed in 1996. The IMF outlook demonstrates the use of *comparable country analysis* in developing discount rates for emerging market countries. The analysis relies on analogies of risk relationships in the marketplace to build up reasonable arguments for a particular project's required rate of return.

The linkage between interest rates, inflation, and currency movements is strong. There is a linkage between a given rate of inflation and the change in the exchange rate necessary to maintain international equilibrium.[20] This relationship is the reason that all participating countries in the Eurodollar maintain minimum trade deficits as a condition of membership in the European Monetary Union (EMU). Stable trade balances breed stable currencies. Not surprisingly, countries that are not as developed and that have more economic instability, more trade imbalances, more perceived political risk, and more inflation have currencies that are under attack.

According to the economic theorem of the law of one price, if there is no variation in the relative prices of goods or services, then the rate of

---

[20] Shapiro, *International Corporate Finance*, 2d ed., p. 111.

change in the exchange rate should equal the difference between the inflation rate of the two countries. In a study of domestic inflation and domestic interest rates for 47 countries over the period 1977–1981, inflation was found to explain most of the difference in nominal interest rates. [21]

Clearly the issue of currency or exchange risk is worth considering. "Currency risk is usually the largest component of bond risk in international bond markets."[22] And currency behavior parallels economic health. The goal of meeting strict Maastricht Treaty criteria for membership in the EMU is credited with participant countries' improved fiscal responsibility. The yields of prospective EMU members have converged steadily, and this is especially apparent in formerly high-yielding countries, such as Spain and Italy. Smaller countries, such as Ireland, are realizing improved yields as a result of improved liquidity in the markets.

At December 1997, prospective EMU countries' long-term interest rates had converged to within about 40 basis points. As one credit analyst put it, "The EMU represents one of the most important economic developments of this century." Nevertheless, yield spreads will continue to reflect concerns about credit quality and political issues.

With this theoretical discussion as a backdrop, let's now turn to a discussion of the application of this theory to development of a present value discount rate for a foreign investment.

Application

The discounted cash flow (DCF) method, which uses the present value of future cash flows to value an investment, may be the primary method available in the valuation of projects in developing countries. Availability of reasonable publicly traded guideline companies may be difficult if not impossible. U.S. companies may prove useful for estimating the normal capital structure for the subject industry. Adjustment to U.S. market multiples may be necessary to account for the issues discussed above, namely income taxes, interest rate differentials, and political risk.

For purposes of this illustration, a DCF method will be used as the sole valuation methodology. A method that considers key economic issues and is practical to apply is desirable. If the estimated cash flows are denominated in the local currency, a discount rate that has been developed considering local country income tax, interest rate, and political risk issues is applied (similar to Methods A and B described above). The resulting DCF analysis will provide a project value in local currency,

[21] Tom Copeland, Tim Koller, and Jack Murrin, *Measuring and Managing the Value of Companies*, 2d ed. (New York: John Wiley & Sons, 1994), p. 358.
[22] "EMU and the Bond Markets of Western Europe," *Credit Analysis Around the World* (Charlottesville, VA: Association for Investment Management and Research, February 10, 1998), p. 11.

and the present value of the project's cash flow can be converted into U.S. dollars using the spot exchange rate. The spot exchange rate is easily obtained from a variety of publications, such as the *Wall Street Journal* and the *Financial Times*.

Another DCF method involves use of forecasted exchange rates. In practice, this analysis is less direct and more cumbersome, since the analyst should obtain forecasted exchange rates for each forecast year. In the DCF analysis using forecasted exchange rates, the appropriate present value discount rate is a U.S.-based discount rate. Here the forecasted exchange rate considers the elements of interest rate and political risk. Arguably, the specific country's income tax rates should be considered in either DCF analysis.

Finally, some analysts feel that the political risk adjustment should be in the cash flows. This method seems to be more cumbersome and lacks clarity on how to consider interest rate and inflation differences. These factors are arguably part of the overall story of political risk issues, as discussed above. The use of adjustments to the cash flow, rather than to the cost of capital, may be considered by multinational companies that choose one global risk threshold rate.

Global Hurdle Rates

The development of an international cost of capital was discussed in the periodical *CFO*,[23] regarding connecting international hurdle rates (discount rates) to investor expectations. The article highlighted several salient considerations to developing a discount rate:

- "You need to earn a return that's based on the risk inherent in the local jurisdiction." The article cited how consistently difficult it is to earn a profit in Brazil, for example, with its various periods of economic turmoil.
- To construct hurdle rates one can "look at the risk differential between countries and mark up the target returns relative to the home country."
- Multinationals with a global perspective are likely to set their hurdle rate in the foreign markets on the basis of the perceived specific foreign risk, but recognize a relationship between the foreign market and the home market.
- A methodology that considers forward-looking data and trends versus backward-looking data is preferred.
- Multinational companies may not want to ignore the impact of diversification when setting discount rate hurdles for foreign investments. Although country-specific risk is recognized, investing simultaneously in many foreign markets will diversify the company's overall risk.
- Multinationals may have an edge over a domestic investor, in that the global company has a diversification benefit.

---

[23] Randy Myers, "GM Remeasures the Bar in Latin America," *CFO: The Magazine for Senior Financial Executives,* May 1998, pp. 77–81.

These highlights from the *CFO* article lend support to a discount rate development methodology that considers market interest rate differentials and political risk analysis, both of which are forward-looking. The article also introduces an issue of diversification into the rate-setting process. This diversification idea is not novel and draws upon modern portfolio theory (MPT) such as the Markowitz model of an efficient frontier.[24] In this model, using computer analysis, an analyst can construct from a universe of stocks a portfolio that offers maximum return at minimum risk. The model inherently recognizes the relationship or covariance of individual stocks. The notion that adding foreign investments to one's asset allocation strategy to lower overall risk is not new. The distinction that should be made is that each individual investment's value is still based on its unique return potential, and the portfolio perspective is an aggregation of individual investments.

The use of multinational companies in a portfolio approach to investing rests upon MPT. One of the principles of MPT is to broaden the universe of security types. With the broader universe, there is a greater opportunity for security types to move out of phase with another. The end result is to create a portfolio based on a global frontier. That portfolio possesses superior return capability at the same risk level.[25]

Most consultants and business valuation analysts approach rate development by considering fair market value and country-specific elements of political risk, interest rate differentials, and income tax rates. However, many multinational companies have taken on the portfolio approach to rate setting, using one global threshold rate. This illustrates the need to evaluate rate setting from a base of facts and circumstances. The application of a global rate suggests the need to consider specific country issues, such as inflation, currency devaluation, turmoil, and taxation in the specific project's cash flows.

An analysis from Standard & Poor's Micropal, a Boston fund tracker, indicated that the correlation between the returns of the international index and the S&P 500 has increased sharply, particularly since 1995. Using a statistical measure of correlation, Micropal discovered that the correlation between the international index and the S&P 500 was 0.64.[26] This correlation is nearly triple a July 1997 correlation measure of 0.23.

While some multinational companies may have adopted a global portfolio approach to discount rate development, relying upon added diversification via a global perspective, recent data suggest that the world is getting smaller. These data also suggest that the diversification aspects of global investing may have significantly decreased.

Considering specific facts and circumstances in valuation of investments is consistent with the fundamental notion of "to whom and for what," which needs to be addressed in the business valuation. Whether

---

[24] Harry Markowitz, "Portfolio Selection," *Journal of Finance*, March 1952, pp. 77–91.

[25] James L. Farrell, Jr., "Portfolio Theory," *Investing and Risk Management,* Vol. I (New York: McGraw-Hill, 1990), pp. 328–339.

[26] Based on the August 26, 1998, issue of the *Wall Street Journal.*

the circumstantial issues are considered in the discount rate or the projected cash flows is a matter of judgment, practicality, and circumstances.

As an illustration of how consideration of facts and circumstances can potentially impact a discount rate, consider an investment evaluation in Mexico under two scenarios: (1) a domestic (U.S.) producer and (2) a multinational producer. The U.S. producer would likely evaluate the investment in Mexico by emphasizing the specific Mexican country issues: political risk, interest rate differential, and income taxes. The multinational producer, with an existing diversified portfolio of operations, may consider only its global threshold rate, since it already has the critical mass in its portfolio to mitigate any Mexican country issues.

The diversified company may choose a lower risk rate because of its specific facts and circumstances, which involve other investments that possess a negative correlation with the Mexican investment. On the other hand, the domestic investor may view the investment as neutral or positively correlating with the Mexican investment. If only these two investors were bidding on the particular asset as potential buyers, it would appear that the global company would offer the higher price. This conclusion assumes that all other things are equal, such as the cash flows forecasted for the investment. This difference in price may be construed as a premium for control, or investment value differential, and it may reflect the different buyers' existing economies of scale, including their cost of capital.

Lack of Perfect Data

There is a notion that estimating discount rates for foreign investments is not an exact science but an art.[27] And the fact that emerging markets require assessment of additional risk components not usually considered in traditional investments[28] needs to be emphasized. In practice, application of sound judgment is the key factor in estimating foreign investment discount rates.

"Financial markets in developing economies are often thin or nonexistent. If no long-term government bond yields are quoted, you need to come up with a substitute. Even if there is a quoted yield, it may not be default-free, as one would usually assume for the debt of developed nations."[29] On the other hand, in developed countries, where government bonds have little or no chance of default, a relatively straightforward comparison between two developed countries' government bonds can be undertaken, provided the duration or time horizon of each bond is similar. For developed countries, inflation largely explains differences in exchange rates. To a lesser extent, the balance of trade and differences in productivity also matter.[30]

---

[27] Copeland, Koller, and Murrin, *Measuring and Managing the Value of Companies*, 2d ed., p. 407.

[28] Roy C. Smith and Ingo Walter, "Risks and Rewards in Emerging Market Investments," *Journal of Applied Corporate Finance,* Fall 1997, pp. 8–17.

[29] Copeland, Koller, and Murrin, *Measuring and Managing the Value of Companies*, 2d ed., p. 404.

[30] Ibid., p. 395.

But for developing countries, an element of default can be present and significant. If government bond yields of the subject developing country are not present, a substitute may be useful. In such situations, government bond yields of other developing countries with similar country risk ratings may be considered. The key is not to consider just one method in estimating a discount rate. This is especially true where data are not abundant. Rather, it is important to work with the variety of market data that exist, including the ever-increasing amount from the Internet or searchable texts, to "pull" risk/return relationships from the market data. For instance, the market return for default risk can be observed by analyzing the interest rate differential between AAA and BAA rated corporate bonds. This yield spread would appear to be a minimal return for a relatively minor amount of perceived default risk. On the other hand, the yield spreads between AAA corporate bonds and high-yield bonds may offer a more significant measure of market-based return required for a more material perceived risk of default.

If the analyst can obtain the government bond yield for a subject developing country, but denominated in dollars, the risk of currency fluctuation has not been considered. An increment of return can be added to the dollar-denominated government bond yield, adjusted for the appropriate time horizon, to consider the currency risk issue. This incremental return could be based on a country's transfer risk differential as compared with the United States, where such transfer risk (as presented by *Country Forecasts*)[31] includes the currency translation issue. Another consideration may involve recognizing that loss in economic value due to currency devaluation is a form of default. Therefore, the analyst may apply market-based default risk data, as discussed above.

Data Sources

Political Risk Data

Political Risk Services, based in Syracuse, New York, publishes *Country Forecasts* (315–431–0511). Besides issuing semiannual country forecasts for all covered countries, the company also provides monthly analyses on a fee basis.

Other sources of political risk data include *Institutional Investor* (212–224–3300) and an occasional edition of *World Trade* (305–358–8373).

The political risk data typically involve various grades assigned to different countries, but no indication of an incremental risk premium is provided. That is where professional judgment comes into play! First, the analyst should distinguish a developed country from a developing country. Using the Political Risk Services rating system, for instance, the analyst may view a developed country risk of turmoil as being "low"

---

[31] Coplin and O'Leary, *Country Forecasts*, July 1997.

while developing countries typically are rated "moderate" or "high" for turmoil. If there is not a material difference between the U.S. benchmark and the country under study, the analyst may not need to analyze political risk further. However, when differences are material, such as when risk of turmoil is moderate or high, the analyst can develop a numeric rating scheme that coincides with the published political risk data.

An example of a framework is to assign a judgment-based 300 basis points for every grade difference in the "investment" category. The investment category may be viewed as most representative of the risk criteria for making an investment. For example, if the United States is rated *A* and the subject country is rated *B*, an incremental risk premium of 300 basis points would be added to the cost of capital. Since the political rating system includes "+" and "−", these can be assigned 100 basis points, such that the difference between *A* and *B*− is 400 basis points. Political Risk Services publishes its ratings on an 18-month and five-year forward-looking basis. The five-year outlook may be most representative, since the typical investment is presumed to have a long-term horizon.

Interest Rate Data

The most common interest rate source is the *Economist*, which includes government bond rates for developed countries and short-term interest rates on developing countries. For developed countries, when a government bond is not available, the analyst may extrapolate a rate on the basis of expected inflation, using inflation rates from Political Risk Services.

Another useful source for interest rate data and yield spreads to U.S. Treasuries is the International Capital Markets section of the *Financial Times*. Data presented in the *Financial Times* include 10-year benchmark spreads (spread versus U.S. Treasury bonds) of developed countries and emerging market spreads, categorized by Europe, Latin America, Asia, Africa/Middle East, and Brady Bonds. A sample of recent rates for emerging market bonds is presented in Exhibit 2–2.[32] In order to use these data properly, the analyst would consider matching maturities and reviewing the spreads over a period of time to obtain a normalized spread. In addition, the analyst would consider if the bonds are denominated in local currency or some other currency, such as the U.S. dollar. In that case, an adjustment for currency risk would be a further consideration.

From the above data, assuming that the only difference between the Mexican and Argentinean government bonds and Brady Bonds (see below) is whether they are quoted in U.S. dollars or local currency, for the same respective countries, the apparent yield spread related to currency is 324 and 341 basis points, respectively.

---

[32] From the September 3, 1998, *Financial Times*.

Exhibit 2–2

Recent Rates for Emerging Market Bonds

	Coupon Rate	S&P Rating	Bond Yield	Spread vs. U.S.
Europe				
Croatia	7.000	BBB–	9.24	+ 4.33
Poland	7.125	BBB–	8.15	+ 3.17
Russia	10.000	CCC	40.83	+35.78
Latin America				
Argentina	9.750	BB	13.25	+ 7.92
Brazil	10.125	BB–	16.43	+11.10
Mexico	11.500	BB	12.47	+ 7.15
Asia				
China	7.750	BBB+	9.11	+ 4.08
Philippines	8.750	BB+	13.42	+ 8.24
Thailand	7.750	BBB–	12.92	+ 7.87
Africa/Middle East				
Lebanon	9.125	BB–	8.73	+ 3.79
South Africa	8.375	BB+	9.50	+ 4.47
Turkey	10.000	B	12.98	+ 7.93
Brady Bonds				
Argentina	5.750	BB	9.79	+ 4.51
Brazil	5.000	BB–	14.22	+ 9.06
Mexico	6.250	BB	9.13	+ 3.91
Venezuela	6.750	B+	11.96	+ 6.72

For developing or emerging market countries, the best source is probably the Internet. The following Web sites have proved to be helpful in the past:

- www.latinolink.com
- www.bradybonds.com

Besides these two sites, it would be wise to employ a variety of search engines. The Brady Bonds site is extremely useful.

Brady Bonds

Search engine terms including the phrases "Brady Bonds" and "emerging market bonds" as well as the country name are good starting points for reference. Brady Bonds were named after Nicholas Brady, who helped design the Brady Bond program when he was secretary of the U.S. Treasury. Brady Bonds were created to help developing nations restructure billions of dollars of defaulted or devalued commercial bank debt in the wake of the Latin debt crisis of the 1980s. The bonds were easier to trade or sell than the loan papers.

By many measures, the Brady program has been a success. The bond markets of Latin America, practically nonexistent in the 1980s, are now among the most active in the world. Between 1993 and 1996, volume of trading in all developing nation debt more than doubled to over $5 trillion per year. Panama's new 30-year bonds yielded just 2.5 percentage points over the 30-year U.S. Treasuries,[33] compared with 5.65 percentage points for Panama's Brady Bonds in July 1996. In approximately only a few years, the Brady Bond market may suffer an eventual demise as $60 billion worth of Brady Bonds are repurchased.[34]

Venezuela's new 30-year bonds were sold at a yield that was just 3.25 percent above the U.S. 30-year Treasury bond.[35] The general trend away from Brady Bonds is likely to follow participant countries' upgrade to investment grade status.

The important thing to remember about Brady Bonds is that they are issued on a number of bases, such as being denominated in dollars or in local currency as well as being guaranteed by the United States from a collateral point of view in interest and/or principal payments. A Brady Bond that has collateral-like guarantees on both principal and interest does not have the full political risk associated with it. Therefore, it is not a great instrument for determining a reasonable yield differential for cost of capital analysis, especially if it is denominated in dollars. The best instrument for analysis is one that is denominated in local currency and has no collateral guarantees in interest and principal.

International Equity Risk Premiums

Another source of data to consider in making an adjustment for country equity risk is Ibbotson Associates' *International Equity Risk Premia*. The 1998 Annual Report published by Ibbotson Associates contains equity risk premium data for a variety of time horizons, such as 1961–1997, 1970–1997, 1978–1997, and 1988–1997. The number of countries covered by each time series varies, with the broadest coverage including 16 countries and starting in 1970. The scope is predominately developed countries in Europe, with additional coverage of Japan, Australia, and New Zealand.

The following additional comments pertain to the international equity risk premium (IERP) study by Ibbotson:

- The IERP is calculated by subtracting the average income return on a riskless asset from the average stock market total return.
- U.S. Treasury securities are assumed to be the riskless asset. However, caution is recommended in that non-U.S. Treasury securities may

[33] Thomas T. Vogel Jr., "Venezuela's Global Bond Issue Is a Big Hit," *Wall Street Journal*, September 22, 1997, p. A18.
[34] Ibid.
[35] Ibid.

possess some default risk that is not considered in the Ibbotson Associates analysis.

- The limitations of data used by Ibbotson may impact comparability of the results.
- IERPs are provided in local currency and U.S. dollars terms.
- Stock market returns are those given by Morgan Stanley Capital International.

Ibbotson Associates recommends that the IERP be calculated using longer time periods. Ibbotson is in the process of obtaining more historical data. To be included in this study, a country must have at least five years of quality equity and risk-free returns.

Comparable Countries

If the analyst cannot find interest rates for a particular country, he or she can develop a comparable universe of countries with similar risk profiles by studying Political Risk Services ratings as well as the inflation outlook and respective government bond rates or yield spreads of these comparable countries.

Country Betas

If individual country betas can be obtained, they can be assimilated into a discount rate development project. However, it would not be wise to add on country-specific beta information as an additional variable. Rather, the analyst should regard it as a substitute or third approach to correlate with Methods A and B, since the country beta would likely overlap interest rate and political risk issues.

Income Tax Rates

Analysts may obtain income tax rates directly from an accounting firm or through their clients. A worldwide corporate income tax summary should be requested. As always, these income tax rates should be reviewed with the client so as to interpret them correctly—especially in certain countries, such as Germany, which have regional income tax structures as well as surcharges.

Computer Models

The starting point to any foreign discount rate development may involve development of a U.S.-based WACC using a traditional WACC model. From that, depending upon the complexity of the assignment, a custom model can be developed to handle Methods A and B or just Method B, if that is the case. When the due diligence investigation reveals no significant political risk differences, and thus Method A is not applicable, the analyst may use a spreadsheet feature called a sensitivity table. Using a two-dimensional sensitivity for the variables—income tax rate and country government bond rate—the analyst may develop a model for any number of countries very efficiently. In this model, it is necessary to impose a linkage between the risk-free rate used in the capital asset pricing model and the cost of debt used in the weighted average cost of capital. Otherwise the model will not work correctly. The relationship of the risk-free rate to the indicated cost of debt for the base U.S. WACC warrants further investigation in order to make the formulas work correctly.

According to Ibbotson Associates, for the period 1926 through 1996, the spread between government bonds and corporate bonds was 60 basis points. This should be viewed as a starting point only. Only after a careful review of the appropriate corporate cost of debt for the subject company can the analyst develop a relationship and an actual differential between the concluded cost of debt and the U.S. government bond rate.

With the above theoretical background and application, the following sample report discussion is provided using a Mexican investment project as an example.

Sample Report Section—Discount Rate Development

Overview

A WACC was developed for XCORP for an investment in Mexico. This analysis took into consideration specific country income tax rates, interest rate structures, and political risk factors.

The WACC is the appropriate cost of capital to apply to a debt-free net cash flow stream. This is because it considers the cost of equity and the after-tax cost of debt, weighted by an appropriate capital structure for the industry in which the business operates.

Five publicly traded companies in the XCORP industry were studied. On the basis of a review of their debt and equity components, a capital structure of 60 percent equity and 40 percent debt was considered appropriate for the business, factoring in the cyclical nature of the industry and capital intensiveness of the business.

Base U.S. WACC

The general method used to estimate a WACC for XCORP began with development of a U.S.-based WACC.

The steps taken in the discount rate development were as follows:

1. The cost of equity or required return on equity was estimated using the capital asset pricing model (CAPM).
2. The current yields on appropriate income securities were analyzed for an indication of the cost of debt.
3. The indicated costs of equity and debt were proportionately weighted, using the appropriate capital structure for an indication of the cost of capital or present value discount rate.

4. The cost of equity—or the required return on equity—was estimated using the CAPM. CAPM is based on the premise that an industry's capitalization rate is equal to the riskless rate of return plus an equity risk premium. The equity risk premium is developed by analyzing the historical relationship between (1) the return required by investors in a particular industry and (2) the average return required by investors in the market as a whole.

Application of the CAPM to estimate the cost of equity involves the following steps:

1. Estimate the riskless rate (R_f), which is the rate of return required by investors in virtually risk-free income securities. The basis for measuring this rate is typically the yield on government notes and bonds. As of the valuation date, that rate approximated 6.89 percent.
2. Estimate the beta coefficient (ß), which relates a specific industry's risk to the average market risk. The betas for the five companies studied range from 1.0 to 1.2, with a median of 1.0. On the basis of this analysis and considering the nature of the subject company, a beta of 1.0 was selected for use in the calculation.
3. Estimate the equity risk premium (R_p), which is the average return the overall market investor requires less the risk-free return. Extensive studies, such as those by Ibbotson Associates, indicate that the equity risk premium has historically averaged about 7.0 percent.

Employing the above, the analyst can estimate the cost of equity (k_e)—the equity return required by investors in a particular industry—as follows:

$$k_e = R_f + ß(R_p)$$
$$= 6.89 + 1.0(7.0)$$
$$= 6.89 + 7.0$$
$$= 13.89$$

The result of the foregoing calculations is an indication of the return required by investors, based on the guideline companies studied.

The cost of debt (k_d) is based on consideration of the industrial bond yields of the five guideline companies studied, which ranged from 7.25 percent to 8.4 percent (Standard & Poor's AAA to BB ratings) at the valuation date. The concluded cost of debt was 7.31 percent, an amount that is tax-deductible for corporations. Income taxes (t) are assumed payable by U.S. corporations at 38.25 percent.

The cost of capital was then calculated by using the weighted average of the cost of equity and the cost of debt from the average capital structure of the guideline companies. The average capital structure was

40 percent debt and 60 percent equity. On the basis of the foregoing, the unadjusted WACC or discount rate considered appropriate for the United States for XCORP was calculated to be 10 percent, as follows:

Cost of Debt	+	Cost of Equity
Percent debt [$k_d \times (1-t)$]	+	Percent equity (k_e)
[0.40 (7.31 × 0.6175)]	+	[0.60(13.89)]
1.81	+	8.33
	=	10.14%
	=	10% (rounded)

Methodology

The general steps associated with the present value discount rate development for XCORP included the creation of a base WACC using U.S. parameters, and the adjustment of the base WACC for the subject-specific factors:

- Country-specific income tax rate
- Interest rate yield structure
- Political risk adjustment factor

Once a U.S.–based WACC was developed, the following two methods were used to estimate a base WACC for the subject:

1. Method A—adjust U.S. WACC for country income tax rate and add political risk factor, if applicable.
2. Method B—adjust U.S. WACC for country income tax rate and interest rate yield differential to United States.

Method A—Political Risk and Specific Tax Rate Adjustment.
Our political risk analysis, based on the January 1997 *Country Forecasts* published by Political Risk Services, indicated that Mexico, as measured by investment and country turmoil, was more risky than the United States. This conclusion is confirmed by the following comparison using the five-year forecast for both countries:

Political Risk Analysis		
Country	Turmoil	Investment
United States	Low	*A*
Mexico	Moderate	*B–*

Political Risk Services (PRS) assigns grades from *A+* to *F* for transfer, investment, and export categories. For purposes of evaluation, the investment rating category was considered the most relevant. Numeric rankings from 1 to 12 were assigned to the investment grade, with a ranking of 1 assigned to a grade of *D–* and a ranking of 12 assigned to a grade of *A+*. In addition, PRS assigns a grade ranging from low to moderate to high for the turmoil characteristic, which was considered in the country risk assessment.

Under this ranking scheme, the United States was assigned a ranking of 11 and Mexico a ranking of 7, a difference of 4. The increased risk of turmoil and higher investment risk were assigned a 400 basis point increment to the U.S. base WACC, adjusted for country-specific income taxes.

With respect to XCORP, the country-specific income tax rate is lower than that of the United States. An income tax rate of 34 percent was concluded. Therefore, the indicated rate using Method A is 14.26 percent, computed as follows:

$$
\begin{aligned}
\text{Country-specific income tax rate impact} \ &= \ \text{Percent debt } [k_d \times (1-t)] + k_e \\
&= \ [0.40(7.31 \times 0.66)] + 8.33 \\
&= \ 1.93 + 8.33 \\
&= \ 10.26\% \\
\text{Add political risk adjustment} \quad\ &\quad\ + 4.00\% \\
&= \ 14.26\%
\end{aligned}
$$

Method B—Yield and Specific Income Tax Rate Adjustment.

As part of our analysis, recent yields on long-term government bonds were compared between the United States and Mexico. The yield differential to the United States for long-term government bonds for Mexico was about 540 basis points higher. The resulting impact on estimated cost of debt (k_d) and cost of equity (k_e) components of the WACC is presented below:

	k_d	k_e
United States	7.31%	13.89%
Add rate differential	5.40	5.40
Total	12.71%	19.29%

The resulting WACC, applying a 540 basis point increase and country-specific income tax rate, is summarized as follows:

$$
\begin{aligned}
&\text{Percent debt } [k_d \times (1-t)] + \text{Percent equity } (k_e) \\
&= \ [0.40(12.71 \times 0.66)] + 0.60(19.29) \\
&= \ 3.36 + 11.57 \\
&= \ 14.93\%
\end{aligned}
$$

Conclusion

As a result of the above analysis, Method B, which considered yield differentials, was given the most weight (75 percent), and Method A, which considered political risk, was assigned a 25 percent weight. This weighting,

Exhibit 2–3

WACC and Weighted WACC Under Methods A and B

Method	Weight	WACC (%)	WACC Weighted (%)
A	0.25	14.26	3.57
B	0.75	14.93	<u>11.20</u>
			14.76
		Rounded	15%

presented in Exhibit 2–3, reflects the fact that most of the political risk information is already accounted for in the country-specific yield structure.

Summary

Therefore, the concluded base rate before considering specific forecast risk issues, for XCORP's contemplated investment in Mexico, is 15 percent.

Analysis of businesses for purposes of valuation inherently requires risk assessment, and recognition of country or political risk is part of the overall due diligence process. Country risk can be a significant and challenging issue to deal with. Taking the perspective that country risk is incremental can help manage the process. The concept of incremental country risk is supported by both academia and the marketplace. However, quantifying country risk is subjective, and there is an inherent lack of perfect data. Nonetheless, diligence in studying market-based data with an objective of observing and measuring risk/return relationships is important and will enhance the valuation's credibility. Market data include both extremes of bull and bear. These extremes warrant recognition so that temporary euphoria or panic in investor behavior does not overly influence observable risk/return relationships from the market. The analyst should strive for normalization of risk/return relationships when adjusting a discount rate for country risk. The globalization of the world's economic environment is a dynamic process. Therefore, the process of developing an international cost of capital should be exploratory, evolutionary, and thought-provoking.

Chapter 3

Equity Risk Premiums

David W. King, CFA, and Roger J. Grabowski, ASA

Introduction

Common stocks are riskier than government securities. Financial theory holds that investors in common stocks expect a return premium over the expected return from government securities as a reward for incurring the extra risk. The *equity risk premium* (ERP) (sometimes referred to as the *market risk premium*) is defined as the extra return (over the expected yield on government securities) that investors expect to receive from an investment in a diversified portfolio of common stocks. In other words:

$$ERP = R_m - R_f$$

where:

R_m = the expected return on a fully diversified portfolio of equity securities

R_f = the rate of return expected on an investment free of default risk

ERP is a forward-looking concept. The ERP is an expectation as of the valuation date for which no market quotes are observable. One can observe return premiums realized over time by referring to historical data (i.e., the realized return approach). Such calculated return premiums, though, are only estimates for the *expected* ERP. Alternatively, one can derive forward-looking estimates for the ERP on the basis of the projections of individual analysts. The goal of either an analysis of historical realized premiums or an analysis of estimates using analysts' projections is to estimate the true *expected* ERP as of the valuation date.

The ERP is a key variable in the application of the income approach to valuation. It is one component of most models for estimating the equity component of the present value discount rate (i.e., the rate of return on equity capital or cost of equity capital). These models include (1) the capital asset pricing model (CAPM), (2) some versions of arbitrage pricing theory (APT), and (3) the build-up method. Estimating the ERP may be more important than most other decisions that the analyst will make in applying these theories. For example, the effect of a decision that the appropriate ERP is 4 percent instead of 8 percent in the CAPM will generally have a greater impact on the concluded present value discount rate than alternative theories of the proper measure of other components—for example, beta.

A recent academic study looked at sources of error in estimating expected rates of return over time and concluded:

> We find that the great majority of the error in estimating the cost of capital is found in the risk premium estimate, and relatively small errors are due to the risk measure, or beta. This suggests that analysts should improve estimation procedures for market risk premiums, which are commonly based on historical averages.[1]

---

[1] Wayne Ferson and Dennis Locke, "Estimating the Cost of Capital through Time: An Analysis of the Sources of Error," *Management Science*, April 1998, pp. 485–500.

There is no universally accepted standard for quantifying ERP. Our research indicates that a wide variety of premiums are used in practice and recommended by academics and financial advisers.

The Realized Return Approach

Practitioners agree that ERP is a forward-looking concept, although many practitioners use historical data to measure it. The *realized return approach* employs the return premium that investors have, on the average, realized over some historic holding period. The underlying theory is (1) that the past provides an indicator of how the market will behave in the future and (2) that investors' expectations are influenced by the historic performance of the market. If periodic (say, monthly) returns are serially independent (i.e., not correlated) and if expected returns are stable through time, then the arithmetic average of historical returns provides an unbiased estimate of expected future returns. A more indirect justification for the historical approach is the contention that, for whatever reason, securities in the past have been priced in such a way as to earn the returns observed. By using the historic ERP in applying the income approach to valuation (e.g., in the discounted cash flow valuation method), one may to some extent replicate this level of pricing.

The selection of which government security to use in measuring the risk-free rate is a function of the expected holding period for the investment to which the present value discount rate (rate of return) is to apply. For example, if one were estimating the equity return on a highly liquid investment and the expected holding period were potentially short term, then the yield on a Treasury bill would be an appropriate instrument to use in measuring the ERP.

In this book, we are directing our observations principally to the valuation of closely held businesses. Those investments are generally thought of as long term. Therefore, there is general consensus that the return on a long-term government bond be used as the benchmark in calculating the ERP. The measure of the risk-free rate is not controversial once the proper term (long term versus short term) of the investment has been determined, because the expected yield to maturity on Treasury securities is directly observable in the marketplace.[2] The differences in approaches, then, hinges on the measure of expected return on stocks.

In applying the realized return method, the analyst selects the number of years to include in the average. One school of thought holds that

---

[2] In applying the ERP in, say, the CAPM, one must use the return on a risk-free security with a term (maturity) that is consistent with the benchmark security used in developing the ERP. For example, in this book we are measuring ERP in terms of the premium over that of long-term government bonds. In the CAPM, $k_e = Rf + (\text{Beta} \times \text{ERP})$. The Rf used as of the valuation date should be the yield on a long-term government bond because the data cited herein have been developed comparing equity returns with the income return (i.e., the yield promised at issue date) of long-term government bonds.

the future is best estimated using a very long horizon of past returns. Another school of thought holds that the future is best measured by the (relatively) recent past.

The highest-quality data, for periods beginning in 1926, are available at the Center for Research in Security Prices (CRSP) at the University of Chicago. Ibbotson Associates has published summaries of returns on U.S. stocks and bonds derived from these data.[3] The year 1926 was selected as the beginning point in order to capture one full business cycle prior to the Great Crash. Historical stock market data are available back to 1871 (there were major changes to regulations on the New York Stock Exchange in the 1860s), and less reliable data are available from various sources back to the end of the eighteenth century. However, in this earliest period, the market consisted almost entirely of bank stocks. And, by the mid-nineteenth century, the market was dominated by railroad stocks.[4] Data for government bonds are also available for these periods.

Exhibit 3–1 presents the realized average annual return premium of stock market returns (relative to the income return on long-term Treasury securities) for alternative periods through 1997.

We measure the realized premium by comparing the stock market returns realized during the period with the income return. Although investors do not know the stock market return when they invest at the beginning of the period, they do know the rate of interest promised on the long-term Treasury bond. Therefore, we are measuring the realized stock market returns relative to the expected returns on bonds expected when they were issued. An investor makes a decision to invest in the

Exhibit 3–1

Realized Return Premium

Period	Arithmetic Average	Geometric Average
20 years (since 1978)	8.5%	7.8%
30 years (since 1968)	5.2%	4.0%
40 years (since 1958)	6.3%	5.2%
50 years (since 1948)	8.1%	6.9%
60 years (since 1938)	8.2%	7.0%
72 years (since 1926)	7.8%	5.8%
156 years (since 1872)	6.2%	4.6%
200 years (since 1798)	5.2%	3.8%

---

[3]*Stocks, Bonds, Bills, and Inflation, 1998 Yearbook* (Chicago: Ibbotson Associates, 1998).

[4] See L. Fisher and J. Lorie, "Rates of Return on Investments in Common Stocks," *Journal of Business*, Vol. 37, No. 1, 1964; J. W. Wilson and C. P. Jones, "A Comparison of Annual Stock Market Returns: 1871–1925 with 1926–1985," *Journal of Business*, Vol. 60, No.2, 1987; G. W. Schwert, "Indexes of Common Stock Returns from 1802 to 1987," *Journal of Business*, Vol. 63, No. 3, 1990; R. Ibbotson and G. Brinson, *Global Investing* (New York: McGraw-Hill, 1993).

stock market today by comparing his or her expected return from that investment with the return in a benchmark security (in this case, the long-term Treasury bond) given the rate of return today on that benchmark security. The investor expects that history will repeat itself and that such a premium return will again be realized (on the average) in the future.

The Selection of the Observation Period

The ERP estimate is sensitive to the period selected for the average. The selection of the year 1926 as a starting point is admittedly arbitrary. That average may be too heavily influenced by the unusually low interest rates during the 1930s to mid-1950s. For example, the average yield on long-term government bonds was only 2.3 percent during the 1940s (the lowest decade on record) and under 3 percent in each year from 1934 through 1955. Yields on government bonds have exceeded 4 percent for most of the nineteenth century and have been consistently higher since the 1960s. Some observers have suggested that the period, which includes the 1930s, 1940s, and the immediate post-World War II boom period, may have exhibited an unusually high average realized return premium. The 1930s exhibited extreme volatility, while the 1940s and early 1950s saw a combination of record low interest rates and rapid economic growth. This combination led the stock market to outperform Treasury bonds by a wide margin.

> The low real rates on bonds may have contributed to higher equity returns in the immediate postwar period. Since firms finance a large part of their capital investment with bonds, the real cost of obtaining such funds increased returns to shareholders. It may not be a coincidence that the highest 30-year average equity return occurred in a period marked by very low real returns on bonds. As real returns on fixed-income assets have risen in the last decade, the equity premium appears to be returning to the 2 percent to 3 percent norm that existed before the postwar surge.[5]

If we disaggregate the years reported by Ibbotson Associates into two equal 36-year subperiods, the first covering the period 1926–1961 and the second covering the period 1962–1997, we get the following comparative figures for stock and bond returns shown in Exhibit 3–2.

The period 1962–1997 has been characterized by a more stable stock market and a more volatile bond market compared with the earlier period. Interest rates, as reflected in the Ibbotson Associates long-term Treasury bond income return statistics, have become more volatile in the later period. The effect is amplified in the volatility of long-term

---

[5] Jeremy Siegel, *Stocks for the Long Run: The Definitive Guide to Financial Market Returns and Long-Term Investment Strategies* (New York: McGraw-Hill, 1994), p. 20.

Exhibit 3–2

Comparative Returns

	1926–1961	1962–1997
Equity premiums over Treasury bond income returns		
Arithmetic average	10.4%	5.2%
Geometric average	7.6%	4.0%
Standard deviations		
Stock market annual returns	24.2%	15.9%
Long-term Treasury bond income returns	0.6%	2.3%
Long-term Treasury bond total returns	5.3%	11.6%

Treasury bond total returns, which include the capital gains and losses associated with interest rate fluctuations.

Further, if one examines the volatility in real (inflation removed) stock returns (as measured by rolling 10-year average standard deviation of real stock returns), one finds that the volatility beginning in 1929 dramatically increased and that the volatility since the mid-1950s has returned to prior levels.[6] Therefore, the data reported by Ibbotson Associates—as measured from 1926 to today—may be biased high.

Examining the longest-term periods (the 200-year period (since 1798) and the 156-year period (1872–1997)), we find that the average real return on stocks has been 8.4 percent over both periods (arithmetic average). This is near 7.9 percent, the average real return on stocks over the past 36 years (since 1962), while the average real return over the past 72 years (since 1926) has been 9.8 percent.

Historical data may also tend to overstate expected returns given the increasing opportunities for international diversification. International diversification lowers the volatility of investors' portfolios, which in theory should lower the required return on the average asset in the portfolio. This would lower the expected return on U.S. securities generally. Therefore, the pattern argues a lower ERP on a forward-looking basis than indicated by historical data. One author has suggested that the increased globalization of financial markets has lowered the expected equity risk premium to about two-thirds of the post-1926 average realized premium.[7]

If the average expected return on stocks has changed through time, then averages using the longest available data become questionable. A short-run horizon may give a better estimate if changes in economic conditions have created a different expected return environment than that of more remote past periods.

---

[6] Laurence Booth, "The Capital Asset Pricing Model + Equity Risk Premiums and the Privately-Held Business." Paper presented at the 1998 CICBV/ASA Joint Business Valuation Conference, September 1998, p. 23.

[7] Rene Stulz, "Globalization of Capital Markets and the Cost of Capital: The Case of Nestle," *Journal of Applied Corporate Finance*, Fall 1995, pp. 30–38..

A drawback of using averages over shorter periods is that because of high volatility of annual stock returns, they are susceptible to large errors in measuring the underlying expected return.

Also, the average of the realized premiums over the past 20 years may be biased because of the general downward movement of interest rates since 1981.

While we can only observe historical realized returns in the stock market, we can observe both expected returns (yield at issue) and realized returns in the bond market. Prior to the mid-1950s, the difference between the yield expected and the realized returns was small because bond yields did not fluctuate very much. Beginning in the mid-1950s until 1981, bond yields trended upward, causing bond prices to generally decrease. Realized returns were generally lower than returns expected when the bonds were issued. Since 1981, bond yields have trended downward causing bond prices to generally increase. Realized returns were generally higher than returns expected when the bonds were issued. If we select the period beginning from the late 1950s or early 1960s to today, we are including a complete interest cycle.[8]

Even if we use longer-term observations, the volatility of annual stock returns is high enough to cause uncertainty about the underlying average premium. For example, the standard error of the realized average return for the entire 72-year period 1926–1997 is approximately 2.5 percent. Even assuming that the 72-year average gives an unbiased estimate, still a 95 percent confidence interval for the unobserved true ERP spans a range of approximately 3 to 13 percent.

The Selection of Which Average to Use— Arithmetic or Geometric?

Return premiums based on the geometric (compound) average are always lower than those based on the arithmetic average. The selection of which average to use is a matter of some disagreement among business valuation practitioners. The arithmetic average receives the most support in the literature,[9] although some authors recommend a geometric average.[10]

The use of the arithmetic average relies upon the assumptions that (1) market returns are serially independent (not correlated) and (2) the distribution of market returns is stable (not time-varying). Under these

---

[8] See Booth, "The Capital Asset Pricing Model . . . ," p. 15.

[9] For example: Paul Kaplan, "Why the Expected Rate of Return Is an Arithmetic Average," *Business Valuation Review*, September 1995, pp. 126–129; *Stocks, Bonds, Bills and Inflation, 1998 Yearbook*, pp. 157–159; Mark Kritzman, "What Practitioners Need to Know About Future Value," *Financial Analysts Journal*, May–June 1994, pp. 12–15; Zvi Bodie, Alex Kane, and Alan J. Marcus, *Investments* (New York: McGraw-Hill, 1989), pp. 720–723.

[10] For example: Aswath Damodaran, *Damodaran on Valuation* (New York: John Wiley & Sons, 1994), pp. 21–22; Tom Copeland, Tim Koller, and Jack Murrin, *Valuation: Measuring and Managing the Value of Companies*, 2d ed. (New York: John Wiley & Sons, 1994), pp. 260–263.

assumptions, an arithmetic average gives an unbiased estimate of expected future returns. Moreover, the more observations one has, the more accurate the estimate will be.

A number of academic studies have suggested that U.S. stock returns are not serially independent; rather, they have exhibited negative serial correlation.[11] One recent study suggests that if stock returns have negative serial correlation, then the best estimate of expected returns would lie somewhere between the arithmetic and geometric averages, moving closer to the geometric average as the degree of negative correlation increases and the projection period lengthens.[12] However, empirical studies indicate a fairly low degree of serial correlation, making the arithmetic average a better estimate.

Minority Ownership Interest Returns or Controlling Ownership Interest Returns?

Do the realized return data result in ERP estimates reflecting minority ownership interest or controlling ownership interest positions? Some practitioners contend that because the data cited above have as their source stock market returns, the data reflect the realized risk premium for minority ownership interest positions. These business valuation practitioners conclude that any present value discount rate derived from the data reflects only a discount rate appropriate for valuing a minority ownership interest position and that a different discount rate should be used for valuing a controlling ownership interest position.

The realized returns are measurements of returns from all stockholders. They include the results from sales of 100-share blocks of stock by one minority ownership shareholder and purchases by another, and they include the results of purchases in tender offer acquisitions of entire companies. These returns are the result of all stock purchases and sales.

Use of the realized return data in the CAPM results in the minimum rate of return necessary for investors to earn a return commensurate with the risk (the cost of capital or hurdle rate). It is well accepted in the field of corporate finance that the rate of return so calculated sets the minimum rate of return the corporation must earn on its investments in order to maintain a company's share price. If investments are made at less than this rate of return, then shareholder value will erode. This is

[11] Eugene Fama and Kenneth French, "Dividend Yields and Expected Stock Returns," *Journal of Financial Economics*, October 1998, pp. 3–25; Andrew Lo and Craig McKinlay, "Stock Market Prices Do Not Follow Random Walks," *Review of Financial Studies*, Spring 1998, pp. 41–66; James Poterba and Lawrence Summers, "Mean Reversion in Stock Prices: Evidence and Implications," *Journal of Financial Economics*, October 1988, pp. 27–59.

[12] Daniel Indro and Wayne Lee, "Biases in Arithmetic and Geometric Averages as Estimates of Long-Run Expected Returns and Risk Premia," *Financial Management*, Winter 1997, pp. 81–90.

because expectations of investors as to the rate of return the corporation must earn have not been met. For example, in assessing the price one corporation would be willing to pay to acquire control of another, the acquiring corporation should set as its minimum hurdle rate the resulting cost of capital.

Does the aggregate market value of a publicly traded company reflect the aggregation of minority ownership values or a controlling ownership value? Why, then, do we see price premiums paid for acquisitions of controlling ownership interests? Do these price premiums reflect the fact that corporations making acquisitions are willing to accept lower rates of return than that cost of capital reflected in, say, the application of the CAPM?

In assessing the valuation of a company's stock using an income approach, one measures the expected cash flows in the numerator and the cost of capital in the denominator. The owner of a small stock holding accepts the expected cash flows given the existing management of the firm. To the extent that management's compensation is tied to increases in the share price of the company (options, shareholdings, etc.), shareholders' and management's interests are wed to each other and the owners' returns will closely reflect the value of controlling that corporation as it exists today.[13]

In assessing the value of an acquisition using the income approach, company management should only pay a price such that the corporation will earn its cost of capital. The cost of capital reflects the risk of the expected cash flows. The denominator is fixed by the expectations of shareholders. The acquiring corporation can pay a price premium to the extent that it can increase the target company's cash flows compared with those being realized under current management.

The cost of capital may change as a result of an acquisition to the extent that the riskiness of the cash flows changes. But the basic method of using the realized return to calculate the cost of capital does not change.[14] This issue was addressed by Ibbotson Associates in the 1998 yearbook:

> The equity risk premium data presented in this publication are derived from data on publicly traded companies, a majority of [which] are minority held. There is no evidence to suggest that the equity risk premium represents a minority interest risk premium. The equity risk premium data make no distinction between majority or minority ownership interests.[15]

---

[13] Roger J. Grabowski, Jeffrey M. Risius, and James P. Kovacs, "Discounted Cash Flow Approach: What Do the Results Represent?" working paper, 1995.

[14] Michael Annin, "Using Ibbotson Associates' Data to Develop Minority Discount Rates," *CPA Expert*, Winter 1997.

[15] *Stocks, Bonds, Bills and Inflation, 1998 Yearbook*, p. 157.

Forward-Looking Approaches

Forward-looking approaches estimate the ERP by subtracting the current risk-free rate from the expected return from the stock market as estimated by investment analysts. A "bottom-up" approach averages the rates of return (weighted by market value) for a large number of individual companies. A "top-down" approach estimates an overall return expected for a stock index. These approaches attempt to directly measure expectations concerning the overall market by using analysts' forecasts of the rate of return on companies in the S&P 500 index.

Bottom-Up Approaches

Merrill Lynch publishes bottom-up expected return estimates for the S&P 500 stock index derived from averaging return estimates for stocks in the S&P 500. Although it does not cover every company in the S&P 500 index, it does cover a high percentage of the companies as measured in market value terms. Merrill Lynch relies on a multistage *dividend discount model* (DDM) to calculate expected returns for several hundred companies, using projections from its own securities analysts. The resulting data are published monthly in the Merrill Lynch publication *Quantitative Profiles*. The Merrill Lynch expected return estimates have indicated an ERP generally ranging from 4 to 5 percent in recent years.

In a dividend discount model, the analyst first projects future company dividends. The analyst then calculates the internal rate of return that sets the current market price equal to the present value of the expected future dividends. If the projections correspond to the expectations of the "market," then the analyst has estimated the rate at which the market is discounting these dividends in pricing the stock. The DDM is a standard method for calculating the expected return on a security.[16] The theory assumes that the value of a stock is the present value of all future dividends. If a company is not currently paying dividends, then the theory holds that it must be investing in projects today that will lead to even greater dividends in the future.

A number of consulting firms use the Merrill Lynch DDM estimates to develop present value discount rates. One author comments on the Merrill Lynch data as follows:

> Two potential problems arise when using data from organizations like Merrill Lynch. First, what we really want is *investor's* expectations, and not those of security analysts. However . . . several studies have proved beyond much doubt that investors, on the average, form their own expectations on the basis of professional analysts' forecasts. The second problem is that there are many professional forecasters besides Merrill

---

[16] See, for example, Sidney Cottle, Roger F. Murray, and Frank E. Block, *Graham and Dodd's Security Analysis*, 5th ed. (New York: McGraw-Hill, 1988), pp. 565–568.

Lynch, and, at any given time, their forecasts of future market returns are generally somewhat different . . . However, we have followed the forecasts of several of the larger organizations over a period of years, and we have rarely found them to differ by more than ± 0.3 percentage points from one another.[17]

Although expected rates of return would be underestimated if the effects of share repurchases are not adequately taken into consideration, personnel from Merrill Lynch have indicated to us that their analysts take share repurchases into account by increasing long-term growth rates in earnings per share. If the effect is not completely modeled, the Merrill Lynch estimates may be biased downward.

It is also possible that the DDM may understate expected returns to the extent that expected dividends are measured based on earnings from assets in place and understates future growth opportunities. But this is most likely a larger problem for the analysis of smaller companies than for large companies, which predominate the S&P 500 index in market value terms.

Value Line projections can be used to produce estimates of expected returns on the market. *Value Line* routinely makes "high" and "low" projections of price appreciation over a three- to five-year horizon for more than 1,500 companies. *Value Line* uses these price projections to calculate estimates of total returns, making adjustments for expected dividend income. The high and low total return estimates are published each week in the *Value Line Investment Survey*. Midpoint total return estimates are published in *Value Line*'s Value/Screen software database. There is some evidence that the *Value Line* analysts' projections are biased toward the high end.[18]

ERP estimates developed from *Value Line* data have been somewhat more volatile than the Merrill Lynch DDM models. In recent years, the indicated equity risk premiums have generally been in the range of approximately 2 to 6 percent.

Several academic studies have been published that employ consensus forecasts of long-run earnings per share growth as a proxy for projected dividends in a DDM.[19] The results suggest that ERP varies over time and the level of ERP is inversely related to the level of interest rates.

One study examined the behavior of analysts' projections from several sources.[20] These included top-down estimates from I/B/E/S (based on analysts' estimates of the aggregate S&P 500 index) and bottom-up projections from I/B/E/S-compiled analysts' estimates of individual companies covered by the S&P 500 index. The authors also compared the

---

[17]Eugene Brigham and Louis Gapenski, *Financial Management: Theory and Practice*, 5th ed. (Philadelphia: The Dryden Press, 1988), p. 227.

[18]David T. Doran, "Forecasting Error of Value Line Weekly Forecasts," *Journal of Business Forecasting*, Winter 1993–1994, pp. 22–26.

[19]Robert Harris and Felicia Marston, "Estimating Shareholder Risk Premia Using Analysts' Growth Forecasts," *Financial Management*, Summer 1992, pp. 63–70; Charles Moyer and Ajay Patel, "The Equity Risk Premium: A Critical Look at Alternative Ex Ante Estimates," working paper, 1997.

[20]See Moyer and Patel.

results with the *Value Line* median projected rates of return (which are generally greater than the market value weighted average projected rate, of return). The authors found that the top-down estimates behaved most consistently with financial theory, while the *Value Line* estimates behaved least consistently. The top-down estimates yielded the lowest average premium (3.3 percent over the 1985–1995 sample period), while the *Value Line* median projected return yielded the greatest average premium (8.8 percent).

Top-Down Approaches

Greenwich Associates is a consulting firm that monitors the financial advisory industry. It publishes an annual survey of several hundred pension plan officers concerning the expected returns for the S&P 500 index for a five-year holding period. This top-down survey has regularly indicated a low ERP, typically in the 2 to 3 percent range.

DRI/McGraw-Hill (DRI), an econometric forecasting firm, regularly makes projections of the S&P 500 index and future dividend yields. Its long-run projections are published in the *DRI/McGraw-Hill U.S. Economic Outlook*. The projections are derived from a large-scale econometric model of the United States and are intended to be consistent with DRI's projections of the overall economy, including inflation, economic growth, and aggregate corporate profits. One can calculate the implied total return on the S&P 500 index from the DRI projections for the index and dividend yields. The ERP derived from DRI has been regularly lower than those from other sources have. The rate of return indicated has been comparable to medium-grade corporate bonds, normally considered less risky than equity.

Exhibit 3–3 summarizes the forward-looking equity risk premium estimates published over the past several years. In the cases of Merrill Lynch, Value Line, and DRI (all of which publish estimates monthly or yearly), the data presented in Exhibit 3–3 are taken from estimates published near the end of the calendar year.

Kidder Peabody formerly published estimates using a dividend discount model, and the results obtained were generally similar to those

Exhibit 3–3

Summary Statistics for 1988–1997

	Range	Mean
Bottom-up approaches		
Merrill Lynch: infinite horizon	3.5% to 5.3%	4.5%
Value Line: 3–5 years	1.8% to 8.8%	4.9%
Top-down approaches		
Greenwich Associates Survey: 5 years	1.2% to 3.9%	2.6%
DRI: long term	−1.5% to 1.9%	0.5%

published by Merrill Lynch. Various alternative sources of forward-looking ERP estimates have come and gone over the years.

The Use of Surveys

One survey of over 100 financial economists at leading universities found that, for long-term investments, one-quarter of the respondents recommended using an ERP 5.0 percent or less, another quarter recommended 7.1 percent or more, and the median recommendation was 6.0 percent. The author of that survey offered his own analysis, suggesting a 3 percent geometric average premium and a 5 percent arithmetic average premium for long-term investments.[21]

Another survey of corporations and financial advisory firms also found a variety of practices among the respondents. Corporate respondents commonly reported using ERP estimates in a 4.0 to 6.0 percent range, while financial advisers reported using estimates more often in the 7.0 to 7.4 percent range (consistent with the Ibbotson Associates long-run arithmetic average).[22]

Other Data Sources

The following are published opinions and guidelines on the ERP. These are not the only sources, but they represent a cross section of opinion on the subject.

The Alcar Group has advocated using forward-looking estimates from a DDM.[23] In practice, Alcar uses the Merrill Lynch DDM data, which in recent years have indicated a range of 4 to 5 percent.[24]

Principles of Corporate Finance, by Richard Brealey and Stewart Myers, recommends using the arithmetic average since 1926.[25]

Financial Management: Theory and Practice, by Eugene Brigham and Louis Gapenski, comments that "the risk premium of the average stock . . . cannot be measured with great precision . . . However, empirical studies suggest that [the market risk premium] has generally ranged from 3 to 6 percent during the last 20 years."[26] The authors recommend the Merrill Lynch DDM as a good indicator.[27]

---

[21] Ivo Welch, "Views of Financial Economists on the Equity Premium and Other Issues," working paper, 1998.

[22] Robert Bruner et al., "Best Practice in Estimating the Cost of Capital: Survey and Synthesis," *Financial Practice and Education*, Spring–Summer 1998, pp.13–28.

[23] Alfred Rappaport, *Creating Shareholder Value* (New York: The Free Press, 1986), p. 58.

[24] From discussions with Alcar personnel. Alcar recommended risk premiums are published quarterly in the newsletter *Alcar Software Review* and are incorporated into Alcar's APT! software product.

[25] Richard Brealey and Stewart Myers, *Principles of Corporate Finance*, 4th ed. (New York: McGraw-Hill, 1991), p. 131 and note, p. 194.

[26] Brigham and Gapenski, *Financial Management: Theory and Practice*, p. 195n.

[27] Ibid., pp. 226–227.

Valuation: Measuring and Managing the Value of Companies recommended a 5 to 6 percent equity risk premium based on a long-run geometric average. In the examples the authors have used a 5.5 percent premium.[28]

Damodaran on Valuation: Security Analyses for Investment and Corporate Finance, by Aswath Damodaran, recommends an equity risk premium of 5.5 percent based on the geometric average since 1926.[29]

The Search for Value: Measuring the Company's Cost of Capital, by Michael Ehrhardt, recommends a long-term arithmetic average, but recognizes that practitioners use geometric averages and forward-looking methods.[30]

Graham and Dodd's Security Analysis uses an "equity risk premium" of 2.75 percent over the yield on Aaa industrial bonds for valuing the aggregate S&P 400 index, which approximates a 10-year historical average;[31] this translates to a premium of approximately 3 percent over long-term Treasury bonds. The authors reproduce the opinion of one security analyst who recommended an equity risk premium over the S&P Composite Bond yield of 3.5 to 5.5 percent in 1978 and 3.0 to 3.5 percent in 1983.[32] This translates to equity risk premiums of approximately 4.5 to 7.0 percent in 1978 and 4.0 to 6.0 percent in 1983 over long-term Treasury bonds.

In *Stocks for the Long Run,* Jeremy Siegal comments that "as real returns on fixed-income assets have risen in the last decade, the equity risk premium appears to be returning to the 2 percent to 3 percent norm that existed before the postwar surge."[33]

In *The Quest for Value,* G. Bennett Stuart recommends a 6 percent return premium, based on a long-run geometric average difference between the total returns on stocks and bonds.[34]

Expected Returns and the Size Effect

The realized return premiums summarized above are averages. Several authors have studied how the realized returns have varied across the various firms composing the universe of companies included in the averages. These studies have discovered that realized returns and the resultant premiums have varied with the size of the firm. Generally this relationship has shown that the realized returns and the resultant premiums for the largest companies have been less than the average, while

[28]Copeland, Koller, and Murrin, *Valuation: Measuring and Managing the Value of Companies*, 2d ed., pp. 260–261.

[29]Damodaran, *Damodaran on Valuation*, pp. 21–23.

[30]Michael Ehrhardt, *The Search for Value: Measuring the Company's Cost of Capital* (Cambridge, MA: Harvard Business School, 1994), pp. 61–64.

[31]Cottle, Murray, and Block, *Graham and Dodd's Security Analysis*, 5th ed., p. 573.

[32]Ibid., pp. 83–85.

[33] Siegel, *Stocks for the Long Run*, p. 20.

[34] G. Bennett Stewart, *The Quest for Value* (New York: HarperBusiness, 1991), pp. 436–438.

the realized returns and resultant premiums for the smaller firms have been greater than the average. This variation in realized returns based on size is not fully explained by beta.

Ibbotson Associates has documented the size effect by dividing the universe of New York Stock Exchange (NYSE) stocks into deciles on the basis of market value. That is, Ibbotson Associates calculates the market capitalization of each NYSE company (shares outstanding times market price per share) using the information in the CRSP database each quarter and ranks the companies from largest market capitalization to smallest market capitalization.

The top 10 percent of the largest companies (i.e., those with the greatest stock market capitalization) are included in the first decile, the next 10 percent of the largest companies (in terms of market capitalization) are included in the second decile, and so forth. The smallest 10 percent of the companies (in terms of market capitalization) are included in the tenth decile. The number of companies included in each decile at each quarter end is the same. Companies added during the quarter are assigned to the appropriate portfolio after two months. Obviously the number of companies included in each decile changes as the number of companies included in the CRSP database changes. The decile portfolios are rebalanced each quarter.

From monthly returns, Ibbotson Associates calculates the average annual returns of each decile portfolio. The beta is calculated using the monthly returns for each decile portfolio. Ibbotson Associates then calculates the expected return for each decile portfolio using the CAPM— that is, multiplying the overall realized equity risk premium based on the S&P 500 index times the beta of the decile portfolio plus the risk-free rate. The results demonstrate that the returns realized for each decile portfolio are not fully explained by beta.

The long-term returns in excess of those predicted by applying the CAPM are displayed in Exhibit 3–4.

Graphically these results are displayed in Exhibit 3–5.

Ibbotson Associates has tested the results to determine the effect of changing the benchmark used to calculate the market portfolio (i.e., the realized return premium) from the NYSE to the S&P 500 stock index. Those results of changing the benchmark still support the relationship between size and realized return.

Ibbotson Associates also tested alternate methods of calculating beta. Betas displayed in Exhibits 3–4 and 3–5 are based on a single variable regression method of calculating beta. Ibbotson Associates recalculated the betas using the sum beta method of estimating beta. That method attempts to provide a better measure of beta for small stocks by taking into account the lagged price reaction of stocks of small companies to movements in the stock market. The results indicate that, although the sum beta method results in larger betas for the smaller-size deciles, the sum beta when applied to the CAPM still does not account for all the returns in excess of the riskless rate found historically in small stocks.

PricewaterhouseCoopers LLP (PwC) has published studies that corroborate the relationship between company size and average rates of

Exhibit 3–4

**Long-Term Returns in Excess of the CAPM
for Decile Portfolios of the NYSE (1926–1997)**

Decile	Beta [a]	Cutoff ($MM)	Actual Return in Excess of Riskless Rate[b] (%)	CAPM Return in Excess of Riskless Rate [c] (%)	Size Premium (Return in Excess of the CAPM) (%)
1	0.9		6.70	7.00	(0.30)
2	1.04		8.49	8.07	0.42
3	1.09		9.10	8.45	0.65
4	1.13		9.80	8.76	1.04
5	1.16		10.56	9.00	1.56
6	1.18		10.63	9.18	1.45
7	1.24		11.20	9.60	1.60
8	1.28		12.26	9.91	2.36
9	1.35		13.02	10.46	2.56
10	1.46		16.63	11.27	5.36
Midcap, 3–5	1.11	945 to 4,014	9.57	8.64	0.92
Lowcap, 6–8	1.22	261 to 945	11.13	9.46	1.68
Microcap, 9–10	1.37	Under $261	13.97	10.68	3.30

[a] Betas are estimated from monthly portfolio total returns in excess of the 30-day U.S. Treasury bill total return versus the S&P 500 total returns in excess of the 30-day U.S. Treasury bill, January 1926–December 1997.

[b] Historical riskless rate is measured by the 72-year arithmetic mean income return component of 20-year government bonds (5.19 percent).

[c] Calculated by multiplying the realized equity risk premium by beta. It is the historical realized equity risk premium measured by the arithmetic mean total return of the S&P 500 (12.96 percent) minus the arithmetic mean income return component of 20-year government bonds (5.19 percent).

SOURCE: *Stocks, Bonds, Bills and Inflation, 1998 Yearbook* (Chicago: Ibbotson Associates, 1998), p. 142. Annual updates by Roger G. Ibbotson and Rex A. Siquefield. Used with permission. All rights reserved.

DATA: Center for Research in Security Prices, University of Chicago, Graduate School of Business.

return as reported by Ibbotson Associates. The latest such study covers the period 1963 to 1997.[35] The data begin in 1963, because the database developed by PwC uses the intersection of the CRSP data and the data contained in Standard & Poor's Compustat database (which contains company-specific financial data). Compustat began in 1963 (the Compustat database does include earlier data for companies that were added to the Compustat database in 1963 or later).

Ibbotson Associates measures "size" on the basis of market value of equity only. There are reasons, however, for seeking alternative measures of size.

---

[35]The study is available via Ibbotson Associates' cost of capital home page (valuation.ibbotson.com). Earlier versions of the study appeared in the following articles: Roger J. Grabowski and David W. King, "New Evidence on Size Effects and Equity Returns," *Business Valuation Review*, September 1996 (covering the period 1963–1994), pp. 103–115; and Roger J. Grabowski and David W. King, "Size Effects and Equity Returns: An Update," *Business Valuation Review*, March 1997, pp. 22–26.

Exhibit 3–5

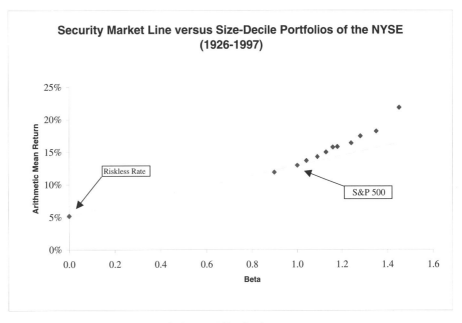

Security Market Line versus Size-Decile Portfolios of the NYSE (1926-1997)

Source: *Stocks, Bonds, Bills and Inflation, 1998 Yearbook*

First, researchers may unwittingly introduce a bias when ranking companies by "market value" of equity.[36] Market value is not just a function of "size"; it is also a function of discount rate. Therefore, some companies will not be risky (high discount rate) because they are small, but instead will be "small" (low market value) because they are risky. Use of fundamental accounting measures (such as net sales or total assets) helps isolate the effects that are purely due to the small financial or operating size in the historical record.

Second, market value of equity is an imperfect measure of the size of a company's *operations*. Companies with large sales or total assets may have a small market value of equity if they are highly leveraged.

PwC defines size using eight different measures:

1. Market value of equity
2. Book value of equity
3. Market value of invested capital (debt plus equity)
4. Total assets
5. Net income
6. Earnings before interest, taxes, depreciation, and amortization (EBITDA)
7. Net sales
8. Number of employees

[36]Jonathan Berk, "A Critique of Size Anomalies," *Review of Financial Studies*, Vol. 8, No. 2 (1995), pp. 275–286.

The study screens the universe of companies to exclude: (1) companies lacking five years of publicly traded price history, (2) companies with sales below $1 million in any of the prior five fiscal years, and (3) companies with a negative five-year average EBITDA. Companies included have been traded for several years, have been selling at least a minimal quantity of product, and have been able to achieve some degree of positive cash flow from operations. This screening process was in a response to the argument that the "small cap" universe may consist of a disproportionate number of high-tech companies, start-up companies, and recent IPOs and that these unseasoned companies may be inherently riskier than companies with a track record of viable performance.

The study considers only companies with a history of profitable operations. (Companies with poor earnings performance and other high-risk characteristics are separated into a "high financial risk" portfolio.) Without isolating the effects of high financial risk, the results might be biased for smaller companies to the extent that highly leveraged and financially distressed companies tend to have both high returns and low market values.

Further, whereas Ibbotson Associates divides the market into 10 deciles, PwC divides the market into 25 portfolios.

Overall, the study finds support for the inverse relationship between company size and average rates of return. As a sampling of the results, we reproduce the four graphs below (Exhibits 3–6 through 3–9) displaying the observed relationships for the 25 portfolios:

Exhibit 3–6

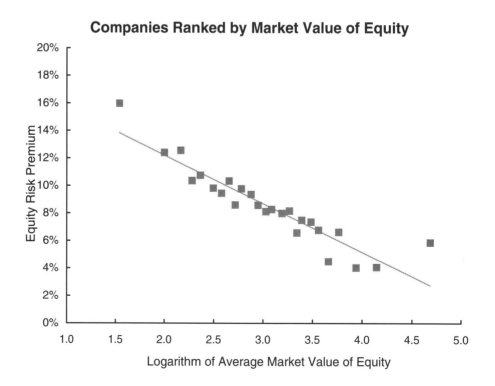

Exhibit 3–7

Companies Ranked by Book Value of Equity

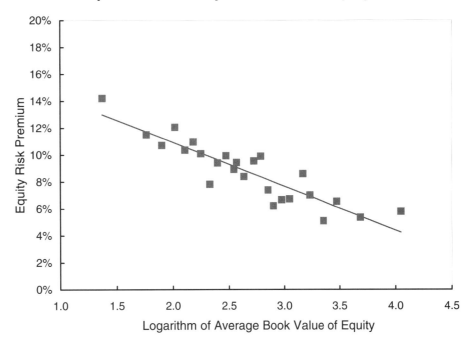

Exhibit 3–8

Companies Ranked by Total Assets

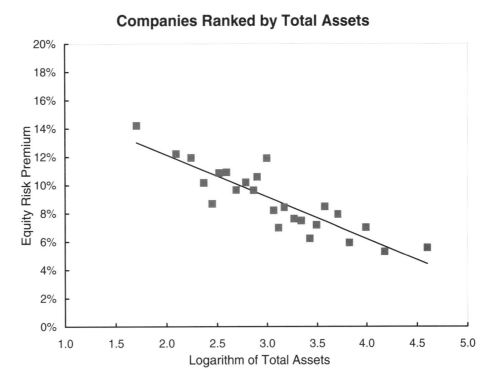

Exhibit 3–9

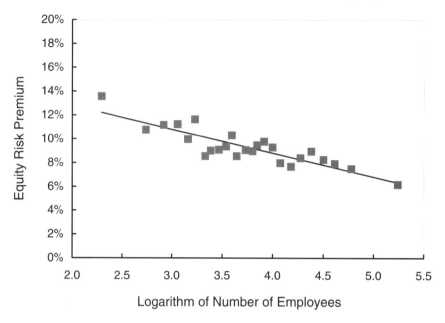

Companies Ranked by Number of Employees

Observed Equity Risk Premiums

The PwC results indicate that the actual returns are greater than those expected by applying the CAPM. This is true regardless of whether the betas for the portfolios (1) are calculated using ordinary least squares applied to monthly return data, (2) are calculated using a sum beta technique applied to monthly return data, or (3) are calculated using ordinary least squares applied to annual data.

The four graphs in Exhibits 3–10 through 3–13 display actual observed rates of return for the 25 portfolios compared with those predicted by the CAPM.

Criticisms of the Small Stock Effect

Several criticisms have been raised about the validity of the small stock effect.

January Effect. The *January effect* is the empirical regularity that rates of returns for small stocks have historically tended to be higher in January than the other months of the year. The existence of a January effect, however, does not present a challenge to the size/expected return relationship, unless it can be established that the effect is the result of a bias in the measurement of returns. Some academics have speculated that the effect may be from a bias related to tax-loss selling.

Exhibit 3–10

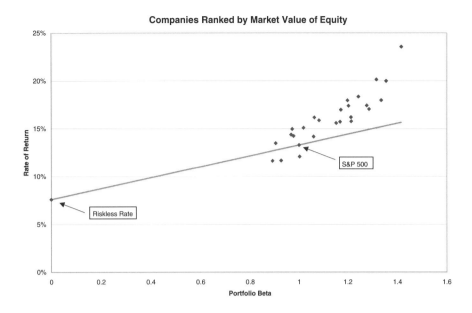

Exhibit 3–11

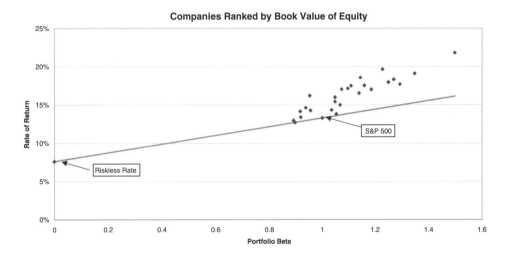

Investors who have earned a capital loss on a security may be motivated to sell their shares shortly before the end of December in order to
realize the capital loss for income tax purposes. This will create a preponderance of "sell" orders for such shares at year end. If so, year-end
closing prices are likely to be at the "bid" rather than the "ask" price.
(Moreover, there may be some temporary downward pressure on prices
of these shares.) The prices of these stocks will only appear to recover in
January, when trading returns to a more balanced mix of buy and sell
orders (i.e., more trading at the ask price).

   How does this cause small stocks to have higher apparent returns?
Stocks that are losers will tend to have depressed stock prices. Also,

Exhibit 3–12

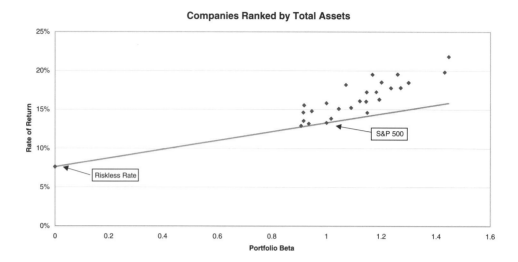

Companies Ranked by Total Assets

Exhibit 3–13

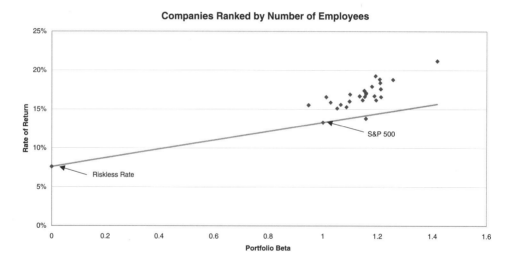

Companies Ranked by Number of Employees

stocks for which prices are quoted at the bid price will tend to have lower apparent market values than stocks quoted at the ask price. These two effects may lead to a bias when we use the market value of equity as our measure of size. If losers have both (1) depressed stock prices and (2) a tendency to sell at the bid at year end, then there will be a tendency for such companies to be pushed down in the rankings according to market value. At the same time, winners will be pushed up. Thus, portfolios composed of small market value companies will tend to have more losers with returns in January that are distorted by tax-loss selling.

Even then, this argument vanishes if one uses a nonvalue measure (such as net sales, total assets, or number of employees used by PwC) to measure size. As long as the size measure is not based on market value, there will be no tendency for firms with depressed stock prices to be ranked lower than other firms. There will be no tendency for small stock portfolios to include a preponderance of bid prices. In fact, the PwC study demonstrates a size effect using alternative measures of size.

Bid/Ask Bounce Bias.   There is an argument that the existence of a bid/ask spread adds a bias to all stock returns, but particularly so to portfolios of less liquid (generally smaller) companies that have higher bid/ask spreads. The bias comes about because the movement from a bid to an ask price creates a measured rate of return that is higher in absolute value than a movement from the same ask price to the same bid price. Since trades occur randomly at either the bid or the ask, a little bit of bias can creep into measured returns. This bias can be especially pronounced if one is measuring rates of return on a daily basis. Most studies (e.g., Ibbotson Associates and PwC) calculate returns monthly at the portfolio level, and then compound the portfolio returns for each of the 12 months of the year to get an annual rate of return. This procedure does much to eliminate possible "bid/ask bounce" bias from the data.

This is a valid point that deserves some consideration. Most studies of the small stock effect use the CRSP database to measure rates of return. To measure rates of return, CRSP generally uses the closing price, which will be either a bid or an ask. But if there are no trades on a given day, CRSP will use the average of the bid and ask price. Note that the most illiquid stocks (those with the highest bid/ask spreads) will be the least likely to trade on a given day. For these stocks, CRSP will be using the bid/ask average, which automatically ameliorates the bias to some extent.

The bid/ask bias has only a trivial impact on the observed size/expected return relationship. Average bid/ask spreads are less than 4 percent of underlying stock price for the smallest decile of the New York Stock Exchange. Spreads of around 4 percent could give rise to biases in measured returns that are only a few basis points at most (assuming that annual returns are being compounded from monthly portfolio results, as in the PwC study). Yet the size/expected return relationship is manifest even for midsize public companies for which the bid/ask spread averages less than 1.5 percent.

Geometric Versus Arithmetic Averages.   It has been pointed out that geometric average return premiums are less than arithmetic average return premiums. It has been suggested that by using geometric averages, one would correct for the alleged bid/ask bounce bias. This argument is completely spurious: The difference between the two averages does not arise from bid/ask bounce. Geometric averages are always less than arithmetic averages as a matter of mathematical law.

Infrequent Trading and Small Stock Betas.   It has been argued that betas for smaller, less frequently traded stocks are mismeasured—in particular, they tend to be too low. If small stock betas were sufficiently high, then the small stock premium may disappear after correcting for the true high betas of the small stock portfolios. This possibility has been offered as a rebuttal to the use of a small stock premium in calculating discount rates.

With a little bit of thought, one should come to a very different conclusion. If small stocks have high returns because they have high betas, and if methods of measuring betas for smaller companies produces betas that are too low, then in the context of the CAPM some sort of adjustment is necessary in order to conclude a discount rate of the right magnitude. A small stock premium is one way of correcting for the bias.

As an empirical matter, the size effect is still there even if one adjusts returns using improved beta estimates. PwC reported portfolio betas that were measured from regressions of annual return data, for which the infrequent trading problem is not an issue—the small stock effect was still evident.

Transaction Costs. It has been argued that because of high bid/ask spreads and other transaction costs, an investor in publicly traded small stocks would not be able to realize returns as high as we observe in the historical record. According to one theory, small stocks earn high returns in order to compensate investors for high transaction costs. However, in valuing a business, one typically applies a present value discount rate to cash flows that do not reflect the buyer's or seller's transaction costs. It would be inconsistent to also use a present value discount rate that reflects a rate of return on a net of transaction cost basis.

Delisted Return Bias. Tyler Shumway has published some evidence that the CRSP database omits delisting returns for a large number of companies.[37] This creates a potential bias, because stocks generally experience negative returns upon delisting. Since delisting is concentrated in firms with small market values, the bias has been offered as a partial explanation of the observed size effect.

First, the Shumway data revealed that the possible bias was trivial for all but the very smallest companies, yet the historical size effect is evident in midcap companies. Therefore, this bias would explain little of the observed historical relationship.

Second, PwC revised its methodology to take into account the Shumway evidence. Shumway reported that for delisted companies for which he could find data, the average delisting rate of return was approximately minus 30 percent. The new PwC calculations assume a rate of return of –30 percent upon delisting for any company for which CRSP lacks delisting return data. PwC discovered that this adjustment did not affect its results by much. Even for the very smallest (twenty-fifth) portfolio, the adjustment lowered the observed average return by less than 1 percent. For the rest of the portfolios, the adjustment was trivial. This should not be surprising: The PwC data set excluded losers, which would be the most likely companies to delist for negative reasons.

---

[37]Tyler Shumway, "The Delisting Bias in CRSP Data," *Journal of Finance*, March 1997, pp. 327–340.

(For the separately calculated "high financial risk" portfolio, the PwC calculations lowered observed returns by about 150 basis points.)

Small Stock Returns Are Unreliable. It has been argued that because small stock returns are unpredictable, investors would not require higher rates of return. It is true that investors in small stocks do not always earn returns higher than those earned by investors in large stocks, even over periods of many years. We find it odd that this would be offered as a reason not to use a small stock premium. By simple definition, one cannot expect risky companies always to outperform less risky companies.

Some have argued that markets have changed and that there is no longer any such thing as a size premium. For example, in the last 20 years, small capitalization stocks have not outperformed large capitalization stocks. In fact, large capitalization stocks have outperformed small capitalization stocks in each of the last several years.

Ibbotson Associates has noted that the size premium is cyclical. Most market returns (including large and small capitalization stocks) have no historical pattern. This is not true of the size premium, however. It is not unusual for the size premium to follow trends of small capitalization stocks consistently outperforming large capitalization stocks for several years, followed by small capitalization stocks consistently underperforming large capitalization stocks for the next several years.

Given the cyclical nature of the size premium, it is not surprising that, in recent years, large capitalization stocks have outperformed small capitalization stocks. One would actually expect time periods of small stock under- or overperformance moving forward.

Summary and Conclusion

Estimating a reasonable ERP is one of the most important issues in cost of capital estimation. We recommend consideration of a variety of alternative sources, including the examination of realized returns over various time periods and forward-looking estimates.

What is a reasonable estimate of ERP? We should give consideration to long-run historical arithmetic averages. The Ibbotson Associates post-1925 historical arithmetic average of 7.8 percent,[38] however, provides an ERP estimate that is at the high end of the range of data from the various sources. Averages over more recent long-run time periods and over even longer time periods suggest a lower estimate for ERP (5+% to 6+% arithmetic average). We should also give consideration to forward-looking approaches. These *ex ante* estimates tend toward the range of 3 to 5 percent. The survey of planners in major corporations indicates that they tend to use equity risk premiums in the 4 to 6 percent range, while financial advisers often use equity risk premiums of 7 percent

---

[38]*Stocks, Bonds, Bills, and Inflation*, 1998 Yearbook (Chicago: Ibbotson Associates, 1998).

or more. The survey of financial economists at major universities tended to recommend equity risk premiums in the 5 to 7 percent range. The reference and textbook authors recommend equity risk premiums in the 3 to 8 percent range.

After considering the evidence, it appears that a reasonable long-term estimate of the ERP (as of 1998) should be in the range of 4 to 6 percent. Obviously, this conclusion is time-dependent and should be reconsidered in future periods as the stock market level and interest rates change.

Evidence for the small stock effect generally comes from historical data. The Ibbotson study measures returns since 1926, using market value of equity to measure size. The PricewaterhouseCoopers study measures returns since 1963, using eight alternate measures of size. Both studies support the existence of a size effect.

Chapter 4

Discounts for Lack of Marketability—Empirical Evidence Related to Pre-IPO Pricing

Steven D. Garber, CFA, ASA, and Jeffrey A. Herbst, Esq.

Introduction

Business valuation professionals have been trying to isolate and quantify the impact of lack of marketability on the value of closely held, or relatively illiquid, securities for over 30 years. A majority of the studies over that period of time have focused on differences in pricing between freely traded securities (in the public capital markets) and their restricted (but otherwise identical) counterparts. The restrictions to free trade associated with these securities typically last for a period of up to two years. The ongoing series of "restricted stock studies," conducted by several different firms and valuation practitioners over the years, spans the time frame from 1969 until the present.

These restricted stock studies have been useful in providing empirical evidence to support discounts for lack of marketability. However, one of the inherent weaknesses in using restricted securities as a benchmark is that the transferability restrictions generally lapse, or disappear, after a given period of time (historically, two years—subsequent to 1996, one year). In contrast, most closely held stocks have no meaningful prospects for liquidity (i.e., a "permanent restriction"). This comparison begs the question: Should the lack of marketability discount be higher for those securities that do not have an easily identifiable time frame associated with their liquidity restrictions? Or, more specifically, does the lack of marketability evidence generated from the restricted stock studies understate the discount for lack of marketability in closely held securities?

With this constraint in mind, a second series of studies has evolved over several years that focuses on the comparison of common stock pricing at the time of an initial public offering (IPO) versus the pricing in arm's-length transactions occurring prior to the IPO. The two principal studies in this area have been conducted by Robert W. Baird & Company and by Willamette Management Associates. The studies, performed independently and using slightly different analytical methodologies, cover the time period 1980 through 1995.

This chapter will focus on Willamette Management Associates' study of these pre-IPO closely held stock transactions and the implied discounts associated with the differences in common stock pricing pre- and post-IPO. It will also discuss the implications of the results as they relate to the discount for lack of marketability.

Use of Empirical Evidence and Lack of Marketability Discounts—Regulatory Oversight and a Standard of Care

In the valuation of closely held securities, the application of a discount for lack of marketability may be the single most significant adjustment to value. In addition, it is an easily identifiable component of, or adjustment to, the final conclusion of value—making it a somewhat easy "target" for a high level of scrutiny. Because of this, any empirical evidence used to substantiate a marketability discount for a closely held security may be subject to an elevated level of contrarian review and scrutiny.

Although the discount for lack of marketability is an important component of almost every valuation related to a minority ownership interest in a closely held company or security, there are several situations that demand increased levels of evidentiary support. These include, but are not limited to, the following:

1. Federal income and transfer taxation compliance, primarily related to gift or estate tax matters.
2. Securities and Exchange Commission (SEC) accounting compliance, primarily related to "cheap stock" or executive compensation issues.
3. Litigation and shareholder disputes, often involving issues related to equitable distribution and fair value.

In each of these situations, the reviewing party (the Internal Revenue Service for federal income and transfer taxation compliance; the Securities and Exchange Commission; and the judge and/or jury for litigation) should be satisfied that:

1. The empirical valuation evidence exists (generally in the public domain) and can be re-created.
2. Analyses have been performed that relate the subject company's valuation characteristics to the valuation characteristics of the underlying empirical data.
3. The conclusions reached as a result of the use of the empirical evidence are valid, supportable, and relevant.

In this regard, the IRS, the SEC, and various courts have accepted and relied upon the series of restricted stock studies conducted over the past 30 years. More recently, the pre-IPO studies have gained acceptance as they become more widely recognized in the business valuation community—and in the respective arenas of oversight and review. The pre-IPO studies have added an additional layer of empirical evidence that supports the levels of lack of marketability discounts recognized in the restricted stock studies.

In the 1995 Tax Court memorandum opinion from *Mandelbaum* v. *Commissioner*,[1] the Tax Court directly addressed the issue of the discount for lack of marketability. As part of its decision, the Tax Court discussed the use and validity of the pre-IPO studies such as those compiled by Willamette Management Associates.

In a Tax Court opinion filed on June 30, 1998 (*Estate of Artemus D. Davis* v. *Commissioner*),[2] the judge considered the evidence on lack of

---

[1] *Mandelbaum* v. *Commissioner*, T.C. Memo 1995–255 (June 13, 1995).

[2] *Estate of Artemus D. Davis* v. *Commissioner*, 110 T.C. 35, 1998 U.S. Tax Ct. LEXIS 35 (June 30, 1998).

marketability discounts, as demonstrated by the Willamette Management Associates pre-IPO study, in determining an appropriate discount for lack of marketability. This type of validation and acceptance encourages business valuation analysts to use such pre-IPO studies in conjunction with the restricted stock studies.

To prepare for contrarian scrutiny, the analyst should review and analyze the characteristics of the subject company relative to the characteristics of the companies cited in the empirical evidence. In other words, naively applying the median indications of the lack of marketability discount may not pass muster. Rather, the analyst should clearly delineate and define why the subject company's lack of marketability discount should be higher, lower, or similar to the conclusions of the empirical study, based upon subject company characteristics. The factors that should be taken into consideration include:

- The size of the company
- The profitability of the company
- The existence of a put option or stock redemption mechanism
- The payment of dividends
- The existence of an "internal market" for shares or a track record of security sales
- Any restrictive covenants, terms, or conditions
- The possibility of an IPO or other exit strategy
- The distribution and ownership of shares

All these items may be considered—including, but not limited to, an accounting of where the subject company fits into the spectrum of companies included in the various studies referenced. Such analyses can justify the use of a discount for lack of marketability above, below, or similar to the central tendencies cited in each of the lack of marketability studies.

It will be easier to substantiate conclusions when substantial relevant empirical evidence to support critical valuation conclusions exists. The pre-IPO studies, and the empirical evidence upon which they are based, are important components in the process to estimate the appropriate discount for lack of marketability.

Summary of Restricted Stock Studies

Exhibit 4–1 summarizes the results of the most frequently cited lack of marketability studies based upon restricted stocks.

As can be seen, the series of restricted stock studies that cover a time period of over 25 years indicates consistent discounts for lack of marketability in the range of 25 to 35 percent. Below, one can see how these compare with the indicated lack of marketability discounts derived from the pre-IPO studies.

Exhibit 4–1

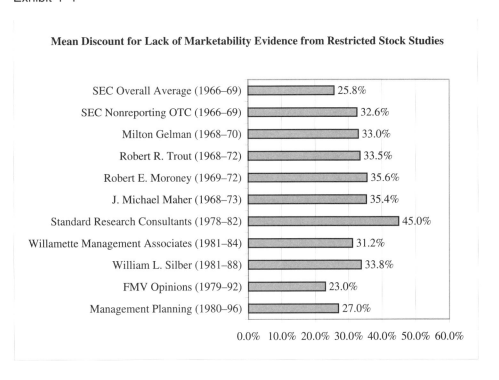

Mean Discount for Lack of Marketability Evidence from Restricted Stock Studies

Summary Results of the Robert W. Baird & Company Study

Exhibit 4–2 summarizes the results of the Robert W. Baird & Company (Baird) pre-IPO study related to quantifying the discount for lack of marketability. The Baird study—spanning over 15 years of empirical evidence, more than 1,500 transactions reviewed, and over 200 qualifying transactions—indicates a stubborn consistency in the discount for lack of marketability of slightly over 40 percent. This level of discount is generally above that indicated by the various series of restricted stock studies (which consistently indicate discounts for lack of marketability in the range of 25 to 35 percent).

This result should not be surprising, since the studies involving restricted stock deal with securities that are only "temporarily" restricted in terms of liquidity. On the other hand, there was uncertainty as of the date of the pre-IPO transaction as to whether the securities in the pre-IPO studies would ever have an easily identified exit vehicle. This uncertainty in timing, including the possibility that there would never be an easily identified exit vehicle, places the closely held security at more risk than the restricted security (with easily identified limits on illiquidity).

Exhibit 4–2

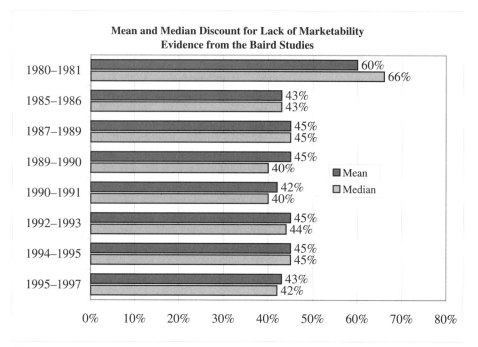

Mean and Median Discount for Lack of Marketability Evidence from the Baird Studies

SOURCE: John D. Emory, "The Value of Marketability as Illustrated in Initial Public Offerings of Common Stock, November 1995 Through April 1997," *Business Valuation Review*, September 1997, pp. 123–131.

Summary Results of the Willamette Management Associates Study

Exhibit 4–3 summarizes the results of the Willamette Management Associates pre-IPO study related to quantifying the lack of marketability discount. Similar to the Baird study, the Willamette Management Associates pre-IPO study provides indications of a discount for lack of marketability consistently above 40 percent. In fact, as indicated by the median discounts associated with the lack of marketability, that figure is consistently over 50 percent. This evidence, when looked at in summary fashion, corroborates the conclusions of the Baird study—that is, the discounts for lack of marketability associated with closely held securities are likely to be higher than the discounts attributed to the liquidity constraints placed on restricted securities.

Baird Study versus Willamette Management Associates Study

Although the underlying premise and motivation for these two independent studies may have been similar, there are some very distinct dif-

Exhibit 4–3

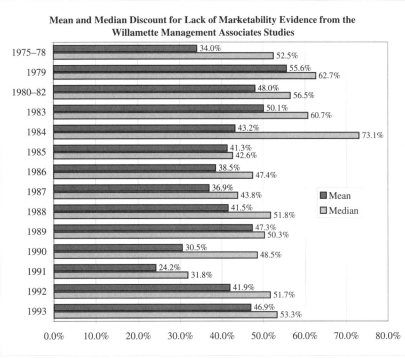

Mean and Median Discount for Lack of Marketability Evidence from the Willamette Management Associates Studies

SOURCE: Willamette Management Associates, unpublished studies.

ferences in the analytical methodology between the two studies. The fact that some of the data studied are from the same transactions does not diminish the independence of the conclusions derived from each study.

However, to gain a greater understanding of some of the analytical differences and similarities between the respective studies, Exhibit 4–4 presents a summary of the more significant factors that impact each. There are subtle, but important, differences in the methods used for the two respective series of studies. However, each captures the critical information necessary to analyze the differences in common share prices on a marketable (IPO) versus nonmarketable (pre-IPO) basis.

Willamette Management Associates Pre-IPO Study Methodology

The Willamette Management Associates study considered all public offerings listed in the *IPO Reporter*.[3] The *IPO Reporter* annually publishes information on all completed initial public offerings excluding closed-end funds. Eliminated from each of these studies were transactional data from financial institutions, natural resource companies, offerings priced at $1 or less per share, and offerings of units or warrants. This is

---

[3] *Going Public: The IPO Reporter* (New York: Investment Dealers' Digest, annual).

Exhibit 4–4

Comparison of Analytical Methods of Willamette and Baird Studies

Analytical Factor	Baird & Company	Willamette Management Associates	Comments
Time frame of studies	1980–1997	1975–1993	Both span a significant number of years, encompassing several stock market cycles and various levels of IPO activity.
Source documents	Prospectuses	Complete registration statement (SEC Form S-1 or S-18)	Prospectus required to disclose only transactions with affiliated parties. S-1 and S-18 require disclosure of all private transactions.
Timing of private transactions used, prior to IPO	5 months	36 months	
Use of affiliated/related party transactions	Yes	Only if believed to be arm's-length transaction	Baird states, "In all cases, the transactions were to have been at fair market value and ultimately would have had to be able to withstand judicial review, particularly in light of the subsequent public offering."
Use of stock options granted	Yes	No	Similar to above, the pricing of options would have had to withstand SEC review.
Adjustments to pricing	No	Yes, for timing and market conditions, based on industry pricing and price/earnings ratios	The Willamette study attempts to account for differences in timing of transactions and market conditions.

because these transactions were likely to have characteristics that were unique and not sufficiently explanatory to a broad population. The private transactions analyzed took place during the 36 months prior to the IPO. If a company had more than one transaction that met the study's criteria, all such transactions were included.

For each transaction for which meaningful earnings data were available in the registration statement as of both the private transaction date and the IPO date, the price/earnings pricing multiple of each private transaction was compared with the subsequent IPO price/earnings pricing multiple. Because some of the companies had no meaningful earnings as of the private transaction date and/or the IPO date, the population of transactions compared on a price/earnings multiple basis was only a small subset of the entire universe of IPOs.

Also, because the private transactions occurred over a period of up to 36 months prior to the IPO, Willamette Management Associates made certain adjustments to reflect differences in industry market conditions between the time of each private transaction and the time of each subsequent IPO. Price/earnings multiples were adjusted for differences in the industry average price/earnings multiples between the time of the private transaction and that of the IPO.

The formula used to derive the discount for the private transaction price from the IPO price was as follows:

$$\text{Adjusted Percentage P/E Discount} = \frac{PE_o - PE_p\left(\frac{IPE_o}{IPE_p}\right)}{PE_o}$$

where:

PE_o = price/earnings multiple of IPO
PE_p = price/earnings multiple of private transaction
IPE_o = industry average price/earnings multiple at IPO date
IPE_p = industry average price/earnings multiple at private transaction date

The summary results of the Willamette Management Associates studies described above were set forth previously in this chapter. The average lack of marketability discount varied from period to period. However, in all cases, the indicated lack of marketability discount was higher than the average discount indicated in the studies of restricted stock—again, the conclusionary result one would expect.

Willamette Management Associates Pre-IPO Study—A Closer Look

The key steps in developing the underlying data for the Willamette Management Associates pre-IPO study were as follows:

1. Identify successfully completed IPOs.
2. Eliminate companies with unique characteristics (e.g., banks, oil and gas companies, closed-end funds, REITs).
3. Obtain registration documents (SEC Form S–1, Form S–18, Prospectus, etc.).
4. Identify opening IPO price.
5. Identify prior arm's-length transactions (e.g., private placements, repurchases, sales of restricted stock).
6. Calculate price/earnings pricing multiples at time of IPO and prior transactions (eliminate companies with negative earnings).
7. Adjust for changes in P/E pricing multiples of the relevant industry.
8. Compare adjusted P/E pricing multiple at time of IPO and prior transaction's adjusted P/E pricing multiple.

Based upon these criteria, Exhibit 4–5 presents a closer look at the underlying data.

Exhibit 4–5

Data Characteristics of Willamette Management Associates
Discount for Lack of Marketability Study

	1993	1989–1993	1975–1993
Number of completed IPOs	820	2,295	6,058
Number of companies used in analysis	51	141	348
Number of transactions	110	263	614
Premium indications	10	40	88
Discount indications	100	223	526
Minimum discount	–68.2%	–73.8%	–142.3%
Maximum discount	93.0%	94.9%	99.0%
Mean discount	46.9%	40.1%	41.6%
Median discount	53.3%	48.5%	50.6%
Standard deviation	33.9%	39.2%	41.5%

A great majority of the total number of transactions are eliminated for one of two reasons: (1) the absence of valid arm's-length prior transactions in the subject company's closely held common shares or (2) the absence of positive earnings. As a result, only approximately 6 percent of the number of companies that completed IPOs yielded useful transactions for inclusion in the Willamette Management Associates studies. Because several transactions were often considered for a single company (i.e., common stock transactions at different points in time prior to the IPO), the number of transactions used in the Willamette Management Associates pre-IPO study was fairly consistent at approximately 12 percent of the number of transactions reported by IPOs. Using these same criteria over the years has yielded a database including more than 600 transactions.

Discount for Lack of Marketability—Critical Factors

As mentioned earlier in this chapter, in the 1995 Tax Court case of *Mandelbaum* v. *Commissioner,* the Court directly addressed the issue of the size of a stock price discount that is attributable to the lack of marketability. More specifically, the Court recognized the validity of the pre-IPO studies and delineated several factors that should be considered in the estimation of the appropriate discount for lack of marketability.

The specific factors outlined by the Tax Court in *Mandelbaum* include:

1. Financial statement analysis
2. The subject company's dividend policy

3. The nature of the subject company and its history, industry position and economic outlook
4. The subject company's management
5. The amount of control in the subject block of shares
6. The restrictions on the transferability of the stock
7. The holding period for the stock
8. The subject company's redemption policy
9. The cost associated with making a public offering

We attempted to analyze the data from the Willamette Management Associates pre-IPO study as they relate to these critical factors. Many of the factors cannot be easily or directly identified for analysis purposes. These include the company's management, the restrictions on the transferability of the stock, the company's redemption policy, and the cost of an IPO.

Although we did not perform an in-depth analysis of the respective companies' financial performance, the selection criteria for the qualified transactions filtered out companies that were not profitable. This process provides a "minimalist" financial performance baseline for comparison purposes.

With regard to dividend policy, the number of companies that pay dividends and are included in the database is insignificant. As a result, no analysis of the correlation between dividend policy and the magnitude of the discount for lack of marketability was performed.

We take a look at the impact of the remaining three factors in the discussion that follows. We address the amount of control in the subject block of shares in the discussion about "Block Size." We address the holding period of the stock in the section titled "Discount for Lack of Marketability—Time Frame." Finally, we look at the impact of the industry in which the company operates.

Discount for Lack of Marketability—Block Size

We analyzed the data from each of the eligible transactions to determine whether there was a relationship between (1) the magnitude of the discount for lack of marketability and (2) the size of the block of shares involved in the transaction. The size of the block for each transaction was calculated as a percentage of total common shares outstanding.

On the basis of our analysis, there is not a material difference in the observed lack of marketability discounts between the various block sizes. However, it should be noted that a great majority of the transactions represented blocks of shares accounting for less than 3 percent of the total shares outstanding. We would expect little difference in the discounts for blocks of shares representing small minority ownership positions, since shareholders of small minority ownership positions typically have little or no influence on strategic direction, distribution of economic income, or other important decisions of the subject company.

As the size of the blocks of shares increased to a level that could theoretically carry a certain amount of "influence," one might expect to see less of a lack of marketability discount (since certain strategic or economic benefits may accrue to the shareholder). We did not observe this phenomenon in larger blocks. In fact, the discounts were distributed in a similar manner over all block sizes of shares transacted.

Exhibit 4–6 illustrates the indicated lack of marketability discounts, relative to the transactional block size, over the entire time period covered by the Willamette Management Associates pre-IPO study. It should be noted that it is difficult to isolate one characteristic of a transaction from the effects of other factors or characteristics of the transaction. More specifically, we can attempt to isolate the effect of the size of the block on the discount for lack of marketability. However, we cannot eliminate other, equally critical influences, such as timing of the transaction, profitability of the company, and many other characteristics of the transaction.

Discount for Lack of Marketability—Time Frame

We analyzed the database for transactions to determine whether there was a relationship between (1) the magnitude of the lack of marketability discount and (2) the length of time between the IPO date and the date of the prior transaction. We measured the time frame in the number of days between the two events.

As expected, there appears to be a relationship between the magnitude of the discount for lack of marketability and the period of time prior to the IPO that the private transaction took place. The correlation is primarily related to transactions that took place less than approximately 120 days prior to the IPO versus those that took place at a time frame greater than the 120-day period. The discounts for lack of marketability were less for the shorter period of time (less than 120 days),

Exhibit 4–6

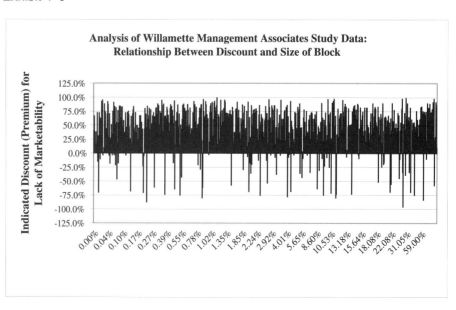

but not overwhelmingly so. This makes some intuitive sense: As companies begin to get serious about the possibility of going public, they tend to be somewhat larger and more profitable than before, and they generally attempt to "put their house in order" when the possibility of an IPO becomes more real.

We attempted to mitigate the impact of the time frame by (1) adjusting for changes in the industry price indexes and (2) adjusting for changes in the industry price/earnings multiple over time. Because of these adjustments, the difference in the size of the discount over time is marginal—indicating a slightly smaller lack of marketability discount on transactions that occurred in the very short time prior to the IPO.

A much more surprising relationship was the greater variance in the magnitude of the lack of marketability discounts as the time frame increased. For the time frame of less than 180 days, there were almost no transactions that took place at a "premium" to the IPO price. As the time frame stretched beyond one year, many of the transactions actually took place at a "premium" to the IPO price. One explanation for this may be that the greater the time frame between the private transactions and the IPO, the greater the risk of the occurrence of unanticipated events. The subject company is exposed to (1) external risks (product market risk, technology risk, capital market risk, etc.), (2) internal risks (management risk, financial risk, product risk, etc.), and (3) any other event that may occur in the normal passage of time. The greater the time frame, the greater the risk, and the greater the variation in the size of the lack of marketability discount.

Uncertainty is one of the primary reasons that the lack of marketability discount exists. The greater holding period creates more risk and uncertainty. The data illustrate the higher level of uncertainty (and risk) associated with the longer holding period.

Exhibit 4–7 illustrates the indicated discounts, sorted by the number of days between the prior arm's-length transaction and the IPO.

Discount for Lack of Marketability—Industry

We analyzed the magnitude of the lack of marketability discount as it relates to the industry of the subject company. Over the 18 years covered by the Willamette Management Associates study (to this point), the qualified transactions included in the study have represented a multitude of industries. The industries represented include manufacturing, wholesale trade, retail trade, finance, insurance, real estate, and various types of service industries.

No single industry seemed to dominate the qualified transactions overall, but as may be expected, certain years were often represented more heavily by a particular industry. This can be accounted for by trends in marketplace activity and sometimes by the existence of multiple qualified transactions for a single company's IPO.

There appeared to be no direct correlation between the magnitude of the lack of marketability discount and the industry. Each industry that was represented by IPOs for multiple companies tended to exhibit discounts for lack of marketability independent of the industry itself.

Exhibit 4–7

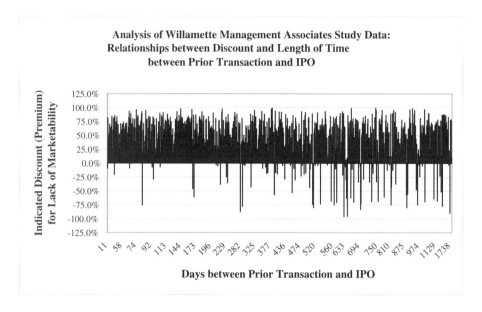

This conclusion may be somewhat counter to the hypothesis that increased risk equates to an increased lack of marketability discount. Given that hypothesis, one may expect that certain industries that are inherently more risky (such as high-technology or other rapidly evolving industries) would demand higher discounts for lack of marketability than those considered more stable (such as banking, retail food stores, certain manufacturing sectors, or other more mature industries). We did not find that to be the case in the selected database of qualified transactions.

Common Critiques of the Willamette Management Associates Pre-IPO Study

Over the years that Willamette Management Associates has used the pre-IPO study in support of the estimation of the lack of marketability discount, the work has been the subject of certain criticisms. In the following discussion, we will attempt to respond to some of these criticisms.

The results are impossible to verify because Willamette Management Associates will not provide the underlying data or calculation. The analyses are performed in response to individual client situations at great expense and are proprietary. However, (1) they are based entirely on publicly available data, and (2) all the calculations can be replicated when needed, as the methodology is set forth in detail in several books and articles published by Willamette Management Associates professional staff.

There is a self-selection bias in the determination of "qualifying transactions," resulting in an overestimation of the discount for lack of marketability by excluding "troubled" companies. The Willamette Management Associates excludes, by definition, companies that fail, or fail to go public. This is obvious because only companies that go public create a benchmark of liquidity for minority ownership interest shares. Conversely, companies that do not go public are useless for the purpose of deriving a marketable stock price. In order to estimate the lack of marketability discount, one should have a benchmark for comparison (i.e., a marketable price to compare with the nonmarketable price).

The fact that our study includes only "successful" companies may actually bias the lack of marketability discount downward. One would expect a "troubled" company to be less liquid than a "successful" company, with fewer options for liquidity resulting in a greater lack of marketability discount.

An argument has been made that the less successful company may trade at a price below the price realized in an earlier transaction (presumably resulting in a premium, or negative lack of marketability discount). This may be true at first glance. However, since we adjust the pricing for changes in the price/earnings multiple, the resulting lack of marketability discount is more reliable. In other words, the exclusion of "troubled" companies, while necessary and logical, does not necessarily lead to an overestimation of the lack of marketability discount.

Many of the transactions are not arm's-length transactions. A comprehensive effort is made to eliminate non-arm's-length transactions. Each of the transactions included in the database has also passed the scrutiny of the SEC. Although the level of effort we put forth to verify the validity of the arm's-length nature of the pre-IPO transaction is subject to challenge, the number of non-arm's-length transactions that may arguably have been included would not skew the results.

Summary

The lack of marketability discount is one of the more important adjustments that business valuation analysts incorporate in the appraisal process for minority ownership interests in closely held companies. The impact of this adjustment on the final estimation of value is usually significant, and its selection and application should be well documented and supported. The pre-IPO studies have added an additional layer of empirical evidence to support lack of marketability discounts, supplementing the restricted stock studies that have been relied upon for years.

The results of the pre-IPO studies have corroborated the intuitive thinking that these discounts should be at a level slightly above those indicated by the restricted stock studies. (The restrictions lapse for restricted stock in a well-defined period of time, whereas the inherent lack of marketability associated with the closely held securities has an undetermined period of "restriction" on its marketability.) As more years (and multiple series of studies) are added to the already existing evidence, the empirical support related to the lack of marketability discount will become stronger.

The valuation analyst should incorporate the available data and analysis in the selection and application of the appropriate lack of marketability discount. As the review and scrutiny of business valuations intensify, the standard of care associated with the analysis, selection, and application of lack of marketability discounts should increase. The addition of the evidence associated with the pre-IPO studies serves to strengthen the empirical evidence upon which valuation analysts can rely.

Chapter 5

Discounts Seen in Private Placements of Restricted Stock: The Management Planning, Inc. Long-Term Study (1980–1996)

Robert P. Oliver, ASA, and Roy H. Meyers, CFA, ASA

Introduction

Thorough research and analysis of capital market evidence is fundamental to the support and development of business valuation conclusions. Many chapters in this book illustrate the critical nature of this concept. Our firm's experience and success in prevailing in business valuation contests regularly reinforces our belief that diligent analysis of pricing parameters obtained from the public market interaction of multitudes of willing buyers and willing sellers is essential to the business valuation process. Too often analysts rely on out-of-date research, performed by others, that includes data and conclusions they cannot themselves check for reliability. With these thoughts and concepts as driving forces, in 1980 we embarked on a long-term project to do our own analysis of private placements of restricted stock, so as to use these data in support of lack of marketability discounts that are applicable to noncontrolling ownership interests.

It is common for analysts to apply valuation discounts in order to estimate the fair market value of closely held business interests, where the freely traded values of those business interests have been estimated by reference to publicly traded securities. This practice has long been accepted by practitioners, the Internal Revenue Service, the courts, and consumers of valuation services, not to mention actual investors. These valuation discounts, the most common of which is the lack of marketability discount, are typically of significant magnitude in a business valuation conclusion. The effort, analysis, and explanation put forward in a typical valuation report with respect to the lack of marketability discount are often minimal compared with other aspects of the valuation (industry analysis, analysis of valuation pricing multiples, etc.).

The insufficient attention given to data and analysis in support of lack of marketability discounts in many valuation analyses probably stems from two sources: (1) court decisions and (2) the availability of a few published—but much older—studies on restricted stock discounts. The courts, most often the U.S. Tax Court, have been asked by petitioners and respondents to render judgment on lack of marketability discounts. The valuation reports and testimony provided in many of these cases offered minimal empirical evidence on the matter of marketability discounts, leaving the judge to choose between the two opinions advanced by the opposing analysts.

A number of restricted stock studies have been available to the business valuation profession, as listed in Exhibit 5-1, along with pertinent statistics from the studies. These studies have been thoroughly discussed by other commentators, notably Dr. Shannon Pratt and Chris Mercer. The table in Exhibit 5-1 provides summary information on certain of these restricted stock studies, but it is not the purpose of this chapter to analyze or comment on these studies in depth. We note them mainly to point out that they are based on what is now fairly dated data. The most recent data studied, in the Silber article, include private placement transaction data through 1988. The study prior to that one, the

Exhibit 5–1

Previously Published Restricted Stock Studies

Date Published	Author	Number of Transactions	Period Studied	Median Discounts	Average Discounts
1972	Milton Gelman [a]	89	1968–1970	33.0%	33.00%
1973	Robert E. Moroney [b]	146	1968–1972	33.0%	35.60%
1976	J. Michael Maher [c]	34	1969–1973	—	35.40%
1977	Robert R. Trout [d]	60	1968–1972	—	33.45%
1983	Standard Research Consultants [e]	28	1978–1982	45.0%	—
1991	William L. Silber [f]	69	1981–1988	—	33.75%
1996	Willamette Management Associates [g]	33	1981–1984	31.2%	—

[a] Gelman, Milton, "An Economist-Financial Analyst's Approach to Valuing Stock in a Closely Held Company," *Journal of Taxation*, June 1972, p. 353.

[b] Moroney, Robert E., "Most Courts Overvalue Closely Held Stocks," *Taxes*, March 1973, pp. 144–155.

[c] Maher J. Michael, "Discounts for Lack of Marketability for Closely Held Business Interests," *Taxes*, September 1976, pp. 562–571.

[d] Trout, Robert R., "Estimation of the Discount Associated with the Transfer of Restricted Securities," *Taxes*, June 1977, pp. 381–385.

[e] Pittock, William F., and Charles H. Stryker, "Revenue Ruling 77-276 Revisited," *SRC Quarterly Reports*, Spring 1983, pp. 1–3.

[f] Silber, William L., "Discounts on Restricted Stock: The Impact of Illiquidity on Stock Prices," *Financial Analysts Journal*, July–August 1991, pp.60–64.

[g] Shannon P. Pratt, Robert F. Reilly, and Robert P. Schweihs, *Valuing a Business: The Analysis and Appraisal of Closely Held Companies*, 3d ed. (New York: McGraw-Hill, 1996), p. 343.

Willamette Management Associates study, includes private placement data through 1984. The transactional data in the other published studies are even older.

In connection with a Tax Court litigation matter, we had a need to review in detail the transactional data and discounts in the Maher and Moroney studies. The opposing expert witness had relied upon these studies. His lack of marketability discount of over 50 percent was based, in part, on the Maher and Moroney studies. Our dissection of these two studies revealed that the private placement transactions with the larger discounts generally involved companies that were losing money or that subsequently filed for bankruptcy. Data from these unprofitable companies had a distorting effect, especially because the subject company in the litigation was very successful and very profitable. The distortion reveals the danger in relying on research performed by others. The opposing expert witness in this particular trial had this concept pointed out to him, too late in the game and much to his chagrin.

In view of these factors, we decided to prepare our own comprehensive and thoroughly researched study of private placements of restricted stocks on a long-term basis.

The Relevance of Restricted Stock Discounts

The American Society of Appraisers, in its *ASA Business Valuation Standards*, defines the term *marketability discount* as "an amount or percentage deducted from an equity interest to reflect lack of marketability."

The lack of marketability of privately held or closely held businesses and equity interests is readily apparent. With the possible exception of a few very large closely held companies with active ESOP plans, there is typically no historical track record of transactions in the equity securities of a private company and no ready market for private company common stock. Looked at another way, the investing public, securities analysts, and others take for granted the ready liquidity available to participants in the public stock markets and do not question why that ready liquidity is available. Huge amounts of capital, the stock markets, an extensive legal and regulatory framework (the SEC, jurisprudence, case precedent), the entire securities industry (registered broker-dealers, their capital, and trained employees), the free flow of information (annual reports, 10Ks, 10Qs), industry and company research reports, media coverage (newspaper and magazine articles on economic and industry conditions and individual companies, television business news, Internet resources) among other things, interact to provide investors with the nearly instant liquidity they take for granted.

Virtually none of the above-mentioned infrastructure or information is available to the owners of privately held securities. The analysis of private placements of restricted stock shows what happens to values, by way of discounts, when the benefit of ready marketplace liquidity is withheld, even if for a relatively short period of time.

Restricted stock is stock issued by a publicly traded company that is restricted from trading on any of the organized stock exchange markets. The shares may be restricted from trading (1) because they are unregistered or (2) because they are legally prevented from being freely traded since they do not meet the requirements of the Securities Act of 1933, as amended (the Act). The Act contains a provision commonly referred to as SEC Rule 144, which sets time and volume limitations on the sale of shares. Requirements under Rule 144, prior to April 29, 1997, generally resulted in a two- to three-year holding period before shares could be sold in the public market. Effective April 29, 1997, unregistered shares subject to Rule 144 generally were subject to an initial one-year holding period instead of the two-year holding period formerly in effect. The purpose of a restricted stock study such as ours is to compare (1) the per share prices paid in private placements of restricted stock with (2) the same company's freely traded, stock market price. Our study shows that in the vast majority of cases, restricted shares are privately placed at a lower price than the concurrent publicly traded price of the same stock. The difference in price, or discount, stems from the burden of the holding period, and resultant lack of liquidity, placed on the restricted stock. The restricted shares, it should be remembered, can be expected to have marketability after the initial two- to three-year holding period (a one- to two-year holding period for shares privately placed after April 29, 1997) and the various other Rule 144 requirements are met. In contrast, there is little likelihood that the typical privately held security will ever have the ready liquidity of a public stock or access to the infrastructure that supports . our efficient public stock markets. Nonetheless, research and understanding of the discounts in private placements of restricted stock provide a good starting point for estimating the size of discounts for lack of marketability. The discounts in our private placement study vary in magnitude. In this chapter we examine a large number of factors that may influence the size and range of the discounts we have found.

Finding Private Placement Transactions

The private placement of restricted stock is a means by which corporations raise capital. This alternative is selected when, for reasons related to control issues, costs, or timing, it is not advantageous or practical to raise new equity capital in the already established market for a company's stock. Over time, we have found three publications to be excellent sources of private placement activity. All are now published by Securities Data Publishing (SDP), located in New York. (They were formerly published by Dealer's Digest, Inc.) Up until 1989, we reviewed *Investment Dealers Digest*. When *Investment Dealers Digest* reduced its coverage of private placements in 1989, we first switched to *Private Placement Letter* and, later, to *Private Equity Week*. Using these three publications as a source, we reviewed all the private placements that were reported from January 1, 1980, to December 31, 1996. In selecting the transactions for further analysis, we established the following initial tests, or screening:

- The company selling stock in a private placement should make its financial statements available to the public.
- The company should have a publicly held and actively traded common stock "counterpart" equal in all other respects to the unregistered stock.
- Sufficient data on the private transaction should be readily available.
- The publicly traded common stock counterpart should be selling at a price of at least $2 per share.
- The company should be a domestic corporation.
- The company should not be characterized as being in the "developmental" stage at the time of the transaction.

An actively traded counterpart publicly held stock is essential so that the spread between the private placement price and the public trading price is a reliable measure of the value differential between (1) a restricted security that cannot be traded and (2) an actively and freely traded security.

We also required a fair amount of information about each transaction and the company issuing the stock in order to conduct our study. The necessary transaction information includes the date of the transaction, the number of shares privately placed, the price at which the stock was sold, price and trading volume information prior to the transaction, the total number of shares outstanding, the presence or absence of registration rights, and the location of the trading market. Company financial statements for at least three years prior to the transaction date were examined for financial condition, sales volume, net income, dividend payments, and other specific factors pertaining to each guideline company.

The benchmark trading price of $2 per share was selected on the theory that low-priced stocks are purchased for pure speculation, in that small rises in price can produce large percentage gains. We believe the presence of this speculative influence is especially great in low-priced stocks (after all, the purchase of any common stock could be deemed speculative). We wanted to reduce any effect this speculative factor may have on our discount conclusions.

Many of the private placement transactions uncovered involved securities issued by private or foreign companies. Some transactions included securities such as warrants, debt, and preferred stock; for example, common stock with warrants attached was issued. These situations preclude a direct comparison between the publicly traded price of the issuing company's common stock and the shares privately placed. Therefore, they were not used in our study.

By using the SDP publications and our preliminary criteria, we developed a list of 231 transactions.

Most of the transactions in the group of 231 occurred at discounts from the public market price. In some of the cases, there was no difference between the private transaction price and the public market price. A small number of the private placement transactions involved prices that were higher than the public market price.

In order to obtain the most meaningful group of private placement transactions that would have the most relevance to business valuation analysts, we established three additional tests that had to be met by each transaction:

- If the company issuing the restricted shares lost money in the year prior to the transaction, it was excluded.
- All start-up companies were excluded. We also excluded companies with less than $3 million in sales volume.
- Some of the transactions involved restricted shares; however, the terms of the transaction conferred on the holder the right to register the shares for public trading. These transactions were excluded.

Private placements made by profitable and actively traded companies were deemed essential. This is because the vast majority of the privately held companies valued by a typical analyst are successful and profitable firms. The owners of successful and profitable firms are the ones who generally have estate tax planning problems or significant estates and estate tax liabilities. Companies that are losing money and experiencing problems need valuation services less frequently.

Trades involving shares of publicly traded companies with less than $3 million in sales were excluded owing to their inherently risky nature. Usually valuation practitioners encounter companies that are established and successful and do not have the investment characteristics associated with newly formed companies.

The registration rights referred to in the last bullet point above generally involve piggyback rights, demand mandatory rights, or at-will registration rights. The ability to register and then sell the shares provides an enhanced element of marketability that is absent from the other transactions. As will be discussed later, a separate analysis of the transactions with registration rights indicates that the discounts associated with these are lower than in those transactions not involving registration rights.

After the transactions were submitted to these three additional tests, a list of 53 transactions remained. Exhibit 5-2 identifies the transactions, the discount involved, and all the factors about which we obtained additional data—revenues, sales volume, trading volume, and many other factors.

The following broad observations can be made about the final 53 transactions included in the study:

- The average lack of marketability discount was about 27 percent.
- The median lack of marketability discount was about 25 percent.
- These median and average lack of marketability discounts are slightly lower than the median (28 percent) and the average (29 percent) discounts of the entire prescreen group of 231 transactions.
- Only one of the 53 transactions occurred at a price equal to the market price.
- The remaining 52 transactions all occurred at lack of marketability discounts ranging from a low of 3 percent to a high of 58 percent.

Given the substantial amount of research and analysis involved up to this point, we could have stopped here with our study. However, because one of the goals of our study was to develop a new and comprehensive body of knowledge that would facilitate the examination of the influence of specific factors on the size of restricted stock discounts, we did not stop at this point. The older restricted stock studies cited in this chapter have been criticized because they report only the discounts seen in the private placement transactions without the accompanying company or market data needed to evaluate factors influencing the size of the discounts.

In 1971, the Securities and Exchange Commission (SEC) commissioned and published *The Institutional Investors Study* (the "SEC Study"). This report analyzed the purchases, sales, and holdings of se-

Exhibit 5–2

Analysis of Private Sales of Unregistered Common Stock January 1, 1980 - December 31, 1996

Date	Company	Location of Market	Revenues $000)	Revenue Growth	Revenue Stability	Earnings ($000)	Earnings Growth.	Earnings Stability	Dollar Amount of Trading Volume ($000)	Block Size Divided by Trading Volume	Block Size Divided by Shares Out- standing	Quarters to Sell Block (Trading Volume)	Quarters to Sell Block (1% Limi- tation)	Dribble Out	State of Market	Price Stability	Debt Ratio	Shares Out- standing (000)	Annual Trading Volume (000 Shares)	Block Size (000 Shares)	Market Price per Share ($)	Value of Block ($000)	Total Market Capital- ization ($000)	Dividends	Discount
3/6/85	Air Express International Corp.	A.S.E.	292,952	3.2%	0.22	184	-67.2%	0.08	11,746	42.6%	19.4%	22	19	19	113	12.0	1100%	3,680	1,678	714	7.00	4,998	25,760	0.00	0.0%
10/19/93	AirTran Corp.	O.T.C.	124,331	39.9%	0.94	6,740	101.9%	0.90	91,854	13.5%	19.6%	7	20	7	110	12.0	94%	7,053	10,206	1,379	9.00	9,998	63,477	0.00	19.4%
10/30/80	Anaren Microwave, Inc.	O.T.C.	8,306	9.6%	0.78	428	-6.7%	0.24	13,452	14.1%	14.1%	7	14	7	122	28.6	120%	1,423	1,416	200	9.50	1,250	13,517	0.00	34.2%
12/14/82	Angeles Corp.	O.T.C.	28,273	54.8%	0.82	3,095	-4.6%	0.08	67,102	3.3%	13.8%	2	14	2	113	8.4	238%	1,160	4,793	160	14.00	1,800	16,242	0.15	19.6%
3/4/96	ARC Capital	O.T.C.	19,394	72.8%	0.74	942	166.0%	0.03	31,858	8.8%	14.9%	5	15	5	129	35.0	91%	9,423	15,929	1,400	2.00	2,275	18,846	0.00	18.8%
10/30/85	AW Computer Systems, Inc.	O.T.C.	4,261	-1.7%	0.00	354	4.9%	0.00	1,256	343.9%	36.9%	179	37	37	109	22.6	145%	3,119	335	1,152	3.75	1,843	11,698	0.00	57.3%
7/12/83	Besicorp Group, Inc.	O.T.C.	3,964	70.7%	0.75	265	14.3%	0.03	85,810	4.1%	5.6%	2	6	2	158	98.6	79%	13,381	18,184	750	4.719	1,500	63,145	0.00	57.6%
4/8/91	Bioplasty, Inc.	O.T.C.	7,872	16.9%	0.62	399	129.3%	0.38	52,674	31.8%	38.6%	17	39	17	115	44.9	76%	2,851	3,454	1,100	15.25	11,550	43,478	0.00	31.1%
5/14/93	Blyth Holdings, Inc.	O.T.C.	9,282	16.3%	0.64	99	-13.0%	0.04	170,065	3.8%	6.6%	2	7	2	104	58.6	30%	5,603	9,718	371	17.50	4,452	98,053	0.00	31.4%
2/5/84	Byers Communications Systems, Inc.	O.T.C.	21,180	-40.8%	0.79	546	2236.7%	0.90	7,940	81.4%	46.1%	42	46	42	111	6.6	N.A.	701	397	323	20.00	5,007	14,027	N.A.	22.5%
1/10/95	Centennial Technologies, Inc.	A.S.E.	8,213	46.3%	0.87	464	139.5%	0.94	20,655	3.3%	2.5%	2	2	2	99	35.0	38%	3,005	2,295	75	9.00	656	27,045	0.00	2.8%
8/8/95	Chantal Pharmaceutical Corporation	O.T.C.	7,215	5.2%	0.23	406	N.M.	0.70	248,704	3.6%	5.9%	2	6	2	124	51.0	33%	16,821	28,023	1,000	8.875	4,900	149,286	0.00	44.8%
9/17/91	Choice Drug Systems, Inc.	O.T.C.	24,881	66.5%	0.89	555	-5.1%	0.29	9,837	48.3%	22.4%	25	22	22	131	23.6	234%	4,470	2,071	1,000	4.75	3,375	21,233	0.00	28.9%
4/1/81	Crystal Oil Co.	A.S.E.	273,294	17.2%	0.57	9,113	143.2%	0.42	99,313	33.1%	4.8%	17	5	5	129	27.3	574%	19,541	2,827	937	35.13	24,990	686,475	0.27	24.1%
3/12/86	Cucos, Inc.	O.T.C.	6,802	60.4%	0.87	272	26.9%	0.77	3,458	71.3%	19.6%	37	20	20	124	20.4	73%	1,735	477	340	7.25	2,003	12,579	0.00	18.8%
9/23/94	Davox Corporation	O.T.C.	33,756	20.2%	0.65	385	7.8%	0.01	5,191	35.9%	9.8%	19	10	10	105	24.6	99%	5,412	1,483	533	3.50	999	18,942	0.00	46.4%
1/13/88	Del Electronics Corporation	O.T.C.	6,492	1.9%	0.10	240	-17.5%	0.08	801	83.3%	19.6%	43	20	20	112	4.0	124%	940	221	184	3.625	394	3,406	0.00	41.0%
2/28/96	Dense Pac Microsystems, Inc.	O.T.C.	18,006	14.9%	0.70	1,698	10.4%	0.08	337,181	1.7%	5.4%	1	5	1	132	42.4	42%	16,748	51,874	900	6.50	4,500	108,862	0.00	23.1%
7/1/92	Edmark Corp.	O.T.C.	5,963	26.2%	0.92	364	55.6%	0.57	256	929.3%	19.4%	483	19	19	104	10.5	23%	1,964	41	381	6.25	2,000	12,275	0.00	16.0%
11/10/81	Electro Nucleonics	O.T.C.	34,959	22.9%	0.97	1,791	117.6%	0.68	44,188	3.2%	3.6%	2	4	2	106	21.4	40%	3,044	3,500	111	12.625	1,055	38,435	0.00	24.8%
9/22/95	Esmor Correctional Services, Inc.	O.T.C.	24,273	66.6%	0.90	1,543	240.2%	0.95	40,722	14.0%	11.3%	7	11	7	126	34.0	150%	4,408	3,541	497	11.50	3,852	50,692	0.00	32.6%
3/27/91	Gendex Corp.	O.T.C.	54,508	28.7%	0.71	2,901	226.4%	0.99	37,395	16.0%	10.9%	8	11	8	110	11.5	170%	3,667	2,493	400	15.00	5,000	55,005	0.00	16.7%
10/31/86	Harken Oil & Gas, Inc.	O.T.C.	8,689	42.8%	0.88	204	55.8%	0.13	9,437	30.4%	10.5%	16	11	11	121	19.0	33%	12,811	4,441	1,351	2.125	1,999	27,223	0.00	30.4%
9/2/83	ICN Pharmaceuticals, Inc.	N.Y.S.E.	38,774	-15.2%	0.87	2,967	38.0%	0.11	169,628	6.2%	13.3%	3	13	3	138	23.9	50%	7,508	16,155	1,000	10.50	9,400	78,834	0.00	10.5%
3/16/92	Ion Laser Technology, Inc.	O.T.C.	3,194	48.4%	0.92	123	161.1%	0.71	2,268	72.9%	16.5%	38	16	16	111	22.0	30%	3,384	764	557	2.96875	975	10,046	0.00	41.1%
2/14/94	Max & Erma?s Restaurants, Inc.	O.T.C.	43,273	13.1%	0.87	1,371	145.4%	0.87	25,148	5.4%	4.4%	3	4	3	107	18.8	144%	3,552	2,874	156	8.75	1,192	31,080	0.00	12.7%
5/8/86	Medco Containment Services, Inc.	O.T.C.	73,615	53.8%	0.89	3,931	97.9%	0.84	340,716	34.7%	21.1%	18	21	18	125	12.8	56%	13,960	8,465	2,941	40.25	99,994	561,890	0.00	15.5%
11/20/85	Newport Pharmaceuticals, Intl., Inc.	O.T.C.	10,469	39.1%	0.87	647	47.6%	0.00	351,495	2.7%	9.4%	1	9	1	115	30.2	67%	9,001	31,244	850	11.25	5,950	101,259	0.00	37.8%
3/5/96	Nobel Education Dynamics, Inc.	O.T.C.	44,154	15.9%	0.76	3,906	180.4%	0.34	118,048	12.6%	24.4%	7	24	7	134	32.1	179%	4,095	7,936	1,000	14.875	12,000	60,913	0.00	19.3%
4/11/93	Noble Roman?s, Inc.	O.T.C.	9,103	-8.9%	0.47	491	1.1%	0.06	1,798	84.1%	13.2%	44	13	13	104	17.0	3505%	3,151	496	417	3.625	1,251	11,422	0.00	17.2%
6/1/87	North American Holding Corporation[a]	O.T.C.	36,677	158.0%	0.84	2,921	N.M.	0.63	22,264	19.4%	5.4%	10	5	5	122	22.1	135%	6,933	1,936	375	11.50	3,000	79,730	0.00	30.4%
5/31/83	North Hills Electronics, Inc.	O.T.C.	3,384	25.4%	0.79	439	48.9%	0.81	19,478	29.8%	26.6%	15	27	15	148	52.7	72%	1,317	1,176	350	16.563	3,675	21,812	N.A.	36.6%
11/14/91	Photographic Sciences Corporation	O.T.C.	16,434	19.8%	0.76	729	32.7%	0.06	16,022	61.8%	22.4%	32	22	22	122	27.2	124%	5,347	1,942	1,200	8.25	5,000	44,113	0.00	49.5%
8/18/93	Presidential Life Corporation	O.T.C.	209,008	0.3%	0.00	23,967	-30.0%	0.00	115,868	39.1%	18.3%	20	18	18	105	17.0	968%	28,613	13,434	5,250	8.625	38,063	246,787	0.00	15.9%
12/21/89	Pride Petroleum Services, Inc.	O.T.C.	65,898	5.8%	0.26	544	543.0%	0.31	98,249	29.0%	38.5%	15	38	15	126	18.0	3650%	11,174	14,830	4,300	6.625	21,500	74,028	0.00	24.5%
6/17/91	Quadrex Corp.	O.T.C.	33,169	-6.4%	0.66	347	-28.4%	0.41	87,590	9.4%	11.6%	5	12	5	111	44.2	265%	8,608	10,617	1,000	8.25	5,000	71,016	0.00	39.4%
2/21/80	Quality Care, Inc.	O.T.C.	28,225	72.9%	0.74	514	156.0%	0.68	10,296	46.6%	24.4%	24	24	24	120	7.0	180%	2,461	1,287	600	8.00	3,150	19,689	0.00	34.4%
12/11/80	Ragen Precision Industries, Inc.	O.T.C.	29,750	13.3%	0.75	861	35.1%	0.61	35,687	6.6%	10.4%	3	10	3	133	26.0	168%	1,918	3,021	200	11.813	2,000	22,653	0.00	15.3%
3/17/92	REN Corporation-USA [b]	O.T.C.	53,427	108.9%	0.88	1,830	-17.0%	0.02	69,065	94.6%	43.2%	49	43	43	106	19.8	255%	12,722	5,816	5,500	11.875	53,625	151,074	0.00	17.9%
10/1/92	REN Corporation-USA[c]	O.T.C.	53,427	108.9%	0.88	1,830	-17.0%	0.02	84,332	20.1%	10.4%	10	10	10	111	36.1	255%	11,293	5,816	1,171	14.50	12,003	163,749	0.00	29.3%
5/24/91	Rentrak Corp.	O.T.C.	33,942	35.1%	0.70	822	10.4%	0.60	30,710	99.7%	49.8%	52	50	50	105	30.0	218%	5,926	2,960	2,950	10.375	20,650	61,482	0.00	32.5%
11/20/85	Ryan?s Family Steak Houses, Inc.[d]	O.T.C.	31,995	56.2%	0.87	3,345	72.0%	0.90	156,722	3.7%	3.6%	2	4	2	115	13.6	18%	6,930	6,814	250	23.00	5,250	159,390	0.00	8.7%
3/21/85	Ryan?s Family Steak Houses, Inc.[e]	O.T.C.	31,995	56.2%	0.87	3,345	72.0%	0.90	63,155	12.1%	6.9%	6	7	6	113	14.4	18%	6,480	3,715	450	17.00	7,250	110,160	0.00	5.2%
6/30/88	Sahlen & Associates, Inc.	O.T.C.	54,949	227.9%	0.81	2,064	159.3%	0.54	48,467	17.2%	19.5%	9	19	9	85	26.1	300%	16,561	18,686	3,222	2.59375	6,057	42,955	0.00	27.5%
3/6/85	Starrett Housing Corp.	A.S.E.	105,147	-1.8%	0.01	5,195	-21.3%	0.02	14,794	36.8%	5.7%	19	6	6	113	12.4	219%	5,256	816	300	18.13	3,000	95,291	0.00	44.8%
6/12/85	Sudbury Holdings, Inc.	O.T.C.	118,068	0.6%	0.17	1,635	170.7%	0.65	25,755	162.0%	124.8%	84	125	84	123	26.6	1429%	3,767	2,902	4,700	8.875	22,325	33,431	N.A.	46.5%
6/21/83	Superior Care, Inc.	A.S.E.	36,399	83.0%	0.93	336	17.9%	0.21	45,821	21.2%	19.3%	11	19	11	149	42.2	116%	7,326	6,660	1,415	6.88	5,660	50,403	0.00	41.9%
2/15/84	Sym-Tek Systems, Inc.	O.T.C.	20,079	39.2%	0.92	780	53.3%	0.34	11,816	12.3%	7.1%	6	7	6	111	13.4	207%	1,200	690	85	17.125	995	20,550	0.00	31.6%
8/22/84	Telepictures Corp.	O.T.C.	74,186	73.9%	0.86	6,057	84.7%	0.81	95,531	18.1%	16.1%	9	16	9	92	6.6	259%	6,194	5,538	1,000	17.25	15,250	106,849	0.00	11.6%
2/29/96	Unimed Pharmaceuticals, Inc.	O.T.C.	7,412	10.8%	0.74	625	66.3%	0.09	28,614	34.9%	22.3%	18	22	18	131	21.0	53%	6,271	4,016	1,400	7.125	8,400	44,681	0.00	15.8%
1/31/84	Velo-Bind, Inc.	O.T.C.	23,466	16.6%	0.85	841	146.3%	0.65	6,285	45.9%	15.6%	24	16	16	114	14.5	39%	1,923	653	300	9.625	2,325	18,509	0.00	19.5%
7/30/80	Western Digital Corp.	O.T.C.	20,603	24.7%	0.32	678	-26.4%	0.00	110,857	13.4%	29.4%	7	29	7	112	22.7	295%	8,491	18,669	2,500	5.938	7,825	50,417	0.00	47.3%
2/22/91	50-Off Stores, Inc.	O.T.C.	78,123	23.7%	0.87	2,816	502.9%	0.80	76,392	8.5%	15.1%	4	15	4	106	23.7	120%	5,378	9,549	810	8.00	5,670	43,024	0.00	12.5%

NOTES:
[a] Class A common stock.
[b] October 1, 1992.
[c] March 17, 1992
[d] November 20, 1985.
[e] March 21, 1985.
N.M. Not meaningful.
N.A. Not available.

curities by financial institutions. Among other things, the SEC study analyzed the discounts seen in private placements of restricted stock as well as factors that appear to correlate with the size of the discounts seen. The factors that the SEC study identified as having some influence on private placements are noted below:

- **The size of the issuing company as measured by its sales.** Companies with the smallest sales volumes tended to have the greatest discounts, while companies with larger sales volumes tended to have lower discounts.
- **The size and pattern of earnings.** Stocks of companies with lower earnings tended to have greater discounts than companies with higher earnings. Also, companies with erratic patterns of earnings tended to have greater discounts than companies with more stable earnings.
- **The dollar amount of sales of securities.** Companies with the lowest dollar amounts of sales of their securities generally accounted for most of the transactions with higher discounts; these companies accounted for only a small portion of transactions involving lower discounts.
- **Trading market.** Discounts were greatest on restricted stocks with identical unrestricted securities traded over the counter, followed by those with unrestricted counterparts listed on the American Stock Exchange, and then by those with unrestricted counterparts listed on the New York Stock Exchange.
- **Resale agreement provisions.** Discounts were related to the resale constraints applicable to the restricted security. Essentially, any provision (piggyback rights, registration rights, etc.) that reduced the time or expense involved in reselling the stock tended to reduce the discount.

We examined the possible influence of these factors, as well as other factors, on the magnitude of the discounts found in our restricted stock study. Any definitive relationships between specific factors and the size of discounts can be used to more definitively establish the lack of marketability discount applicable to a particular closely held security. The results of a comprehensive restricted stock study such as ours can also be used in valuing securities of publicly held companies that are restricted from resale under Rule 144 and related federal securities laws. In fact, the Internal Revenue Service Revenue Ruling 77-287, "Valuation of Securities Restricted from Immediate Resale" (included as Exhibit 5-3), promulgates guidelines for the valuation of such securities. It is apparent that the restricted stock study was heavily influenced by the results of the SEC study with respect to private placement transaction discounts.

Exhibit 5–3

Revenue Ruling 77-287

SECTION 1. PURPOSE.

The purpose of this Revenue Ruling is to amplify Rev. Rul. 59-60, 1959-1 C.B. 237, as modified by Rev. Rul. 65-193, 1965-2 C.B. 370, and to provide information and guidance to taxpayers, Internal Revenue Service personnel, and others concerned with the valuation, for Federal tax purposes, of securities that cannot be immediately resold because they are restricted from resale pursuant to Federal securities laws. This guidance is applicable only in cases where it is not inconsistent with valuation requirements of the Internal Revenue Code of 1954 or the regulations thereunder. Further, this ruling does not establish the time at which property shall be valued.

SEC. 2. NATURE OF THE PROBLEM.

It frequently becomes necessary to establish the fair market value of stock that has not been registered for public trading when the issuing company has stock of the same class that is actively traded in one or more securities markets. The problem is to determine the difference in fair market value between the registered shares that are actively traded and the unregistered shares. This problem is often encountered in estate and gift tax cases. However, it is sometimes encountered when unregistered shares are issued in exchange for assets or the stock of an acquired company.

SEC. 3. BACKGROUND AND DEFINITIONS.

.01   The Service outlined and reviewed in general the approach, methods, and factors to be considered in valuing shares of closely held corporate stock for estate and gift tax purposes in Rev. Rul. 59-60, as modified by Rev. Rul. 65-193. The provisions of Rev. Rul. 59-60, as modified, were extended to the valuation of corporate securities for income and other tax purposes by Rev. Rul. 68-609, 1968-2 C.B. 327.

.02   There are several terms currently in use in the securities industry that denote restrictions imposed on the resale and transfer of certain securities. The term frequently used to describe these securities is "restricted securities," but they are sometimes referred to as "unregistered securities," "investment letter stock," "control stock," or "private placement stock." Frequently these terms are used interchangeably. They all indicate that these particular securities cannot lawfully be distributed to the general public until a registration statement relating to the corporation underlying the securities has been filed, and has also become effective under the rules promulgated and enforced by the United States Securities & Exchange Commission (SEC) pursuant to the Federal securities laws. The following represents a more refined definition of each of the following terms along with two other terms-"exempted securities" and "exempted transactions."

(a)   The term "restricted securities" is defined in Rule 144 adopted by the SEC as "securities acquired directly or indirectly from the issuer thereof, or from an affiliate of such issuer, in a transaction or chain of transactions not involving any public offering."

(b)   The term "unregistered securities" refers to those securities with respect to which a registration statement, providing full disclosure by the issuing corporation, has not been filed with the SEC pursuant to the Securities Act of 1933. The registration statement is a condition precedent to a public distribution of securities in interstate commerce and is aimed at providing the prospective investor with a factual basis for sound judgment in making investment decisions.

(c)   The terms "investment letter stock" and "letter stock" denote shares of stock that have been issued by a corporation without the benefit of filing a registration statement with the SEC. Such stock is subject to resale and transfer restrictions set forth in a letter agreement requested by the issuer and signed by the buyer of the stock when the stock is delivered. Such stock may be found in the hands of either individual investors or institutional investors.

(d)   The term "control stock" indicated that the shares of stock have been held or are being held by an officer, director, or other person close to the management of the corporation. These persons are subject to certain requirements to SEC rules upon resale of shares they own in such corporations.

(e)   The term "private placement stock" indicates that the stock has been placed with an institution or other investor who will presumably hold it for a long period and ultimately arrange to have the stock registered if it is to be offered to the general public. Such stock may or may not be subject to a letter agreement. Private placements of stock are exempted from the registration and prospectus provisions of the Securities Act of 1933.

(f)   The term "exempted securities" refers to those classes of securities that are expressly excluded from the registration provisions of the Securities Act of 1933 and the distribution provisions of the Securities Exchange Act of 1934.

(g)   The term "exempted transactions" refers to certain sales or distributions of securities that do not involve a public offering and are excluded from the registration and prospectus provisions of the Securities Act of 1933 and distribution provisions of the Securities Exchange Act of 1934. The exempted status makes it unnecessary for issuers of securities to go through the registration process.

SEC.4 SECURITIES INDUSTRY PRACTICE IN VALUING RESTRICTED SECURITIES.

.01   Investment Company Valuation Practices. The Investment Company Act of 1940 requires open-end investment companies to publish the valuation of their portfolio securities daily. Some of these companies have portfolios containing restricted securities, but also have unrestricted securities of the same class traded on a securites exchange. In recent years the number of restricted securities in such portfolios have increased. The following methods have been used by investment companies in the valuation of such restricted securities:

(a)   Current market price of the unrestricted stock less a constant percentage discount based on purchase discount;

(b)   Current market price of unrestricted stock less a constant percentage discount different from purchase discount;

(c)   Current market price of the unrestricted stock less a discount amortized over a fixed period;

(d)   Current market price of the unrestricted stock; and

(e)   Cost of the restricted stock until it is registered.

The SEC ruled in its Investment Company Act Release No. 5847, dated October 21, 1969, that there can be no automatic formula by which an investment company can value the restricted securities in its portfolios. Rather, the SEC has determined that it is the responsibility of the board of directors of the particular investment company to determine the "fair value" of each issue of restricted securities in good faith.

.02   Institutional Investors Study. Pursuant to Congressional direction, the SEC undertook an analysis of the purchases, sales and holding of securities by financial institutions, in order to determine the effect of institutional activity upon the securities market. The study report was published in eight volumes in March 1971. The fifth volume provides an analysis of restricted securities and deals with such items as the characteristics of the restricted securities purchasers and issuers, the size of transactions (dollars and shares), the marketability discounts on different trading markets, and the resale provisions. This research project provides some guidance for measuring the discount in that it contains information, based on the actual experience of the marketplace, showing that, during the period surveyed (January 1, 1966 through June 30, 1969), the amount of discount allowed for restricted securities from the trading price of the unrestricted securities was generally related to the following four factors.

(a)   Earnings. Earnings and sales consistently have a significant influence on the size of restricted securities discounts according to the study. Earnings played the major part in establishing the ultimate discounts at which these stocks were sold from the current market price. Apparently earnings patterns, rather than sales patterns, determine the degree of risk of an investment.

(b)   Sales. The dollar amount of sales of issuers' securities also has a major influence on the amount of discount at which restricted securities sell from the current market price. The results of the study generally indicate that the companies with the lowest dollar amount of sales during the test period accounted for most of the transactions involving the highest discount rates, while they accounted for only a small portion of all transactions involving the lowest discount rates.

(c) Trading Market. The market in which publicly held securities are traded also reflects variances in the amount of discount that is applied to restricted securities purchases. According to the study, discount rates were greatest on restricted stocks with unrestricted counterparts traded over-the-counter, followed by those with unrestricted counterparts listed on the American Stock Exchange, while the discount rates for those stocks with unrestricted counterparts listed on the New York Stock Exchange were the smallest.

(d) Resale Agreement Provisions. Resale agreement provisions often affect the size of the discount. The discount from the market price provides the main incentive for a potential buyer to acquire restricted securities. In judging the opportunity cost of freezing funds, the purchaser is analyzing two separate factors. The first factor is the risk that underlying value of the stock will change in a way that, absent the restrictive provisions, would have prompted a decision to sell. The second factor is the risk that the contemplated means of legally disposing of the stock may not materialize. From the seller's point of view, a discount is justified where the seller is relieved of the expenses of registration and public distribution, as well as of the risk that the market will adversely change before the offering is completed. The ulitmate agreement between buyer and seller is a reflection of these and other considerations. Relative bargaining strengths of the parties to the agreement are major considerations that influence the resale terms and consequently the size of discounts at which restricted stocks are sold. Several such provisions follow, all of which, other than number (3), would tend to reduce the size of the discount:

(1) A provision giving the buyer an option to "piggyback", that is to register restricted stock with the next registration statement, if any, filed by the issuer with the SEC;

(2) A provision giving the buyer an option to require registration at the seller's expense;

(3) A provision giving the buyer an option to require registration, but only at the buyer's own expense;

(4) A provision giving the buyer a right to receive continuous disclosure of information about the issuer from the seller;

(5) A provision giving the buyer a right to select one or more directors of the issuer;

(6) A provision giving the buyer an option to purchase additional shares of the issuer's stock; and

(7) A provision giving the buyer the right to have a greater voice in operations of the issuer, if the issuer does not meet previously agreed upon operating standards.

Institutional buyers can and often do obtain many of these rights and options from the sellers of restricted securities, and naturally, the more rights the buyer can acquire, the lower the buyer's risk is going to be, thereby reducing the buyer's discount as well. Small buyers may not be able to negotiate the large discounts or the rights and options that volume buyers are able to negotiate.

.03 Summary. A variety of methods have been used by the securities industry to value restricted securities. The SEC rejects all automatic or mechanical solutions to the valuation of restricted securities, and prefers, in the case of the valuation of investment company portfolio stocks, to rely upon good faith valuations by the board of directors of each company. The study made by the SEC found that restricted securities generally are issued at a discount from the market value of freely tradable securities.

SEC. 5. FACTS AND CIRCUMSTANCES MATERIAL TO VALUATION OF RESTRICTED SECURITIES.

.01 Frequently, a company has a class of stock that cannot be traded publicly. The reason such stock cannot be traded may arise from the securities statutes, as in the case of an "investment letter" restriction; it may arise from a corporate charter restriction, or perhaps from a trust agreement restriction. In such cases, certain documents and facts should be obtained for analysis.

.02 The following documents and facts, when used in conjunction with those discussed in Section 4 of Rev. Rul. 59-60, will be useful in the valuation of restricted securities:

(a) A copy of any declaration of trust, trust agreement, and any other agreements relating to the shares of restricted stock;

(b) A copy of any document showing any offers to buy or sell or indications of interest in buying or selling the restricted shares;

(c) The latest prospectus of the company;

(d) Annual reports of the company for 3 to 5 years preceding the valuation date:

(e) The trading prices and trading volume of the related class of traded securities 1 month preceding the valuation date, if they are traded on a stock exchange (if traded over-the-counter, prices may be obtained from the National Quotations Bureau, the National Association of Securities Dealers Automated Quotations (NASDAQ), or sometimes from broker-dealers making markets in the shares);

(f) The relationship of the parties to the agreements concerning the restricted stock, such as whether they are members of the immediate family or perhaps whether they are officers or directors of the company; and

(g) Whether the interest being valued represents a majority or minority ownership.

SEC. 6. WEIGHING FACTS AND CIRCUMSTANCES MATERIAL TO RESTRICTED STOCK VALUATION.

All relevant facts and circumstances that bear upon the worth of restricted stock, including those set forth above in the preceding Sections 4 and 5, and those set forth in Section 4 of Rev. Rul. 59-60, must be taken into account in arriving at the fair market value of such securities. Depending on the circumstances of each case, certain factors may carry more weight than others. To illustrate:

.01 Earnings, net assets, and net sales must be given primary consideration in arriving at an appropriate discount for restricted securities from the freely traded shares. These are the elements of value that are always used by investors in making investment decisions. In some cases, one element may be more important than in other cases. In the case of manufacturing, producing, or distributing companies, primary weight must be accorded earnings and net sales; but in case of investment or holding companies, primary weight must be given to the net assets of the company underlying the stock. In the former type of companies, value is more closely linked to past, present, and future earnings while in the latter type of companies, value is more closely linked to the existing net assets of the company. See the discussion in Section 5 of Rev. Rul 59-60.

.02 Resale provisions found in the restriction agreements must be scrutinized and weighted to determine the amount of discount to apply to the preliminary fair market value of the company. The two elements of time and expense bear upon this discount; the longer the buyer of the shares must wait to liquidate the shares, the greater the discount. Moreover, if the provisions make it necessary for the buyer to bear the expense of registration, the greater the discount. However, if the provisions of the restricted stock agreement make it possible for the buyer to "piggyback" shares at the next offering, the discount would be smaller.

.03 The relative negotiation strengths of the buyer and seller of restricted stock may have a profound effect on the amount of discount. For example, a tight money situation may cause the buyer to have the greater balance of negotiation strength in a transaction. However, in some cases the relative strengths may tend to cancel each other out.

.04 The market experience of freely tradable securities of the same class as the restricted securities is also significant in determining the amount of discount. Whether the shares are privately held or publicly traded effects the worth of the shares to the holder. Securities traded on a public market generally are worth more to investors than those that are not traded on a public market. Moreover, the type of public market in which the unrestricted securities are traded is to be given consideration.

Sec.7. Effect on Other Documents.

Rev. Rul, 59-60, as modified by Rev. Rul. 65-193, is amplified.

SOURCE: REV. RUL. 77-287, 1977-2, C.B. 319.

Analysis of the Relationships between Specific Factors and the Size of Discounts

This section examines the detailed transactional data we identified and analyzed. A total of 24 factors were considered in attempting to explain the discounts. They are grouped below according to the strength of correlations or relationships between the factors and the size of the discounts.

We emphasize that the relationships seen among the various factors and the size of the discounts can be described as observed tendencies and not mathematical correlations. In examining the relationships between each factor and the discounts in each private placement transaction, we found it useful to group the 53 transactions into four quartiles. The example in Exhibit 5-4 illustrates how this quartile methodology was used in examining the relationships between the size of revenues and discounts. The first quartile includes the largest 25 percent of the companies in terms of revenues. The second quartile contains 25 percent of the companies ranking next in terms of size of revenues, and so on. With 53 companies, the top three quartiles each have 13 companies and the fourth quartile has 14 companies.

When considering the revenue factor, it is clear from Exhibit 5-4 that companies with the largest revenues have the smallest private placement discounts. The median discounts of each quartile are progressively higher as revenue declines. Revenue appears to be a factor that explains differences in the size of discounts.

This quartile method and the related computations of average and median discounts per quartile were generally used with respect to the remaining 23 factors. Of the 24 factors, 21 have been characterized as falling into one of the following three groups:

- Factors with the most explanatory power
- Factors with some explanatory power
- Factors with little explanatory power

Factors with the Most Explanatory Power

Seven factors were found to be well correlated with the size of discounts, as discussed below and summarized in Exhibit 5-5.

Size of Revenues.   Companies with higher revenues tended to be associated with lower discounts than companies with lower revenues. To measure revenues, we used revenues in the latest fiscal year preceding the private placement transaction.

Size of Earnings..   Companies with higher earnings were clearly associated with lower discounts, as presented in Exhibit 5-5. Earnings for the fiscal year prior to the transaction date were used to measure earnings.

Exhibit 5–4

Relationship Between Revenues and Discount

Company	Revenues ($000)	Discount Percentage	Median Discount
Air Express International Corp.	292,952	0.0%	
Crystal Oil Co.	273,294	24.1%	
Presidential Life Corporation	209,008	15.9%	
AirTran Corp.	124,331	19.4%	
Sudbury Holdings, Inc.	118,068	46.5%	
Starrett Housing Corp.	105,147	44.8%	
50-Off Stores, Inc.	78,123	12.5%	17.9%
Telepictures Corp.	74,186	11.6%	
Medco Containment Services, Inc.	73,615	15.5%	
Pride Petroleum Services, Inc.	65,898	24.5%	
Sahlen & Associates, Inc.	54,949	27.5%	
Gendex Corp.	54,508	16.7%	
REN Corporation–USA[a]	53,427	17.9%	
REN Corporation–USA[b]	53,427	29.3%	
Nobel Education Dynamics, Inc.	44,154	19.3%	
Max & Erma?s Restaurants, Inc	43,273	12.7%	
ICN Pharmaceuticals, Inc.	38,774	10.5%	
North American Holding Corporation[c]	36,677	30.4%	
Superior Care, Inc.	36,399	41.8%	
Electro Nucleonics	34,959	24.8%	24.8%
Rentrak Corp.	33,942	32.5%	
Davox Corporation	33,756	46.4%	
Quadrex Corp.	33,169	39.4%	
Ryan?s Family Steak Houses, Inc.[d]	31,995	8.7%	
Ryan?s Family Steak Houses, Inc.[e]	31,995	5.2%	
Ragen Precision Industries, Inc.	29,750	15.3%	
Angeles Corp.	28,273	19.6%	
Quality Care, Inc.	28,225	34.4%	
Choice Drug Systems, Inc.	24,881	28.9%	
Esmor Correctional Services, Inc.	24,273	32.6%	
Velo-Bind, Inc.	23,466	19.5%	
Byers Communications Systems, Inc.	21,180	22.5%	
Western Digital Corp.	20,603	47.4%	31.4%
Sym-Tek Systems, Inc.	20,079	31.6%	
ARC Capital	19,394	18.8%	
Dense Pac Microsystems, Inc.	18,006	23.1%	
Photographic Sciences Corporation	16,434	49.5%	
Newport Pharmaceuticals, Intl., Inc.	10,469	37.8%	
Blyth Holdings, Inc.	9,282	31.4%	
Noble Roman?s, Inc.	9,103	17.2%	
Harken Oil & Gas, Inc.	8,689	30.4%	
Anaren Microwave, Inc.	8,306	34.2%	
Centennial Technologies, Inc.	8,213	2.8%	
Bioplasty, Inc.	7,872	31.1%	
Unimed Pharmaceuticals, Inc.	7,412	15.8%	
Chantal Pharmaceutical Corporation	7,215	44.8%	32.7%
Cucos, Inc.	6,802	18.8%	
Del Electronics Corporation	6,492	41.0%	
Edmark Corp.	5,963	16.0%	
AW Computer Systems, Inc.	4,261	57.3%	
Besicorp Group, Inc.	3,964	57.6%	
North Hills Electronics, Inc.	3,384	36.6%	
Ion Laser Technology, Inc.	3,194	41.1%	

[a] October 1, 1992.

[b] March 17, 1992.

[c] Class A common stock.

[d] November 20, 1985.

[e] March 21, 1985.

Exhibit 5–5

Factors with the Most Explanatory Power

The Factors	First Quartile	Second Quartile	Third Quartile	Fourth Quartile	Indicated Correlation
Revenues (From highest to lowest)	17.9%	24.8%	31.4%	32.7%	Higher revenues, lower discount
Earnings (From highest to lowest)	16.7%	23.1%	31.6%	40.2%	Higher earnings, lower discount
Market/Price Per Share (From lowest to highest)	30.4%	24.5%	19.6%	23.3%	Lower price, higher discount
Price Stability (From lowest to highest)	31.4%	32.5%	19.5%	18.1%	Lower stability, higher discount
Number of Quarters of Trading Volume (From highest to lowest)	32.5%	24.5%	29.3%	19.2%	More quarters, larger discount
Rule 144 Dribble Out (More time to less time)	28.9%	29.3%	24.1%	21.4%	More time, larger discount
Value of Block (From highest to lowest)	19.4%	22.5%	30.4%	31.0%	Higher value, lower discount

Market Price per Share. We found that the companies with the highest per share trading prices had lower private placement transaction discounts than companies with lower trading prices per share. Recall that we had a minimum price criterion of $2 per share in order to eliminate stocks we considered cheap speculative vehicles.

Price Stability. We constructed an index of price stability on the basis of the standard deviation of the stock trading price over the 12 months preceding the date of the transaction. A higher index number corresponds to greater price stability. Our analysis found that higher price stability was associated with lower discounts.

Number of Quarters of Trading Volume. In deriving this statistic, the number of shares in each block was divided by the average weekly trading volume for the publicly traded counterpart security for the previous year. This approximates the number of three-month periods that it would take to dispose of each block under the trading volume limitation of the dribble-out. The data clearly show that more quarters, or more time to sell the block, results in larger discounts.

Rule 144—Dribble-Out. We computed the number of three-month periods required to sell each block on the basis of both the 1 percent or the average volume limitations of Rule 144. The number of shares in each block was divided by an amount equal to the greater of 1 percent of the shares outstanding or the average weekly trading volume to determine the number of shares that would be permitted to be disposed of every three months through the public market following the required holding period. The data show that more time required in order to sell results in larger discounts.

Value of Block. Using the quartile method, we ranked the blocks from those with the highest value, based on the private placement price paid, to the lowest. Larger companies that might attract more investor interest generally issue higher-valued blocks. Larger value block sales are associated with lower discounts.

Factors with Some Explanatory Power

Seven factors were found to be somewhat correlated with the size of discounts, as discussed below and summarized in Exhibit 5-6.

Revenue Growth Rate. Investors, it would seem, are generally attracted to companies with good growth rates. Using up to 10 years of revenues prior to the private placement transaction date, we computed the compound annual growth rate of revenues of each guideline company. The guideline companies were ranked by quartile from highest to lowest revenue growth rate. With the exception of the first quartile, there is a progression of discounts from lower to higher as revenue growth rates declined.

Earnings Growth Rate. Using up to 10 years of earnings figures (as available), we calculated compound annual growth rates of earnings. The two quartiles with higher growth rates have lower discounts than the two quartiles with lower growth rates.

Revenue Stability. We constructed an index of revenue stability on the basis of the reported revenue over the 12 months preceding the transaction date. Higher revenue stability was somewhat associated with lower discounts.

Block Size/Trading Volume. For each of the transactions, we computed the size of the block placed as a percentage of the annual trading volume of the counterpart stock for the year preceding the placement transaction. We thought that very large blocks of stock relative to annual trading volume would have larger discounts than relatively smaller blocks. This seems to be the case to some degree.

Block Size (Number of Shares). Here, we simply ranked the number of shares sold in each private placement transaction from the largest to the smallest blocks. The fourth quartile, representing small blocks, had the lowest discount.

Earnings Stability. We used, if available, as many as 10 years of earnings history (reported earnings before extraordinary items) to compute the variance of the annual earnings. As presented in Exhibit

Exhibit 5–6

Factors with Some Explanatory Power

The Factors	First Quartile	Second Quartile	Third Quartile	Fourt Quartil	Indicated Correlation
Revenue Growth Rate (From highest to lowest)	28.9%	19.6%	24.1%	29.4%	High growth, low discount
Earnings Growth Rate (From highest to lowest)	22.5%	16.0%	36.6%	30.4%	High growth, low discount
Revenue Stability (From highest to lowest)	28.9%	18.8%	32.5%	36.2%	High stability, low discount
Block Size/Trading Volume (From highest to lowest)	32.5%	24.5%	29.3%	19.2%	Larger block, larger discount
Block Size (Number of Shares) (From highest to lowest)	24.5%	29.3%	30.4%	21.1%	Larger block, larger discount
Earnings Stability (From highest to lowest)	15.5%	30.4%	28.9%	34.6%	Higher stability, lower discount
Annual Trading Volume (From highest to lowest)	27.5%	17.9%	24.8%	34.3%	Higher volume, lower discount

5-6, the most stable earnings are associated with lower restricted stock discounts.

Annual Trading Volume. Annual trading volume is measured by the number of shares traded in the calendar year prior to each transaction. Logically, higher trading volume might indicate more liquidity and lower discounts. With the exception of the first quartile, as trading volume declines, the discounts increase from the second to the third to the fourth quartile.

Factors with Minimum Explanatory Power

We found that a total of seven factors had little correlation with the size of the discounts. The following seven factors, also presented in Exhibit 5-7, fell into this category:

Dollar Amount of Trading Volume. We calculated the dollar amount of trading volume (annual trading volume times market price) of each guideline company and the size of the private placement discount. We expected that lower trading volume would be associated with

Exhibit 5–7

Factors with Minimum Explanatory Power

The Fact	First Quartile	Second Quartile	Third Quartile	Fourth Quartile	Indicated Correlation
Dollar Amount of Trading Volume (From highest to lowest)	23.1%	27.5%	30.4%	29.6%	Not significant
Shares Outstanding (From highest to lowest)	24.5%	30.4%	28.9%	23.6%	Not significant
Quarters to Sell Block (1% Limitation) (From highest to lowest)	32.5%	18.8%	19.6%	27.6%	Not significant
Debt Ratio (From highest to lowest)	24.1%	31.6%	34.2%	19.5%	Not significant
Block Size Divided by Shares Outstanding (From highest to lowest)	32.5%	18.8%	19.6%	27.6%	Not significant
State of Market (From strongest to weakest)	24.1%	31.1%	29.3%	17.6%	Not significant
Market Capitalization (From highest to lowest)	23.1%	30.4%	27.5%	27.1%	Not significant

higher discounts. The lower discount in the first quartile meets with our hypothesis but the remaining data do not.

Shares Outstanding.   This statistic simply ranks, by quartile, the number of shares outstanding of each guideline company at or near the placement transaction date. Larger numbers of shares might indicate greater liquidity and lower discounts. We did not find this to be the case.

Quarters to Sell Block (1 Percent Limitation).   We computed this factor by dividing the number of shares sold in each transaction by 1 percent of the shares outstanding prior to each transaction. The resulting calculation measures the number of quarters required to sell the block. With the exception of the first quartile, with the largest number of required quarters, the transactional data are not in accord with our anticipated conclusion.

Market Capitalization. We calculated the total market capitalization on the basis of the shares outstanding prior to the private placement. No clear relationship is seen.

Debt Ratio. A standard calculation of total liabilities divided by net worth was used to compute this ratio. Weaker financial condition may be associated with higher risk and higher discounts. There appears to be no relationship between the discounts seen in the four quartiles.

Block Size Divided by Shares Outstanding. We divided the number of shares privately placed by the number of shares outstanding prior to the transaction. There appears to be no significant correlation between the size of the block and the size of the discount.

State of Market. There are bull markets and there are bear markets and the private placement transactions have occurred in both. We computed the percentage increase or decrease in the S&P 400 in the year prior to the transaction date as a measure of the state of the market at the time of the transaction. We thought discounts may be lower in rising markets when demand for stock was strongest. The data show no significant relationship along these lines.

Of the 24 factors, 3 did not lend themselves to the quartile method of analysis. They are discussed as follows.

Dividends. Receipt or nonreceipt of dividends by investors is often discussed as a factor with a potential influence on lack of marketability discounts. We would like to have examined the significance of this factor based on the data uncovered in our restricted stock study. As presented on Exhibit 5-2, only 2 of the 53 guideline companies paid dividends. For three of them (those labeled NA), we could not determine if dividends were paid or not. The vast majority of the companies in the study did not pay dividends. With these data, we cannot draw any conclusions with respect to the dividend factor.

Chronology. Although not shown here in this chapter, we did rank the transactions chronologically by date. After grouping the chronological data in several different ways, we were unable to draw any meaningful conclusions about the influence of the transaction date on the size of the discount.

Stock Exchange Influence. As noted earlier, the SEC study found that NYSE stocks had lower discounts than ASE stocks, which in turn had lower discounts than OTC traded stocks. The vast majority of the transactions in our study involved companies traded over the counter. Five of the companies were traded on the American Stock Exchange and one was traded on the New York Stock Exchange. This distribution of data does not permit any meaningful analysis of the influence of the location of the exchange on discounts.

Exhibit 5–8

Private Sales of Unregistered Common Stock with Registration Rights

Revenue	Net Income	Transaction Date	Company	Number of Shares Sold	Private Sale Price Per Share ($)	Market Price Per Share ($)	Discount[a]
46,781	4,417	6/28/95	Robotic Vision Systems, Inc.	1,110,000	9	19.875	54.7%
48,766	8,503	7/24/95	Republic Waste Industries, Inc.	5,400,000	13.25	22.125	40.1%
23,318	1,613	12/14/94	Plasma-Therm, Inc.	1,500,000	4.25	6.25	32.0%
131,780	4,604	2/8/95	Optical Coating Laboratory, Inc.	288,224	5.50	8.00	31.3%
58,630	3,189	10/03/95	CPAC, Inc.	1,500,000	11	14.50	24.1%
58,630	3,189	12/28/95	CPAC, Inc.	632,000	11	14.125	22.1%
29,871	3,643	4/26/95	Thermo Remediation, Inc.	500,000	13.25	16.625	20.3%
24,371	1,258	2/28/94	Leather Factory, Inc., The	40,000	5	6.25	20.0%
219,663	4,257	9/30/94	Ameridata Technologies	824,742	12	14.875	19.3%
443,989	38,626	3/31/92	Ashland Coal, Inc.	1,550,000	31	38.375	19.2%
12,244	707	4/24/95	NTN Communications, Inc.	600,000	4.36	5.0625	13.9%
235,397	9,743	1/21/94	Jason Incorporated	200,000	11	12.75	13.7%
214,674	37,144	2/28/95	Penn Corp. Financial Group, Inc.	3,500,000	14.29	16.00	10.7%
1,050,558	21,635	9/15/92	Smithfield Foods, Inc.	1,000,000	17	18.50	8.1%
48,766	8,503	9/7/95	Republic Waste Industries, Inc.	5,000,000	20.24	22.00	8.0%
25,426	410	6/27/94	Shared Technologies, Inc.	1,062,000	3	3.25	7.7%
57,155	5,457	6/24/91	Production Operators Corp.	590,000	17	18.25	6.8%
12,978	1,043	6/15/92	Transmedia Network, Inc.	507,989	10	11.00	9.1%
219,663	4,257	12/15/94	AmeriData Technologies, Inc.	885,000	10	10.625	5.9%
58,074	28,982	5/17/91	Meditrust	3,795,445	23	23.625	2.6%
8,362	2,513	5/1/92	Swift Energy Company	990,000	7	6.625	-5.7%
126,029	2,604	7/13/92	Maverick Tube Corporation	562,616	5	5.00	0.0%
720,683	34,966	5/9/91	Thermo Electron Corp.	500,000	40	39.50	-1.3%
13,178	479	6/10/95	Unapix Entertainment, Inc.	300,000	4.25	4.1875	-1.5%
20,504	2,126	7/5/95	Pacific Rehabilitation & Sports Medicine, Inc	210,527	9.50	9.25	-2.7%
114,475	6,552	11/20/86	C.O.M.B. Co.	2,589,000	20	19.00	-5.3%
11,646	665	6/28/91	Summit Technology, Inc.	865,000	21	19.50	-7.7%
						Median	9.1%
						Average	12.8%

[a] Denotes a premium.

The Influence of Registration Rights on Discounts

One of the criteria by which we selected our guideline company group of 53 transactions was to exclude any privately placed shares issued with registration rights. Exhibit 5-8 is a comprehensive list of the transactions we found from 1980 through 1996 that had registration rights. There were 27 private placements involving stocks with registration rights.

The analysis of these transactions indicates what an investor may be willing to pay for a block of stock of a public company with some form of impaired marketability but with liquidity and marketability more assured nonetheless because of the registration rights. As seen in

Exhibit 5-8, the private placement transactions with registration rights generally take place at discounts from the freely traded prices of the publicly traded counterparts but at considerably smaller discounts than those of similar transactions involving stock without registration rights.

The median and average discounts of the transactions in Exhibit 5-8 are 9.1 percent and 12.8 percent, respectively. These discounts are much lower than the median discount of 25 percent and the average discount of 27 percent obtained from the study of 53 private placement transactions without registration rights. This difference shows the immense benefit of greater or more imminent liquidity.

Observations and Conclusions

Valuation analysts and consumers of valuation services generally agree that valuation opinions derived from capital market evidence are preferred. The lack of marketability discounts seen in private placement studies are an excellent foundation for estimating lack of marketability discounts for privately held business interests. Numerous court decisions have accepted the relevance of restricted stock studies as a reliable indicator of lack of marketability discounts.

The Management Planning restricted stock study includes, in the final analysis (so far) only 53 private placement transactions (not counting the supplemental list of 27 transactions with registration rights). The preparation of this analysis has, however, required thousands of hours of research and involved the review and cross-checking of many thousands of documents and bits of information. These transactions are, after all, mainly private transactions.

Emphasis should be placed on one additional point. The purchasers of the restricted shares in the transactions in our study have considerable assurance that, after the requisite holding period, they will be able to sell their shares in a public market. Even with this most desirable of exit strategies, sophisticated willing buyers demanded and obtained an average discount of 27 percent. These buyers have, it should be noted, a complete spectrum of investment options. The willing buyer of privately held common stock has no public market exit strategy and should, *ceteris paribus*, demand and obtain a larger lack of marketability discount than the average of 27 percent determined in our study.

Part II

Special Applications

Chapter 6

S Corporations— Premium or Discount?

Gary R. Trugman CPA, ABV, CBA, ASA, CFE, MVS

Introduction

Business valuation analysts eventually face the question of what to do about income taxes when valuing an entity that has elected to be treated as an S corporation under the Internal Revenue Code. Some analysts believe that having S corporation status adds value to the ownership interest, since the entity does not pay income taxes. Other analysts believe that having S corporation status reduces the value of an ownership interest. This is because taxes on corporate profits are a personal liability of the shareholder whether or not the shareholder receives distributions in an amount sufficient for the individual to pay the income taxes when they come due. In this chapter, we will explore the never-ending question: Does an S election add a premium or bring about a discount to the business value?

What Is an S Corporation?

Although this is not a treatise on income tax laws, a good place to begin a discussion about the value of an S corporation is to understand the rules regarding this type of entity. The term *S corporation* means a corporation for which an election to be taxed under Subchapter S of the Internal Revenue Code is in effect for that year.[1] To be classified as a corporation for purposes of Subchapter S, a corporation has to meet all the following requirements:

- The corporation must be a domestic corporation.
- It must not have more than 75 shareholders.
- Only individuals, decedents' estates, estates of individuals in bankruptcy, and certain trusts may be shareholders. Partnerships, corporations, and many types of trusts may not be shareholders.
- No shareholder may be a nonresident alien.
- The corporation may have only one class of stock, but different voting rights are allowed.[2]

A corporation can elect to become an S corporation by filing the appropriate form with the Commissioner of the Internal Revenue. This election can also be revoked, voluntarily or involuntarily, under certain circumstances. Once elected, a corporation will remain an S corporation until such time as a revocation takes place.

An S corporation is a pass-through entity. This means that the profits and losses are passed through to the shareholders, and any income tax that is payable will be paid by the shareholders, and not by

---

[1] Code Sec. 1361(a)(1).
[2] Code Sec. 1361(b).

the corporation. The original purpose of an S election was to allow these corporations to be treated as if they were partnerships, while continuing to allow the shareholders the legal protection of operating in a corporate form.

Being an S corporation provides the shareholders with certain income tax benefits. These include, but are not limited to, the following:

- Avoiding controversy with the Internal Revenue Service about the reasonableness of compensation for shareholder/employees.
- Avoiding the accumulated earnings tax if dividends are not paid to the shareholders.
- Avoiding double taxation upon sale of the corporation's assets (other than those assets that may be subject to the built-in gains tax—see discussion below).

Although there are certain income tax advantages to electing S status, there are also certain disadvantages. Any gain on the sale of assets that the corporation recognizes within the 10 years after the election is made to convert from a regular coporation, also known as a *C corporation*, to an S corporation is taxed as if the asset was purchased at the time of the conversion to S status. This is known as the built-in gains tax. Not only does the corporation pay income tax on this gain, but the shareholders will also be taxed on the income that flows through after corporate taxes are paid. This constitutes double taxation.

Another tax consideration relating to the S election is the shareholder's income tax basis in the corporation's stock. In a C corporation, the income tax basis is generally the purchase price of the stock. In an S corporation, the shareholders will constantly be adjusting the income tax basis of their shares. The S corporation shareholders will increase their basis for all earnings reported by the company that are not distributed. An example of a simplified S corporation tax basis calculation follows:

	S election fair market value	$ 1,000,000
+	Profit—year 1	500,000
−	Distributions—year 1	(200,000)
=	Stock tax basis—end of year 1	$ 1,300,000
+	Profit—year 2	800,000
−	Distributions—year 2	(400,000)
=	Stock tax basis—end of year 2	$ 1,700,000

The tax implication of the adjusted basis is that the amount of income tax that is paid by the shareholder upon the eventual sale of the corporate stock will depend on whether the sale is for an amount greater or lesser than the tax basis. Although a tax basis adjustment, in and of itself, does not affect the value of the corporate stock, the shareholder's after-tax return will be affected. Investment decisions may vary depending upon the shareholders' goals relating to a particular investment. This will be discussed later in the chapter.

The rules relating to the tax treatment of S corporations, as with all other tax rules, are complex. There is no need to delve any deeper into the rules for purposes of this chapter. Suffice it to say that when an analyst is involved with the valuation of an S corporation, professional tax advice may be necessary.

Valuation Issues

In the valuation of an equity interest in an S corporation, two main issues arise. First, do the income tax advantages of the S election create value? This issue gets carried one step further by raising two key questions:

1. Value to whom?
2. How do we account for any incremental value in the valuation process?

The second issue is, if we value an S corporation by relying on the financial data from non–S corporation entities, what adjustments are necessary in the valuation process?

Many analysts believe that an S corporation should be valued in the same fashion as they would value a regular or C corporation. This is because:

- C corporations operate in the same economic environment as S corporations.
- S corporations may lose their S status in the future and convert to C corporations.
- Most measures of corporate performance used in valuation models, such as growth and discount rates, are derived from C corporations; therefore, S corporations should be valued as C corporations to maintain consistency with these measures.[3]

According to the Internal Revenue Service:

> S corporations lend themselves readily to valuation approaches comparable to those used in valuing closely held corporations [C corporations]. You need only to adjust the earnings from the business to reflect estimated corporate income taxes that would have been payable had the Subchapter S election not been made.[4]

Some analysts believe that the income tax benefits of having made an S election should increase the value of the entity. Many of the fundamental issues that affect the valuation process should be considered,

---

[3] William E. Simpson and Peter D. Wrobel, "Income Tax Issues in Valuing S Corporations," *CPA Expert*, Spring 1996, pp. 1–2.

[4] *IRS Valuation Training for Appeals Officers* (Chicago: CCH Incorporated, 1998), p. 7–12.

as well, for the determination of whether or not an S corporation election adds value. Some of these factors include:

1. Standard of value
2. Control versus minority ownership interest
3. Distributing versus nondistributing
4. Holding period of the investment
5. Time value of S corporation benefits

Standard of Value

The standard of value in any business valuation assignment affects the final estimate of value. Valuing an entity that has elected S status is no different. Let's consider the difference between fair market value and investment value.

A common definition of fair market value is found in Revenue Ruling 59–60. This revenue ruling defines fair market value as

> . . . the price at which the property would change hands between a willing buyer and a willing seller when the former is not under any compulsion to buy and the latter is not under any compulsion to sell, both parties having reasonable knowledge of relevant facts. Court decisions frequently state in addition that the hypothetical buyer and seller are assumed to be able, as well as willing, to trade and to be well informed about the property and concerning the market for such property.[5]

This definition of fair market value is widely used in valuation practice. Also implied in this definition is (1) that the value is to be stated in cash or cash equivalents and (2) that the property will have been exposed on the open market for a long enough period of time to allow the market forces to interact in order to establish the value.

Investment value may be defined as the "value to a particular investor based on individual investment requirements, as distinguished from the concept of market value, which is impersonal and detached."[6] Although this definition comes from real estate terminology, a similar application is used in business valuation. Investment value may differ from fair market value for a number of reasons. Among these reasons are:

1. Differences in estimates of future earning power
2. Differences in perception of the degree of risk
3. Differences in tax status
4. Synergies with other operations owned or controlled[7]

---

[5] Rev. Rul. 59–60 (1959–1 C.B. 237).

[6] *The Dictionary of Real Estate Appraisal*, 3d ed. (Chicago: Appraisal Institute, 1993), p. 190.

[7] Shannon P. Pratt, Robert F. Reilly, and Robert P. Schweihs, *Valuing a Business: The Analysis and Appraisal of Closely Held Companies*, 3d ed. (New York: McGraw-Hill, 1996). p. 25.

If the purpose of the valuation assignment is to estimate the fair market value of a controlling ownership interest in an S corporation for purchasing, selling, or merging the corporation, the corporation's tax structure may have little or no impact on value. If the most probable "willing buyer" is an ineligible shareholder (e.g., a C corporation), then that shareholder will not pay for income tax benefits that it cannot take advantage of. Therefore, in this case corporate income taxes should be a part of the valuation analysis. Conversely, if the "willing buyer" qualifies for the S election, that buyer may be willing to pay the seller for income tax benefits that will eventually be received, and it may be appropriate to assume no corporate income taxes in the determination of the benefit stream to the investor.

An important component of estimating fair market value is the determination of who will be the "willing buyer." This point became evident in the *Estate of Samuel Newhouse,*[8] where it was demonstrated that different classes of investors would pay different amounts under the fair market value scenario. Following this logical foundation, an analyst may need to make certain assumptions about the income tax attributes of the most likely purchaser. However, care should be exercised not to fall into a tax trap by identifying a specific buyer. The Tax Court has gone on record to state:

> We need not identify directly who the buyer would be or even what class of investors the buyer would belong to. The "willing buyer" is supposed to be a hypothetical amalgam of potential buyers in the marketplace. Although we have, in prior opinions, identified types of hypothetical buyers, we did so only to determine which valuation approach, among several reasonable approaches, would result in the highest bid, and therefore the one most acceptable to a willing seller. The question is not so much "who" but "how."[9]

The financial characteristics (including the tax attributes) of the most likely purchaser of the property are an important element in examining the highest and best use of the property. During periods of industry consolidation, companies are offered greater amounts (higher premiums) than they may get from "nonsynergistic" buyers. If the seller expects that his or her company will sell to one of the consolidators, then the company's fair market value may appropriately include a price premium for consolidation (but not for S status, since that election would likely not be available to the buyer). This argument can be carried one step further by stating that when an analyst reviews market data, a examination is generally made as to who is buying these companies. Therefore, it is not uncommon to consider the issue of who is the most likely willing buyer.

For smaller companies, the likelihood of the S election to continue and the corresponding value implications are more easily understood.

[8] *Estate of Samuel Newhouse*, 94 T.C. 193 (Feb. 28, 1990).
[9] *Estate of Mueller* v. *Commissioner*, TC Memo 1992–284 at 1415, 63 TCM 3027–16 (citations omitted).

Small businesses are frequently purchased by an individual or a group of individuals who will continue to operate the company as an S corporation. In these situations, the continuity of an S election may be a reasonable assumption. However, small businesses do not always automatically qualify as S corporations after they are purchased. As the melting pot of the United States continues to grow, a large influx of nonresident aliens is flooding the marketplace creating new possible purchasers of businesses. It may no longer be the most likely scenario that the S election will continue after the acquisition.

Larger corporations are even more problematic than small corporations when the analyst has to make assumptions about the tax attributes of the most likely willing buyer. Larger entities are more likely to be purchased by a C corporation, a move that would immediately negate the S election. Therefore, it may be reasonable to assume that the target company will not be able to continue its S corporation tax status.

Purpose of the Assignment

In addition to the standard of value, the purpose of the assignment may also cause the analyst to consider the extent to which the S corporation affects business value. For example, if the business valuation is being performed to estimate fair market value in a matrimonial litigation, it may be considered unfair to the nonowner spouse to make the assumption that the S election will change. However, since matrimonial courts are courts of equity, it may be equally unfair to the business owner not to recognize that taxes have to be paid on corporate income—and that they are paid at the personal level even if the S corporation pays no dividends.

When the standard of value is investment value, the analyst should consider whether the specific buyer would cause a revocation of the S election. The specific buyer's goals regarding rates of return and whether he or she wants current cash flow or capital appreciation should be considered when analyzing the consequences of the S status on business investment value. More often than not, valuations of an entire business being performed for transactional purposes (1) use pretax earning streams and then (2) adjust for the buyer's expected income tax status rather than the seller's historical tax structure.

Business valuations are performed for a wide variety of purposes. The impact of the S election on business value depends on the purpose of the assignment.

Control Versus Minority Ownership Interest

If the business interest being valued is a minority ownership interest—that is, the ownership interest does not enjoy the prerogatives of control—then a direct comparison with values of other minority ownership interests often is the most appropriate method of valuation.[10] In essence,

---

[10] Pratt, Reilly, and Schweihs. *Valuing a Business: The Analysis and Appraisal of Closely Held Companies*, 3d ed., p. 525.

if the minority ownership interest cannot effect a change in the company's income tax structure, no such change should be assumed.

An argument could be made that a minority ownership shareholder could, in fact, cause a change to an S election by selling the shares to a nonqualified shareholder of the S corporation. This violation of the rules regarding ownership could change the tax status involuntarily. However, an analyst should also consider the likelihood of the shareholder's action. It would seem that the minority shareholder would have to have special motivations to intentionally kill the S election for the balance of the shareholders. Considering special motivations of a buyer or seller may violate the definition of fair market value.

Although the minority ownership shareholder can cause the S election to be involuntarily terminated, it is not an obvious assumption. The facts and circumstances of the situation dictate whether or not to make such an assumption.

Distributing versus Nondistributing

The S corporation status may be favorable or unfavorable depending upon whether the corporation distributes its earnings to its shareholders. If only some, or possibly none, of the earnings are distributed, the result can be extremely unfavorable to the investor.

For example, let's assume that ABC Corp. and XYZ Corp. are similar companies, both operating with valid S elections under the tax law. Let's further assume that ABC Corp. can distribute all its earnings, since its cash flow is adequate for all its capital requirements. XYZ Corp., however, has to reinvest most of its earnings and can distribute only some of them. The results presented in Exhibit 6–1 illustrate the potential problem for the investors.

This example illustrates the fact that the shareholders of ABC Corp. are clearly better off than XYZ shareholders, at least when it comes to the net distributions that they received during the year. Shareholders of XYZ Corp. paid more personal income taxes than they received in distributions, leaving them in a negative cash flow position for the year.

Exhibit 6–1

S Corporations		
	ABC Corp.	**XYZ Corp.**
Pretax income	$ 600,000	$ 600,000
Corporate income tax	0	0
Net income	$ 600,000	$ 600,000
Distributions	$ 600,000	$ 200,000
Personal income tax (at 40%)	240,000	240,000
Net distributions	$ 360,000	$ (40,000)

But what happens if these same two corporations had been regular (C) corporations, instead of S corporations? Exhibit 6–2 illustrates the impact. In the case of the C corporation, the shareholders of ABC Corp. realize a $216,000 net distribution from the company. However, when comparing this with the $360,000 net distributions that they received as an S corporation, the shareholders did not do as well as they could have if the company was an S corporation. The shareholders of XYZ Corp. actually did better than ABC shareholders by being owners of a C corporation in that year. Whereas shareholders' cash flow was negative $40,000 in an S corporation, cash flow was $0 in a C corporation. In the C corporation situation, the company did not distribute any of the earnings because it required the same $400,000 that it retained in Exhibit 6–1.

As discussed earlier in this chapter, a shareholder's income tax basis in the S corporation is increased by any profits that are retained by the corporation. In Exhibit 6–1, although the shareholders of XYZ Corp. had a negative cash flow, their tax basis increased by $400,000 ($600,000 net income less $200,000 in distributions). This will reduce the amount of income taxes payable when the shareholders eventually sell their shares.

The questions that should be considered are: (1) When will a sale most likely take place? (2) What income tax rate will be paid on the assumed capital gain at the time of the sale? Changing income tax rates, timing issues, and a myriad of other factors come into play here.

The valuation implications of this situation depend upon the facts and circumstances of the subject valuation. Most business valuations are performed by considering only corporate level income taxes, without consideration of personal taxes, but it may be inappropriate to ignore personal income taxes when valuing an S corporation. The investor in the real world makes investment decisions on the basis of the net benefit to him or her. This issue has been argued about for years in the case of the built-in gains attributable to the appreciation of real estate held in a C corporation. So why shouldn't a similar argument be made here?

Exhibit 6–2

C Corporations

	ABC Corp.	XYZ Corp.
Pretax income	$ 600,000	$ 600,000
Corporate income tax (at 40%)	240,000	240,000
Net income	$ 360,000	$ 360,000
Distributions	$ 360,000	$ 0
Personal income tax (at 40%)	144,000	0
Net distributions	$ 216,000	$ 0

It is readily accepted that an investor in common stock of any corporation makes an economic investment for three reasons. They are:

1. Immediate cash flow (dividends)
2. Future cash flow (capital appreciation)
3. A combination of 1 and 2 above

The total expected return to the shareholder consists of a part that is currently taxable and a part that is tax-deferred until the time of sale. Under the current tax law, the deferred portion may be subject to favorable capital gains tax rates. Although the present value discount rate used in the application of a discounting model ignores personal income tax rates, the investor does not.

Exhibit 6–1 illustrates that ABC Corp. is more valuable to the investor than XYZ Corp., based solely on the distributions made to the shareholders. The XYZ Corp. shareholders receive distributions and immediately turn around and pay them out, and more, as personal income taxes. The capital appreciation component has been excluded so far in this example but needs to be considered in estimating the true value of the investment. The analyst should make some assumptions regarding when the residual will be received.

Using the same fact pattern as above, it can be demonstrated that the only true difference in value to the shareholders is the present value of the cash that can be retained by the shareholders. Exhibits 6–3 and 6–4 assume that at the end of the year, the corporations are sold. ABC Corp. is sold for $1 million. XYZ Corp. is sold for $1.4 million (it is assumed that the reinvested funds added a dollar for dollar value, with no leveraging on the amount of reinvestment). In Exhibit 6–4, XYZ Corp. is sold for $1.36 million (less reinvestment took place as a C corporation).

According to Exhibit 6–3, the shareholders end up with the same amount of money in their pockets if the reinvestment of net income increases the value on a dollar for dollar basis. Management would hopefully leverage the reinvestment to increase the value of the company by an even greater amount. Therefore, although the shareholders in ABC Corp. had originally appeared better off than the shareholders of XYZ Corp., they may not have been.

Exhibit 6–4 demonstrates the impact of the sale on the shareholders of the C corporations.

The results reflected in Exhibits 6–1 through 6–4 allow us to draw the following conclusions:

1. As owners of an S corporation, the shareholders of ABC Corp. were better off than the shareholders of XYZ Corp. with regard to current cash flow.
2. As owners of an S corporation, the shareholders of ABC Corp. were only marginally better off than the shareholders of XYZ Corp. if an immediate sale took place. Any increase in value was, at most, attributable to the present value of the distributions and tax payments.

Exhibit 6–3

S Corporations

	ABC Corp.	XYZ Corp.
Shareholders' tax basis	$ 200,000	$ 200,000
Adjustments to basis:		
+ Net income	600,000	600,000
− Distributions	(600,000)	(200,000)
Adjusted tax basis	$ 200,000	$ 600,000
Sales price	1,000,000	1,400,000
Capital gain	$ 800,000	$ 800,000
Capital gains tax (at 20%)	$ 160,000	$ 160,000

Net Proceeds in the Shareholders' Pockets

	ABC Corp.	XYZ Corp.
Distribution	$ 600,000	$ 200,000
Ordinary income tax	(240,000)	(240,000)
Sales proceeds	1,000,000	1,400,000
Capital gains tax	(160,000)	(160,000)
Net proceeds in shareholders' pockets	$1,200,000	$1,200,000

Exhibit 6–4

C Corporations

	ABC Corp.	XYZ Corp.
Shareholders' tax basis	$ 200,000	$ 200,000
Adjustments to basis:		
+ Net income	0	600,000
− Distributions	0	0
Adjusted tax basis	$ 200,000	$ 200,000
Sales price	1,000,000	1,360,000
Capital gain	$ 800,000	$1,160,000
Capital gains tax (at 20%)	$ 160,000	$ 232,000

Net Proceeds in the Shareholders' Pockets

	ABC Corp.	XYZ Corp.
Distribution	$ 360,000	$ 0
Ordinary income tax	(144,000)	0
Sales proceeds	1,000,000	1,360,000
Capital gains tax	(160,000)	(232,000)
Net proceeds in shareholders' pockets	$1,056,000	$1,128,000

3. As owners of a C corporation, the shareholders of ABC Corp. were better off than the shareholders of XYZ Corp. with regard to current cash flow.
4. As owners of a C corporation, the shareholders of XYZ Corp. were better off when a sale took place.
5. The shareholders of both ABC Corp. and XYZ Corp. were better off when they were S corporations when considering the sale.
6. The shareholders of ABC Corp. were better off as owners of an S corporation when no sale took place.
7. The shareholders of XYZ Corp. were better off as owners of a C corporation when no sale occurred.

The conclusions reached in the above example indicate that the increase to value for being an S corporation does not happen in every situation. However, there does seem to be an indication that the shareholders did better in these scenarios if an S election was in place.

Exhibits 6–5 and 6–6 include similar illustrations as Exhibits 6–3 and 6–4. However, this time, leveraging is assumed to take place. This is probably more realistic, as one would expect there to be more than a dollar for dollar benefit from investment into the company.

Exhibit 6–5 reflects a sales price of $1.8 million resulting in the shareholders of XYZ Corp. coming out in a better position than the shareholders of ABC Corp. Exhibit 6–6 also reflects the benefits of leveraging, demonstrating that the shareholders of XYZ Corp. are better off than the ABC Corp. shareholders. The conclusion that can be reached from the illustration is that leveraging ultimately provides a considerably better return to the shareholders of XYZ Corp. when they elected S status. Therefore, not having the benefit of full distributions in the current year is more than offset if the nondistributed funds are reinvested with good leveraging.

Although the individual shareholders have the opportunity to leverage their investment portfolio as they periodically receive distributions, they may not be able to receive the same level of return on their investment as the nondistributed earnings that are reinvested into the leveraged company. Clearly, returns will vary according to the facts and circumstances surrounding the investments. However, if the returns were not expected to be better in the business enterprise, then the shareholders would be better off purchasing a well-diversified portfolio of public securities.

If the shareholders have control of the company, they will generally do everything possible to ensure that distributions are made in sufficient amounts to cover the personal income taxes. They do not want to reach into their own pockets to pay income taxes on profits that they did not receive. However, shareholders of a C corporation will usually take the opposite position, since they generally want to avoid paying income tax on dividend distributions. In fact, the Internal Revenue Service generally scrutinizes these companies either because they do not pay dividends or because the shareholders disguise the dividends as compensation. As a result, a dividend model based on actual dividends paid may overstate the value of an S corporation and understate the value of a C corporation.

Exhibit 6–5

S Corporations

	ABC Corp.	XYZ Corp.
Shareholders' tax basis	$ 200,000	$ 200,000
Adjustments to basis:		
+ Net income	600,000	600,000
– Distributions	(600,000)	(200,000)
Adjusted tax basis	$ 200,000	$ 600,000
Sales price	1,000,000	1,800,000
Capital gain	$ 800,000	$1,200,000
Capital gains tax (at 20%)	$ 160,000	$ 240,000

Net Proceeds in the Shareholders' Pockets

	ABC Corp.	XYZ Corp.
Distribution	$ 360,000	$ 200,000
Ordinary income tax	(240,000)	(240,000)
Sales proceeds	1,000,000	1,800,000
Capital gains tax	(160,000)	(240,000)
Net proceeds in shareholders' pockets	$1,200,000	$1,520,000

Exhibit 6–6

C Corporations

	ABC Corp.	XYZ Corp.
Shareholders' tax basis	$ 200,000	$ 200,000
Adjustments to basis:		
+ Net income	0	0
– Distributions	0	0
Adjusted tax basis	$ 200,000	$ 200,000
Sales price	1,000,000	1,720,000
Capital gain	$ 800,000	$1,520,000
Capital gains tax (at 20%)	$ 160,000	$ 304,000

Net Proceeds in the Shareholders' Pockets

	ABC Corp.	XYZ Corp.
Distribution	$ 360,000	$ 0
Ordinary income tax	(144,000)	0
Sales proceeds	1,000,000	1,720,000
Capital gains tax	(160,000)	(304,000)
Net proceeds in shareholders' pockets	$1,056,000	$1,416,000

Since shareholders of an S corporation will frequently attempt to pass through dividends to themselves in an amount at least equal to the estimated tax obligation, the actual dividend distributions may appear to be attractive. This could give the appearance that a company is a great dividend payer. It makes the investment appear as if it has excellent liquidity. The opposite is true with the shareholders of a C corporation. They will generally do everything possible to avoid dividends. Because of this, the C corporation would appear to be less liquid than the equivalent S corporation. This contrasting position of the shareholders makes dividend-paying capacity a more attractive method to assess the value of the S corporation. Particularly in a controlling ownership interest valuation, even Revenue Ruling 59–60 suggests the use of dividend-paying capacity as opposed to actual dividends paid.

David C. Dufendach raises an interesting point about these returns.[11] He states:

> Research has shown that the slope of the actual security market line is less than predicted by the CAPM. [Eugene F. Brigham and Louis C. Gapenski, *Financial Management: Theory and Practice*, 6th ed. (Fort Worth, TX: The Dryden Press, 1991), pp. 156–157.] Riskier stocks have lower required returns than predicted, whereas less risky stocks suffer from higher required returns. One possible explanation is that riskier stocks provide relatively more of their return in the form of non-taxable price appreciation. One study suggests that this is the case. [Thomas E. Copeland and J. Fred Weston, *Financial Theory and Corporate Policy*, 2d ed. (New York: Addison Wesley Longman, 1983), p. 513. Refers to a study by I. Friend and M. Puckett, "Dividends and Stock Prices," *American Economic Review*, September 1964, pp. 656–682.] If true, then investors who wish to avoid current tax liability on dividend income would prefer higher risk/lower dividend stocks, driving down their required return below that predicted by the CAPM. Another study supported this view, implying that dividends are undesirable (presumably because of their immediate taxability), and that stocks with higher dividends are penalized in the form of higher required returns. [Ibid., pp. 515–516. Refers to a study by R. Litzenberger and K. Ramaswamy, "The Effect of Personal Taxes and Dividends on Capital Asset Prices: Theory and Empirical Evidence," *Journal of Financial Economics*, June 1979, pp. 163–196.]

The various studies cited by Dufendach lead to the conclusion that, given all other risk factors being equal, a stock that pays dividends, causing an immediate income tax consequence, is worth less than a stock that provides capital appreciation, which is tax-deferred and then possibly taxed at more favorable rates. The factor that causes the difference in value is apparently personal income taxes. We accept the premise that a prudent investor considers personal income taxes in investment decisions. Otherwise, if all else were equal, why would anyone

[11] David C. Dufendach, "Valuation of Closely Held Corporations: 'C' v. 'S' Differentials," *Business Valuation Review*, December 1996, pp. 176–179.

buy tax-free bonds? Therefore, we should not ignore the personal tax effect of the investment. The difficulty is estimating which income tax rates to use.

Corporate or Personal Income Tax Rate

One of the difficulties that the analyst faces is the determination of which set of income taxes is appropriate to use in valuing the S corporation. The determination will most likely depend on the standard of value. However, this exercise can be more trouble than it is worth.

If the standard of value is fair market value, the appropriate income tax rates should be those rates that will be applicable in the hands of the willing buyer. The problem is that we do not know who that specific buyer will be. Will it be an individual, another S corporation, or a C corporation? Once again, there is no distinct answer. Depending upon the facts and circumstances, the analyst may be able to make an assumption about the most probable willing buyer (or category of buyer).

If the standard of value is investment value, the analyst should consider the income tax rates of the specific buyer. In this instance, the analyst is estimating value to a particular buyer. This makes the task a little bit easier.

Once the standard of value has been identified, the analyst is still faced with the dilemma of which rates to use. If corporate income tax rates are used, the analyst, with or without the help of the local CPA, can calculate the income taxes from the sliding rates applicable at the time. However, if personal rates are to be used, this calculation can become even more complicated because of factors such as personal exemptions, itemized deductions, phase-out rules, and other income or losses from unrelated activities that could affect the income tax rates that may be applicable. The analysis could become convoluted.

The practical application of income tax rates is up to the analyst. If the rates can be calculated in a relatively straightforward manner, the analyst should do so. If personal income tax rates are involved, most analysts believe that there is little to be gained by factoring in personal exemptions and itemized deductions. If the analyst represents a specific potential buyer who is an individual, these items may be taken into consideration if they are material. Common sense and reasonableness should prevail.

Holding Period of the Investment

Many analysts feel that both S and C corporations should be valued on an after-tax basis. Many analysts subscribe to the premise that "after-tax" means after corporate income tax and not after personal income taxes to the individual. Since yield and direct capitalization rates are derived from an analysis of market evidence, usually after corporate income taxes but before personal income taxes, more comparability can be achieved by applying corporate income tax rates. Adjusting the income returns for personal income taxes would make the discount rate selection more difficult.

This is particularly true since rates of return reported in the empirical literature are based on returns to the investor before personal taxes are paid.

Some analysts adjust the benefit stream of an S corporation to the amount left over after the payment of dividends. It is fairly common to see dividends paid by S corporations in the amount no more than that necessary to pay the personal income tax obligation associated with the S corporation's taxable income. In that way, shareholders have the money they need to meet their income tax obligation and the S corporation retains the balance for corporate purposes. The problem with this approach to estimating the appropriate S corporation's earnings stream is that the shareholders of an S corporation increase their income tax basis in the S corporation for the balance of the net income on which the tax has already been paid but not distributed. Therefore, comparability cannot truly be achieved between the S corporation shareholders and the C corporation shareholders.

A related consideration is that S corporation shareholders are permitted to take subsequent distributions from the S corporation without current tax implications. Shareholders' undistributed taxable income from previous years is available for distribution tax-free, since the shareholders have already paid tax on the profit in the year that it was earned. This also causes a significant difference in the timing of the cash flows between the shareholders of these different types of entities.

The timing differences can be caused by the shareholders' deferring distributions until a later year when they feel that the cash flow will permit them to do so. They may not have been able to distribute the profits immediately because of reinvestment needs of the entity.

An argument can be made that the difference between a perpetual S corporation and a C corporation is the present value of the annual corporate income tax savings. The analyst should face the question in each business valuation regarding an S corporation of what the holding period of the investment will be while the corporation keeps its S election. Some analysts believe it may be instructive to assume that a corporation will lose its S election at some point.[12]

This means that the interest in the corporation being valued will be an S corporation for certain years and convert to a C corporation for its remaining life. Therefore, the value of this entity can be measured as the present value of the S corporation benefit stream for N periods plus the present value of the C corporation benefit stream in the years $N + 1$ into perpetuity. When N years of S corporation benefits are greater than or equal to zero, the value can be expressed as:

$$\text{Value at time zero} = \left[\sum_{n=0}^{N} \frac{E(1 + g)^{n-1}}{(1 + d)^n} \right] + \left[\frac{\left(\dfrac{E(1 - t)(1 + g)^N}{d - g} \right)}{(1 + d)^N} \right]$$

[12] Robert E. Duffy and George L. Johnson, "Valuation of 'S' Corporations Revisited: The Impact of the Life of an 'S' Election under Varying Growth and Discount Rates," *Business Valuation Review*, December 1993, pp. 155–167.

where:
N = number of years S corporation status is retained
n = number of years in the life of the corporation, such that $0 \leq n$
$\leq \infty \leq N$
E = initial level of benefit stream before corporate income taxes
(reported at the end of year 1, at $n = 0$, $E = 0$)
g = growth rate in the benefit stream
d = present value discount rate
t = corporate income tax rate

If $N = 0$, the S election is lost immediately, resulting in C corporation earnings for the entire period. This would result in income taxes being paid at the corporate level for the entire holding period, thus reducing the available cash flow that can be distributed or reinvested into the company. When $N = \infty$, the opposite is true. The cash flow represents S corporation earnings that are expected to continue into perpetuity. Exhibit 6–7 illustrates the impact of this concept, demonstrating that the value of the company varies in a nonlinear fashion. The estimated life of the S election has a direct impact on its value. In this example, value indications vary between \$330,000 for a perpetual C corporation and \$500,000 for a perpetual S corporation. This example demonstrates that the value of an S corporation, without regard to personal income taxes and income tax basis adjustments, results in a premium over the C corporation value—because of the tax savings at the corporate level.

Exhibit 6–7 also demonstrates the size of the discount/premium related to S corporation status. The greater the life of the S corporation, the lower the discount from C corporation value, or the greater the premium attributable to the S election. Varying the growth rate of the benefits stream will impact the size of the discount or premium.

Timing of the Valuation

When the fair market value of the shares of stock in a corporation is estimated, theoretically, it does not matter who the shareholder is. In addition, the income tax implications of a sale of the interest by that shareholder should not be considered. Personal income taxes generally have no impact in the valuation of corporate stock (assuming that the shareholder is an individual). Obviously, not all shareholders are individuals, and not all shareholders are taxpaying entities. Pension plans, for example, do not pay taxes on gains in their investment portfolio. Therefore, the value of a share of IBM is no different if an individual owns it or if a pension plan owns it.

At this point, we have come almost full circle in our discussion about willing buyers. The investing public calculates rates of return on an after-corporate-tax basis. Since different classes of investors have different tax structures, the required rates of after-shareholder-tax return will vary among the classes. In estimating an appropriate discount rate for the net cash flow of an S corporation versus a C corporation, it is reasonable to

Exhibit 6–7

Valuation of S/C Hybrid Corporation Income

ASSUMPTIONS:

Present value discount rate	20%	Corporate income tax rate	34%	
Growth rate	0%	Benefit stream	$100,000	
Direct capitalization rate	20%			

Number of Years S Earnings Received	Present Value of Year n Earnings	Present Value of Taxed Residual	Sum of PV of N Years Earnings and Residual	Discount from S Value	Premium over C Value
0	$ 0	$ 330,000	$ 330,000	34.00%	0.00%
1	83,333	275,000	358,333	28.33%	8.59%
2	69,444	229,167	381,944	23.61%	15.74%
3	57,870	190,972	401,620	19.68%	21.70%
4	48,225	159,144	418,017	16.40%	26.67%
5	40,188	132,620	431,681	13.66%	30.81%
6	33,490	110,516	443,067	11.39%	34.26%
7	27,908	92,097	452,556	9.49%	37.14%
8	23,257	76,747	460,463	7.91%	39.53%
9	19,381	63,956	467,053	6.59%	41.53%
10	16,151	53,297	472,544	5.49%	43.20%
25	1,048	3,459	498,218	0.36%	50.98%
50	11	36	499,981	0.00%	51.51%
75	0	0	500,000	0.00%	51.52%
100	0	0	500,000	0.00%	51.52%
∞	0	0	500,000	0.00%	51.52%

Perpetual C Corp. Value	$330,000	Perpetual S Corp. Value	$500,000

SOURCE: Robert E. Duffy and George L. Johnson, "Valuation of 'S' Corporations Revisited: The Impact of the Life of an 'S' Election under Varying Growth and Discount Rates," *Business Valuation Review*, December 1993, pp. 155–167.

assume that there is an increased risk relative to the net cash flow of the S corporation that the enterprise may at some point in time pay taxes and have a lower cash flow. This could be justification for a different discount rate for the two entities. The question to be raised is, by how much?

Since all S corporations are privately held, it becomes difficult, if not impossible, to quantify the exact level of adjustment to the present value discount rate. Mathematical quantification cannot be used as readily as it is for the conversion of pretax and after-tax discount rates. Analysts continue to struggle with the notion of whether the corporate cash flows from an S corporation are after tax. Analysts have argued that there should be a tax equivalency made to reflect the personal income taxes that will have to be paid by S corporation shareholders.[13]

The reality of the situation is that personal income taxes will be paid whether or not distributions are made to the shareholder. It seems reasonable to consider these taxes in a similar fashion as corporate income taxes. Either way, the government is going to get paid. There is not going to be a benefit to the shareholder other than as an adjustment to his or her basis in the corporate stock.

Arguments have been raised for years regarding the built-in gains tax. Up until recently, the position of the Tax Court has been that no discount would be permitted for a built-in gains tax, even though investors in the real world consider them in making investment decisions. In the *Estate of Artemus D. Davis* v. *Commissioner*,[14] part of the discount for lack of marketability was attributed to the built-in gains tax. This could influence future valuations of S corporations, particularly those that have exposure to the built-in gains tax in the postconversion period. The issue then arises as to the S election having a possible discount associated with it because of the taxes that potentially could be paid at the corporate level.

If the valuation conclusion is to be based on the value to the willing seller, a valuation in the hands of the current owner of the investment in an S corporation may result in a more realistic valuation. This may be a consideration for the assignment when a transaction will not occur (e.g., a divorce valuation). However, that is clearly not fair market value. Personal income tax rates may vary depending on too many factors that have nothing to do with the investment. An analyst cannot be expected to consider items such as personal exemptions and itemized deductions. Certainly, the smaller S corporations can be affected by these items. Larger S corporations may not be influenced by these items because the shareholders are more likely to be in higher income tax brackets where these items do not matter. Does this mean that analysts should have two standards, one for small companies and one for large companies?

Conclusion

If the reader has learned anything from this chapter, it is probably that the question of an S corporation adding a premium or a discount to the value of an investment does not have an easy answer. Although there appears to be a possible benefit if the willing buyer can continue the S election into the future, there is no guarantee that this will happen. Consideration should be given to all the factors that influence value in making a determination.

---

[13] See George G. Cassiere, "The Value of S-Corp Election—The C-Corp Equivalency Model," *Business Valuation Review*, June 1994, pp. 84–91.

[14] *Estate of Artemus D. Davis* v. *Commissioner*, 110 T.C. 35 (1998).

The premium or discount issue should be examined on a case-by-case basis, because there is no other way to do it. For example, if the assignment calls for a valuation in which the willing buyer is known to qualify as an S corporation shareholder, the various attributes discussed in this chapter may lead to a premium or discount.

The answer depends on a variety of factors. Here, the most important factors are analyzed: income tax rates, leverage, holding period, timing, and control versus minority ownership interest. The S election may add value (a premium) if the entity will be sold in the short term. It may also add value if the individual income tax rates are lower than the C corporation income tax rates. Additional shareholder value can also be realized if the corporation cannot distribute profits in the year the profits are earned, but the corporation can distribute these previously taxed profits soon thereafter. The shareholder can benefit from the distribution.

A discount may result if no earnings are distributed. This is particularly true since these earnings will be taxed to the shareholder regardless of whether cash flow permitted a distribution to be made. A discount may also occur if the corporate income tax rates are lower than the individual income tax rates. This is because greater distributions will be required to allow the shareholders to pay their personal income taxes.

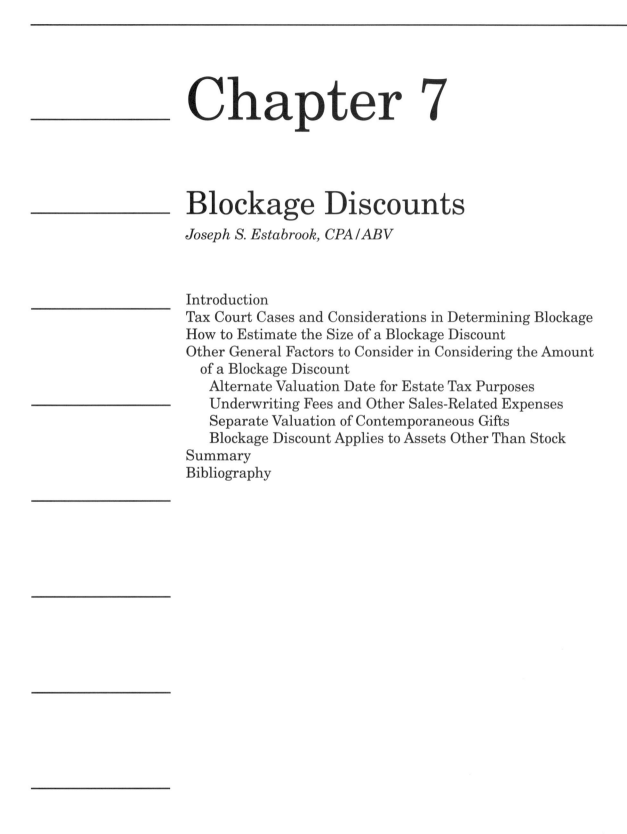

Chapter 7

Blockage Discounts

Joseph S. Estabrook, CPA/ABV

Introduction

A blockage discount is a deduction from the actively traded price of a stock because the block of stock to be valued is so large relative to the volume of actual sales on the existing market that the block could not be liquidated within a reasonable time without depressing the market price. Blockage discounts are considered in many business valuation assignments, especially for estate and gift tax purposes.

For estate tax purposes, the value of every item of property included in a decedent's gross estate is its fair market value at the date of death. This is true except that an executor can elect the alternate valuation date, which is six months after the date of death. Similarly, the value of a gift is its fair market value on the date of the gift. Under Section 20.2031-1(b) of the Estate Tax Regulations,[1] fair market value is defined as the price at which the property would change hands between a willing buyer and a willing seller, neither being under any compulsion to buy or to sell and both having reasonable knowledge of relevant facts. Furthermore, the fair market value of the property is not to be determined by a forced sales price. When the property to be valued is a marketable security, such as a stock or a bond, the value is the fair market value per share, which is the mean between the highest and lowest quoted selling prices on the valuation date.[2]

Under certain circumstances, however, the value of a share of stock determined on the basis of selling or bid and asked prices may not reflect its fair market value. The size of the block of stock may be a factor in determining whether the bid and asked prices reflect the fair market value of the stock.[3] Section 20.2031-2(e) of the Estate Tax Regulations recognizes this point:

> In certain exceptional cases, the size of the block of stock to be valued in relation to the number of shares changing hands in sales may be relevant in determining whether selling prices reflect the fair market value of the block of stock to be valued. If the executor can show that the block of stock to be valued is so large in relation to the actual sales on the existing market that it could not be liquidated in a reasonable time without depressing the market, the price at which the block could be sold as such outside the usual market, as through an underwriter, may be a more accurate indication of value than market quotations. Complete data in support of any allowance claimed due to the size of the block of stock shall be submitted with the return (Form 706 Estate Tax Return or Form 709 Gift Tax Return). On the other hand, if the block of stock to be valued represents a controlling interest, either actual or effective, in a going business, the price at which other lots change hands may have little relation to its true value.

---

[1] It should be noted that the Gift Tax Regulations for the valuation of stocks and bonds under 25.2512-2 mirror the Estate Tax Regulations under 20.2031–2. For purposes of this chapter, the reasoning of any regulation referred to under the Estate Tax Regulations should/would also apply for gift tax purposes.

[2] Reg. Sec. 20.2031-2(b)(1).

[3] *Estate of Myrtle M. Sawade*, T.C. Memo 1984-626.

Sales of small blocks of stocks do not provide conclusive evidence regarding the discount for a large block of the same stock.[4] Blockage is not a law of economics, a principle of law, or a rule of evidence. If the value of a given number of shares is influenced by the size of the block, this is a matter of evidence and not of doctrinaire assumption.[5] The Estate Tax Regulations require the taxpayer to show:

1. That the block of stock is so large that it could not be liquidated in a reasonable time without depressing the market.
2. That the number of shares ordinarily traded on the market must be so small, in comparison to the block, that even if the block is divided into smaller blocks, there would be a depressed sales price; this would have to be true even if the block was gradually sold through the market over a reasonably long period of time.
3. Whether the length of time needed to gradually dispose of the block is "reasonable," based on the facts and circumstances of each case.

The courts have determined that there is no presumption of blockage. The taxpayer must affirmatively provide evidence that the sales in the marketplace at or near the valuation date are not representative of the value of the subject block of stock. The block of stock being valued should be large in comparison to the volume of sales being traded on the exchange where it is listed. Rather than simply assuming that the entire block will be dumped on the market at one time, the analyst should consider sensible alternatives. The analysis should take into account the effect on the price, based on the assumption (1) that the block could not be sold on the market at its quoted price and (2) that the block would be fed out into the market under prudent practices of liquidation over a reasonable period of time. There is no definition of what a reasonable period of time is. It depends on the facts and circumstances of each case.

Blockage discounts should not be confused with other valuation discounts, specifically restricted stock discounts. Blockage is a separate and distinct concept. This concept relates essentially to the laws of supply and demand and the depressive effect on the price of selling. Restricted stock discounts relate to prohibiting the sale of the shares of stock for a defined holding period. The restrictions can introduce substantial valuation discounts that are of a magnitude much greater than blockage discounts. Revenue Ruling 77-287 deals with the valuation of restricted stocks. This revenue ruling states that the problem is to determine the difference in fair market value between (1) shares that are registered with the SEC and are actively traded and (2) the unregistered/restricted shares. Court cases over the years have not always

---

[4]*Phipps v. Commissioner*, 127 F.2d 214 (29 AFTR 209), 1942.

[5]*Safe Deposit & Trust Co. of Baltimore v. Commissioner, 35 B.T.A. 259 (1937).*, 127 F.2d 214 (29 AFTR 209).

distinguished between restricted stock and large blocks of stock. When performing case research on blockage discounts, the analyst should be acutely aware of the difference in these two concepts.

Tax Court Cases and Considerations in Determining Blockage

The concept of blockage was rejected by the Internal Revenue Service for many years until the courts first adopted it in the late 1930s (see Exhibit 7-1). In 1937, the Board of Tax Appeals made a landmark decision that "blockage is not a law of economics, a principle of law or a rule of evidence,"[6] but is based on the facts and circumstances of each case. The concept of blockage was finally recognized by the Internal Revenue Service in 1958, when it issued Federal Tax Regulations under Sections 2031 and 2512. Even though the Internal Revenue Service has issued regulations,[7] they are not conclusive as to objective guidance on how to actually identify and quantify a blockage discount.

With the burden of proof on the taxpayer to provide factual and objective proof of the existence of a blockage discount, analysts look to the court case decisions for guidance. Even with numerous court decisions on the subject over the last 60 years, there is still no conclusive objective method that can be applied in every case. The only thing certain is that the testimony of an expert witness will be considered along with the facts and circumstances of the case. Since each decision has been based on the specific facts and circumstances of the case, a large range of discounts has been decided by the courts. Even though the reported discounts in some cases have been as high as 50 percent, it appears that a restricted stock lack of marketability discount was included in the total blockage discount accepted by the court.

A pure blockage discount is typically substantially less than the lack of marketability discounts arrived at through the restricted stock studies.[8] Pure blockage discounts typically fall within a range of 0 to 15 percent, most often in the lower end of that range. Again, it is important to stress (1) that each case is based on its specific facts and circumstances and (2) that the use of averages or an analysis based on anything other than the specific facts and circumstances is perilous. Furthermore, if there is appropriate justification for a discount that is higher than the

---

[6] Ibid.

[7] Federal Tax Regulations 20.2031-2(e) and 25.2512-2(e).

[8] See, for example, Milton Gelman, "An Economist-Financial Analyst's Approach to Valuing Stock of a Closely Held Company," *Journal of Taxation*, June 1972, pp. 353–354; Robert R. Trout, "Estimation of the Discount Associated with the Transfer of Restricted Securities," *Taxes*, June 1977, pp. 381–385; Robert E. Moroney, "Most Courts Overvalue Closely Held Stocks," *Taxes*, March 1973, pp. 144–154; and Shannon P. Pratt, Robert F. Reilly, and Robert P. Schweihs, "Discount for Lack of Marketability" (Chapter 25) in *Valuing Small Businesses and Professional Practices*, 3d ed. (New York: McGraw-Hill, 1998), pp. 445–475.

Exhibit 7–1

Relevant Case History of Blockage Discounts

Case Name	Citation	Issues
Helvering v. *Safe Deposit and Trust Company of Baltimore*	35 BTA 259, 263 (1937)	Landmark decision that "blockage is not a law of economics, a principle of law or a rule of evidence," but is based on the facts and circumstances of each case.
Bull v. *Smith*	119 F.2d 490 (CA-2,1941)	Standard of value not a forced sale but what "a skillful broker could, within a reasonable period, have realized for the stock."
L.C. Phipps v. *Commissioner*	127 F.2d 214 (10th Cir., 1942)	Established that "evidence of sales of small blocks of stock is not a criterion of the value of a large block of same stock."
Estate of Christie v. *Commissioner*	T.C. Memo 1974-95 (1974)	Petitioner suggested that an arithmetical average of discounts allowed in previous court cases be used: "The suggestion is too simplistic to require detailed comment."
Rushton v. *Commissioner*	498 F.2d 88 (5th Cir., 1974)	Permits a blockage discount for gift tax purposes only upon "a showing that the block of stock to be valued with reference to each separate gift . . . without consideration of companion" gifts.
Estate of Kopperman v. *Commissioner*	T.C. Memo 1978-475 (1978)	Whether a blockage exists is "solely a question of fact and petitioner bears the burden of proof."
Estate of Sawade v. *Commissioner*	T.C. Memo 1984-626 (1984)	Petitioner valued shares as if each block was dumped on the market in one transaction. Expert "did not consider the alternative of disposing of the stock in small amounts over a reasonable period of time;" blockage discount not allowed.
Robinson v. *Commissioner*	T.C. Memo 1985-275 (1985)	Court evaluated declining market prices, public knowledge of sale of block, and broker discount pressure in valuing stock obtained pursuant to exercise of stock option determined under section 83(a).
Adair v. *Commissioner*	T.C. Memo 1987-494 (1987)	Distinguishes between a restricted stock marketability discount and a blockage discount and allowed both discounts to be taken against the same block of stock.
Mitchell v. *Commissioner*	T.C. Memo 1990-617 (1990)	Court rejected petitioner's experts findings since expert "did not provide any specific facts on which to base such a discount."
Estate of Friedberg v. *Commissioner*	T.C. Memo 1992-310 (1992)	Court discusses a number of different factors to be considered in arriving at an appropriate blockage discount.
Estate of Wright v. *Commissioner*	T.C. Memo 1997-53 (1997)	Allowed a blockage discount after Court rejected respondent's evidence of a control premium.
Estate of Artemus D. Davis v. *Commissioner*	110 T.C. No. 35 (1998)	Blockage discount was not allowed since "Petitioner has the burden of establishing that a blockage/or SEC rule 144 discount should be applied . . . we find that the Petitioner has failed to satisfy that burden."
Estate of Mario E. Bosca v. *Commissioner*	T.C. Memo 1998-251 (1998)	IRS improperly valued transferred voting stock as a single block of 50%, rather than as 2 separate blocks of 25%. Amount of premium reduced based on 2 separate blocks.
Estate of Dorothy B. Foote v. *Commissioner*	T.C. Memo 1999-37 (1999)	The petitioner's failure to show the market price of the stock on valuation date created an inaccurate reflection of the true value of the block of stock. Relative size of the block at issue in relation to the amount of stock outstanding (plus the trading volume and the fact that the entire block was sold within a reasonable period of time) suggests only a minimal blockage discount warranted. Court accepted respondent's expert's opinion of a 3.3% blockage discount.

The cases listed in this table are not all inclusive. Additional analysis of relevant cases can be found in the Bureau of National Affairs, Inc., *Tax Management Series*, Portfolio 831-2d, B-301 to B-305.

suggested range, it should be presented and a bigger blockage discount should be applied.

Despite the lack of a definitive model, an analysis of court decisions and pertinent valuation literature has shown a pattern of factors that should be considered in order to support the determination of a blockage discount:[9]

1. The percentage of shares represented by the subject block of stock relative to the number of shares outstanding of the company.
2. The share size of the subject block of stock relative to the daily, weekly, quarterly, and annual volume of shares of the subject stock traded.
3. The volatility of the price of the subject stock and the actual price changes in the stock under recent and preceding market conditions.
4. The size of trading "float" of the stock, relative to the number of shares outstanding.
5. How much daily volume could be increased without affecting price and how long it would take to dribble out the stock into the market.
6. Whether the stock trades on a recognized national stock exchange, on Nasdaq, over the counter, or on a regional exchange.
7. The trend of the price and financial performance of the subject stock relative to the general equity markets for the periods preceding the valuation date.
8. The dividend yield of the subject company as compared with industry and general market equity yields.
9. The current economic outlook for the company, its industry, and the national and regional economy.
10. The existence of recent large block trades or major secondary offerings of the subject stock or the guideline companies.
11. The existence of significant news or articles on the company or industry that may have affected stock price behavior.
12. The total number of shareholders in the company and how many are institutional investors and their proportion of ownership.
13. Any special features or attributes of the stock—voting/nonvoting, different classes, and so forth.
14. How many analysts follow the stock and whether there have been any recent changes in their recommendations.
15. How many market makers there are and who they are.

---

[9] Philip W. Moore, "Blockage Redux," *Trusts and Estates*, February 1992; J. Michael Julius, "Blockage Discounts and Restricted Stocks," *Mercer Capital Value Added*, Vol. 6, No. 3, 1994.

How to Estimate the Size of a Blockage Discount

The valuation analyst should perform a due diligence analysis by considering the factors previously enumerated. This will allow for the preparation of a detailed opinion—an opinion that substantiates the fact that the block of stock could not be disposed of within a reasonable period of time after the valuation date without depressing the market. Since the burden of proof is on the taxpayer, the valuation analyst's report should fully explain the process and methods used. The report should be similar to a standard valuation report, which includes the basic elements of the valuation assignment such as the name of the client, definition and size of the interest being valued, date of the valuation, purpose of the valuation, and applicable standard of value.

The valuation report should also include an implicit or explicit discussion of the following facts or present supporting exhibits specific to the blockage discount:

1. Daily trading prices, volume, and number of trades for a reasonable period before and after the valuation date.
2. Analysis of the volatility of the trading price in relation to trading volume.
3. Discussion of the stock market on which the shares are traded.
4. Number and volume of block trades during the same period.
5. Daily, monthly, quarterly, and annual average volume of trades.
6. Total number of shares outstanding, how many stockholders the company has, and what percentage of stock each stockholder owns.
7. How much the daily volume could be increased without affecting price.
8. Fundamental performance trends and overall condition of the economy, the subject company, and its industry.
9. Discussion of how many analysts follow the stock and if there have been recent changes in their consideration.
10. Discussion of how many market makers there are for the stock and who they are.
11. Schedule of analysts, market traders, and corporate officers interviewed and discussion of the facts obtained from the interviews.
12. Detailed exhibits showing the method and calculation of the blockage discount.

The court case decisions have demonstrated that all the facilities available for the disposition of the block of stock over a reasonable period of time should be considered. There are procedures for selling large blocks of stock that are governed by the individual exchanges on which the stock is traded, and they include:[10]

---

[10]The Bureau of National Affairs, Inc., *Tax Management Series,* Portfolio 831–2d, p. A–13; Rules of Board of Governors, New York Stock Exchange, Rule 391–Rule 396.

1. The sale to an underwriting syndicate for resale to the public—*secondary distribution*. The stock is offered for sale *off the floor* of the exchange at a price not exceeding the last sales price of the stock on the floor of the exchange at the time of the offering.

2. A *special offering* by which a broker may buy the entire block and resell it or offer it. The offering is at a fixed price by one or more members of the exchange acting as a principal or agent for the sale of the stock *through* the exchange, with special commissions paid by the seller to other members of the exchange who accept the offering for a particular account.

3. *Exchange distributions*, where one member acting as a principal or as an agent sells a block to other members of the exchange that have solicited purchases—and the price of the stock cannot be stabilized during the period of sale.

4. *Private placement* of the stock, which does not involve any public offerings. Securities regulations control when a sale of stock is exempt from registration and can be sold as a private placement.

5. Sales made in smaller lots over a reasonable period of time.

A determination should be made as to which procedure would be most feasible to dispose of the stock over a reasonable time period. As part of the due diligence process, experts such as market makers, traders, investment analysts, brokers, and investment bankers should be interviewed. Through the interview process, the proper information is gathered to allow for ample substantiation as to why a particular technique was either chosen or disregarded. This is an important step in the valuation process.

If it is determined that one of the first four steps is the most reasonable, then the amount of the discount is based on the difference between (1) the hypothetical sales price and (2) the actual trading price on the date of the valuation. (See the section below on other factors to consider for a discussion of what expenses of sale can be considered in ascertaining the appropriate discount.)

If none of the first four procedures are feasible or make the most sense under the facts and circumstances, then the blockage discount is based on the technique of hypothetically selling the stock in smaller lots over a reasonable period of time. From an analysis of the trading volume and discussions with the market makers and traders, a determination is made as to (1) the number of additional shares required over and above normal trading volume and (2) over what length of time they could be fed into the market—without depressing the stock price. An appropriate present value discount rate is arrived at to reflect the appropriate amount of risk involved. The net present value of the cash flow proceeds based on the various sale dates is calculated to arrive at the fair market value of the block of the stock, as of the valuation date.

Exhibit 7-2 is an example of a block in which a reasonable time period to dispose of the stock would be over a three-week period, with a portion of the block being sold in a scheduled public offering. The block represents 3.687 percent of the outstanding shares of the subject company. On the basis of the specific facts and circumstances of the case, the

Exhibit 7–2

Estate of a Decedent A
Valuation of 650,000 Shares of ABC, Inc.
Considering a Blockage Discount
as of December 28, 1995

Total number of shares to be liquidated:	650,000	
Number of shares to be traded daily:	10,000	
Reasonable number of trading days to liquidate 170,000 shares	40	
Discount rate (prime @ 12/28/95 of 8.5 + 5%), first 170,000 shares	13.50%	0.000369863
Public offering risk premium	3.00%	
Discount rate for public offering, 480,000 shares	16.50%	0.000452055
Mean share value at date of death	$21.9375	
Total mean share value at date of death:	$14,259,375	
Date of death:	12/28/95	

Date	Trading Dates	Period	Shares Traded	Mean Share Value Share Value	Mean Share Value Cumulative Trade	Mean Share Remaining Balance	Mean Share Cumulative Balance
Liquidation of first block of 170,000 shares:							
12/29/95	12/29/95	1	0	$21.9375	$0	$14,259,375	$0
12/30/95		2	0	$21.9375	0	14,259,375	0
12/31/95		3	0	$21.9375	0	14,259,375	0
01/01/96	Holiday	4	0	$21.9375	0	14,259,375	0
01/02/96	01/02/96	5	0	$21.9375	0	14,259,375	0
01/03/96	01/03/96	6	0	$21.9375	0	14,259,375	0
01/04/96	01/04/96	7	0	$21.9375	0	14,259,375	0
01/05/96	01/05/96	8	0	$21.9375	0	14,259,375	0
01/06/96		9	0	$21.9375	0	14,259,375	0
01/07/96		10	0	$21.9375	0	14,259,375	0
01/08/96	01/08/96	11	0	$21.9375	0	14,259,375	0
01/09/96	01/09/96	12	0	$21.9375	0	14,259,375	0
01/10/96	01/10/96	13	0	$21.9375	0	14,259,375	0
01/11/96	01/11/96	14	0	$21.9375	0	14,259,375	0
01/12/96	01/12/96	15	0	$21.9375	0	14,259,375	0
01/13/96		16	0	$21.9375	0	14,259,375	0
01/14/96		17	0	$21.9375	0	14,259,375	0
01/15/96	01/15/96	18	10,000	$21.9375	219,375	14,040,000	219,375
01/16/96	01/16/96	19	10,000	$21.9375	219,375	13,820,625	438,750
01/17/96	01/17/96	20	10,000	$21.9375	219,375	13,601,250	658,125
01/18/96	01/18/96	21	10,000	$21.9375	219,375	13,381,875	877,500
01/19/96	01/19/96	22	10,000	$21.9375	219,375	13,162,500	1,096,875
01/20/96		23	0	$21.9375	0	13,162,500	1,096,875
01/21/96		24	0	$21.9375	0	13,162,500	1,096,875
01/22/96	01/22/96	25	10,000	$21.9375	219,375	12,943,125	1,316,250
01/23/96	01/23/96	26	10,000	$21.9375	219,375	12,723,750	1,535,625
01/24/96	01/24/96	27	10,000	$21.9375	219,375	12,504,375	1,755,000
01/25/96	01/25/96	28	10,000	$21.9375	219,375	12,285,000	1,974,375
01/26/96	01/26/96	29	10,000	$21.9375	219,375	12,065,625	2,193,750
01/27/96		30	0	$21.9375	0	12,065,625	2,193,750
01/28/96		31	0	$21.9375	0	12,065,625	2,193,750
01/29/96	01/29/96	32	10,000	$21.9375	219,375	11,846,250	2,413,125
01/30/96	01/30/96	33	10,000	$21.9375	219,375	11,626,875	2,632,500
01/31/96	01/31/96	34	10,000	$21.9375	219,375	11,407,500	2,851,875
02/01/96	02/01/96	35	10,000	$21.9375	219,375	11,188,125	3,071,250
02/02/96	02/02/96	36	10,000	$21.9375	219,375	10,968,750	3,290,625
02/03/96		37	0	$21.9375	0	10,968,750	3,290,625
02/04/96		38	0	$21.9375	0	10,968,750	3,290,625
02/05/96	02/05/96	39	10,000	$21.9375	219,375	10,749,375	3,510,000
02/06/96	02/06/96	40	10,000	$21.9375	219,375	$10,530,000	$3,729,375

Totals:	170,000	729,375	$ 3,729,375

Fair market value (NPV of cash flows from 12/29/95-2/6/96)   3,690,329

Blockage discount on 170,000 shares (difference) $ 39,046

Liquidation of second block of 480,000 shares in public offering:

Date	Trading Dates	Period	Shares Traded	Mean Share Value Share Value	Mean Share Value Cumulative Trade	Mean Share Remaining Balance	Mean Share Cumulative Balance
02/07/96	02/07/96	41	480,000	$21.9375	$10,530,000	$0	$14,259,375

Fair market value (present value from 12/29/95 thru 2/7/96)   10,336,675

Blockage discount on 480,000 shares (difference) $ 193,325

Total blockage discount $ 232,371

Total fair market value as of December 28, 1995 $ 14,027,004

blockage discount represents a 1.63 percent discount from the share price at the date of the valuation.

Another method of estimating a blockage discount suggests that there are two separate and distinct cost components of blockage that should be measured.[11] The first cost component is *price pressure*. This can be defined as the impact on stock price when a large block of stock depresses the market and lowers the price that can be obtained for the stock. The second cost component is *market exposure*. This is the cost associated with bearing the risk of holding a position in the marketplace without the ability to close the position, for a specified period of time. The appropriate blockage discount is that combination of price pressure and market exposure that produces the least cost to the seller of the block. Using this approach appears to satisfy both requirements of the tax regulations: (1) that the taxpayer show that the length of time is reasonable, and (2) that the sale of smaller blocks of stock would depress the sales price.[12]

In estimating price pressure, the factors listed earlier should be taken into consideration. The valuation analyst should analyze the daily price volatility in relation to trading volume over at least a three- to six-month period (longer if deemed appropriate) in order to identify the amount of additional price movement that is created by the trading of the additional shares. From this analysis, the amount of the excess volatility or negative pricing pressure created by selling the shares is estimated.

Market exposure is estimated by calculating the cost of buying a put option on the subject company shares (1) at a strike price equal to the traded sales price at the valuation date (date of death or gift), (2) exercisable in the number of days determined under the different trading period scenarios, (3) based on the results of the analyst's due diligence. The cost of the put option is determined under a conventional option model (e.g., the Black-Scholes option pricing model). Such a model takes into consideration the five variables of stock price, exercise price, risk-free rate, time to expiration, and volatility (all on an annualized basis).

Exhibit 7-3 is an example of the blockage discount based on both price pressure and market exposure. In this example, the stock price is $40, the block size is 500,000 shares, and the average daily trading volume is 25,000 shares. An analysis of the normal price volatility of ABC, Inc., is made and is compared with the excess volatility at various levels of trading volume. The average percent price decline is the price pressure discount for each trading volume scenario. The cost of the put option is based on the calendar day equivalent of the trading volume days. The cost of the put compared with the stock price is the market exposure discount. The combination of the two discounts that gives the lowest possible total discount would be the reasonable length of time that the block would be sold—and would equal the blockage discount.

[11] William H. Frazier, "The Use of Capital Gains Tax Liability When Employing an Asset-Based Approach to the Valuation of a C Coporation and 'Pure' Blockage" (presentation to the Valuation Study Group), April 25–28, 1996.

[12] Federal Tax Regulation 20.2031-2(e).

Exhibit 7–3

Estate of Decedent A

ABC, Inc.

Blockage Discount Example

Considering Price Pressure and Market Exposure

Stock price	$40.00	
Block size	500,000	shares
Average daily trading volume	25,000	shares

Price Volatility	Selling Period	Excess Volume		Excess Volatility Created (a)	ABC Price At End of Period	Average % Price Decline	
	10 Days	200%	50,000	1.75%	$33.50	9.30%	
	20 Days	100%	25,000	0.75%	$34.41	7.60%	
	30 Days	67%	16,667	0.45%	$34.94	6.70%	
	40 Days	50%	12,500	0.25%	$36.19	5.00%	
	60 days	33%	8,333	0.10%	$37.67	2.90%	
	80 Days	25%	6,250	0.005%	$38.43	2.00%	

Price Pressure

Days to sell block	10	20	30	40		60	80
Additional shares sold daily	50,000	25,000	16,667	12,500		8,333	6,250
Average daily excess volume	200.00%	100.00%	67.00%	50.00%		33.00%	25.00%
Discount	9.30%	7.60%	6.70%	5.00%	11.43%	2.90%	2.00%

Market Exposure

Calendar days = to trading days	14	28	42	56	84	112
Averaged days	7	14	21	28	42	56
Cost of put	$1.65	$2.33	$2.84	$3.27	$3.98	$4.57
Discount	4.13%	5.83%	7.10%	8.19%	9.95%	11.43%

| **Total of two components** | 13.43% | 13.43% | 13.80% | 13.19% | 12.85% | 13.43% |

| **Blockage discount** | | | | | **12.85%** | |

a. Based on due diligence analysis of trading volume and price volatility.

SOURCE: William H. Frazier, "The Use of Capital Gains Tax Liability When Employing an Asset-Based Approach to the Valuation of a C Corporation and 'Pure' Blockage," presentation to the Valuation Study Group, April 25–28, 1996.

Other General Factors to Consider in Considering the Amount of a Blockage Discount

Alternate Valuation Date for Estate Tax Purposes

Under Internal Revenue Code Section 2032(a), the executor of an estate can elect an alternate valuation date that is six months after the decedent's death. The election should decrease the gross estate and estate tax. Its purpose is to permit a reduction in the amount of estate tax that would otherwise be payable if the gross estate had suffered shrinkage in its aggregate value in the six months following the date of death. If an alternate valuation date is selected, the use of a blockage discount could be prevented. Depending on the facts and circumstances at the alternate valuation date, the factors that could have justified a blockage discount at the date of death may not be present at the alternate valuation date.

In the *Estate of Van Horne*,[13] the executor elected to value the estate as of the alternate valuation date. The decedent owned 56,454 shares of the William Wrigley, Jr. Company. The executor sold 42,416 shares of the total at a discount during the six-month period before the alternate valuation date. The executor argued that the remaining 14,038 shares should be valued on the basis of a blockage discount, taking into consideration the total shares of 56,454. The Ninth Circuit Court of Appeals affirmed the Tax Court's findings that only those shares remaining in the estate on the alternate valuation date may be considered for a blockage discount. The remaining shares could have been disposed of in an orderly manner at no less than the market price. The Appeals Court also noted that the market had been in a decline at the date of death but was now in a state of recovery at the alternate valuation date. "Because the market in Wrigley stock was rising, the estate would not have been required to accept less than the market price in order to sell the remaining shares." The executors failed to substantiate their burden of proof that the remaining 14,038 shares, which represented only 0.36 percent of total Wrigley stock, warranted a blockage discount.

Underwriting Fees and Other Sales-Related Expenses

In an estate tax valuation, the question arises: Can the hypothetical underwriting and sales-related expenses be taken into consideration in estimating the amount of the blockage discount? Revenue Ruling 83-30 states that underwriting fees necessarily incurred in marketing a large block of stock are deductible as an estate administration expense under Code Section 2053(a)(2), and are not considered in estimating the

---

[13] *Estate of Van Horne* v. *Commissioner*, 720 F.2d 1114 (9th Cir. Nov. 22, 1983).

blockage discount to be accorded in valuing the stock under Section 2031.[14] It further states that the appropriate value for blockage purposes is the price that the public would pay to the underwriter, not the price the underwriter would pay to the estate, net of the underwriting fees.

In *Gillespie III* v. *U.S.*,[15] the Second Circuit Court of Appeals affirmed a lower court decision that adhered to the principles under Revenue Ruling 83-30 that allowed a blockage discount, but without further reduction for hypothetical underwriting fees and other sale-related expenses. The purpose of the Revenue Ruling appears to be to prevent an estate from taking a double deduction under both Sections 2053(a)(2) and 2031. Not withstanding the Internal Revenue Service position and relevant court cases, the economic argument remains that selling costs are a relevant factor taken into consideration by willing sellers and buyers.

Separate Valuation of Contemporaneous Gifts

The question arises: Can multiple gifts of the same stock made at the same time be aggregated for purposes of estimating a blockage discount? Regulation 25.2512-2(e) states that the size of the block of stock included in each separate gift is relevant in determining whether the stock selling price reflects fair market value. In *Rushton* v. *Commissioner*,[16] the Fifth Circuit Court of Appeals affirmed the Tax Court decision that, for blockage purposes, several gifts made on the same day to several donees should be viewed separately, rather than in the aggregate.

In TAM 9719001, the Internal Revenue Service precluded a blockage discount in the gifting of the same stock to nine different trusts. The taxpayer argued that the gifts should be aggregated as a single transfer, since all nine trusts had the same trustee. The Internal Revenue Service noted that the trustee holds only legal title while the beneficiaries are the equitable owners of the trust assets, and that the valuation should be based on the beneficiaries and not the trustee. The reasoning of the Internal Revenue Service and court cases appears to be consistent with the position taken in Revenue Ruling 93–12.[17] This ruling allows the consideration of a minority ownership interest discount in valuing each gift as an independent transfer—without regard to the identity of the donor or donee or the aggregation of any separate gifts.

Blockage Discount Applies to Assets Other Than Stock

Blockage discounts can also be taken into consideration in the valuation of collections of art, antiques, and so on. In *Calder* v. *Commissioner*,[18]

[14] Rev. Rul. 83-30, 1983-1 CB 224, IRC Sec. 2031.
[15] *Gillespie, III* v. *U.S.*, 73 AFTR2d 94-2374 (2nd Cir. Apr. 13, 1994).
[16] *Rushton* v. *Commissioner*, 498 F.2d 88 (5th Cir., 1974).
[17] Rev. Rul. 93–12, 1993–1, C.B. 202.
[18] *Calder* v. *Commissioner*, 85 TC 713, Nov. 6, 1985.

there is a discussion of the blockage discount that was agreed to by the Internal Revenue Service in the estate of Alexander Calder, a well-known artist. A substantial blockage discount was allowed on the estate tax return in the valuation of 1,226 works of art that were distributed to the widow of Alexander Calder. As in the valuation of a blockage discount for stock, the facts and circumstances dictate the amount of blockage for these types of assets.

Summary

Blockage discounts can be one of the most controversial aspects of a business valuation assignment. They have been misunderstood and misapplied too often. This chapter identified the leading Tax Court cases, highlighted the most important factors for the analyst to consider, and presented several acceptable valuation procedures for the analyst to consider when estimating a blockage discount.

Bibliography

Barron, Robert A. "Control and Restricted Securities: Some Comments on the Discount Valuation of Publicly Traded Stock for Federal Estate Tax Purposes, Part 2," *Securities Regulation Law Journal*, Vol. 24, No. 2, Summer 1996.

"Blockage and Restricted Stock," *Tax Management, Inc.* Washington: Bureau of National Affairs, Inc., Portfolio 831-2d, 1998.

Frazier, William H. "The Use of Capital Gains Tax Liability When Employing an Asset-Based Approach to the Valuation of a C Coporation and 'Pure' Blockage," (presentation to the Valuation Study Group), April 25–28, 1996.

Hawkins, George B. "Selling Out to a Public Company, Buyer-Blockage, Restricted Shares, and Value: The Stated Price Versus Reality," *Banister Financial, Inc., Fair Value*, Vol. 6, No. 1, Spring–Summer 1997.

Holthausen, Robert W., Richard W. Leftwich, and David Mayers. "The Effect of Large Block Transactions on Security Prices: A Cross-Sectional Analysis," *Journal of Financial Economics*, July 1987.

Julius, J. Michael. "Blockage Discounts and Restricted Stocks, Parts I and II," *Mercer Capital Value Added*, Vol. 6, No. 2, 1994.

Moore, Philip W. "Blockage Redux: The Challenge Posed by Blockage," *Trusts and Estates*, February 1992.

"Multiple Gifts of Stock Are Separate for Blockage Discount Purposes," *Journal of Taxation*, August 1997.

Schlenger, Jacques T., Robert E. Madden, and Lisa H.R. Hayes. "Blocks of Stock Are Aggregated When Determining Estate Tax Values," *Estate Planning*, May/June 1994.

Wise, Richard M. "Discounts in Arriving at Share Values of Closely-Held Corporations," *The Journal of Business Valuation* (proceedings of the 2nd Joint Business Valuation Conference of The Canadian Institute of Chartered Business Valuators and the American Society of Appraisers), 1991, pp. 127–148.

Zaritsky, Howard M. "Sauce for the Goose? IRS Rejects Discount Based on Aggregating Separate Gifts," *Estate Planning*, August–September 1997.

Zwiebel, Jeffrey. "Block Investment and Partial Benefits of Corporate Control," *Review of Economic Studies*, 1995-62, pp. 161–185.

Chapter 8

The Valuation of Family Limited Partnerships

Charles L. Elliott, CFA, ASA

Overview

The use of family limited partnerships (FLPs) by the legal community as effective vehicles in estate and gift tax planning programs has reached extraordinary heights in the last decade, bordering on the popularity of "estate freezes" in the 1970s and early 1980s. The estate freeze movement was dealt its death knell by legislation [Internal Revenue Code 2036(c)] that was so broadly written as to result in prospective applications well beyond the original intent of its drafters. As a consequence, Section 2036(c) was repealed and replaced with new legislation (Chapter 14 of the Internal Revenue Code), effective October 1990. Chapter 14 embodies the new regulations, or ground rules, that govern whether or not various provisions of partnership agreements can be considered in the process of valuing partnership interests. Specific commentary on Chapter 14 appears later in this chapter.

The early sections of this chapter are intended to provide the reader with perspective before specifically embarking on the task of valuing limited partnership interests.

The Rationale behind FLPs

There is a vast array of reasons to explain the attractiveness of the partnership format, particularly with respect to the needs and requirements of family units:

1. Through the creation of an FLP, mom and dad have the ability to indirectly transfer interests in family-owned assets without losing control over them. In addition, the possible problems related to direct gifts of securities (stocks and bonds)—namely, profligacy on the part of children—can be avoided by gifts of limited partnership interests. This is because the parents control the distribution of the cash flow generated by the partnership. The ability of the offspring to sell the limited partnership interest gifted to them is also extremely limited.

2. A high degree of protection against creditors can be achieved through a partnership. Typically, a partner's creditor is legally unable to get to the assets of a partnership. The creditor is also unable to cause distributions to be made to the debtor partner. This would not be the case if the assets in the partnership were owned directly by the debtor instead of being held within the partnership.

3. Clearly, the partnership form satisfies the objective of keeping the assets in the family. Typically, partnership agreements afford either the partnership or other partners (or both) the opportunity to acquire the ownership interest of a partner wishing to assign his or her interest to a third party (1) at the same price and (2) on

157

the same terms as agreed upon with the third party. Similarly, provisions of partnership agreements can ensure that partnership interests do not stray from family control in instances of divorce, bankruptcy, death, and similar circumstances.

4. Another important advantage relates to the avoidance of problems pertaining to undivided or fractionalized interests when one property is gifted to several individuals. This is particularly relevant in regard to real estate properties. The alternative is to transfer the entire property to a partnership and then gift a limited partnership interest to various donees.

5. When family-owned assets (real estate, securities, other partnership interests, interests in family businesses, etc.) are placed in a partnership, the advantages of economies of scale and diversification may also be achieved.

6. The partnership form is extremely flexible. The partnership agreement can provide broad investment and business powers. By agreement of all partners, or as required by the partnership agreement, the agreement can be amended to facilitate changed objectives and purposes of the partners. In addition, the partners may terminate the partnership, depending upon the provisions of the partnership agreement.

7. Because partnerships are pass-through entities, they do not pay income tax. Clearly, this is not true of C corporations for two reasons. First, the corporation is subject to corporate income taxation (both on a federal and state level). Second, shareholders are taxed on dividends, both as to ordinary income and realized capital gains. In addition, partnerships are not subject to franchise and related taxes whereas corporations are so taxed in most jurisdictions.

8. The gifting or transfer of an ownership interest in a limited partnership may be made at a lower value than that interest's pro rata share of net asset value. The reason is that the limited partnership interest is likely to be noncontrolling and nonmarketable. This rationale, which has been applicable to minority ownership interests in privately owned corporations for a long period of time and has been acknowledged by the Internal Revenue Service, is equally applicable to limited partnership ownership interests with similar characteristics.

An important event in facilitating the use of an FLP in estate planning programs has been the reversal of the Internal Revenue Service's position with regard to "family attribution." Prior to February 1993, the IRS aggregated ownership interests of family members in an entity (privately owned corporations or partnerships) in arriving at the minority or controlling ownership status of an interest. For instance, if the patriarch gifted 20 percent interests in his company's stock to each of his five children, the gift was viewed as one gift of 100 percent. Therefore, the value of each gift was its pro rata share of the value of 100 percent of the common stock of the company. No minority ownership interest or lack of marketability discounts were allowed.

However, the IRS suffered numerous defeats in Tax Court on this position, culminating with the *Bright* case.[1] After the *Bright* case, the IRS reaffirmed its intent to continue to pursue the family attribution policy. However, in 1993, it issued Revenue Ruling 93–12 explicitly abrogating this position. Revenue Ruling 93–12 recognized that the fair market value standard assumes a transaction between a hypothetical buyer and a hypothetical seller and that the specific identity of either party is irrelevant.

Therefore, valuations for gift and estate tax purposes are now based on the property actually transferred without regard to the identity of the buyer of the property or his or her relationship to the seller. Under this new interpretation, the IRS treats the gifting of a 20 percent stock interest in a company to each of five children not as a single gift of 100 percent, but rather as gifts of what really was transferred: five separate gifts of 20 percent each, subject to discounts to reflect (1) lack of control and (2) lack of marketability.

Clearly, this reversal of policy has profound implications for the gifting or other transfers of various interests in limited partnerships, as it does for similar real or hypothetical transactions involving common stock of privately owned companies, as partnership interests are also entitled to discounts reflecting lack of control and illiquidity.

Chapter 14 of the Internal Revenue Code

As mentioned earlier, Chapter 14 was enacted in the fall of 1990 as a replacement for the repealed Section 2036(c). The objective, however, was the same—to eliminate perceived abuses in regard to the valuation of common or preferred stocks and partnership interests in privately owned entities. Obviously, the valuation analyst is not acting as an attorney and therefore should not be determining the applicability of the provisions of Chapter 14 or any other statute, for that matter. The valuation analyst should rely on guidance from the client's attorney for direction pertaining to these issues. However, the analyst should be familiar with the "whys" and "wherefores" of the legal framework of the valuation, including the pertinent partnership statutes of the state in which the partnership under valuation is domiciled.

The following comments on Chapter 14 are presented here only as an overview of some of the important provisions that are at issue. Again, the estate planning attorney should provide the ultimate interpretations of the provisions of Chapter 14, the partnership agreement, and the partnership statutes of the pertinent state.

The two critical parts of Chapter 14 that relate to valuation considerations are Sections 2703 and 2704. Section 2703 states that the value of the partnership interest will be determined without regard to:

---

[1] *Estate of Mary Frances Smith Bright* v. *United States*, 658 F.2d 999 (5th Cir. 1981).

1. Any option agreement, or other right to acquire or use the interest, at a price less than fair market value.
2. Any restriction on the right to sell or to use the interest. However, Section 2703 will not apply to any option, agreement, right, or restriction that meets each of the following requirements:
   a. It is a bonafide business arrangement.
   b. It is not a device to transfer property to members of the decedent's family for less than full and adequate consideration.
   c. At the time of the inception of the restriction or agreement, its terms are comparable to similar arrangements entered into by persons in an arm's-length transaction.

The thrust of Section 2704 is on lapsing rights and liquidation and withdrawal rights. This section states that any provision in the agreement that restricts a partner's ability to liquidate or withdraw his or her interest is not to be considered when valuing the interest. The facts should be analyzed. The restrictions might be ignored if the individual who is transferring the interest controls the company or the partnership (along with family members), or if the restriction lapses or can be eliminated by the transferor or family member after the transfer has been made (e.g., by amending the partnership agreement). However, if the restriction is no more restrictive than that allowed under applicable state statutes, then the restrictions would not be disallowed.

The Partnership Beginner's Kit for the Valuation Analyst

Exhibit 8-1 provides a checklist of documents and information that the analyst should have in order to commence the valuation assignment.

The beginning point in valuing a limited partnership interest is the critical review of the partnership agreement ("the Agreement"). It is the provisions of the Agreement in conjunction with the state partnership statutes and the basic characteristics of a limited partnership interest (its rights, or lack of rights, and its limitations) that enable the analyst to estimate a lower value for the partnership interest than its pro rata share of net asset value (NAV)—the fair market value of the assets minus the liabilities.

Business Purpose

The partnership will fail the tests put forth in Section 2703 if the business purpose is not real and well stated. Clearly, adequate business purpose is the responsibility of the attorney who draws up the Agreement, but the valuation analyst may wish to raise a question on this point if he or she believes it is warranted.

Exhibit 8–1

FLP Document Checklist

For a Partnership That Is Just Being Formed

1. The final or proposed partnership agreement.

2. Documentation of the assets being contributed to the partnership.

3. Valuations of real estate and similar assets. The analyst should obtain market values of publicly traded securities that are being contributed.

4. Determination of whether certain assets (other partnership interests, stock in a privately owned company, etc.) to be contributed to the partnership need to be valued separately and prior to the formation of the partnership. The analyst should request the information necessary to make each of those valuations.

5. Balance sheet as of the valuation date.

6. Income statement for the stub period through the valuation date.

7. Pro forma income and expense statement for the partnership once it is effective.

8. The general partner's anticipated policies regarding:
   a. Prospective distributions to the partners.
   b. The Section 754 election.

For a Partnership That Is Ongoing

1. Most of the same information requested for a partnership that is just being formed.

2. Partnership tax returns for a reasonable period of time or for the life of the partnership, if its history is short.

3. The history of distributions made to the partners.

Contributions

The valuation analyst should know and understand how the partnership is to be capitalized. The analyst should be aware of the circumstances in which additional capital contributions (cash calls) may be required.

Management Prerogatives

The agreement should articulate management responsibilities and authority, which are typically granted exclusively to the general partner(s). It should also disclose limitations placed on the general partner and the basis upon which he or she can be removed (if, in fact, the general partner can be replaced).

Most important, the Agreement should speak to the inherent characteristics attributable to the limited partners. Ordinarily, the limited partners have no liability (beyond the requirements of the Agreement) to provide additional capital, no role in the management of the partnership, and no ability to unilaterally dissolve the partnership.

Distributions to the Partners

Typically, distributions will be at the discretion of the general partner. However, there may be language that defines "cash flow" and indicates that the general partner may establish reserves for current or future needs of the partnership, basing any distribution decision on "net cash flow."

Transferability of Limited Partnership Interests

There is normally a provision in the Agreement (possibly in the form of a right of first refusal on the part of the partnership and then to the individual partners) restricting transfer of a limited partnership interest to anyone other than a family member (a third party). The critical element here is that a partner cannot sell or transfer a partnership interest. He or she can sell only a transferee/assignee interest. The reason is that no one can cause another to be one's partner. In essence, the analyst is valuing an assignee interest. An assignee has no voting rights whatsoever; he or she has only an economic interest (the right to receive his or her pro rata share of distributions made to all the partners).

Section 754. The partnership agreement may be silent regarding the Section 754 election. It may say that the availability of the election is strictly at the discretion of the general partner or the tax matters partner. The Agreement may state that if a partner or assignee requests a Section 754 election, the general partner is obligated to honor the request. The significance of whether or not the Section 754 election is available upon the transfer of a partnership interest is discussed later in this chapter.

Dissolution/Liquidation. The partnership agreement is likely to spell out several events that will cause the dissolution of the partnership:

1. Reaching the designated term (the date at which the partnership is to be liquidated as indicated in the agreement).
2. Upon the death, bankruptcy, or other demise of the general partner. However, the limited partners normally can vote to reconstitute and continue the partnership under certain conditions.

3. By vote of a prescribed percentage of the partners.
4. The occurrence of any circumstance that, by law, would require that the partnership be dissolved.

Clearly, the key sections of a typical partnership agreement (along with the fundamental characteristics of a limited partnership interest as defined in state partnership statutes), which are designed to be an effective estate planning tool, serve to:

1. Exclude the limited partners from participation in the management of the partnership, including decisions pertaining to distributions to be made to the partners.
2. Restrict the transferability of a limited partnership interest.
3. Provide the general partner with exclusive managerial power to operate and manage the partnership.
4. Distance the limited partners from the assets of the partnership thereby preventing the limited partners from having access either to partnership assets or to their own capital contributions.

Control in the Context of Limited Partnership versus a Corporation

The percentage ownership of the corporation that gives an owner the right to unilaterally sell, merge, liquidate, or effect similar transactions is called a supermajority interest. In some states, a simple majority is all it takes; other states require two-thirds or an even greater percentage.

If the supermajority owner sells his or her stock to another person or entity, that buyer will stand exactly in the same shoes as the previous owner. He or she will have the same ability as the previous owner to determine operating policies, establish his or her own salary, set dividend payouts, hire and fire employees, and the like. The new owner will also have the ability to unilaterally sell, merge, or liquidate the corporation, as did the former owner.

If the same supermajority ownership in an FLP represents control because of various provisions of the Agreement, the situation is dramatically different. The owner of this interest cannot pass on his or her controlling attributes to another through sale or other means of transfer, for the reason expressed earlier. An owner of a partnership interest cannot actually sell his or her partnership interest. The owner can only transfer an assignee interest to another, because he or she cannot pass partner status to anyone. In the context of an FLP in which all the partners are family members, one can only assume that the hypothetical, nonfamily assignee would believe that he or she would remain an assignee.

It is possible for an agreement to provide that a supermajority ownership position would enable the holder to dissolve the partnership, to replace the general partner, and to determine distributions. However, such provisions would be at cross-purposes with the objectives of the typical FLP. In normal circumstances, the general partner of an FLP will unilaterally control all the operations of the partnership.

In addition, the partnership agreement is likely to require 100 percent vote of all partners to dissolve it and a high ownership percentage to replace the general partner. As a consequence, the ownership of even a high percentage of the limited partnership interests in an FLP may be worth no more than the equivalent of a minority interest in the stock of a corporation. In addition, in the context of a sale (actual or hypothetical), a limited partnership interest has only the status of an assignee (with the attendant consequences that have already been described) regardless of the percentage ownership of the partnership.

Valuation Parameters

Having established this framework, we are now ready to discuss various valuation parameters applicable to the valuation of assignee limited partnership interests in FLPs. We are limiting our discussion to partnerships comprised of the assets most commonly owned by FLPs—namely, securities and real estate. It should be noted that, by definition, the value of the underlying assets of partnerships determines its net asset value. However, we are valuing a limited partnership interest in the FLP, not direct ownership in the individual assets.

In making valuation judgments, analysts are constantly looking for reliable, empirical evidence—a surrogate—in the public markets upon which to base their opinions.

The public stock market provides such a basis when one is valuing the stock of a privately owned company. By comparing the operating performance of a subject company in relation to a group of guideline companies with stocks that are publicly traded, the appraiser is able to determine if the subject, privately owned company is (1) a good buy or a bad buy, and (2) an outperformer or an underperformer. Knowing how guideline publicly traded stocks sell, based upon various valuation parameters (e.g., price/earnings and price/book value multiples and yields), provides the necessary perspective on which to base a valuation judgment.

Premised upon a combination of (1) the operating performance of the private company relative to the guideline publicly traded companies and (2) the valuation parameters observed in the public market, the valuation analyst is able to explain and defend a value for the stock of the private company as if it were publicly traded. This is exactly the process that investment bankers utilize when pricing initial public offerings. In this illustration, the analyst would apply a lack of marketability discount to the as-if-publicly-traded value in order to arrive at the minority ownership interest/nonmarketable value to be attributed to the stock of the private company.

In the same fashion, the valuation analyst should find a basis from which to form his or her opinion in regard to securities and real estate FLPs (or partnerships comprised of combinations of these assets).

Security Partnerships

FLPs comprised of publicly traded stocks and other securities are clearly asset-oriented. One has merely to price each security in the portfolio and add up the totals. Accordingly, the most logical reference point when valuing a securities FLP is closed-end investment companies. It is best to use closed-end investment companies that are comprised of publicly traded securities akin to the security classes that match the securities portfolio held by the FLP, such as domestic stocks, foreign stocks, municipal bonds, corporate bonds, or government bonds. Typically, closed-end funds have sold at price discounts from their net asset values per share, though not all funds sell at discounts all the time.

Explanations for the discount phenomenon range from expense-related reasons to the presence of a capital gains tax liability imbedded in some funds. Statistical efforts (regression and similar analysis) have not provided a definitive explanation for the price discount. In regard to the question of the imbedded capital gains liability, many funds sell at large price discounts from net asset values whether they have small tax liabilities or large tax liabilities.

In any regard, the ranked profile of discounts/premiums (the *investment company discount/premium*) in relation to NAVs observed in the public market serves as a proxy for the minority ownership interest discount. Exhibits 8-2 and 8-3, which rank discounts from NAVs (and premiums to NAV) for groups of closed-end stock and municipal bond funds, also indicate financial data about each fund in each grouping.

For the stock funds, the data include NAVs, market prices, the indicated dividend rates, yield based both on NAVs and market prices, net assets, and three-year total rates of return. The information provided for the closed-end, municipal bond funds is very similar, except that the average S&P credit rating and average maturity are also presented.

The key question is how the security portfolio owned by the subject FLP compares to the portfolios managed by the closed-end funds. The following provides guidance and perspective as to various characteristics of a securities portfolio that are likely to increase or decrease the investment company discount:

1. The primary difference is likely to be that the securities portfolio owned by the FLP is not professionally managed, whereas the closed-end funds are. If the FLP portfolio is professionally managed, then (all things being equal, which they never are) the price discount from NAV may approximate the median discount for the closed-end fund grouping. The absence of professional management would clearly drive the discount higher.

Exhibit 8–2

Closed-End Funds--Domestic Equity Portfolios
As of April 1, 1999
Ranked by Percent Premium (Discount)

Company	Exchange Symbol	04/01/99 NAV	04/01/99 Market Price	Percent Premium (Discount)	Percent Indicated Rate [a]	Indicated Rate/ NAV	Yield [b c]	Net Assets (Millions)	3-Year Average Total Return
Baker Fentress	BKF	$19.97	$15.00	(24.9) %	0.41	2.1 %	2.8 %	$776	16.9 %
Central Securities [d]	CET	29.82	23.81	(20.1)	0.88	3.0	3.7	468	14.3
Adams Express	ADX	33.59	27.31	(18.7)	0.49	1.5	1.8	1,531	21.2
Morgan Grenfell Small Cap	MGC	10.86	8.88	(18.3)	0.00	0.0	0.0	120	27.7
Tri-Continental [d]	TY	34.90	29.00	(16.9)	0.46	1.3	1.6	3,231	23.1
Royce Value [d]	RVT	13.34	11.38	(14.7)	1.90	14.2	3.7	527	6.3
Liberty All-Star Growth	ASG	12.29	10.69	(13.0)	0.00	0.0	0.0	156	19.6
Salomon Brothers	SBF	19.60	17.94	(8.5)	0.14	0.7	0.8	1,696	28.6
Liberty All-Star Equity [d]	USA	14.00	12.88	(8.0)	0.00	0.0	0.0	1,253	19.7
Blue Chip Value	BLU	10.12	9.75	(3.7)	0.05	0.5	0.5	158	25.9
Gabelli Equity [d]	GAB	11.70	11.81	1.0	1.17 [e]	10.0	0.5	1,207	19.6
Alliance All-Market Advantage	AMO	47.28	48.81	3.2	0.88	1.9	1.8	95	41.2
Source Capital	SOR	43.01	45.00	4.6	N/A	N/A	N/A	331	18.8
Average				(10.6) %		2.9 %	1.4 %	$888	21.8 %
75th percentile				(18.3) %		2.3 %	2.0 %	$1,253	25.9 %
Median				(13.0) %		1.4 %	1.2 %	$527	19.7 %
25th percentile				(3.7) %		0.4 %	0.4 %	$158	18.8 %

[a] Excludes captial gains.
[b] Indicated rate divided by market price.
[c] Yields obtained from Morningstar Principia Pro; the apparent dividend rate is calculated based upon the yield.
[d] Fund is leveraged.
[e] Actual 1998 indicated rate excluding capital gains.

SOURCE: *Morningstar Mutual Funds,* September 6, 1998, through January 21, 1999; *Barron's,* April 5, 1999; *Standard & Poor's Stock Guide,* March 1999; and *Morningstar Principia Pro,* January, 1999.

2. The investor in the closed-end fund is a beneficiary of stringent regulation imposed by the Securities and Exchange Commission (SEC). The limited partner in the securities partnership is afforded no such protection.

3. The portfolio of the FLP may be undiversified compared with the closed-end funds. The assets of the FLP portfolio may be concentrated in a relatively few investments. Though there may be numerous securities in the subject FLP portfolio, some may be outsized while other positions are extremely small.

Exhibit 8–3

Closed-End Funds--Municipal Bond Portfolios
As of April 1, 1999
Ranked by Percent Premium (Discount)

Company	Exchange Symbol	04/01/99 NAV	04/01/99 Market Price	Percent Premium (Discount)	Indicated Rate [a]	Indicated Rate/ NAV	Yield [b]	Net Assets (Millions)	3-Year Average Total Return	Average Credit Quality	Average Effective Maturity (years)
Managed Municipals	MMU	$12.18	$10.81	(11.2) %	$0.59	4.8 %	5.5 %	$368	4.5 %	AA	22.4
Van Kamp Am Cap Value Muni [c, d]	VKV	15.42	14.25	(7.6)	0.81	5.3	5.7	2,022	12.3	AA	21.1
Smith Barney Intermediate Municipal	SBI	10.52	10.00	(4.9)	0.53	5.0	5.3	88	6.8	AA	10.0
MSDW Qual Income [c, e]	IQI	16.01	15.25	(4.7)	0.93	5.8	6.1	534	11.9	AA	18.0
Nuveen Municipal Value	NUV	10.20	9.81	(3.8)	0.51	5.0	5.2	623	7.0	AA	10.8
Munivest [c, d]	MVF	10.00	9.69	(3.1)	0.59	5.9	6.1	746	12.6	AA	18.8
Van Kamp Am Cap Muni [c, d]	VKQ	16.54	16.25	(1.8)	0.96	5.8	5.9	918	13.7	AA	9.9
Nuveen Performance Plus Muni [c]	NPP	15.26	15.00	(1.7)	0.90	5.9	6.0	922	5.9	AA	8.3
Municipal High-Income	MHF	9.66	9.56	(1.0)	0.58	6.0	6.1	197	12.2	A	21.3
Colonial High-Income Municipal	CXE	8.39	8.38	(0.2)	0.50	6.0	6.0	264	11.2	BBB	23.5
MuniYield [c, d]	MYD	15.37	15.50	0.8	0.96	6.2	6.2	612	14.1	A	6.9
MFS Municipal Income	MFM	8.43	8.56	1.6	0.53	6.3	6.2	333	12.8	BBB	18.7
Nuveen Quality Income Muni [c]	NQU	15.61	16.38	4.9	1.03	6.6	6.3	850	11.5	AA	5.6
MSDW Municipal Opportunities	OIA	8.76	9.31	6.3	0.60	6.8	6.4	186	12.2	BBB	20.0
Average				(1.9) %		5.8 %	5.9 %	$619	10.6 %	A	15.4
75th percentile				(4.5) %		6.2 %	6.1 %	$824	12.5 %	AA	20.8
Median				(1.7) %		5.9 %	6.1 %	$573	12.0 %	AA	18.4
25th percentile				0.6 %		5.4 %	5.7 %	$281	8.1 %	BBB	9.9

[a] Excludes capital gains.

[b] Indicated rate divided by market price.

[c] Fund is leveraged.

[d] Fund may be open-ended by supermajority shareholder vote.

[e] Fund may be open-ended by 80% shareholder vote.

SOURCE: *Morningstar Principia Pro*, January 1999; *Barron's*, April 5, 1999; and *Standard and Poor's Stock Guide*, March 1999.

4. A closed-end fund may be subject to specific investment objectives and limited to investing in particular investment vehicles. On the other hand, the portfolio of the FLP may reflect no defined investment policy, discipline, or objective, which is also a reflection of the lack of professional management. The portfolio may simply represent a hodgepodge of miscellaneous securities. It may have no definable investment character.

5. The quality of the investments in the FLP portfolio (speculative versus investment grade) is another dimension that would affect where the portfolio should be placed in the ranked discount from NAV scale.

6. If the securities FLP has been in place for a reasonable length of time, then total return performance compared with the performance of individual funds in the appropriate fund grouping would be a significant factor.

7. In regard to fixed income portfolios, all the aforementioned criteria would apply in distinguishing the FLP portfolio from the comparable fund grouping. In addition, the average maturity of the bond portfolio is a significant factor. The longer the average maturity or duration, the greater the price volatility and risk.

Armed with valuation information with regard to the closed-end funds derived from the public market, the valuation analyst is prepared to make discerning judgments as to the size of the discounts to be taken from the aggregate asset value of the securities component of the FLP. Again, the investment company discount becomes the proxy or substitute for the minority ownership interest discount applicable to the value of the limited partnership interest, before application of a lack of marketability discount. Exhibit 8-5 (presented later in this chapter, in the sample case) incorporates the investment company discount to the securities component of a hypothetical securities/real estate partnership.

Real Estate Partnerships

Not too many years ago, valuation analysts had few benchmarks to use as valuation reference points for limited partnership interests, particularly real estate partnerships. Typically, the net asset value of the partnership was estimated and the resulting value discounted to reflect (1) minority ownership interest and (2) lack of marketability. These discounts were derived from the vast number of studies conducted over the years regarding nonmarketable, minority ownership interests in corporations, not partnerships.

About 1980, an informal market (ultimately to be known as the secondary market for limited partnership interests) made its appearance. As is frequently the case, entrepreneurs are constantly on the lookout for new opportunities, identifying situations where a void must be filled. The secondary market commenced as a response to the enormous number of offerings of publicly syndicated partnerships in the late 1970s and early 1980s. No provisions were made to enable unit holders to buy or sell interests in the respective partnerships. It was this liquidity void that the creators of the secondary market were attempting to fill.

The secondary market is comprised of three different types of participants. The first group operates as market makers (over-the-counter dealers). There are about nine firms that regularly conduct transactions in limited partnership units on either a principal or an agency basis. Another group of firms refers to themselves as "exchanges." In reality, however, they simply operate a service through various brokerage firms in an attempt to match prospective buyers and sellers. The third group is composed of those who buy and sell for their own account or for partnerships established to own interests in publicly syndicated partnerships.

It is clear that all the participants in this market have strong preferences for partnership units in publicly syndicated deals (as opposed to privately syndicated partnerships). They prefer real estate–oriented partnership units, "seasoned" partnerships—those in existence for many years with established track records—and income-producing, cash-flowing, and distributing partnerships.

During the early years of the secondary market's existence, information was limited regarding the basis upon which partnership units were priced. The author of this chapter completed several studies on pricing in the secondary market over a seven-year period, based upon discussions with market makers, "exchange" executives, and those managing their own accounts. The working range of price discounts from net asset value was 20 to 40 percent in 1987, 20 to 40 percent in 1990, and 30 to 50 percent in 1993.

Just as the secondary market was conceived as a result of a need to fill the liquidity void for partnership units, the information void was filled by another entrepreneur. In 1990, Partnership Profiles, Inc. (PP) was established. PP issues a bimonthly publication (*Partnership Spectrum*) that offers general commentary about what is happening in the secondary market for limited partnership interests. The publication reports on developments at a vast number of specific partnerships and provides trading information on a large number of partnerships, divided into groups (lodging, conventional, triple-net lease, oil and gas, equipment leasing, etc). The reported information for each two-month period for these partnership units includes the range of trading prices, the number of trades and total number of units traded, the current yield, and unit values (net asset values).

Of particular value to the analyst is *Partnership Profiles*, a publication providing fundamental operating and financial information on hundreds of partnerships, derived from filings with the Securities and Exchange Commission. Operating data for the last five years are provided, including the cost basis of properties owned, percentage leverage, gross revenues, net income, cash flow, working capital, and the history of distributions to partners. In addition, there are descriptions of properties and dispositions as well as substantial commentary regarding fundamental information about the partnership properties and explanations about the financial statements.

Clearly, as a result of the dramatic expansion of operating and financial information about partnerships whose units trade in the secondary market, valuation analysts are able to function like stock and bond market investment analysts who evaluate and assess the relative merits of securities on the basis of the wealth of information available on corporations whose stocks are publicly traded. From the aforementioned operating and financial information and pricing and trading data, the analyst is able to calculate various valuation parameters for a group of secondary market partnerships similar to the subject partnership. Valuation parameters that can be determined include price to net asset value, price to cash flow, yield based on distributions, degree of leverage, and percentage of cash flow paid out as distributions to partners.

From the input from the secondary market and Partnership Profiles, Inc., the following conclusions are drawn regarding the basis upon which pricing of limited partnership units in the secondary market is determined.

It is clear that the most significant driver of the pricing of partnerships in the secondary market is cash distributions and therefore yield. Keep in mind that the great majority of partnerships trading in this market are real estate–related. Other factors that influence pricing include:

1. The type of real estate assets owned by the partnership.
2. The amount of financial leverage inherent in the partnership's capital structure.
3. Underlying cash flow coverage of yearly distributions made to partners.
4. The caliber of the information flow from the partnership and the general partner.
5. Whether or not the assets of the partnership are well diversified.
6. The reputation, integrity, and perceived competence of the management/general partner.
7. Liquidity factors:
   a. How often a partnership interest trades.
   b. The number of investors in the partnership.
   c. The time period until liquidation.
   d. The universe of interested buyers.
   e. Whether the partnership is publicly or privately syndicated.
   f. The presence of rights of first refusal.

Periodic reviews of pricing of distributing and nondistributing equity partnerships support the proposition that nondistributing equity partnerships generally sell at higher price discounts from net asset values than do distributing equity partnerships. This conclusion is in line with what one would logically expect. In addition, nondistributing equity partnerships are characterized by a higher degree of leverage than is associated with distributing equity partnerships.

Exhibit 8-4 presents various valuation parameters for both nondistributing and distributing equity partnership units trading in the secondary market. Nondistributing equity partnerships consistently embody higher leverage (the two factors are interrelated, since high leverage indicates the necessity to use cash flow to fund debt service as opposed to making distributions to partners). Further, nondistributing equity partnerships sell at higher discounts from NAV than do distributing, equity partnerships. The price discount from NAV for the nondistributing equity partnerships at the twenty-fifth ranked percentile and the price discount from NAV for the distributing equity partnership at the seventy-fifth ranked percentile have been consistent for several years. Reflecting the improved prospects for real estate investments and the broader acceptance and maturity of the secondary market, the median yield on distributing equity partnerships has declined to about 6.5 percent from about 9.0 percent three to four years ago.

A lack of marketability discount in the range of 30 to 40 percent, based on the multitude of studies pertaining to pricing of restricted stocks and other stock market–related sources, may be applicable for a noncontrolling partnership interest in a securities FLP. However, this

Exhibit 8–4

The Secondary Market for Limited Partnership Interests
Equity Real Estate Partnerships
As of April 1, 1999

	Nondistributing Partnerships [a]			
	Discount from NAV	Cash Flow/ NAV	Price/ Cash Flow	Leverage
75th percentile	43.6 %	10.3 %	8.5 x	69 %
Median	37.7	9.7	6.4	56
25th percentile	33.0	7.7	6.1	50

	Distributing Partnerships [b]					
	Discount from NAV	Cash Flow/ NAV	Price/ Cash Flow	Payout Percentage	Yield	Leverage
75th percentile	37.4 %	9.8 %	11.4 x	86.1 %	9.7 %	45 %
Median	31.7	8.5	8.8	60.5	7.3	33
25th percentile	20.4	6.1	6.8	40.3	4.0	18

[a] 14 partnerships.

[b] 33 partnerships.

SOURCE: *Partnership Spectrum* and *Partnership Profiles.*

conclusion is not supported by data on trades in the secondary market of limited partnership interests in real estate FLPs. The reason is that the secondary market for real estate FLPs is a "thin" market. It does not offer the liquidity of the New York Stock Exchange or Nasdaq. As a consequence, there is an element of illiquidity already imbedded in the pricing of real estate FLP units in the secondary market.

Subjectively, the lack of marketability discount applied to an ownership interest in a FLP derived from the secondary market, while significant, is probably less than the 30 to 40 percent lack of marketability discount premised on restricted stock transactions of publicly traded stocks. Various sources in the secondary market have suggested that an additional yield of about 200 basis points may be required to account for the impaired liquidity of the secondary market. This translates into a range of lack of marketability discounts to be applied to the value of non-controlling ownership interests in real estate FLPs of 15 to 25 percent.

The Section 754 Election

Section 754 of the Internal Revenue Code provides for the transferee or the substituted limited partner to write up the cost basis of the limited partnership interest transferred to the partner to what he or she paid for it, as opposed to inheriting the cost basis of the previous owner of the interest. This is particularly important to the acquirer of a partnership interest if the cost basis of the selling partner is very low. Without the election, the new owner inherits the cost basis of his or her predecessor and is saddled with any imbedded capital gains liability. If a Section 754 election is made and the cost basis is written up to what was paid for the acquired limited partnership interest, then the assignee of the partnership interest enjoys a free "step up" in the basis of his or her investment. Since the Section 754 election is not mandated, the decision to grant or withhold the election is normally at the total discretion of the general partner. Accordingly, there is an element of uncertainty as to whether the general partner will provide the election when a limited partnership interest is transferred. Therefore, the valuation analyst may wish to consider both the net asset value of the FLP and the adjusted net asset value (NAV reduced by the built-in capital gains liability) in his or her analysis.

Both the NAV and the adjusted NAV should be subjected to the investment company discount or the secondary market discount (as appropriate) as well as the applicable lack of marketability discount. The resulting values could then be weighted to reflect the probability that the partnership would or would not be granted a 754 election. When the partnership is comprised of assets with very low cost basis, the result may be a few additional, but legitimate, discount points.

Illustrative Case

Let's put the information presented in this chapter to work by valuing two 20 percent assignee, limited partnership interests in Jinx, Ltd. Since we have kept the facts and circumstances simplified, discounts have been rationalized in a general way. In an actual valuation assignment, the analyst should spend more time and effort developing the detailed reasons for the chosen valuation parameters (see, for example, *Mandelbaum*).[2]

The facts and assumptions in this example are the following:

1. Jinx, Ltd., is an FLP comprised of two general partners (mom and dad) and four limited partners (mom, dad, son, and daughter). Each of the two general partners has a 1 percent interest. Mom and dad own the balance of the limited partnership interest and intend to gift a 20 percent limited partnership interest to each child.
2. The FLP has $10 million in assets at appraised or market values. There are no liabilities. As a consequence, the $10 million in asset value is also the net asset value (NAV) of the partnership.

---

[2] *Bernard Mandelbaum et al.* v. *Commissioner*, T.C. Memo 1995-255.

3. The partnership assets are comprised as follows:
   a. A nondiversified, unmanaged stock portfolio of less than blue chip quality—market value of $3 million, cost basis of $1.5 million.
   b. An unmanaged, municipal bond portfolio comprised of BBB rated long bonds—market value of $2 million, cost basis $2 million.
   c. Non-income-producing ranch land—market value of $3 million, cost basis of zero.
   d. Commercial real estate—market value of $2 million, cost basis of $1.5 million.
4. The likelihood of receiving a Section 754 election is determined to be 75 to 80 percent.
5. The following judgments are made regarding the discounts (the investment company discount and the secondary market discount) to be applied to the limited partnership value represented by each asset component of the partnership:
   a. Stocks and municipal bonds: Utilize the discount at the seventy-fifth percentile (18.3 percent for stocks and 4.5 percent for municipal bonds) of the ranked discount profile for the closed-end stock and municipal bond funds, as indicated in Exhibits 8-2 and 8-3, to reflect that the partnership's portfolios are not professionally managed, are nondiversified, and are of less than high quality.
   b. Non-income-producing ranch land: Use the discount at the fiftieth percentile (37.7 percent) of the ranked discount profile for the nondistributing partnerships, shown in Exhibit 8-4, to reflect that no income is likely to be produced by the property but recognizing that there is no indebtedness against it.
   c. Income-producing, cash-flowing, commercial property: Utilize the midpoint (7.7×) between the twenty-fifth percentile (6.8×) and the median (8.8×) of ranked price/cash flow multiples and the midpoint (8.5 percent) between the seventy-fifth percentile (9.7 percent) and the median (7.3 percent) of the ranked yields for the distributing partnerships in Exhibit 8-4, to reflect the fact that the property is generating reasonable cash flow and there is no indebtedness against the property, but recognizing that the commercial real estate portfolio is totally concentrated in a single, income-producing property. Value the interest at the midpoint of the values produced by the multiple of cash flow and the required yield.

Exhibit 8-5 incorporates all the aforementioned facts, assumptions, and prescribed valuation judgments. The fair market value of each 20 percent limited partnership interest in Jinx, Ltd., is $1.35 million (rounded), on an assignee, noncontrolling, nonmarketable ownership interest basis, which compares with its pro rata share of net asset value of $2 million.

Exhibit 8–5

Illustrative Case

	Cost	Market Value	Adjusted Market Value [a]	Valuation Discount Applied [b]	Multiplier [c]	Market Value	Valuation at the Partnership Level After Imposition of Discounts [d]	
							Adjusted Market Value	
Securities								
Stocks	$1,500,000	$3,000,000	$2,700,000	18.3%	0.817	$2,451,000	$2,205,900	
Bonds	2,000,000	2,000,000	2,000,000	4.5%	0.955	1,910,000	1,910,000	
Total stocks and bonds						4,361,000	4,115,900	
Less lack of marketability discount of 30%						(1,308,300)	(1,234,770)	
						$3,052,700		$2,881,130
Real estate								
Ranch	0	$3,000,000	$2,400,000	37.7%	0.623	$1,869,000	$1,495,200	
Commercial	1,500,000	2,000,000	1,900,000	-	-	1,565,176 [e]	1,465,176 [f]	
Total real estate						3,434,176	2,960,376	
Less lack of marketability discount of 20%						(686,835)	(592,075)	
						2,747,341		2,368,301
Discounted values at the partnership level						$ 5,800,041		$ 5,249,431

Discounted market value (754 election provided)	$5,800,041 x	0.775	=	$4,495,032
Discounted adjusted market value (no 754 election provided)	5,249,431 x	0.225	=	1,181,122

The value of 100% of the partnership, on an assignee/noncontrolling/nonmarketable basis

$5,676,154
x 0.2

The value of a 20% partnership interest, on an assignee/noncontrolling/nonmarketable basis

$1,135,231

[a] After imposition of tax liability, which effectively assumes "no 754 election provided."

[b] See text for explanation of the discount taken for each asset category.

[c] 1.000 minus the investment company discount or the secondary market discount, as applicable.

[d] Either the investment company discount or the secondary market discount, as applicable.

[e] ($160,000 cash flow x 7.8) + ($160,000 cash flow divided by 0.085), averaged.

[f] $1,565,176 minus capital gains tax liability of $100,000.

Summary

In summary, FLPs merit the attention they have received as effective estate and tax planning vehicles. By carefully analyzing and applying the available valuation benchmarks, the valuation analyst is able to develop credible and defendable values for partnership interests in FLPs.

Chapter 9

In-Process R & D

Lawrence B. (Larry) Gooch, ASA

In-process R&D (IPRD) is a term of art in financial accounting that refers to product development that has not yet reached the point where it is technically complete—that is, the design and testing are not yet finished. Under purchase accounting, IPRD acquired in an acquisition is valued and written off against goodwill. A direct deduction of the goodwill is made without a concomitant earnings write-off. Thus, future amortization of goodwill is lowered with a corresponding increase in reported earnings. For those investors who prefer earnings rather than cash flow, a rosier picture is painted.

Not surprisingly, companies making acquisitions involving R&D want to ensure that all IPRD is identified and valued. In many acquisitions, the write-off of IPRD has exceeded 80 percent of the purchase price. The SEC has been skeptical about the size of the IPRD write-offs and frequently challenges the magnitude and validity of such positions.

The purpose of this chapter is to describe the estimation of the fair market value of IPRD, as part of a going concern, a process that is usually conducted for purchase price allocation purposes. Our discussion begins with methodology. As will be discussed, the income approach is the most common method of estimating the value of IPRD. An integral part of the income approach to valuation is the concept of contributory assets used in conjunction with IPRD. To isolate the expected income attributable to the IPRD, it is necessary to recognize a return on the value of the contributory assets. The mechanics of this methodology are explained in some detail. As a validation of the IPRD valuation, reconciliation with the purchase price is discussed. Finally, several examples are provided of IPRD valuations in different industry contexts.

Methodology

In valuation practice, three approaches are available to estimate asset value: cost, market, and income.

The cost approach is based upon the principle of substitution. The value of an asset is estimated according to the cost to re-create it. Although this approach may be applicable to new tangible assets such as buildings, where the technology of construction and the resources to accomplish duplication are readily available, IPRD tends to be leading edge and represents technology not yet readily reproducible. The ability to reproduce the technology embodied in the IPRD is not generally available. In a valuation sense, the IPRD may be thought of as scarce. The scarcity of the technology may enhance its value such that it has more value than the costs incurred to develop it. Frequently, timing is critical in high-tech fields where huge premiums are awarded by the marketplace for being first. For these reasons, the cost approach is generally not a good measure of IPRD value.

The market approach is based upon the principle of supply and demand with a view to sales of comparable assets. These sales, if contracted between independent parties with reasonable knowledge, tend to constitute a "market." Unfortunately, because IPRD assets are usually leading edge, it is unlikely, but not impossible, that reliable data describing sales of similar technology will be found. However, the search for comparable sales should be undertaken. When comparable sales are found, the difficulty is usually comparability. The reason for this difficulty is that comparable sales often include other assets, such as existing technology and trade names, that blur the ability to isolate the price paid for IPRD. Even if IPRD were the sole asset, there would still be comparability issues such as the cost to complete the product and what functionality and reliability is represented by the IPRD.

Because of the difficulties associated with the application of the cost and market approaches, the valuation approach of choice for IPRD tends to be the income approach. The income approach also has its share of difficulty. However, it is generally believed by most analysts in the IPRD field to be the most reliable approach and to be consistent with the way IPRD is actually purchased and sold.

The income approach is based upon the principle of anticipation. The biggest difficulty in applying the income approach is the inherent problems of projecting economic income for a new product, assessing the risk of the product's failure, and isolating the contribution of IPRD from other assets (especially existing technology) necessary for the production of the income stream.

Contributory Assets

Whether the product is hardware, software, a new drug, or a medical device, the projected economic income from the new product is the result of many assets working in concert. These include fixed assets, working capital, trade name and/or existing technology, and other intangible assets, such as software, distribution systems, and assembled workforce.

Fixed assets such as buildings and equipment are needed to manufacture the product and house the sales and administrative functions necessary to sell and distribute the product.

Most products require working capital in the form of receivables, inventories, and payables in order for the product to be part of a going-concern business.

Even though technology may be the dominant asset in precipitating the sale of IPRD, the existence of a trade name can facilitate or enhance the sales process. The trade name often provides the buyer with the assurance of quality and reliability, whether the product is tangible or intangible.

Other intangible assets may also be involved with product sales and development. Some may be identifiable, such as software or an assembled workforce. Lastly, other existing technology may be an integral part or base of the IPRD. In other words, the IPRD may be an improvement, enhancement, or refinement of existing developed technology.

Thus, in attributing a projected income stream to IPRD, it should be recognized that other assets contributing to the production of income require a return on investment. Under an income approach to valuing IPRD, it is first necessary to identify all the operative assets necessary to exploit the IPRD. In many cases, this requires a valuation of the contributory assets, while in other cases, it may be necessary only to identify a royalty rate, a rent, or a finance charge. For this purpose, contributory assets can be segregated into the following classifications:

- Nonwasting
- Wasting
- Other technology

To account for these contributory assets, it is convenient to assume that we take capital charges against the income stream for their use.

Nonwasting Assets

Many of the assets contributing to the production of income from technology are nonwasting. For IPRD valuation purposes, these assets include working capital, land, trade name, and assembled workforce. Because these assets are not wasting, we need only identify a return of capital. To estimate what an appropriate return is, we can hypothecate that these assets are effectively "borrowed" from an outside party. In the case of working capital, we can hypothecate that it is borrowed from a financial institution and that interest is charged on the borrowing. The capital charge is then a function of the amount borrowed and the financing rate.

Accordingly, we would first determine the amount of working capital necessary to support the business operations of the product. This is standard financial analysis. In terms of the interest rate to apply to arrive at the working capital charge, there are three possibilities: (1) the straight borrowing rate of the firm, (2) a weighted average cost of capital for the working capital, or (3) the weighted average cost of capital of the firm.

The first choice implicitly assumes that we could borrow 100 percent of our working capital needs. This may be possible if we could borrow 75 percent of the amount of receivables and inventory, and if accounts payable represented 25 percent of receivables and payables. On the other hand, if we concluded that we could not borrow 100 percent of our working capital needs, then the unfinanced portion would bear the firm's cost of equity. The third choice—using the firm's weighted average cost of capital (WACC)—applies only if the WACC is used as the return for all assets including the IPRD.

Technically, using the WACC for all assets is inaccurate, because each asset has different risk characteristics. However, it is a simplifying assumption that can approximate the more technically correct analysis—that is, using distinct rates of return for each asset class. The firm's rate of return for IPRD tends to be approximately correct because more of the firm's total income is typically allocated to less risky assets, leaving less income for the IPRD. Thus, the lower income allocated to IPRD tends to offset the relatively lower discount rate assigned to the IPRD, yielding value conclusions that may approximate the more technically correct analysis of using distinct rates of return for each asset class. If the rates of return for the asset classes are widely disparate—for example, 8 percent for working capital and 40 percent for IPRD—then it is probably better to use distinct rates of return for each asset class.

Land is considered a nonwasting asset and may even be an appreciating asset. In many parts of the country, land leases are common and rental percentages can be observed. Some analysts would argue that the rental rate for land should be a real rate rather than a nominal rate. However, if land is leased for a long period of time, the lessor never sees the appreciation. Our experience is that ground leases tend to reflect nominal interest rates.

Conceptually, the capital charge for a trade name is straightforward. It is simply the appropriate royalty rate for the trade name. The reality, however, is that an assessment must be made of the importance of the trade name in the overall sales process. For a truly *de novo* product, the trade name may be of little importance. For products with little technical differentiation, the trade name could be very important —more so than the technology. If the trade name applies to a family of other products with little or no technical differentiation between them, a royalty rate might be inferred from the situation and applied in the subject IPRD valuation. Sometimes a trade name can be viewed akin to a performance bond. It gives the buyer confidence that the product is bona fide and that a reputable company stands behind it. A performance bond can typically be obtained for 1 to 2 percent of the sales price.

The assembled workforce is a human capital intangible asset that is often identified in acquisitions. Typically an assembled workforce is valued through a cost approach based upon the cost to recruit and the cost to assimilate the workforce. Theoretically the compensation of an employee is at the market rate but there is a benefit in that the workforce is assembled and organized. Once a workforce is in place, the asset is often thought of as self-sustaining and hence is considered to have an indefinite life. Thus, the capital charge against the IPRD income stream to account for the contributions of the assembled workforce would be the rate of return times the assembled workforce value. The rate of return should be the firm's equity rate, since an assembled workforce could not be collateralized, or the firm's WACC, if that rate is being used for all assets.

The recap of capital charges for nonwasting assets is as follows:

Asset	Capital Charge Rate		
Net working capital	Debt rate	or	WACC
Land	Ground lease rate	or	WACC
Trade name	Royalty rate	or	WACC
Assembled workforce	Equity rate	or	WACC

Wasting Assets

The capital charge for wasting assets is more complex because it needs to provide for both a return on capital and a return of capital. Typically, the major wasting assets classes are improvements to real estate and equipment. However, it could also include intangible assets, such as software and noncompete agreements.

The rental rate to be charged against the IPRD income stream to account for the contributions of the fixed assets can be computed in several ways. One way is as a level rent over the economic life of the asset. If the expected remaining life of the fixed assets is greater than the expected remaining life of the IPRD, then the level rent assumption is reasonable and the capital charge formula can be developed as follows:

Level Rent Capital Charge[1]

$$R_L = \frac{V}{(1-t) \times ADF_e} \times \left[1 - \left(\frac{ADF_t}{L_t} \times t \right) \right]$$

where:
R_L = level rent
V = value of contributory asset
t = income tax rate
ADF_t = present value of $1/year depreciation over income tax life
ADF_e = present value of $1/year rent over economic life
L_t = income tax life

The rent calculated by the formula above would be analogous to the charge made by a leasing company. The rate of return could be specific for either the asset or the firm's WACC. In the former case, a weighted rate could be computed for the asset based upon its average loan to value ratio—typically on the order of 50 to 60 percent for fixed assets.

If the IPRD has a life that extends beyond the life of some of the fixed assets, a problem arises. This is because, presumably, inflation would cause their replacement to be more expensive (except in the case of computers where the converse could be true). One way to handle this problem is to use a graduated rent formula. The graduated rent formula increases at a chosen rate—usually the assumed inflation rate. The graduated rent formula follows:

Graduated Rent[2]

$$R_G = \frac{V \times (k-g) \times \left[1 - \left(\frac{ADFt}{L_t} \times t \right) \right]}{(1-t) \times \left[1 - \left(\frac{1+g}{1+k} \right)^{L_e} \right]}$$

[1] Lawrence B. Gooch, "Capital Charges and the Valuation of Intangibles," *Business Valuation Review*, March 1992, pp. 5–21.

where:

R_G = graduated rent (year 1)
V = value of contributory asset
k = cost of capital
g = growth rate (inflation)
t = income tax rate
ADF_t = present value of $1/year depreciated over income tax life
L_t = income tax life
L_e = economic life

The application of capital charges to the IPRD income stream to account for the contribution of wasting assets has many nuances and basically comes down to applying the capital charges in an appropriate way given the valuation circumstance. There are many permutations to this process, and there is no substitute to a logical analysis of the matching process. Some of the nuances involved in estimating the capital charge for fixed assets are whether they are fixed or variable relative to sales volume, whether they are at capacity, and whether they have a salvage value.

The formulas provided for level and graduated rent are both based upon a rent before tax akin to a leasing company's charge to a lessee. If the charges are taken after tax, the factor $(1 - t)$ in the denominator disappears, making the formulas somewhat simpler. The authors have preferred before-tax charges because they correspond to actual charges that would be incurred from a leasing company. Imagine the profit and loss statement (P&L) of a leasing company. What rent do they need to charge to recover the cost of the asset? This cash flow analysis can be emulated in a spreadsheet such that the lessor has a zero net present value on the asset at the leasing company's cost of capital.

Existing Technology

As was mentioned before, it is most common for IPRD to be found in tandem with existing technology. For example, a new version of software builds upon the previous version. The existing technology is the building block for the IPRD.

There are several methods used to estimate the value of existing technology. One method is based upon the proposition that the new version represents a turnover in technology in the product. Thus, if a new software product has 500,000 lines of code and the IPRD accounts for 100,000 lines of code, then maybe one-fifth of the value or royalty should be attributed to the IPRD. Another method is to estimate the value of the existing technology and develop a royalty rate consistent with that value. The royalty rate is then deducted from the IPRD income stream to provide a return on the value of the existing technology.

---

[2] Ibid.

The preferred method is to hypothecate the probable reasoning between the licensor and licensee. Assuming that the licensor owns the rights to the existing technology, the licensee must develop the improvements to regenerate the product and undertake the business risk to make the product successful, and thus, a significant profit must exist for the licensee. The hypothecated royalty rate to the licensor would depend on how much capital was being invested by the licensee and the risk inherent in achieving the projected income stream of the new product. If the investment by the licensee was small and the risk of failure low, then that would argue for a substantial royalty (in comparison to profits) for the licensor of the existing technology. If, on the other hand, the IPRD investment was large and the risk of failure significant, this would argue for a relatively low royalty rate to the licensor of the existing technology.

IPRD is normally viewed as a stream of successive generations emanating from an existing technology or platform. Thus, it is typical that the royalty rate for existing technology is stepped down through succeeding generations as more and more of the income stream from future products is attributable to future IPRD spending in comparison to the existing technology.

Exhibit 9–1 graphically expresses the relationship between the royalty rate for existing technology and the investment characteristics of the IPRD. Although Exhibit 9–1 may suggest that IPRD be assigned a pro rata amount of the profit of the new product, based upon the licensee's investment ratio for the IPRD, it does not work that way in practice. This is because the licensee is taking a preponderance of the risk. Even though he or she provides only one-third of the investment, the licensee may get two-thirds of the profit split. These are the kinds of relationships that are observed in the case of patents and trade names. The general rule of thumb is that the licensor of the existing technology gets one-quarter to one-third of the profit. This is because the licensee is in a leveraged position while the licensor is more or less in a bond position—that is, requires a fixed rate of return.

Estimating In-Process Cash Flows

Rather than estimating the cash flows to be derived from IPRD in isolation, the preferred approach is to project cash flows for the entire business over the expected life of the base technology inherent in the IPRD. Thus, if we are valuing a software technology: What is its total expected life span? It could be very short, because it is related to hardware that is expected to be superseded, or it might be long, if it is a leading operating system or spreadsheet program.

Typically, an acquirer is buying the rights to a series of products that are derived by successive improvements. It's a product tree, but trees don't last forever. An analogy might be the process followed by manufacturers of cars or airplanes. We are asking the question: How long will the base design be around until a totally new model is developed from

Exhibit 9–1

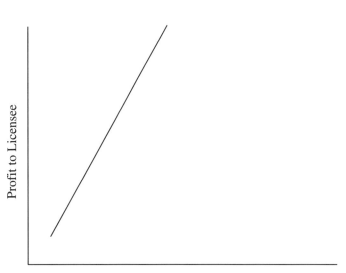

Royalty Rate Economics
Existing Technology

Profit to Licensee (y-axis)

IPRD Investment/Total Product Investment

scratch, even if the name of the base design continues on with the new model?

We suggest projecting cash flows for the entire company over this period because a return on certain assets, such as fixed assets and workforce, should be allocated to the collective cash flows they support. Exhibit 9–2 graphically depicts the company's projected sales by relevant category—existing, in-process, and future. As can be seen, at time $t = x$, the fixed assets of the company will be supporting both existing and IPRD products.

Ideally, it is desirable to develop a projection that is consistent with the actual purchase price. This is not to suggest that a projection be reverse-engineered, but rather that a projection be logically developed that is internally consistent with the price paid for the entire collection of assets of the business. If the IPRD valuation is being done subsequent to an acquisition, it might be helpful to obtain any analysis that was presented to the board of directors. If these projections were the basis of the company's purchase, then it would be presumed that they represent the company's unbiased (for financial reporting) view.

Estimating Useful Life of In-Process Technology

IPRD represents the stream of products (new versions) that are predicated on the base technology. The base technology may be the existing technology or the IPRD if it is totally *de novo* and separate from any

Exhibit 9–2

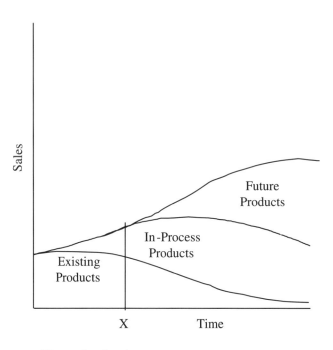

Projected Sales by Category

X = valuation date

existing technology. Again we are viewing the value of the IPRD as the present value of this base technology over and above its existing value and returns to other assets, such as working capital, fixed assets, trade name, and assembled workforce.

Estimating the remaining useful life of the in-process technology is usually based upon a combination of *ex post* and *ex ante* analyses. A review would be made of any historical precedents—active and inactive products to ascertain how long they have lasted or their current age. *Ex ante* analysis could be made based upon discussions with industry experts and/or research of any projections of life that may exist. Special attention should be given to factors that might cause functional or economic obsolescence, such as anticipated changes with interdependent computer hardware. Although opinions are subjective, a survey of opinions would be considered relatively objective, especially if individuals who would be considered knowledgeable in the subject industry rendered the opinions.

Sometimes useful life is elusive because, by constant modification, the product has an indefinite life. In this case, useful life might be viewed to cease when existing and in-process technology are no longer expected to provide any contribution to the subject business cash flow. Mathematically, when the existing and in-process capital investment is expected to turn over once in real dollars, then it may be assumed that a life cycle has transpired.

Revenue Projection

Sales projections have to be put in context in order to be comprehended. For instance, when cellular phone technology was first introduced, purchase prices for franchises were valued on how much was paid per capita. When microwave ovens were introduced, the backdrop was penetration of households.

Whether we are talking about the Internet or pharmaceuticals, the ultimate market should be investigated. For instance, the automotive market in the United States is considered to be fully developed, since the number of cars registered virtually equals the number of licensed drivers.

The size of the market in many cases will be a function of the price level. As penetration increases, economies of scale are achieved and prices drop, thus increasing the potential market.

In terms of computers, the price has been declining (on a functionality basis) at a rate of more than 15 percent per year. The computer may someday become as ubiquitous as the telephone. Projections should not ignore this relationship.

In making projections, we have to be aware of the ultimate potential of the genre of products with which the subject technology competes. Clearly for many high-tech products, the future market is considered to be orders of magnitude larger than the current market. In embryonic industries with large potential, the value of technology is almost a lottery. We know the market is big and when the market matures, the dominant companies will have some normal market shares of a large market (in units). The price level is the unknown element.

Obviously supporting documentation that explains the basis of an independent projection of the size of the market is important.

In any given industry there are usually only three or four survivors who end up with the lion's share of the market and make most of the profit. Depending upon circumstances—that is, number of competitors— what is the likelihood that the subject company and technology will be successful? What positions in the industry does management's projection represent (e.g., is a 35 percent market share reasonable)? Does it make sense from the subject company's historical performance and potential of the subject IPRD? If a company has not been a market leader and significant competition is expected, it may not make sense to have a sales projection that suggests a leading position for that company.

Projecting Expenses

Depending upon the product—hardware, software, pharmaceutical, medical device, and so on—cost of sales can vary significantly. Cost of sales for software and patented pharmaceuticals can be very low. The gross margin on hardware is going to depend upon whether the technology offers any differentiation from competition. If not, margins may depend upon being the low-cost producer. In this case one would not expect a large IPRD value.

Selling and advertising expenses can be somewhat discretionary in a particular year. Close attention should be paid to whether selling expense is normal in a particular year or whether there was a campaign or hiatus in selling expenses.

How do general and administrative expenses (G&A) vary as volume changes? Usually G&A is only partly fixed in nature with another part that is variable. Thus, as sales become very large, the reduction in the percentage of G&A will tend to become asymptotic at a fixed percentage of revenue.

If a return on and of fixed assets is being used as a capital charge, the charge must be structured such that it allows for both replacement and expansion of capacity.

In estimating engineering and R&D expenses, these percentages will typically be different for existing, IPRD, and future technology. For existing technology, all that may be required is a maintenance level of engineering (technical support) with no real R&D. For IPRD, there should be some remaining R&D and engineering may be heavier until the product matures.

Cost of Capital

Besides the difficulty of projecting revenue and expenses, estimating the appropriate cost of capital is generally complex. QED[3] performed a study that represents a 1987 survey of venture capitalists and their expected rates of return by stage of financing. They defined various stages of development starting from seed and progressing through multiple stages to a "cash-out." Rates of return varied from approximately 60 percent at the start-up stage to 30 percent at the IPO or cash-out stage.

Another alternative to simply changing the rates of return as an investment in R&D reaches various stages is to allow for discrete probabilities of success. This may be more applicable to pharmaceutical products where there are established patterns of passing clinical trials. Exhibit 9–3 depicts an outcome tree where odds for success can be computed on various outcomes. Exhibit 9–4 describes the probabilities of the possible outcomes. Please be mindful that the probabilities used in Exhibit 9–3 and computed in Exhibit 9–4 are illustrative only.

For any particular case, these probabilities would have to be carefully analyzed from the facts and circumstances involved in that case. In the subject example, there was only a 24 percent probability that the

---

[3] James L. Plummer, *QED Report on Venture Capital Financial Analysis* (Palo Alto, CA: QED Research, Inc., 1987).

product would be approved for sale. How do simple rates of return compare with a combination of probability and rate of return? Exhibit 9–5 illustrates the balance between the concepts. Depending upon the projection horizon, a 15 percent rate of return with a 25 percent probability of success results in approximately a 40 to 50 percent rate of return, if the horizon is about 10 years.

In fact, a Monte Carlo simulation could be designed that took into consideration possible outcomes, including success of entry and market position—that is, high market share, high margin to low market share, low margin. The rates of return to use in the discounted cash flow analysis could be more in line with rates of returns earned by smaller existing

Exhibit 9–3

Outcome Tree

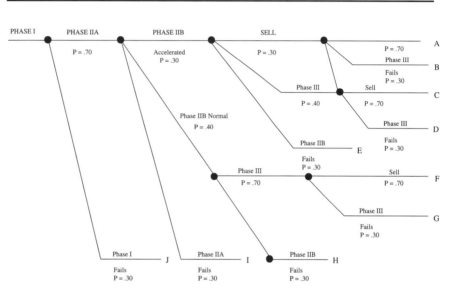

Exhibit 9–4

Calculation of Probabilities
of Clinical Outcomes
Fat Buster

Outcom	Phase I	Phase IIA	Phase IIB	Sell	Phase III	Calculation of Probability	Probabilities of Outcome	Sell
A	Yes	Yes	Yes	Yes	Yes	70 x .30 x .30 x .7	0.0441	Yes
B	Yes	Yes	Yes	Yes	Fail	.7 x .3 x .3 x .3	0.0189	No
C	Yes	Yes	Yes	No	Yes	.7 x .3 x .3 x .7	0.0588	Yes
D	Yes	Yes	Yes	No	Fail	.7 x .3 x .3 x .3	0.0252	No
E	Yes	Yes	Fail			.7 x .3 x .3	0.0630	No
F	Yes	Yes	Yes	No	Yes	.7 x .3 x .7 x .7	0.1372	Yes
G	Yes	Yes	Yes	No	Fail	.7 x .4 x .7 x .3	0.0588	No
H	Yes	Yes	Fail			.7 x .4 x .3	0.0840	No
I	Yes	Fail				.7 x .3	0.2100	No
J	Fail					.3	0.3000	No

Exhibit 9–5

Equivalent Single Rates of Return

	Year 3	Year 5	Year 10	Year 20
15% rate of return				
50% probability	45%	32%	23%	19%
25% probability	82%	52%	32%	23%
10% probability	148%	82%	45%	29%
25% rate of return				
50% probability	57%	44%	34%	29%
25% probability	98%	65%	44%	34%
10% probability	169%	98%	57%	40%

publicly traded companies in the industry—that is, small cap rates of return.

Dr. Stewart C. Myers, in his presentation at the 1995 American Society of Appraisers Advanced Business Valuation Conference in Boston, made the following observations about the cost of capital in R&D–intensive companies:

- R&D intensity increases the risk of companies.
- Betas are typically very high for pure R&D companies (his data suggested betas of 1.5 to 2.0 or higher).
- Conventionally measured WACC is too low for R&D.
- Rates of return requirements fall as a product matures.
- An R&D investor is in a leveraged position because costs of R&D are largely fixed. Macro risks are amplified because of fixed costs.
- Venture capital returns are skewed—many failures, few successes.
- Venture capitalists succeed because they identify losers early and make it big on the few that actually succeed.

The remarks of Dr. Myers were particularly directed at the pharmaceutical and biotech industries.

The type of cost of capital or rate of return that is appropriate will depend on the particular circumstances. If probabilities of success (or failure) can be estimated, then this hybrid discounting technique is preferable to the single rate, which is difficult to associate or match up with the underlying risk.

If probabilities of failure cannot be estimated, then the *de novo* product rates of return should undoubtedly be higher than 30 percent after tax. The actual rate of return selected should consider how far along the development is and the perceived confidence of success or failure. If the product is embryonic, the rate of return might well be as high as 50 percent after tax. If the IPRD is just an improvement on an existing well-established product line, then rates of return should probably be pegged at the firm's cost of capital plus a premium depending on the perceived additional risk.

The three examples below illustrate some of the theories and concepts involved in valuing IPRD.

Example 1

The Bull Moose Pharmaceutical Company has several products in the pipeline. Fat Buster is a *de novo* product that breaks up cholesterol and triglycerides. It has phenomenal potential, but clinical testing has not commenced. Clinical trials are normally conducted in three phases, which can take up to four years to conduct. In each successive clinical trial, a larger number of participants are tested. If a proposed drug shows extraordinary promise, clinical tests can be accelerated by going to a larger participant population.

The outcome tree in Exhibit 9–3 presents Phase IIB accelerated and Phase IIB normal. In the normal trials there would be less intensive testing and less cost before evaluating whether to go to Phase III. In some cases, the outcome of Phase IIB may allow the product to come to market before Phase III is undertaken. The company has estimated the probability of passing clinical trials as presented in the outcome tree in Exhibit 9–3 and in Exhibit 9–4.

The company has expanded the possible outcomes for success—that is, outcomes A, C, and F, as presented in Exhibit 9–4—by allowing for the possibility of different market shares, different cost of sales, and different G&A, shown in Exhibit 9–6. Capital charges were computed to provide for returns on net working capital, fixed assets, trade names, and assembled workforce. Net working capital charges were based upon net working capital to sales ratio of 15 percent and pretax finance charge of 10 percent. The net working capital charge is accordingly estimated at 1.5 percent times sales.

Exhibit 9-6

Expanded Successful Outcomes

Outcome	Market Share	COGS/Sales	G&A/Sales
A1	.50	.20	.08
2	.33	.30	.09
3	.25	.40	.10
C1	.33	.30	.09
2	.25	.40	.10
3	.20	.40	.10
F1	.33	.30	.09
2	.25	.40	.10
3	.20	.40	.10

Land for the manufacturing plant and warehouse is estimated at $10 million and annual land lease rates are observed at 10 percent of market value. A fair rental rate for the land is $1 million per year. The manufacturing/distribution building cost is estimated at $50 million. Other estimates are a 14 percent cost of capital, a 5 percent long-term growth rate, and a 30-year life on the building. Recall that the graduated rent formula is:

$$R_G = \frac{V \times (k - g) \times \left[1 - \left(\dfrac{ADFt}{L_t} \times t \right) \right]}{(1 - t) \times \left[1 - \left(\dfrac{1 + g}{1 + k} \right)^{L_e} \right]}$$

$\dfrac{ADF_t}{L_t}$ for a building under the modified accelerated cost recovery system (MACRS) is 0.182 using a 40 percent income tax rate. The graduated rent is:

$$\frac{50,000 \times (0.14 - 0.05) \times [1 - (0.182 \times 0.4)]}{(1 - 0.4) \times \left[1 - \left(\dfrac{1 + 0.05}{1 + 0.14} \right)^{30} \right]}$$

$$RG_{BLDG} = 7,599 \text{ (in \$000s)}$$

The cost of the equipment (M&E) required for the new product is estimated at $40 million. The graduated rent formula is similar to that for the building except for life and present value of depreciation.

The life of the equipment is 10 years and it can be depreciated at 7-year MACRS. The present value of depreciation is 68.78 percent of cost.

$$RG_{M\&E} = \frac{40,000 \times (0.14 - 0.05) \times [1 - (0.6878 \times 0.4)]}{(1 - 0.4) \times \left[1 - \left(\dfrac{1 + 0.05}{1 + 0.14} \right)^{10} \right]}$$

$$RG_{M\&E} = 7,757 \text{ (in \$000s)}$$

The combined annual fixed asset charge is:

Land	$ 1,000,000
Building	7,599,000
Equipment	7,757,000
Total	$16,356,000

Because we used the graduated rent formula, we should increase the fixed asset rents at the assumed rate of inflation, which is 5 percent. It is noteworthy that rents can be put into a spreadsheet as a percent of sales when they are supporting both old and new technology. As old technology sales decline and new technology increases, the rent shifts from the old to the new technology. For our example here we merely assume that all the fixed assets support the new technology.

Assumptions

The market for drugs that can break up (clean out) cholesterol is estimated at $1.3 billion and growing at $100 million per year. The share of the market for Fat Buster will depend on its efficacy and timing of entry. In outcome A1, we assumed it is first on the market and gains the lion's share (50 percent) even after several competitors also break into the market. In outcome A1, we estimated cost of goods sold (COGS) at 20 percent, while in outcome A3, we estimated a terminal market share of 25 percent with a COGS of 40 percent. Usually the leading product has the highest margin. R&D clinical testing cost estimates are usually more easily projected than income projections. Selling and G&A are estimated on the basis of past experiences for similarly successful products. The capital charges have already been discussed.

The cost of capital for the firm is estimated from traditional techniques, since the unusual risk is being considered in the probabilities.

Analysis

In Exhibit 9–7, the outcome of A1 is calculated in a spreadsheet. The outcome value is $1.088 billion, but since the probability of this outcome is only 1.47 percent (one-third of 4.41 percent for outcome A), the expected value is $16.004 million. Similarly, all the outcomes are calculated and their expected values estimated as presented in Exhibit 9–8.

Thus, the IPRD value of Fat Buster is $79.2 million. Remember that some outcomes were in excess of $1 billion. Outcome A1 had a 120 percent rate of return while outcome C3 had a 60 percent rate of return.

Exhibit 9–7

Bull Moose Pharmaceutical Company
Product—Fat Buster
Analysis of IPRD
$000s

Outcome	A1
Value	$1,088,693
Rate of return	14%
Probability	1.47%
Expected value	$16,004

	Year 1	Year 2	Year 3	Year 4	Year 5	Year 6	Year 7	Year 8	Year 9	Year 10
Potential revenue			$1,300,000	$1,400,000	$1,500,000	$1,600,000	$1,700,000	$1,800,000	$1,900,000	$2,000,000
Market share			1.00	0.75	0.50	0.50	0.50	0.50	0.50	0.25
Product revenue			$1,300,000	$1,050,000	$750,000	$800,000	$850,000	$900,000	$950,000	$500,000
Cost of goods sold			260,000	210,000	150,000	160,000	170,000	180,000	190,000	100,000
Gross profit			1,040,000	840,000	600,000	640,000	680,000	720,000	760,000	400,000
R&D	$6,000	$16,000	78,000							
Selling			156,000	126,000	90,000	96,000	102,000	108,000	114,000	60,000
G&A			104,000	84,000	60,000	64,000	68,000	72,000	76,000	40,000
EBITDA			702,000	630,000	450,000	480,000	510,000	540,000	570,000	300,000
Capital charges										
Net working capital			19,500	15,750	11,250	12,000	12,750	13,500	14,250	7,500
Fixed assets			16,356	17,174	18,032	18,934	19,881	20,875	21,919	23,015
Trade name			26,000	21,000	15,000	16,000	17,000	18,000	19,000	10,000
Assembled workforce			10,000	10,000	10,000	10,000	10,000	10,000	10,000	10,000
Profit before tax			630,144	566,076	395,718	423,066	450,369	477,625	504,831	249,485
Income tax			252,058	226,430	158,287	169,226	180,148	191,050	201,933	99,794
Net income			378,086	339,646	237,431	253,840	270,222	286,575	302,899	149,691
Present value factor	0.9366	0.8216	0.7207	0.6322	0.5545	0.4864	0.4267	0.3743	0.3283	0.2880
Present value	(5,620)	(13,145)	272,476	214,713	131,663	123,476	115,302	107,264	99,450	43,112
Sum of present value			$1,088,693							

Exhibit 9–8

Calculation of Expected Value by Outcome for Fat Buster ($000)

	Possible Outcomes	**Market Success**	**Joint Probability**	**Expected Value**
A1	Pass all trials	High market share	.0147	$16,004
2		Medium market share	.0147	6,883
3		Low market share	.0147	4,893
B	Fail phase III		.0189	(354)
C1		High market share	.0196	10,064
2		Medium market share	.0196	4,502
3		Medium market share	.0196	3,019
D	Fail phase III		.0252	(597)
E	Fail phase IIB		.0630	(768)
F1	Pass all	High market share	.0457	22,451
2		Medium market share	.0457	10,487
3		Low market share	.0457	7,039
G	Fail phase III		.0588	(1,395)
H	Fail phase IIB		.0840	(1,024)
I	Fail phase IIA		.2100	(1,180)
J	Fail phase I		.3000	(843)
Sum of all outcomes				**$79,181**

Thus, this format for evaluating risk is ideal for technologies with a relatively low probability of success where specifying high rates of return would be extremely problematic.

Example 2

The Jolt Company has pioneered a new, large weight-bearing frame made from high-performance plastics that can be used in multiple applications such as electric transmission and microwave towers. The product offers lightweight, high-shear strength, small footprint, and ease of assembly, since it does not use conventional fasteners such as bolts or adhesives. The frame is also corrosion resistant and has less signal interference. Currently, the cost of high-performance frames is greater than for conventional steel frames, but the difference is nearly offset by its lower cost of assembly.

In its first two years of full-scale production, The Jolt Company generated the financial performance, shown in Exhibit 9–9.

Currently, the Jolt Company has an R&D project under way that will improve the current product by enabling the use of lower-cost raw materials. This new technology, if successful, will enable Jolt to produce

Exhibit 9–9

Jolt Company Historical Financial Performance
($000)

	1999	2000
Transmission towers	10,488	20,627
Communication towers	7,008	16,877
Total	17,496	37,504
Cost of goods sold	15,746	30,753
Gross profit	1,750	6,751
R&D	1,815	2,397
SG&A	3,675	6,513
Operating income	(3,740)	(2,159)

the frames at a significant cost savings. The new technology is a derivative of the existing technology, and the product will use the existing patented fastening scheme—an interlocking arrangement that is easy to assemble and requires no traditional fasteners.

The existing technology required $15 million and 5 years to develop. Approximately $6 million has already been spent on the new technology, and it is estimated that another $4 million will be required to complete development.

One way of valuing the new technology is to isolate the incremental business that will be generated by the new technology. Exhibit 9–10 projects this incremental business. Note that revenue, cost of sales, gross profit, and so on, are incremental to the new technology.

The existing technology sales are off to a good start and are expected to be commercially successful. At the current stage of development, a 22.5 percent rate of return is considered to be appropriate, given the success already noted. Development to date on the new technology has demonstrated that it has similar properties to the existing technology but is less expensive. The remaining development costs are principally for testing and certification of the new material.

No problems are anticipated, but there is some uncertainty about the amount of the cost savings and the incremental sales that are expected to be generated. For this reason, a higher rate of return is applicable to the incremental business attributed to the new technology. We have added a 5 percent premium, giving us a rate of return of 27.5 percent on the incremental business.

From Exhibit 9–10, the present value of the new business is $22.9 million. This compares with the $6.0 million we have spent to date on this technology. The new technology, however, is a successor to the existing technology and we would not be able to use it unless we hypothetically obtained a license from the owner of the existing technology.

Exhibit 9–10

Incremental Business Expected to Be Generated by New Technology ($000s)

							Terminal
Incremental	2001	2002	2003	2004	2005	2006	Year

Rate of return: 27.50%
Estimated value: $ 22,902

Incremental	2001	2002	2003	2004	2005	2006	Terminal Year
Revenue	—	50,000	100,000	150,000	225,000	300,000	350,000
Cost of sales	—	35,000	69,000	102,000	150,750	198,000	227,500
Gross profit	—	15,000	31,000	48,000	74,250	102,000	122,500
R&D	4,000	1,000	1,000	1,000	1,000	1,000	1,000
SG&A	1,000	7,500	15,000	22,500	33,750	45,000	52,500
Operating profit	(5,000)	6,500	15,000	24,500	39,500	56,000	69,000
Income taxes at 40%	(2,000)	2,600	6,000	9,800	15,800	22,400	27,600
Net income	(3,000)	3,900	9,000	14,700	23,700	33,600	41,400
Depreciation	1,666	3,333	3,333	3,333	3,333	3,333	3,000
Capital expenditures	20,000	20,000	2,000	2,000	2,000	2,000	4,000
Change in working capital	—	6,250	6,250	6,250	9,375	9,375	6,250
Free cash flow	(21,334)	(19,017)	4,083	9,783	15,658	25,558	34,150
Present value factor	0.8856	0.6946	0.5448	0.4273	0.3351	0.2628	1.0728
Present value	(18,893)	(13,209)	2,224	4,180	5,247	6,717	36,636
Sum of present value	22,902						

The question becomes what the royalty rate would be if it were established on the basis of hypothetical arm's-length negotiations between the owner of the existing technology and a separate owner of the new technology. Typical rules of thumb indicate that the licensor gets one-fourth to one-third of the incremental profit. However, at a royalty of 30 percent of the operating profit, the present value of the new technology is only $379,000. Clearly this is not enough incentive for the licensee to agree to the license.

In the subject case, it is our observation that the royalty would have to be set to provide a significant incentive to take on the risk of completing development and paying a fixed royalty. From the existing technology licensor's standpoint, without the new technology his profits are limited, and by signing the license, he gets a fixed percentage of sales. Using 10 percent of operating profits as a royalty for the existing technology, the licensee (i.e., the hypothetical IPRD owner) receives $15.4 million out of the total incremental value of $22.9 million, or about two-thirds. This analysis is presented in Exhibit 9–11.

This return appears to be acceptable. It is equivalent to a royalty on incremental sales of 2 percent. The royalty on actual sales could be computed by factoring this royalty rate by the relationship of incremental sales to actual sales.

In this example we did not substitute capital charges for fixed assets and working capital. Because (1) our analysis was over a sufficiently long period of time and (2) terminal period sales were projected to increase at a constant rate, it was reasonable for us to use free cash flow.

Exhibit 9–11

Valuation of In-Process R&D
Incremental Business
Expected from
New Technology
($000s)

Rate of return		27.50%					
Royalty on existing technology		10.00%					
Estimated value		$ 15,394					

Incremental	2001	2002	2003	2004	2005	2006	Terminal Year
Revenue	—	50,000	100,000	150,000	225,000	300,000	350,000
Cost of sales	—	35,000	69,000	102,000	150,750	198,000	227,500
Gross profit	—	15,000	31,000	48,000	74,250	102,000	122,500
R&D	4,000	1,000	1,000	1,000	1,000	1,000	1,000
SG&A	1,000	7,500	15,000	22,500	33,750	45,000	52,500
Operating profit	(5,000)	6,500	15,000	24,500	39,500	56,000	69,000
Royalty on existing technology		650	1,500	2,450	3,950	5,600	6,900
Income taxes at 40%	(2,000)	2,340	5,400	8,820	14,220	20,160	24,840
Net income	(3,000)	3,510	8,100	13,230	21,330	30,240	37,260
Depreciation	1,666	3,333	3,333	3,333	3,333	3,333	3,000
Capital expenditures	20,000	20,000	2,000	2,000	2,000	2,000	4,000
Change in working capital	—	6,250	6,250	6,250	9,375	9,375	6,250
Free cash flow	(21,334)	(19,407)	3,183	8,313	13,288	22,198	30,010
Present value factor	0.8856	0.6946	0.5448	0.4273	0.3351	0.2628	1.0728
Present value	(18,893)	(13,480)	1,734	3,552	4,453	5,834	32,195
Sum of present value	15,394						

Example 3

Building Works is a software company specializing in computer-aided design of buildings and improvements. The company has been in business for nearly 10 years and has several software products that automate the design of commercial properties, such as offices, apartments, and shopping centers.

The products have gone through several generations of updates, including Windows 95 and Windows 98. Substantial effort has been expended in preparing new versions to run on Windows 2000. Building Works 2002 is the last generation expected to be run on the Viper 1000 series hardware. Building Works 2004 is a future product that is expected to be totally redesigned to run on a new line of hardware being developed by Viper. The financial performance is projected in Exhibit 9–12. The value of the Building Works Company is estimated to be $19.8 million.

A valuation is needed of the existing (commercially feasible) technology and the IPRD. A reasonable amount should be estimated for goodwill, which represents products not relating to software products but based upon the firm's other technical know-how.

The contributory assets consist of existing technology, working capital, fixed assets, assembled workforce, and a trade name. The trade name is not the critical intangible in the sale of the software, since the buyers are professionals who are making an informed purchase. A 2 percent royalty rate attributable to the trade name is deemed appropriate, based on the financial credibility of Buildings Works as a firm that will be around to support the product.

Exhibit 9–12

**Financial Projections for
Building Works Software
($000)**

	1999	2000	2001	2002	2003	2004	2005	Terminal Year
Discount rate		20%						
Company value		$19,848						
Revenue								
Building Works 98	8,000	2,000						
Building Works 2000		9,000	12,000	3,000				
Building Works 2002				10,000	14,000	4,000		
Building Works 2004						11,000	16,000	
Total	8,000	11,000	12,000	13,000	14,000	15,000	16,000	17,000
Cost of sales	960	1,320	1,440	1,560	1,680	1,800	1,920	2,040
Gross profit	7,040	9,680	10,560	11,440	12,320	13,200	14,080	14,960
R&D								
BW98	500							
BW2000	2,000	2,100	600					
BW2002			2,200	2,300	700			
BW2004					2,400	2,500	800	
							2,600	2,700
Total R&D	2,500	2,100	2,800	2,300	3,100	2,500	800	2,700
Selling expense	1,408	1,936	2,112	2,288	2,464	2,640	2,816	2,992
G&A	640	659	679	699	720	742	764	787
Operating profit	2,492	4,985	4,969	6,153	6,036	7,318	9,700	8,481
Income taxes at 40%	997	1,994	1,988	2,461	2,414	2,927	3,880	3,392
Net income	1,495	2,991	2,981	3,692	3,621	4,391	5,820	5,089
Depreciation	150	160	170	180	190	200	210	220
Capital expenditure	120	120	120	120	120	120	120	120
Change in net working capital	-	450	150	150	150	150	150	150
Free cash flow	1,225	2,711	2,691	3,392	3,311	4,071	5,490	4,749
Present value factor	0.9129	0.7607	0.6339	0.5283	0.4402	0.3669	0.3057	1.7983
Present value	1,118	2,062	1,706	1,792	1,458	1,493	1,678	8,540
Sum of present value	19,848							
Trade name present value	88	100	91	82	74	66	59	367
Trade name value	927							

Working capital is estimated to be slightly less than two months of (15 percent) sales, and the interest rate is the firm's borrowing rate. This equates to a capital charge of 1.2 percent (0.15 × 0.08). A study has been done on the cost to recruit and assimilate the Building Works workforce. The cost is estimated at $1 million. At the firm's equity rate of 20 percent, the annual charge is $200,000.

Land is valued at $500,000 and the annual land lease rates are estimated at 10 percent. Land rent is thus $50,000 per year. Buildings are valued at $2 million and are estimated to have an economic life on a composite basis of 40 years. Equipment is valued at $1 million and is estimated to have a 12-year life. Assuming an income tax rate of 40 percent and fixed asset rate of return of 12 percent on the building and 13 percent on the equipment, level rents can be computed according to the following formula:

$$R_L = \frac{V}{(1-t) \times ADF_e} \times \left[1 - \left(\frac{ADF_t}{L_t} \times t \right) \right]$$

Assume the present value of MACRS depreciation for buildings is 25 percent and 72 percent for equipment.

Building rent is estimated as follows:

$$R_L = \frac{2000}{(1-0.4) \times 8.244} \times [1 - (0.25 \times 0.4)]$$

$$R_L = 363 \text{ (in \$000s)}$$

Equipment rent is estimated as follows:

$$R_L = \frac{1000}{(1-0.4) \times 5.92} \times [1 - (0.72 \times 0.4)]$$

$$R_L = 200 \text{ (in \$000s)}$$

The combined rent for fixed assets is as follows:

Land	$ 50,000
Buildings	363,000
Equipment	200,000
Total	$613,000

Since the fixed assets are used by all products, their rent must be shared by existing, in-process, and future products. For the sake of simplicity, we have split fixed asset rent, assembled workforce, and general and administrative expenses on the basis of sales. This is arbitrary, but sales is a reasonable basis on which to allocate charges, since most expenses are related to sales activity directly or indirectly.

Exhibits 9–13, 9–14, and 9–15 represent the value of technology, which we have discounted at a higher rate (25 percent) than the company cash flow.

Our discounted cash flow of the company at 20 percent yielded a value of $19.8 million. Previously, we have stated (or assumed) the following asset values:

Net working capital[4]	$1,200,000
Fixed assets	3,500,000
Assembled workforce	1,000,000
Trade name[5]	750,000
Total nontech/goodwill assets	$6,600,000

---

[4]Estimated as sales times 15 percent times borrowing rate.

[5]Estimated as sales times 2 percent times the tax rate times present value factor at 25 percent.

Exhibit 9–13

Valuation of Building Works 1998 Software
In-Process R&D before Technology Royalties ($000)

								Terminal
Discount rate		25%						
Company value		$2,294						
Revenue	1999	2000	2001	2002	2003	2004	2005	Year
Building Works 98	8,000	2,000						
Building Works 2000								
Building Works 2002								
Building Works 2004								
Total	8,000	2,000						
Cost of sales	960	240						
Gross profit	7,040	1,760						
R&D								
BW98	500							
BW2000								
BW2002								
BW2004								
Total R&D	500							
Selling expense	1,408	352						
G&A	640	132						
Capital charges								
Net working capital	96	24						
Fixed assets	613	111						
Trade name	160	40						
Workforce	200	36						
Technology royalty								
Operating profit	3,423	1,065						
Royalty income								
Income taxes at 40%	1,369	426						
Net income	2,054	639						
Free cash flow	2,054	639						
Present value factor	0.8944	0.7155	0.5724	0.4579	0.3664	0.2931	0.2345	
Present value	1,837	457	—	—	—	—	—	
Sum of present value	2,294							

The following additional intangible values from Exhibits 9–13, 9–14, 9–15, and 9–16 are as follows:

Existing technology BW 1998 (Ex. 9–13)	$2,294,000
In-process R&D BW 2000 (Ex. 9–14)	2,820,000
In-process R&D BW 2002 (Ex. 9–15)	2,053,000
Future products BW 2004 (Ex. 9–16)	5,613,000
Total	$12,780,000

Thus, the value of separately identified assets and goodwill (future products) is equal to about $19.4 million (or approximately the same as our overall company valuation of $19.8 million). Adjusting discount rates and having more precision in capital charges would enable us to reconcile the values, but this is reasonably close.

Exhibit 9–14

Valuation of Building Works 2000 Software
In-Process R&D before Technology Royalties ($000)

	1999	2000	2001	2002	2003	2004	2005	Terminal Year
Discount rate		25%						
Company value		$2,820						
Revenue								
Building Works 98								
Building Works 2000		9,000	12,000	3,000				
Building Works 2002								
Building Works 2004								
Total		9,000	12,000	3,000				
Cost of sales		1,080	1,440	360				
Gross profit		7,920	10,560	2,640				
R&D								
BW98								
BW2000	2,000	2,100	600					
BW2002								
BW2004								
Total R&D	2,000	2,100	600					
Selling expense		1,584	2,112	528				
G&A		539	679	161				
Capital charges								
Net working capital		108	144	36				
Fixed assets		502	613	141				
Trade name		180	240	60				
Workforce		164	200	46				
Technology royalty								
Operating profit	(2,000)	2,743	6,572	1,668				
Royalty income								
Income taxes at 40%	(800)	1,097	2,629	667				
Net income	(1,200)	1,646	3,943	1,001				
Free cash flow	(1,200)	1,646	3,943	1,001				
Present value factor	0.8944	0.7155	0.5724	0.4579	0.3664	0.2931	0.2345	
Present value	(1,073)	1,178	2,257	458	—	—	—	
Sum of present value	2,820							

One aspect of technology value has been overlooked: The in-process technology embodied in BW 2000 and BW 2002 is dependent on existing technology. If truly segregating the value between existing and in-process products, a royalty would be necessary to compensate the hypothetical licensor. After scrutinizing the financial impact, we assigned a 5 percent royalty on sales to the most recent noncurrent technology (one generation removed) and a 2.5 percent royalty on technology two generations removed.

The results are provided in Exhibits 9–17, 9–18, and 9–19. The impact of the royalties shifted the value as follows:

	Before Royalties ($000)	After Royalties ($000)
BW 1998	2,294	2,898
BW 2000	2,820	2,706
BW 2002	2,053	1,563

Exhibit 9–15

Valuation of Building Works 2002 Software
In-Process R&D before Technology Royalties ($000)

Revenue	1999	2000	2001	2002	2003	2004	2005	Terminal Year
Discount rate		25%						
Company value		$2,053						
Building Works 98								
Building Works 2000								
Building Works 2002				10,000	14,000	4,000		
Building Works 2004								
Total				10,000	14,000	4,000		
Cost of sales				1,200	1,680	480		
Gross profit				8,800	12,320	3,520		
R&D								
BW98								
BW2000								
BW2002			2,200	2,300	700			
BW2004								
Total R&D			2,200	2,300	700			
Selling expense				1,760	2,464	704		
G&A				538	720	198		
Capital charges								
Net working capital				120	168	48		
Fixed assets				538	720	198		
Trade name				200	280	80		
Workforce				176	235	65		
Technology royalty								
Operating profit			(2,200)	3,168	7,033	2,227		
Income taxes at 40%			(880)	1,267	2,813	891		
Net income			(1,320)	1,901	4,220	1,336		
Depreciation								
Capital expenses								
Change in net working capital								
Free cash flow			(1,320)	1,901	4,220	1,336		
Present value factor	0.8944	0.7155	0.5724	0.4579	0.3664	0.2931	0.2345	
Present value	—	—	(756)	871	1,546	392	—	
Sum of present value	2,053							

Thus, the royalties shifted value out of in-process technology into existing technology. (Note: We could have used a higher royalty rate and shifted more value. As described earlier, this analysis is part of estimating what arm's-length parties would do.)

Finally, note in Exhibit 9–16 that the value of future products not yet on the drawing board is $5.6 million, or about 28 percent of the total company value. This is goodwill. The amount of goodwill will depend on the life of the existing and in-process technology. The longer their lives, the smaller the goodwill. In this example, the lives were short—producing significant goodwill.

Exhibit 9–16

Valuation of Building Works Future Products ($000)

Discount rate		25%						
Company value		$5,612						

Revenue	1999	2000	2001	2002	2003	2004	2005	Terminal Year
Building Works 98								
Building Works 2000								
Building Works 2002								
Building Works 2004						11,000	16,000	
Total						11,000	16,000	17,000
Cost of sales						1,320	1,920	2,040
Gross profit						9,680	14,080	14,960
R&D								
BW98								
BW2000								
BW2002								
BW2004					2,400	2,500	800	
							1,800	2,700
Total R&D					2,400	2,500	2,600	2,700
Selling expense						1,936	2,816	2,992
G&A						544	764	787
Capital charges								
Net working capital						132	192	204
Fixed assets						450	613	613
Trade name						220	320	340
Workforce						147	200	200
Technology royalty								
Operating profit					(2,400)	3,751	6,575	7,124
Income taxes at 40%					(960)	1,500	2,630	2,850
Net income					(1,440)	2,251	3,945	4,274
Depreciation								
Capital expenses								
Change in net working capital								
Free cash flow					(1,440)	2,251	3,945	4,274
Present value factor	0.8944	0.7155	0.5724	0.4579	0.3664	0.2931	0.2345	1.0658
Present value	—	—	—	—	(528)	660	925	4,555
Sum of present value	5,612							

Summary

The valuation of in-process R&D is a sensitive topic. The two most important issues to be considered are (1) projected income stream during the expected remaining life of the IPRD and (2) the isolation of, and the capital charges attributable to, contributing assets, including existing technology. Again, the guiding light is the probable bargaining between hypothetical arm's-length buyers and sellers.

Complicating IPRD valuations are the difficulty of projecting revenues for new technology and determining an appropriate scheme for handling the issues of risk and uncertainty.

Exhibit 9–17

Valuation of Building Works 1998 Software
In-Process R&D after Technology Royalties ($000)

								Terminal
Discount rate		25%						
Company value		$2,898						
Revenue	1999	2000	2001	2002	2003	2004	2005	Year
Building Works 98	8,000	2,000						
Building Works 2000								
Building Works 2002								
Building Works 2004								
Total	8,000	2,000						
Cost of sales	960	240						
Gross profit	7,040	1,760						
R&D								
BW98	500							
BW2000								
BW2002								
BW2004								
Total R&D	500							
Selling expense	1,408	352						
G&A	640	132						
Capital charges								
Net working capital	96	24						
Fixed assets	613	111						
Trade name	160	40						
Workforce	200	36						
Technology royalty								
Operating profit	3,423	1,065						
Royalty income		450	600	400	350	100		
Income taxes at 40%	1,369	606	240	160	140	40		
Net income	2,054	909	360	240	210	60		
Free cash flow	2,054	909	360	240	210	60		
Present value factor	0.8944	0.7155	0.5724	0.4579	0.3664	0.2931	0.2345	1.0658
Present value	1,837	650	206	110	77	18	—	—
Sum of present value	2,898							

Bibliography

Aaron, Anthony. "Purchase Price Allocation in the High Technology Industry: Valuing Purchased Research and Development," presented at the American Society of Appraisers Advanced Business Valuation Conference, Boston, November 2, 1995.

Aaron, Anthony, and Brent Uken. "The Valuation of Research and Development in Purchase Business Combinations in the Software Industry," *Software Executive Alert* (a publication of Ernst & Young LLP), 1995.

Financial Accounting Standards Board Interpretation No. 6, "Applicability of FASIS Statement No. 2 to Computer Software."

Exhibit 9–18

Valuation of Building Works 2000 Software
In-Process R&D after Technology Royalties ($000)

Discount rate 25%
Company value $2,706

Revenue	1999	2000	2001	2002	2003	2004	2005	Terminal Year
Building Works 98								
Building Works 2000		9,000	12,000	3,000				
Building Works 2002								
Building Works 2004								
Total		9,000	12,000	3,000				
Cost of sales		1,080	1,440	360				
Gross profit		7,920	10,560	2,640				
R&D								
BW98								
BW2000	2,000	2,100	600					
BW2002								
BW2004								
Total R&D	2,000	2,100	600					
Selling expense		1,584	2,112	528				
G&A		539	679	161				
Capital charges								
Net working capital		108	144	36				
Fixed assets		502	613	141				
Trade name		180	240	60				
Workforce		164	200	46				
Technology royalty		450	600	150				
Operating profit	(2,000)	2,293	5,972	1,518				
Royalty income					500	700	200	
Income taxes at 40%	(800)	917	2,389	807	280	80		
Net income	(1,200)	1,376	3,583	1,211	420	120		
Free cash flow	(1,200)	1,376	3,583	1,211	420	120		
Present value factor	0.8944	0.7155	0.5724	0.4579	0.3664	0.2931	0.2345	
Present value	(1,073)	985	2,051	555	154	35	—	
Sum of present value	2,706							

Myers, Stewart C. "Risk and Return in R&D Intensive Companies," presented at the American Society of Appraisers Advanced Business Valuation Conference, Boston, November 2, 1995.

Pittock, William, and John Capecci. "Valuing In-Process Research & Development," presented at the American Society of Appraisers Advanced Business Valuation Conference, San Francisco, October 24, 1997.

Statement of Financial Accounting Standards No. 2, "Accounting for Research and Development Costs."

Statement of Financial Accounting Standards No. 86, "Accounting for the Costs of Computer Software to Be Sold, Leased, or Otherwise Marketed."

Exhibit 9–19

Valuation of Building Works 2002 Software
In-Process R&D after Technology Royalties ($000)

								Terminal
Discount rate		25%						
Company value		$1,563						
Revenue	1999	2000	2001	2002	2003	2004	2005	Year
Building Works 98								
Building Works 2000								
Building Works 2002				10,000	14,000	4,000		
Building Works 2004								
Total				10,000	14,000	4,000		
Cost of sales				1,200	1,680	480		
Gross profit				8,800	12,320	3,520		
R&D								
BW98								
BW2000								
BW2002			2,200	2,300	700			
BW2004								
Total R&D			2,200	2,300	700			
Selling expense				1,760	2,464	704		
G&A				538	720	198		
Capital charges								
Net working capital				120	168	48		
Fixed assets				538	720	198		
Trade name				200	280	80		
Workforce				176	235	65		
Royalty 98				500	700	200		
Royalty 2000				250	350	100		
Operating profit			(2,200)	2,418	5,983	1,927		
Income taxes at 40%			(880)	967	2,393	771		
Net income			(1,320)	1,451	3,590	1,156		
Depreciation								
Capital expenses								
Change in net working capital								
Free cash flow			(1,320)	1,451	3,590	1,156		
Present value factor	0.8944	0.7155	0.5724	0.4579	0.3664	0.2931	0.2345	
Present value	—	—	(756)	664	1,315	339	—	
Sum of present value	1,563							

Part III

Special Issues Related to Specific-Purpose Valuations

Chapter 10

The Business Appraiser's Role in Estate Planning

S. Stacy Eastland and John W. Porter

Introduction

The estimation of the fair market value of an interest in property that is being transferred, either by gift or at death, is the foundation upon which our federal estate and gift tax system is built. The U.S. Supreme Court has often held that succession taxes, inheritance taxes, and estate taxes are constitutional levies by the federal government only if they are applied in a manner that is merely an excise tax at the transfer of property at death.[1] Therefore, only that property that is *transferred* as a result of a taxpayer's death or by gift during the taxpayer's life can be subjected to taxation under the federal estate and gift tax system. The tax cannot be a "wealth tax" or "property tax" on the intrinsic value of an asset to the decedent or donor at the time the transfer occurs; rather, it should be a tax on the value of the asset transferred.[2]

In an estimation of the value of any asset that is transferred, the legal rights and interests inherent in that property should first be determined under state law (unless federal law supersedes state law). After that determination is made, the federal tax law takes over to determine how such rights and interests will be taxed.[3] The valuation of property for transfer tax purposes is based upon the "price at which the property would change hands between a willing buyer and a willing seller, neither being under any compulsion to buy or to sell and both having reasonable knowledge of relevant facts."[4]

Because of this test, there are two primary components of federal estate and gift tax valuation: (1) understanding the state law rights being transferred from the hypothetical willing seller to the hypothetical willing buyer, and (2) estimating the fair market value of those interests. As the expert who applies sound valuation principles to estimate the fair market value of the property interests being transferred, whether by gift or at death, the valuation analyst serves a key role in the estate planning process.

Valuations from Qualified and Respected Analysts Should Be Obtained at the Appropriate Estate Planning Stage

The great majority of Internal Revenue Service challenges in the transfer tax area focus on disputing a taxpayer's valuation of hard to value, or *inactively traded* assets such as partnership interests or closely held corporations. Assuming a supportable legal framework for an estate

[1] See for example, *Knowlton* v. *Moore*, 178 U.S. 41 (1900); *New York Trust* v. *Eisner*, 256 U.S. 345 (1921).
[2] See I.R.C. §§2033, 2035–38, 2040(c), 2044, and 2501.
[3] *United States* v. *Bess*, 357 U.S. 51 (1958); *Morgan* v. *Commissioner*, 309 U.S. 78 (1940).
[4] Treas. Reg. §20.2031-1(b); Treas. Reg. §20.2512-1.

planning transaction with an inactively traded asset, the only way for a taxpayer and the IRS to differ on the amount of the tax owed is for each to claim a different value for the asset transferred. If such a dispute arises and progresses to litigation, the result is determined after a "battle of the experts."

The taxpayer should not rely on an accountant or on someone else who is not qualified as an appraiser to value a business interest. The taxpayer generally has the burden of presenting credible evidence in order to prove the taxpayer's valuation position.[5] For valuation disputes in court proceedings arising in connection with examinations commencing after July 22, 1998, the burden of proof in a court proceeding may shift to the IRS in certain cases where the taxpayer presents "credible evidence" with respect to the valuation issues.[6] However, without a well-reasoned valuation from a qualified analyst, the taxpayer has virtually no basis to dispute what may prove to be an unrealistic IRS valuation claim. Likewise, the IRS has much less of an obligation to show proof of its valuation position. The taxpayer's valuation analyst should be reputable, qualified, and independent. After all, the analyst may be the taxpayer's expert witness in the event of an audit and any related litigation. If a qualified appraisal has not been obtained before filing the estate or gift tax return, the taxpayer will ultimately have to pay for such a valuation when the valuation dispute arises.

The existence of a well-reasoned valuation from a qualified analyst can in some cases prevent a valuation challenge. When faced with a taxpayer valuation based on the opinion of a well-respected, independent analyst, the IRS is essentially forced to hire an equally qualified analyst (1) who can credibly attack the valuation opinion of the taxpayer's analyst and (2) who can produce an opinion of value different enough to generate a tax revenue advantage for the government. The IRS is going to allocate resources to pay for valuations if there is an expectation that the allocation will be more than reimbursed. It is difficult for the IRS on a cost/benefit analysis to justify spending the money to challenge a reasonable valuation from a qualified expert that is based upon widely used valuation methods. This cost/benefit analysis can and should work to the advantage of taxpayers who use timely, well-reasoned valuations.

Examples of situations involving inactively traded assets that warrant contemporaneous valuations include:

1. For inactively traded assets contributed to a family partnership or a closely held corporation, a valuation should be obtained at the time the entity is created. This will help to head off the argument that a gift was made when an entity was created.

---

[5] T.C.R. 142(a); *Welch* v. *Helvering*, 290 U.S. 111, 115 (1933).

[6] I.R.C. §7491. For the burden of proof to shift, the taxpayer must satisfy the following conditions: (1) the taxpayer must comply with the substantiation and recordkeeping requirements of the Internal Revenue Code and the regulations, (2) the taxpayer must cooperate with reasonable requests by the IRS for witnesses, information, documents, meetings and interviews, (3) taxpayers other than individuals must have a net worth of less than $7 million.

2. When creating an entity with a preferred interest (e.g., a "freeze" partnership), obtain a contemporaneous valuation in order to determine the appropriate interest rate for the preferred interest.

3. When making a gift of partnership interests, closely held stock, or an undivided interest in real estate, obtain a valuation at the time of the gift. The appraisal can be filed with the gift tax return to begin the three-year statute of limitation for transfers adequately disclosed on a gift tax return.[7]

The Valuation Analyst's Credibility Is Key

One of the most important qualifications that an analyst can possess is credibility. The analyst's role is to estimate the fair market value of the property interest being valued, giving consideration to all relevant facts, and to support that valuation with appropriate data and analysis. Although the analyst should be confident in his or her methodology and conclusions, the analyst should not become an advocate for the taxpayer's position. In other words, the independent analyst cannot simply adopt the taxpayer's analysis or opinion of value. Once the finder of fact believes that the analyst has become the taxpayer's "advocate" and not an independent expert engaged to apply appropriate valuation methodology to estimate the fair market value of the property interest being valued, the analyst will lose credibility.

Judge Beghe recently stated in *Martin Ice Cream Company v. Commissioner* that "experts are not supposed to be 'hired guns'; they lose their usefulness and credibility to the extent that they become mere advocates for the side that hired them."[8] When credibility is lost, the analyst's conclusions will no longer be considered helpful to the finder of fact in the valuation dispute, and they will be disregarded. Consider the following passage from Judge Hamblin's opinion in *Jacobson v. Commissioner*:

> In closing, we once again observe with some dismay the disparity in the reports of the experts in this case. We have previously remarked that we sense some degree of advocacy on one or both sides when such diversions of opinion as to value occurs in the reports of apparently qualified realtors-appraisers. If this is the case, the experts can be viewed only as hired guns of the side that retained them, and this not only disparages their professional status but precludes their assistance to the Court in reaching a proper and reasonably accurate conclusion.[9]

---

[7]I.R.C. §6501(c)(9).
[8]*Martin Ice Cream Company* v. *Commissioner*, 110 T.C. 189 (1998).
[9]*Jacobson* v. *Commissioner*, 58 T.C.M. (CCH) 645, 650 (1989).

The Valuation Analyst Should Understand and Apply the Fair Market Value Standard

In preparing valuations for estate and gift tax purposes, many analysts fail to focus on the correct definition of fair market value. For federal estate and gift tax purposes, fair market value has long been defined as "the price at which the property would change hands between a willing buyer and a willing seller, neither being under any compulsion to buy or to sell and both having reasonable knowledge of relevant facts."[10] "All relevant facts and elements of value as of the applicable valuation date shall be considered."[11] For purposes of estimating the fair market value of property being valued, the identity and intentions of the recipient of the property is irrelevant. "The standard is an objective test using hypothetical buyers and sellers in the marketplace, and is not a personalized one which envisions a particular buyer and seller."[12]

This point has also been emphasized in the updated edition of *IRS Valuation Training for Appeals Officers*. That IRS training course stresses the hypothetical willing buyer and seller, and states unequivocally that "it is irrelevant who are the real seller and buyer."[13] However, if the interest being valued is a partial interest in property, the identity of the owner of the interests that are not being transferred and the effect of such ownership on the value of the property being transferred is highly relevant.[14]

Dealing with Legal Issues

One of the more difficult questions in valuation work is how to deal with legal issues that are in dispute in the context of a valuation. Examples of such issues include the effectiveness of a buy-sell agreement and the rights of an owner of a partial interest in property. Examples of such partial interests include undivided interests in real estate, limited partnership interests, and ownership of less than all the shares of a corporation. Each of these ownership interests carries with it a different bundle of rights and obligations under applicable state law.

Understanding the rights that a hypothetical seller can transfer, and the rights that a hypothetical buyer can receive, is critical to the valuation analysis. The analyst's role is to estimate the price at which a

---

[10] Treas. Reg. 20.2031-1(b).

[11] Ibid.

[12] *LeFrak* v. *Commissioner*, 66 T.C.M. (CCH) 1297, 1299 (1993). See also *Estate of Bonner* v. *United States*, 84 F.3d 196 (5th Cir. 1996). ("We are precluded from considering evidence submitted by the government regarding who actually received the assets.")

[13] *IRS Valuation Training for Appeals Officers* (Chicago: CCH Incorporated, 1998).

[14] See Treas. Reg. 20.2031-1(b).

property interest being valued would change hands between a willing buyer and a willing seller, both having reasonable knowledge of relevant facts. Relevant facts include all the attributes attached to the property being transferred, including any legal rights or obligations attached to the property. For example, is the hypothetical buyer of a partnership interest automatically entitled to become a partner? Or is the buyer limited to the status of a mere assignee (with no management rights, limited or no information rights, and no right of withdrawal)? See Chapter 8 for further discussion of this subject.

Most analysts, however, are not qualified to render a legal opinion, and they should not try to do so. Where questions of law exist, the appraiser should rely on the opinion of qualified counsel as to the likely understanding of the rights and privileges attached to the interest being valued. For example, if a buy-sell agreement exists for a closely held entity and its application is uncertain, the analyst generally should not opine on whether the buy-sell agreement is valid. A knowledgeable owner of the interest being valued—whether a buyer or seller—would likely consult with an attorney to analyze his or her rights in connection with the enforceability of such a buy-sell agreement, since the legal issue may have a significant impact on the value of the property interest.[15] It is not necessary to obtain a conclusive determination of the legal issue, but, as the Tax Court stated in *Newhouse*, "it is a likely understanding of the rights and privileges . . . that will influence the terms of the sale, not whether we resolve this dispute over New York law."[16]

A Team of Experts?

When an asset or a closely held business is valued, the need for more than one expert often arises. The valuation of an undivided interest may include an analysis of local law regarding the rights of an undivided interest owner, and an analyst who can analyze both the 100 percent value of the property and the sales of comparable undivided interests. If the property is income-producing, then a business valuation analyst may analyze the value on a "going-concern basis." If environmental problems exist, then an environmental engineer may be consulted to determine the cost of remediation or the effect of the problem on the property's fair market value. For a closely held business, experts such as business valuation analysts or investment bankers will be useful. If the business itself contains inactively traded assets that require special expertise, those assets can be separately valued by specialists (e.g., real estate appraisers, personal property appraisers, industry experts, accountants, company advisers).

---

[15] See, for example, *Estate of Newhouse* v. *Commissioner*, 94 T.C. 193, 231 (1990) ("a hypothetical willing buyer would have had the counsel of several advisors of formidable reputation").

[16] Ibid.

The Estate Planning Professional Should Hire the Valuation Analyst

Working with valuation analysts is an everyday event for most estate planning professionals. On the other hand, working with analysts can be something of a rarity for most taxpayers, many of whom have dealt with appraisers only in the purchase of their home. In addition, the attitude of many taxpayers is that, although valuation analysts are a necessary component of the estate planning process, they necessarily complicate the timing and expense of estate planning transactions.

In most cases, the estate planner, not the taxpayer, should hire the analyst for an estate planning transaction. The estate planning professional can offer guidance to both the taxpayer and the analyst as to how similar transactions have been handled in the past by the IRS and the courts. Involvement of the attorney estate planner early in the process will also provide the taxpayer with a compelling argument that any unused reports or correspondence is attorney work product.

Remember That Anything Committed to Writing May Be Discoverable

Any document in the valuation analyst's final work paper file, including correspondence, notes, and drafts of valuations, is subject to being discovered during the audit process or in subsequent valuation litigation.[17] Experienced valuation analysts should know this. However, it never hurts for the estate planner to remind the analyst. Once again, consider who the audience may ultimately be and understand that the analyst's final work paper file may be reviewed by the examining agent, appeals officer, district counsel, or ultimate finder of fact in estate or gift tax litigation.

The Analyst, the Taxpayer, and the Taxpayer's Representatives Need Not Retain Drafts of Valuations

There is generally no benefit for the estate planner, the client, or the valuation analyst to keep drafts of a valuation once the finished product

---

[17] For the purpose of "ascertaining the correctness of any return, making a return where none has been made, or determining the liability of any person for any internal revenue tax," the IRS is authorized (1) to examine any books, papers, records, or other data that may be relevant or material to such inquiry, and (2) to summon the person liable for tax or required to perform the act, or any officer or employee of such person, or any person having possession, custody, or care of books of account containing entries relating to the business of the person liable for tax or required to perform the act, or any other person the IRS may deem proper to produce such books, papers, records or other data. I.R.C. §7602(a).

has been completed. The valuation and the analyst's work papers should contain all relevant information that is necessary to support the valuation. Drafts of valuations may not be subject to the attorney-client privilege or the attorney work product privilege. Generally, once the valuation analyst is designated as an expert in litigation, any privilege that existed as to those drafts is lost. A document request from an examining agent or district counsel is likely to include a request for all drafts of any valuations. Drafts that differ in any way from the finished product could be used in an attempt to embarrass or impeach the analyst's results. The valuation analyst, on examination, may be asked to explain the reason for each difference between the draft and the final product.

The Valuation Should Be in a Form That Fully Sets Forth the Analyst's Conclusions and Is Admissible in Court

Even when a valuation will initially be used only to estimate the fair market value of an asset in connection with the filing of an estate or gift tax return, the valuation report should be in a form that will allow the report to be introduced in subsequent tax litigation. Preparation of a complete report with this potential end use in mind will avoid the need to have the analyst prepare a new or revised report in the event the matter proceeds to trial. Rule 143(f) of the U.S. Tax Court sets forth the requirements for the expert's report, and provides:

> The report shall set forth the qualifications of the expert witness and shall state the witness' opinion and the facts or data on which that opinion is based. The report shall set forth in detail the reasons for the conclusion, and it will be marked as an exhibit, identified by the witness, and received in evidence as the direct testimony of the expert witness, unless the Court determines that the witness is not qualified as an expert. Additional direct testimony with respect to the report may be allowed to clarify or emphasize matters in the report, to cover matters arising after the preparation of the report, or otherwise at the discretion of the Court...An expert witness's testimony will be excluded altogether for failure to comply with the provisions of this paragraph, unless the failure is shown to be due to good cause and unless the failure does not unduly prejudice the opposing party, such as by significantly impairing the opposing party's ability to cross-examine the expert witness or by denying the opposing party the reasonable opportunity to obtain evidence in rebuttal to the expert witness's testimony.[18]

In most Tax Court cases, the valuation report will serve as the expert's direct testimony. Unless permitted by the Court, no oral direct testimony from the valuation analyst will be admitted regarding his or her valuation. It is, therefore, imperative that the valuation contain all

---

[18]T.C.R. 143(f).

facts, data, and reasoning on which the valuation analyst bases the valuation conclusion. The valuation methodology should be rational and understandable. If a part of the valuation is based upon third-party contacts, those contacts should be identified. If a part of the appraisal is based upon comparable sales or statistical data, the sales and statistical data should be identified and included in the report. Although the inclusion of this material may make the report more cumbersome, it will allow the reader to fully understand all the reasons for the analyst's valuation conclusion. Put yourself in the position of the uninformed reader of the report who is attempting to use the valuation to determine the fair market value of property: Does the valuation contain all the information in a clear, rational and logical manner to allow the reader to fully understand and decide whether the analyst's conclusions are correct?

When Partial Interests Are Valued, the Discounts Should Be Appropriately Tied to the Specific Attributes of the Interest in the Valuation Entity

In estimating the fair market value of a partial interest in a closely held business, analysts often rely on various studies to determine the discounts for (1) lack of control and (2) lack of marketability. These studies, which help the analyst quantify and select the appropriate minority ownership interest discount, include (1) studies of tender offers (control price premiums) and (2) studies of closed-end investment funds. Studies that help the appraiser quantify and select the appropriate discount for lack of marketability include: (1) studies of restricted (letter) stock transactions, and (2) studies of private transactions prior to initial public offerings.

Unfortunately, many inexperienced analysts blindly apply the results of these studies without actually comparing the attributes of the stock reflected in the studies to the interest being valued. All too often an analyst will simply average the results of the studies and apply the resulting valuation discount to the percentage value of the interest being valued. A report that takes this approach may strike the Internal Revenue Service and the courts as a useless "cookie cutter" approach.

Simply relying on these commonly cited valuation studies without tying the studies to the specific attributes of the entity being valued is usually not sufficient. It is practically impossible to prescribe a single standard or formula that must be applied in arriving at fair market value in each case. The analyst should carefully consider all relevant factors regarding the entity. The weight to be accorded each factor will be different depending upon the facts, circumstances, and perspective of the case at hand. For example, in *Mandelbaum* v. *Commissioner*, Judge Laro provided a list of 10 nonexclusive factors that should be considered when valuing unlisted stock. Judge Laro stated:

Ascertaining the appropriate discount for limited marketability is a factual determination. Critical to this determination is an appreciation of the fundamental elements of value that are used by an investor in making his or her investment decision. A non-exclusive list of these factors includes: (1) The value of the subject corporation's privately traded securities vis-à-vis its publicly traded securities (or, if the subject corporation does not have stock that is traded both publicly and privately, the cost of a similar corporation's public and private stock); (2) an analysis of the subject corporation's financial statements; (3) the corporation's dividend paying capacity, its history of paying dividends, and the amount of its prior dividends; (4) the nature of the corporation, its history, its position in the industry, and its economic outlook; (5) the corporation's management; (6) the degree of control transferred with the block of stock and the value; (7) any restrictions on the transferability of the corporation's stock; (8) the period of time for which an investor must hold the subject stock to realize a sufficient profit; (9) the corporation's redemption policy; and (10) the cost of effectuating a public offering of the stock to be valued, e.g., legal, accounting, and underwriting fees.[19]

Judge Laro then examined each of these factors to determine whether the factor favors an above-average or below-average lack of marketability discount. Although those criteria may not fit each valuation situation, the criteria demonstrate that the Tax Court desires more than simple blind reliance on the "average" result of valuation discount studies. Careful thought should be given by the valuation analyst as to how the interest being valued compares with the companies analyzed in each published study that was relied upon.

Conclusion

The valuation analyst plays a critical role in estate planning. Valuations from qualified and respected analysts should be obtained early in the estate planning process. Most analysts are unqualified to render a legal opinion and should not try to do so. When questions of law exist, the analyst should rely on the opinion of qualified counsel as to the likely understanding of the rights and privileges attached to the interest being valued. When appropriate, additional experts can be added to the team to focus on particular legal, environmental, or industry issues that affect the valuation.

The estate planning attorney rather than the taxpayer should engage the analyst in order to keep the process focused and to protect any attorney-client privilege that may be available to the taxpayer. Anything committed to writing may be discoverable, so the valuation analyst should be careful about producing draft reports and saving obsolete documents. Similarly, the taxpayer and the taxpayer's

---

[19]*Mandelbaum* v. *Commissioner*, 69 T.C.M. (CCH) 2852, 2864 (1995).

representatives should not retain obsolete documents, including drafts of valuations.

The business valuation report should be complete—that is, it should fairly set forth the analyst's conclusions—and it is admissible in court. When valuation adjustments must be made, the rationale for applying discounts should be based on the specific attributes of the interest in the entity being valued.

Chapter 11

Valuation Issues Unique to ESOPs

Gregory K. Brown

Introduction

Uses and Applications

An employee stock ownership plan (ESOP) may borrow money and enter transactions with related parties to acquire the employer's securities in what would be prohibited transactions for other types of qualified plans. As a result, an ESOP may serve as a financing vehicle for the employer. ESOPs serve a variety of corporate objectives beyond the primary objective of providing employees with a retirement benefit.

ESOPs also serve as a technique of corporate finance. In particular, ESOPs can serve the following corporate finance objectives:

- Capital formation
- Solving ownership succession issues
- Refinance existing debt
- Estate planning and charitable giving
- Financing an acquisition or a divestiture

Statutory Requirements

ESOPs must satisfy several statutory requirements. An ESOP must:

1. Be a defined contribution plan that is a stock bonus plan or a combination stock bonus and money purchase pension plan.
2. Meet all the tax qualification requirements applicable to retirement plans in general.
3. Be designed to invest primarily in qualifying employer securities.
4. Meet the participant voting requirements, give participants the right to demand that benefits be distributed in the form of employer securities, and require the employer to repurchase those securities if they are not readily tradable on an established securities market.
5. Meet the benefit distribution requirements for ESOPs.
6. Meet the nonallocation requirements applicable to tax-deferred rollover transactions (see below).
7. Meet the requirements relating to certain gratuitous transfers of qualified employer securities.
8. Meet certain miscellaneous requirements under Internal Revenue Service regulations.

Types of ESOPs

There are essentially two types of ESOPs: nonleveraged and leveraged. The nonleveraged ESOP in its simplest form is a stock bonus plan into which the employer contributes stock and takes a tax deduction.

Alternatively, the employer contributes cash to the nonleveraged ESOP, and the ESOP trustee takes the cash and buys employer securities within a reasonable period of time.

In a leveraged situation, the ESOP uses its prohibited transaction exemption to borrow money either from the employer or a shareholder or from a third party with a payment guarantee provided by the employer or the shareholder. The ESOP uses the proceeds of its loan to purchase employer securities from either the company or its shareholders. After that initial purchase, the employer makes annual contributions to the ESOP in an amount sufficient to allow the ESOP to amortize its acquisition indebtedness in a timely manner.

Each year, as the employer contributions are made to the ESOP, shares purchased with the acquisition indebtedness are released from a loan suspense account. This is accomplished according to one of two permissible formulas (principal only or principal and interest methods). In this way, the shares are allocated to the accounts of eligible participants, pro rata, based on compensation until the ESOP loan has been entirely repaid and all shares have been released from the loan suspense account and allocated to the accounts of eligible participants.

Special Considerations

Permissible Employer Securities

An ESOP is permitted to own common stock issued by an employer that is readily tradable on an established securities market. If the company's common stock is not readily marketable, the ESOP can own stock that has a combination of the greatest voting power and the greatest dividend rights. Also permitted is noncallable preferred stock if it is convertible at a reasonable price at any time into the qualified common stock described above. Securities issued by any member of a controlled group of corporations are treated as employer securities for all members of the controlled group.

The IRS and the courts have not interpreted the phrase "designed to invest primarily." The phrase implies that an ESOP must permit the plan trustees to invest or hold a majority of the plan's assets in employer securities. The ESOP's purpose is to serve as an employee benefit plan, and no "bright line" quantitative test for compliance with this phrase applies.

ESOP Tax Incentives

Under the Internal Revenue Code, several attractive taxation incentives are available both to employer corporations and to selling stockholders in connection with ESOP formations and financing. The primary ESOP-related income taxation incentives are as follows (these points are discussed in more detail below):

1. Periodic contributions to the ESOP are a tax-deductible expense to the corporation, whether they are made in cash or in stock.
2. Selling stockholders can roll over proceeds of sales of stock to the ESOP tax-free, deferring the income or capital gains tax on the sale until the securities purchased with the proceeds are ultimately sold; this is often called a Section 1042 rollover.
3. Dividends paid on ESOP-owned employer securities can be tax-deductible to the corporation.

Periodic Contributions to the Plan Are Tax-Deductible

Coporate contributions to an ESOP are a tax-deductible expense to the corporation, regardless of whether the contributions are made in cash or in stock.

Cash contributions can be used to buy the corporation stock from existing stockholders or, in the case of a leveraged ESOP, to make payments on ESOP stock acquisition debt. In the latter case, the economic effect is that the acquisition loan principal repayments, as well as the loan interest, become tax-deductible expenses to the corporation.

If the contribution to the ESOP is made in employer corporation stock (either treasury stock or authorized but unissued shares), then there is some dilution to the existing stockholders. However, the effect on cash flow generally is positive. Since the ESOP contribution is a deduction from taxable income, it usually results in a lower corporate income tax expense with no corresponding cash outlay.

The annual employer contribution normally can be 15 percent of eligible payroll. However, in some cases, it may be as high as 25 percent of the corporation's annual payroll.

Tax-Deferred Rollovers

A shareholder selling stock to an ESOP can reinvest the proceeds on a tax-free rollover basis if the ESOP owns stock with at least 30 percent of the corporation's value immediately after the sale. To qualify for the tax-free rollover, the shareholder must invest the proceeds in stock, debt, or options of domestic operating corporations within a 15-month period beginning 3 months before the date of the sale. Further, notice of the Section 1042 election must be filed on the appropriate form during the taxable year of the sale.

As long as the ESOP maintains its 30 percent ownership, additional sales of stock to the ESOP, in any amount, are eligible for the Section 1042 tax-free rollover treatment.

Deductible Dividends

A corporation may deduct dividends paid on securities that are held by a leveraged ESOP maintained by the corporation or controlled group member, provided that the dividends paid are:

1. Not pursuant to an evasion of taxation which the Internal Revenue Service has interpreted as requiring that the amount of dividend be financially reasonable.
2. In cash directly or through the ESOP to ESOP participants or their beneficiaries or used to repay an ESOP loan.

Dividends paid to ESOP participants or their beneficiaries are deductible only if they are paid in cash directly or through the ESOP within 90 days after the end of the plan year in which the dividends are paid. The corporation paying the dividends is entitled to take a deduction in the year in which the ESOP participants or beneficiaries have a corresponding income inclusion.

The corporation may also deduct dividends that are used to make loan repayments in the case of a leveraged ESOP. This deduction applies only to dividends paid on employer securities (whether or not allocated to participants' accounts) actually acquired with the proceeds of the loan that is being repaid. Thus, dividends paid on other shares in the ESOP that were not acquired with the loan proceeds are not eligible for this deduction.

Distributions, Diversification, and Put Options

Unless the participant elects otherwise, the distribution of his or her vested account balance will begin within one year after the end of the plan year during which employment is terminated because of normal retirement, disability, or death. If the participant resigns or is dismissed, distributions must begin within one year after the end of the fifth plan year after termination. Unless the participant elects otherwise, his or her account balance must be distributed in substantially equal periodic payments (not less frequently than annually) over a period not exceeding five years.

If a participant has an account balance exceeding $500,000, the distribution may take place over a period not exceeding five years plus one year for each $100,000 (or fraction thereof) by which a participant's account balance exceeds $500,000. The $100,000 and $500,000 limits are adjusted for cost-of-living increases.

These distribution requirements may be extended until the end of the plan year in which the entire ESOP loan is repaid. This exception may require separate accounting within a participant's account for non-leveraged shares and for allocations from ESOP loans that become due at different times.

A participant who is entitled to receive a distribution may demand that the benefits be distributed in the form of employer securities. Absent a demand for a stock distribution by a terminated participant or beneficiary, benefits may be distributed in cash.

If the corporation only permits employees to own shares, the ESOP may distribute all benefits in cash without granting participants the right to demand stock.

Employees who are at least 55 years old and have completed 10 years of participation in the ESOP may elect to diversify up to 25 percent of their plan account into investments other than employer securities. Diversification increases to 50 percent after the employee reaches age 60. This requirement, in effect, accelerates the corporation's repurchase liability whenever older employees elect to exercise their option to diversify.

The mandatory distribution of vested stock, along with the related put option, creates an economic and a legal liability on the part of the employer. The corporation's ability to meet this liability is an important aspect of the financial feasibility of any ESOP formation. The company's ability to meet its repurchase obligation may affect the value of the securities sold or contributed to the ESOP.

Voting Rights

If the company has publicly traded securities, each participant can direct the voting of the securities allocated to his or her account. When the company does not have publicly traded securities, voting rights pass-through is required only for corporate mergers, consolidations, sales of all or substantially all of the corporation's assets, recapitalization, reclassifications, liquidations, dissolutions, or similar transactions.

S Corporations/C Corporations

Prior to 1998, only employers taxed as C corporations were permitted to have ESOPs. Effective for tax years beginning after December 31, 1997, the Internal Revenue Code was modified to permit qualified plan trusts to be S corporation shareholders.

An S corporation is a corporation for state law purposes that generally is not required to pay federal income tax. (See Chapter 6 for a discussion of valuation aspects of S corporations.) Many, but not all, states provide S corporations with similar treatment. The shareholders must pay tax on their proportionate share of the S corporation's income. This means that S corporation income is not subject to the two layers of tax applicable to a C corporation's income: a tax on corporate earnings payable once by the corporation, and a second tax payable by the shareholders when these earnings are distributed as dividends or liquidation proceeds.

Independent Appraiser Requirements

Both ERISA and the Internal Revenue Code require that an ESOP have an independent valuation conducted annually. The purpose of this rule is to protect the ESOP participants and beneficiaries and to ensure that they are treated fairly.

Internal Revenue Code Requirements

An ESOP must have all valuations of securities acquired after 1986 made by an independent appraiser. An "independent appraiser" means an appraiser meeting the requirements similar to the requirements under the charitable contribution regulations.[1] A translation of those regulations to the ESOP context would mean that the ESOP independent appraiser should be a person who does not perform any other service to a party whose interest may be adverse to the ESOP and who would meet an objective standard of impartiality.

The Internal Revenue Service has issued plan examination guidelines that address the issue of the requirement for an independent appraiser of closely held ESOP stock. In those guidelines, the Internal Revenue Service states that an appraiser is *not* independent if:

1. The appraiser is the taxpayer that maintains the ESOP (or a member of the controlled group).
2. The appraiser is a party to the transaction in which the ESOP acquired the property.
3. The appraiser is employed by the taxpayer maintaining the ESOP.
4. The appraiser is regularly used by any entity described in 1 through 3 above.

The guidelines include an example that an employer's accounting firm could perform the valuation as long as (1) the valuation was performed by a separate division of the accounting firm that holds itself out to the public as an appraiser and (2) a majority of the division's appraisals are for entities other than the employer or entities related to the employer.

ERISA Requirements

The Department of Labor (DOL) regulations defining the term *adequate consideration* provide that the fiduciary making the valuation decision must itself be independent of all parties to the transaction or the fiduciary must rely on the report of an appraiser who is independent of all parties to the transaction. The DOL believes that this is the only way to protect plan participants from conflicts of interest. Under the department's proposed regulations, an appraiser is considered independent of all parties of a transaction only if a plan fiduciary has chosen the appraiser and has a right to terminate that appointment and the plan is thereby established as the appraiser's client. Absent such circumstances, the appraiser may be unable to be completely neutral in the exercise of its function. The independence of an appraiser is not adversely affected solely because the plan sponsor pays the appraiser's fee, however.

Independent Appraiser Role as a Nonfiduciary

An independent appraiser is just that, an appraiser. The role of the appraiser is to provide financial data and input to a fiduciary that is

---

[1] Internal Revenue Code Sec. 170 (a)(1).

required by law and the documents to make its decision on behalf of the participants. The fiduciary is responsible for value and fairness, *not* the appraiser. Thus, it would behoove the appraiser not to exceed his or her role and unwittingly become the fiduciary by trying to provide investment advice and recommendations to the fiduciary who is otherwise responsible. This falls under the legal maxim "no good deed shall go unpunished." There are a number of published decisions that indicate that an appraiser is not a fiduciary for purposes of the fiduciary duty provisions of the Employee Retirement Income Secuirty Act of 1974, as amended (ERISA). Although this may be reassuring to many valuation analysts, it should not provide unfettered comfort.

The law indicates that the fiduciary is determined not by label but by function. This may involve the function of the person described in the relevant plan documents or may be determined by the person's behavior. For example, a person may become a fiduciary with respect to a plan by reason of rendering investment advice for a fee or other direct or indirect compensation. This investment advice could involve any property of the plan if there is a written or unwritten mutual agreement, arrangement, or understanding that the person's services will serve as a primary basis for investment decisions with respect to plan assets. Providing investment advice to the plan on such matters as investment policies or strategies, overall portfolio composition, or diversification of plan investments could imply that the appraiser is a fiduciary.

Imagine that an analyst has delivered the valuation report and his or her conclusions as to value and fairness to the fiduciary. The fiduciary then raises questions as to methodology, assumptions, and conclusions and asks the analyst whether he or she should close the transaction. Whether to close the transaction is a question that the appraiser should refuse to answer on the grounds that providing such an answer may involve the rendering of investment advice for a fee and start the appraiser down the slippery slope to becoming a "fiduciary." It is a legal duty and responsibility of the trustee to make such a decision and inappropriate for the valuation analyst to do so.

A Typical Leveraged ESOP Transaction

The fundamental characteristics of the basic leveraged ESOP transaction is that the ESOP borrows money to buy securities either from a selling stockholder or from the company itself. The financing is provided (1) by the selling stockholder, (2) from a third party that loans the money to the employer and the employer in turn loans the money to the ESOP, or (3) directly from the third party to the ESOP with a corporate guarantee. In any instance, the only collateral the ESOP is permitted to provide, even if it owns other assets, are the company securities purchased with loan proceeds.

The company then makes annual cash contributions to the ESOP in an amount sufficient to amortize the stock acquisition loan. In addition to the cash contributions, dividends on the leveraged shares may be used to amortize the stock acquisition loan.

The company contributions that are used to repay acquisition indebtedness are limited each year to 25 percent of aggregate ESOP participant compensation plus, for C corporations only, interest payments. The dividends must be financially "reasonable."

Illustrative Example

The XYZ Company is a C corporation and has three shareholders: Brown, Smith, and Jones. These three founding shareholders want to retire and make their personal estates more liquid. Although they will accept the highest offer they receive for their company, the three founders would prefer that their loyal employees purchase the company from them. A committee of employees is formed to consider the purchase of the entire company, possibly through a leveraged ESOP. The XYZ Company funds the committee's retention of an attorney, an administrative adviser, and a financial adviser, all of whom will analyze the financial and legal feasibility of a leveraged ESOP buyout.

After careful analysis, the financial adviser believes the fair market value of all the outstanding equity of XYZ Company is $11 million. This value estimate is confirmed by an expression of interest offered by several potential corporate acquirers that are interested in bidding for control of XYZ Company.

However, because of the tax-deferred rollover advantages available to them under Internal Revenue Code Section 1042, the founders have agreed to accept an offer from the ESOP to buy the company for $10 million. Accordingly, because of this Section 1042 tax attribute available to the three selling shareholders, the ESOP is able to outbid the corporate acquirer's alluring offer price.

To finance this transaction, a commercial lender has made a commitment for the required $10 million financing over a seven-year net level payment amortization schedule. Exhibit 11-1 presents a summary of the salient facts regarding the ESOP leveraged acquisition of the outstanding stock of the XYZ Company:

Exhibit 11–1

Exhibit 11-1
XYZ Company Hypothetical Fact Set

Annual revenues	$20,000,000
Earnings before interests and taxes (EBIT)	$ 3,000,000
Payroll eligible for ESOP contributions	$ 6,000,000
Combined federal and state income tax rate	40%
Loan interest rate for ESOP loan	8.5%

Exhibit 11-2 presents the projected income statement for XYZ Company, assuming both conventional acquisition financing and acquisition financing through an ESOP. The exhibit also presents the loan amortization schedule and after-tax costs to XYZ Company of servicing the stock acquisition loan, assuming conventional acquisition financing and acquisition financing through an ESOP.

The ESOP committee's administrative adviser has analyzed the potential cash requirements for the liability to repurchase the stock of the vested terminated ESOP participants made under the mandatory put option associated with employee terminations and with participants' election to diversify investments after age 55 and 10 years of participation. The administrative adviser has estimated that the $628,000 cash available annually, after debt service, should be adequate to cover the estimated repurchase liability.

The ESOP advisers have determined that XYZ Company could make tax-deductible contributions of up to 25 percent of eligible payroll, plus interest payments. With projected annual payroll expense of $10 million, the maximum allowable annual deduction of $2.5 million is more than adequate to cover the $1,954,000 annual ESOP contribution required to amortize the ESOP stock acquisition debt.

A comparison of a conventionally financed acquisition and an ESOP-financed acquisition reveals that the use of an ESOP provides the following:

1. Founders Brown, Smith, and Jones will receive a tax-deferred rollover by selling their stock to the ESOP and reinvesting the proceeds in a diversified securities portfolio.
2. Because the annual contributions to the ESOP are tax-deductible, both principal and interest on the ESOP payment are paid with pretax dollars.
3. Because of the tax advantages available to the selling shareholders, the employees were able to purchase the XYZ Company at a price that was $1 million less than the bids that were being contemplated by the other corporate acquirers.

In this case, the ESOP not only facilitated the acquisition, but also made it feasible for the employees to purchase the company. As is often the case, financing the transaction without the benefits of the ESOP would be extremely difficult.

Multiple Investor Leveraged ESOPs

Often companies using ESOPs for leveraged acquisitions must create several different classes of securities in order to attract and satisfy all the diverse parties to the transaction. These parties often include the party supplying the bulk of the acquisition financing, a management group, and the ESOP itself.

Exhibit 11–2

XYZ Company: Conventional Acquisition
Financing versus ESOP Acquisition Financing ($000s)

Projected Income Statements

Conventionally Financed Acquisition		Leveraged ESOP Acquisition	
Company revenues	20,000	Company revenues	20,000
Operating profit (EBIT)	3,000	Operating profit (EBIT)	3,000
Interest	1,000	ESOP contribution	1,954
Taxable income	2,000	Taxable income	1,046
Income taxes	800	Income taxes	418
Net income	1,200	Net income	628
Nondeductible portion of debt service	1,054	Nondeductible portion of debt service	0
Cash available after debt service	146	Cash available after debt service	628

Acquisition Loan Amortization

	Conventionally Financed Acquisition					Leveraged ESOP Acquisition				
Year	Total Payment	Principal	Interest	Value of Deductions	After-Tax Cost	Total Payment	Principal	Interest	Value of Deductions	After-Tax Cost
1	2,054	1,104	850	344	1,710	1,954	1,104	850	782	1,172
2	2,054	1,197	757	303	1,751	1,954	1,197	757	782	1,172
3	2,054	1,299	655	262	1,792	1,954	1,299	655	782	1,172
4	2,054	1,410	544	218	1,836	1,954	1,410	544	782	1,172
5	2,054	1,529	425	170	1,884	1,954	1,529	425	782	1,172
6	2,054	1,660	294	118	1,936	1,954	1,660	294	782	1,172
7	2,054	1,801	153	61	1,993	1,954	1,801	153	782	1,172
Total	14,378	10,000	3,678	1,476	12,902	13,678	10,000	3,678	5,474	8,204

Analytical projections:
1. The $10 million acquisitive loan is amortized over seven years, with net level payments.
2. The 8.5% interest rate is available for both the ESOP loan and conventional financing.
3. A 40% combined federal and state income tax rate is appropriate.

On the basis of a fair allocation of the total business value among the different securities classes, as well as on the basis of ERISA regulations regarding the employer securities eligible for ESOP ownership, the structure of such securities is bounded only by the financial creativity of the parties involved in the ESOP, the company, other participants, and their respective financial advisers. Permissible securities can include one or more classes of common stock, traditional and/or convertible debt or preferred stock, stock options, and various junior classes of securities. Also, voting rights may be assigned to the various classes of securities in a number of ways. (See Chapter 12.)

A convertible debt or preferred security is, in essence, a combination of a traditional debt instrument or preferred stock combined in an option. In many cases, it is difficult to find convertible securities in the public market that are adequately comparable in terms of economic characteristics to the convertible securities created for use in leveraged ESOP acquisitions. Thus, for valuation purposes, it may be useful to disaggregate these convertible securities into their financial components— that is, traditional debt or preferred stock plus a common stock option—and to value each component separately.

Special Valuation Issues in ESOPs

ERISA requires ESOPs to pay no more than "adequate consideration" when investing in employer securities. This means that the plan trustees and fiduciaries must estimate, in good faith, the fair market value of employer securities in accordance with the proposed regulation issued by the U.S. Department of Labor. Although there is some controversy as to whether this proposed regulation has been withdrawn, most ESOP practitioners still consider it carefully in discharging their responsibilities. Therefore, valuation implications of this proposed regulation are worth talking about.

The Valuation Advisory Committee of The ESOP Association (TEA) has provided important guidance with respect to the valuation of ESOP securities to be considered by ESOP fiduciaries sponsoring corporations and professionals rendering advice to these plans. This guidance is in the form of a publication, *Valuing ESOP Shares*, [2] which covers the following topics:

1. The DOL proposed regulation and its implications for valuation
2. Commonly accepted practices for estimating the fair market value of closely held stock for ESOP purposes
3. Four special valuation positions adopted by the Valuation Advisory Committee:
   a. Discount for lack of marketability
   b. Repurchase liability
   c. Premium for control
   d. The effects of leverage

ESOP Stock Valuation Factors

The DOL proposed regulation defines *fair market value* as:

> The price at which an asset would change hands between a willing buyer and a willing seller when the former is not under any compulsion to buy and the latter is not under any compulsion to sell and both

---

[2]*Valuing ESOP Shares* (Washington, DC: The ESOP Association, 1994). Reference to this published resource and to other published positions of The ESOP Association and the Valuation Advisory Committee is highly recommended.

parties are able, as well as willing, to trade and are well informed about the asset and the market for such asset.[3]

The DOL proposed regulation requires the fair market value of a security (1) to be estimated as of the date of the transaction involving the asset; (2) to be estimated without considering transactions resulting from other than arm's-length negotiations, such as distress sales; (3) to reflect the application of "sound business principles of valuation"; and (4) to be recorded in a document meeting the requirements of the proposed regulation.[4]

When the security being valued is the stock of a closely held employer, the DOL proposed regulation requires that the written document include an assessment of all "relevant factors" plus an assessment of all the factors outlined in Revenue Ruling 59-60. In addition, some ESOP-specific factors need to be taken into account.

For example, an assessment needs to be made as to whether the seller is able to obtain a control premium from an unrelated third party with regard to the block of securities being valued. This assessment depends upon (1) whether actual control (both in form and in substance) is passed to the purchaser with the sale, or will pass to the purchaser within a reasonable time pursuant to a binding agreement in effect at the time of the sale, and (2) whether it is also reasonable to assume that the purchaser's control will not be dissipated within a short period of time subsequent to acquisition.

In addition, the marketability (or lack thereof) of the securities needs to be taken into account. The extent to which the put rights (which are a mandatory component of the ESOP shares) are enforceable, as well as the company's ability to meet its obligations with respect to the put rights, should be taken into account when estimating the magnitude of the discount for lack of marketability.

Control Versus Minority Ownership Basis for Valuation

The basis for the ESOP valuation will differ depending upon whether or not the block of ESOP shares subject to valuation carries elements of control. Generally, a buyer of a controlling economic interest will pay a premium for the stock because the buyer expects to make changes that enhance the income-generating aspects of the business or in some other way improve the economic situation for the business. This premium is evidenced by a higher price relative to what would be paid for a minority ownership interest position in the business.

However, valuation analysts often differ in their application of an ownership control premium to a block of stock being purchased by an

---

[3]"Regulation Relating to the Definition of Adequate Consideration: Notice of Proposed Rulemaking," 29 CFR Part 2510, May 17, 1988.

[4]This definition and requirements (with the exception of the requirement for written documentation) follow the established guidelines for estimating fair market value found in Rev. Rul. 59-60.

ESOP. Most analysts agree that an ESOP should be able to pay whatever a hypothetical third-party buyer would pay for the block of stock being purchased. In other words, most analysts recognize that fair market value is not influenced solely by a certain percentage of ownership (e.g., greater than 50 percent), but instead is estimated by what a willing buyer would pay to a willing seller.

In estimating what a hypothetical third party would pay, analysts should give recognition to the facts and circumstances of the case, including any limitations that may be imposed on an ESOP as the buyer of the stock. Many of the unusual aspects of an ESOP where elements of ownership control may be present result from the fact that the ESOP does not generally represent an active investor that is willing or able to make certain changes that could maximize the value of the stock. However, an ESOP fiduciary is required to monitor the activities of the board of directors and senior management in order to ensure that value is being preserved and, when necessary, to ensure that corrective actions are being taken to improve value. This applies whether the fiduciary representing the ESOP is directed by an administrative committee made up of company management or of employees.

For example, management may be taking excessive compensation or maintaining certain perquisites that the third-party buyer purchasing control of the company would eliminate. The ESOP, represented by its fiduciary, may be reluctant to force such a change unless it feels itself in jeopardy for not attempting to force such a change. If the appraiser believes the ESOP fiduciary is unlikely to force such a change, then the level of the ownership control premium paid for the purchase of the stock would likely be lower than what would be paid by a hypothetical third-party buyer.

Alternatively, some analysts believe the ESOP should pay a control premium reflecting what a hypothetical third-party would pay, without considering possible limitations applicable to the ESOP as the buyer. If, by virtue of holding the block of stock, the ESOP in aggregate has the ability to affect corporate transactions through electing board members, then the value of stock at the time of the purchase by the ESOP can reflect those changes. This is because, upon obtaining ownership control, the ESOP could sell the block of stock to a third-party buyer that could fully realize the benefits of control or could cause a liquidation, if such a sale or liquidation would result in the highest value.

Notwithstanding these differences in approach, certain general guidance may be offered regarding factors to consider when valuing ESOP noncontrolling ownership interests. In addition to all other considerations that are otherwise relevant when estimating the value of a subject block of stock, the following are some factors to consider when estimating the appropriate ownership control premium, if any:

1. The financial attributes inherent in the particular block of stock.
2. The degree of control: effective, operating, and absolute.
3. The aggregate percentage interest purchased or held by the ESOP, regardless of whether the sellers constituted a minority or controlling interest.

4. The potential for control, such as binding agreements with other shareholders that could result in the passing of control to the ESOP.
5. The distribution of the total stock ownership.
6. The empirical evidence of control premiums actually paid in similar transactions.
7. Any value enhancement that may result from the passing of control (e.g., effective use of leverage, elimination of excess compensation paid to selling shareholders, sale of undervalued assets).
8. Any value enhancement due to a put right.
9. The right to an obligation under the employer's articles of incorporation, bylaws, and state law.

Lack of Marketability Discount

Another controversy in ESOP share valuation is whether, or to the extent to which, some discount should be applied for lack of marketability. Certainly the fair market value of ESOP-owned stock depends in part on its marketability. Marketability is the ability of the stock to be sold and turned into cash quickly.

On one end of the marketability spectrum, there are relatively few potential buyers for shares in most closely held corporations (especially of minority ownership positions). It may take months (or years) to market these shares and receive payment. On the other end of the marketability spectrum, shares in publicly traded corporations have almost instant marketability on an organized exchange and high liquidity, since the seller can receive cash within three business days.

In many ESOP valuations, the market value estimate is based on market comparisons with publicly traded guideline companies. The value conclusion obtained from this valuation method is on a marketable, minority ownership premise, sometimes referred to as an "as if freely traded value" or "publicly traded equivalent value." If this is the preliminary premise of value, then a discount for lack of marketability may be appropriate to estimate the fair market value of shares in a closely held company. Nonetheless, other generally accepted valuation methods may implicitly incorporate the consideration of lack of marketability. ESOP valuation analysts, therefore, should not apply some standard discount for lack of marketability without fully understanding the premise of value to which the discount for lack of marketability will be applied.

The economic factor that generally distinguishes ESOP shares from non-ESOP shares in a closely held corporation is the put option requiring the employer corporation to repurchase the distributed employer securities.

In the DOL proposed regulation, a written assessment of the marketability of shares held by an ESOP is required. The proposed regulation states the following with respect to a discount for lack of marketability:

Where the plan is the purchaser of securities that are subject to "put" rights and such rights are taken into account in reducing the discounts for lack of marketability, such assessment shall include consideration of the extent to which such rights are enforceable, as well as the company's ability to meet its obligation with a respect to the "put" rights (taking into account the company's financial strength and liquidity).[5]

The effect of the ESOP put option is to generally enhance the marketability and liquidity of the plan participant's ownership interest and, hence, to reduce or eliminate the appropriate discount for lack of marketability. ESOP valuation analysts should evaluate the features of the put option, including payment terms, as well as the employer's record in redeeming shares. Ultimately, the amount of the discount applied, if any, is a function of the ESOP analyst's professional judgment. It should be noted, in this respect, that the Tax Court has held that, despite the existence of a put option in an ESOP, ESOP fiduciaries should apply a lack of marketability discount in estimating the value of stock to be sold to an ESOP.

Another economic feature unique to an ESOP is the repurchase liability that arises from the ESOP put option. The repurchase liability tends to increase over time as shares are allocated to a participant's account and vest, and as the value of the employer's securities increases. The repurchase liability arising from the terms of the ESOP does not normally affect the discount for lack of marketability unless the ability to repurchase the stock is impaired or the employer's ability to honor the put option is in question.

The DOL proposed regulation makes it clear, however, that the employer's financial ability to meet its put obligations should be considered when assessing an appropriate discount for lack of marketability. The financial position of the ESOP trust should also be considered with respect to the lack of marketability issue. If the ESOP trust has excess cash, then it may repurchase the shares distributed to participants rather than having the shares repurchased by the employer.

The principal economic factors that influence the discount for lack of marketability with regard to ESOP-owned employer securities are summarized below:

1. The provision of the ESOP plan documents, including the put rights.
2. The financial strength and solvency of the employer.
3. The size of the share block owned by the ESOP.
4. The degree of liquidity.
5. The borrowing capacity of the employer.
6. The repurchase liability and funding thereof.
7. Any past repurchase experience of ESOP shares by the employer corporation.

---

[5]Ibid.

8. The form and timing of payment by the employer corporation to the selling shareholders.
9. The overall priority of acknowledged and contingent financial plans that may conflict with achieving liquidity for plan participants over time.
10. The valuation in leveraged ESOPs.

Post-transaction ESOP Debt

The impact of the ESOP debt on the company's securities is often explicitly considered by the ESOP valuation analyst, and such debt naturally tends to reduce the value of the company's equity. Whether the analyst is using guideline publicly traded companies or discounted economic income valuation methods, the valuation of the company following the formation of the ESOP should reflect the reduction in cash flow from the repayment of ESOP debt. Several valuation procedures can be taken into account for this purpose, of which the most common include:

1. Valuing the overall business, using either the discounted economic income method or the guideline publicly traded company method, on a debt-free basis, and then subtracting the tax-adjusted value of the ESOP debt.
2. Inserting the specific debt service requirement into the economic income projection of the company on a pretax basis, thus accounting for the associated income tax savings. This valuation procedure is easiest to apply, and a discounted economic income valuation analysis can account for the temporary nature of the ESOP debt.

Further, ESOP leverage increases the financial risk of the company by increasing its fixed cash flow obligations, which heightens the possibility that fluctuations in the company's operating results could cause financial distress. Leverage may also force the employer corporation management to focus primarily on current cash flow, rather than on longer-term economic benefits, thereby restricting discretionary investments in capital equipment, marketing, research and development, or other areas that require up-front cash outlays. These issues should be considered in the valuation of leveraged ESOP-owned companies.

ESOP as Seller

A number of factors unique to ESOPs add layers of complication to the sale of an ESOP company.

For example, many have questioned whether an offer that is slightly higher than the most recent appraisal will require that the ESOP fiduciary make the sale. However, under a joint statement issued by the

Internal Revenue Service and the Department of Labor, the mere fact that the offer may be higher than the current valuation does not mean that the ESOP fiduciary must sell. This is because the ESOP fiduciary must consider whether the participants would maximize their retirement benefits over the long term by selling and reinvesting in a diversified portfolio or in realizing the expected increments in value arising from the activities of the employer.

In addition, many ESOP valuations are performed on a minority ownership interest basis, whereas an offer is typically for all outstanding stock of the corporation and should reflect an ownership control premium for all outstanding stock. Thus, an offer that is only slightly higher than a minority ownership interest value may not reflect the economic reality of the situation.

Another factor that the ESOP will need to consider in assessing an offer is whether the 10 percent premature distribution excise tax would be applicable to the sale. This tax arises if, after a Section 1042 transaction, the ESOP proposes to dispose of the shares to a third party within three years of the Section 1042 transaction. An exception does apply in a stock for stock merger, but cash transactions will generate this excise tax, which will ultimately be borne by the buyer and thus cause the buyer to reduce its offering price. After the three-year period, the tax obligation expires. Obviously, this is a factor that the ESOP fiduciary must take into account.

Still another factor for the ESOP fiduciary to consider is ESOP indebtedness and thus shares remaining in the loan expense account. The only way for the full value of these shares to be realized is for the employer to make its scheduled contributions and for the shares to be released and allocated to participants' accounts. If there is a premature sale—that is, a sale before all outstanding indebtedness is paid—the participants may realize only the net sales proceeds from the shares in that loan expense account. Thus, the size of the price premium offered over the cost of the shares is quite relevant.

In this respect, until recently the Internal Revenue Service took the position that participants might not be able to realize the full net benefits from the loan expense account in the year of the sale or for several years thereafter. Because many of the participants may not be employed in the ensuing years, they might never realize the full benefit from the loan expense account.

From the view point of the fiduciary, he or she should view a sale offer in terms of maximizing retirement benefits for participants and beneficiaries. Both the Internal Revenue Service and the DOL have clearly stated that it is impermissible for the fiduciary to consider job retention by the employees in making the decision as to whether to sell the shares. Moreover, whether the fiduciary is taking directions from the participants or not, the fiduciary is obliged to maximize retirement benefits without regard to job retention or to coercion by management to accept or resist the offer.

Chapter 12

Use of Alternative Equity Securities in the Capital Structure of ESOP Companies
Chester A. Gougis

Introduction

Most companies that set up employee stock ownership plans (ESOPs) have a fairly simple capital structure: one class of common stock, which is the security sold to the ESOP. In recent years, however, many companies have begun to use different types and classes of equity securities in their ESOPs and other employee benefit plans. Companies have elected to use more complex securities to achieve various objectives related to taxation, compensation, corporate governance, and financial flexibility.

U.S. tax laws allow C corporations to use a broad range of security types in ESOPs. Securities that can be sold to a leveraged ESOP include all employer securities with the highest dividend and voting rights of all classes of common stock.[1] In addition, an ESOP may purchase equity securities that are convertible into such a class of stock. Given this wide array of possible securities, companies have been very creative in designing complex securities that meet the basic legal requirements for ESOP securities. These complex securities also have special features to meet specific corporate finance objectives.

Types of Complex Securities Used in Employee Stock Ownership and Other Benefit Plans

In this section, we describe some of the complex equity securities that have been sold to ESOPs. In addition, we discuss some of the ways in which these securities meet various corporate objectives.

Standard Convertible Preferred Stock

Standard convertible preferred is the most commonly used complex security in ESOPs. By *standard*, we simply mean convertible preferred stock that has dividend rates, call features, and conversion rights that are similar to those issued in the public markets by the typical public company issuer. A convertible preferred security gives the holder the ability to convert the preferred shares into a fixed number of common shares, thereby participating along with common shareholders in the growth of the company.

Before conversion, the preferred shares receive a higher dividend over a certain period of time. In exchange for this larger and more secure dividend, the purchaser of a convertible preferred security pays a price higher than the common stock for the security. The conversion premium is a measure in percentage terms of how much higher a price is required for the superior dividend rights. Dividend rates on newly

---

[1]It is noteworthy that contributions of stock to nonleveraged ESOPs do not have some of these limitations.

issued public convertible preferred securities generally range from a few basis points below to 400 basis points above the rates on medium-term Treasury notes, and conversion premiums at the time of issuance range from 15 to 30 percent.

Call protection is typically offered for two to five years. This call protection guards the convertible preferred security holder from having his or her financial advantage taken away during that period.

Many of the other complex securities issued to ESOPs are variations on standard convertible preferred stock. The differences often involve special features that are added to address specific tax or compensation-related needs.

Floor Put Convertible Preferred Stock

One of the most common variations in ESOPs from the standard convertible preferred security is the *floor put convertible preferred*. This type of security has essentially the same structure as the standard convertible preferred stock described above, with one key additional feature—a floor put. The floor put feature gives employees the right to sell the stock back to the company for at least face value when they are cashed out of the plan. This feature increases the downside protection for employees and insulates them from the negative impact of rising interest rates and/or a falling common stock price. This feature is very common in public company ESOP convertible preferred securities.

High-Yield Convertible Preferred Stock

High-yield refers to convertible preferred stock most often issued by companies with a highly leveraged capital structure. Typically these securities have a higher yield and often a higher conversion premium than standard convertible preferred stock. The higher conversion premium may reflect the fact that these highly leveraged companies often have the expectation of faster growth in equity value because of the impact of repaying debt in a highly leveraged capital structure.

Super Common Stock

The term *super* describes common stock that has superior rights over regular common stock. These rights most often include higher dividend rates than regular common stock and/or higher voting rights than regular common stock.

Tracking Stock

Tracking stock is a class of security the value of which tracks the value of a particular subsidiary or other entity. Two of the first and most widely known examples of tracking stock are the General Motors E Class and H Class securities, which tracked the value of the company's EDS and Hughes Electronics subsidiaries.

Many varieties of tracking stock incorporate different features that cause the stock to track the value of the underlying subsidiary. For example, in some tracking securities, dividends may be payable only out of the surplus of earnings of the tracked subsidiary. In other cases, the stock may be convertible or exchangeable directly into the stock of the underlying subsidiary under some circumstances. Alternatively, sale or liquidation of the subsidiary can trigger conversion into regular parent common stock on the basis of the value realized in the sale of the subsidiary.

Fixed Dollar Convertible Preferred Stock

Fixed dollar convertible preferred stock is convertible into a fixed dollar value of the common stock rather than into a fixed number of shares of common stock. This type of stock is similar to nonconvertible preferred in that its value does not increase and decrease with the value of the common stock until it has been converted. Because of this feature, such securities are often automatically converted upon allocation into ESOP participants' accounts in order to provide some appreciation.

Performance Stock

Performance stock is a special class of common or preferred stock that is convertible into the regular common stock of the company at a conversion ratio that varies with the performance of the company. For example, the performance shares may be convertible into one share of common stock if five-year compound annual growth in earnings per share is above a certain target, and convertible into only one-tenth of a share otherwise. This type of stock is more often used in nonqualified employee incentive stock plans than in traditional ESOPs.

Reasons for Choosing Complex Securities

ESOP Debt Repayment Requirements

One of the most common reasons companies offer a different type of security from an ESOP is to allow the ESOP to receive a higher dividend than other stockholders. Dividends paid on ESOP stock can be used to repay ESOP borrowings. This may be important to companies whose requirements for ESOP debt repayments exceed the limits set by Internal Revenue Code Section 415. These provisions basically limit contributions to leveraged ESOPs to a maximum of the amount of interest due on ESOP debt plus 25 percent of eligible payroll. If the total of allowable contributions plus dividends on the ESOP common stock is insufficient to meet the ESOP debt repayment requirements, then one solution may be to offer the ESOP a stock with higher dividends.

Many privately owned companies pay no dividends at all on their regular common stock. This is due to the income tax disadvantages of paying dividends to their individual shareholders. As a result, any required dividend payments to the ESOP can be accomplished by offering the ESOP a different security.

Either convertible preferred or a class of common stock paying higher dividends (*super common stock*) can be used to accomplish this goal. For many private companies, super common stock is the selected vehicle because of the requirements of Section 1042, the provision of the Internal Revenue Code that allows owners of privately held businesses to defer the gain on the sale of stock to an ESOP under certain conditions. The conditions of a Section 1042 transaction can be met when (1) the selling shareholders first exchange their regular common stock for super common stock and (2) then sell this new super common stock to an ESOP. There may be negative income tax consequences to a similar transaction involving convertible preferred. As a result, many private companies choose to use super common stock rather than convertible preferred stock.

Taxation Issues

ESOPs become somewhat tax-inefficient compensation vehicles when the value of the ESOP shares allocated to employee accounts significantly exceeds the original purchase price of those shares. This is because the amount deductible as compensation expense relates to the original purchase price of the shares. For example, suppose a company makes a stock contribution to an ESOP of $1 million. That contribution is used to repay loan principal. And that repayment of loan principal allows for the allocation of 100,000 shares of company stock. This contribution effectively gives the company a tax valuation of the stock contributed of $10 per share, which is approximately the price at which the ESOP originally purchased the shares. But what if the current market value of the stock has appreciated and is now worth $15 per share? In this case, the company is contributing stock worth $1.5 million and receiving only a $1 million deduction. The company would have received a higher income tax deduction by simply contributing the shares directly to an employee benefit plan rather than making the contribution to the ESOP.

One way to mitigate this problem is by using one of the complex securities described above. Because convertible preferred stock is a hybrid fixed income/equity instrument, it often appreciates less quickly in the early years than does regular common stock. As a result, the gap between the income tax valuation of the stock and the market valuation may be smaller. A security that has a fixed dollar conversion feature completely avoids this issue. However, such a security may also fail to provide any equity-like appreciation potential until it is converted.

Compensation Issues

ESOPs are first and foremost compensation vehicles. As a result, companies establishing ESOPs have looked to complex securities to more

closely match the compensation objectives of the plan. In many companies, the ESOP becomes the employees' primary retirement benefit. One
of the advantages of such an ESOP is that it aligns the interests of the
employees with those of the company's owners and motivates the employees to help the company succeed. However, in some cases, companies want to limit the degree to which employees' compensation and/or
retirement benefits are linked to company performance. The concern is
that external factors like the economy, interest rates, and stock market
performance may cause too much volatility in the value of the ESOP
stock allocated to employee accounts.

Securities such as convertible preferred stock help solve this problem by creating a more stable and less volatile security to offer to the
ESOP. In many cases, such convertible preferred stock has floor redemption value, which helps ensure that the value will never fall below
the original price at which the ESOP purchased the stock. The higher
dividends associated with "super dividend" securities may also decrease
the volatility of this type of security and make it appealing for use in
ESOPs.

Another issue of concern to some larger companies is the fact that
an ESOP that purchases stock of a large diversified company may not
provide an incentive targeted enough to motivate the employees of a
specific division or subsidiary of the company. Today's large companies
often have disparate subsidiaries with no clear business relationships
among them. As a result, the performance of the company's regular
common stock may seem unrelated to the performance of a particular
subsidiary.

Some companies have addressed this problem by issuing tracking
stock to employees of that subsidiary. Because the tracking stock is a security of the parent company, it is a qualified employer security for
ESOP purposes. The stock of the subsidiary company is generally not a
qualified employer security eligible for purposes of Section 1042 capital
gains tax deferral.

Despite the fact that the tracking security is issued by the parent
corporation, its value will be more closely linked to the underlying business unit that it tracks. As a result, the benefits provided by the ESOP
to employees of that business unit are more closely linked to the performance of that entity.

Impact of Post-transaction Dilution

Complex securities may also help address one of the most difficult issues in ESOP valuations—the post-transaction dilution in value in
leveraged ESOP transactions. In an ESOP transaction involving significant leverage, the ESOP contributions needed to service the debt often
represent a significant increase in benefits relative to normal historical
levels. These higher contributions will therefore have a significant negative impact on the equity value of the company after the transaction.
The impact of the ESOP contributions will diminish as the ESOP debt
is repaid. This post-transaction decline in value, though familiar to

ESOP structuring professionals, is often hard to communicate to employees and owners.

The use of complex securities with a higher dividend than regular common stock can help mitigate this problem. To the extent that debt service can be met through dividends, not contributions, the valuation impact on the stock purchased by the ESOP may be lessened. This is true because, although the company's obligation to contribute funds to the ESOP to repay debt is valuable, it is not an intrinsic characteristic of the security owned by the ESOP. Therefore, it is not taken into account in valuing the security. On the other hand, dividend rights are intrinsic characteristics of the security and should be taken into account in the valuation. These dividends will increase the value of the ESOP security and reduce the negative impact of the company's contribution obligation on value.

Corporate Governance Issues

Corporate governance issues can also play a role in the decision to use a complex security in ESOP transactions. In the late 1980s, many public companies believed that ESOPs could play a useful role in their takeover defense strategies. Tax laws require that leveraged ESOPs receive stock that is (or is convertible into) the class of stock with the highest voting rights. However, this does not prevent the ESOP from receiving better voting rights than other types of securities. As a result, convertible preferred securities may receive better voting rights than typical publicly traded convertible preferred. Alternatively, in private companies the ESOP may be offered a special class of common stock with superior voting rights relative to ordinary common stock.

The assumption behind offering the ESOP a security with higher voting rights is that the ESOP will tend to support the existing management or shareholder group. However, the ESOP fiduciaries that control the vote of the ESOP's shares have an obligation to vote in the best interests of the participants. This duty may not necessarily coincide with the desires of the existing management, especially in a takeover situation. In addition, recent court cases (most notably, the *Polaroid* case)[2] have suggested that ESOP trustees in some circumstances have a duty to override participants' instructions when the economic benefits to the participants are clear. As a result, the corporate governance benefits of offering an ESOP securities with higher voting rights are uncertain.

Valuation Issues for Complex ESOP Securities

The use of complex securities in the capital structures of ESOP companies presents several interesting valuation issues. Some complex securities, such as traditionally structured convertible preferred stock, may

---

[2]*Martin* v. *NationsBank*, C.A. No. 1:92-CV-1474-HTW (N.D. Ga. 1993).

be easily valued by reference to guideline publicly traded securities. There are a large number of corporate issues of convertible preferred stocks with a wide range of credit risk and dividend yields. As a result, it is often easy to find comparative publicly traded securities of companies with similar credit risk and conversion rights. The valuation characteristics (yield, conversion premium, etc.) of these comparative publicly traded securities can be used to estimate the value of a standard convertible preferred security used in an ESOP. Alternatively, well-developed theoretical formulas have been developed to estimate the value of standard convertible preferred securities on the basis of their dividend rate conversion rights and the dividend and volatility of the underlying common stock.

However, many of the convertible preferred securities used in ESOPs have some of the unusual features described above. As a result, sufficiently comparative publicly traded securities are not likely to exist. This is also true for many of the other complex securities used in ESOPs. Therefore, theoretical models are typically relied upon to estimate the value of these complex securities.

Most complex securities can be viewed as hybrid securities, combining characteristics of two or more less complex securities. Convertible preferred stock, for example, can be viewed as the combination of (1) a fixed income security plus (2) an option to purchase the underlying common stock into which it is convertible. The exercise price of the option can be viewed as the conversion price of the convertible preferred security. Most of the other complex securities can be viewed as combinations of securities or rights, which can be more easily valued separately. The sum of these components of value can be used as a benchmark for valuing the complex security.

Exhibit 12-1 illustrates how some of the complex securities often seen in ESOPs can be viewed as combinations of more easily valued securities.

It should be noted that this additive approach to valuing complex securities is a slightly imprecise methodology. For example, valuing a convertible preferred security as the sum of (1) a straight preferred and (2) an option to buy the common at the exercise price will tend to slightly overvalue the security. This is because the "option" can be exercised only by converting the security. This conversion is effectively equivalent to selling the fixed income component of the security at par.

On the other hand, valuing the convertible preferred instead as the sum of (1) the common stock plus (2) the present value of the additional dividend stream received on the preferred may understate the value. This is because it may not fully capture the value of the downside protection that the preferred offers. Similarly, the additive approach to valuing certain other complex securities may slightly overvalue them. Nevertheless, this approach to value may be the best practical alternative to valuing certain complex securities.

Exhibit 12–1

Exhibit 12-1
Comparison of Complex Securities
to Alternative Traditional Securities

Complex Security		Traditional Security	Valuation Methodology
Convertible preferred		Straight preferred	Call option on the underlying common
	or	Common stock	Present value of dividend stream
Super dividend common		Common stock	Present value of dividend stream
Super voting common		Common stock	Value of extra voting rights
Tracking stock		Straight preferred	Call option on tracking entity
Performance stock		Common stock	Complex option on additional shares of common
Floor put convertible		Straight preferred	Call option on the underlying common
	plus	Put option	Put option on the convertible preferred

Summary

As companies desire to use ESOPs to more closely fit their corporate governance, individual taxation, and compensation needs, the use of complex securities in the capital structure of ESOP companies is likely to increase. Beyond standard convertible preferred securities, complex ESOP securities include floor put convertible preferred stock, high-yield convertible preferred stock, super common stock, tracking stock, and performance stock.

The increasingly intricate design of these securities will continue to challenge the valuation professional in both executing and communicating the results of these more complex valuation engagements.

Chapter 13

Valuation for Ad Valorem Taxation

Claire H. Donias, FASA

Introduction

Ad valorem taxation is a fiscal system of taxation imposing levies on property according to the value of such property. Strictly speaking, customs duties are a form of such taxation. However, the most common usage of the term *ad valorem taxation* is for property taxation. Property taxes are imposed by local jurisdictions on property within their bailiwick. Such jurisdictions may be cities, counties, or states, or specially created public agencies empowered to levy property taxes for their operational and other needs.

Because ad valorem taxation takes place at the local level, there is wide diversity in the property taxation statutes. Typically the statutes are established at the state level, and the various taxing jurisdictions within each state follow standards and guidelines established by state bodies—such as assessment boards, tax commissions, and boards of equalization—with respect both to administrative procedures and to valuation methodology and practice. In many states, centrally developed procedures are guidelines only; local assessing authorities may exercise their independence if they disagree with the state guidelines.

In some jurisdictions, more than one taxing authority, each independent of the others, may levy ad valorem taxes on the same property. There are situations where as many as six different taxing authorities estimate value and tax the same property: county, city, school district, port authority, sewage and sanitation district, library district, parks and recreation district, flood control district, and so forth. Each one of these taxing authorities may estimate a different value for the same property at the same time. The property owner may reach an agreement on value with one authority, only to have to argue with another taxing authority about the value that is appropriate for that other authority's purpose.

Occasionally, the significance of the taxation revenue to the jurisdictional authority's budget may prolong a valuation dispute far beyond what would be indicated by the technical aspects of the two parties' valuation methods. If the local assessor is an elected official, as often is the case, then politics may interfere with traditional valuation theories for ad valorem taxation. This is because the corporate property owner or taxpayer does not vote.

The most common type of property subject to ad valorem taxation is real estate. Other tangible property, such as machinery and equipment, fixtures, or chattels, is taxable in most states. Intangible property is taxable in a very few states (e.g., Florida). Some states (e.g., Washington and California) explicitly exclude intangible property from taxation. However, assessors often attempt to include the value of intangible property as part of the value of tangible property if it "enhances the value of real property."

There are more, by far, real property taxpayers than any other kind. This is because there are far more personal residences than there are factories or office buildings. As a result, ad valorem taxation regulations and procedures are geared more toward the valuation of simple real estate than the valuation of a major industrial complex. Sometimes, for a complex valuation case to be understood at the initial level of review, it has to be reduced by the taxpayer to the most basic terms, whether or not it is susceptible to such reduction. Quite often, however, assessors in small jurisdictions that do not have enough properties of a special purpose or type to justify the employment of a full-time valuation specialist in such properties (e.g., oil and gas) may retain an outside consultant to assist them.

In cases of properties that operate in more than one jurisdiction and that require the valuation of the entire operating property as a whole ("unitary property," such as a utility or a railroad), a state agency usually performs a valuation of the entire property using business valuation methods. The value of the portion lying within any assessment jurisdiction in the state is allocated on the basis of some acceptable but arbitrary formula.

The standard of value that is the basis for levying the tax also differs from state to state, not only with respect to terminology or nomenclature but, most important, with respect to substance. There are terms such as *cash value, true cash value, full cash value, actual value, market value, fair value, base year value,* and so forth, with which the valuation analyst should be familiar. The analyst should understand the conceptual basis of the value definition in the particular jurisdiction of the assignment.

In some states, the standard is the cost incurred in the acquisition of the property. In other jurisdictions, the standard may be unrecovered cost. In yet other jurisdictions, the standard may be replacement cost less depreciation, narrowly defined (or worse, not defined at all). For the most part, however, and regardless of the actual terms used, the standard of value is market value, or fair market value, as valuation analysts generally understand it. Nonetheless, the appropriate standard of value should be defined at the outset.

This chapter will not deal with the ordinary cases of simple real property valuation. The chapter will deal, instead, with situations that typically lead to controversy between taxpayer and assessing authority. It will cover situations where all approaches to value may be used without statutory limitation to a specific methodology or formula. These situations typically involve industrial properties subject to functional and economic obsolescence.

These are properties that should be approached from the unitary, or business valuation, perspective, since obsolescence (especially economic) usually affects all property units, tangible or intangible, taxable or not. The premise of value, then, will consider the assessable assets as parts of a going-concern business enterprise. And the standard of value we will consider is fair market value. This premise of value makes ad valorem taxation assignments a natural fit with the skill of the advanced business valuation professional.

Definition of Value

A typical definition of fair market value is the amount at which property would equitably change hands between a willing seller and a willing buyer, when neither is acting under compulsion, and when both have reasonably complete knowledge of the relevant facts concerning the property and its utility.

The definition uses the conditional tense: "...property *would* equitably change hands...." The valuation analyst expresses the opinion that *if* the property were to change hands, the conclusion of value would be the amount at which the transaction would take place. It is not necessary that a sale transaction has actually taken place or that it is even contemplated. The definition presupposes or assumes a transaction and that is the basis for the value that is estimated.

It should be noted that the property exchange in the definition is between *a* willing buyer and *a* willing seller. The indefinite article is used because the value estimated should apply to the typical or average buyer and seller, not to a specific one who may be motivated by facts and circumstances not commonly present in the marketplace. If such uncommon factors and circumstances are present, the value is no longer fair market value—but a subjective worth, a concept that is not the basis of valuation for ad valorem taxation.

Fair market value also requires the absence of *compulsion* on the part of both the seller and the buyer. Again, a party to the transaction that is acting under duress or compulsion is not the typical or average buyer or seller. It may be argued that prices prevailing in a buyers' market or in a sellers' market are not typical. However, it should be remembered that if the conditions present in the marketplace affect all buyers or sellers equally, the prices that prevail are the reflection of typical market forces at that specific time.

The parties to a transaction where fair market value applies should also be well informed about the subject of the transaction. They are expected to have conducted an adequate due diligence investigation and be aware of any unusual features, good or bad, of the subject property. The *reasonable knowledge* expectation in the fair market value definition extends to management expertise in the case of a business enterprise. If for some reason the business enterprise that is the subject of the transaction is not being run competently and as a result its operating assets do not enjoy a fair rate of return, then the analyst should make certain assumptions. For example, the analyst may assume competent management and the kind of return that such management can produce. However, such an assumption should be well researched and documented and should not be just an expedient means of justifying a hypothetical value.

"Reasonably well-informed parties acting without compulsion" implies a transaction that is fair to both parties. The use of the word *fair* in the value term does imply exactly that. However, very frequently the word *equitably* is added in the definition to emphasize this point.

Alternatively, the phrase "and with equity to both" is added at the end of the definition.

Premise of Value

The premise of value is just as important in ad valorem valuations as the standard of value. The valuation analyst estimates not only the fair market value of the subject property but also the status of the property under which such value applies. In the case of industrial facilities, the property or operating assets are almost always considered for ad valorem valuation as parts of a going-concern business enterprise. For example, a large air compressor may have a certain value FOB the dealer's shipping dock, but an entirely different value as part of a going-concern business enterprise. This is because the value as part of a going-concern business will consider the cost of freight, foundations, installation, piping and electrical connections and controls, and start-up.

By the same token, if the business enterprise is in a slumping industry and cannot generate an adequate return for the compressor at the original cost, including all those going-concern elements, the compressor may be worth even less than the value FOB the dealer's shipping dock. Quite often the concept of the asset being part of a going-concern enterprise is further stressed by adding the phrase "for continued use in place as acquired and installed" to make sure that the asset is not considered apart from the business enterprise and its current use.

Valuation Date

The valuation date is the date to which the analyst's opinion of value applies. It is not the date on which the analyst conducts the valuation or the valuation report is submitted. The last two dates may be considerably removed in time from the valuation date. Very seldom are valuations performed prospectively or as of a future date. If they are, they are labeled as hypothetical or prospective valuations and are of little relevance for ad valorem taxation purposes.

Most ad valorem property valuations are made as of a date in the past. In making such a valuation, the analyst should view the property under the conditions prevailing as of that prior time period.

The analyst should consider only the information that was known or "knowable" as of that time and nothing else. This is true even if the analyst knows that events that transpired since then would have a material impact on the value. Even if events that transpired since then have revealed a condition that may have existed before the valuation date, if the condition was not known or suspected as of the valuation date, then it is not normally taken into consideration in the valuation. The hypothetical buyer and seller are expected to be reasonably well informed of prevailing conditions but not clairvoyant.

This concept of time may appear to be at odds with some important valuation concepts, especially in real estate appraisal, that assume adequate exposure in the marketplace. The temptation here is to allow consideration of information that may have become available within the exposure time appropriate to the subject property type after the valuation date. However, that is not the corollary to the definition. The valuation date is at the end of the appropriate market exposure period, not at the beginning.

In the case of some major industrial plants that have been shut down, the market exposure period may be even longer than one year. In some cases, the analyst may estimate that it would take more than one year to sell the plant. The analyst may wish to take that delay into account. This could be accomplished by discounting the price of a presumed sale a year or more after the valuation date back to the valuation date. However, even in this situation, the factors entering into the valuation analysis are only those that are known to exist as of the valuation date, not a year or more later.

Valuation Approaches

Traditionally, the three approaches to property valuation have been cost, market, and income, usually in that order. Theoretically, the order should be reversed. In the analysis of industrial operating assets, the value of which depends on the ability of the enterprise or industry to generate a fair rate of return, the income approach should come first, followed by the market approach, and then the cost approach. These three valuation approaches are briefly described below.

Under the income approach, investors or prospective buyers (as contemplated in the fair market value definition) decide how much they can afford to pay for an asset. Knowing the asset, the intended use, the period of time the asset is expected to be useful, and the rate of return expected on the investment, each buyer decides to pay a certain amount. The value of the asset to the buyer is the present worth of the future economic benefits that he or she anticipates (generally, the classic definition of value).

As a prudent investor, the buyer then looks at the market, by checking the prices of comparable or guideline assets in the marketplace, to see if he or she can acquire the same asset for less. If identical or sufficiently similar assets are not trading in the marketplace, the buyer can use the nearest comparable data and make adjustments for any elements of dissimilarity. This is the market approach.

Instead of buying the asset in the market in a ready-made condition, so to speak, the prudent investor also wants to make sure that he or she cannot build it at a lower cost. To do this, the buyer estimates the cost of replacing the asset in new condition. He or she then makes allowances or adjustments for the fact that the contemplated asset (the asset subject to appraisal) is not new but is suffering from various forms of depreciation and obsolescence. This is the cost approach.

Valuation theory and practice provide that all three approaches should be considered in every assignment. It should be noted, however, that "considered" does not mean "applied." All assets are not susceptible to valuation by all three approaches at all times. For example, a church property is not valued by capitalization of the contents of the Sunday collection plate, or a public library by analyzing the prices at which comparable libraries are trading in the market.

Frequently, there is so much dissimilarity between the subject asset and its market counterparts that the necessary adjustments are too significant and make certain valuation approaches unreliable. On the other hand, certain assets, such as some intellectual property and goodwill, defy attempts at estimating their fair market value by using the cost approach.

As a rule, the cost approach and the market approach may be more appropriate in the valuation of fixed or tangible assets, whereas the market approach and the income approach are more appropriate in the valuation of business enterprises and intangible assets. This is a general rule because it has many exceptions. Moreover, in practice, a valuation assignment typically involves the use of more than one valuation approach, and each approach may entail more than one valuation method. However, as discussed in more detail later, one form or another of income (or anticipated economic return) is a major consideration in each of the three valuation approaches, including the cost approach.

Assets Subject to Valuation

This discussion will first address assets subject to ad valorem taxation, which consist of land and improvements, buildings and structures, and machinery and equipment—or simply land, buildings, and equipment—all as part of a going-concern business enterprise. Initially, the subject going concern will be a one-facility industrial enterprise. The discussion will then address operating assets owned by a multiplant enterprise situated in one taxing jurisdiction only. A variation of this scenario is the railroad or utility enterprise with assets scattered over a number of jurisdictions. The assets will be assumed to have economic utility—in other words, not objets d'art or other collectibles that are acquired for the pride of ownership rather than the intent to derive a financial return from their use.

When operating assets are valued as parts of a going-concern business enterprise, only those assets that are used and necessary for the operation of the going concern should be included. Unrelated, excess, idle, or nonoperating assets should be excluded and valued under a separate premise of value, if they are subject to taxation at all. This principle would also apply to assets held for future use, such as land for expansion. This is true if the assets held for future use do not in any way contribute to the profitability of the subject enterprise as of the appraisal date. A simple test to be applied in this regard is to check if removal or disposal of the asset would affect the business operation. If the answer is no, then the asset should not be considered as part of the business enterprise. This is true for both taxable and nontaxable assets if, as will be discussed later, total enterprise profitability is used to quantify any economic obsolescence that may be present.

The analyst's first task, then, is to analyze and categorize the enterprise assets as either operating or nonoperating. Nonoperating assets will be valued for sale or disposal. Operating assets will be valued for continued use in place. Assets valued for sale or disposal should be valued in the form or condition in which the sale or disposal will take place.

For example, if an air compressor is no longer of use or is not in use but is still sitting on its foundation, with all its connections intact, then it should probably be valued as if crated and awaiting shipment. Its value would be the price that it will bring in the used market, either through sale to a dealer or a private party or at auction. However, from such price should be deducted the cost of dismantling, crating, and other expense to be incurred in bringing the asset to the salable condition.

The Valuation Process

For ease of presentation of the subject, with all its computations and adjustments, the concepts and methodologies are best illustrated through a hypothetical case study. This case study is presented to highlight specific points and is not intended to represent an exhaustive valuation analysis. The facts are as follows:

- Tangible assets of a manufacturing facility ("the Facility") are subject to ad valorem taxation at a rate of 2 percent of their fair market value. Such assets include land, buildings, equipment, supplies, and spare parts.
- The Facility is owned 87.5 percent by a multiplant conglomerate; a foreign corporation owns 12.5 percent. It is organized as a C corporation in the state where it is located, and it is subject to income taxation at statutory corporate rates.
- It has been in operation for many years, and it has reached stabilized levels of activity long ago; its growth in sales now barely outpaces inflation.
- The plant is not the most modern, but it is adequate for its current level of activity and no expansion is planned.
- The Facility manufactures a consumer product sold under a brand name that is owned by its parent. It sells the product direct to the trade, but it also sells some products to affiliates of its corporate group, which then resell them.

- Because of economic downtrends worldwide, the Facility's industry is in a slump and no recovery is expected in the foreseeable future.
- The corporate parent provides certain services to all its subsidiaries at a corporate charge based on a formula equally applicable to all. Such services include research and development, industrial relations, engineering and plant design, legal and tax services, market research, advertising, and public relations. The Facility cannot operate on its own without these services.

The Facility's latest balance sheet, which coincides with the lien date (or valuation date), shows a gross investment in fixed assets of nearly $75 million, depreciated to a little more than $45 million. In addition, there is a cost of $1.7 million of supplies and spare parts. (See columns 1, 2, and 3 in Exhibit 13-1.)

By state law, the Facility annually reports all its taxable property to the local assessor by year of acquisition and by historical cost incurred. The assessor processes the cost data by applying trend factors and depreciation factors (i.e., percent-good factors) provided by the state Bureau of Assessment Standards to the depreciable property. Land values are updated periodically by market investigations. The Facility's last tax bill was based on the data in Exhibit 13-2, as the assessor's work papers show.

When questioned to explain the difference in land value between cost new today and fair market value, the assessor explained that cost new represented the price prevailing in the market as of the lien date for the land parcel of the Facility. However, as part of a going-concern business enterprise, fair market value also included interest during construction (one year at 8 percent), property taxes during the year of construction (at 2 percent), and entrepreneurial profit (at 25 percent). In fact, interest during construction, taxes, and entrepreneurial profit, at the same rates, has been added by the assessor to buildings and equipment as well, before depreciation was applied. Cost new included only the direct cost.

The assessor also stated that the value of the land, which had significantly increased from prior years, was based on development activity in the vicinity where technology parks were being built. The subject parcel's highest and best use would be for a technology park.

Both the land value increase and the introduction of the entrepreneurial profit element by the assessor nearly doubled the property tax due compared with the prior year. The owners of the Facility decided to appeal and retained an independent valuation analyst.

The analyst found not only that the entrepreneurial profit concept had been misapplied but also the Facility's assets were subject to considerable functional and economic obsolescence that had not yet been incorporated into the analysis. The analyst proceeded to consider all three approaches to value but soon realized that assets such as those under assessment do not frequently change hands in the marketplace. The analyst found a few sales of shutdown plants, but they either were too far removed in time, when the industry was not in a slump, or were

Exhibit 13-1

Subject Facility Balance Sheet ($000s)

	Per Corporate Books			4	5	6	7	8	9	10	11	12	13	14	15	16
	1	2	3	Reclassi-fication	Nonenter-prise Assets	Enter-prise Assets	Repro-duction Cost	Replace-ment Cost	Depreci-ation	Depre-ciated Cost	Functional Obsolescence	Value in Use	Fair Market Value of Enter-prise Assets	Nonenter-prise Assets	Fair Market Value of Tax-able Assets	Assessor's Value of Taxable Assets
	Actual Cost	Depre-ciation	Net Book Value													
Current assets																
Cash	1,320	-	1,320	-	-	1,320	1,320	1,320	-	1,320	-	1,320	1,320	-	-	-
Accounts receivable	14,241	-	14,241	-	-	14,241	14,241	14,241	-	14,241	-	14,241	11,384	-	-	-
Inventories: Raw materials	4,165	-	4,165	(3,000)	-	1,165	1,340	1,340	-	1,340	(500)	1,340	1,071	-	-	-
Goods	5,822	-	5,822	-	-	5,822	7,685	7,685	-	7,685	-	7,185	5,744	-	-	-
Supplies	943	-	943	-	-	943	1,084	1,084	-	1,084	(90)	1,084	867	-	867	943
Spare parts	765	-	765	-	-	765	880	880	-	880	-	790	632	-	632	765
Prepayments	895	-	895	-	-	895	895	895	-	895	-	895	715	-	-	-
Subtotal	28,151	-	28,151	(3,000)	-	25,151	27,445	27,445	-	27,445	(590)	26,855	21,733	-	1,499	1,708
Fixed assets																
Land	7,083	-	7,083	-	(1,200)	5,883	28,000	14,100	-	14,100	-	14,100	14,100	3,000	17,100	35,500
Buildings	14,708	(3,677)	11,031	-	-	11,031	19,856	17,800	(4,450)	13,350	(900)	12,450	9,217	-	9,217	17,228
Equipment	52,949	(25,739)	27,210	-	-	27,210	63,539	54,008	(26,254)	27,754	(1,200)	26,554	19,658	-	19,658	49,391
Subtotal	74,740	(29,416)	45,324	-	(1,200)	44,124	111,395	85,908	(30,704)	55,204	(2,100)	53,104	42,975	3,000	45,975	102,119
Other assets																
Investments	-	-	-	3,000	(3,000)	-	-	-	-	-	-	-	-	-	-	-
Long-term notes	400	-	400	-	-	400	400	400	-	400	-	400	324	-	-	-
Intangible assets	-	-	-	-	-	-	4,500	4,500	-	4,500	-	4,500	3,641	2,400	-	-
Subtotal	400	-	400	3,000	(3,000)	400	4,900	4,900	-	4,900	-	4,900	3,965	2,400	-	-
Total assets	103,291	(29,416)	73,875	-	(4,200)	69,675	143,740	118,253	(30,704)	87,549	(2,690)	84,859	68,673	5,400	47,474	103,827
Current liabilities																
Current debt portion	2,310		2,310	(2,310)												
Accrued expenses	13,356		13,356	-	-	13,356	13,356	13,356	-	13,356	-	13,356	13,356			
Accrued taxes	623		623	-	(6)	617	617	617	-	617	-	617	617			
Subtotal	16,289		16,289	(2,310)	(6)	13,973	13,973	13,973	-	13,973	-	13,973	13,973			
Business enterprise	87,002	(29,416)	57,586	-	(4,194)	55,702	129,767	104,280	(30,704)	73,576	(2,690)	70,886	54,700			
Long-term liabilities																
Long-term debt	11,515	-	11,515	2,310	-	13,825	13,825	13,825	-	13,825	-	13,825	13,825			
Deferred taxes	917	-	917	-	-	917	-	-	-	-	-	-	-			
Subtotal	12,432	-	12,432	2,310	-	14,742	13,825	13,825	-	13,825	-	13,825	13,825			
Minority interest	9,321	(3,677)	5,644	-	(524)	5,120	14,493	11,307	(3,838)	7,469	(336)	7,133				
Shareholder equity	65,249	(25,739)	39,510	-	(3,670)	35,840	101,449	79,148	(26,866)	52,282	(2,354)	49,928				
Liabilities and equity	103,291	(29,416)	73,875	-	(4,200)	69,675	143,740	118,253	(30,704)	87,549	(2,690)	84,859				

Exhibit 13–2

Tax Bill Data ($000)

Asset Category	Historical Cost	Cost New Today	Fair Market Value
Supplies	943	983	943
Spare parts	765	765	765
Land	7,083	26,335	35,500
Buildings	14,708	17,981	17,228
Equipment	52,949	60,112	49,391
Totals	76,448	106,136	103,827

sales of obsolete plants sold for demolition or alternative use. Therefore, the market approach, applied directly to the taxable assets only, would not produce reliable value indications.

A properly applied cost approach would have to consider both the functional and economic obsolescence of the assets. Both of these forms of obsolescence are measurable for the most part through an investigation of the earning capacity of the Facility. Furthermore, the operating assets were parts of a going-concern business enterprise. And whenever the operating assets were sold, they were sold as parts of an entire going-concern business. Therefore, the analyst would have to estimate the value of the entire going-concern business first and then arrive at the value of its component parts, including the operating assets under assessment.

The analyst began with the income approach. This is because certain elements of the income approach, such as rates of return, would also be needed in the application of the cost approach. A review of the Facility's income statement, shown in Exhibit 13-3, indicated that a number of reclassifications and adjustments would be needed before the value of the business enterprise could be estimated. (All dollar numbers from here on are in thousands. Column letters refer to Exhibit 13-3.)

Reclassifications (Column B)

The cost of material was increased by the cost of freight into the plant and was decreased by discounts received and the income from scrap sales. These are material-related costs and expenses and should be included in the cost of sales.

Depreciation expense was removed from both the cost of sales and the expenses in order to arrive at a measure of operating income—or earnings before depreciation, interest, and taxes (EBDIT). EBDIT is one true measure of the profitability of a business enterprise. And it is one of the valuation parameters typically used in the application of the market approach in the case of a business enterprise.

Exhibit 13–3

Subject Facility Income Statement ($000)

	A	B	C	D
	Per Annual Report	Reclassi- fications	Valuation Adjustment	Adjusted
Revenue				
Sales: third parties,	133,275	-	-	133,275
affiliates	13,160	-	3,290	16,450
Returns, discounts, etc.	(5,565)	-	(125)	(5,690)
Net revenue	140,870	-	3,165	144,035
Cost of sales				
Beginning inventory	8,361	-	-	8,361
Purchases	23,245	305	-	23,550
Direct labor	30,124	-	-	30,124
Factory overhead	48,257	(3,864)	-	44,393
Ending inventory	(11,695)	-	-	(11,695)
Cost of sales	98,292	(3,559)	-	94,733
Expenses				
Freight in	665	(665)	-	-
Freight out	5,857	-	-	5,857
Commissions	6,664	-	165	6,829
Advertising	93	-	207	300
Other selling expense	3,228	-	-	3,228
Occupancy expense	1,269	(365)	-	904
Office salaries	1,437	-	-	1,437
Professional services	546	-	-	546
Taxes and insurance	6,831	-	(816)	6,015
Royalty expense		-	7,638	7,638
Miscellaneous	3,969	-	-	3,969
Corporate allocation	3,400	-	(1,420)	1,980
Total expenses	33,959	(1,030)	5,774	38,703
Operating income	8,619	4,589	(2,609)	10,599
Other expense (income)				
Depreciation/amoritization	-	4,229	-	4,229
Interest, net	1,054	-	(1,054)	-
Sales of assets	(420)	-	420	-
Scrap sales/discounts	(360)	360	-	-
Total other expense	274	4,589	(634)	4,229
Earnings before taxes	8,345	-	(1,975)	6,370
Income taxes	3,338	-	(790)	2,548
Net income after taxes	5,007	-	(1,185)	3,822
Minority interest	626	-	(626)	-
Net income	4,381	-	(559)	3,822

Valuation Adjustments (Column C)

The Facility is considered as an autonomous and independent going concern. As such, it would have no affiliation with its corporate parents and it will direct all its sales to the trade at regular prices. The discounts offered to the affiliates were restored, including the provision for the associated returns, discounts, and allowances.

If affiliate sales were destined to the trade, commissions would also apply and the related expense should be included. Also, if the facility were to be considered as an autonomous and independent enterprise, it would have to do its own advertising, which is estimated at $300.

It is a common convention in valuations for ad valorem taxation purposes to capitalize income before consideration of property taxes. This is because the taxes are a function of value, and the value has not yet been determined. Allowance for property taxes is made by increasing the rate of return by a component equal to the percentage of the tax. If pretax income is capitalized, the entire tax percentage is added to the pretax rate of return. If after-tax income or cash flow is capitalized, the after-tax equivalent of the property tax component is added to the after-tax rate of return. For example, assume that pretax income before property taxes is $160, the property tax rate is 2 percent of value, and the pretax rate of return is 14 percent. Adding the two rates produces a direct capitalization rate of 16 percent, which, when applied to the $160 income, yields a value of $1,000.

If the property tax rate of 2 percent is applied to that property value, it would result in a property tax of $20. Deducting this tax from the $160 income before property and income taxes, and capitalizing at the 14 percent rate of return, would yield the same $1,000 value. Use of after-tax income and rates of return would produce the same result.

An autonomous and independent going concern would have no affiliation with the parent corporation that owns the brand name. Use of the brand name is essential in selling the product, but the subject Facility does not own the name. The subsidiary company could license use of the name from the parent, which is now granting licenses to third parties at a royalty fee of 5.3 percent of sales. Imputing such a charge to the sales of $144 million increases expenses by $7,638.

The Facility benefits from the services provided by the parent, but an analysis indicates that such benefit is worth $1,980, not the $3,400 charge it now pays under the formula.

Adjusted Income (Column D)

After the reclassifications and valuation adjustments, operating income—or EBDIT—was increased to $10,599 and, after allowing for depreciation and income taxes but disregarding property taxes, net income after taxes was reduced to $3,822.

Minority interest considerations are disregarded for ad valorem valuation purposes. This is because the entirety of the assets of the Facility are subject to property tax, paid by the facility, rather than the individual interests of its two stockholders.

Net Cash Flow

The analyst decided to use net cash flow as the appropriate measure of economic income for valuation purposes. Net cash flow is defined in this context as net income after income taxes plus tax depreciation and amortization expense, less additions to working capital and less capital additions to plant and equipment. Net cash flow can be capitalized either through the discounted cash flow method or through the single-period direct capitalization method. For the sake of simplicity, and, most particularly since a steady-state or stabilized level of operations has already been achieved, the single-period direct capitalization method is selected.

A review of financial statements of publicly held companies in the same industry as the Facility indicates that companies the size of the Facility maintain working capital at a level equal to 8 percent of the increase in sales. At the Facility's sustained growth rate of 3.5 percent, net working capital addition this year should have been $390 [(144,035 − (144,035 / 1.035))(0.08) = 390].

A review of capital expenditures for plant and equipment by the Facility, as well as its industry in general, indicates that such expenditures amount to approximately 4 percent of gross depreciable assets. Using the cost approach, the analyst estimated that the replacement cost new of such assets is $17,800 + $54,008 = $71,808, and the annual capital expenditures at 4 percent of that cost would be $2,872.

Net cash flow then is $3,822 + $4,229 − $390 − $2,872 = $4,789. Year-to-year change in that amount is expected to parallel the compound annual expected growth rate of approximately 3.5 percent.

Rate of Return

Traditionally, a rate of return for any investment is considered to encompass the pure cost of money or risk-free rate, plus a component that is adequate to compensate the investor for the risks inherent in the subject investment. Valuation analysts often estimate the appropriate rate of return through the capital asset pricing model (CAPM) and the weighted average cost of capital (WACC). The CAPM relates to the return applicable to the equity portion of an investment. The WACC applies to the rate of overall return for both equity and debt capital in an enterprise or a project.

Other parts of this book cover the CAPM and WACC concepts and methodologies in more detail than is warranted in this chapter. Suffice it to say that the analyst conducted a search of the market for publicly traded companies similar to the Facility in their line of business and in size. From the financial and other information these publicly traded companies are required to release, the analyst was able to extract a number of factors, ratios, and relationships that prevail in the Facility's industry as represented by this group of guideline companies. Significant among these factors were the following:

- The rate of return on equity in the Facility's industry over the last 30 years was 13 percent. To this, the analyst added 2 percentage points for specific company risk. This is because the analyst considered the Facility somewhat riskier as an investment owing to the fact that (1) its product line was less diversified than the public companies', (2) it did not own its own brand name, (3) it did not provide for all the management and administrative functions through its own resources, and (4) it was a single-plant enterprise and thus more vulnerable to disruption of operations. The analyst arrived at a rate of 15 percent for the return on equity.

- The analyst found that the prevailing debt to equity ratio in the industry was 30–70; an investor in the Facility would be able to leverage his or her investment up to 30 percent of total capital through borrowings.
- The interest rate for such borrowed funds would be 8 percent. Since any interest expense would be deductible for income tax purposes, the net after-tax cost of the interest would be considered.
- The analyst found that the typical level of working capital in the industry was 8 percent of sales.

At a combined federal and state income tax rate applicable to the Facility of 40 percent, the WACC is computed at 12 percent: $[(0.3 \times 8.0 \times 0.6) + (0.7 \times 15.0 \times 1.0) = 11.94]$. From the cost approach, the analyst found that at value in use (Column 12 in Exhibit 13-1), the taxable assets represented only 65 percent of total assets. Thus the property tax rate of 2 percent should be added to the rate of return, only 65 percent of that tax rate should apply. Also, since property taxes are deductible for income tax purposes, only the after-tax cost of the property tax component should be added: $2.0 \times 0.65 \times 0.6 = 0.78$. The present value discount rate, then, for the income approach is $12.0 + 0.78 = 12.78$ percent.

Business Enterprise Valuation

Since the Facility had reached stabilized operations and no significant changes in sales and earnings were anticipated in the foreseeable future, the analyst selected the single-period direct capitalization method to value the business enterprise. Had the analyst selected the discounted cash flow (DCF) method, the results would not have been different if the same valuation parameters—such as beginning net cash flow, expected growth rate, and present value discount rate—had been used.

Using the present value discount rate of 12.78 percent, the expected long-term growth rate of 3.5 percent, and the beginning net cash flow of $4,789, the direct capitalization valuation method yields the following:

$$\text{Business enterprise value} = \frac{\$4,789 \times 1.035}{0.1278 - 0.035} = \$53,412$$

This value indication for the business enterprise is at the invested capital (i.e., long-term debt plus stockholders' equity) level. The only liabilities that are excluded from the value estimate are those that are incurred in the normal course of business (such as current liabilities), but after the reclassification of the current portion of the long-term debt. By definition, then, adding the current liabilities to the business enterprise value would yield the fair market value of all the assets employed by the subject business enterprise that generate economic income.

In the investigation of the market and the industry, the analyst found that market pricing multiples of the publicly traded companies in the Facility's peer group could be used in valuing the Facility. Adjustments were made to the pricing multiples to account for dissimilarities between the Facility and its peers such as those that prompted the analyst to add 2 percentage points to the equity rate of return in the income approach. The selected pricing multiples, all on an invested capital basis, were 15 times net income, 7.5 times cash flow, and 5 times EBDIT.

It should be noted at this point that valuation of the entire business enterprise, which represents the value of all the operating assets, implies the presence of ownership control of the enterprise. The analyst should adjust reported stock trading prices of the publicly traded companies for the ownership control premium that would have been paid if one desired to buy the entire company, or at least a controlling ownership interest in it.[1]

Using the above multiples and the values in Column D of Exhibit 13-3, the analyst concluded the following enterprise value indications:

Measure of Economic Income	Financial Fundamental		Pricing Multiple		Value Indication
Net income	3,822	×	15.0	=	57,330
Cash flow	8,051	×	7.5	=	60,383
EBDIT	10,599	×	5.0	=	52,995

The analyst was more inclined to rely on the EBDIT-derived value and weighted that value twice in concluding a value of $55,926 through the market approach. The reason for this greater reliance on the EBDIT-derived value was the fact that EBDIT is considered to be the best measure of the profitability of this enterprise. EBDIT is the level of earnings before introduction of discretionary elements of cost or expense of enterprise operations. For example, depreciation expense for tax and/or accounting purposes depends upon the method and the expected lives selected by management or allowed by the Internal Revenue Service. Also, the amount of interest expense is a function of the degree of leverage that the ownership of the enterprise decided to use. And income taxes depend on the amounts charged for depreciation and interest. For valuations at the controlling ownership interest or business enterprise level, therefore, where such decisions are within the purview of the owners, capitalization of EBDIT is a preferable method.

---

[1]The concept of minority ownership or majority ownership stock prices and ownership control premium considerations are discussed in more detail in Shannon P. Pratt, Robert F. Reilly, and Robert P. Schweihs, *Valuing a Business: The Analysis and Appraisal of Closely Held Companies*, 3d ed. (New York: McGraw-Hill, 1996).

With the two value indications obtained through the income and market approaches of $53,412 and $55,926, respectively, the analyst concluded a business enterprise value of $54,700. By definition, this value is after a reduction of current liabilities. Adding the current liabilities (from Column 12 of Exhibit 13-1) to the business enterprise value yields the fair market value of the operating assets of the business enterprise in the aggregate, or $54,700 + $13,973 = $66,173.

Valuation of Operating Assets

In addition to the valuation of the operating assets in the aggregate, or the "unitary method" as it is sometimes called, through the valuation of the entire enterprise by the income and market approaches, the analyst applied the cost approach. The analyst began with the Facility's balance sheet as of the valuation date (columns 1, 2, and 3 of Exhibit 13-1) and then made some reclassifications for valuation purposes (Column 4):

1. The analyst deducted $3,000 from raw materials inventory, considering that amount to be in excess of the Facility's usual operating levels. In fact, it is the result of a purchase in anticipation of a price hike in raw materials. The price hike did not take place, but the Facility had not yet worked off the excess by the valuation date. The analyst reclassified this excess as an investment.
2. The analyst removed the current portion of long-term debt from the current liabilities and added it to the long-term portion. In this manner, the analyst could insert an additional entry, normally not found in balance sheets prepared in accordance with generally accepted accounting principles, to show the value of the business enterprise on an invested capital basis. This procedure had nothing to do with the cost approach as such, but was in preparation for the income and market approaches that the analyst expected to apply.

The analyst then segregated the operating from the nonoperating assets of the facility. It was discovered that a parcel of land adjacent to the subject facility's property had been bought several years earlier when management speculated on an expansion program. With the entire industry in a recession as of the valuation date, no expansion was anticipated in the foreseeable future. Therefore, the land, which was vacant and was used occasionally for storage because it was available, was not necessary for the conduct of the Facility's business operations. It could be classified as an investment, but it was definitely a nonoperating asset. The excess inventory that had been reclassified as an investment was also a nonoperating asset. The remaining operating assets, presented in Column 6 of Exhibit 13-1, were all used and necessary for the Facility's business operations.

The analyst estimated the reproduction cost, in new condition, of the Facility's assets. Since the unitary method of valuation was being used, and since the operating assets were considered as parts of a going concern, the analyst estimated the reproduction cost of all operating assets, not only the assets under assessment. In this way, all operating assets could be considered as parts of a going concern on the same basis.

Although companies typically report inventories at "lower of cost or market," the reported cost is only the direct manufacturing cost, usually the amount that corresponds to the cost of sales level of the income statement. The valuation of inventory as part of a going concern would have to be performed under the "full costing" principle—where general and administrative expense, as well as carrying costs or return on funds employed, should be considered. Such "full costing," but at varying levels, was applied to all items of inventory, including supplies and spare parts.

As did the assessor, the analyst found that the land occupied by the Facility was considerably more valuable than industrial land. The assessor's value of the land, as if vacant and available for its highest and best use but before addition of interest during construction and entrepreneurial profit, was reasonable. However, in light of the market prices of the land, a manufacturing plant such as the subject was not the vacant land's highest and best use.

The analyst also estimated the reproduction cost of buildings and equipment assuming similar surface areas, methods of construction, equipment types and capacities, and so on.

The $400 long-term note receivable (conversion of an account receivable to a long-term note as a result of a customer's financial difficulties) carried interest at a market rate, and interest was being paid on schedule. Therefore, no adjustment was necessary.

The Facility owned no intellectual property. Its corporate parent, which also owned the brand name, performed all research and development. Any customer account value would be more attached to the brand loyalty than to the Facility. The Facility did have, however, its own sales and distribution network, an assembled workforce, and all its systems and procedures in place—including supplier and financial relationships, licenses, permits, and so forth. The analyst estimated the reproduction cost of all these intangible assets at $4,500.

The next step in the valuation process was to estimate the replacement cost in new condition. In the case of the current assets and the intangible assets, reproduction and replacement costs were the same. There was a big difference, however, in the case of all three categories of fixed assets.

The analyst considered replacement at the plant level, rather than at the individual asset level. Upon replacement, the plant would be located in an area where suitable land would be available at a price nearly half that of the land at the current location. A new plant would also require less area; it would consolidate the required floor space in fewer buildings than had been constructed over the years in the current location. Also, the cost per square foot in larger buildings was lower than the cost in smaller buildings.

Capacity considerations also enter into the estimate of replacement cost of equipment. Production machinery was installed in the current plant over the years as operations expanded, but the increase in capacity was made at small increments. As a result, there exists a large number of small capacity production units. Upon replacement, capacity would be replaced by larger units, and the cost per unit of capacity would be lower.

A point to be made here is that in estimating both the reproduction and the replacement cost, the analyst included not only (1) the cost of freight and installation and (2) engineering and architectural fees but also (3) the cost of interest during construction and (4) a return on the amount invested during the period that the plant was not operational. This interest and return represented, in other words, the entrepreneurial profit that the assessor had added to the actual costs of construction.

It should be remembered that unlike residential housing tracts, industrial facilities are not built on speculation. Any profit to be made from the construction and installation of assets in an industrial facility built on a turnkey contract is included in the cost of the contract. Building cost estimates from various services—Marshall Valuation Service, Means, and others—are based on the unit method and typically include contractor's overhead and profit.

In this case, the analyst estimated that a replacement plant would take 18 months to build. Land would be bought at the beginning of that period and any investment in it (its cost) would require a return, and property tax payments, during the entire period. The building amount would be spent at the rate of two-thirds during the first year and one-third during the following six months. Equipment would be bought and installed at the rate of one-third during the first year and two-thirds during the last six months. The return required during this period would be capitalized and included in the overall replacement cost of the plant. The rate of return is the WACC, which was computed under the income approach, increased by the full amount of the property tax rate. This is because all plant assets are taxable and capitalized property taxes are not tax-deductible: $12 + 2 = 14$ percent. The related computations were as shown in Exhibit 13-4.

Depreciation presented in Column 9 of Exhibit 13-1 includes only physical depreciation due to wear and tear and reduced life expectancy. It applies with the replacement cost rather than to the reproduction cost.

Functional obsolescence presented in Column 11 relates to the higher operating costs in the existing buildings and equipment as compared to their replacement counterparts. For example, if the buildings were replaced with larger units and were arranged in such a manner as to optimize material flow, not only heating, lighting, and maintenance expense would be lower, but materials handling cost would be reduced as well. The difference in such costs and expenses, on an after-tax basis, capitalized over the remaining useful life of the existing buildings, is the amount of functional obsolescence shown. Similarly for equipment, the fewer but higher-capacity production units would require fewer operators and power. The capitalization of these savings in the replacement units over the remaining life of the existing equipment is shown as functional obsolescence.

The functional obsolescence due to excess construction is the difference between reproduction and replacement cost, and it could have been

Exhibit 13–4

Replacement Cost Computations ($000)

Construction Period	Year 1	Year 1.5	Total
Land—cost incurred	11,637	–	11,637
Return	1,571	892	2,463
			14,100
Buildings—cost incurred	10,353	5,176	15,529
Return on 10,353	699	1,398	2,097
Return on 1,398		174	174
			17,800
Equipment—cost incurred	16,840	33,680	50,520
Return on 16,840	1,137	1,214	2,351
Return on 33,680		1,137	1,137
			54,008

shown separately if reproduction cost were the starting point. Since computations began with replacement cost in this case, that element of obsolescence has already been accounted for.

It was also found that inventories of finished goods included some product that was considered obsolete and unsalable. Also, spare parts included certain old model parts that were still on hand but were for machinery already replaced and for which there is no further use. The data for value in use in Column 12 of Exhibit 13-1 include all the adjustments for physical depreciation and for functional obsolescence.

The value in use of all the facility assets in the aggregate is $84,859. Yet, from the unitary approach, it was estimated that the fair market value of all these assets in the aggregate is $68,673. This means that if the facility had to replace all its assets today, even in the obsolete state that they are in, it would have to pay far more than it can justify on the basis of the return that it can earn from the use of the assets. As parts of the going-concern business enterprise to which they belong, then, the operating assets are not worth their replacement cost. They are subject to economic obsolescence.

Faced with such economic obsolescence, the analyst first reexamined all work papers and notes to see if any identifiable individual assets or asset categories were solely responsible for the lack of adequate profitability of the subject business enterprise. This reexamination did not result in any such findings. Therefore, the lack of adequate profitability is due to external sources, and the operating assets are indeed subject to economic obsolescence. Such obsolescence affects all the assets employed. This is because it cannot be identified and attributed to any individual assets. The obsolescence should be spread equally among all assets and asset categories. The figure of $84,859 for value in use should be reduced to the fair market value figure of $68,673—an overall reduction of 19.07 percent. Multiplication of the value-in-use figure of every operating asset by a factor of 0.8093 (100.00 − 19.07 = 80.93) results in the fair market value of each asset, using the cost approach.

By statutory or administrative dicta in some jurisdictions, the value of land, once entered on the assessment rolls, cannot change. In such cases, the adjustment for economic obsolescence may be made only to the asset categories other than land and allocation of obsolescence within the category may be made only to those assets that are allowed to be adjusted according to the dicta. A similar concept might apply to the cash in the current asset category.

The adjustments in the case of the Facility are made and the results are presented in Column 13 of Exhibit 13-1. In this presentation, no economic obsolescence was made to cash and to land values.

Nonoperating assets identified earlier are not subject to the economic obsolescence determined above. This is because, by definition, they do not contribute to the profitability of the enterprise (or the lack thereof), and they can be disposed of without affecting the operations or value of the enterprise. Their fair market value would be that which they can command in the marketplace upon disposal.

Nonoperating assets identified earlier include the parcel of land bought for possible expansion and the excess raw materials inventory. The land parcel was bought for $1,200 but its value today, vacant and available, is $3,000. Since it is already vacant and available, no demolition or other preparation costs have to be deducted. The excess inventory is reported at its actual cost of purchase, not including freight. If it were to be sold in the market as of the valuation date, however, it would bring less. The analyst estimated that a 20 percent discount would apply. These asset values are presented in Column 14. Column 15 shows the fair market value of all assets subject to assessment, and Column 16 presents the corresponding values originally assigned by the assessor.

As can be seen from the last two columns in Exhibit 13-1, the difference between the assessor's values and the analyst's fair market value conclusions are significant—more than $56 million. At the property tax rate of 2 percent, the difference represents more than $1,127 in additional property tax, making it worthwhile for the Facility to appeal its tax bill.

Analysis and Observations

A two-to-one difference in values raises eyebrows and suspicions of incompetence or advocacy. Upon analysis of the facts in the illustration, however, the causes of the difference may be identified and ascribed to a number of factors.

There seem to exist four major areas of disagreement or difference in treatment between the assessor and the analyst: (1) entrepreneurial profit, (2) land value, (3) use of reproduction rather than replacement cost method by the assessor, and (4) sole reliance by the assessor on an incomplete cost approach.

Entrepreneurial profit is a subject that deserves a chapter of its own, if one judges by the its recurrence in major property tax disputes. Some real estate appraisal texts (e.g., *The Appraisal of Real Estate*[2]) mention entrepreneurial profit as one element of the cost approach. However, there seems to be a dearth in the valuation literature of specific discussion of the concept, where and how it applies, and how it is measured. Aggressive assessors have applied the concept arbitrarily.

Basic accounting defines profit generally as the difference between selling price and all costs and expenses. Financial theory holds that profit is what is available to an investor as the return on the investment used to generate the profit. If the entrepreneurial activity of replacement of an asset—in this case, the entire plant—is entitled to a profit, that profit should be the return on the investment used in the replacement activity. This investment included the debt and equity capital used to build or buy the plant. The debt capital receives interest income during construction and the equity capital receives, or is entitled to receive, the equity return that is proper in the circumstances. Both of these were estimated in the income approach by the analyst and were blended into a single rate (WACC) of 12 percent.

The assessor first applied an interest rate of 8 percent to all capital, debt and equity, and then added a 25 percent profit on top of that; the total compounded return (since the assessor estimated a year as the necessary construction period) is 35 percent ($1.08 \times 1.25 = 1.35$). When put in this context, the assessor's entrepreneurial profit assumption approaches usurious rates in most states, not a reasonable rate of return on investment for an industrial plant.

Of the $56 million difference in values, the portion that results from the difference in entrepreneurial profit treatment is more than $20.5 million, before applying economic obsolescence.

The next major difference is due to the inclusion by the assessor of the value of the land under the plant as if it was vacant and available for alternative use. What the assessor failed to consider was the cost of making the land vacant and available. The assessor's approach should recognize not only the cost of demolition but also the loss of the value of all other assets currently existing that would not survive a move or be of equal value in an alternate use. The entire value of the inefficiently designed buildings would be lost, by definition, since the buildings were admittedly not functioning at their highest and best use as part of a technology park.

The third major difference comes from the assessor's trending the Facility's reported original costs. Such trending produces a reproduction rather than a replacement cost. Just as important, trending of book costs without verification of the existence of the assets assigns values to what are known as "ghost" assets—that is, assets that were replaced but were never removed from the books. This occurs when a major asset is reported for accounting purposes as a single item even though it is an assembly or group of component parts. When only one of the parts is

---

[2]*The Appraisal of Real Estate*, 11th ed. (Chicago: Appraisal Institute, 1996).

replaced, the replacement is reported as an addition but the record is not relieved of the original cost of the replaced item. This problem is partly because of the taxpayer's inability to provide the assessor with denuded records. But responsible valuation procedures such as capacity replacement cost estimates cure this problem generally, or an inspection (even on a sampling basis) can highlight the severity of the situation and call attention to necessary measures for its solution. The perfunctory trending of accounting records misses this step and the result is an overestimate.

The fourth area of difference is the lack of consideration by the assessor of any form of obsolescence. Some jurisdictions use "percent-good factor" tables that combine trending and depreciation in one factor. In the description of the factors by the issuing agency, usually the state bureau of assessment standards, the claim is made that the tables include "normal" obsolescence. The statement by itself is a contradiction in terms, because nothing is normal about obsolescence, especially economic obsolescence. Industry recessions or general economic downtrends cannot be forecast in advance, let alone with any degree of accuracy that will allow their tabulation.

Some states have guidelines regarding the use of unitary valuations where the assets are parts of an integrated assembly and are employed jointly in the achievement of a common economic goal. Disregarding the status of such assets produces a "fractional appraisal," something that is not acceptable in modern valuation theory and practice. When a plant is not generating a fair rate of return at the value in use level on all the assets employed, and the fair market value of the assembled entity is less than the value in use of all its assets, a downward adjustment is appropriate to reflect this fact. The sum of the values of the parts cannot exceed the value of the whole.

Another area of disagreement between assessors and taxpayers generally is the consideration of intangible assets. Some assessors argue that any intangible assets in a unitary property are actually part of the tangible property if they enhance its value. However, a more carefully reasoned viewpoint is beginning to emerge.

In California at least, a new rule was added to Title 18 of the Administrative Code recognizing intangible assets as separate, nontaxable property. The California Assessment Standards Board is in the process of issuing *Assessors Handbook 502* on advanced valuation, in which the same concepts will hopefully be enunciated and explained more fully. It is expected that other states will follow California's example.

Direct Valuation Procedure

Occasionally, the valuation of a major asset as part of a going concern may not be possible using the unitary method. This is because of the lack of sufficient financial information or the reluctance of the taxpayer to make such information available. In such cases a direct valuation procedure, taking into account most if not all elements of obsolescence, is possible by use of financial theory and analysis.

Consider, for example, a heavy extrusion press owned by the General Services Administration but installed at a manufacturing company's plant and used for the most part by the company for its own production needs. The valuation is needed for possessory interest purposes. Assume that the replacement cost in new condition of the press and all ancillary parts and equipment is $20 million. The normal economic life of the press is 25 years and its current age is 14 years. The WACC in this case is estimated to be the same 12 percent as determined earlier. The repair and maintenance record of the press is available and shows a nearly straight-line increase in maintenance expense over the life of the press. With this information, it is possible to estimate the fair market value of the press in use as part of a going concern.

One valuation perspective is that whoever buys the press for $20 million in new condition does so because he or she is satisfied that during its 25-year anticipated life it will produce such benefits, or income, that will allow recovery of the $20 million investment at the 12 percent expected rate of return. The sum of the present worth of each year's economic income will be equal to the purchase price. If such income can be estimated for each year, the value of the press at age 14 is equal to the present worth of the income during the remaining 11 years. In California, the *Assessors Handbook 581* and *Handbook 581A* contain tables and explanatory text for use of this concept.

This valuation perspective is based on the assumption that the income imputable to the press during the 25 years of its life will be uniform and equal year to year. The problem of valuation becomes a matter similar to the amortization of a $20 million loan at 12 percent through 25 level annual payments; and the value at age 14 is the present worth of an annuity of 11 payments at 12 percent. For example, the $20 million press investment can be recovered through 25 payments of $2.55 million each. The present worth of 11 payments of $2.55 million at 12 percent is $15.14 million and that is the value of the press at age 14.

The assumptions used in this example seem to make economic sense at first glance. However, the example also shows that with only 44 percent of its life remaining, the press still has a value equal to 61 percent of its cost new. The value calculation ignores the matter of increasing repairs and maintenance of the press. The press may still have 11 years of service and revenue generation but each subsequent year's revenue produces less and less on a net basis after consideration of the increasing maintenance costs. In fact, an increase in operating expenses, assuming no external causes of obsolescence and reduction of revenue, is what will bring about the end of the life of the press—when the revenue generated through the service it provides is entirely offset by the cost and expense of providing the service.

Therefore, the income, or net income, generated by the press is highest in the beginning year and zero in the last year. If the cost of repairs and maintenance has been increasing in a straight line over the life of the press, the reduction in net income will be expected be in a straight line also. In that case, the first year net income would be $3,587,600, decreasing in a straight line by $143,500 per year to $1,578,600 by the end of year 14, and to zero by the end of year 25. (Note that if the asset has reached age 14, statistically at least, its remaining life would be expected to be more than 11 years. However, remaining life is not addressed at this time for ease of presentation.[3]) The value of the press at that time will actually be $5.54 million rather than the $15.14 million concluded on the assumption of level and uniform income over the entire 25-year life.

Conclusion

Ad valorem taxation for property tax purposes is an area where financial analysis and concepts of business valuation can and should play an important role. Business valuation is playing an increasingly important role in assessors' concepts of unitary valuation and in the proper consideration of the operating assets as parts of a going-concern business enterprise.

With formal concepts of business valuation gaining ground in the taxation arena generally, assessors will begin to pay more attention to financial and economic theory in the matter of the valuation of the operating assets of major industrial properties. And they will recognize that the valuation of such properties differs significantly from that of residential real estate or even office buildings.

[3]For a more detailed analysis of this subject, see Claire H. Donias, "Appraisal of Major Machinery and Equipment," *Valuation* (journal of the American Society of Appraisers), November 1981, pp. 84–99.

Chapter 14

Economic Damages: Use and Abuse of Business Valuation Concepts

John R. Phillips, CPA/ABV, CFA, and Michael Joseph Wagner, Esq., CPA

Introduction

The estimation of economic damages often requires or may benefit from the use of business valuation procedures. This is particularly true when the litigation involves business lost profits. However, there are some differences between calculating economic damages in a disputed matter and traditional business valuation. This chapter will explain some of these differences as well as many of the similarities between estimating the value of a business and estimating economic damages.

Economic damages are usually calculated as the difference between (1) what a plaintiff business would have earned "but for" the legal violations of the defendant and (2) what the plaintiff business will actually earn. Therefore, unlike traditional business valuation assignments, the damages/valuation analyst typically performs at least two damage analyses or valuations. One analysis is what the company is worth (or would earn) "but for" the legal violations. The second analysis is what the company is worth (or would earn) in the actual world given the impacts of the legal violations on the plaintiff's business.

The discounted cash flow method is probably the most common method used to calculate a plaintiff's lost profits. Typically, a damages expert estimates the difference between (1) the plaintiff's cash flow or other measure of economic income in the "but for" world and (2) the plaintiff's cash flow or economic income in the "actual" world. The difference between these two estimates of economic income is discounted to a present value either at the date of the legal violation or at the estimated date of judgment. In other words, discounted cash flow analysis is used as frequently in economic damage calculations as it is used in business valuation.

On the other hand, economic damages calculations differ from business valuation analyses in the use of *ex post* information in the calculation of economic damages. Courts have permitted the use of a "book of wisdom" of economic information not available until after date of injury. Arguably, the use of information available after the date of injury provides a more accurate estimate of the plaintiff's loss. Therefore, information between the date of injury and the trial date is often considered in developing assumptions as to what would have happened to the plaintiff's business if the legal violations had not occurred.

Another difference between economic damages calculations and a traditional business valuation analysis is the nature of the written report. In many state jurisdictions, no reporting of an expert witness opinion is required. In this type of jurisdiction, the attorney who retains a damages expert should give that expert guidance as to the nature of the report, if any, that the attorney expects. In most federal courts, there is a requirement for experts to submit a report. The content of the expert's report is controlled by the Federal Rules of Civil Procedure No. 26. There is no legal requirement that a business valuation used in a damages report comply with The Appraisal Foundation's *Uniform Standards of Professional Appraisal Practice* or the standards of any other professional organization.

A much-confused concept in economic damages is the income tax effects of the present value discount rate applied against the "but for" estimated economic earnings required to make the plaintiff whole. The general rule in business valuation, to use pretax discount rates to present value pretax cash flows and to use after-tax discount rates to present value after-tax cash flows, is *not* automatic in economic damages calculations. This is because, in most instances, the award of economic damages is a taxable event to the plaintiff. Therefore, to make the plaintiff whole, the analyst should consider the impact of the payment of income taxes on the damages award.

One important consideration when using business valuation methods to estimate economic damages is the duration of the damage period. If the damages expert determines that the loss to the plaintiff is permanent, then traditional business valuation methods may be appropriate to estimate the lost profits to the plaintiff. However, if the damage period is limited in time, then business valuation techniques may not be appropriate, since such valuation methods usually contemplate that the business will continue in perpetuity.

Often, economic damages do not last forever. The plaintiff may have been delayed or lost some current business. However, the plaintiff is often assumed to be able to mitigate future damages and catch up at some future point to where he or she would have been even if the defendant had not violated the plaintiff's legal rights. The damages expert should make an assumption as to whether the plaintiff can recover and how long it will take the plaintiff to recover to the level of profitability in the actual world that the plaintiff would have achieved in the "but for," undamaged world.

Value the Whole or Just a Part?

Economic damages calculations frequently focus on just part of a business, the part alleged to be damaged or lost. Consider the example of a multiproduct manufacturer who has problems with a supplier of a critical part on only one of the many products that the manufacturer makes. The damaged product line makes up only 20 percent of the manufacturer's business. The entire business of the manufacturer is not damaged. Although a material portion of the manufacturer's business is impacted, it is usually not necessary or appropriate to value the entire business. In contrast, business valuations often focus broadly on the whole business.

However, business valuation methods can be used even when the defendant's actions or inaction affects only a portion of the plaintiff's business. An estimate of the damage suffered by only one of a manufacturer's many products can be accomplished by analyzing the discounted cash flow of that one product line of the company.

A common mistake can occur when valuing only the damaged or lost part of a business. For example, elements of expense or capital investment may be left out or exaggerated. As a result, the plaintiff may attempt to claim that damages equal the gross profit on lost sales, improperly ignoring incremental selling and general and administrative expenses, as well as incremental investment.

Business valuation methods provide useful reasonableness checks on damages. A fair use of business valuation methods to estimate damages is to prepare two models of the entire business: one actual and damaged, the other but-for the violation and undamaged. The undamaged entity may be modeled by making an adjustment for the incremental damages on the actual financial statements of the damaged company. By comparing the two sets of financial statements, a damages expert may conclude whether the undamaged statement of operations and the undamaged financial position of the whole company appear reasonable.

For example, the expert can conclude whether profit margins and turnover for the undamaged entity fall within a reasonable range for the industry. Similarly, the damages expert can conclude whether the undamaged entity provides for sufficient capital investment to support the projected sales growth, in comparison with the industry.

It is usually helpful to compare the future projections for the damaged and undamaged companies. One worthwhile test is to see whether the projections differ only to the extent that the plaintiff is unable to mitigate or avoid damages, without incurring undue burden or risk, after the cessation of the violations and the receipt of a compensatory award for past damages. Although the plaintiff has the duty to mitigate or avoid damages, the defendant bears the burden of proving the reasonable extent of mitigation. In line with mitigation, the damages expert should reach a conclusion regarding the period required for the plaintiff's recovery.

The damages estimate's limitation on future performance contrasts with a business valuation projection of future performance in perpetuity. In the example above, when we compare the damaged and undamaged future financial statements, at some future date they converge, leaving no further damages. Justifying the projection of damages in perpetuity, as in a discounted cash flow analysis for a business valuation, requires proof that the plaintiff's business has been destroyed. In this circumstance, damages may be limited to the fair market value of the business on the date of loss.[1]

Use All Valuation Approaches?

Business valuation standards emphasize that all approaches should be considered and the reasons for the inclusion or absence of each approach should be explained. By instinct, valuation analysts want to estimate

---

[1] Robert L. Dunn, *Recovery of Damages for Lost Profits*, 5th ed. (Westport, CT: Lawpress Corporation, 1998), p. 500.

damages using an asset-based, market, and income approach. To make matters worse, the valuation analyst may weight the damages approaches mechanically by the asset-based, market, and income approach.

Depending on the facts available to the damages expert, more than one approach may be used to estimate damages, but there is no legal requirement to do so. As a reasonableness check on the primary damages calculation, a damages expert may use a secondary approach. This secondary approach will be described only as a reasonableness check and not as an alternative damages figure to be awarded by the trier of fact.

Damages studies do not focus on valuation approaches. In a civil suit, the trier of fact focuses on three elements of proof:

1. That a violation of a legal right has occurred.
2. That this violation caused damages to occur.
3. That the amount of the damages caused by the violation has been estimated with reasonable accuracy.

Business valuation methods are relevant to estimating the amount of the damages. However, the key question to address in estimating the amount of damages is: Do the assumptions and methods used accurately portray the full extent of the changes caused by the violation, consistent with the findings of fact and law by the court? The business valuation methods, by which these changes are reduced to a present value of damages, or a fair market value, are part of—but not the principal focus of—the examination.

What do we mean by the terms *valuation approach* and *damages approach*? Business valuation approaches include all the methods available to benchmark the financial statements to present or fair market value. These may include any of the methods used under the asset-based approach to valuation, the market approach, and the income approach, such as the direct capitalization and discounted cash flow methods. On the other hand, damages approaches include the methods used to demonstrate the fact and amount of injury.

There are three basic categories for damages approaches:

1. The before and after approach.
2. The yardstick approach.
3. The economic modeling approach.

As examples of the before and after approach, a damages expert may compare the plaintiff's experience during the damage period to the plaintiff's prior experience, to the plaintiff's subsequent experience, or to the defendant's subsequent experience.[2] As examples of the yardstick approach, a damages expert may compare the plaintiff's experience during the damage period to the plaintiff's experience at other undamaged locations or in other undamaged product markets, to the comparable experience of others, to industry averages, or to projections prepared prior to the violations.[3]

[2] Dunn, *Recovery of Damages for Lost Profits*, 5th ed., pp. 396–401, 416–421.
[3] Ibid., pp. 401–416, 422–427.

Consider two business valuation analysts, A and B. Analyst A estimates damages by asking the plaintiff, "How much did you lose?" The plaintiff tells analyst A the amount lost and A incorporates this amount into an asset-based, a market, and an income approach to damages. On the other hand, Analyst B estimates damages using two different benchmarks: (1) by comparing sales of plaintiff's undamaged product lines with sales of the damaged product lines, and (2) by comparing plaintiff's actual sales before and after the damage period with the sales of undamaged competitors. Analyst B calculates damages by valuing the earnings differences from each damages approach using only one method—that is, the discounted cash flow method.

Do we consider analyst A's work more compelling than Analyst B's because A considered all business valuation approaches? Of course not. Analyst A simply relied upon plaintiff's word, which is fine so long as the reliance is admitted, and the plaintiff proves that portion of the damages calculation to the satisfaction of the court. On the other hand, Analyst B provided some independent, objective measures of injury that either supported or refuted the plaintiff's claims. The methods used to reduce the injury to present value or fair market value are not of primary importance. Business valuations implicitly assume that income statements and statements of financial condition may be objectively prepared or adjusted to include everything of value to the satisfaction of all parties. Business valuations focus more on the methods used to benchmark the adjusted financial statements to market value than on the adjustments themselves.

In contrast, in a damages calculation, the business valuation methods are only one part. A damages calculation places more emphasis on the methods and evidence used to measure the amount and fact of damages. Damages analysis focuses on how much of the income statement or statement of position should be included in damages. Business valuation comes second. Therefore, in assigning weight to different business valuation approaches, the damages expert places more emphasis on the source and strength of the evidence of loss, rather than feeling compelled to give at least some weight to each of the asset-based, market, and income approaches to value.

Value before or after Taxes?

The Rule of Thumb

In theory, investors estimate the market value of a business after adjusting for any taxes payable by the business. In other words, investors value only the net after-tax cash flows available to them. In a business valuation, to calculate this net after-corporate-tax value using a direct capitalization or a discounted cash flow method, the analyst discounts after-tax cash flows by after-tax rates of return. In some cases, the analyst may discount before-tax cash flows by before-tax rates of return.

However, after-tax values and after-tax rates of return can be observed readily in markets. Either way, in a business valuation, the income tax status of the cash flows always matches the income tax status of the discount or capitalization rate.

In contrast to the after-tax market value of a business, a damages award typically includes the taxes payable on the award. In other words, because most damages awards are taxable to the plaintiff, in order to restore the after-tax loss of value sustained by the plaintiff, the damages award should include both the after-tax loss of value and the taxes payable (if any) on the award. One way that this is achieved in practice is to mismatch the tax status of cash flows and discount rates. The approach may appear to be counterintuitive, but it is theoretically sound.

Exhibit 14–1 illustrates how this rule of thumb works. At the top of the right column, we assume that one year after the date of trial, lost profits before tax are projected to equal $100. If income taxes will be paid at a marginal rate of 40 percent at the end of this year, after-tax lost profits will equal $60. Next, assume that the company's lost project was expected to earn an after-tax rate of return of 12 percent, at the bottom of the second column from the left. As shown at the top of the column, the after-tax rate of return has been converted to a pretax reinvestment rate for the project. Now, what before-tax amount should be awarded at trial to reimburse the plaintiff for the $60 after-tax loss suffered one year after trial? The amount, $89.29, at the top of the left column, should be awarded. You can check the amount by following the calculation along the arrows from $89.29.

Income taxes will be paid on the award at 40 percent, resulting in a net after-tax award of $53.57, at the bottom of the first column. In turn, this amount would be invested at a before-tax reinvestment rate of 20 percent to produce $64.29 before taxes at the end of the year, at the top of the third column. At the end of the year, income taxes are paid only on the increase in value from $53.57 to $64.29 [$40\% \times (\$64.29 - \$53.57) = \$4.29$]. The amount that remains after income tax at the end of the year is $60 ($64.29 – $4.29), equal to the loss to be reimbursed, the projected after-tax loss at the end of the year.

Exhibit 14–1

Pretax versus After-Tax Damage Analysis

		Taxable Award for Future Loss			Lost Profits Damages
	Amount Awarded Today	Rate of Return	Future Value of Award in 1 Year		Future Loss in 1 Year
Pretax amount	$ 89.29	20.00%	$	64.29	$ 100.00
Income tax rate	40.00%	40.00%		40.00%	40.00%
After-tax amount	$ 53.57	12.00%	$	60.00	= $ 60.00

Exhibit 14–2

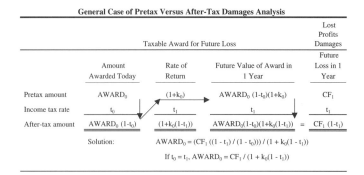

General Case of Pretax Versus After-Tax Damages Analysis

| | | Taxable Award for Future Loss | | Lost Profits Damages |
	Amount Awarded Today	Rate of Return	Future Value of Award in 1 Year	Future Loss in 1 Year
Pretax amount	$AWARD_0$	$(1+k_0)$	$AWARD_0\,(1-t_0)(1+k_0)$	CF_1
Income tax rate	t_0	t_1	t_1	t_1
After-tax amount	$AWARD_0\,(1-t_0)$	$(1+k_0(1-t_1))$	$AWARD_0(1-t_0)(1+k_0(1-t_1))$ =	$CF_1\,(1-t_1)$

Solution: $AWARD_0 = (CF_1\,((1-t_1)\,/\,(1-t_0)))\,/\,(1+k_0(1-t_1))$

If $t_0 = t_1$, $AWARD_0 = CF_1\,/\,(1+k_0(1-t_1))$

Now in Exhibit 14–2, we substitute variable names in place of the previous amounts. Working through the algebra, we solve for the before-tax amount of the award, at the bottom of Exhibit 14–2. In our example, if income tax rates do not change, then the before-tax amount of the award equals the amount of the future before-tax loss, discounted by the after-tax rate of return. This is the rule of thumb for damages: "Discount before-tax cash flows by after-tax rates of return." You may also have heard the rule of thumb stated more crudely, "Never consider income taxes in damages."

Complications to the Rule of Thumb

This rule of thumb is almost always followed in state superior courts and in federal courts. One author on the income tax treatment of damages cites the following passage from *Hall* v. *Chicago & N.W. Railway Company*,[4] to explain the legal reasoning that supports the rule of thumb.

> It is a general principle of law that in the trial of a lawsuit the status of the parties is immaterial. Thus, what the plaintiff does with an award, or how the defendant acquires the money with which to pay the award, is of no concern to the court or jury. Similarly, whether the plaintiff has to pay a tax on the award is a matter that concerns only the plaintiff and the government. The tort feasor has no interest is such questions. And if the jury were to mitigate the damages of the plaintiff by reason of income tax exemption accorded him, then the very Congressional intent of the income tax law to give an injured party a tax benefit would be nullified.[5]

Following the rule of thumb "Never consider income taxes in damages" is adequate for the run-of-the-mill, commercial damages case. However, depending on the facts and circumstances, the court may weigh evidence concerning the real economic effect of income taxes,

---

[4]*Hall* v. *Chicago & N.W. Railway* Company, 5 Ill. 2d 135, 125 N.E. 2d 77 (1955), 50 ALR 2d 661.

[5]Gerald D. Martin, *Determining Economic Damages* (Costa Mesa, CA: James Publishing, 1996), pp. 8-1–8-3.

irrespective of the common legal practice. Legal counsel may want to consider the opportunity to argue for exceptions to the rule. Keep in mind that a damages award based on this rule of thumb will resemble the actual economic loss, plus actual income taxes payable on the award, only when certain assumptions are met.

First, as noted in the formulas at the bottom of Exhibit 14–2, a damages award based on this rule of thumb resembles the actual economic loss, plus actual income taxes payable, only when permanent income tax rates remain constant over time. However, tax laws and permanent income tax rates sometimes change.

In *Polaroid Corporation* v. *Eastman Kodak Company*,[6] Kodak presented the argument that the plaintiff's damages calculations overcompensated Polaroid for its economic loss, because of the change in income tax rates during the damage period. Kodak's experts pointed out that the plaintiff's pretax losses would have been taxed at higher permanent rates than existed at the date of trial. Plaintiff actually would pay less in income tax than the amount of tax included in the pretax award, providing Polaroid with a windfall of approximately $80 million. The court rejected Kodak's argument; however, in the future, when large amounts are at stake, defense counsel will likely again consider making this argument for an exception to the rule.

Second, to complicate the rule of thumb, damages are not always taxable. Damages awards for personal physical injuries are exempt from income tax.[7] For business, in those rare instances where the taxpayer can support the treatment of damages as a recovery of capital, then damages are exempt from income tax to the extent of the taxpayer's basis in the lost capital asset.[8]

Third, our analysis of the rule of thumb assumed that the plaintiff was a C corporation. In Exhibit 14–1, when the plaintiff is a C corporation, the after-tax rates of return are the same ones used in business valuation. In other words, the rates of return are those available to investors in the financial markets after corporate income taxes. However, if the plaintiff in Exhibit 14–1 is an individual, a partnership, or an S corporation, the rates of return earned on investments in the market may be viewed as before personal income taxes. The true after-tax rate of return for an individual *may* best be expressed after deducting personal income taxes as well as corporate income taxes.

Fourth, not all areas of law treat taxes in this same way. For example, damages for personal injury are treated differently if brought under a federal statute than if brought under state law. In *Norfolk & Western Railway Co.* v. *Liepelt*,[9] the Supreme Court ruled that, in calculating damages in a Federal Employer's Liability Act (FELA) case, earnings should be estimated on an after-tax basis.[10] In *Jones & Laughlin Steel*

[6] *Polariod Corporation* v. *Eastman Kodak Company*, 16 U.S.P.Q. 2d 1481 (D. Mass., 1990, as corr. 1991).
[7] *1998 U.S. Master Tax Guide* (Chicago: CCH Incorporated, 1997), ¶702, p. 193.
[8] Robert W. Wood, *Taxation of Damage Awards and Settlements* (San Francisco: Tax Institute, 1991), p. 4-4.
[9] *Norfolk & Western Railway Co.* v. *Liepelt*, 444 U.S. 490 (1980).
[10] Martin, *Determining Economic Damages*, p. 8-2.
[11] *Jones & Laughlin Steel Corp.* v. *Pfeifer*, 462 U.S. 523 (1983).

Corp. v. *Pfeifer*,[11] the court ruled that, since earnings are estimated in after-tax terms, the discount rate should be the after-tax rate of return.[12]

Note that, in the FELA cases above, the personal injury awards are exempt from federal income tax. However, the interest income accumulating on the award is taxable. Therefore, in *Shaw* v. *U.S.*,[13] the Ninth Circuit Court of Appeals ruled that, since income taxes are deducted from earnings, the award should be increased to pay the income taxes on it. In another example, recall that the after-tax rates of return for damages to an individual *may* be best expressed after deducting personal taxes as well as corporate taxes. However, in *Trevino* v. *U.S.*,[14] the Ninth Circuit ruled that tax-free municipals are a suspect surrogate for after-tax yield.[15] Remember that these cases all involve personal injuries and tax-exempt damage awards.

Finally, a more direct way to ensure that a plaintiff is made whole is to estimate all the cash flows on an after-tax basis, use an after-tax discount rate to bring the cash flows to present value, and then gross up the after-tax damages amount to a pretax damage award using the current effective or marginal income tax rate of the plaintiff. It is not correct to assume that if the economic damages award is before taxes, you can completely ignore income taxes by using pretax cash flows and discount these cash flows at a pretax discount rate in order to make the plaintiff whole. Although this appears to make sense intuitively, it is not supported in practice: the plaintiff will not be in the same position after paying taxes on the damages award as he or she would have been if the legal violation had never occurred. However, let us return to the typical, taxable lost profits claim and the rule of thumb.

A Typical Lost Profits Claim

For the typical lost profits claim, the damages award is taxable and the court will typically follow the rule of thumb "Discount before-tax cash flows by after-tax rates of return." Given these restrictions, what is the correct way to define both the pretax loss and the after-tax rate of return? We will address this question with another example, below.

Exhibit 14–3 shows an income and cash flow statement for a hypothetical lost project. The loss is assumed to occur in a single period, one year after the date of trial. The example is constructed so that the after-tax net present value of the project at the date of trial is $1,200. The cost of debt is 8 percent and cost of equity is 15 percent.

We can solve for the correct definition of cash flow by starting with the after-tax definitions of cash flow and the after-tax cost of capital typically used by business valuation professionals. There are several possi-

---

[12] Harold R. Dilbeck, "The Time Value of Money," *Litigation Services Handbook*, Peter B. Frank, Michael J. Wagner, and Roman L. Weil, eds. (New York: John Wiley & Sons, 1997), p. 38.2.

[13]*Shaw* v. *U.S.*, 741 F.2d 1201 (9th Cir. 1984).

[14] *Trevino* v. *U.S.*, 804 F.2d 1201 (9th Cir. 1986).

[15] Martin, *Determining Economic Damages*, p. 8–3.

Exhibit 14–3

Lost Project Example

Statement of Cash Flows	Assumptions	For the Period Ending at the Date of	
		Trial	Future Loss
Cash flow from operating activities			
Revenue			$ 10,000
Cash operating costs			$ (7,001)
Depreciation			$ (750)
Earnings before interest and tax (EBIT)			$ 2,249
Interest expense			$ (24)
Earnings before tax			$ 2,225
Taxes	$t_c = 40\%$		$ (890)
Net income			$ 1,335
Add back depreciation			$ 750
Increase (decrease) in working capital			$ —
Subtotal—cash flow from operations			$ 2,085
Cash flow from investing activities			
Proceeds from sale of fixed assets			$ —
Investment in fixed assets			$ (750)
Subtotal—cash flow from investing			$ (750)
Cash flow from financing activities			
Debt	$k_d = 8\%$	$ 300	$ (300)
Equity	$k_e = 15\%$	$ 900	$ (1,035)
Subtotal—cash flow from financing		$ 1,200	$ (1,335)
Net cash flow		$ 1,200	$ —

ble combined definitions of cash flow and cost of capital that will produce a correct after-tax value. However, we have selected the most common definitions.

First, for the definition of the after-tax rate of return, let us select the after-tax weighted average cost of capital ($WACC_{AT}$). Written in symbols, we combine the cost of debt (k_d), the cost of equity (k_e), the market value of debt (D), and the market value of equity (E) in the formula for $WACC_{AT}$:

$$\text{WACC}_{AT} = \left[k_d(1 - tax\ rate) \times \frac{D}{D + E} \right] + \left[k_e \times \frac{E}{D + E} \right]$$

Business valuation professionals typically use the following after-tax definition of net cash flow, that is the earnings before interest and tax (*EBIT*) times the quantity, 1 minus the income tax rate, plus depreciation, minus the increase in working capital, plus any decrease in working capital, and minus the required future capital investment. Below, written in algebraic symbols, we combine *EBIT*, depreciation (*depr*), the decrease (increase) in working capital (*WC*), and future investment (*I*) in the formula for after-tax net cash flow:

$$\text{After-tax net cash flow} = \left[EBIT\ (1-t) \right] + depr \pm WC - 1$$

However, for damages, we need a definition for the before-tax net cash flow in order to follow the rule of thumb. To create this definition, we divide both sides of the equation above by 1 minus the income tax rate $(1-t)$. The result is the equation for before-tax net cash flow.

$$\text{Before-tax net cash flow} = EBIT + \frac{depr}{(1-t)} \overset{\pm}{\mp} \frac{WC}{(1-t)} - \frac{I}{(1-t)}$$

The formula is considerably simplified if we make two assumptions. First, let us assume, as in our example in Exhibit 14–3, that the lost project encompasses a complete operating cycle. Then the net change in working capital is equal to zero. Second, let us assume, as in Exhibit 14–3, that the amount of depreciation is equal to the amount of required future investment. Then these terms cancel one another. After making these assumptions, all that remains of the formula above is:

Before-tax net cash flow = Earnings before interest and tax (EBIT)

Now we can apply these formulas to our example in Exhibit 14–3 and demonstrate that they work. In Exhibit 14–4, we discount earnings before interest and tax, $2,249, by the weighted average cost of capital, 12.45 percent. The result is the proper amount of a before-tax damages award, $2,000. In Exhibit 14–4, after income taxes are paid on the award at 40 percent, the after-tax proceeds from the damages award, $1,200, exactly match the after-tax present value of the lost project at the date of trial in Exhibit 14–3. In other words, given our assumptions, the plaintiff is placed in the same position as if the legal violation had never occurred.

This is not the only way that damages may be correctly computed. In the example above, we assumed that the marginal capital for the lost project was comprised of both debt and equity in this particular blend.

Exhibit 14–4

Present Value of Future Lost Profits

Calculation of Damages Award	Assumptions	For Period Ending at Date of	
		Trial	Future Loss
Before-tax loss			
Earnings before interest and tax			$ 2,249
Add depreciation / $(1-t_c)$			$ 1,250
Decrease (increase) in working capital / $(1-t_c)$			$ —
Less cash flow for future investing activities / $(1-t_c)$			$ (1,250)
Before-tax net cash flow			$ 2,249
After-tax discount rate			
Weighted average cost of capital (WACC)			
= k_e [Equity / (Debt + Equity)] + k_d $(1-t_c)$ [Debt / (Debt + Equity)]	WACC = 12.45%		
Value of award		$ 2,000	
Less taxes on award	t_c = 40%	$ (800)	
After-tax proceeds from award		$ 1,200	
Repay debt		$ (300)	
Repay equity		$ (900)	
Net gain (loss) from loss and award		$ —	

Under different facts and circumstances, an analyst might find that the marginal capital for the lost project was comprised entirely of the lost market value of equity. The choice of an equity value versus an enterprise (or invested capital) value is a question of fact to be determined by the expert. If an equity value is appropriate, then the after-tax cost of capital is equal to the cost of equity (k_e) alone. The definition of the before-tax loss will remain the same; however, when discounted by the cost of equity alone, the amount of the award will usually be lower.

In addition, we could have started with different definitions for the cost of capital and the after-tax net cash flow that, after adjustment to a before-tax basis, produce the same amount. Examples of possible matched pairs of definitions for the cost of capital and the after-tax net cash flow are presented in Exhibit 14–5. Note that in Exhibit 14–5 investment includes working capital. We leave it as an exercise for the reader to adjust these definitions to a before-tax basis.

Value Only the Future? Know Only the Past?

Value Only the Future?

Damages claims differ from business valuations in another respect. In a typical business, one values only the future economic benefits associated with the business at an agreed date of value. On the other hand, to compute damages, one must determine both the past and the future losses, and then determine the total amount of loss as of the date of trial. This raises a host of issues that are not considered in a typical business valuation assignment.

First, economists disagree about how past damages should be han-

Exhibit 14–5

**Alternative Definitions
of Cash Flow and Cost of Capital**

Definition of Cash Flow	Definition of Cost of Capital
[Earnings before interest and tax (EBIT) x (1 - tax rate)] + depreciation +/- investment	$k_d (1 - t) [D / (D + E)] + k_e [E / (D + E)]$
Net Income + depreciation +/- investment + [(1 - tax rate) x interest expense]	Same as above.
Net Income + depreciation +/- investment + interest expense	$k_d [D / (D + E)] + k_e [E / (D + E)]$
Net income + depreciation +/- investment +/- debt principal	k_e

k_d = Marginal cost of debt, market yield to maturity
k_e = Marginal cost of equity
D = Market value of debt
E = Market value of equity
t = Marginal income tax rate

dled. There are two competing schools of thought on this subject. One school claims that damages should be valued as of the date of injury. This type of calculation is called *ex ante* damages. *Ex ante* means "from before."

To compute total damages, to the value at the date of injury, the analyst may add interest damages, at the prejudgment interest rate, up to the date of trial. Within this school, there is disagreement about what the prejudgment interest should be. One faction argues that the defendant's unsecured borrowing rate is the correct prejudgment interest rate.[16] Another faction argues that the short-term risk-free rate is the correct prejudgment interest rate.[17] Now back to the second school of thought.

The second school claims that damages should be valued at the date of trial.[18] This type of calculation is called *ex post* damages. *Ex post* means "from after." *Ex post* damages use all information available to the date of trial and replicate the lost cash flow from the project up to the date of trial. In an *ex post* damages calculation, we calculate the actual loss in each year and add interest damages at the prejudgment interest rate up to the date of trial. Each of these approaches is illustrated in Exhibit 14–6.

The economic argument for *ex post* damages can be presented with the following example. The solution is found in the put/call parity table, which for our purposes we will call the damages payoff table, in Exhibit 14–7. The first column of the damages payoff table shows that, on the date of injury, the *ex ante* and the *ex post* damages comprise the same

Exhibit 14–6

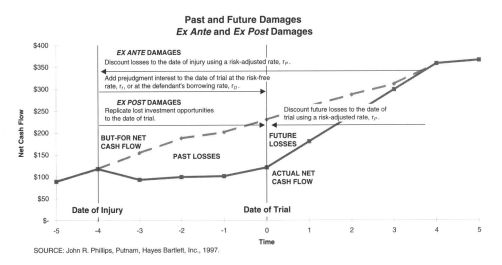

SOURCE: John R. Phillips, Putnam, Hayes Bartlett, Inc., 1997.

---

[16] James M. Patell, Roman L. Weil, and Mark A. Wolfsen, "Accumulating Damages in Litigation: The Roles of Uncertainty and Interest Rates," *Journal of Legal Studies*, Vol. XI, June 1982, pp. 341–364.

[17] Franklin M. Fisher and R. Craig Romaine, "Janis Joplin's Yearbook and the Theory of Damages," *Journal of Accounting, Auditing and Finance*, Winter 1990, pp. 145–157.

[18] Konrad Bonsack, "Damages Assessment, Janis Joplin's Yearbook, and the Pie-Powder Court," *George Mason University Law Review*, Fall 1990, pp. 1–26.

amount, $5. The amounts at the date of trial, however, may be quite different. At the date of trial, *ex ante* damages will be equal to $5 with interest at the prejudgment interest rate. At the date of trial, *ex post* damages will be equal to the value of the lost project, Y_t, an amount arrived at under a separate analysis.

The actual amount of damages collected by the plaintiff will be different too. The middle column of Exhibit 14–7 shows the amount of damages collected if the actual value of the lost project is less than the amount of *ex ante* damages. In this case, because we assumed that only the actual benefits from the lost project would be available to pay damages, the maximum amount that can be collected will be Y_t. This is exactly the amount of *ex post* damages, but less than (or equal to) the amount of *ex ante* damages. The economic effect is the same as if the plaintiff receiving *ex ante* damages had written a put option on the value of the lost project with an exercise price equal to *ex ante* damages. If the actual value of the lost project is less than *ex ante* damages, then the put option is exercised against the plaintiff with *ex ante* damages.

The third column of Exhibit 14–7 shows the payoff if the actual value of the lost project is greater than the amount of *ex ante* damages. In this case, the *ex ante* plaintiff received only the amount of *ex ante* damages, no matter how large the value of the lost project has actually become. The economic effect is the same as if the plaintiff with *ex ante* damages gave the defendant a call option on the value of the lost project. If the actual value of the lost project is greater than *ex ante* damages, then the defendant exercises the call option by paying *ex ante* damages, $5 r_f, and pocketing the difference, $Y_t - \$5\ r_f$, the call option payoff.

On the other hand, if the plaintiff received *ex post* damages, the defendant would pay Y_t and no profit would remain for the defendant. Because of the uncertainty of collection, given these assumptions, the value at the date of injury of *ex post* damages is always greater than the value of *ex ante* damages. In addition, unlike *ex ante* damages, *ex post* damages do not provide a call option payoff to the defendant, an incentive to commit the wrongful act in spite of the payment of *ex ante* damages.

Consider Only Information at the Date of Value?

When conducting business valuations, analysts exclude consideration of any information not made public prior to the valuation date. This makes sense, because market values are determined this way. Damages calculation is different. There is a debate among academics on this topic, but typically damages are determined by giving some weight to all information available at the date of trial. Evidence for the existence and amount of damages unfolds from the date of the damage forward.

Valuation procedures are abused in litigation when damages experts dogmatically exclude information made public after the valuation date. In one instance, a valuation analyst valued a company on a liquidation basis as of the date of injury and refused to consider subsequent evidence. Within that subsequent period, the company was sold at a premium price. The subsequent events revealed that the liquidation assumption used by

Exhibit 14–7

Ex Ante Damages Versus *Ex Post* Damages

Problem

The defendant has stolen a business opportunity from the plaintiff. On the day
of the theft, the fair market value of plaintiff's lost opportunity was $5. By the date of
trial, at time T, the defendant will have received the actual economic benefits from
plaintiff's business opportunity. At the date of trial, the actual benefits can take on
any value, Y_T, but the actual benefits comprise the defendant's only asset from which
damages will be paid.

The court may award either *ex ante* damages, which are equal to the value of
plaintiff's lost opportunity on the date of loss plus prejudgment interest, or *ex post*
damages, which are equal to the actual benefits that result from the lost opportunity.
Which damages award will be fairest to the plaintiff?

Solution: Damages Payoff Table

	At the Date of Injury	At the Date of Trial: If $Y_T \le 5\,r_f^T$	At the Date of Trial: If $Y_T > 5\,r_f^T$
Ex ante damages plus interest	$5	$5\,r_f^T$	$5\,r_f^T$
Less written put option	$-P_Y(5\,r_f^T)$	$-(5\,r_f^T - Y^T)$	0
Value of *Ex ante* damages	$5 - P_Y(5\,r_f^T)$	Y^T	$5\,r_f^T$
Call option	$C_Y(5\,r_f^T)$	0	$(Y^T - 5\,r_f^T)$
Value of *Ex Post* damages	$5	Y^T	Y^T

T = The number of years between the date of injury and the date of trial.

r_f^T = 1 + the prejudgment interest rate, compounded for T years.

$5 = The fair market value of lst business opportunity at the time of injury.

$5\,r_f^T$ = The amount of *ex ante* damages payable at the date of trial, equal to the fair
market value of the lost opportunity at the date of injury plus prejudgement
interest compounded to the date of trial.

Y_T = The amount of *ex post* damages payable at the date of trial, equal to the
value of the actual economic benefits that result from the lost project by the
date of trial.

$P_Y(5\,r_f^T)$ = The value of a put option written against the value of the lost business
opportunity, with an exercise price of $5\,r_f^T$ and an expiration date of T.

$C_Y(5\,r_f^T)$ = The value of a call option written against the value of the lost business
opportunity, with an exercise price of $5\,r_f^T$ and an expiration date of T.

the analyst at the date of injury was probably incorrect.

In disputes concerning the fair market value of failed mergers and
acquisitions, a common abuse of business valuation theory is to claim
that no documents should be produced from the period after the transaction has closed, because none of this information was available as of
that date. For example, the seller of a subsidiary business or product

line might argue that he or she should not have to produce any financial records prepared after the closing because they were unavailable at the date of value. However, prior to the date of value, the financial statements and books of the seller, particularly internal statements used to manage product lines or segments of the business, are typically loaded with accrual estimates for revenue, product returns, marketing and selling expenses, and distribution expenses. After the date of value, the subsequent reversals and corrections of these accrual estimates are available only on the books of the seller and cannot be known by the buyer unless produced in discovery. Once they are produced, an expert can estimate whether the errors in the accruals were material and either were known or should have been known or knowable by the seller at the close of the transaction.

Projected or Expected Cash Flows

There are areas of potential abuse that apply both to business valuation and to economic damages. One such abuse is to value projected cash flows without reflecting the true likelihood that these projections actually can be achieved. To comply with the assumptions used in the economic model for present value, the *projected* cash flows being discounted should be adjusted to reflect the *expected values* of the future cash flows

Exhibit 14–8

Risk Parity
Expected Cash Flow, Expected Rate of Return, and Time
ex Post Damages

Fact Pattern

In period 0, the Defendant destroyed the Plaintiff's opportunity to pursue the lost project, after Plaintiff had invested $500, but before any product development had been conducted. The trial is held at the end of period 3. The statutory prejudgment interest rate is 5%. How would *ex post* damages be calculated?

					Projected Cash Flows at Date of Trial				
	Phase I				Phase II				
Ex Post Damages at Date of Trial:	0	1	2	3	4	5	Terminal Value		
	Date of Injury		Date of Trial						
Projected Cash Flows	$ (514)	$ 100	$ 200	$ 300	$ 400	$ 500	$ 3,333		
x Probability of Success at Time 3	100%	20%	20%	20%	20%	20%	20%		
Expected Value of Cash Flows at Time 3	$ (514)	20	40	60	80	100	667		
x Present Value Factor for 15%		100.00%	100.00%	86.96%	75.61%	65.75%	65.75%		
Present Value of Lost Project at Time 3		$ 20	$ 40	$ 52	$ 60	$ 66	$ 438		
Prejudgment Interest at 5%		$ 1	$ -						
Total Damages at Date of Trial			$ 678						
	$514	20	40	60	80	767			
		87%	76%	66%	57%	50%			
	$514	17	30	39	46	381			

from the project. The effect is illustrated in the example in Exhibit 14–8.

In Exhibit 14–8, the projected cash flows do not equal the expected value of the cash flows, because Phase I, the product development, had only a 20 percent chance of success. If the plaintiff offers the projected cash flows as evidence of loss at trial, and the actual success of the product development cannot be determined without speculation, then the projected cash flows should be reduced to their expected value. The plaintiff can exaggerate economic damages by assuming the product development in Phase I was successful and ignoring other possibilities.

Differences in Reporting Requirements

Expert opinions concerning economic damages have reporting requirements that are set by the court. State and federal courts have different rules. Each court may have local rules that differ from other jurisdictions. The most uniform and widely used rules are applied in federal courts. These rules are specified in the Federal Rules of Civil Procedure (FRCP).

Under the FRCP, an expert in economic damages or business valuation should provide a written report that describes the opinions that the expert will offer at trial. Generally, the rules require that the expert list all the opinions to be rendered at trial and all the bases for these opinions in the report. A literal reading of the rules requires that each and every reason that the expert has for each opinion must be explained; otherwise the expert runs the risk of not being allowed to testify about any unlisted reason at trial. The bases for an expert's opinion may include all the assumptions the expert is making to reach his or her conclusions. The bases may also include all the facts that support the assumptions used in reaching the expert's conclusions. If the only basis for the expert's opinion is the judgment of the expert, then this should be disclosed.

The FRCP also requires that the report contain a list of all the documents considered by the expert in reaching his or her opinions. The operative word in this requirement is "considered." This is a broader concept than documents "relied upon." Documents considered should include any that the expert looked at in connection with the assignment. There is no requirement that the documents be produced with the report, particularly if they are documents that have been previously produced by one of the parties to the litigation.

Frequently documents produced by parties in litigation are stamped with a unique number so that each document can be uniquely identified. One typical numbering system is called the Bates Stamp. If the documents considered by the expert are Bates-stamped, then a listing of a description of the documents and the documents' Bates Stamp numbers will satisfy the disclosure requirement. If the damages expert has considered documents not produced by a party but collected by the expert instead, there should be a sufficient description of the documents so that the opposing side can understand what the expert did consider in reaching his or her opinions. It is a good practice to produce these documents with the expert report, particularly if the documents are not publicly available, so that a proper foundation can be made for the expert opinions.

The FRCP also requires disclosure of a list of all cases in which the expert has testified in either deposition or trial in the last 4 years and any publication authored by the expert in the last 10 years. Finally, the expert is required to disclose how much he or she has been paid to prepare the report. Some attorneys and experts interpret this last requirement to require only a disclosure of the billing rate of the expert.

There is no legal requirement, in either the FRCP or any state rules of civil procedure, that expert reports comply with the *Uniform Standards of Professional Appraisal Practice* (USPAP) put forward by The Appraisal Foundation, or with the standards propounded by other professional organizations, such as the American Institute of Certified Public Accountants (AICPA), the American Society of Appraisers, the Institute of Business Appraisers, and the National Association of Certified Valuation Analysts. The question of how professional standards should be addressed in litigation has been a topic of concern for all these organizations. For example, the AICPA Professional Standards provide an exemption from other standards for work prepared for litigation. The AICPA exempted experts in litigation from other standards because experts in litigation are subject to thorough examination by all the parties at interest. In contrast to the litigation setting, other AICPA standards apply to situations in which parties may use a report without the opportunity to fully examine the expert.

A similar debate is currently taking place in the business valuation profession. Many business valuation analysts are concerned about the provisions in USPAP, especially those concerning departing from compliance. Many valuation analysts are also concerned that USPAP and appraisal standards, in general, do not clearly distinguish between, or define, (1) a business valuation that constitutes an appraisal, subject to USPAP and other professional appraisal standards, and (2) a business valuation prepared for a financial analysis that does not constitute an appraisal, or is not subject to these standards.

Certain portions of the recordkeeping provisions in the Ethics Rule of USPAP, as follows, also concern analysts:

> The workfile must include . . . true copies of any written reports, . . . summaries of any oral reports or testimony, or a transcript of testimony . . . An appraiser must retain the workfile for a period of at least five (5) years after preparation or at least two (2) years after final disposition of any judicial proceeding in which testimony was given, whichever period expires last . . . .[19]

It is not common practice for damages experts to keep copies of their reports, their prior deposition transcripts, or trial testimony transcripts,

---

[19] Appraisal Standards Board, "Second Exposure Draft of Proposed Revisions to USPAP" (Washington, DC: The Appraisal Foundation, June 23, 1998), pp. 7–8.

after the final disposition of a litigation matter. By final disposition, we mean that the parties have reached a binding settlement, or the court has issued a verdict and judgment and no avenues remain for appeal. Documents are always retained with matters that are pending; however, these are confidential because of the ongoing nature of the disputes. Typically, document retention is governed by the client's instructions and by confidentiality agreements. It appears, however, that in the absence of any legal proscription against the release of these documents, any damages study that an expert claims to have prepared in accordance with USPAP will be kept available in compliance with the Ethics Rule. In any subsequent litigation, opposing counsel will certainly demand that these documents be produced.

In the case of an expert report concerning economic damages, although the substantive requirements of USPAP may be useful or constitute good practice, they are not required. The principal problem with compliance with USPAP in an expert report on damages is that some of USPAP's specific requirements may be less relevant, or of a lower priority, than the principal issues of fact to be decided by the trier of fact. For example, under the proposed revisions to USPAP, Standards Rule 10–2 requires that both appraisal reports and restricted use appraisal reports "identify and state a description of the business equity appraised."[20] In contrast to USPAP, the inclusion of this information in an expert report on damages is a matter of judgment, not a requirement.

An occasional abuse of business valuation practices has been to make an unspecified blanket claim that an opposing expert's damage study fails to meet professional standards because it does not comply with USPAP. However, in this circumstance, the general failure to comply with USPAP may often be trivial. This is because any report that does not explicitly state its compliance with USPAP is, by definition, not in compliance with USPAP.

In contrast, a better use of USPAP in rebuttal may be to point out how specific omissions or departures have resulted in a substantive error. Consider, for example, an expert whose selection of comparable sales transactions grouped together prices of entire enterprises with prices for equity and with prices of differing collections of assets, including various intangible assets. This expert failed to follow the requirements of USPAP Standards Rule 9–1, to carefully define the property being valued, and the failure to follow this practice in the expert's selection of comparable sales produced a misleading analysis. In this case, one could demonstrate that the failure to define the property produced a substantive error, not just a failure to comply with USPAP. In our experience, if the standards required by USPAP are appropriate, they will speak for themselves.

---

[20] Ibid., pp. 82, 84.

Use Legal Precedent?

Many business valuations are prepared for taxation-related purposes. The tax preparers who engage business valuation experts are themselves experts in tax law. Tax preparers rightfully try to be advocates for their clients' legal positions and interpretations of tax law. As a result, business valuations prepared for tax purposes tend to emphasize legal precedent as justification for various factual positions, such as the amounts taken for discounts. For example, a business valuation prepared for tax purposes may apply a minority ownership interest discount, a lack of marketability discount, a key person discount, and a small size discount, and cite cases wherein these discounts were allowed. However, in a damages report it may be more effective to provide empirical evidence that the discounts are of an appropriate size and are independent and additive, so that the aggregate discount used in the report is reasonable.

Generally, when prepared for taxation-related purposes, business valuations that result in lower values also result in lower taxes. Not surprisingly, there is a suspicion that arguments for valuation methods and forms of discounts that result in uniformly lower values and lower taxes may tend to be popular in taxation-related appraisals. However, this sort of implied advocacy creates problems in damages testimony if the damages expert offers to provide services for both plaintiffs and defendants. There is no bias that can work for both parties.

Assume that a damages expert is proving a damages estimate for a plaintiff in litigation. Prior inconsistent testimony or approaches used when working for a defendant in a previous litigation can be used effectively by the current defendant's attorney in an effort to impeach the damages expert. If the damages expert is ever taking an opposite position or using an inconsistent approach, then there should be a good reason for the change and it should be explained. The change may not be an inconsistency because of the different factual situations of the two cases. The inconsistency may be deliberate as a result of the further learning of the damages expert, and the fact is that if the expert had this knowledge in the earlier case, the expert may have done things differently.

Different jurisdictions may have different statutes or case law that impact the appropriate measure of damages in a particular litigation. It may be appropriate to discuss what statutes or case law impact your choice of damages approaches or measures. Analysts may use case precedent to understand the required legal tests, but should use empirical data to determine the fact and amount of damages.

There is very little case law or statutory authority as to what is an acceptable method or approach to calculate economic damages. The method or approach used by the damages expert is generally considered by the courts to be a fact question that is unique to the fact situation of the case in question. The courts are reluctant to generalize rules as to how to compute economic damages because there are so many unique factual situations that make it nearly impossible to arrive at rules that will always work.

The U.S. Supreme Court in the *Daubert* decision has given guidance to federal judges to not permit expert testimony that is "junk science."[21] The *Daubert* decision has been used to exclude damages expert testimony because the method or approach of the expert was considered inappropriate science. The science of damages calculation is a soft science. It may be a blend of economics, statistics, marketing, accounting, and finance. There are no peer-reviewed journals related to damages calculation except, perhaps, in the area of employment damages. Therefore, it is difficult for a federal judge to know whether the expert's peers generally accept a damage expert's approach or assumptions. Very rarely is a damages expert's opinion excluded under *Daubert*. In addition, not all state courts follow *Daubert* but may instead have their own guidelines for admission of scientific evidence.

On March 23, 1999, the U.S. Supreme Court broadened the "gatekeeping" obligation of trial judges in federal cases set forth in Daubert to all testimony based on "technical" and "other specialized" knowledge.[22] *Kumho* clearly holds that the four factors listed in *Daubert*— testing, peer review, error rates, and acceptability in the relevant scientific community—are not a definitive list or test. The inquiry of the judge must be flexible and tied to the facts of a particular case. However, *Kumho* makes it clear that *Daubert* type inquiries as to the reliability of damages or valuation expert testimony are permitted.

Conclusion

Economic damages often require or may benefit from the use of business valuation methods. Both disciplines rely heavily on income approach methods.

This chapter discussed many of the important differences. Damages experts need not consider more than one approach or method and need not limit their examination to data that were available prior to the valuation date. The preparation of the work product of an economic damages assignment is not necessarily governed by the *Uniform Standards of Professional Appraisal Practice*, but more likely is governed by the legal rules of the jurisdiction in which the testimony will be heard.

Damages are usually suffered during a distinct period of time, so the damage analysis does not usually rely on the perpetuity assumption that is typically part of a business valuation analysis. Furthermore, the treatment of taxes in the analysis could be radically different.

Any business valuation analyst who is asked to express an opinion regarding economic damages should be careful to recognize the many differences between these two disciplines.

---

[21] *Daubert* v. *Merrill Dow Pharmaceuticals, Inc.*, 509 U.S. 579 (1993).

[22] *Kumho Tire Company, Ltd., et al.* v. *Patrick Carmichael, etc., et al.*, No. 97–1709; 1999 WL 152455 (U.S.), Mar. 23, 1999.

Chapter 15

Fair Value for Oppressed and Dissenting Shareholders

Anne C. Singer and Jay E. Fishman, ASA, CBA

Introduction

It is well recognized that minority ownership shareholders in closely held corporations[1] are exposed to certain risks of minority ownership. These risks stem from the illiquidity of their stock and from their lack of control. Minority investors in closely held corporations can be "locked into" an investment from which they may receive no compensation, dividends, or other distributions and have no voice in management.

The risks to which such minority ownership shareholders are exposed include the possibility that the majority ownership shareholder may take actions over which they have no control, with which they do not agree, and that they fear will reduce the value of their ownership interest. Such actions include mergers with another corporation, the sale or other disposition of substantially all the corporate assets, and significant changes in the corporate bylaws.

In addition, if minority ownership shareholders are employed by, or have management roles in, the corporation, the controlling ownership shareholders may (1) terminate the minority shareholders' service as employees, directors or officers of the corporation, (2) reduce or eliminate their salary, (3) completely "freeze out" minority shareholders, or (4) otherwise "oppress" them. Minority shareholders are also sometimes subjected to mismanagement, fraud, or illegality by the majority shareholders.

Recognizing (1) that minority shareholders in closely held corporations are generally subject to decisions made by the majority shareholders, and (2) that they do not have a ready public market for their stock, many states have enacted statutes that provide minority shareholders with remedies for "oppressive action," fraud, and mismanagement by the majority (hereinafter called *oppressed shareholders' statutes* or *dissolution statutes*). Moreover, all states have also enacted dissenters' rights statutes. These statutes provide an appraisal remedy for minority shareholders who do not agree with significant actions of the majority affecting their economic interests and who wish to sell their stock as a result.

Although these two types of statutes differ in the triggering mechanisms, the procedural implementation, and the amount of discretion residing in the court in imposing a remedy, the remedies for both categories of ills include the payment of *fair value* for the minority shareholder's stock.

For dissenters, the purchase of their stock for fair value is usually the only remedy. For minority shareholders, seeking a remedy for oppression, fraud, mismanagement, or similar problems, a fair value purchase is the most common remedy. However, courts usually have a panoply of remedies within their discretion.

---

[1] Closely held corporations are those whose stock is "not generally traded in the securities market." F. Hodge O'Neal and Robert B. Thompson, *O'Neal's Oppression of Minority Shareholders*, 2d ed. (St. Paul, MN: West Group, 1997), §1.01 n.1. The term is usually used to distinguish the corporation with only a few shareholders from the publicly held corporation.

The fair value remedy is crucial for oppressed and dissenting shareholders because they rarely, if ever, have a ready market for their stock on the open market, as do stockholders in publicly traded companies. As stated by one court, the fair value remedy effectively provides a marketplace for the sale of the minority shareholder's stock.[2]

Fair value is a legal term used in the vast majority of dissenters' rights[3] and oppressed shareholders' statutes. However, the term is virtually never legislatively defined. Therefore, the definition has been left to judicial interpretation. Since fair value is a judicially defined term, the analyst should be familiar with applicable relevant statutes and case law. As will be discussed later in this chapter, judicial interpretation of the term *fair value* can be inconsistent both within and among various states.

This chapter will discuss: (1) what a dissenter's case is; (2) what an oppressed shareholder's case is; (3) fair value as a standard of value; (4) the appropriate valuation date and its significance in a fair value case; and (5) common methods for estimating fair value.

This chapter is not intended to be a comprehensive survey of the law in all 50 states. Accordingly, New Jersey statutes, which are generally typical of statutes in this area, are used as an example. However, as appropriate, the statutes and cases of other states, particularly Delaware, are discussed to show the variation that exists in this area of the law. Needless to say, it is important for any analyst to understand the meaning of fair value in the jurisdiction in which he or she practices. This will likely entail seeking legal advice as to the application of the fair value standard.

The Dissenter's Fair Value Case

Minority shareholders who believe that certain fundamental or extraordinary corporate changes voted by the majority shareholder will adversely affect them have available statutory rights as dissenters. Currently, the statutes of all states permit such shareholders to dissent from the majority shareholder's action and thereby compel the corporation to purchase their stock, a remedy commonly called the *appraisal remedy*.

The first dissenters' rights statutes were enacted in the early twentieth century. The statutes were enacted to ameliorate the rule of unanimity existing at common law[4] requiring the unanimous consent of shareholders for statutorily enumerated extraordinary corporate transactions, such as mergers. Before the enactment of such statutes, each

---

[2] *Orchard* v. *Covelli*, 590 F.Supp. 1548, 1557 (W.D. Pa. 1984), aff'd, 802 F.2d 448 (3d Cir. 1986).

[3] Not all states have adopted the fair value standard in dissenters' cases. See the discussion accompanying notes 35–37 *infra* and list of state statutes in John D. Emory Jr., "The Role of Discounts in Determining 'Fair Value' under Wisconsin's Dissenters' Rights Statutes: The Case for Discounts," 1995 Wis. L. Rev. 1155, 1164, n. 50 (1995).

[4] *Common law* refers to the body of law that is derived through judicial decisions and judgments, as opposed to *statutory law*, which is enacted by legislatures, or *regulations*, which are promulgated by administrative bodies.

shareholder effectively had veto power and could prevent fundamental corporate actions. However, in states where the rule of unanimity was abolished, objecting shareholders were bound by majority shareholder decisions, sometimes to their detriment.[5]

The statutes, which were enacted to protect dissenting minority shareholders who no longer could depend upon the rule of unanimity, vary as to which corporate actions will trigger dissenters' rights. For example, in Delaware, only a merger or consolidation triggers dissenters' rights.[6] However, under the statutes of most states, including New Jersey, dissenters' rights are triggered by a variety of actions, such as a merger, a sale, lease, exchange, or other disposition of all or substantially all of the corporate stock.[7]

Typically, to initiate the dissenters' rights remedy, shareholders must give notice in advance of the vote to the corporation that they intend to demand payment for their shares if the proposed action is approved. The stockholder must then make written demand for payment within 20 days of the mailing of notice, advising that the corporate action was approved.[8] A shareholder making such demand is called a *dissenting shareholder*. Upon demanding payment, the dissenting shareholder ceases "to have any rights of a shareholder, except the right to be paid the fair value of his shares...."[9]

For example, the applicable New Jersey statute provides that the corporation must mail to each dissenting shareholder the balance sheet and surplus statement of the corporation as of the latest available date and profit and loss statements for a 12-month period ending on the date of the balance sheet. The corporation may, at the time of this mailing, make a written offer to buy the dissenting shareholders' shares at a specified price, deemed to be the fair value.[10] If no agreement as to fair value is reached within the statutory time period, the dissenting shareholder may serve a demand on the corporation that it commence an action to determine fair value.[11] Once the action is initiated, the court may appoint a valuation analyst to estimate fair value.[12]

---

[5] See Annotation to Section 13.01, Model Business Corporation Act (the "Model Act"), at 13-8 (3d ed. 1995 Supp.) The Model Act was first adopted in 1969 by the Committee on Corporate Laws of the Section of Business Law of the American Bar Association. It was prepared by members and consultants to the committee, who are experts in the field of corporate law. As the name suggests, the Model Act has served as a model for many state legislatures, and some states have adopted it virtually verbatim.

[6] 8 Del. Code Ann. §262 (1996 Supp.).

[7] N.J.S.A. §14A:11-1 (1998 Supp.); see also Model Act, §§13.02 et seq. and annotation thereto containing comparison of state statutes.

[8] N.J.S.A. §14A:11-2.

[9] N.J.S.A. §14A:11-3(2).

[10] N.J.S.A. §14A:11-6.

[11] N.J.S.A. §14A:11-7.

[12] N.J.S.A. §14A:11-8.

The Oppressed Shareholder's Fair Value Case

An oppressed shareholder case is, in effect, a "corporate divorce." Such cases provide a remedy to a minority shareholder[13] in a closely held business who seeks a remedy for the majority shareholder's fraud, illegality, mismanagement, oppression, or similar reason.[14] Courts have recognized that such remedies are necessary for shareholders in closely held corporations because of the "special nature" of these corporations. This "special nature" includes the following characteristics:

1. Shareholders usually expect to be active participants in management.
2. When dissention arises, the majority shareholder is likely to have the power to undermine or disappoint the minority shareholder's expectations and prevent the minority shareholder from obtaining a fair return on his or her investment.
3. The lack of a ready market for the minority shareholder's stock means that he or she may be locked into an investment that no longer provides an adequate return or that the shareholder no longer wants for other reasons.[15]

Oppression is a legal term that has most often been defined to mean that a minority shareholder's reasonable expectations have been disappointed.[16] These may be expectations of employment, participation in management, or any other reasonable expectations. The New Jersey Supreme Court has held that even nonmonetary expectations of shareholders can be considered.[17]

Oppression covers actions taken against a minority shareholder in his or her capacity as director, officer, employee, or shareholder.[18] Oppression does not necessarily connote any fraud, mismanagement, or other wrongdoing.[19] Indeed, under the statutes of some states, an action

---

[13] Note that the term *minority shareholder* in this context may, according to some courts, include a 50 percent shareholder who is not in control of the corporation. *Bonavita* v. *Corbo*, 300 N.J. Super. 179, 187–88, 692 A.2d 119 (Ch. Div. 1996); *Balsamides* v. *Perle*, 313 N.J. Super. 7, 712 A.2d 673 (App. Div. 1998), *cert. granted*, 156 N.J. 425, 719 A.2d 1023 (1998); *Martin* v. *Martin's News Service, Inc.*, 9 Conn. App. 304, 518 A.2d 951 (1986).

[14] See O'Neal and Thompson, *O'Neal's Oppression of Minority Shareholders*, 2d ed., §7.13, p. 79.

[15] Ibid., §7.15, p. 89.

[16] For example, *Brenner* v. *Berkowitz*, 134 N.J. 488, 506, 634 A.2d 1019, 1028 (1993); *Meiselman* v. *Meiselman*, 309 N.C. 279, 307 S.E.2d 551 (1983); *Exadactilos* v. *Cinnaminson Realty Co., Inc.*, 167 N.J. Super. 141, 400 A.2d 554 (L.Div. 1979), *aff'd*, 173 N.J. Super. 559, 414A.2d 994 (App. Div.), *cert. denied*, 85 N.J. 112, 425 A.2d 273 (1980). Other courts have held that oppressive conduct is (1) conduct that is "burdensome, harsh and wrongful or (2) a breach of fiduciary duty of good faith and fair dealing by majority shareholders to minority shareholders. See, for example, *Kisner* v. *Coffey*, 418 So.2d 58, 61 (Miss. 1982).

[17] *Brenner* v. *Berkowitz*, 134 N.J. at 509, 634 A.2d at 1029.

[18] For example, N.J.S.A. §14A:12-7(1)(c); O'Neal and Thompson, *O'Neal's Oppression of Minority Shareholders*, 2d ed., §7.13, p. 81.

[19] For example, *Stumpf* v. *C.S. Stumpf & Sons, Inc.*, 67 Cal. App. 3d 230, 20 Cal. Rptr. 671 (1975) (no mismanagement or misconduct occurred, but only extreme hostility); *Gianotti* v. *Hamway*, 239 Va. 14, 387 S.E.2d 725, 730-31 (1990); *Compton* v. *Paul K. Harding Realty*, 6 Ill. App. 3d 488, 285 N.E.2d 574, 581 (1972) (oppression is not synonymous with illegal or fraudulent conduct); *Application of Topper*, 107 Misc.2d 25, 433 N.Y.S.2d 359, 362 (1980).

based on shareholder oppression may effectively become a no-fault cause of action.[20] According to one commentator, courts will be especially likely to find oppression when minority shareholders who have been involved in running the business are excluded. In addition, if a minority shareholder is permitted to continue to receive a salary or other return from the business, courts are less likely to find oppression.[21]

Although courts usually have a panoply of equitable remedies available, including corporate dissolution, the most common remedy afforded minority shareholders is an award of fair value for their stock.[22]

This buyout remedy effectively provides a marketplace for the sale of the minority shareholder's shares. It accomplishes two purposes: It (1) provides the minority shareholder with a fair return on his or her investment while (2) alleviating the continuation of a forced association no longer desired by antagonistic parties. Thus, it benefits the individual owners and the corporation itself.[23]

Under the statutes of many states, including New Jersey,[24] a minority shareholder must prove oppression, fraud, illegality, or mismanagement before the court can order a remedy or determine fair value. Under the statutes of some states and the Model Act, once a minority shareholder petitions for dissolution of the corporation on the basis of oppression or related grounds, the majority shareholder can automatically elect to purchase the shares of the petitioning shareholder for fair value.[25] The effect of this election is to convert the case into a simple stock purchase in which allegations of oppression or wrongdoing are no longer at issue.[26] In some states, the choice to purchase a minority shareholder's stock is irrevocable, absent court approval.[27] In other states, the corporation may elect not to proceed with the purchase if it is dissatisfied with the value eventually set by the court for the stock.[28]

The payment of fair value to an oppressed shareholder has been recognized as a complete and just remedy for oppression.[29] The Delaware

---

[20] See note 25 *infra* and accompanying text.

[21] O'Neal and Thompson, *O'Neal's Oppression of Minority Shareholders*, 2d ed., §7.13, p. 81.

[22] New Jersey courts also have the discretion to allow the minority shareholder to buy the stock of the majority, although this remedy is uncommon and will be permitted only in unusual circumstances. *Muellenberg* v. *Bikon Corp.,* 143 N.J. 168, 183, 669 A.2d 1382 (1996).

[23] *Meiselman* v. *Meiselman,* 309 N.C. 279, 307 S.E.2d 551, 558-60 (1983).

[24] *Brenner* v. *Berkowitz,* 134 N.J. at 506, 510, 634 A.2d at 1027, 1030 (mere discord between shareholders is not sufficient to obtain a remedy); *Muellenberg* v. *Bikon Corp.*, supra, 143 N.J. at 182; 669 A.2d at 1389 (triggering event is necessary).

[25] For example, Rev. Model Act, §14.34 (1995 Supp.); Alaska Stat. §10.06.628(b) (1998); N.Y. Bus. Corp. Law §§1104-a, 1118 (McKinney's 1998 Supp.); Cal. Corp. Code §2000 (West 1995).

[26] For example, *Friedman* v. *Beway Realty Corp.*, 87 N.Y.2d 161, 638 N.Y.S.2d 399, 661 N.E.2d 972, 976 (1995); *In re Cristo Bros.*, 64 N.Y.2d 975, 489 N.Y.S.2d 35, 489 N.E.2d 176 (1985) (rejects plaintiff's argument that defendant should not be able both to deny oppression and to purchase minority's stock).

[27] For example, N.Y. Bus. Corp. Law §1118.

[28] Cal. Corp. Code §2000.

[29] *Muellenberg* v. *Bikon Corp.*, 143 N.J. 167, 182, 669 A.2d 1382, 1389 (1996) (claims of oppression are typically remedied by a buyout of the minority shareholder's stock); *Meiselman* v. *Meiselman*, 309 N.C. 279, 307 S.E.2d 551 (1983); *Berger* v. *Berger*, 249 N.J. Super. 305, 592 A.2d 321(Ch. Div. 1991); *Matter of Wiedy's Furniture Clearance Center*, 108 A.D.2d 81, 487 N.Y.S.2d 901, 904 (1985); *Maddox* v. *Norman*, 669 P.2d 230 (Mont. Sup. Ct. 1983); *Stefano* v. *Coppock*, 705 P.2d 443, 446 (Alaska Sup. Ct. 1985) (buyout fairly compensates oppressed shareholder); Comment to Section 14.34 of Rev. Model Act, Vol. 3, at 14-155 (3d ed. 1995 Supp.) (the rights of the minority shareholder "are fully protected" by paying the full value of his or her shares while permitting the majority shareholders to continue the business).

Supreme Court has said that fair value "measures 'that which has been taken from [the shareholder], *viz.*, his proportionate interest in a going concern.'"[30]

Fair Value as a Standard of Value

A clear and concise understanding of the appropriate standard of value is a key to any credible business appraisal. Indeed, as Pratt, Reilly, and Schweihs have indicated, the failure to adhere to the appropriate standard of value can be a primary reason for the wide variances between two business valuations.[31] Nowhere is this principle more significant than in the application of the fair value standard in connection with oppressed and dissenting shareholder matters.

As we mentioned previously, fair value is rarely legislatively defined. As a result, there can be confusion about the meaning of fair value in the context of these assignments. Moreover, even when the courts have addressed this issue, legal precedents can be vague or contradictory and therefore offer inadequate guidance as to the application of the fair value standard. For example, New Jersey's dissenters' rights statute[32] and its oppressed shareholder statute use the term *fair value* repeatedly, but they do not define the term or state how it is to be applied. Thus, as in most jurisdictions, the definition of fair value is left to judicial interpretation. Similarly, the dissenters' rights section of the Model Act does not provide any direction as to how fair value is to be determined, although it contains a definition. This definition states:

> "Fair value," with respect to a dissenter's shares, means the value of the shares immediately before the effectuation of the corporate action to which the dissenter objects, excluding any appreciation or depreciation in anticipation of the corporate action unless exclusion would be inequitable.[33]

The definition contained in the Model Act has variations among states' dissenters' rights statutes. Although some states have adopted that identical definition, other states use the definition without the final phrase "unless exclusion would be inequitable."[34] Variations that are

---

[30] *Matter of Shell Oil Co.*, 607 A.2d 1213, 1218 (Del. 1992) (citations omitted), quoting *Tri-Continental Corp.* v. *Battye*, 74 A. 2d 71, 72 (Del. 1950); see also *Beerly* v. *Dept. of Treasury*, 768 F. 2d 942 (7th Cir. 1985) (purpose of an appraisal is to give a shareholder the cash equivalent of what he or she has given up).

[31] Shannon P. Pratt, Robert F. Reilly, and Robert P. Schweihs, *Valuing Small Businesses and Professional Practices,* 3d ed. (New York: McGraw-Hill, 1998), p. 512.

[32] The New Jersey statute, N.J.S.A. §14A:11-1(a)(i)(A)(1998 Supp.), and the statutes of certain other states exclude from the fair value remedy shareholders in publicly traded companies.

[33] Model Act, §13.01(3).

[34] The statutes of approximately 27 states contain the same definition of fair value. See, for example, Wis. Stat. §180.1301(4)(West 1997 Supp.). Approximately 14 other states, including New Jersey, N.J.S.A. §14A:11-3, use the same general concept of fair value without the final phrase "unless exclusion would be inequitable." See listing of statutes in Emory, "The Role of Discounts in Determining 'Fair Value' Under Wisconsin's Dissenters' Rights Statutes: The Case for Discounts," at 1165, n. 52.

similar to the Model Act require consideration of "all relevant factors."[35] Still others use entirely different terms, like "fair cash value,"[36] "value,"[37] or even "fair market value."[38]

It seems clear that fair value can differ from fair market value. Fair market value is a term that has a well recognized meaning to valuation analysts. Fair market value may be defined as:

> The amount at which the property would change hands between a willing buyer and a willing seller when the former is not under compulsion to buy and the latter is not under any compulsion to sell, both parties having reasonable knowledge of the relevant facts.[39]

Because fair market value refers to the price at which stock would be bought and sold in the marketplace, the estimation of the value of a minority shareholder's stock under this standard may include (1) a discount for lack of marketability and (2) a discount for minority ownership interest. A lack of marketability discount reflects the fact that sale of a minority ownership interest is difficult because only a small pool of potential buyers exists. A minority ownership interest discount reflects the lack of control of a minority shareholder. One heavily litigated issue with regard to the meaning of fair value is whether calculation of fair value of a minority shareholder's stock should include these valuation discounts—that is, (1) a discount for lack of ownership control (i.e., a minority ownership interest discount) and (2) a discount for lack of marketability or liquidity—and, conversely, whether a control premium should be included in the valuation of a majority shareholder's stock.

This issue largely revolves around the appropriate level of value sought by the particular jurisdiction in a particular case. The concept of levels of value is a fundamental principle of business valuation theory. Different business valuation methods produce different relative levels of value through the implicit or explicit use of valuation discounts and premiums.[40]

Levels of value are used to understand the relationship between the attributes of the interest being valued and the various indications of value produced by the methods applied to reach a conclusion of value. For example, (1) if the interest that is being valued is a minority ownership interest and (2) if the valuation methodology derives an indication of value on the basis of acquisitions of controlling ownership

---

[35] Delaware and Oklahoma exclude any element of value arising from the corporate action that led to the exercise of dissenter's rights, but state that in determining fair value, "all relevant factors" must be considered by the court. 8 Del. Code Ann. §262(h) (1996 Supp.); 18 Okla. Stat. Ann. §1091(H) (West 1999 Supp.).

[36] Ohio Rev. Code Ann. §1701.85(C) (Page's 1997 Supp.) (defined in the same way as fair market value); La. Rev. Stat. Ann. §12:131C(2) (West 1998 Supp.).

[37] Kan. Stat. Ann. §17-6712 (1997 Supp.).

[38] Cal. Corp. Code §1300(a) (West 1998 Supp.).

[39] REV. RUL. 59-60; Jay E. Fishman, Shannon P. Pratt et al., *Guide to Business Valuations,* 8th ed. (Fort Worth, TX: Practitioners Publishing Co., 1998), ¶205.04.

[40] Daniel R. Van Vleet and Frederick W. Axley, "Fair Value in Dissenting Stockholder Disputes," in *Financial Valuation: Businesses and Business Interests*, 1997 Update, Robert F. Reilly, Robert P. Schweihs et al., eds. (New York: Warren, Gorham & Lamont, 1997), p. U9A-11.

interests, then (3) the analyst should address the issue of the derivation of value for a controlling ownership interest—and its use in estimating the value of a minority ownership interest. Typically, the analyst would acknowledge that this methodology would first produce a pro rata enterprise level of value. Consideration should be given to an adjustment downward to reflect the minority position of the ownership interest that is being valued. It is in this regard that fair value may differ from fair market value. This is because valuation of minority ownership interest may entail consideration of discounts both for minority ownership interest and for lack of marketability. Discounts are part of the "willing buyer, willing seller" concept that defines fair market value, in contrast to fair value (the valuation standard included in most appraisal and buyout statutes).

In considering this issue, many courts have concluded that discounts should not apply to valuations of stock in dissenters' rights or in oppressed shareholder cases when the minority shareholder's stock is being sold not to a third party but to the other shareholders or to the company. According to one pair of commentators, a discount for lack of marketability is inappropriate in dissenters' actions. This is because the statute itself requires the corporation to purchase a dissenter's stock, thereby "creating the economic equivalent of a market."[41]

Likewise, a minority ownership interest discount is not appropriate because the purchaser is either the corporation or the majority shareholder(s). Accordingly, the purchaser is not one who will have no control—the rationale for applying a minority ownership interest discount—rather, the effect of the purchase is to increase the control of the purchasing shareholders.

As stated by one court:

> The rule justifying the devaluation of minority shares in closely-held corporations for their lack of control has little validity when the shares are to be purchased by someone who is already in control of the corporation. In such a situation, it can hardly be said that the shares are worth less to the purchaser because they are noncontrolling.[42]

Further, such discounts are objectionable because they require courts to engage in speculative inquiries.[43]

As one commentator has pointed out, it is incongruous for the majority shareholder to oppress the minority shareholders, or to control the timing of a valuation by voting on a merger, and then obtain the benefit of a discount at the minority shareholders' expense.[44] The Delaware

---

[41] Paul Much and Louis A. Paone, "Fair Value of Dissenters' Shares Debated," *National Law Journal*, May 10, 1993, pp. 17, 22; see also Siegel, "Back to the Future: Appraisal Rights in the Twenty-First Century," 32 HARV. J. ON LEGISLATION 79, 1995, pp. 137–38 (disapproving both types of discounts).

[42] *Brown* v. *Corrugated Box Co., Inc.*, 91 Cal. App. 3d 477, 154 Cal Rptr. 170, 175–76 (1979), quoted in *Balsamides* v. *Perle*, 313 N.J. Super.7, 28, 712 A.2d 673, 683 (App. Div. 1998), cert. granted, 156 N.J. 425, 719 A.2d 1023 (1998).

[43] See American Law Institute, *Principles of Corporate Governance: Analysis and Recommendations*, §7.22 comment e, at 324 (1994).

[44] Murdock, "The Evolution of Effective Remedies for Minority Shareholders and Its Impact upon Valuation of Minority Shares," 65 NOTRE DAME L. REV. 425, 1990, pp. 486–487.

Supreme Court has held that "the application of a discount to a minority shareholder is contrary to the requirement that the company be viewed as a 'going concern.'"[45] The Delaware courts have usually rejected application of ownership control premiums and minority ownership interest and lack of marketability discounts.[46] The Maine Supreme Court has recognized that utilizing discounts would encourage majority squeeze-outs.[47] Other courts have also refused to apply such discounts, both in dissenters' rights and in oppressed shareholder cases.[48]

On the other hand, a number of courts valuing dissenters' stock have applied one or both types of discounts.[49] For example, New York courts may apply a discount for lack of marketability but not a discount for minority ownership interest. Whether any discount is applied in estimating fair value is a legal determination about which the valuator should seek legal advice.[50]

The Valuation Date

An appraisal is an estimate of value "of a specifically defined asset at a given point in time."[51] The point in time selected, whether statutorily mandated or otherwise, is critical.

Most state statutes provide that when a dissenting shareholder's stock is to be purchased, fair value is determined as of the day prior to the meeting of shareholders at which the action dissented from was opposed.[52] The New Jersey statute provides: "In all cases, fair value shall exclude any appreciation or depreciation resulting from the proposed action."[53] Thus, the dissenting shareholder neither gets credit for any gain nor is penalized for any loss that results from the action from which he or she dissented.

---

[45] *Cavalier Oil Corp.* v. *Harnett*, 564 A.2d 1137, 1145 (Del. 1989) (rejecting both minority ownership and lack of marketability discounts).

[46] For example, *Rapid-American Corp.* v. *Harris*, 603 A.2d 796 (Del. 1992) (but allows a control premium to be added at the corporate level to compensate shareholders for the company's control of subsidiaries); *Cavalier Oil Corp.* v. *Harnett*, 564 A.2d 1137 (Del. 1989); *Weinberger* v. *UOP, Inc.*, 457 A.2d 701 (Del. 1983).

[47] *In re McLoon Oil Co.*, 565 A.2d 997, 1005 (Me. 1989).

[48] For example, *Foy* v. *Klapmeier*, 992 F.2d 774, 780-81 (8th Cir. 1993); *Hunter* v. *Mitek Indus.*, 721 F. Supp. 1102 (E.D. Mo. 1989); *In re McLoon Oil Co.*, 565 A.2d 997 (Me. 1989) (dissenters' rights: neither discount); *Rigel Corp.* v. *Cutchall*, 511 N.W. 2d 519 (Neb. 1994); *Walter S. Cheesman Realty Co.* v. *Moore*, 770 P.2d 1308, 1312 (Colo. Ct. App. 1988) (dissenters' rights: no minority discount); *Ronald* v. *4-C's Elec. Packaging, Inc.*, 214 Cal. Rptr. 225 (Cal. Ct. App. 1985); *Charland* v. *Countryview Golf Club, Inc.*, 588 A.2d 609 (R.I. 1991) (oppression case: neither discount); *Balsamides* v. *Perle*, 313 N.J. Super. 7, 712 A.2d 673 (App. Div. 1998) (oppression case: neither discount applied).

[49] For example, *Hernando Bank* v. *Huff*, 609 F. Supp. 1124 (N.D. Miss. 1985), *aff'd*, 796 F.2d 803 (5th Cir. 1986) (minority discount); *Perlman* v. *Permonite Mfg. Co.*, 568 F. Supp. 222 (N.D. Ind. 1983), *aff'd*, 734 F.2d 1283 (7th Cir. 1984) (both types of discounts); *Stanton* v. *Republic Bank*, 144 Ill. 2d 472, 581 N.E.2d 678 (1991) (both types of discounts); *Armstrong* v. *Marathon Oil Co.*, 513 N.E.2d 776 (Ohio 1987) (both types of discounts); *Independence Tube Corp.* v. *Levine*, 179 Ill. App. 3d 911, 535 N.E.2d 927 (1989) (both types of discounts).

[50] *Blake* v. *Blake Agency, Inc.*, 107 A.D.2d 139, 486 N.Y.S.2d 341, *appeal denied*, 65 N.Y.2d 609, 494 N.Y.2d 1028, 484 N.E.2d 671 (1985).

[51] Jay E. Fishman, "Valuation Terminology and Methodology," in *Financial Valuation: Business and Business Interests,* James H. Zukin, ed. (New York: Warren, Gorham & Lamont, 1990), pp. 2–6.

[52] For example, N.J.S.A. §14A:11-3(3)(a).

[53] N.J.S.A. §14A:11-3(3)(c).

The Delaware Supreme Court has held that the language limiting consideration of postmerger changes in value bars only consideration of speculative elements of value created by the merger. It does not bar consideration of elements of future value, including the nature of the enterprise, "that are known or susceptible of proof as of the date of the merger and not the product of speculation...."[54]

Under the New Jersey statute applicable to oppressed shareholders, the purchase price of any shares sold "shall be their fair value as of the date of the commencement of the action...plus or minus any adjustments deemed equitable by the court...."[55]

The establishment of a valuation date, whether it be in a dissenters' rights case or an oppressed shareholder case (or any valuation case), is significant. This is because only those facts known or knowable on the valuation date should be considered. Simply stated, "An investor's required return and the amount of available benefits usually is estimated at a single point in time. Also, the estimate of value is based solely on the information that is discernable and predictable at the valuation date."[56]

Courts have accepted and reiterated this principle. For example, one court stated that, "valuation of securities is 'in essence a prophecy as to the future,' but this prophecy must be based upon facts available at the critical [valuation] date."[57] The Seventh Circuit Court of Appeals has stated that elements of future value are part of the entitlement of the investors "when 'known or susceptible of proof as of the [valuation] date....'"[58] The court continued:

> Here the subsequent events...were no more than speculation as of the time of the merger...We, like the district court, therefore exclude from consideration the fact that Mobil paid in 1980 more than twice the value implied by the merger in 1979. Only facts known in 1979 count.... Any increment of value attributable to changes after August 1979 [the valuation date] in the market for oil and gas, or to Mobil's willingness to make changes or bear special risks, belongs to [the purchasing] shareholders rather than [the selling shareholders]. The investors in a firm are entitled only to what it is worth as it exists, not as it could become in other hands.[59]

Thus, the choice of valuation date is critical, since it determines in large part what events and financial data in the corporate history may be considered in the valuation determination.

---

[54] *Weinberger* v. *UOP, Inc.*, 457 A.2d 701 (Del. 1983); *see also Cede & Co.* v. *Technicolor, Inc.*, 684 A.2d 289 (Del. 1996).

[55] N.J.S.A. §14A:12-7(8).

[56] Fishman, Pratt et al., *Guide to Business Valuations*, ¶210.04; see also ¶405.03.

[57] Rev. Rul. 59-60, quoted in *Blass* v. *United States*, 344 F. Supp. 669, 670 (E.D. Ark. 1972).

[58] *Metlyn Realty Corp.* v. *Esmark, Inc.*, 763 F.2d 826, 838 (7th Cir. 1985).

[59] Id. at 838. See also *Kastenbaum* v. *Falstaff Brewing Corp.*, 514 F. Supp. 690, 698 (5th Cir. 1976) (elements to be considered in determining the value of a business are the prospects that profits will continue in to the future, "considering all circumstances existing and known as of the date of the valuation"); *Gratto* v. *Gratto*, 272 N.J. Super. 140, 639 A.2d 390 (App. Div. 1994); *Bogosian* v. *Woloohojian Realty Corp.*, 923 F.2d 898 (1st Cir. 1991).

Fair Value Methodology

Historically, the valuation methods employed to estimate fair value have been heavily influenced by judicial precedents emerging from Delaware. Delaware is the state where the issue of fair value has been frequently litigated. In addition, Delaware's holdings have been followed in other jurisdictions. Although Delaware case law suggests that "all factors and elements which reasonably might enter into the fixing of value"[60] are relevant, until 1983, Delaware courts relied heavily on a mechanistic method known as the "Delaware Block Method." This method was adopted by a number of other states.[61]

Under that method, the analyst (1) derives separate values using methods that rely on earnings and/or dividends, net assets, and market value, (2) weights each of these three methods depending upon the type of business being valued (the weight being a percent and the total of the three factors adding up to 100 percent), (3) multiplies the percentile weighting factor by the calculated value of each method, and (4) adds the results together. Traditionally, the earnings or dividend methods have generally used pricing multiples derived from publicly traded guideline companies. If the subject company is publicly traded, the market approach would be based on some measure of the market price of the company's stock.

In 1983, the Delaware Supreme Court decided the case of *Weinberger* v. *UOP, Inc.*,[62] in which a minority shareholder had objected to a "freeze-out merger"[63] and shares were being valued. *Weinberger* held that the Delaware Block Method was "clearly outmoded" because it "excludes other generally accepted techniques used in the financial community."[64] Although *Weinberger* appeared to eliminate use of the Delaware Block Method in favor of other accepted valuation methods, the Delaware Supreme Court has since seemed to interpret *Weinberger*

[60] *Tri-Continental Corp.* v. *Battye*, 74 A.2d 71, 72 (Del. 1980).

[61] See, for example, *Brown* v. *Hedahl's QB&R, Inc.*, 185 N.W.2d 249 (N.D. 1971); *Leader* v. *Hycor, Inc.*, 479 N.E. 2d 173 (Mass. 1985).

[62] *Weinberger* v. *UOP, Inc.,* 457 A.2d 701 (Del. 1983).

[63] A freeze-out merger is one in which a minority shareholder's interest in a corporation is involuntarily eliminated when controlling shareholders create a dummy corporation, transfer their stock to that corporation, and then agree to merge the old corporation with the new one. The new corporation thereby acquires the assets and liabilities of the original corporation, with the majority owning the stock of the surviving corporation. The minority shareholders no longer have any equity interest in the new business and have the right to receive only cash for their shares in the original company. Although freeze-out mergers may be thought to create special valuation problems, because minority shareholders subject to a freeze-out merger do not have a choice as to whether to sell their stock, this is not the case. Although the valuation does not take into account any increased value or synergies that may result from the merger, an ousted shareholder bears no costs or risks of the future enterprise and so should not share in its possible rewards. But see *Mills* v. *Electric Auto-Lite Co.*, 552 F.2d 1239, 1248 (7th Cir. 1977) (stating that an undervaluation can occur in a freeze-out situation).

[64] 547 A.2d at 713. See also *Stringer* v. *Car Data Systems, Inc.*, 314 Or. 576, 841 P.2d 1183, 1189 (1992) (fair value includes "all relevant factors"); *Schechter* v. *Watkins*, 395 Pa. Super. 363, 577 A.2d 585, 592 (1990) (in a forced buyout, the jury is instructed to consider any factor deemed appropriate).

as not abolishing the Delaware Block Method, but only "relaxing" its exclusivity as a valuation method.[65] Certainly, other valuation methods are much more common today. Thus, in Delaware and other states, courts may base their valuation determination on any method accepted in the financial community.

Most courts in both dissenters' cases and oppression cases have held that fair value means the value of the business as a going concern, rather than liquidation value.[66] According to the Delaware Supreme Court, "The basic concept for value under the appraisal statute is that the stockholder is entitled to what has been taken from him, viz., *his proportionate interest in a going concern.*"[67] The discounted cash flow method is one frequently utilized method to arrive at the value of a going concern[68] and was, in fact, the method used by the experts in *Weinberger.* This method estimates the present value of a corporation's projected future cash flow. Other appropriate methods for calculating the value of a going concern are the capitalized earnings method (in which the analyst uses historical earnings for a period of time, perhaps five years, and then uses a multiple to capitalize the income stream into the future) and multiples derived from guideline companies. In sum, at the present time most states allow any method commonly used by the financial community to estimate the value of a going concern as a means to estimate fair value.

Conclusion

Although oppressed shareholders' cases and dissenters' rights cases may differ as to the triggering mechanism, the procedural implementation, and the amount of judicial discretion available in devising a remedy, a common remedy available to both oppressed and dissenting shareholders is the payment of fair value for their minority shares. Since fair value is a judicially mandated concept and therefore subject to judicial interpretation, the analyst should be familiar with the relevant statutes and case law that discuss this standard of value in the jurisdiction where the action commenced.

An area of contention concerning the meaning of fair value is the applicability of certain valuation adjustments, including (1) a discount for minority ownership interest and (2) a discount for lack of marketability or (3) an ownership control premium. Since fair value is a legal determination, the analyst should seek the opinion of counsel in coming to a clear understanding of the fair value standard as it is applied in the relevant jurisdiction

---

[65] *Rosenblatt* v. *Getty Oil Co.*, 493 A.2d 929, 940-41 (Del. 1985); see also *Leader* v. *Hyco, Inc.*, 479 N.E.2d 173 (Mass. 1985) (continuing to hold, after *Weinberger*, that the Delaware Block Method was an appropriate method of valuation, although not the exclusive method).

[66] For example, *New Jersey Sports & Exposition Authority* v. *Del Tufo*, 230 N.J. Super. 616, 554 A.2d 878 (1989); *Application of Vision Hardware Group, Inc.*, 669 A.2d 671, 677 (Del.Ch. 1995); *Blake* v. *Blake Agency, Inc.*, 107 A.D.2d 139, 486 N.Y.S.2d 341 (1985). See also Model Stat. Close Corp. Supp. §42(b)(1) (saying going-concern value must be considered); but see Cal. Corp. Code §2000 (fair value should be determined based on liquidation value, but court may consider the possibility of sale of business as a going concern).

[67] *In re McLoon Oil Co.*, 565 A.2d at 997, 1003 (emphasis in original).

[68] For example, *In re Radiology Assoc., Inc.*, 611 A.2d 485, 490, 496 (Del.Ch. 1991); *Weinberger* v. *UOP*, 457 A.2d 701, 712 (Del. 1983).

Finally, most courts have held that the premise underlying fair value is the entity as a going concern and not its value in liquidation. The methods used in determining the fair value of a minority shareholder's stock are those commonly used in the financial community. These include the discounted cash flow method, the capitalization of earnings method, and other methods that comprise the body of accepted business valuation methodology.

Chapter 16

Fairness Opinions

M. Mark Lee, CFA, and Gilbert E. Matthews, CFA

Overview

Definition of Fairness Opinion

A fairness opinion is a letter, prepared by a knowledgeable financial advisory firm (generally an investment banking firm or an entity specializing in valuations), that states whether or not a transaction—or the consideration or financial terms of a transaction—is fair. Fairness is assessed from a financial point of view, to one or more parties as of a specific date, based on certain assumptions, limitations, and procedures.

Fairness opinions have two purposes: (1) to provide a decision maker with essential information and (2) to act as an element of proof that the decision maker used reasonable business judgment in making a decision on behalf of others. An opinion of fairness, from a financial point of view, expresses the financial adviser's conclusion that the exchange of the consideration given and received in the proposed transaction falls within a range within which the parties to the transaction might reasonably agree on the basis of financial factors.

The limiting phrase "fair, from a financial point of view" serves to indicate the scope of the experience and professional qualifications of the investment bank or valuation firm giving the opinion. It is not opining as to whether the transaction is fair from a legal viewpoint, nor is it recommending the transaction from the point of view of the corporation. It is the responsibility of the board of directors to determine whether the transaction is appropriate as a business decision, and the board of directors engages counsel to advise it on legal matters.

Importance in Litigation

Acting with informed business judgment when considering a proposed transaction can often be the central issue in litigation against boards of directors of public or private corporations and general partners of limited partnerships making decisions on the behalf of others. In *Smith* v. *Van Gorkom*, the Supreme Court of the State of Delaware ruled that the board of directors of Trans Union Corporation did not seek adequate information or take sufficient time when it approved a cash-out merger of the company into the Marmon Group. Although the directors were experienced and reputable and were not charged with acting with malice, they were adjudged liable to the plaintiff stockholders for damages. The Court arrived at this decision notwithstanding the fact that the merger price represented a substantial premium over the market price of Trans Union's stock, that the transaction was at arm's length, and that the board had relied on its chairman for the financial fairness of the transaction.[1]

The Supreme Court of the State of Delaware wrote in evaluating the conduct of the Trans Union board:

---

[1] *Smith* v. *Van Gorkom*, 488 A.2d 858 (Del. 1985).

Representation of the financial interest of others imposes on a director an affirmative duty to protect those interests and to proceed with a critical eye in assessing information. . . . Despite the foregoing facts and circumstances, there was no call by the Board, either on September 20 or thereafter, for any valuation study or documentation of the $55 price per share as a measure of the fair value of the Company in a cash-out context.

Although the Court added that it was not holding that an outside valuation study was required as a legal matter in order to support a finding that the board made an informed business judgment, the Trans Union directors clearly would have been in a better position to convince the Court that they had made an informed business decision if they had commissioned one. The case was settled for payment of $23.5 million to the plaintiff class.

When Fairness Opinions May Be Advisable

Fairness opinions are often used by businesses in the following situations:

1. By independent directors and fiduciaries in a transaction between the company and a related party.
2. By the seller in the sale of a company for cash and/or securities.
3. By the seller in the sale or spin-off of material assets, divisions, or subsidiaries.
4. By the purchaser in the acquisition of a company, if material to the acquirer.
5. By the purchaser in the acquisition of material assets, divisions, or subsidiaries.
6. By the purchaser in the buybacks of outstanding securities.
7. By the limited partners regarding contributions to, or sale of assets by, a partnership.
8. By the trustees in the acquisition or divestiture of securities or businesses by nonprofit organizations and charities.
9. For bond trustees when required by the indenture.
10. For regulatory agencies in the conversion of nonprofit medical organizations or mutual bank or insurance companies to for-profit stock corporations.

Standards of Financial Fairness

Fairness Opinions—The Legal Context

The minimum level of financial fairness in a proposed transaction is a function of the amount that dissenting shareholders to the transaction could reasonably expect to obtain in a statutory appraisal action. The

valuation methods allowed for computing this amount and the applicability of certain valuation discounts vary from state to state. Since fair
value is a judicially mandated concept and therefore is subject to judicial interpretation, which can be inconsistent both within and among
various states, the analyst should be familiar with the relevant statutes
and case law that discusses the standard of value in the state where the
company is incorporated. (See Chapter 15.) However, because more public corporations are incorporated in Delaware than in any other state,
and many other states follow its lead, this chapter will focus primarily
on fairness and dissenters' rights in Delaware. A recent Delaware decision from the bench stated that, although the appraisal remedy was not
available to the plaintiff, directors had:

> a fiduciary duty . . . to pay shareholders who are cashed out the fair
> value of their stock as that term is defined in appraisal cases . . . . [2]

In light of this standard, a financial adviser should not render a positive fairness opinion in a transaction if the consideration is materially
below the price that the shareholders would be awarded in an appraisal
action. This is true whether or not the structure of the transaction permits shareholders to avail themselves of the appraisal remedy.

Dissenters Rights in Delaware. The remedy of a stockholder
dissenting from a cash-out merger under Delaware law is a statutory
appraisal proceeding to determine the fair value of the shares owned. A
cash-out merger is the forced sale of the corporation's stock for a non-
negotiable amount of cash, securities, or assets other than common
stock.

Fair value in an appraisal action is not the same as *fair market
value*. It is described in *Tri-Continental Corp.* v. *Battye* as follows:

> The basic concept of value under the appraisal statute is that the stock-
> holder is entitled to be paid for that which has been taken from him,
> viz., his proportionate interest in a going-concern. By value of the stock-
> holder's proportionate interest in the corporate enterprise is meant the
> true or intrinsic value of his stock which has been taken by the merger.
> In determining what figure represents this true or intrinsic value, the
> appraiser and the courts must take into consideration all factors and
> elements which reasonably might enter into the fixing of value. Thus,
> market value, asset value, dividends, earnings prospects, the nature of
> the enterprise and any other facts which were known or which could be
> ascertained as of the date of merger and which throw any light on fu-
> ture prospects of the [acquired] corporation are not only pertinent to an
> inquiry as to the value of the dissenting stockholders' interest but must
> be considered by the agency fixing value.[3]

---

[2] *Metropolitan Life Issuance Co.* v. *Aramark Corp.*, Del. Ch. C.A. No. 16142 (Feb. 5, 1998) (transcript).
[3] *Tri-Continental Corp.* v. *Battye,* 74 A.2d 71 (Del. 1950).

Under 8 Del. C. §262(h), the Court of Chancery should determine the fair value of the shares exclusive of any element of value arising from the accomplishment or expectation of the merger. The objective is to provide the dissenting shareholders with their proportionate share of fair value in the going concern on the date of the merger, rather than the value that is determined on a liquidation basis.[4] However, the shareholders are entitled in a statutory appraisal to no more than going-concern value, but not to a premium resulting from the transaction.[5] Thus, the dissenting shareholder's value excludes cost savings, synergies, or benefits of restructuring planned by the buyer. However, in *Cede & Co.* v. *Technicolor, Inc.*, the Delaware Supreme Court ruled that because the relevant valuation date is the merger date, actions planned by an acquirer should be taken into account in a second stage merger. This second stage merger is a transaction in which the shareholders' shares not acquired in an initial tender or exchange are squeezed out in a subsequent merger, provided that the plan is sufficiently fixed at the merger date.[6]

Normally, neither ownership control premiums nor minority ownership interest discounts should be considered when determining the value of a stockholder's interest in the corporation in appraisal actions. Typically, discounts for lack of marketability are also not permitted. In *Cavalier Oil Corporation* v. *Harnett*, the Delaware Supreme Court wrote:

> Cavalier's argument that the only way Harnett would have received value for his 1.5% stock interest was to sell his stock, subject to market treatment of its minority status, misperceives the nature of the appraisal remedy. Where there is no objective market value available, the appraisal process is not intended to reconstruct a pro forma sale but to assume that the shareholder was willing to maintain his investment position, however slight, had the merger not occurred. Discounting individual share holdings injects into the appraisal process speculation on the various factors which may indicate the marketability of minority shareholdings. More important, to fail to accord to a minority shareholder the full proportionate value of his shares imposes a penalty for lack of control, and unfairly enriches the majority shareholders who may reap a windfall from the appraisal process by chasing out a dissenting shareholder, a clearly undesirable result.[7]

Although valuation premiums and discounts normally may not be applied at the stockholder level, they may be applied at the company level. For example, *Tri-Continental Corp.* v. *Battye* ruled that an investment company discount is permissible for a closed-end fund. When a parent company has a majority or controlling ownership interest in its subsidiaries, the value of control of the subsidiary may be considered to arrive at the value of a parent company.

---

[4] *Bell* v. *Kirby Lumber*, 413 A.2d 137 (Del. 1980).

[5] Ibid.

[6] *Cede & Co.* v. *Technicolor, Inc*, 684 A.2d 289 (Del. 1996).

[7] *Cavalier Oil Corporation* v. *Harnett*, 564 A.2d 1137 (Del. 1989).

In *Rapid-American* v. *Harris*, the Delaware Supreme Court ruled that an ownership control premium at the parent company level should be included in an appraisal to compensate stockholders for the parent company's 100 percent interest in three subsidiaries. This decision leads to the anomaly that a business conducted through a subsidiary is entitled to an ownership control premium, but an identical business conducted through a division is not.[8]

Delaware Block Valuations.   Until 1983, the traditional method in Delaware for determining the value of dissenters shares was the Delaware Block Method. Using this method, the Chancery Court determined market value, asset value, and earnings or investment value, and then weighted the results to determine fair value. Market value was the trading price of stock in the marketplace, excluding any impact of the transaction from which the stockholder is dissenting. Asset value, or net asset value, was the market value of the firm's assets on a going-concern basis, less liabilities. Earnings or investment value was the value of historical earnings of the company, generally capitalized using a price/earnings multiple, based on the capitalization rates of the common stocks of similar companies. (Since the capitalization rate is developed independent of the subject company's price/earnings multiple, this value is distinct from market value.) As discussed below, the Delaware Block Method is no longer regularly used in Delaware. However, it has not disappeared in some other jurisdictions.

In the opinion of the authors, the Delaware Block Method is flawed in that it necessarily understates fair value. The conclusion as to fairness ought to focus not on a blending of the three approaches, but on the highest of them. For example, if you have a silver dollar that is worth $1 as currency, $5 if melted, and $10 to a coin dealer, it is worth $10.

Valuations under *Weinberger* v. *UOP, Inc.*   In the landmark Delaware case *Weinberger* v. *UOP, Inc.*,[9] the use of the Delaware Block Method as the only means of determining value was declared obsolete. The plaintiff alleged, among other things, that The Signal Companies, Inc., which owned 50.5 percent of UOP, Inc., had unfairly used its majority stock ownership position in UOP to cash out UOP's minority shareholders at the grossly inadequate price per share of $21. In addition, the plaintiff argued that Signal had abused its majority ownership position by causing the board and management of UOP, which it controlled, to disseminate proxy information to minority stockholders that misrepresented and failed to disclose how the merger price was established.

The plaintiff's expert had determined fair value using two approaches: (1) acquisitions of comparable companies, and (2) a discounted cash flow analysis—both determining enterprise value. The defendants' expert used the Delaware Block Method. In 1981, the Court of Chancery

---

[8] *Rapid-American* v. *Harris*, 603 A.2d 796 (Del. 1992).
[9] *Weinberger* v. *UOP, Inc.*, 457 A.2d 701 (Del. 1983).

rejected the plaintiff's valuation as being contrary to logic and to Delaware law, and ruled for the defendants on all counts.

In 1983, this decision was reversed in part by the Delaware Supreme Court, negating the Court of Chancery's rejection of plaintiff's expert's discounted cash flow valuation as a matter of law. The Supreme Court noted that the discounted cash flow method was the method that had been used by two UOP directors in evaluating the merger. The Court stated that, to the extent that the Delaware Block Method excluded other generally accepted approaches and methods used by the financial community, it was clearly outdated.

The Court further ruled:

> Accordingly, the standard "Delaware block" or weighted average method of valuation, formerly employed in appraisal and other stock valuation cases, shall no longer exclusively control such proceedings. . . . Only the speculative elements of value that may arise from the "accomplishment or expectation" of the merger are excluded.

The Delaware Block Method seldom has been used in subsequent Delaware decisions.

Delaware Court Valuations in Stock-for-Stock Mergers.
Mergers in which common stock of one company is exchanged for common stock of another are viewed differently from sales for cash or for cash and debt. This is because the stockholders will have a continuing economic interest in the surviving firm. The landmark case describing the standard of value in these mergers for Delaware corporations is *Sterling* v. *Mayflower Hotel Corp.*[10] In this decision the Supreme Court of Delaware wrote:

> A merger ordinarily contemplates the continuance of the enterprise and of the stockholder's investment therein, though in an altered form . . . In [this] case the stockholder of the merged corporation is entitled to receive directly securities substantially equal in value to those held before the merger. . . .

The primary issue is the exchange ratio of the value contributed by each share to the merger versus the value received. If the merging companies have similar capitalization rates, the exchange ratio computation should compare the bases of value of the constituent companies. For example, the exchange ratios in the case of Strawberry Corporation merging with Raspberry, Inc., could be computed as in Exhibit 16–1. In this case, the bases of value tend to indicate an exchange ratio of approximately 1 share of Strawberry Corporation for 0.55 to 0.66 shares of Raspberry, Inc.

Occasionally, plaintiffs contend that an exchange is unfair because share market value received by the common stockholders is less than

---

[10] *Sterling* v. *Mayflower Hotel Corp.*, 93 A.2d 107 (Del. 1952).

Exhibit 16–1

Exchange Ratios

Exchange Ratio Basis	Strawberry Corporation	Raspberry, Inc.	Ratio of Strawberry to Raspberry
Market price	$46.83	$84.64	0.55x
Asset value per share	$18.73	$28.21	0.66x
Historical earnings per share (excluding nonrecurring items)			
1999	$2.68	$4.56	0.59x
2000	$2.94	$5.25	0.56x
Latest 12 months	$3.12	$5.64	0.55x
Projected earnings per share			
2001	$3.30	$5.77	0.57x
2002	$3.69	$6.35	0.58x
Dividends per share			
2000	$0.75	$1.50	0.50x

the asset or liquidation value given up. *Sterling* v. *Mayflower Hotel Corp.* showed why this objection is not valid:

> If plaintiffs' contention should be accepted it would follow that upon every merger of a subsidiary into its parent corporation that involves a conversion of a subsidiary's shares into shares of the parent, the market value of the parent stock issued to the stockholders of the subsidiary must equal the liquidating value of the subsidiary's stock. On its face this proposition is unsound, since it attempts to equate two different standards of value. In the case of many industrial corporations, and also in the instant case, there is a substantial gap between market value and the liquidation value of the stock; and to apply to the merger of such corporations the proposition advanced by plaintiffs would be to bestow upon the stockholder of the subsidiary something which he did not have before the merger and could not obtain—the liquidating value of his stock.

In some mergers, the capitalization rates of the merging companies will be different and the analysis will focus more directly on comparing the market value received in the combined firm in exchange for the market value given up. Moreover, in mergers that are not "mergers of equals" (companies of similar size), the value of the shares offered to stockholders of the smaller company will almost always be greater than the smaller company's market value to induce approval of the merger.

For example, in the stock-for-stock acquisition by DuPont of the minority shares in Remington Arms Co., the Court in *Citron* v. *E.I. DuPont de Nemours & Co.* considered the fact that Remington shareholders received a premium. The Court also noted that the cash value was significant to shareholders who immediately sold the shares they received and that the DuPont stock was a higher-quality security.[11]

Appraisal Rights in Other Jurisdictions. It cannot be overemphasized that the legal standard for dissenters' rights and for fairness in one jurisdiction may be different than in another. For example, a number of states permit the application of (1) minority ownership interest and (2) lack of marketability discounts in a statutory appraisal. As discussed later in this chapter, the value of the dissenters' shares in these jurisdictions may be discounted materially from the amount that would be determined elsewhere.

Among the states that permit discounts are New York, Kentucky, Oregon, Colorado, and Georgia. Ohio has an unusual appraisal standard —fair market value of the shares, generally their public market price, is the amount awarded on an appraisal. This standard has little relation to actual fairness.

Despite a fairness opinion's accuracy from an economic or financial point of view, a court can accept or reject it *as a matter of law*. This occurs when a court considers the fairness opinion to be inconsistent with the valuation standard used or the valuation methods prescribed in the jurisdiction. It is therefore incumbent on the financial adviser to inquire as to the relevant statutory and case law when necessary.

Determinants of the Range of Financial Fairness

In arriving at a conclusion with respect to a transaction involving cash or debt, a financial adviser ordinarily will derive a range of fairness. An imprecise definition of a range of fairness is that the upper end is the highest price that a reasonable buyer would pay, and the lower end is the lowest price that a reasonable seller would accept, after consideration of all relevant factors. It is, of course, possible that a buyer would overpay and exceed the upper end of such range. There are numerous historical examples, often in a bidding contest, where an acquirer paid more than anticipated by the financial advisers to the seller. Many such instances were followed by bankruptcy of the acquiring entity, as in the case of Federated Department Stores.

Several factors enter into determining the range of financial fairness. The basic question that has to be answered is: Will the shareholder be better off after the transaction than before it? Legal standards may set a floor on fairness for the seller, but the facts of a situation may lead to increasing the lower end of the fairness range. For example, in an appraisal under Delaware law, selling shareholders cannot share in any of

[11] *Citron* v. *E.I. DuPont de Nemours & Co.*, 584 A.2d 490 (Del. 1990).

the benefits arising from the challenged transaction. Nonetheless, fairness may require that a portion of the synergies and cost savings be attributed to the seller if such benefits could be achieved in an alternative transaction.

In a cash transaction, the selling shareholder has to look at whether the price is within the fairness range and what alternatives exist. In a stock-for-stock deal, it is necessary to consider the relative benefits of owning the respective securities.

Financial fairness to a buyer presents different issues. The primary concern is estimating the upper end of the fairness range, considering the impact of the transaction on the acquirer. It is necessary to look at the pro forma effect on a buyer, including potential cost savings and synergies, as well as related expenses, to determine whether the shareholders will benefit from the transaction.

Other Matters to Be Considered

Structural Fairness.   Most fairness opinions address only the fairness, from a financial point of view, of the consideration offered in a transaction. Directors may be better served if a fairness opinion addresses the fairness of the transaction taken as a whole rather than simply the consideration offered.

A situation in which the consideration is fair—but the transaction could be unfair—arises when inside shareholders receive materially greater consideration than public shareholders, but the latter receive an amount within the fairness range. A similar situation could come about through differences in consideration paid to various classes of stock, differences in treatment of certain shareholders within a class, or an excessive premium being paid to controlling shareholders. Differences in consideration among various shareholders should be analyzed to determine if they are justifiable.

A financial adviser should not render an opinion that the consideration is fair if he or she has reason to believe that the transaction taken as a whole is unfair.

Non-Arm's-Length Transactions.   Fairness opinions are particularly important (and contentious) in non-arm's-length transactions, such as a going-private transaction. In these situations, the analyst giving the opinion frequently also functions as a financial adviser with respect to the terms of the transaction and may assist in negotiations.

Unlike the typical arm's-length transaction, in which there is usually a presumption of fairness, the financial adviser in a going-private transaction normally starts with a presumption of unfairness—a presumption that has to be dispelled for the transaction to proceed. A board of directors addressing a proposed non-arm's-length transaction will customarily appoint a committee of independent directors (usually called a *special committee*) in an effort to shift the burden of proof if the fairness issue is litigated. The special committee will hire independent counsel and an independent valuation firm to render a fairness opinion. It will also be responsible, if necessary, for negotiations with the acquiring party.

The due diligence for preparing the fairness opinion has to be conducted with greater than ordinary skepticism. Since management is likely to be a beneficiary of the deal, it may take a conservative view of the company's prospects. It is often helpful to review forecasts made prior to the gestation of the proposal and to see any information provided to parties that are being asked to assist in financing.

Because of disclosure requirements established by the Securities and Exchange Commission (SEC), it may be inadvisable for a financial adviser to disclose a range of fairness to the special committee. Unfortunately, the SEC requires that, if such information is given to a special committee, disclosure is required in a proxy statement. It is difficult to negotiate with a controlling shareholder for a higher price within a fairness range if such range would have to be revealed publicly at a later date.

Discussions between a special committee and its financial adviser could be more open and constructive if disclosure were limited to describing (1) negotiations with the controlling shareholder and (2) an explanation and description only of the ultimate fairness opinion—as rendered to the special committee and the full board of directors. Advice of counsel is particularly useful during this process.

Stock-for-Stock Transactions. Fairness in a stock-for-stock transaction is based on relative measures and not on the absolute price of the shares being received. Even if the value of the shares being received is below the fairness range for a cash deal, a board of directors may, in its business judgment, decide that it prefers a nontaxable deal. This would be the case if the board believes that the equity being received is attractive. The fact that the shareholders have a continuing economic interest, as discussed above in *Sterling* v. *Mayflower Hotel Corp.*, affects the legal standard of fairness.

Even if a cash offer is made at a somewhat higher price, a stock-for-stock deal may be fair. However, if the cash offer is materially higher than a stock offer and near the upper end of a fairness range, it may become difficult to render a fairness opinion on the stock proposal.

Comparing Different Forms of Consideration. It is easy to determine which of two cash offers is more fair. However, the decision can be less clear if one is comparing a cash offer to a securities offer. In *Citron* v. *Fairchild Camera Corp.*, the Court ruled that a board of directors, in its collective business judgment, could elect to take a cash offer with a value lower than a preferred stock offer from a different bidder.[12] It is therefore possible that two offers, one in cash and the other in equity, can both be fair, regardless of which is higher. The decision as to which offer to accept should be made by the board. Similarly, two equity offers can both be fair, and it is for the directors to decide which to recommend. The role of the financial adviser in assisting the board in its deliberations will depend upon the scope of the assignment.

---

[12] *Citron* v. *Fairchild Camera Corp.*, 569 A.2d 53 (Del. 1989).

Legally, there is a substantive distinction between situations that would result in a change of control, where a board is required to quantify noncash consideration to compare it objectively to a cash offer[13] and situations in which there is no change of control, where a board can elect to favor a transaction that it believes is consistent with its long-range objectives.[14]

Inadequacy Opinions. Valuation analysts are sometimes requested to render an "inadequacy opinion" in response to an unsolicited bid for a company. Because such opinions normally are needed in a short time frame, they are usually provided by a valuation firm with a historical relationship to the target company. There are no established legal standards as to what inadequacy is, but it is clear that *inadequate* is not synonymous with *unfair*. A price in the low portion of a fairness range can be deemed inadequate. However, it would appear that a cash price above the midpoint of a fairness range should be deemed adequate.

The Fairness Opinion Process

Generally, the fairness opinion process has the following steps:

1. The decision maker and his or her advisers conclude that a potential transaction requires a fairness opinion.
2. The decision maker interviews financial advisers and explains the facts and circumstances of the potential transaction.
3. Potential financial advisers evaluate the nature of the proposed transaction and check for conflicts of interest.
4. The selected financial adviser forms an engagement team (which may include an industry specialist).
5. The team carries out:
   - A transaction review
   - Qualitative analyses, including due diligence
   - Quantitative analyses
   - Pricing analyses
6. The team consults with the decision maker and with other appropriate parties, both in carrying out its analyses and in obtaining information.
7. If appropriate (particularly in non-arm's-length transactions), the financial adviser assists in negotiations.
8. The team prepares an internal memorandum to an internal review committee, which then questions the team and decides whether to issue the opinion.
9. A presentation is made to the decision maker.

---

[13] *Paramount Communications, Inc.* v. *QVC Network, Inc.,* 637 A.2d 34 (Del. 1994).
[14] *Paramount Communications, Inc.* v. *Time Inc.,* 571 A.2d 1140 (Del. 1990).

10. If the opinion is to be publicly disclosed, the financial adviser and the decision maker prepare a written description of the role of the financial adviser.
11. If a proxy statement or similar document is to be distributed, the financial adviser reviews the document, provides required information regarding the opinion, and updates the opinion prior to mailing.
12. The final written opinion is issued.

Selection of the Financial Adviser

The decision maker usually selects the financial adviser on the basis of two criteria: (1) professional experience and (2) personal relationships. If the decision maker has retained a financial adviser in an arm's-length transaction, that adviser is usually selected to render the fairness opinion. This is true even though the adviser may have a financial interest (i.e., a contingent fee) in the transaction.

Although some commentators have frowned on this apparent conflict of interest, it is still a common practice. It is a common practice under the theory that the financial adviser brokering the deal knows the most about it. In many situations, an independent opinion may be requested. In these cases, the decision maker may interview a number of prospective financial advisers to present their qualifications and terms for providing the fairness opinion.

In a non-arm's-length transaction, it is more likely that an independent party will be retained for the fairness opinion. However, there are occasions when the controlling party may select the "opinion giver." This is often the case in partnership transactions, where an independent party rarely represents the outside limited partners. In such a situation, the financial adviser should remain aware that the opinion should address the fairness to the noncontrolling interests.

Evaluating the Engagement

Qualifying the Engagement. A fairness opinion engagement differs in many ways from a valuation engagement. In hiring the financial adviser, the decision maker—at a minimum—is attempting to demonstrate the exercise of reasonable business judgment in making a fiduciary decision. Depending on the facts, the engagement may require special industry knowledge, transactional experience, or testimony experience, as well as a detailed understanding of the business valuation and the fairness opinion process. Furthermore, the financial adviser may have a conflict of interest because of past or current relationships with one of the parties and/or direct involvement in the transaction. Therefore, a financial adviser should consider refusing an engagement because of lack of specific experience or material conflicts. The alternative could be costly and embarrassing litigation.

An engagement may have significant litigation and reputation exposure owing to such factors as poor planning, litigious shareholders, or unequal treatment of minority stockholders.

Defining the Engagement. Once a financial adviser accepts an assignment to opine on a potential transaction, the next issue is defining the engagement. The value of companies and their securities is always dependent on the specific situation. Before a valuation assignment or fairness opinion can begin, the following questions should be answered:

1. What is the consideration being exchanged?
2. What is the opinion date?
3. What legal valuation standard is applicable and how is it applied?
4. What are the limitations imposed, if any?

It is also necessary to define the scope of the assignment, such as the extent of any services in addition to the rendering of an opinion.

The Consideration to Be Exchanged

Economic Value of Common Stock. The consideration to be exchanged affects the valuation methods to be employed. Most fairness opinions involve the purchase, sale, or exchange of equity interests, such as common stock. If a corporation is profitable and has prospects of generating additional income, its value is dependent on its earning power, and the methods that value earning power will be emphasized in the valuation. These include analyses of publicly traded companies in the same or similar industries, analyses of acquisitions of companies in the same or similar industries, and discounted cash flow calculations. To the extent that a company has excess assets, their value should also be taken into account.

If the company has little or no earning power, but it has asset value, then the methods that estimate net asset value on a going-concern basis should be emphasized.

Marketability of Common Stock. Publicly traded shares are passive minority ownership interests in a company. Marketable common stock is salable in the open market; either on an exchange or over the counter. Marketability can be affected by the size and breadth of the market for the shares. Marketability of common stock can be an important factor in determining value in many jurisdictions—and may be relevant in a fairness determination.

Minority ownership interests in closely held corporations—or restricted minority ownership interests in public corporations—cannot be legally sold in the open market; they can be sold only in private placements. These blocks have the added risk of lack of ready marketability, in that their owners may not be able to sell at a time of their choice (1) to take advantage of high prices or (2) to avoid anticipated price declines. This added risk causes a discount for lack of marketability to be applicable to these shares. The discount normally leads to the shares being valued (1) materially below the market price of equivalent freely traded minority shares and (2) at a greater discount from the value of control blocks.

Ownership Control Premium and Minority Ownership Interest Discount. Control blocks are active ownership interests. Depending on the size of the block held, an owner of a control block can direct day-to-day operations of the corporation, liquidate or redeploy assets, or sell, merge, or liquidate the entire corporation. To the extent that these powers represent the potential for added income or capital appreciation, the value of control blocks on a per share basis will be greater than the value of marketable minority ownership interests. This increase in value is often called the ownership control premium.

The term *ownership control premium* can be ambiguous, since it is used in two different ways: (1) it is sometimes calculated on the basis of the difference between the price paid for control and the market price of publicly traded shares, and (2) it is sometimes the difference between the price paid for a control block and that block's pro rata share of the aggregate value of the company. The payment of an ownership control premium to a major shareholder may be fair to the other shareholders, provided that, under the facts and circumstances, it is a reasonable percentage of the total value of the company.

Public companies' common stock generally trades in the marketplace at a price that reflects a minority ownership discount. The amount, or even the presence, of a minority ownership discount, however, varies widely. The market price may reflect the fact that the corporation is already large and well run, that there are unusually favorable prospects for the company and its industry, or that a deal is anticipated.

There are occasions when shares trade at prices that value a company at a higher level than a reasonable acquirer would pay. And it is erroneous to assume that the market price of publicly traded shares necessarily includes a minority ownership interest discount. Moreover, as with a discount for lack of marketability, the relevancy of a minority ownership interest discount to fairness is a function of the relevant state law.

Not all restricted interests in public corporations will be priced lower than the market price of similar publicly traded interests. Control blocks will often sell at a price premium. Private stock sales reflecting either (1) major capital infusions to generate significant earnings or (2) strategic alliances may be priced above the market price, if the transaction has not been disclosed. Similarly, private sales of stock in highly speculative industries may be priced at or above the current market price because of the limited stock available for purchase on the open market.

Other Legal Rights and Stockholder Agreements. Corporate charters may also contain special allocations of dividends, assets, and earnings. Each of these can have an effect on relative value of different classes. Side agreements by stockholders—whether in the form of buy-sell agreements, voting trusts, or estate planning devices—can have much the same effect of increasing or reducing the value of common stock by altering its rights to control, income, appreciation, and marketability.

The Opinion Date. The value of common stock may be quite different at different dates. Stock prices will vary depending upon the economic conditions, interest rates, and outlook as perceived by investors at any given time. During periods of economic expansion and low interest rates, values will be high. Conversely, during periods of economic contraction or high interest rates, common stock prices will be relatively low. As a result, even though an acquisition or a going-private transaction may be fair during the planning stages, it may become unfair two to six months later because of a change in economic circumstances, market conditions, adverse events specific to the company (or to the acquirer if it is offering securities), or changes in the company's (or acquirer's) prospects.

For transactions that do not require shareholder approval, the fairness opinion is normally dated on or shortly before the date that the transaction is finalized. When a fairness opinion is included in a proxy statement, it is advisable that it be updated to a date proximate to the mailing date. Some valuation analysts continue to monitor companies between the mailing date and the shareholder vote and to withdraw an opinion if material changes have occurred. For example, Bear, Stearns & Co. withdrew a fairness opinion given to Far West Financial Corporation in 1984 when a takeover battle caused a substantial increase in the market value of a major investment position subsequent to the proxy mailing.

The Legal Standard of Value and Its Application. As discussed above, the standard of value for a particular transaction can change depending on the jurisdiction. As a financial adviser, the analyst should rely on counsel to explain the appropriate standard of value and its application.

Limitations Imposed. Sometimes the activities of the financial adviser may be limited by the client, by the other party to the transaction, or by law. The cause may be either the nature of the proposed transaction or the desire to speed up the process or reduce the fee. For example, a bidder may demand an answer by a certain date, and tender offer rules also limit response time. If constraints limit the scope of the activities of the financial adviser, the constraints should be disclosed in the opinion letter. Courts do not look favorably on opinions produced in record time or opinions that lack independence. Generally, the minimum time required to produce a fairness opinion is approximately two weeks —unless the adviser has a prior familiarity with the situation or the time constraints are beyond the control of the client. In accepting a constrained assignment, an adviser should be cognizant of the heightened litigation risk.

The Role of the Engagement Team

The role of the engagement team is to review the proposed transaction, to prepare a memorandum or submission to an internal review committee recommending acceptance or rejection, and to act as an intermediary between the internal committee and the client. The team often will perform the following analyses:

1. A transaction analysis that summarizes the proposed transaction, including the parties, the proposed terms, and an assessment of the risk and opportunities involved.
2. A qualitative analysis of the consideration to be exchanged in the transaction. If equity is part of the consideration, the qualitative analysis may include an analysis of the issuer and/or securities in question, which would include the history, nature, operations, and outlook of the corporation as well as its environment, and the rights and privileges of the securities to be exchanged.
3. A quantitative analysis of the consideration to be exchanged, which in the case of common stock consists of an analysis of the issuer's financial statements and projections as well as the income and asset claims of the securities.
4. A pricing analysis of the consideration to be exchanged, which in the case of common stock consists of one or more of the following:
    a. Reviewing market prices, prior sales, and firm arm's-length offers for the issuer and its stock.
    b. Computing the appropriate relationship of the market value of the common stock to the market value of underlying assets less all liabilities.
    c. Comparing the performance and common stock prices of guideline public companies, in relation to the issuer's performance and the proposed transaction price for its common stock, with market values of the common stock expressed in the form of ratios, such as:
        *   Aggregate market value of the issuer's capital (often defined as the market value of the common equity plus debt and preferred stock less cash) to:
            revenues
            EBITDA (earnings before interest taxes, depreciation, and amortization)
            EBIT
        *   Price/earnings
        *   Price/book value (if book value is relevant)
        *   Dividend yields (for minority interests)
    d. Comparing the performance and acquisition prices of comparable companies in relation to the issuer's performance and the proposed transaction price.
    e. Computing net asset value.
    f. Preparing a discounted cash flow calculation.

Qualitative Analysis and Due Diligence.   Qualitative analysis usually consists of tours of the facilities and essential management interviews with respect to the company and, if relevant, the other party to the transaction. Interviews with management involve discussions about the history, operations, environment, and prospects for the company.

Follow-up interviews should be conducted if important questions subsequently develop. During visits to significant manufacturing facilities or other facilities, the financial adviser should be alert to material negatives and positives, potential problems and opportunities, and questions that elicit contradictory, angry, or negative responses. However, the financial adviser generally is not expected to be an expert on the operations of a company.

It is important to understand the bases for a company's projections and the sensitivity of the projections to the respective assumptions. To the extent that the prospective transaction may generate cost savings and other synergies, these benefits should be discussed and quantified.

The sources of information that should be reviewed include (1) written company materials (including SEC filings, if any); (2) publicly available secondary sources; (3) due diligence, possibly including calls to suppliers, customers, or other companies in the industry, if appropriate; (4) other information required for the specific study; (5) press releases; and (6) security analysts' reports on the company and its industry and, if relevant, the other party to the transaction and its industry. If a proxy statement or other document is to be distributed, it should be reviewed as well.

Quantitative Analysis.   Quantitative analysis is used to analyze the subject company's past financial statements, interim statements, and projections in order to understand its income potential, assets, liabilities, and financial condition. The typical ratios to be calculated include:

1. Profit margins
2. Profit trends
3. Capital structure ratios, such as leverage ratios and fixed charges coverage
4. Liquidity ratios, such as the current ratio, quick asset ratio, receivables, and inventory turnovers
5. Rates of return on assets and equity
6. Industry ratios

Financial statements should be adjusted to eliminate any nonrecurring or special items that may distort the earning power of the corporation. Similar adjustments should be made to data of guideline companies. These items can include profits from discontinued lines of business, litigation awards or costs, one-time write-offs, profits from favorable refinancing, or changes in accounting methods. The effects of nonoperating assets should be removed from the financial statements, and these assets should be analyzed separately.

In consolidated financial statements, losses from one operation can obscure the profits of another. Therefore, divisional financial statements should be reviewed. Private corporations' financial statements may need further adjustments, since they are frequently run to minimize taxes, not to maximize profits.

Financial budgets and projections should be reviewed to understand management's expectations for the company. The analysis should take into consideration the company's budgeting or forecasting methods, its past budgeting or forecasting accuracy, and the reasonableness of the assumptions—given past performance and current and expected business conditions.

Pricing Analyses. Any pricing analysis may be used to value a company as long as it is a standard procedure used by the financial community. The most common techniques, as discussed above, are market analysis, public company analysis, acquisition analysis, computation of net asset value, and computation of discounted cash flow value. A full discussion of each of these techniques is beyond the scope of this chapter. However, a few observations may be useful.

Market Value. The market price of a common share of a public company traded in a free and active market is one of the best indicators of its value. However, market prices can be affected by one-time events such as the stock market declines of 1987 and 1998, extraneous rumors, announcements, or even the pending transaction that is the subject of the opinion. Furthermore, market prices may be unreliable because of either the low price or the low trading volume of the stock. Daily or weekly price and share volume should be reviewed (1) in comparison with the proposed transaction price and (2) in comparison with either market indexes or the market prices of shares of stock of guideline public companies. In addition, even in the case of public companies, the financial adviser should review other offers for the company and/or its stock and prior written valuations.

The Problem with Acquisition Price Premiums. A common error in attempting to estimate the acquisition value of an interest in the stock of a company is to compute the average historical price premium in similar acquisitions and apply it to the market price. Historical price premiums over market are a biased sample; the universe includes situations in which a buyer was willing to pay a premium over market. However, it obviously cannot include situations in which the stock is considered by prospective acquirers to be fully priced in the market, and therefore no bid is made.

Moreover, the price premium that a buyer would pay in an acquisition results from the buyer's valuation. The price premium is not the cause, but the effect. Acquisition price premiums depend on the specific factors of each transaction.

Analysis of Guideline Public Companies. The guideline company method is a primary method of valuation. Courts and financial advisers often have different views of the role of public companies in the determination of value. Despite the existence of tens of thousands of public companies, it is getting harder to find close proxies for a company as public companies broaden their businesses.

Many financial advisers have expanded their criteria for selecting guideline companies, believing that these comparisons provide useful information. However, some courts have chosen to question this method because of the lack of direct comparability of the public companies and to rely more heavily on the discounted cash flow method. Nevertheless, methods require significant judgment and interpretation. Even with somewhat less comparative companies, the guideline publicly traded company method can be more reliable than many discounted cash flow calculations.

Analysis of Guideline Acquisitions. The guideline acquisition method is essentially similar to the guideline company method and is subject to many of the same strengths and questions. There are two important differences, however, that should be noted.

First, acquisition prices normally include an ownership control price premium. The extent or dearth of acquisition activity in a particular industry can affect the analyst's conclusion as to the applicability of a control price premium in a prospective transaction.

Second, acquisitions are valued as of the date that the terms of the deal were agreed to, whereas guideline companies are valued as of a current market date. In utilizing multiples paid in acquisitions, the analyst should give consideration to relevant changes in market and industry conditions subsequent to the date at which the acquisition was evaluated.

The Harmonic Mean. Pricing the subject company on the basis of market-derived multiples of public companies and acquisitions requires using either summary statistics or individual company-to-company comparisons.

Most people automatically use the arithmetic mean to summarize these pricing multiples. However, arithmetic means of pricing multiples with price in the numerator are often distorted because they are effectively weighted toward the higher multiples. The median—the midpoint of the group—is a better measure of central value. However, it has the disadvantage of eliminating the information contained in the remaining pricing multiples.

In many instances, the best measure of central value is the harmonic mean (H), which is derived from the arithmetic mean of the reciprocals of the market-derived pricing multiples. It is calculated as follows:

$$H = n / \Sigma(1/m)$$

where:
H = harmonic mean
n = number of companies for which ratios are computed
m = pricing multiple of a guideline company
$\Sigma(1/m)$ = sum of the reciprocals of the guideline companies' pricing multiples

With respect to price/earnings multiples, the harmonic mean calculates an average on the basis of earnings/price multiples. This is identical to the method of calculating an average yield on a group of debt securities, since yield is simply the dividend/price multiple. Another way of describing the harmonic mean is that it gives equal weight to equal dollar investments in securities whose multiples are being averaged. In contrast, the arithmetic mean gives a pricing multiple of 20×, which is twice the weight of a multiple of 10×. To give proper weighting, the harmonic mean should be used for multiples in which price is in the numerator.

The following example may be useful. Assume that Company A sells at a market price of $20 per share, has earnings of $2 per share, and a dividend of $2 per share. Assume that Company B sells at a market price of $25 per share, has earnings of $1.25 per share, and a dividend of $1.25. The dividend yields are 10 percent and 5 percent, respectively. The average yield is 7.5 percent. The price/earnings multiples of the two companies are 10 times and 20 times, respectively. The arithmetic mean of these two numbers is 15. The harmonic mean is calculated by taking the reciprocals of 10× and 20× (0.10 and 0.05), averaging them (0.075), and then taking the reciprocal of 0.075 to get a harmonic mean price/earnings multiple of 13.3×.

Looking at this in a different way, if one has an equal amount invested in each stock, what is the price/earnings multiple of the portfolio? If one spends $1,000 to buy 50 shares of Company A earning $2 per share, the underlying earnings would be $100 (50 times $2.00). If one spends $1,000 to buy 40 shares of Company B earning $1.25 per share, the underlying earnings would be $50 (40 times $1.25). With $2,000 invested in a portfolio earning a total of $150, the portfolio's price/earnings multiple is 13.3×—that is, the harmonic mean.

If, instead, one wished to purchase $100 of the underlying earnings in each company, one would still buy 50 shares of Company A for $1,000, but it would be necessary to spend $2,000 to buy 80 shares of Company B. The total cost of the portfolio would be $3,000 for $200 in earnings. The price/earnings multiple of this portfolio is 15×, the same as the arithmetic mean.

The harmonic mean gives equal weight to equal dollar investments, whereas the arithmetic mean gives greater weight to stocks with higher price/earnings multiples.

Discounted Cash Flow (DCF). In the 1980s and 1990s, DCF analysis gained widespread acceptance as a preferred valuation method because of its apparent objectivity and mechanical nature. However, as of this writing, several potential problems with this method have to be addressed when using DCF analysis for fairness opinions.

DCF is based on the premise that the value of an equity interest is the present value of its future net cash flows (1) for 5 to 10 years plus (2) its *terminal value* (the interest's value at the end of the projection period).

Projected net cash flows. Net cash flow is defined as the amount of cash available to an equity interest after all the company's operating expenses and investment needs, such as capital expenditures and incremental working capital, have been met and all senior obligations and claims, if any, have been satisfied. These cash flows may be projected on either a *leveraged* or an *invested capital* basis.

Leveraged cash flow projections incorporate the costs of senior financing through deducting the projected after-tax cost of interest and other financing costs from each year's operating cash flow, adding the funds available through additional financing, and subtracting the funds required to meet future financing payments. The net annual cash flows and the terminal value are present-valued, using the cost of common equity capital (k_e) as the present value discount rate.

Invested capital cash flow projections do not incorporate the cost of financing in the projection. The present value of the annual cash flows and the terminal value are calculated using the weighted average cost of capital (WAAC) as the present value discount rate. Any existing senior financing is subtracted from the present value of the invested capital annual cash flows and the terminal value in order to estimate the value the common equity.

Estimation of the present value discount rates. Academically, the cost of common equity capital (k_e) is estimated using the capital asset pricing model (CAPM) as follows:

$$k_e = R_f + B \times (RP_m - R_f) + RP_s + RP_u$$

where:

R_f = risk-free rate of return of U.S. Treasury securities
B = beta, a measure of volatility relative to other assets
RP_m = common stock market rate of return
RP_s = a risk premium for small equity capitalization stocks
RP_u = alpha, the return for company-specific risk

The weighted average cost of capital (WACC) is calculated as follows:

$$WACC = k_e \times W_e + k_d \times (1 - t) \times W_d$$

where:

k_e = cost of common equity capital, determined above
W_e = percent of total capital represented by equity
k_d = pretax cost of debt
W_d = percentage of total capital represented by debt
t = marginal income tax rate

Although the CAPM is widely accepted academically, and its application has been approved by some courts, it should be recognized that the model may be flawed in some applications. Beta can be difficult to determine and is not infrequently a matter of contention. Moreover, there is disagreement in the academic community over the relevance of beta. Some practitioners also disagree with how the small company risk premium is typically determined.

An analyst's own experience and judgment as to the capitalization rates required by investors should be used to test the reasonableness of the cost of capital calculated using the CAPM model. Experienced valuation analysts are well aware of the high targets set by venture capital investors, and are aware of returns expected by their clients in M&A

transactions. It is preferable to use the present value discount rates required in the real world when such rates are justified by knowledge and experience.

Estimation of terminal value. The terminal value (*TV*) can be calculated by using either a market-derived pricing multiple or a growth model. The most commonly used is the Gordon Growth Model shown below.

$$TV = [NCF \times (1 + g)]/(k - g)$$

where:

NCF	=	normalized net cash flow in the terminal year
g	=	expected annual long-term growth rates in *NCF*
k	=	the cost of capital, either k_e or the WACC, as appropriate

In using the Gordon Growth Model, the analyst should be aware that a distorted result can be obtained when the expected growth rate is close to the cost of capital. If the expected growth rate is equal to the cost of capital, the calculated terminal value is infinite.

Valuation analysts sometimes estimate terminal value by taking a multiple of EBIT or EBITDA in the final year. Often, the current pricing multiple for guideline companies is used. However, the valuation analyst should consider whether an adjustment is necessary, for example, because the current pricing multiple is based on a current growth rate that may decline as an industry matures.

The present value of the terminal value is calculated by discounting it by the appropriate direct capitalization rate.

Alternative scenarios. Companies often produce forecasts using different sets of assumptions. Alternatively, valuation analysts may consider the impact of changes in certain assumptions on a company's projections. It can be helpful to perform DCF calculations on the basis of the various scenarios and to consider the relative likelihood of each scenario.

DCF problems. There are several potential problems with the DCF method. The first problem is whether management or the financial adviser reasonably can be expected to project future performance over the following 5 to 10 years. These projections are necessarily based on numerous assumptions. Many public companies have trouble projecting next year's earnings accurately. To the extent that the projection incorporates new or untested actions, it would tend to be less reliable. However, if (1) the projections are based on reasonable assumptions, (2) management has been reasonably accurate in its prior projections, and (3) the projections are reasonable given past performance, then they may be analytically useful. Certain industries can be projected with reasonable confidence (e.g., cable TV, regulated utilities), while others are much more difficult to project (e.g., airlines, computers).

The second problem is the "horizon problem"—that is, the impact of the number of years in the projection. The outer years are obviously more difficult to project. If a projection has higher growth rates than the discount rate, each added projection year will increase the DCF value. The impact of the horizon should be reviewed.

The third problem is the selection of the terminal value. Often 80 percent or more of the DCF value is the present value of the terminal value. The terminal value is a function of the projection for the final year of the forecast, which is necessarily subject to the highest margin of error. Small changes in the final year forecast, in the terminal multiple, in the present value discount rate, or in the expected growth rate used in the Gordon Growth Model can have a major impact on the DCF value. Given the importance of the terminal value in the DCF method, some commentators have noted that the method is simply taking the present value of capitalized earnings 5 to 10 years in the future using a guideline company or acquisition approach. The impact of alternate terminal values should be reviewed.

The fourth problem is the method used to calculate the present value discount rate. Although the CAPM has been widely accepted for portfolio applications, there is growing doubt about its accuracy for calculating present value discount rates applicable to individual companies. The WACC used in calculating the present value discount rate is affected by the assumed level of debt in the capital structure. Some practitioners use an industry average capital structure, others use the actual capital structure for the firm, and still others use an acquisition capital structure.

Despite these potential problems, a DCF calculation may be useful if it is one of several valuation methods employed. It can be helpful as a check on other methods. A method that implies a valuation greater than the calculated value based on discounted cash flow should be examined carefully.

Asset Value.   Net asset value generally refers to the value of both the company's tangible and intangible assets. However, the definition is changing. There are generally four methods of estimating net asset value.

The first method, used in financial statements under GAAP, values the assets on the basis of their historical cost net of depreciation and amortization. This approach is of little use in fairness opinions, with the limited exception of industries such as insurance, in which book value has a direct relation to earning power.

The second method is valuing assets in use, estimating their value as part of a profitable going concern. The assets are valued by their revenue-producing ability or at their depreciated replacement cost (including the cost of assemblage). This method may not be realistic if the going concern cannot produce the assumed revenues.

The third method is liquidation. This approach values the assets assuming the break-up of the company and either (1) the orderly liquidation or (2) the auction of its assets, with related tax consequences.

The fourth method is disaggregation. This method assumes that the company is broken into smaller units, some of which are valued as going concerns, others of which are liquidated.

Formula Pricing.   In some industries, there are rules of thumb that are widely applied—for example, value per subscriber for a cable television company. To the extent that such guidelines are widely used in an industry and have a justifiable economic basis, they can be used as a confirmatory method for a fairness opinion and in litigation. For example, in *Neal* v. *Alabama By-Products Corp.,* the Court used a value per recoverable ton of coal reserves.[15]

Developing the Conclusion

The engagement team is usually responsible for the preliminary conclusion of whether a transaction is fair from a financial point of view. The decision should be based on thorough analysis, informed judgment, and common sense. If the team decides to recommend the issuance of a fairness opinion, the team normally will present its conclusion before an internal review committee, which typically makes the final decision about issuing the opinion. Whenever possible, adequate information about the proposed transaction should be given to committee members in advance of the meeting. In large or complex transactions, a well-reasoned memorandum to the committee can be a helpful document if there is subsequent litigation.

Presenting the Opinion

After the internal review, the financial adviser usually makes an oral presentation to the decision maker. The presentation typically covers the following topics: (1) a description of the transaction and the scope of the opinion requested, (2) a description of the procedures used and factors considered, (3) a summary of the significant findings, (4) a discussion of the assumptions and limitations, and (5) the conclusion.

Frequently the presentation is accompanied by tables and charts relevant to the conclusion. If the conclusion is positive, a form of the opinion letter may be presented to the board and its legal counsel. If a proxy statement or similar document is filed with the SEC, any documents presented to the special committee or to the board are required to be filed as exhibits. However, absent a federal requirement, there is no Delaware requirement that the analyses underlying a fairness opinion must be disclosed,[16] and we are not aware of any such disclosure requirement in any other state.

The Final Opinion Letter

Normally, the opinion letter summarizes the following information:

1. The date of the letter.
2. The addressee, usually the decision maker.

---

[15] *Neal v. Alabama By-Products Corp.*, Del. Ch., C.A.. No. 8292 (Aug. 1, 1990), reprinted in 5 M&A & Corp. Gov. L. Rptr. 238.

[16] *Matador Capital Management Corp. v. B.B.C. Holdings, Inc.,* Del Ch. C.A. No. 16758 (Nov. 25, 1988).

3. A summary description of the transaction that is the subject of the opinion.
4. The assignment of the financial adviser.
5. Material relationships, if any, between the financial adviser and any of the parties to the transaction.
6. A description of the factors considered and procedures used by the financial adviser to carry out the assignment, including:
   a. Materials reviewed
   b. Facilities visited
   c. Meetings and interviews with senior management and any others
   d. Review of market data, appraisals, and offers
   e. The guideline company analysis
   f. The guideline acquisition analysis
   g. The discounted cash flow calculation
   h. Other analyses, if any
7. A statement of the scope and limitations of the assignment, including:
   a. Reliance on representations of management and the decision maker
   b. Reliance on projections prepared by management
   c. Reliance on public company data
   d. Reliance on information provided by others, including consultants, if any
   e. Reliance on market and economic conditions as of the date of the opinion
   f. Time constraints, if any
   g. Other contingent and limiting conditions.
8. The statement of opinion.
9. The signature.
10. Limitations on use of the opinion letter.

The final opinion letter is usually signed as of the date of the decision, if the transaction is expected to close promptly. If the opinion will be included in a proxy statement, it should be dated at or shortly before the mailing date. A sample opinion is presented in Exhibit 16–2.

Exhibit 16–2

Form of Opinion Letter

May 1, 1999

Board of Directors
Strawberry Laboratories, Inc.
11 Tyler Drive
Lakeville Industrial Park
Lakeville, VT 00001

Dear Directors:

We understand that Strawberry Laboratories, Inc. ("Strawberry") is considering entering into an Agreement and Plan of Merger pursuant to which Merger Sub, Inc. ("Merger Sub"), a wholly owned subsidiary of Fantastic PLC ("Fantastic"), will commence a tender offer for all of Strawberry's outstanding common stock for $20.00 per share in cash, net to the seller, to be followed as soon as practicable by a merger of Strawberry and Merger Sub, pursuant to which each share of Strawberry (other than shares owned by Strawberry, Fantastic, Merger Sub or dissenting shareholders) will be converted into the right to receive the cash consideration per share paid in the tender offer (collectively, the "Transaction").

You have supplied us with a draft of the Agreement and Plan of Merger by and among Fantastic PLC, Merger Sub, Inc., and Strawberry Laboratories, Inc., dated as of May 31, 1999, in substantially the form to be executed by the parties (the "Merger Agreement").

You have asked us to render our opinion as to whether the Transaction is fair, from a financial point of view, to the public stockholders of Strawberry.

In the course of our analyses for rendering this opinion, we have:

1. reviewed the Merger Agreement;

2. reviewed Strawberry's Annual Reports on Form 10-K for the fiscal years ended June 30, 1994 through 1998, its Quarterly Reports on Form 10-Q for the periods ended September 27 and December 27, 1998, and its unaudited interim financial statements for the periods ended March 29, 1998, and March 28, 1999;

3. reviewed certain operating and financial information provided to us by management relating to Strawberry's business and prospects, including its budgets for the years ending June 30, 1999 and 2000;

4. met with Strawberry's senior management to discuss its operations, historical financial statements, and future prospects;

5. visited Strawberry's facilities in Lakeville, Vermont;

(continues)

Exhibit 16–2

6. reviewed the historical market prices and trading volume of the common stock of Strawberry;

7. reviewed publicly available financial data and stock market performance data of public companies that we deemed generally comparable to Strawberry;

8. reviewed the terms of recent acquisitions of companies that we deemed generally comparable to Strawberry; and

9. conducted such other studies, analyses, inquiries, and investigations as we deemed appropriate for the purposes of this opinion.

In rendering our opinion, we have relied upon and assumed, without independent verification, the accuracy and completeness of all financial and other information that was available to us from public sources and all the financial and other information provided to us by Strawberry or its representatives. We have further relied upon the assurances of the management of Strawberry that they are unaware of any facts that would make the information Strawberry or its representatives provided to us incomplete or misleading.

With respect to the projected financial results, we have assumed that they have been reasonably prepared on bases reflecting the best currently available estimates and judgment of the management of Strawberry. We do not express an opinion or any other form of assurance on the reasonableness of the underlying assumptions. In arriving at our opinion, we have not performed or obtained any independent appraisal of the assets of Strawberry.

Our opinion is necessarily based on economic, market, financial, and other conditions as they exist on, and on the information made available to us as of, the date of this letter.

Based on the foregoing, it is our opinion that the Transaction is fair, from a financial point of view, to the public stockholders of Strawberry.

The opinion expressed herein is provided for the information and assistance of the Board of Directors of Strawberry concerning its consideration of the Transaction. Our opinion does not constitute a recommendation to the stockholders of Strawberry as to whether or not to tender their shares in the tender offer or vote in favor of the merger.

Very truly yours,

ABC Securities

Chapter 17

Solvency Opinions

David Light, Bryce May, Richard May, John Miscione, and John O'Brien

Purpose of Solvency Analysis

The desire for, and reliance on, solvency opinions has grown significantly over the past three decades along with the increase in the number of leveraged buyouts (LBOs). An LBO is a form of corporate restructuring whereby a company is acquired through borrowed funds. Although an LBO may be an effective way for parties with limited capital to gain control of an enterprise, the resulting level of debt may place an undue financial burden on the business, thereby increasing the likelihood of financial distress and threatening the going-concern status of the business.

In fact, as the number of leveraged transactions has increased, so has the number of subsequent reorganizations and liquidations. These occurrences can injure both pre- and post-LBO creditors. In an attempt to limit their losses, creditors and bankruptcy trustees have used the fraudulent conveyance laws to avoid fraudulent transfers that are financed with debt.[1]

Financial consultants often perform a solvency analysis to determine whether, following some type of leveraged transaction ("the transaction"), the company that incurred the leverage is left with (1) positive equity, (2) the ability to repay its debts as they come due, and (3) adequate capital to operate its business. These three requirements form the foundation for solvency analysis. After performing a solvency analysis the analysts can, if warranted, write a solvency opinion with regard to the transaction. Typically, a solvency opinion may be requested by the directors of a company or by the lender to the transaction. The purpose of such an opinion is to assure the directors and/or lender that the leveraged transaction is not likely to harm the other creditors of the company by forcing a bankruptcy or liquidation.

Brief Definition of Solvency Analysis and Description of Tests for Solvency

A solvency analysis attempts to determine whether a transaction will create any one of the three financial conditions that can lead to claims that a fraudulent transfer exists at the time of a debt financing or a transaction.

The three conditions studied in a solvency analysis are defined in Section 548 of the U.S. Bankruptcy Code, the Uniform Fraudulent Transfers Act, and the Uniform Fraudulent Conveyance Act (the "fraudulent conveyance laws"). According to Section 548 of the Bankruptcy Code, a transfer may be voided if a business entity:

---

[1] Edward I. Altman, *Corporate Financial Distress and Bankruptcy,* 2d ed. (New York: John Wiley & Sons, 1993).

(i) was insolvent on the date that such transfer was made or such obligation was incurred, or became insolvent as a result of such transfer or obligation;

(ii) was engaged in business or a transaction, or was about to engage in business or a transaction, for which any property remaining with the debtor was an unreasonably small capital; or

(iii) intended to incur, or believed that the debtor would incur, debts that would be beyond the debtor's ability to pay as such debts matured.

"insolvent" means—

(A) with reference to an entity other than a partnership and a municipality, financial condition such that the sum of such entity's debts is greater than all of such entity's property, at a fair valuation, exclusive of—

(i) property transferred concealed, or removed with intent to hinder, delay, or defraud such entity's creditors; and

(ii) property that may be exempted from property of the estate under section 522 of this title.[2]

To summarize, a solvency analysis determines if at the time of the transaction (giving effect to the transaction) any of the following conditions exist:

1. A company is insolvent (the *balance sheet test*).
2. A company is engaged in (or is about to engage in) a business or a transaction for which it has unreasonably small capital (the *adequate capital test*).
3. A company is incurring debts that would be beyond its ability to pay as such debts matured (the *cash flow test*).

These three tests together are here identified as the *solvency tests*. It is important to note that in order to be considered solvent, a company must pass all three tests.[3]

The occurrence of bankruptcy after a leveraged transaction does not necessarily prove that the company was insolvent immediately after the transaction, or that a fraudulent conveyance did occur. The opposite is equally true: The absence of a bankruptcy after a transaction does not guarantee that the company would have passed the solvency tests.

Thus, it is apparent that the solvency tests are *legal standards*, which, if *not* passed by a company after a transaction, expose the company,

---

[2] U.S. Bankruptcy Code, Section 548.

[3] For a thorough discussion of the legal framework for solvency and fraudulent conveyance, see: J. Queenan, "The Collapsed Leveraged Buyout and the Trustee in Bankruptcy," *Cardozo Law Review*, December 1989, pp. 1–49.

selling shareholders, its lenders, and its directors to liability under the fraudulent conveyance laws *in the event of a bankruptcy*. Obviously if no bankruptcy or loss occurs, then neither the pre- nor the post-transaction creditors are damaged, so no legal action would be taken to trigger an examination of the solvency tests by a court.

A major risk to secured creditors loaning into a transaction that is later considered a fraudulent conveyance is that the loan and security interests could also be considered fraudulent. An important decision on this point is *United States* v. *Tabor Court Realty Corporation,*[4] which voided the lender's security interests, even though the loan was to the company rather than to the buyer or seller directly.

Selling shareholders are subject to subordination of debts owed to them by the company incurred as part of their sale proceeds if the transaction is found to be a fraudulent conveyance, and in fact may have to put money back in from proceeds already received. Directors and controlling shareholders are also subject to liability for breach of their fiduciary duties if a fraudulent conveyance is found.

Balance Sheet Test

The balance sheet test determines whether, at the time of the transaction, a company's asset value was greater than its liability value. As a first step in conducting the balance sheet test, the assets of the company are valued as a going concern as of the date of the transaction. Then the value of the company's liabilities is subtracted from the asset value. The balance sheet test is passed if the sum of the value of the company's assets is greater than the sum of the value of its liabilities.

For purposes of this analysis, a valuation of the company should be performed. As an example, let us assume that $5.5 million is the fair market value of the company's assets. We would then subtract the value of the company's post-transaction liabilities ($4 million) included in the assumed opening balance sheet. In this example, the result is an excess of fair market value of assets over liabilities of $1.5 million. Therefore, the company passes the balance sheet test.

Exhibit 17-1 highlights the results of the balance sheet test. Notice that the value of current liabilities is added to the market value of the enterprise capital of the company. The reason is that current liabilities are part of working capital, and therefore have already been accounted for as part of the ongoing working capital level in the operating value of the business. Since we deduct these out of value as part of the liabilities, we should add them to the fair market value of the company's enterprise capital above in order to get an estimate of the value of the left-

---

[4] *United States* v. *Tabor Court Realty Corp.*, 803 F.2d 1288 (3d Cir. 1986), *cert. denied*, 483 U.S. 1005 (1987).

Exhibit 17–1

ABC Auto Supply, Inc.
Present Fair Salable Value Analysis

Pretransaction enterprise value	$ 5,500,000
Plus: current liabilities	4,000,000
Present fair salable value	9,500,000
Liabilities	
Current liabilities	4,000,000
Debt Financing	
Senior secured debt	2,000,000
Revolving line of credit	750,000
Subordinated debt	1,250,000
Total liabilities	8,000,000
Excess (deficit) of fair value	$ 1,500,000

hand side of the balance sheet—the value of the assets.

Cash Flow Test

The cash flow test determines if a business entity incurred debts that would be beyond the debtor's ability to pay as such debts matured. Conclusions about the ability to pay debts are based on analyses of a series of projections of future financial performance of the business that are created by varying some key operating characteristics of the business (typically including, but not limited to, revenue growth and profit per dollar of sales). Similar to what should be done in evaluating company projections for a discounted cash flow (DCF) valuation, the analyst should judge which scenarios are reasonable in light of the company's past performance, current economic conditions, and future prospects.

In the cash flow test, future post-transaction debt payments of a company are computed and scheduled by due date. Then a projection of the amount of liquidity available to the company to meet its debt requirements is estimated from each set of projections. To calculate a company's liquidity available for debt repayment, the analyst could project each of the following for the company for several periods after the transaction: (1) any excess cash on hand, (2) free cash flows earned during each period, and (3) the company's borrowing availability on each due date to pay its debts. A comparison would then be made between the amount of debt payments required during each period and the liquidity available to satisfy such requirements.

A company will pass this test in any projected period if it can pay its debts as they come due either through cash accumulated on its prior earnings or through free cash flow earned in the period, or by having enough borrowing availability to pay its debts. As an example:

1. Cash on hand is considered in conjunction with the borrowing availability (item 3 below) so that cash is allowed to go to $0 in certain scenarios as long as there is credit available.
2. Free cash flow is defined as net income plus noncash charges, plus or minus cash required to fund the company's operating assets, capital expenditures, and dividends (if any).
3. Borrowing availability is the amount of unused credit under the company's credit line that can be borrowed without causing an event of default.

As one projects further into the future, borrowing ability may also consist of the ability to relever the company to take advantage of the prior debt repayments that have been made.

As presented in Exhibits 17-5 through 17-7 at the end of this chapter, the company in our example passes the cash flow test in each of the scenarios examined except the final year of Scenario III. The failure in the final year is due to the balloon payment of an unsecured shareholder subordinated debenture. As mentioned above, this failure is probably acceptable since the payment of the subordinated debt could be rescheduled or restructured in order to prevent an immediate cash shortfall or a violation of a loan covenant.

The Adequate (Reasonable) Capital Test

The adequate capital test determines if a business entity was engaged in a business or a transaction for which it had unreasonably small capital. This test is related to the cash flow test in that if a company has adequate capital, it will be able to pay its debts as they come due and have the capital to run its business under a wide range of financial circumstances and economic conditions.

The adequate capital test is intended to determine whether a company is *likely* to survive, assuming reasonable business fluctuations in the future. In other words, recognizing that all projections about the future are uncertain, one would like to be able to estimate the likelihood that the newly leveraged company has enough cushion in its post-transaction capital structure to withstand a typical amount of fluctuation in financial results.

Unlike the cash flow test, which looks directly at whether the company is able to meet its scheduled debt obligations as they come due, the adequate capital test is intended to analyze the company's robustness to the general economic uncertainty that all businesses face. That is, given its new capital structure, can the company survive if its actual performance is slightly below its projections, or if it takes slightly longer to achieve certain assumed changes in the business?

One key measure of a company's reasonable capital is the availability of committed credit, given a variety of projected levels of performance. One would typically test the availability of committed credit under the lending covenants that were negotiated as part of the leveraged transaction.

Projected Cash Flow Sensitivity Analysis

When a cash flow sensitivity analysis is used to determine adequate capital, the projected future financial performance of the company is analyzed in a variety of scenarios and the sufficiency of its cash and credit to meet its business needs is assessed. In addition to comparing the cash needs relative to its revolver limit, as is done in the cash flow test, one would analyze whether the company would pass each of the *covenants* on its term debt under a variety of presumed performance scenarios. Assessment can then be made of whether the company would have access to its committed credit when needed.

The results of this test will demonstrate under what circumstances the company would trigger a default under its lending covenants. The scenarios tested should include (1) management's best estimate of the future, (2) no change from recent historical performance, and (3) some reasonable variations of revenue growth and profit margin assumptions.

Black-Scholes Option Pricing Analysis

In order to address possible issues of bias in the selection of appropriate scenarios for capital adequacy, an alternative and less subjective technique is often used: Black-Scholes option pricing default analysis. This analysis can provide a specific numerical estimate of the company's expected probability of defaulting on its debt obligations given the nature of its business and its capital structure. Before we look at the specific assumptions and implementation of the default analysis, it is useful to review some general theory regarding bankruptcy.

Bankruptcy. Bankruptcy occurs when a company is unable to meet a legal obligation to its debtors. The obligation may be an actual cash payment (e.g., an interest payment) or it may be technical (e.g., a required minimum coverage ratio). Several important points about bankruptcy should be noted:

- The declaration of bankruptcy may be partly voluntary on the part of the company, or it may occur involuntarily because of lender perceptions. Either way, it is difficult to predict bankruptcy.
- Bankruptcy occurs at a point in time. The fact that a company is

bankrupt today does not mean that it was bankrupt yesterday. If a company is not currently bankrupt, one can only ask about the *probability* of its bankruptcy in the future.

- It is important to distinguish perceptions about the *value* of the company (used for the balance sheet test) from perceptions about the *probability* of bankruptcy. However, in order to estimate the probability of bankruptcy, it is necessary to have an estimate of the company's value.

- With a relatively simple model, it is possible to estimate the probability that bankruptcy will occur. This can be done by estimating either the probability that assets will be worth less than required debt payments at maturity or, alternatively, the probability that asset values will be less than the face value of debt owed at any time during the debt amortization period. The latter probability is a conservative estimate of bankruptcy, since it captures all instances where the asset value falls below the face value of debt, regardless of the length of time during which this condition persists. In other words, a case where asset value falls to less than the face value of debt for only a single day would, in actuality, not cause either bankruptcy or default. However, this second model captures all such instances, regardless of how brief.

Until a company actually fails to meet its obligations and formally enters bankruptcy, it may be hard to estimate precisely the probability that bankruptcy will occur. If a company does not have the cash to make an interest payment, it can often acquire cash by selling assets or new securities. Similarly if a company is about to enter technical default, management may elect certain accounting conventions that can eliminate or defer the violation, or it may be possible to raise cash from new sources.

Thus, the occurrence of bankruptcy may be in part voluntary on the part of management, or it may stem from the lender's perception—right or wrong—that the company is in hopeless straits. Either way, it is difficult to formally model the occurrence of bankruptcy, and it is often difficult to tell whether a company is in fact bankrupt at any point in time prior to the formal declaration of bankruptcy.

Despite the difficulty of knowing whether a company is about to enter bankruptcy, these models can be used to give a range of probabilities of technical default where the fair salable value of assets does not exceed liabilities. It is important to distinguish two issues:

1. What is the *value* of the company's assets at the time of the transaction?
2. Given the value of the company's assets, what is the *likelihood* that at some future date the company will enter bankruptcy?

One should realize that even if the value at which the assets were transferred was adequate and the company was not insolvent at the time of the transaction, bankruptcy might occur at a later date. The question then is: Was there sufficient capital on a post-transaction basis to *reasonably expect* that the company could survive in the normal course of business? Rather than a strict "bankrupt" or "not bankrupt" state, the question of bankruptcy is more usefully thought of as a continuum, with the *probability of bankruptcy* depending on several factors, including the value of a company's assets as a percentage of debt.

Implementation of the Default Analysis. Suppose that the value of the company is estimated accurately. If one adopts a very simple model of bankruptcy, it is possible to estimate a range of likelihood that bankruptcy will occur. For this default model, one can consider two different definitions of bankruptcy. One can say bankruptcy has occurred if (1) the fair salable value of assets falls below the value of the debt at a specific future maturity date (i.e., the company has inadequate capital at a specific future date) or (2) the fair salable value of assets falls below the level of debt at any time over the life of the debt. These two calculations provide bounds on the likelihood of bankruptcy. A very important feature of this technique is that it captures the entire spectrum of possible future performances of the business.

Using these two definitions of bankruptcy (or default), one can call upon the same assumptions that were used by Black and Scholes in their derivation of the option pricing model to estimate the probability of bankruptcy.

This model views the assets of the company as behaving like a stock, on average increasing because of reinvestment and decreasing because of dividends and payments to debtholders, but also moving randomly up and down. The expected growth in asset value would equal the unleveraged discount rate. The amount of debt owed by the company is assumed to increase at the cost of debt. The maturity is estimated as the average duration of all debt. The random up and down movements of the assets' value are estimated in terms of a *standard deviation*, but in this case considering volatility of the assets rather than of the equity. This is a measure of the likelihood of "unexpected" movements. If the standard deviation is small, the assets are very likely to grow at close to the estimated growth rate. If the standard deviation is large, the assets will still be expected to grow at the same growth rate, but with substantial margin for error (both up and down).

The specific inputs into a Black-Scholes default analysis model are:

1. **Asset value.** An estimate of the fair salable value of the company's assets as of the transaction date. This would most likely equal the actual transaction price for the enterprise.
2. **Expected growth in assets.** The unleveraged equity rate of return required by investors in the company.
3. **"Expiration date" or time for debt repayment.** This is the time frame during which the model estimates the probability of bankruptcy, often estimated as the duration of debt, meaning the weighted average of the present value of interest and principal payments of all debt. In other words, duration accounts for both timing and amount of payments. For senior debt, subordinated

debt, noncompete payments, and capital leases, the timing and interest rates are known. For the timing of the revolver payments, one can use projected revolver balances based on management's projected income statement or vary the timing according to alternative scenarios.

4. **Value of the debt.** This is the face amount of debt on a post-transaction basis. This debt amount is assumed to grow at the cost of debt.

5. **Volatility of assets.** This is an estimate of the expected annual standard deviation of future asset returns for the company. Standard deviation is a common measure of expected uncertainty or risk. Since the standard deviation measures the extent to which the company can be expected to vary from its mean growth rate, a larger standard deviation means that there is a greater probability of bankruptcy. The company's expected asset volatility can be estimated from analysis of historical volatility of its actual asset returns or those of public companies in similar industries.

The above inputs are used to calculate two probabilities that can be used to estimate reasonable bounds for the probability of default. In the first calculation, one estimates the probability that the company's asset value will be less than the value of debt at the expiration date of the debt. This considers only a single point in time, without regard to whether the asset value fell below the value of debt during the interim period, and so is likely to understate the actual probability of default.

The second calculation gives the probability that the company's asset value will fall below the value of debt (at some interim period) *at any time* before the expiration date. Suppose that there is a debt repayment schedule under which the outstanding value of debt grows at some specified rate per year (think of this as the interest rate on zero coupon debt). Then given the value of debt today, one is asking for the probability that at some time between now and the expiration date, the asset value "hits" the barrier value of debt at that interim time.

This second analysis will produce a higher probability of default, since it captures all cases where the asset value is below the value of debt at the expiration date, plus some additional cases where the company, if given the opportunity, would have bounced back from its interim drop in asset value.

Obviously, whether the company is able to bounce back in reality depends on how long it remains below the value of debt threshold, how deeply it falls below this threshold, and the tolerance of its creditors. Clearly some cases that are counted as defaults in the second test may not actually result in either default or bankruptcy. Therefore, the second probability can be thought of as an upper bound on the probability of default for a company.

Typically, whenever either model produces a probability of default that is above 50 percent (making bankruptcy more likely than not), one could argue that the company fails the adequate capital test. An example of how these results might be reported is shown below.

The results of the two default probability tests, run on data as of the transaction date, show that:

1. At the expiration date of the debt, there was a 20 percent chance that the company's assets would be less valuable than its capital debt plus accrued interest.
2. At *any time* before the expiration date of the debt there was a 40 percent chance that the company's asset value would fall below its then capital debt plus accrued interest balance.

The range of probabilities calculated using the Black-Scholes approach gives an unbiased assessment of the likelihood of default. Thus, this implementation of the adequate capital test is an important data point that can support or refute conclusions reached on the basis of other solvency tests.

Sensitivity Methodology

In order to make a determination as to whether a company has adequate capital and is likely to be able to pay its debts as they come due, one should examine the company's financial performance under a range of possible performance scenarios. Obviously, no formula can be given here as to how much adjustment should be made to each variable. However, some general guidelines can be laid out. One should always test management's best estimate projections. Another important scenario to test is a "no changes" approach that would represent zero sales growth and zero profit margin improvement. Typically, one would adjust the following variables, both individually and in tandem: sales growth; gross profit margin; selling, general, and administrative expenses; and depreciation and capital expenditures. Below is a brief description of three scenarios that are shown later as an example.

Scenario I: Management's Best Estimate

Scenario I looks at what would happen to the company if it met the base case management projections. These projections are assumed to be the management's best estimate of the company's most likely future performance.

Scenario II: Inflationary Sales Growth and Original Projected Profit Margins

In Scenario II, projected revenue growth is trimmed back from management's best estimate, but operating profit margins (EBITDA margin) are kept at the original projection levels as in Scenario I.

Scenario III: No Changes

In Scenario III, one can assume that there is essentially no change to the balance sheet working capital items or the income statement throughout the projection period. The goal of this scenario is to examine the performance of the business assuming no changes in revenues, profit margins, and working capital turnover rates from their pretransaction levels. This is a conservative scenario if the company had been experiencing both improving margins and positive sales growth in recent years, in which case "no change" would be a reduction from historical trends. This can be an aggressive scenario if the company has been experiencing deteriorating sales or margins. If the company were deteriorating, a more pessimistic scenario from "no change" would be warranted.

Key Variables of Historical and Projected Operations

The following example comes from a company in the auto parts and supply business. Key variables influencing the company's ability to generate cash flow for debt repayment were its (1) level of sales and growth in sales; (2) gross profit margin; (3) selling, general, and administrative expense level; and (4) asset and liability turnover ratios.

For purposes of the cash flow test, a sensitivity analysis was performed that determined whether the company could have survived if the management projections were not met as planned. The key assumptions under each scenario are highlighted in Exhibits 17-2, 17-3, and 17-4.

Exhibit 17–2

Management's Best Estimate

	Historical Performance January				Projected Performance January						
	1995	1996	1997	1998	1999	2000	2001	2002	2003	2004	2005
Income statement											
Sales growth	1.50%	0.80%	5.10%	5.00%	5.50%	4.50%	4.50%	4.50%	4.50%	4.50%	5.00%
Gross profit margin	40.60%	41.00%	39.20%	37.70%	41.00%	41.00%	41.00%	41.00%	41.00%	41.00%	41.00%
SG&A expense as a % of sales	39.60%	39.00%	36.80%	35.50%	36.90%	36.60%	36.50%	36.40%	36.30%	36.20%	36.30%
Income tax rate	7.30%	22.50%	-0.10%	0.60%	29.30%	38.60%	38.60%	38.60%	38.60%	38.60%	38.60%
EBITDA margin	1.00%	1.90%	2.30%	2.20%	4.10%	4.40%	4.50%	4.60%	4.70%	4.80%	4.70%
EBIT margin	0.00%	1.00%	1.30%	1.50%	3.20%	3.50%	3.60%	3.70%	3.80%	3.90%	3.80%
Balance sheet											
Accounts receivable turnover	1,088.0	1,040.0	903.5	605.8	626.0	641.0	656.6	660.2	677.0	694.6	677.0
Inventory turnover	2.3	2.6	2.7	3	2.9	3	2.9	3	2.9	2.9	2.9
Accounts payable turnover	5.4	6.7	5.2	5.3	5.3	5.5	5.5	5.6	5.5	5.5	5.5

Exhibit 17–3

Inflationary Growth

	Historical Performance January				Projected Performance January						
	1995	1996	1997	1998	1999	2000	2001	2002	2003	2004	2005
Income statement											
Sales growth	1.50%	0.80%	5.10%	5.00%	2.70%	2.70%	2.70%	2.70%	2.70%	2.70%	2.70%
Gross profit margin	40.60%	41.00%	39.20%	37.70%	41.00%	41.00%	41.00%	41.00%	41.00%	41.00%	41.00%
SG&A expense as a % of sales	39.60%	39.00%	36.80%	35.50%	36.90%	36.60%	36.50%	36.40%	36.30%	36.20%	36.30%
Income tax rate	7.30%	22.50%	-0.10%	0.60%	29.30%	38.60%	38.60%	38.60%	38.60%	38.60%	38.60%
EBITDA margin	1.00%	1.90%	2.30%	2.20%	4.10%	4.40%	4.50%	4.60%	4.70%	4.80%	4.70%
EBIT margin	0.00%	1.00%	1.30%	1.50%	3.20%	3.50%	3.50%	3.60%	3.70%	3.80%	3.70%
Balance sheet											
Accounts receivable turnover	1,088.0	1,040.0	903.5	605.8	626.0	641.0	656.6	660.2	677.0	694.6	677.0
Inventory turnove	2.3	2.6	2.7	3	2.9	3	2.9	3	2.9	2.9	2.9
Accounts payable turnover	5.4	6.7	5.2	5.3	5.3	5.5	5.5	5.6	5.5	5.5	5.5

Exhibit 17–4

No Change From Historical

	Historical Performance January				Projected Performance January						
	1995	1996	1997	1998	1999	2000	2001	2002	2003	2004	2005
Income statement											
Sales growth	1.50%	0.80%	5.10%	5.00%	0.00%	0.00%	0.00%	0.00%	0.00%	0.00%	0.00%
Gross profit margin	40.60%	41.00%	39.20%	37.70%	37.70%	37.70%	37.70%	37.70%	37.70%	37.70%	37.70%
SG&A expense as a % of sales	39.60%	39.00%	36.80%	35.50%	35.50%	35.50%	35.50%	35.50%	35.50%	35.50%	35.50%
Income tax rate	7.30%	22.50%	-0.10%	0.60%	29.30%	38.60%	38.60%	38.60%	38.60%	38.60%	38.60%
EBITDA margin	1.00%	1.90%	2.30%	2.20%	2.20%	2.20%	2.20%	2.20%	2.20%	2.20%	2.20%
EBIT margin	0.00%	1.00%	1.30%	1.50%	1.30%	1.20%	1.20%	1.10%	1.10%	1.00%	1.00%
Balance sheet											
Accounts receivable turnover	1,088.0	1,040.0	903.5	605.8	605.8	605.8	605.8	605.8	605.8	605.8	605.8
Inventory turnover	2.3	2.6	2.7	3	3	3	3	3	3	3	3
Accounts payable turnover	5.4	6.7	5.2	5.3	5.3	5.3	5.3	5.3	5.3	5.3	5.3

Sensitivity Analysis Outcomes

At the end of each sensitivity analysis, the following outcomes were measured:

1. Free cash flow versus scheduled debt payments
2. The amount of unused committed credit lines
3. Compliance with loan agreement covenants

The output of these tests is presented in Exhibits 17-5 through 17-7.

Exhibit 17–5

Management's Best Estimate

	January						
	1999	2000	2001	2002	2003	2004	2005
Cash flow tests	Pass	Pass	Pass	Pass	Pass	Pass	Pass
Covenants							
Interest coverage	Pass	Pass	Pass	Pass	Pass	Pass	Pass
Net worth	Pass	Pass	Pass	Pass	Pass	Pass	Pass
Debt to capital base	Pass	Pass	Pass	Pass	Pass	Pass	Pass
Current ratio	Pass	Pass	Pass	Pass	Pass	Pass	Pass

Exhibit 17–6

Inflationary Growth

	January						
	1999	2000	2001	2002	2003	2004	2005
Cash flow tests	Pass	Pass	Pass	Pass	Pass	Pass	Pass
Covenants							
Interest coverage	Pass	Pass	Pass	Pass	Pass	Pass	Pass
Net worth	Pass	Pass	Pass	Pass	Pass	Pass	Pass
Debt to capital base	Pass	Pass	Pass	Pass	Pass	Pass	Pass
Current ratio	Pass	Pass	Pass	Pass	Pass	Pass	Pass

Exhibit 17–7

No Change from Historical

	January						
	1999	2000	2001	2002	2003	2004	2005
Cash flow tests	Pass	Pass	Pass	Pass	Pass	Pass	**Fail**
Covenants							
Interest coverage	Pass	Pass	Pass	Pass	Pass	Pass	Pass
Net worth	Pass	Pass	Pass	Pass	Pass	Pass	Pass
Debt to capital base	Pass	Pass	Pass	Pass	Pass	Pass	Pass
Current ratio	Pass	Pass	Pass	Pass	Pass	Pass	**Fail**

Conclusions for Our Example

The results of the sensitivity analysis suggest that the company would have passed each of the standard solvency tests on a post-transaction basis. This is true even in the case of the "no change" scenario, which would represent a significant break from the increasing sales and higher margin trends that the company had experienced immediately before the transaction.

In addition, when the Black-Scholes analysis incorporated estimates of the fair market value of the company using the actual purchase price paid and the actual capital structure established to assess default risk, the analysis resulted in a range of probabilities of default from 12 percent to less than 35 percent. This analysis, which incorporates downside possibilities for future company performance that are below the "no change" scenario, would strongly confirm that the company had adequate capital after giving effect to the transaction.

Summary and Conclusion

A properly performed solvency analysis examines, on a pre- and post-transaction basis, the financial condition of a company that is entertaining the possibility of a leveraged transaction. The fraudulent conveyance laws provide the framework for analysis. Three tests must be passed in order to conclude that the company is not placing undue stress on the going-concern status of the enterprise. They are the *balance sheet test*, the *adequate capital test*, and the *cash flow test*. It is important to remember that these tests provide legal standards that, if not met, could result in the unwinding of the transaction. The law allows for the invocation of the fraudulent conveyance laws for up to one year (certain states extend this term for up to two years) from the date of the transaction.

The prediction of bankruptcy is extremely difficult, and no empirical model or legal standard can accurately predict the future viability of an enterprise. A solvency analysis attempts to assure the parties involved in a leveraged transaction that, as a result of the transaction, the company is not being subjected to undue financial distress. A solvency

Chapter 18

How Valuations Affect Transactions: Psychological Powers of Financial Numbers

Robert S. Socol and Robert Lawrence Kuhn

Value of Valuations
Psychological Factors
    Valuation as Metric
    Valuation as Certainty
    Valuation as Self-Esteem
    Valuation as Manipulator
Myths of Value
    Myth 1—Value Is Clear
    Myth 2—Value Is Consistent
    Myth 3—Value Is Constant
    Myth 4—Value Is Only for Transactions
Valuation in Transactions
    Valuation in Mergers and Acquisitions
    Valuation in Private Placements
    Valuation in Initial Public Offerings (IPOs)
    Valuation in ESOPs
    Valuation in Buy-Sell Agreements
Conclusion

Business valuations are not simply mathematical analyses. And value estimates of operating assets, business enterprises, and debt or equity securities are not just abstract numbers. Rather, business valuations are designed to support some specific practical application, usually (1) a transaction of some kind or (2) the prospect of such a transaction. This chapter will explore how business valuations and value conclusions affect transactions, particularly the subtle impact of valuations and value estimates on the psychological component of transactions.

Other chapters in this book discuss the analytical and systematic aspects of performing business valuations. We take the following next step: How do valuations—both the process and the result—affect and alter the transactions to which they relate? What are the ways in which the estimation of a seemingly hypothetical number can change or modify the qualitative—as well as the quantitative—aspects of a business or security sale transaction?

From a valuation analyst's perspective, the anticipated transaction may be (1) advisory (as in a merger or acquisition), (2) adversarial (as in a divorce, Internal Revenue Service dispute, or shareholder litigation), or (3) determinative (as in a buy-sell agreement). Such business valuations, respectively, may be characterized as negotiable, contentious, or definitive. However, they all are dependent, to a greater not lesser degree, on the psychological factors encompassing the business valuation. This chapter focuses on business valuations for business transaction purposes.

Value of Valuations

Whether for public or private companies, valuations play a critical role in transactions. For companies whose securities are publicly traded, valuations by independent third parties give a certain degree of protection to executives and board members. For privately owned companies, shareholders are almost always psychologically and emotionally too close to the companies to assess properly what is usually the major component of their net worth.

A seller who expects a certain value can compare his or her needs and expectations to what the valuation analyst estimates is likely to be achieved in the market. If market value is sufficiently below expectations, then the shareholder can avoid the hassle, disruption, and exposure of marketing the company until value and expectations are better aligned.

What makes a business valuation appropriate to be relied upon for transactional purposes? A business valuation, properly conducted, will show the owner of a company:

- How the company compares with its peers, in terms of financial and operational performance.
- What is going on in the company's industry environment, including trends and competitive pressures.

- What is going on in the M&A marketplace, relative to the overall financial and credit markets.
- What is going on in the M&A marketplace, relative to comparative companies in the same or a similar industry.

Valuations, to provide benefits in transactions or potential transactions, should be broad-based. A rigorously analyzed and thoroughly documented valuation will show the owner how his or her company would look in the eyes of a buyer. That is, the valuation should indicate how the buyer would assess the company in terms of its value enhancers and risk considerations. If the owner is not ready to sell, this assessment may still be helpful in positioning the company for sale at a later date.

Indeed, there are steps that business owners can take, over time, to mitigate the risks that may be depressing the subject business value. One typical condition in many small to midsize privately held companies is an excess dependence on the key shareholder. For example, owners who want to seriously prepare for a future business sale may learn from the valuation process that they could hire additional sales personnel to service the customers whom they have been personally handling. It is surprising how often owners will brag to buyers about their own indispensability, even after the business seller has been told that such rhetoric may actually reduce the business sale price offer.

Psychological Factors

Valuation as Metric

Business valuations, theoretically, are envisioned to be a critical measure of a fundamental operating asset or business enterprise characteristic—a clean metric. Business valuations are envisioned as a "stamp on the goods," so to speak, a seal of approval—as to the best estimate of the value of a bundle of operating assets or of a business enterprise. What could be simpler, or less ambiguous (certainly to a layperson), than a single number (or even a range of numbers) placed on the value of the subject business enterprise?

The problem, of course, comes in reconciling the fair market value estimate with transactional reality. What, in fact, is transactional reality? In theory, the best transactional reality is, classically, what an independent, willing buyer will pay an independent, willing seller, with sufficient information known to all parties. But what does this mean in the practical world of business valuations and acquisitive transactions?

Business valuations may be either a decision-making metric or a definitive-determining metric, depending on the purpose of the valuation. A business valuation for a prospective seller in an M&A assessment is "decision making." This is because the business valuation is a means to an end. On the other hand, in a buy-sell agreement, the business valuation is "definitive determining." That is, the business valuation itself is the end result.

In each case, however, the valuation is always more than just a numerical conclusion. Valuations carry surprisingly strong psychological baggage. Often the impact is subconscious. This is the fascinating part.

Valuation as Certainty

The greatest *weakness* of business valuations is that their conclusions are expressed in numbers. Does this assertion sound strange? Calling "numbers" a "weakness" may seem an odd thing for finance professionals to profess. This is because it is commonly assumed that the greatest *strength* of business valuations is that, contrary to much of what occurs in the chaotic world of business organizations, they *are* expressed in numbers.

The problem, of course, is one of artificial certainty. Business valuations are calculated and expressed as numbers. To the nonprofessional, the quantitative conclusion conveys the illusion of accuracy, as well as the confidence of precision. Business valuations, as transactional market participants know well, are concluded by various analytical methods. And these various analytical methods often yield somewhat contradictory results.

The final estimation of value, usually based as much on the individual analyst's experience and expertise as it is on analytical rigor and robust science, synthesizes—or blends—the varying value indication results into an overall value conclusion. This value conclusion, because it is quantitative, is what appears definitive to some of the more naive parties who rely upon business valuations.

One way that valuation professionals can ameliorate this problem is by limiting the number of significant digits in their valuation. To express a business valuation conclusion to the last odd dollar or even thousands of dollars, based on the output of a discounted cash flow analysis with an otherwise rounded present value discount rate, is ludicrous. *It is not paradoxical to assert that business valuations can be made more accurate by being made less precise!* It is often better to err on the side of uncertainty by rounding or ranging to as few significant digits as is practical, given the purpose and objective of the subject business valuation.

Valuation as Self-Esteem

Valuation is perhaps the strongest psychological measure of a business owner's overall perception of his or her bundle of operating assets or business enterprise. One of the most powerful—yet subtle—effects of a business valuation is its impact on the business owner's self-esteem, and the consequent potency of that self-esteem to alter business sale/purchase transactions.

Virtually all M&A professionals can offer war stories about how private business owners would rather sell their business for a purchase expressed as a large face value even though the payment terms stretch over many years. This is true even if such a business sale structure yields a significantly lower present value, or "cash equivalency value." This preference for the big face value business sale price seems to be just to make the "story at the club" more attractive (or more jealousy provoking).

Similarly, many business owners will commission a valuation of their own companies after the announcement of the sale of a company that is owned by friends or colleagues. This interest in a business valuation may be the owners' unconditioned response to a temptingly high sale price for the friends' company.

Valuation as Manipulator

Circular reasoning is the intellectual bane of business valuations. How easy it is to assume an end-result value and choose valuation methods, value indication, weightings, economic income projections, and present value discount rates to back into the already-assumed value. Although intellectually—and professionally—dishonest, this circular reasoning is sometimes difficult to avoid. The best antidote to the process is to recognize the poison.

Another temptation for valuation professionals is to factor into their assessment the wishes or goals of their clients. Let's assume that a client of an investment bank seeks a business valuation in order to determine whether or not to sell the business. If the investment bankers are thinking strictly for their own interests—which is both to get the sale mandate and to maximize the likelihood of a completed transaction—then the business valuation presents a subtle tension. On the one hand, if the business valuation conclusion is too low, then the client does not "go to market." On the other hand, if the business valuation conclusion is too high, then the client "goes to market" but becomes disappointed with the offers and ultimately decides not to close the business sale transaction.

It is easy to see how a business owner would be unhappy with a business purchase offer of $18 million given a business valuation conclusion of $20 million. However, the same business owner would be pleased with a business purchase offer of $17 million after receiving a business valuation estimate of $15 million. If the investment bankers can "get away" with a business valuation estimate of $15 million and still get the client to "go to market," then that is their best strategy.

But what is in the business owner client's best interest? The answer is simple: At all stages in the transactional process, the truth. A possible exception to that rule (or is it an investment banker's rationalization?) is if an unbiased assessment concludes that the business owner client should sell, then—by tilting the sale game board—the investment banker is truly protecting the client's long-term interests. However this altruistic goal may be accomplished, it may be thwarting the business owner client's short-term desires.

Myths of Value

Nonprofessionals largely assume that operating assets or business enterprise valuations consist of a relatively straightforward set of standardized methods that, much like generally accepted accounting principles, produce a standardized set of value results and valuation reports. This is often a mirage, ideal as it may sound. And it is the responsibility of valuation professionals to explain this common misunderstanding to their business owner clients.

Myth 1—Value Is Clear

How many generally accepted valuation methods are there for estimating business value? Who knows. One of the authors of this chapter enumerated 20 valuation methods.[1] No doubt, there are more business valuation methods than that, especially when one considers all the various procedures within each method. How does the conscientious analyst sort through and determine which valuation methods to use and how to weight their respective value indications? Leaving the rhetorical question unanswered, we note that even within each valuation method there is significant call for the application of professional judgment. For example, the estimation of projected economic income and the calculation of the appropriate present value discount rate are problematic enough.

Myth 2—Value Is Consistent

Forced consistency in business valuations is another flashpoint of potential errors. The worst part of this myth is an assumed degree of replicability of business valuation analyses.

Consistency and replicability are hallmarks of scientific analysis. The problem in transference from scientific analysis to valuation analysis is that the analytical input variables, both known and unknown, are orders of magnitude greater. Therefore, consistency and replicability are much harder to achieve in a valuation analysis than in a scientific analysis.

Certainly, there are generally accepted valuation approaches, methods, and procedures. Industries, generally, have "rules of thumb" that yield ballpark value indications. Some industry rules of thumb rely upon pricing multiples of EBITDA and/or EBIT, others rely upon pricing multiples of revenues and/or gross margin/contribution, and still others rely upon pricing multiples of operational data such as number of cable subscribers or hospital beds.

---

[1] Robert Lawrence Kuhn, "Valuing and Pricing Mergers and Acquisitions I: Practices and Techniques," Volume IV (Mergers, Acquisitions, and Leveraged Buyouts), *The Library of Investment Banking* (New York: McGraw-Hill, 1990).

Such industry rules of thumb, however, cannot constrain the actual valuation. To assume that all telecommunications companies should trade for the same pricing multiples is to invite a high degree of ridicule. In fact, there is often more variation in market-derived pricing multiples among companies within the same industry as there is between two different industries. In fact, companies with consistent earning patterns in two different industries may have a higher correlation of value than companies with inconsistent earning patterns in the same industry.

Myth 3—Value Is Constant

There is nothing constant about value. Once is not forever. Business valuation conclusions change, sometimes with astonishing speed and magnitude. Change is inevitable, and the inevitable change can occur without warning. Exogenous macroeconomic conditions, such as stock market discontinuities or industrial dynamics, and endogenous microeconomic conditions, such as competitive pressures or declining earnings, can trigger a sudden shift in business value.

Myth 4—Value Is Only for Transactions

Although the subject of this chapter is valuations in transactions, it is another myth to assume that business valuations are useful *only* for transactional purposes. Business valuations provide diverse benefits for a host of taxation, financing, litigation, and corporate governance purposes, such as for banking and insurance, intergenerational wealth transfers, and executive stock option grants.

Valuation in Transactions

Valuation in Mergers and Acquisitions

Business valuations are not essential for consummating M&A transactions. Many clients, who are sure that they want to sell, do not want to waste the time and money to estimate some analytical, theoretical, paper valuation. Rather, these clients are concerned only with what prospective buyers will actually pay at the closing table: the amount, terms, and conditions of the business sale consideration.

On the other hand, many prospective business sellers would consider a sale only if their "number is hit." These business owners require a specific minimum amount of after-tax cash and/or other form of sale consideration to induce them to enter into the business sale transaction. Often, it makes no difference to these business owners whether that "number" be logical or fanciful.

We often see business sellers stating that they must get $XX million for their business, regardless of when or how the sale proceeds are actually distributed. We remember one client who "needed" $12 million in order to entice him to sell his business. And that client didn't care that the slow growth rate of his mature company showed that it would take eight years to go from the current $8 million value to the desired $12 million value—present value being of little understanding and no interest. The sad conclusion to this actual client situation is that, owing to industry turmoil while the client demurred, the value of the client's business decreased to $3 million in less than two years.

Business valuation methods are also used on the buy side of an acquisitive transaction to determine how much can or should be paid for an acquisition. On the buy side of a transaction, the client motivations are different. In this case, estimates of initial offer, target price, negotiating range, and maximum price (and terms) are all part of the complex equation of decision making and negotiation strategy.

Business valuations have no less of a psychological effect on buyers than they do on sellers. We recall a large, highly leveraged buyout in the late 1980s in which a growth rate of 12 percent was required just to make the interest payments on the debt. The target company was a retail chain in a mature industry. The client, who was considering whether to take part of the mezzanine financing, was advised that, although the returns seemed spectacular, the price was just too high. The client fortunately decided not to participate in the deal. However, the equity sponsor had just raised a new fund and needed to do a "big deal" in order to justify his existence. Predictably, the deal collapsed within a few years, with heavy recriminations directed at the investment bankers who had pocketed large fees at the closing.

Business valuation can directly affect a transaction when there are internal differences of opinion as to the desirability of the transaction. Take a typical situation in a closely held company with multiple owners. In general, the more owners, the greater the likelihood that one or more will want to sell before the others do.

Unanimity among stockholders is rare when it comes to cashing out. Even with two happy stockholders, it is not uncommon for one stockholder to desire a sale—for a host of reasons from burnout to illness to wanderlust—and the other stockholder to decline. In these cases, business valuation can be a helpful psychological tool in convincing either one or the other: a low valuation conclusion may quiet the seller, and a high valuation conclusion may arouse the nonseller.

Valuation in Private Placements

Business valuation is just one of many aspects involved in the private placement of debt and equity securities. From the sell side, the owner may be raising equity capital either to expand the company's business or to shore up an ailing balance sheet. In either event, the current owner is concerned about the ultimate dilution of a new infusion of cash for equity. However, there may be other factors that outweigh the dilution penalty that the current owner will suffer.

There may be significant business opportunities that the company must act upon immediately. The current equity owner may be confronted with the decision of minimizing dilution at the expense of ulti-mately missing the business opportunity. The need to act quickly may obviate the business owner's ability to get the best price from the equity sponsor. Moreover, the seller may be more concerned with the overall fit of the new minority interest owner than in maximizing the equity sale price. Passing on an equity sale opportunity could lead to a better business result than entering into a venture with a bad partner.

An equity sponsor is typically looking to make investments that will return a minimal "hurdle" rate of return. This hurdle rate expectation requires the buyer to purchase the equity at the right price. Business valuations assist in establishing the "right price," but they are not conclusive in making the investment decision. The equity buyer may ultimately decide to pass on the investment because the selling company's operating philosophy is inconsistent with the buyer's own. Alternatively, the equity buyer may decide to invest in the company at a price that is too high in order to earn the required hurdle rate of return. This may be because the investment provides a platform into a desired industry or market.

In a recent case, a client needed an equity investment to allow his company to grow and take advantage of a significant market opportunity. Coincidentally, an equity investor approached him about the same time. We had a difficult time convincing the business owner to enter into the transaction by selling a piece of his company to the equity group. Although the price offered was attractive and more than the client thought the equity was worth, he was concerned about the potential changes resulting from having a new partner. After much encouragement, the business owner overcame his concerns and the story ends well: The performance of the company has far exceeded anyone's expectations and the equity investor has become a tremendous financial, operational, and strategic resource. The original owner's equity position is worth more now than it would have been had he not given up a piece of the business.

Valuation in Initial Public Offerings (IPOs)

Companies go public for a variety of reasons. Access to the capital markets is important for financing corporate growth, facilitating mergers and acquisitions, obtaining liquidity for the founders, and the like. The financial dynamics of IPOs for certain closely held companies became especially attractive in the mid-1990s. Companies could go public at higher valuations than they could be sold for in private market transactions. In many cases, traditional business valuation methods apparently became irrelevant. Companies could go public at enormous prices regardless of their earnings, or lack thereof. This led to a record number of IPOs in the 1990s.

Leveraged buyout investors were enticed by the high valuations. IPOs offered them the exit vehicle they were looking for to maximize their returns. High-tech companies went public because they needed access to growth capital. Other companies went public for their founder's ego gratification. Being the chairman of a public company meant that the founder had "made it." Still other companies were looking for financial security.

Often, the IPOs were difficult to justify from an investor's perspective. Traditional business valuation methods often yielded values substantially lower than the public offering prices. It is hard to imagine why people invested in some of these IPOs, other than for the emotional and psychological gratification of being able to say they owned the stock. What else can explain the enormous popularity of Internet stocks with small investors?

When valuations are high, why not go public? One client who went public several years ago is now exploring the possibility of going private. Although her company's stock is trading at an extremely high multiple of earnings (much higher than it would be in a private market transaction), she is tired of being in the public "fishbowl." The peace of mind of not worrying about quarterly earnings, investor expectations, and reporting requirements is a tempting offset to any diminution in her wealth by going private.

Valuation in ESOPs

Business owners' motivations behind employee stock ownership plan (ESOP) transactions are varied. These motivations can include rewarding loyal employees, obtaining liquidity for the owners, motivating employees, maximizing personal gain, or any combination of these factors. One of the first thoughts that comes to a business owner's mind after deciding to sell all or a portion of the company's stock is: "What is my stock worth?" A business valuation will help answer this question.

But the business valuation may only be a starting point for the owner. A business owner who wants to reward loyal employees may sell the stock at a value that is less than he or she could receive from an outside third party. If the intent is to motivate the employees, the business owner may decide to sell the stock at the price established by an independent valuation.

A business owner desiring liquidity may have a preconceived idea of the amount of money that he or she needs for financial security. Therefore, the ultimate sales price may have no relation to the inherent value of the business. If maximizing proceeds from sale of the business is the motivating factor for the business owner, the valuation may establish a floor price for the transaction. Alternatively, if one of several owners is selling, the business valuation can provide an equitable solution to a potentially problematic situation.

By law, an ESOP can pay no more than the fair market value of the securities that it is buying. This establishes a ceiling on what an ESOP can pay for stock. However, two valuation professionals can differ as to the fair market value of a security or business and, thereby, as to how high the ceiling may be.

Two recent client engagements illustrate the opposing psychological views of business valuations in ESOP transactions. A small service company had several owners in its almost 75-year history. The current majority owner had spent his entire career at the company. He had attained financial security and wanted to reward his loyal employees. After receiving an independent valuation of his stock, the majority owner determined what he thought was a fair price to sell his stock to the ESOP. This price was below the independent valuation and far below what he believed he could have received from an outside buyer. The psychological gratification of rewarding loyal employees was far more important than the true value of the company in establishing the sales price.

Conversely, the founder of a company that distributes industrial products was exploring succession planning alternatives. He obtained an independent valuation of his business. This value immediately established the floor in the owner's mind as to what he would sell the company for. Although he was financially comfortable prior to the transaction, he wanted to maximize the price at which he would sell his company. The price had become a matter of the owner's ego. He could not sell his company for less than what he thought it was worth.

Valuation in Buy-Sell Agreements

Buy-sell agreements not only facilitate orderly transitions of companies' ownership interests, but also provide a mechanism for departing shareholders, or their estates, to liquidate a substantial portion of their net worth. It is easy to see how these sometimes conflicting purposes can create controversy. A low valuation conclusion can ease ownership transition but may result in a shareholder receiving a much smaller nest egg than originally anticipated (and prompt the IRS to allege that a gift subject to gift tax is being made). A high valuation conclusion, while appealing to a departing shareholder, can cause financial distress to the company.

The valuation for a buy-sell agreement has the potential of causing the demise or sale of the company. Failure to take into consideration the company's ability to finance the buyout—as well as each shareholder's contribution to the company—may result in a value that is unworkable. Once a seller has fixated on a value, it is extremely difficult to negotiate a different sales price. However, it may be possible to alter the terms of the sale. Psychologically, the seller has already counted his or her money. Conversely, the buyer does not want to pay the seller for future value created by the buyer.

A management consulting firm with 25 partners was confronted with a potential liquidity crisis created by the prospect of the retirement of several of its senior partners. Because of the large salaries paid to the retiring partner group, the firm historically operated with a limited amount of cash. An old buy-sell agreement drafted when the firm was founded some 30 years earlier placed an unrealistically high value on the firm. The senior partners clearly anticipated that the firm would honor the terms of the buy-sell. The junior partners were equally adamant in their resolve that the terms of the pricing mechanism in the buy-sell agreement be revised to reflect the current firm operating characteristics and the current market conditions. Honoring the original terms of the agreement would result in burdening the firm with a potentially crippling level of debt. The junior partners had absolutely no desire to work for the rest of their careers in order to fund the senior partners' buyouts.

After two years of sometimes contentious debate, a business valuation was undertaken to estimate a value for the firm and to structure the terms of the buyout. The result was a program that allowed the firm to satisfy the retiring partners, to continue to operate without severe capital constraints, and to not diminish the current compensation to the surviving partners.

Conclusion

Business valuations in transactions are often more than mere support documentation. The estimations of company worth can play a powerful role in shaping a transaction, even affecting whether a transaction occurs. As such, business valuations have profoundly important psychological aspects—factors that are sometimes easy to overlook.

Business valuations are complex estimates that demand substantial number crunching and analytical techniques. However, such quantitative complexity can yield not only results that are inaccurate (even if precise) but, worse yet, results that can affect the transaction in unexpected, unintended, and unhelpful ways.

Financial advisory professionals should visualize the "psychological aura" surrounding business valuations. And financial advisers should assess the behavior-modifying impact of these qualitative and often nonrational factors—while always upholding the twin pillars of professional integrity and client service.

Part IV

Special Issues Related to Valuations in Specific Industries

_____ Chapter 19

_____ # Sports Team Valuation and Venue Feasibility*

John E. (Jack) Kane CFA, ASA

_____

_____

_____

_____

_____

_____

* Richard D. Wolfe, a financial analyst with Kane Reece Associates, Inc., provided research assistance on Chapter 19. He is a 1994 graduate of the Wharton School of Business of the University of Pennsylvania, a candidate for the chartered financial analyst and accredited senior appraiser designations, and a member of the New York Society of Security Analysts.

Cleveland Browns franchise "winner" to pay $530 million for the privilege of starting a National Football League team! Holy cow!

Build it and they will come! Well, maybe? Hopefully?

Introduction

These remarks are fitting lead-ins to this chapter dealing with sports team valuation and venue feasibility. First, sports franchises are big, complex businesses and the number of teams and leagues is growing rapidly on a global scale. How big? Exhibit 19-1 presents the attendance figures for the four professional sports leagues that are the subject of this chapter. As can be seen, many millions of fans pay admissions, and many millions more watch these sporting events on television. Second, there are thousands of venues across the United States, mostly publicly owned. Most venues would be considered economic failures or, at best, marginally successful. From their results of operations, the initial feasibility of most venues appears to have been determined by the "field of dreams" approach.

Phil Rizzuto would have surely applied his famous phrase "Holy cow!" to the price offered for the "naked" National Football League (NFL) franchise for Cleveland—the largest price ever for a professional franchise. The deal was announced on September 9, 1998, in numerous news sources, including ESPN.com. Was the buying group driven by ego, as is often said of major league team buyers? Or was the price based upon sound economics?

As pricey as this deal was, another deal is in the works, as of this writing. Daniel Snyder, a 34-year-old communications executive, has offered $800 million for the NFL Washington Redskins. This deal, if approved by NFL team owners, will carry a record price. In addition to the team, the price also includes the Redskins' home venue—Jack Kent Cooke Stadium.

Professional sports teams are entertainment businesses. The business of entertainment seeks to maximize economic income (1) through the attraction of large audiences and holding and increasing those audiences, and (2) through development and extension of brands in order to expand ancillary revenues. At the end of the day, it is a game of audience ratings and reach. Said another way, it is a popularity, fan loyalty, and availability contest. Pro sports compete with all the other leisure time activities for consumers' discretionary income.

This chapter presents the fundamentals of professional sports team economics and the valuation methods applicable to them. The purpose of the chapter is to provide insight into this specialized valuation niche by examining sports within the context of the entertainment industry, exploring the important value drivers on and off the field.

The success of a sports team, especially from an owner's point of view, has become inextricably tied to the venues in which it plays. As evidence, we have recently witnessed pro teams switching cities, leaving their old venues and great traditions behind (e.g., the Cleveland Browns

Exhibit 19–1

League Attendance
(in millions)

Season	MLB	NHL	NBA	NFL
1970	28.7	8.0	5.8	10.0
1975	29.8	9.8	8.2	10.7
1980	43.0	11.7	10.2	14.0
1985	46.8	12.8	12.2	14.1
1990	54.8	13.8	18.0	14.8
1995	50.5	18.6	21.8	15.8
1996	60.1	19.1	21.6[a]	15.4
1997	63.2	18.8	21.7[b]	15.8

Average Annual Growth Rates

	MLB	NHL	NBA	NFL
1970-80	4.1%	3.9%	5.8%	3.4%
1980-90	2.5%	1.7%	5.8%	0.6%
1990-97	2.1%	4.5%	2.7%	0.9%
1970-97	3.0%	3.2%	5.0%	1.7%

;SOURCE: MLB, NHL, NBA, and NFL leagues.

)Note: All attendance figures include regular season, playoffs, championships, and all-star games.

[a] Playoff attendance estimated at 1.3 million.

[b] Playoff and all-star game attendance estimated at 1.3 million and 20,000, respectively.

becoming the Baltimore Ravens) for new stadiums or arenas, better lease terms, and a better media market.

Two of the many examples of teams moving to greener pastures are (1) the NFL Houston Oilers, now the Tennessee Oilers, and (2) the National Hockey League (NHL) Winnipeg Jets, now the Phoenix Coyotes. In the latter example, Jerry Colangelo, an owner of the National Basketball Association (NBA) Phoenix Suns, purchased the Jets in 1996. Colangelo moved the team to Phoenix and into the state-of-the-art America West Arena. The geographic shift alone has probably doubled the team's value. The Phoenix Suns control the America West Arena and receive more revenue from the arena's naming rights from America West Airlines than the gross revenues the Jets realized in their last year in Winnipeg! This purchase and move is a great case study on the value-enhancing potential of market relocations and of new venues.

The critical importance of venue to a sports business makes venue feasibility analysis a natural topic to be explored in this book.

Questions that will be taken up in this section include:

- What is feasibility?
- Feasible to whom?
- Isn't this real estate? Why should business valuation practitioners be interested?

An overview of feasibility analysis methodology will be presented, and elements of a feasibility study for a Middle Atlantic market area in the hunt for a new NHL franchise will be discussed.

Sports Team Valuation

The Economics of Professional Sports

Our focus here is on the four major leagues—namely, the NFL, NBA, MLB (Major League Baseball), and NHL. The economics of pro sports are primarily driven by four variables: (1) owner/player relationships; (2) laws that are unique to these businesses and league regulations; (3) broadcast and cable television contracts; and (4) venue attributes. The four leagues are currently comprised of 120 franchises. It is safe to say that there are 120 unique sets of value drivers. Thus, the analyst should exercise caution by employing sound analyses based upon sufficient information when using a market transaction valuation method to appraise a team.

Professional sports leagues are the only businesses in which "the owners want regulation and labor—the players want a free market."[1] These great leagues, which are owner associations, have the exclusive power to grant local monopolies, influence player mobility, and decide revenue splits—and, it's legal.

Exhibit 19-2 depicts representative, common-size income statements for each league. The income and expense relationships shown assume the average for the many individual team variables (e.g., local broadcast revenues and venue control). Therefore, the table ratios, although useful for "orders of magnitude comparisons" between revenues and expenses and between leagues, should not be blindly applied to any one team or used in new franchise projections.

Often team operating statements may intermingle other owner business interests and include large compensation packages for the owner(s) and various kinfolk (e.g., deemed dividends related to the payment of discretionary expenses). Careful analysis is required to adjust for nonoperating variables.

Owner/Player Relationships

As can be seen in Exhibit 19-2, player compensation, the largest single team expense, approaches 60 percent of team revenue. This economic

---

[1] Michael K. Ozanian and Stephen Taub, "Big Leagues, Bad Business," *Financial World*, July 7, 1992.

Exhibit 19–2

Professional Sports Leagues
Representative Common-Size Income Statements

	Hockey	Basketball	Football	Baseball
Gate Receipts:				
Home games (net)	51%	38%	16%	38%
Road receipts	0%	0%	11%	3%
Total ticket revenue	51%	38%	27%	41%
Broadcasting and Cable Revenue:				
National broadcasting	13%	25%	60%	15%
Local TV	4%	4%	0%	10%
Regional cable	7%	7%	0%	6%
Local radio	1%	3%	3%	5%
Total broadcasting and cable	25%	38%	63%	36%
Other Revenue:				
Concessions revenue	6%	2%	3%	11%
Advertising / signage	6%	10%	1%	2%
League merchandising	2%	6%	5%	5%
Playoff revenue (net)	4%	4%	0%	2%
Preseason / exhibition	2%	2%	5%	0%
Miscellaneous revenue	4%	3%	0%	3%
Total other revenue	24%	27%	15%	23%
Total Revenue	100%	100%	100%	100%
Team Expenses:				
Players' salaries	53%	57%	60%	57%
Team expenses	9%	9%	12%	7%
Minor league expenses	5%	NA	NA	7%
Scouting expenses	2%	1%	2%	5%
Total team expenses	69%	67%	73%	76%
Business Expenses:				
Sales and marketing	5%	4%	2%	3%
Facility rent / operations	7%	2%	5%	11%
Public relations / promotions	2%	2%	0%	2%
General and administrative	7%	8%	5%	11%
League assessments	3%	2%	4%	2%
Total business expenses	24%	19%	15%	29%
Total Expenses	93%	85%	89%	105%
Reported Operating Cash Flow	7%	18%	11%	-5%

SOURCE: Kane Reece Associates, Inc., estimates.

relationship was not always the case. The history of the relationship between team owners and players is riddled with strikes, lockouts, and lawsuits. Prior to World War II, and for nearly three decades following the war, owners had the power to keep players for their entire careers and to pay them whatever they wished. Teams agreed not to go after each other's players. If it sounded like a cartel, it was. And, in many important ways, it still is.

Early in league development, it was important to protect competitive parity by restricting the movement of players. Thus, the wealthiest owners could not simply raid other teams' talent. To say that the owner/players relationship balance was skewed significantly to the owners is an understatement.

Players' attempts to gain some measure of economic balance relative to the owners literally did not pay off in a material way until the 1970s. Each of the four leagues has eventually settled on some form of free agency and collective bargaining as players' unions gained power.

The question then became: What to do about out-of-control player compensation? Team owners and leagues have tried to stem the tide of rapidly escalating compensation by instituting salary caps and revenue sharing agreements. These measures have enjoyed varying degrees of success. As will be discussed later, large publicly traded media companies now own teams in each sport (except football) and this ownership trend will most likely accelerate.[2] This presents the opportunity to use future career opportunities for players and equity, more likely in the form of stock option programs, to slow the growth of cash compensation and to entice the star players to stay with the team.[3] Readers interested in a concise history of the owner/player relationship, including court cases and milestones, are referred to Harold Vogel's book on entertainment industry economics.[4]

The analyst should research and understand (1) the contribution that each player makes to his team; (2) his contract terms and conditions; (3) his ranking in terms of performance—that is, "stats"—and (4) his level of compensation within the league. Team managers should be consulted to elicit their opinions with respect to each player's current and expected future potential, expected future compensation, and anticipated roster changes. As an example, management may claim that "so-and-so" brings in 5,000 to 6,000 season ticket sales or they expect to trade "so-and-so."

Michael Jordan of the NBA Chicago Bulls exemplifies the power of "marquee" players. His drawing power virtually guaranteed a sellout wherever he played. The value of the Bulls clearly depends upon the contribution of Michael Jordan. Key management and coaches' contracts should also be analyzed and benchmarked within the league.

Both the teams and leagues closely guard the details of personal service contracts. This information falls in the "if I tell you, I may have to kill you" category. The point is, do not think contract information is freely given to an analyst, even by the very team engaging the analyst, let alone by a competing team. With this said, the NHL Players Association Web site (www.nhlpa.com) provides compensation data on

---

[2] The NFL is the only league of the four that does not permit corporate ownership. Today over 50 public companies own interests in MLB, NBA, and NHL franchises.

[3] Each of the four leagues has rules aimed at preventing salary cap violations, including side deals such as movie deals and stock options provided outside the cap. In fact, NBA teams must represent in writing that they have abided by this rule.

[4] Harold L. Vogel, *Entertainment Industry Economics*, 4th ed. (New York: Cambridge University Press, 1998).

each of its members. However, these data are far from the whole story since the many terms and conditions are not shown.

The intent of these analyses is to provide a reasonable basis for projecting team compensation as an input variable into a discounted cash flow (DCF) model. The DCF model, which falls within the income approach, is one of the methods commonly used in valuing a sports franchise. Winning records and star power are key to the financial success of non-NFL teams, especially those in smaller markets. Television contracts and revenue sharing arrangements provide the primary financial cushions for NFL teams. Therefore, (1) the current and anticipated roster and (2) the team record and schedule provide indications of future gate, local television, and ancillary revenues.

Laws and League Regulations

An understanding of the laws and league rules under which the franchises operate is an important part of the sports team valuation process. The analyst should know how the "game is played." It is not the purpose of this discussion to delve into these laws and rules. Rather, the intention is to explain that the laws and rules have a significant impact on the economics of pro sports and, therefore, on sports team valuations. These laws and regulations are numerous and complex, and a league's rules change often. For example, *Sports Business Daily* reported that MLB approved a rule change that allows limited ownership in more than one team.[5] The laws and regulations governing professional sports may be viewed as falling into three categories: (1) organizational, (2) revenue sharing, and (3) owner/player relationships.

Organizational. The leagues enjoy exemptions from certain portions of the antitrust laws. Franchises benefit from tax-deductible write-offs of acquired player contracts. In addition, franchises are frequently subsidized by host cities and or county governments. The antitrust exemptions give the league (i.e., the team owners) the exclusive right to control entry through the franchising process. They also can (1) exercise the right to prevent teams from relocating, (2) fine teams and players for breaking their rules, and (3) arbitrate disputes between teams. These powers—and the many other powers they possess—are for the stated purpose of protecting the competitiveness and integrity of the league and the value of the franchises.

NFL expansion teams benefited from rule changes that include unrestricted free agency (1993) and a salary cap (1994). "In this brave new world, the incumbent teams' edge evaporated. In a game driven ever more by stadium economics, the rookie teams' fancy new stadiums helped put them in the driver's seat. In a tradeoff for the high cost of expansion (e.g., $140 million entry fee) the new owners [of the Carolina Panthers and Jacksonville Jaguars] got quick parity: extra picks in each round of the 1995 and 1996 drafts and, in effect, extra muscle under the

[5] As reported in the *Sports Business Daily*, September 18,1998, p.7.

salary cap. When it came to attracting veteran free agents, they could, in the parlance of silver-screen agent Jerry Maguire, 'show them the money.' "[6] Both teams reached their respective conference's championships two years after joining the league. In addition to paying the entry fee, each team will receive only a one-half share of the all-important television revenues for the first three years. These payments are to compensate incumbent owners for the expansion team head start.

Revenue Sharing. The Sports Broadcasting Act (1961) is another antitrust exemption. This Act allows the leagues the right to negotiate as a cartel with television networks. The leagues evenly divide national television revenues among the teams. "Football clearly remains the quintessential sport for television. The NFL's national television deal, worth $40.5 million per franchise last season (1995–96), could increase by as much as 50% per team by the 1998 season."[7] All football teams received the same amount of television money independent of market size and whether or not they win any games.

League expansion offers additional revenues to owners. The NHL added four teams in 1996. Each expansion club paid $80 million for the privilege to join the league. Each NHL team owner received an equal share of the $320 million. The NBA also sets franchise prices. The last two NBA expansion teams, the Toronto Raptors and the Vancouver Grizzlies, each paid $125 million for their franchise. This compares with $32.5 million that the Orlando Magic and Minnesota Timberwolves each paid to join the NBA in 1990.

The NFL used a bidding process to award a new franchise for Cleveland. The amount of $530 million turned out to be the highest offer. The reported bids ranged from a low of approximately $310 million to the accepted bid of $530 million. The second highest offer was $500 million. Does this set a market price for a naked NFL franchise?

Leagues share licensing revenue and merchandise sales equally among their teams without regard to an individual team's sales. *Financial World* reported that in 1995 the NFL took in $3 billion from licensed goods; the NBA received $3.1 billion; MLB received $1.7 billion; and the NHL received $1 billion.[8] Today team uniforms are no longer an expense but a profit center, as outfitters such as Champion and Starter vie to have their logos prominently displayed on team apparel.

The Dallas Cowboys tried to "go it alone" by entering into a licensing agreement with Nike a few years ago. This is against NFL rules, and the league sued. The suit was eventually dropped when the league entered into its own lucrative deal with Nike.

National television revenues are, and licensing and product sales may be, divided equally among teams in a given league. But there are many other revenue items that are not divided, such as local television and cable rights fees, gate receipts, and concessions. Clearly, the New

---

[6] John Helyar, "NFL's New Expansion Teams Get Fast Access to Talent," *Wall Street Journal*, January 10, 1997, p. A1.

[7] Kurt Badenhausen, Christopher Nikolov, Michael Alkin, and Michael K. Ozanian, "More Than a Game: An In-Depth Look at the Raging Bull Market in Sports Franchises," *Financial World*, June 17, 1997, pp. 40–62.

[8] Debra Sparks, "The Cost of Cool," *Financial World*, June 17, 1997.

York Rangers, located in the largest media market, will command much higher local television rights fees than the Sabers playing in Buffalo, the fortieth largest market.

MLB, the NHL, and (to a lesser extent) the NBA have a great deal of variability in revenues between teams, far higher than among NFL teams. Market size and venue attributes are key determinants of the magnitude of these teams' revenues. The NFL's major revenue sources—gate receipts, national television, and merchandising and licensing—are shared. The other sports do not share regular gate receipts with the visiting team (baseball shares only nominally). Their national television revenues are not as large a proportion of revenues as the NFL's. The other revenues, with the exception of league merchandising revenues, are not shared at all.

Exhibit 19-2 puts the economic implications of revenue sharing in perspective. For some non-NFL teams, the difference among making money, breaking even, and losing money is whether they advance in the playoffs or not. This is particularly true of hockey clubs.

Michael Bauman, writing in the *Milwaukee Journal Sentinel,* examines the revenue disparity in MLB: "...and that despite the 'dramatic' home run chase, the game is still sick."[9]. These leagues, excluding the NFL, are challenged and have been working to alleviate revenue disparity between teams.

Owner/Player Relationships. These rules, as discussed earlier, are extremely complex and vary by league. It is important that the analyst has an understanding of the rules governing free agency and salary caps. In addition, the analyst should understand the economic impact of the rules that directly or indirectly limit player and team mobility. The details of these rules are beyond the scope of this discussion.[10]

Broadcasting and Cable Connection

One has only to look at Exhibit 19-2 to see the importance of television rights fees to professional sports. Television revenues are 60 percent of football's total revenue and even hockey, which has the lowest percentage, still obtains 25 percent of its revenues from TV.

Television provides not only much needed cash, via rights fees, but also team exposure. Television has added millions of fans and helped create new teams and a more even distribution of teams around the country. Television helps build and maintain the teams' powerful brands, which have driven licensing and in-venue advertising revenues.

The top 40 television markets, along with their NBA and NHL teams and their arenas, are presented in Exhibit 19-3. One can readily see the concentration of teams in the top 20 markets. This concentration would hold if MLB and NFL teams were added. Newer franchises have been—and will be—added in rapidly growing Sunbelt cities that have reached critical mass (e.g., the Jacksonville Jaguars of the NFL). Also,

---

[9] As reported in the *The Sports Business Daily*, September 18,1998, p.7.
[10] See Vogel, *Entertainment Industry Economics*, 4th ed.

new franchises will replace franchises that have departed major markets for even greener pastures (e.g., the NHL Minneapolis Wild replaced the team that became the Dallas Stars).

Television rights fees continue to escalate. For example, hockey agreed with ABC/ESPN and their parent Disney for the exclusive national broadcast and cable TV rights for the NHL. This five-year broadcast and cable programming package cost a reported $600 million. The figure is nearly twice as much for the broadcast portion—and over three times as much for the cable TV portion—as were the previous contracts with Fox and ESPN, respectively. What's more surprising is that the price increased despite declining hockey viewership, as measured by A. C. Nielsen. Such is the demand for television content, especially sports content.

NBC and Turner obtained NBA national broadcast rights for $1.75 billion and $900 million, respectively, for four-year deals. Rupert Murdoch and his fledgling Fox network surprised the industry by outbidding CBS for the NFL National Football Conference games. Fox paid $1.58 billion.

Fox and its parent News Corp. have not stopped with television rights to feed their huge appetites for programming. Rather, they have begun purchasing the content. In 1997, News Corp. purchased the Los Angeles Dodgers and Dodger Stadium for $350 million from the O'Malley family. This was the highest price paid for a sports franchise at the time. Disney owns the Anaheim Mighty Ducks hockey team and a 25 percent interest in the California Angels. News Corp. has become one of 52 public companies to own an interest in a pro team.[11] Indeed, team owners, who historically have been wealthy individuals and buying groups, are giving way to corporate buyers, especially media giants.

> Beyond the sheer numbers, the News Corp. deals are emblematic of a deeper change: Sports franchises are quickly becoming the core asset in the sports communications business, and the long-ball hitters are getting into the game. Murdoch's arrival creates a true Murderer's Row of powerful media and entertainment companies in the owner's boxes.[12]

Exhibit 19-4 supports Mr. Johnson's quote, notwithstanding the "Murderer's Row" characterization.

We are all aware of the exponential increase in television channels brought about by the maturation of cable television. Even more channels are on the horizon as digital technology continues to develop and roll out. Programmers are scrambling to become destination channels in a vast multichannel universe. Sports, as live event programming, coupled with the powerful team and league brands and the drawing power of marquee athletes, are seen as "must haves" by general broad-reach networks, such as NBC, and of course by the specialized cable networks and the more than 30 regional cable sports nets.

---

[11] Roy S. Johnson, "Take Me Out to the Boardroom," *Fortune*, July 21, 1997.
[12] Ibid.

Exhibit 19–3

Top 40 Television Markets with NBA and/or NHL Teams

DMA[a] Rank		Households (000s)	Arena	Capacity	Year Opened	NBA Team	NHL Team
1	New York	6,756	Madison Square Garden	19,763	1968	Knicks	Rangers
			Continental Arena, NJ	20,049	1981	Nets	Devils
			Nassau Veterans Memorial Coliseum	16,800	1972		Islanders
2	Los Angeles	5,009	Great Western Forum	17,505	1967	Lakers	Kings
			Arrowhead Pond of Anaheim	17,174	1993		Ducks
			LA Sports Arena	16,021	1959	Clippers	
3	Chicago	3,140	United Center	21,711	1994	Bulls	Blackhawks
4	Philadelphia	2,659	First Union Center	20,444	1996	76ers	Flyers
5	San Francisco/Oakland/ San Jose	2,298	San Jose Arena	18,500	1993		Sharks
			Arena in Oakland	19,500	1966	Warriors	
6	Boston	2,174	Fleet Center	18,600	1995	Celtics	Bruins
7	Washington D.C.	1,928	MCI Center	20,674	1997	Wizards	Capitals
8	Dallas/Ft. Worth	1,899	Reunion Arena	18,042	1980	Mavericks	Stars
9	Detroit	1,782	The Palace of Auburn Hills	22,076	1988	Pistons	
			Joe Lewis Arena	19,983	1979		Red Wings
10	Atlanta	1,675	Georgia Dome	34,000	1992	Hawks	Thrashers[b]
11	Houston	1,624	Compaq Arena	16,285	1975	Rockets	
12	Seattle/Tacoma	1,514	Key Arena	17,072	1995	SuperSonics	
13	Cleveland	1,469	Gund Arena	20,562	1994	Cavaliers	
14	Minneapolis/St. Paul	1,448	Target Center	19,006	1990	Timberwolves	Wild[b]
15	Tampa/St. Pete/Sarasota	1,436	Ice Palace	19,500	1996		Lightning
16	Miami/Ft. Lauderdale	1,386	Miami Arena	15,200	1988	Heat	Panthers
17	Phoenix	1,289	America West Arena	19,023	1992	Suns	Coyotes
18	Denver	1,199	McNichols Sports Arena	17,171	1976	Nuggets	Avalanche
19	Pittsburgh	1,140	Pittsburgh Civic Arena	17,181	1961		Penguins
20	Sacramento/Stockton/ Modesto	1,127	Arco Arena	17,317	1988	Kings	
21	St. Louis	1,109	Kiel Center	19,260	1994		Blues
22	Orlando/Daytona/Melbourne	1,041	Orlando Arena	17,248	1989	Magic	
23	Baltimore	988					
24	Portland	976	Rose Garden	21,538	1995	Trail Blazers	
25	Indianapolis	957	Market Square Arena	16,530	1974	Pacers	
26	San Diego	924					
27	Hartford/New Haven	916	Hartford Civic Center	16,500	1976		
28	Charlotte	840	Charlotte Coliseum	24,042	1988	Hornets	
29	Raleigh/Durham	826	Greensboro Coliseum	11,500	1959		Hurricanes
30	Cincinnati	797					
31	Kansas City, MO	792					
32	Milwaukee	791	Bradley Center	18,717	1988	Bucks	
33	Nashville	789	Nashville Arena	17,500	1996		Predators[b]
34	Columbus	739					Blue Jackets[b]
35	Greenville/Spartanburg	718					
36	Salt Lake City	690	Delta Center	19,911	1991	Jazz	Predators[b]
37	Grand Rapids/Kalamazoo	659					
38	San Antonio	649	Alamodome	20,557	1993	Spurs	
39	Norfolk/Portsmouth	636	Norfolk Scope	10,000	1971		
40	Buffalo	630	Marine Midland Arena	18,500	1996		Sabres

SOURCE: National Hockey League, National Basketball Association, 1998 Cable Fact Book.

[a] DMA = designated market area, defined by Nielsen Media Research
[b] New NHL franchise.
  Predators begin play 1998–1999.
  Thrashers begin play 1999–2000.
  Wild begins play 2000–2001.
  Blue Jackets begin play 2000–2001.

Exhibit 19–4

Entertainment/Media Companies
Owning Professional Sports Franchises and Venues

Company	Professional Sports Franchise	Professional Sports Venue	Programming Assets
Disney	Mighty Ducks (NHL) Anaheim Angels (MLB) 25% interest		ABC ESPN
Comcast	Philadelphia Flyers (NHL) Philadelphia 76ers (NBA)	First Union Center First Union Spectrum	Comcast Sports Net
Cablevision Systems	NY Rangers (NHL) NY Knicks (NBA)	Madison Square Garden	Sports Channel MSG Interest in Fox Sports
Fox (News Corp.)	LA Dodgers (MLB)	Dodger Stadium	Fox Sports
Tribune Company	Chicago Cubs (MLB)		WGN Superstation
Time Warner	Atlanta Braves (MLB) Atlanta Hawks (NBA) Atlanta Thrashers (NHL expansion team)	Turner Field	TBS TNT
Ascent Entertainment Group	Denver Nuggets (NBA) Colorado Avalanche (NHL)	Pepsi Center	Interest in studio and transmission operations
Liberty Media (Tele-Communications Inc.)		Interest in Pepsi Center	Interest in Fox Sports

Fox currently operates 20 regional sports networks around the country. All things being equal, fans root for the teams located in their geographic area. Again, all things being equal, fans would rather watch their team than the teams offered up by the national networks. Fox's strategy is to offer local NBA, NHL, and MLB teams to local audiences.

These sports offer too many games to be limited to national exposure. Competition for the local games is between cable and local television stations. These stations are generally independents that depend on sports programming to differentiate themselves in the market. Most often cable and broadcast split the local schedule. Local TV and cable rights make up between 11 percent and 16 percent of total team revenues.

There is a huge disparity in local broadcast rights fees between teams. The New York Yankees are near the end of a 12-year, $486 million agreement with MSG Network, while the Seattle Mariners were paid $7.5 million for a three-year deal by KIRO-TV. In this case, size does count. This revenue category has potential for growth, especially in large markets with successful franchises.

The importance of understanding the terms and conditions of the contracts between a team or league and the broadcasters and cable programmers, as an essential part of the valuation process, cannot be overstated.

Venue Attributes

Arenas and stadiums built after 1990 represent the state of the art in exploiting real estate of these types as businesses. The attitude of team owners today is: If they are not in a new venue, then they are either (1) pressuring the city for a new one or for extensive renovations on the old venue or (2) planning to move the team. Microsoft billionaire Paul Allen waited for voters to approve a $425 million stadium-financing package before exercising his option to buy the Seattle Seahawks.[13] New venues have become core assets of professional sports teams. The revenues they generate are largely not shared among other league teams.

Thus, a sports franchise that owns or substantially controls its venue is a growing trend. In fact, the majority of NHL teams now either own or control their venues. Control, as used here, relates to splits of the revenues that result from venue operations. A brief discussion of modern arena attributes follows. The same basic points apply to stadiums.

The International Association of Assembly Managers (IAAM) defines an arena as an indoor public assembly facility with fixed and/or portable seats surrounding an open floor area that can be set with different event configurations.[14] Arenas typically have 8,000 to 22,000 seats on one or more tiers with sightlines optimized for basketball and hockey. The arenas used by NHL and NBA teams generally average 20,000 seats.

The modern arena envisioned here always contains luxury suites and considerable premium seating, as well as a mall atmosphere. Premium seating and suites are usually provided on the main concourse or middle level, between the upper and lower tiers of seating. This location brings the expensive seats closer to the action on the floor than did the old "skyboxes." When older facilities are renovated, the suites (the most expensive seating) are often forced into poor locations. The Giants Stadium renovation placed the suites on top of the stadium. They should call these suites "ionosphere boxes." There is nothing like a new, well-designed venue. The United Center in Chicago and the First Union Center in Philadelphia are excellent examples of modern arenas.

New arenas are very customer/fan friendly, and they are becoming destinations in and of themselves. These facilities are characterized by the intensity of use—that is, many ways to generate revenue and frequency of use—so that they are rarely totally dark. They create a mall atmosphere with well-lighted concourses that are conducive to spending. Gone are the dimly lit corridors of the old facilities that created bottlenecks—that is, long, slow-moving lines for purchasing food, drinks, and merchandise. Now spectators do not have to worry about missing the game while waiting to make purchases. Rather, they can continue to watch the action on video monitors throughout the venue.

Venues with 100 events or fewer per year may maintain a small staff of permanent, full-time employees. Conversely, venues with 250 events

---

[13] E. Robinson, "It's Where You Play That Counts," *Fortune*, July 21, 1997.

[14] International Association of Assembly Managers, 4425 West Airport Freeway, Suite 590, Irving, TX 75062-5835, 972-255-8020.

per year can obtain the financial advantages of retaining day-of-event employees on a full-time basis and recapturing their expense by charging event producers less than they might otherwise be charged for less skilled and less reliable temporary employees. The availability of a trained in-house staff is an important intangible asset and a major marketing plus for a venue and another source of revenue. The foregoing is an example of an economy-of-scale benefit that accrues to venues that have both NHL and NBA teams as anchor tenants.

Excluding playoffs, professional hockey and basketball together provide over 85 event dates annually. Typical events in addition to basketball and hockey include concerts, ice shows, circuses and other family shows, and religious and motivational meetings. Other sports include arena football, tennis, indoor soccer, lacrosse, boxing, and professional wrestling. Collegiate and high school teams, in addition to professional teams, will use the facility for regular season games and especially for tournaments.

Motor sports, including tractor pulls, are enormously popular events. Setup for these events requires the trucking in—then out—of tons of dirt! Arena managers are always looking for new events and revenue-producing gimmicks and tie-ins. Tie-ins include corporate sponsored events such as the Virginia Slims Open. The San Jose Arena, home to the NHL Sharks, hosts arena football and roller hockey in the summer months to keep the lights on.

Another arena use is women's professional basketball. The nascent Women's National Basketball Association (WNBA), which began in June 1997 and is sponsored by the NBA, is off to a successful start. According to the WNBA, attendance in the second season increased 50 percent to over 1.6 million, with an average game attendance of 10,869. The league has also attracted broadcasters and national coverage.

The "motherload" in the arena world is the major collegiate tournament games such as (1) the NCAA basketball tournament, especially the Final Four, or (2) professional sports playoffs and championships, such as the NHL contest for the Lord Stanley Cup. The venues benefit from a revenue windfall and national television exposure.

Arenas may also have so-called flat shows, such as conventions and trade shows, and meetings, such as corporate annual meetings. These uses are attracted to arenas because they require a smaller scale than typical convention centers.

An important characteristic of a modern arena is the ability to quickly set up and take down—to run two events on the same day, such as a basketball game in the afternoon and a concert that evening.

Modern venues all have plush restaurants and private banquet rooms that can be in use before, during, and after events, and when the facility is otherwise vacant. These upscale amenities are located on a separate midlevel executive concourse. The fit and finish of these amenities are high-end and businesslike. The First Union Center in Philadelphia has a microbrewery on its main concourse that would rival any freestanding bar/restaurant. These and other amenities, such as interactive computer kiosks and superstores, are designed to get fans to come early, stay late, and of course spend money.

Financial data on venues and professional sports teams are difficult to obtain, since many venues and teams are not owned by public corporations. Even available public financial and operating data are of limited use because teams and arena operations are generally a small part of a large corporation. Ownership of the Florida Panthers is publicly held. However, the data available are not disaggregated to the level required for detailed financial and comparative analysis, and other businesses are included. The Boston Celtics, a public limited partnership, provide reasonable financial detail in their public filings and they are a "pure play" team.

The Cleveland Indians Baseball Company, Inc., went public in June 1998 (Nasdaq: CLEV). In addition to the baseball team, the company manages Jacobs Field, a state-of-the-art baseball venue. The Orlando Predators and arena football team saw its stock buoyed by an announcement that the NFL was granted an exclusive option to purchase equity in the Arena Football League (AFL) (Nasdaq: PRED). This option, reported in a Predator press release dated February 8, 1998, specifically grants the NFL the right to acquire up to 49.9 percent of the AFL, and the option can be exercised over a two-year period. Arena football is seen as complementary by NFL owners since it is played in the summer and can develop fans in small- and medium-size markets. The benefit to venue owners of a successful AFL is arena utilization during the summer.

The United States Baseball League (USBL) is the only public, albeit thinly traded, professional sports league (OTC Bulletin Board: USBL). The USBL is comprised of 13 teams, many of which (e.g., the Atlantic City Seagulls) play in smaller non-NBA markets. Like arena football, they play in the summer.

Exhibit 19-5 presents a statement of revenues for a new arena with both a hockey and basketball team. Our work with professional sports teams and venues and our industry research provide the basis for the data in Exhibit 19-5. The largest sources of new venue revenue are luxury suites and premium seat licenses. In fact, these revenues are higher than total general admission revenues. The analyst is cautioned that financing terms of new venues may require that all or a portion of these revenues be dedicated to debt service. The table also provides a comparison to the IAAM 1996 industry survey for arenas over 12,500 capacity. The 1996 survey is the latest available from the IAAM. Notwithstanding the fact that the survey includes many arenas without professional sports teams, the comparison with a new venue is striking.

The analyst should understand the degree of control, or lack thereof, that a team has over its venue. The degree of control runs from total ownership to being a rent-paying tenant. The venue depicted in Exhibit 19-5 is one with private venue control and two professional teams.

Exhibit 19-6 presents a sample of recent naming rights deals. "Before 1990, only four naming rights deals existed in the four major leagues, none in major league baseball."[15] Today, there are so many

---

[15] D. A. Markiewicz, "Corporations Paying More for Right to Put Their Brand on Sports Arenas," *Star-Telegram* (Arlington, Texas), December 18, 1997.

Exhibit 19–5

Statement of Revenues
New Arena with Hockey and Basketball Teams

	Modern Arena Revenues		IAAM 1996 Industry Profile Survey	
	$000s	% of Total	$000s	% of Total
Premium Seating				
Suites	$ 8,500	21.30%	$1,945	
Superbox seats	1,500	3.80%		
Club seats	7,250	18.10%		
Rights of first refusal	250	0.60%		
	17,500	43.80%	1,945	20.60%
Ticket Rentals				
General seating	3,500	8.70%		
Premium seating	1,000	2.50%		
	4,500	11.20%	1,601	17.00%
Concession Sales				
General seating	4,500	11.20%		
Premium seating	2,000	5.00%		
	6,500	16.20%	1,567	16.60%
Novelty Sales				
General seating	750	1.90%		
Premium seating	250	0.60%		
	1,000	2.50%	308	3.30%
Parking				
General seating	2,000	5.00%		
Premium seating	1,000	2.50%		
	3,000	7.50%	732	7.80%
Advertising	3,000	7.50%		
Naming Rights	1,500	3.70%		
	4,500	11.20%	1,151	12.20%
Other Revenues				
Membership fees	500	1.20%		
Restaurant/superstore operations	1,000	2.50%	552	
Television	500	1.20%		
Ticket incentives	750	1.90%		
Other income	250	0.60%	1,577	
	3,000	7.50%	2,129	22.50%
Total Revenues	$40,000	100.00%	$9,433	100.00%

SOURCE: Kane Reece Associates, Inc., estimates

"naming rights" deals that it was newsworthy when the son of the late Jack Kent Cooke, owner of the Washington Redskins, announced that his new stadium would not carry a corporate brand, but would remain named after his father.

These venues offer corporations the powerful physical presence of their signage and local and national television exposure. They also offer

Exhibit 19–6

Sample of Recent Naming Rights Deals

Name	City	Company	Price (millions)	Term (years)
American Airlines Arena [a]	Miami, FL	American Airlines	$ 42.0	20
Bank One Ballpark	Phoenix, AZ	BancOne Corp	33.1	30
Continental Airlines Arena	East Rutherford, NJ	Continental Airlines	29.0	12
Edison International Field	Anaheim, CA	Edison International	50.0	20
Fleet Center	Boston, MA	Fleet	30.0	15
MCI Center	Washington, DC	MCI	44.0	20
National Car Rental Center [a]	Sunrise, FL	National Car Rental	25.0	10
Pepsi Center [a]	Denver, CO	Pepsi	68.0	20
Raymond James Stadium	Tampa, FL	Raymond James Financial	32.5	13
Staples Center [a]	Los Angeles, CA	Staples, Inc	100.0	20

SOURCE: Press releases, local news sources, trade journals, professional sports teams' Web sites.

[a] New, under construction, or future facility.

the brand a hometown presence. The Staples rights deal in Los Angeles involves payment of $100 million over 20 years. The company's reported motivation was to increase its brand recognition in Los Angeles and on the West Coast. These deals may also include one or more luxury suites and other seating in preferred locations, and use of the facility once or twice a year.

The analyst should review each of the line items of the operating statement to gain an understanding of the revenue and expense split, and analyze the lease between the team and the venue. Even in cases where the venue owner and team(s) owner(s) are related parties, leases between the entities invariably exist and should be analyzed.

The business of sports is rapidly growing, and paradigm shifts are constantly occurring. The analyst should remain current. The next section will address valuation methodology, including a brief discussion on the implications of the federal income tax code.

Valuation Methodology

Analysts approaching a valuation problem should have an understanding of the subject business as well as the market for that business. Sports team valuations offer the analyst the opportunity to value a unique and a truly scarce franchise. Their uniqueness arises from several factors. "First, they tend to be more valuable than other franchises, with values running into the hundreds of millions for some teams. Second, the success of a sports franchise is judged not only in economic terms but also in terms of winning and losing—though winning teams tend to gain in economic terms as well. Third, the strong local connections that these teams have and the intense emotions they evoke in their fans make them different from a typical business."[16]

---

[16] Aswath Damodaran, *Investment Valuation* (New York: John Wiley & Sons, 1996), p. 488.

The three generally accepted approaches to business value—namely, asset-based, income, and market—all have relevance and validity in the valuation of sports enterprises and of their underlying assets. The asset-based approach, however, would have the least relevance in producing a value indication for a team's enterprise value. This is because a team's value arises principally from many intangible assets working together in the enterprise. The costs of obtaining many of these intangibles may bear little resemblance to their value. The asset-based approach is discussed later when the income tax implications of franchise ownership are addressed. Consequently, the primary approaches to estimating the value of a sports franchise are (1) the income approach, which relies on estimates of future economic income to be realized from operating the team, and (2) the market approach, which examines actual purchase and sale transactions. Eventually, after enough data are available, there may be a third approach based upon an auction process such as the one used to award the Cleveland NFL franchise.

Income Approach. The most applicable income approach method for valuing sports properties is the discounted cash flow (DCF) method. This valuation method is preferred because of the uniqueness of sports franchises and the nature of the "willing buyers."

Projections based upon "business as usual" will generally produce understated value indications and/or depend upon a continuing or residual value for much more than 75 percent of the total value indication. The DCF model in this case is generally not mirroring investor behavior.

A DCF method allows the analyst (1) to consider and analyze all the current unique attributes of a franchise's value drivers and (2) to make reasonable assumptions as to how each driver may be maximized. This valuation method gives the analyst the opportunity, and burden, of mirroring the behavior of the typical investor or willing buyer. Each line of a team's operating statement should be benchmarked. The benchmarks reflect the best case for each element of team operations of revenue and expense. In order to analyze likely business scenarios, the analyst can rely on a number of case studies of successful team marketing, the revenue-generating capacity of new venues or improved venue lease terms, and successful league expansions and team relocations. The analyst can then build the valuation case after evaluating the merits of the various business scenarios.

The valuation case should reflect investor intentions, be prudent and possible to attain, and include all expenditures necessary to implement the valuation case. Because of the number and complexity of variables that need to be projected, the practitioner should be particularly sensitive about the potential for client and personal bias. "Bias control" is a critical element of independence. Buyers have a natural downward bias and sellers a natural upward bias when it comes to projecting financial performance. The analyst's own in-depth knowledge of, and experience in, the entertainment industry and thorough analyses of appropriate case studies are salves—but not cures—for bias.

Synergy is the essential ingredient not yet discussed. As we have seen, pro sports ownership has progressed from a tax shelter "hobby" of the rich to a business still dominated by high net worth individuals. Lately, pro sports team ownership has come to attract, directly or indirectly, media corporations that bring synergies and economies of scale. These corporations dominate the market for MLB, NBA, and NHL teams.

Although the NFL is the last holdout prohibiting corporate ownership, individual owners (such as Paul Allen of the Seattle Seahawks) are involved in the media industry. Others would like to join the club. For example, Charles Dolan, chairman of Cablevision Systems Corp. (which owns Madison Square Garden and the Knicks and Rangers), was involved with an investor group (which included comedian Bill Cosby) in bidding for the Cleveland NFL franchise. Cablevision is also a major cable TV system owner with large system clusters in and around New York and Cleveland. Cablevision also has significant programming interests, including sports channels. Mr. Dolan's group was unsuccessful, bidding a reported $500 million.

Sports franchises appear to be more valuable to media companies than to the individual owners. Using a real estate valuation term, the "highest and best use" of these properties may be as part of a media/entertainment matrix. Further, current individual owners, in addition to bidding against consortiums or corporations with deep pockets, face enormous estate planning and succession issues that will eventually cause them to rationalize their investments.

Who are the willing buyers? They are certainly not financial buyers, who seek their returns through leverage and financial engineering. They are strategic buyers who expect synergy and scale economies to increase the value of an acquisition. Just as important, media companies expect their sports investments to enhance the values of their own core assets. Strategic buyers can afford to pay more and do pay more than financial buyers.[17]

The challenge for the analyst is to properly quantify synergies and scale economies, both team related and those associated with the buyer. It is noteworthy that buyers hate to give up synergies and economies in the buying process. Rather, they hope to enhance their returns by keeping them for themselves. Synergies and scale economies that are given up are impounded in the price paid.

In any analysis of future cash flows, an important factor is the selection of the present value discount rate that will be used to bring the projected cash flows to a present value. The present value discount rate, or weighted average cost of capital (WACC), is made up of two components: debt and equity. The capital asset pricing model (CAPM) can be used to estimate the cost of equity capital. The CAPM inputs are readily available, with the exception of the beta used to adjust the equity risk premium and the estimate for the franchise-specific equity risk premium. One cannot observe the movement of sports franchise stocks, because there are not enough pure play or near-pure play companies.

[17] E. K. Jacquet, "Buyout Funds," *Alternative Investments* (Charlottesville, VA: Association for Investment Management and Research, 1998), pp. 28–34.

Therefore, a beta should be developed indirectly. Professional sports are part of the entertainment industry. Thus, a composite risk measure based on betas of firms such as Disney and TimeWarner, coupled with betas of companies that depend on sports for their profitability such as Nike, Reebok, and Russell Athletic, may provide a reasonable beta estimate.

The composite beta, being comprised of the large diversified entertainment and large related industry companies, probably understates the amount of systematic market risk of a given sports franchise. However, at least the procedure gives the analyst a place to start.

Unsystematic risk is the risk that is specific to the franchise being valued. It should be estimated with consideration given to the league in which the subject plays, variability of historical revenues and earnings, venue attributes, and so forth.

Using the DCF method to value a sports franchise is like crossing a minefield. That is, every step along the way is fraught with danger. Nonetheless, the wary analyst can and should cross it.

Market Approach. The valuation analyst has available two methods within the market approach. The first method is the guideline publicly traded company method. In this method, (1) public companies similar to the subject company are selected, (2) publicly available data are gathered and analyzed, and (3) value indications are reached by applying various market-derived pricing multiples to the subject franchise's parameters. The problem with this method, as was discussed earlier, is that sports franchises are usually in private hands—or they are a small part of a public company's business. This valuation method will likely not be appropriate unless and until more sports teams go public.

The preferred market approach method is referred to as either the guideline merged and acquired company method or the market transaction method. Under this method, the analyst collects and analyzes recent guideline market transactions and makes value adjustments on the basis of a comparative analysis between the market transactions and the subject property. In this valuation method, it is important to use actual sale transactions that were consummated on or before the valuation date.

The application of the market transaction method is often analogized to the valuation of real estate. The market for real estate is characterized by frequent sales within a geographic area, reliably known sales prices, and readily discernable attributes of properties sold. This is not the case for sales of sports franchises, which fail on each of these points. These businesses are comprised of a number of different types of tangible and intangible assets. The data on these transactions are typically available only through the press and trade publications; the quality of these data is suspect, and they are often incomplete. However, as public corporations buy sports franchises, they will have an obligation to disclose team acquisitions in their SEC filings as material events. These purchasers will likely disclose as little information as the SEC disclosure rules permit.

The application of the market transaction method to a sports franchise is difficult because of (1) the lack of data on the comparative franchises and (2) the subjectivity of any comparative value adjustments. The unique nature of each franchise requires that complete and valid comparative analyses be performed. A number of factors should be considered in such analyses, including—but not limited to—the following:

- Market size, location, demographics, and growth
- Synergies and scale economies
- Venue—ownership or lease terms, venue revenues, and age
- Local television agreements
- Roster and status of player contracts
- Liabilities and obligations assumed

Examples of the types of adjustments that would need to be made are as follows:

- Differences in market size—particularly important to MLB, NBA, and NHL teams because of their dependence on gate receipts, local television, and in-venue advertising.
- A difference in venue revenue splits—for example, one team retains all parking and concession revenues while the other splits these with the venue owner or municipality.
- Venue amenities—differences in the number and quality of luxury boxes and premium seating.

Given the scarcity of these properties, buyer synergies are often impounded in the transactional purchase prices. This fact alone gives support to the use of the market transaction method to value these unique properties.

The income and market approaches, as discussed, are both valid in arriving at value indications. However, neither approach should be relied upon solely to produce a value conclusion. The proper weighting afforded each approach will depend on the specific facts and the degree that sufficient reliable information is available in order to apply each valuation approach.

Implications of the Federal Income Tax Code. The Internal Revenue Code has always had an impact, good or bad, on businesses—and hence on their values. The business of sports has benefited from the Internal Revenue Code through most of the last 40 years. In fact, in the early going, when sports teams were owned only by wealthy individuals, the income tax benefits of team ownership were usually the only justifications for the investment.

The Revenue Reconciliation Act of 1993 significantly changed the income tax treatment of professional sports teams and not for the better. Sports franchises are now specifically excluded as amortizable intangible assets under Internal Revenue Code Section 197.[18] Therefore, the

---

[18] Internal Revenue Code, Section 197(e)(6).

franchise acquired in the purchase of a professional sports team is not allowed any amortization at all—not even the 15-year amortization afforded virtually every other intangible asset. In addition, national television contracts that are negotiated by the leagues are considered part of the franchise and thus not afforded income tax amortization.

Player contracts are also not considered Section 197 intangible assets. Player contracts can be valued separately and amortized for federal income tax purposes over their remaining useful lives. The Internal Revenue Service generally sets a limitation of 50 percent of the total team purchase price on the value of these assets, except where the specific facts and circumstances would support a higher or lower valuation.[19]

Teams are made up of a number of tangible and intangible assets other than the nonamortizable franchise. In addition to player contracts, other assets may include:

- Fixed assets
- Arena/stadium lease
- Minor league team
- Season ticket holder relationships
- Suite and premium seat holder relationships
- Coaches and management contracts
- Local cable TV, television, and radio contracts
- Advertiser relationships
- Draft rights
- Expansion rights

The three generally accepted asset valuation approaches—that is, the cost, income, and market approaches—all have applicability in the valuation of these individual assets. The proper valuation of these individual assets—plus the inclusion of any current assets acquired—will reduce the amount allocated to the franchise value.

Venue Feasibility

At this point in the discussion, the reader should have a pretty good understanding of the importance of a team's venue to its profitability and value. This section will (1) answer the questions posed in the introduction, (2) outline feasibility analysis, and (3) present excerpts from an arena feasibility study. We cannot avoid the fact that a venue is real estate. A venue is, after all, comprised of dirt, bricks, and mortar—and that's real estate.

The specific case we will discuss here is a venue that has, as owners or anchor tenants, one or (hopefully) two, in the case of an arena, of the teams in the four professional leagues that are the subject of this chapter.

---

[19] Internal Revenue Code, Sections 1056(a) and 1060(e)(2).

We are getting ahead of ourselves. So, let's first define feasibility by borrowing from the real estate valuation literature:

> A real estate project is "feasible" when the real estate analyst determines that there is a reasonable likelihood of satisfying explicit objectives when a selected course of action is tested for fit to a context of specific constraints and limited resources.[20]

The late Dr. Graaskamp certainly had a way with words. Whose objectives and what specific constraints and limited resources? We will address these questions below.

True economic feasibility exists when a project obtains the required rate of return on the full replacement cost of the individual assets employed. Statutory feasibility considers returns that include property tax abatements or exemptions, free sites or favorable lease terms, infrastructure improvements, and security provided by the local government. Subsidized feasibility considers returns at other than full replacement costs.

In virtually every feasible project that we have examined, the city/user has developed the project through a combination of statutory benefits and subsidies. This in no way means that cities always shoulder losses. Indeed, well thought out venues can have significant direct and indirect benefits. This brings us back to the Graaskamp definition. Venue feasibility objectives, from the point of view of a government unit—a city, county or authority—include:

- Key agglomeration element
- Attract professional sports team(s)
- Retain a professional sports team(s)
- Prestige
- Regional and national promotion
- Increase in-market spending (multiplier effect)
- Increase out-of-market spending (multiplier effect)
- Increased taxes
- Part of a downtown revitalization plan
- Promote university athletics

Within the past decade, St Petersburg, Indianapolis, Nashville, Orlando, and St. Louis have built major venues in order to lure franchises. All five cities have been successful in signing permanent tenants (see Exhibit 19-3). A venue's success from a city's point of view should consider the economic multiplier effects, and the social and cultural benefits to a community. Venues provide focus, and the events that occur are a kind of glue for the community, bringing people together and giving them a sense of pride.

[20] J. A. Graaskamp, *A Guide to Feasibility Analysis*, 2nd ed. (Chicago: Society of Real Estate Appraisers (now the Appraisal Institute), 1980), p. 4.

The local economic impact of a venue can be significant. The New Jersey Sports and Exposition Authority Continental Airlines Arena had a direct and indirect impact on the state's economy of $309 million in 1995, according to a May 1996 Deloitte & Touche study.[21] The study results can be summarized as follows:

In-facility revenues	$110.7 million
Out-of-facility revenues	33.3
Total direct impact	144.0
Indirect impact	165.0
Total impact	$309.0 million

The study also indicated that the arena directly and indirectly generated 1,680 full-time equivalent jobs in 1995. Various taxes, which are not included above, are estimated to have raised an additional $25.6 million for state and local municipalities.

Objectives of professional team owners are different from, but allied with, objectives of the community—at least as they relate to feasibility. Team owners are businesspeople driven by the need to maximize economic income and by the need to provide investors with an appropriate rate of return. As we have seen, major corporations are now "playing ball." Their additional objectives include brand expansion and the enhancement of core assets.

Faced with escalating player salary demands, team owners have sought new venues. In fact, between 1988 and 1996, more than 80 percent of NBA and NHL teams (1) moved into new venues, (2) had one under construction, or (3) obtained a commitment from a government entity for a new one. It has been our experience that the deals between team owners and the public agencies are as varied as the number of teams involved. Team owners and leagues often believe that the cities need them more than they need a given city. The team owners, therefore, drive hard bargains when negotiating lease/ownership arrangements and revenue splits.

Why should business valuation analysts be interested in venue feasibility? Complete venue feasibility analysis requires collaboration among professionals. Disciplines including engineering, architecture, finance, law, sports and venue marketing, real estate, and financial analysis should be brought to bear.

Where does the business valuation analyst fit in? The business valuation analyst should have the training and experience to act as the synthesizer of the inputs of the various disciplines involved.

Feasibility analysis is not a valuation, which seeks value in the market of theoretical buyers and sellers. Rather, it makes a "go" or "no-

---

[21] Deloitte & Touche Consulting Group, *New Jersey Sports and Exposition Authority Economic Impact Study of the Meadowlands, Monmouth Park, and Atlantic City Convention Center*, May 1996.

go" recommendation. The problem, then, is to determine true economic, statutory, and subsidized returns based upon given sets of objectives—with consideration of constraints and resource limitations. In addition to the role of synthesizer, the valuation analyst is uniquely suited to develop (1) cash flow projections and (2) various scenarios from the team owner's (or the public authority's) point of view.

Feasibility Analysis Outline

The feasibility analysis outline that follows is largely summarized from Dr. Graaskamp:[22]

- Objectives setting—strategy study
- Market definition
  - Trading area
  - Competition
  - Demographics
  - Household and income growth
  - Economic base
        Major corporate presence
        Employment growth
        Employers with over 500 employees
- Market segmentation
- Legal-political constraints
- Aesthetic-ethical constraints—including environmental impact
- Physical-technical constraints and alternatives
- Financial synthesis of proposed venue
  - Financial feasibility
  - Economic modeling
  - Cash flow projections
  - Financing alternatives
  - Tax strategy
  - Risk evaluation/sensitivity analyses
  - Measures of profitability and returns

Addressing each of the above items is beyond the scope of this discussion. The outline is intended to give the reader an overview of the process. However, financing an expenditure of the amount required to build a new privately owned arena is instructive of how a partnership between a city and private owner can allow each of the parties to reach its objectives. Municipally owned facilities, of course, can be built with revenue or general obligation bonds, assuming voter approval.

A hypothetical, privately owned $250 million arena may be funded as follows:

---

[22] Graaskamp, *A Guide to Feasibility Analysis*, 2nd ed., p.4.

Various types of senior debt	$150 million
Government agency subordinated debt	35
Equity	35
Concessionaire funding	25
Pouring rights	5
Total	$250 million

In this example, let's assume that the franchise credit is strong and that the franchise has successfully operated sports teams. Let's assume that the senior debt was obtained from a single source, a major insurance company. The concessionaire and soft drink providers paid for the right to serve the new arena and for certain improvements. A portion of the equity came from a payment for naming rights. Also, the city turned over very profitable parking operations unrelated to the arena, abated property taxes, provided the arena site at a bargain lease rate, and gave development rights for an adjacent acreage.

Still, in the final analysis, the city was not out of pocket very much money, as no significant new infrastructure work was required. In addition, the city stood to gain substantial amusement and sales tax revenues, as well as the indirect economic benefits. The city also kept two professional teams from relocating. This was an ideal situation where public/private partnerships could work together for the overall benefit of the community.

Certainly not all new venue proposals are warmly received. Witness the proposed move of Robert Kraft's NFL New England Patriots from Foxboro, Massachusetts, to Hartford, Connecticut. The team was to move into a $374 million taxpayer-paid stadium. Critics of the move characterized the new stadium and the lucrative revenue arrangements as a handout to a wealthy team owner and league at the expense of the average taxpayer. The feasibility study was also declared to be too optimistic with respect to the economic benefits of the new venue. The issue is now moot since the team has decided to remain in Foxboro ostensibly because there was no guarantee that the Hartford venue would be ready by 2002.[23] One cannot help but wonder if that was the real reason. The league has been studying for over a year how to help finance stadiums to keep teams in larger markets like Chicago, Boston, and Philadelphia and to bring teams back to cities like Los Angeles.[24] It should be noted that Hartford is the twenty-seventh largest television market, while the Boston DMA, in which Foxboro is located, is the sixth largest market. In order to keep the Patriots from moving, the NFL sweetened its 12-year-old stadium financing aid program. It has agreed to put up $125 million of the $250 million needed for the project in the form of an interest-free load to be paid off from club seat premium revenues that the team

---

[23] Richard Sandomir, "Stadium Financing? NFL Has a New Twist," *New York Times*, May 6, 1999, p. D1.
[24] Ibid, p. D3.

would not have to pay to visiting clubs.[25] The team owners in this league, like none others, have a tradition of sharing revenues. It is clear that the league and the owners see the financing package as adding to their future prosperity. Kraft will need to raise the balance of $125 million for the project. He will then own the venue as opposed to being a tenant in Hartford. Public money is still needed and, according to the article, the Massachusetts Legislature is to vote on a $70 million subsidy for infrastructure. League financing for team operations is not new, but the Patriots package exemplifies how far a league will go to stay the strategic course.

The Hampton Roads Rhinos—A Case Study

Experienced sports franchise investor George Shinn, owner of the NBA Charlotte Hornets, applied for one of four NHL expansion franchises. We know, of course, that he was unsuccessful. Exhibit 19-3 presents the four 1997 expansion franchise winners. However, it is instructive to examine the market and analyze it to see why the application was not successful.

Shinn selected the Hampton Roads area of Virginia as his proposed team's location. If successful, he would have named the team the Hampton Rhinos. He would also have been required to pay an $80 million expansion fee to the NHL, as did each of the winners. A key to his selection of this market area was that an agreement was reached, after much negotiation, with the region's authorities to construct a new arena.

The Hampton Roads market area, as used herein, is the designated market area (DMA), as defined by A. C. Nielson. This market delineation corresponds with television station coverage, and the area perimeter is a reasonable drive time to the proposed arena site. The area comprises 19 counties (i.e., the metropolitan statistical area plus five counties in southeastern Virginia) and 636,000 households, and is the thirty-ninth largest DMA in the United States (see Exhibit 19-3). Hampton Roads itself is comprised of the cities of Norfolk, Virginia Beach, Portsmouth, Hampton, and Newport News. The economy is heavily dependent on the military and tourism. The Norfolk Naval Base, home port of the Atlantic Fleet, is the world's largest naval installation.

Norfolk was willing to handle the burden of a new arena itself, if the new arena were to be built within the city. The site is located between (1) the Scope, an outmoded 10,000-seat venue, and (2) the MacArthur Center, a planned retail mall. The Norfolk Redevelopment and Housing Authority owns the property. The arena was to be the centerpiece of a downtown redevelopment plan. The Scope is home to the Hampton Admirals, a minor league hockey team. The team draws an average of 6,900 fans per game, and tickets cost $8 compared with an average of $34 for NHL games.

---

[25] Ibid, p. D1

The lack of a large enough media footprint as compared with the semifinalist markets was one of the reasons the NHL gave for dropping Hampton Roads for contention. The Washington Capitals are less than 200 miles to the north. This reasoning shows the importance of broadcast revenues to the NHL, which has the least developed broadcast revenue base in major league sports.

At the time, the Fox Television Network had been strongly promoting hockey to a national audience. This was a first, and it promised to help increase the sport's population of fans. Greater popularity would then lead to further team expansion, because of increased broadcast revenues and additional new revenues from corporate support (as the audience grows). Indeed, Shinn had plans to develop a regional cable sports network around the Rhinos and the Hornets.

A second factor that is also extremely important in the selection process is corporate support. The Hampton Roads area is home to only one Fortune 500 company, Norfolk Southern Corp. In addition, it has relatively few firms with more than 500 employees. A large base of corporations is critical to the feasibility of a modern arena. The reason is that such companies have the financial resources to (1) purchase luxury suites and other premium seating, (2) sponsor events, (3) bid for naming rights, and (4) become in-venue advertisers.

A third factor is the market area's income. The Hampton Roads market had a relatively low income level compared with the other markets in contention. Obviously, it is desirable to fill the arena at compensatory ticket prices and have high "per caps." *Per caps* is the per capita spending on concessions. This spending varies, rather predictably, by market and by type of event.

Exhibit 19-7 presents various demographic statistics and projections provided by CACI Marketing Systems (CACI). The exhibit compares the Norfolk (Hampton Roads) DMA with the Commonwealth of Virginia and with the United States. The 1996 median age for the Norfolk DMA is much younger than for the commonwealth or the United States, owing to the large military presence. This should bode well for professional sports arena attendance. However, the analyst should also consider income.

A fourth factor is a market's household growth. Teams are attracted, as are broadcast networks, to rapidly growing areas. Indeed, virtually all professional team expansion has been in the rapidly growing Sunbelt. The Norfolk DMA, though ranked thirty-ninth in broadcast terms, is ranked seventy-ninth in terms of household growth by CACI. This low relative growth rate is tied to the slowdown in military spending.

The fifth and final factor in the feasibility analysis relates to the seeming lack of resolve to support the construction of a new venue. A review of the relevant articles in the *Virginian-Pilot* over a seven-month period showed that the cities that make up Hampton Roads were not of a single mind with respect to a new arena. They were openly concerned over (1) funding and taxation issues and (2) where the stadium would actually be built.

Professional teams are the anchor tenants and are key to the feasibility of the type of venue considered in this discussion. However, as important as professional teams are, local business leader support and the

Exhibit 19–7

Demographics
Comparison of Norfolk DMA
with Virginia and the United States

Year	Norfolk DMA	Virginia	U.S.	Compound Average Annual Growth Rates		
				Norfolk DMA	Virginia	U.S.
Population (000s)						
1980	1,368	5,347	226,542			
1990	1,622	6,187	248,710	1.7%	1.5%	0.9%
1996	1,743	6,693	265,295	1.2%	1.3%	1.1%
2001	1,853	7,112	278,802	1.2%	1.2%	1.0%
Households (000s)						
1990	579	2,292	91,947			
1996	625	2,476	98,239	1.3%	1.3%	1.1%
2001	664	2,627	103,293	1.2%	1.2%	1.0%
Families (000s)						
1990	420	1,629	64,518			
1996	456	1,767	68,968	1.4%	1.4%	1.1%
Median Age						
1990	30.3	32.6	32.9			
1996	31.8	34.2	34.3			
1996 Per Capita Income				% v. U.S.	% v. U.S.	
	$14,589	$17,589	$16,738	87.0%	105.0%	
Median Household Income						
1996	$32,350	$36,850	$34,650	94.0%	107.0%	
2001	$29,516	$33,863	$33,189	89.0%	102.0%	
1996 Average Disposable Income						
Total	$30,211	$34,809	$33,213	91.0%	105.0%	
Householder < 35	$25,568	$29,698	$29,095	88.0%	102.0%	
35-44	$34,711	$39,778	$38,643	90.0%	103.0%	
45-54	$40,574	$45,876	$43,775	93.0%	105.0%	
55-64	$32,807	$36,598	$34,976	94.0%	105.0%	
65+	$20,784	$22,410	$21,850	95.0%	103.0%	

SOURCE: *Sourcebook America* (CACI Marketing Systems, 1996).

political resolve of a community can often overcome the lack of a team. The Nashville Arena (DMA 33) and the Memphis Pyramid (DMA 42) are examples of markets about the size of Hampton Roads that built modern facilities, both within the last three years, without a professional team as an anchor. Nashville was awarded an expansion team, and the Predators began playing in the 1998–1999 season.

The premise of this section was that the feasibility of a modern venue is tied directly to having a professional sports team as an anchor tenant or owner. The Hampton Roads case lends support to venue attributes, which include location and corporate density, and to the broadcast and cable connection as value drivers. As can be seen, professional sports are played off the field as much or more than on.

Concluding Remarks

Sports are an important part of the media/entertainment matrix. It is a growth industry that will continue to diversify geographically. There will be a continued emergence of new teams and leagues and new ways to attract audiences and to deliver sports content to them.

This discussion presented some of the intricacies of sports economics. The recent dominance of public media companies and high net worth individuals with ties to the media as buyers of franchises was discussed. This trend will continue. Venue attributes were shown to be a key value driver. Team relocations—and the number of venues under construction or being renovated—evidenced the importance of venues to teams.

Team valuations depend heavily on (1) the market transaction method and (2) the discounted cash flow method. Weightings of these valuation methods should be determined on a case-by-case basis. The quality and sufficiency of data and a relative risk assessment are the major determinants of the weighting afforded each valuation approach and method.

Feasibility was defined, and the objectives of host cities and team owners were discussed. The business valuation analyst's role in feasibility analysis was also examined. The feasibility analysis process was outlined. Finally, elements of an economic feasibility study were presented. The study excerpts presented (1) the highlights of the process, (2) the insights into league selection criteria, and (3) the team value drivers.

Chapter 20

Valuing Automobile Dealerships

James L. (Butch) Williams, CPA/ABV, CVA, CBA

Overview

The valuation issues associated with automobile dealerships, in many respects, mirror those of most industries. However, the automobile dealership industry also possesses many unique characteristics requiring specialized knowledge by the valuation professional. With unique terminology that distinguishes this industry from others, an abundance of historical and forecasted performance data, and a strong reliance on the national and local economies, the valuation of automobile dealerships requires a thorough examination of the dealership by an analyst knowledgeable in the industry.

What Are the Major Reasons for Valuation?

Although automobile dealerships can be valued for almost any reason, the following discussion summarizes the more common purposes for valuation:

1. **Dealer succession.** Since the automobile dealer is usually the franchise owner, the various manufacturers (General Motors (GM), Ford, Chrysler, Toyota, Nissan, Mercedes, etc.) impose stringent requirements regarding succession ownership. The valuation of a dealership for estate and gifting purposes is very common. And it provides unique issues to the valuation professional. Because of the franchise relationship, the issue of valuing goodwill also takes on special significance.

2. **Merger and acquisition.** Most dealerships (and franchises) are transacted directly between existing dealers. Nonetheless, an increasingly larger number of transactions are now involving publicly traded companies. Valuations are utilized by purchasers for due diligence purposes to help ensure that a fair price is determined for the target entity.

3. **Sale of dealership or franchise.** Similarly, the selling dealer is well advised to obtain an accurate estimation of value before placing the dealership or franchise in line for sale.

4. **Marital dissolution.** Individual state laws affect the way most dealerships are valued in divorce situations. However, the valuation professional is frequently called upon to educate the court on the unique ownership and operational issues confronting the dealership owner and their impact on value.

5. **Litigation.** Areas of litigation vary widely. Most litigation matters requiring the services of a valuation professional involve shareholder disputes. Accordingly, fair value and fair market value (depending on jurisdictional law) opinions are needed to resolve these matters of dissent. In addition, valuations are used in

disputes with manufacturers, usually in the form of lost profits computations.

6. **Income tax elections.** The seller or purchaser in establishing value prior to a dealership transaction often relies upon the valuation professional. In addition, the valuation professional is often called upon to estimate values for purposes of asset allocation in the transaction. The estimation of the value of a dealership at the time of electing S corporation status is another example of a valuation service for income tax purposes.

Understanding the Industry

The valuation analyst is required under professional standards (American Institute of Certified Public Accountants (AICPA), American Society of Appraisers (ASA), the Institute of Business Appraisers (IBA), National Association of Certified Valuation Analysts (NACVA), *Uniform Standards of Professional Appraisal Practice* (USPAP), etc.) to obtain an adequate knowledge of the subject company's industry. Fortunately for the practitioner, the automobile industry is one of the largest in the world, and a significant amount of information is available.

Although a detailed description of the typical automobile dealership is not practical in this chapter, a review of the publications and resources listed in the bibliography is recommended. However, a brief overview of the unique attributes of an automobile dealership is useful.

Multiple Businesses in One

Possibly one of the most misunderstood and least appreciated aspects of the automobile dealership is the complexity of the business. Whereas most companies involve one or two lines of business, the automobile dealership is composed of at least five businesses in one company. The typical dealership is divided into several departments, each including very separate and distinct management requirements.

Closest in similarity are the new vehicle department and the used vehicle department, although the methods for acquiring and merchandising these two types of vehicles vary dramatically. In recent years, margins on new vehicles have significantly decreased, and the contribution to the gross profit of the dealership has correspondingly declined. Gross profit from used vehicles, on the other hand, has increased in recent years.

The parts department includes both retail and wholesale activities, and it can represent a sizable investment of financial resources by the dealership. Proper coordination of this department with the service department can have a large effect on dealership profitability. As "front end" (vehicle sales) gross profits have declined in recent years, the "back end" (parts and service) operations have become increasingly more important. In addition, a dealership with strong "back end" operations is better able to financially weather economic downturns resulting from manufacturer strikes, rising interest rates, global crises, and other events. These events negatively impact consumer confidence and vehicle purchases. When vehicle purchases decrease, dealership income from parts and service increases as consumers spend their dollars to repair rather than replace their existing vehicles.

The finance and insurance (F&I) department of the dealership is the operation requiring the least overhead and producing the largest gross profit. Curiously, it is often the area of the dealership receiving the least attention by management. Directly impacted by demographics and the product lines of the dealership, the F&I income can be very significant.

In addition to the five departments prevalent in almost every dealership, many dealerships operate a body shop department. Although this department is often linked with the service department, the body shop department is unique. The relationship with the various insurance companies is critical to the success of this department, and a major investment in facility and equipment is also required.

Larger dealerships may have separate departments (or separate companies) for lease and rental sales, and they may also have a "buy here, pay here" lot targeting lower-value, used vehicle sales.

Managing these varied functions requires skilled handling of personnel and physical facilities, inventory control, and money management. Relationships with the manufacturer and key vendors are also very important to the success of the dealership. To place the importance of skilled management in proper perspective, it is interesting to note that most well-run dealerships operate, on average, on after-tax net income of less than 2 percent of total revenues. With such a narrow level of return on sales, there is not much room for management error.

Dealership Accounting

The automobile dealership industry is fairly standardized in its accounting. As part of the franchise agreement, the dealer agrees to use and to report to the manufacturer under that manufacturer's standard accounting system. In this way, the manufacturer can more accurately compare a particular dealership with its peers. Each dealership is provided with a standardized accounting manual that describes how each type of dealership transaction is to be reported. Therefore, with very few exceptions, most dealerships within a particular manufacturing "family" (GM, Ford, etc.) will have substantially identical reporting of financial information. This consistency provides a significant tool for the valuation analyst.

Although automobile dealership accounting substantially follows generally accepted accounting principles (GAAP), it does possess several unique features that the valuation professional should be aware of. A few of the more prominent, unique accounting features are listed below.

LIFO Inventory Method. An often-employed method of inventory valuation in the automobile industry is the last-in, first-out (LIFO) method. LIFO is adopted to reflect the matching of revenue and expense, and it can result in substantial income tax savings for the dealership. Because of the significant investment in inventories by the dealership, this inventory accounting method (depending on the number of years it has been used) can reflect a dramatic reduction in the net value of the assets of the entity.

The reporting of the LIFO reserve (a value amount often exceeding $1 million) is usually found in one of two places on the dealership's balance sheet. The most prevalent method of presentation reports the reserve as a contra-asset account reducing the inventory in the "current assets" section of the balance sheet. This inventory category can include new vehicles, used vehicles, and/or parts.

Another, less frequently used method of presentation is to record the entire reserve in the "equity section" of the balance sheet. The dealer that prefers to show the dealership inventory not reduced by the LIFO reserve, in order to avoid appearing "out of trust" with the financial institutions financing the vehicles, often uses this method. Hence, the inventories are recorded at original cost (not reduced by the LIFO reserve in the asset section), and this figure compares favorably with the inventory amount financed by the financial institutions.

The important point to note is that the valuation professional should make adequate inquiries to determine if the dealership is using the LIFO method of inventory valuation. This is because the LIFO reserve may not be readily apparent on the financial statement prepared for the manufacturer.

Liability for Chargebacks. Chargebacks consist of amounts charged by the finance and insurance companies, including charges for credit life and extended warranty contracts, back to the dealership for contracts terminating prior to maturity. The dealership earns commissions from the vendors on these contracts at the time of sale. In turn, the dealership is charged for any loss of income to the vendor when the customer prematurely ends the contract (via the sale of an owned vehicle, refinancing or paying off the original contract, terminating the insurance contract, etc.).

Most dealerships record these amounts as expenses as they are incurred, so the estimated liability is not accrued on the dealership's financial statements. Depending on the level of "paper" (outstanding finance and insurance contracts) associated with the dealership, the outstanding contingent liability could be significant. For example, if a dealership has $30 million of outstanding paper and has a historical chargeback rate of 0.8 percent, then a contingent liability of $240,000 could be associated with the value of the entity. The chargeback rate could vary widely among dealerships. Demographics, dealer philosophy, and many other factors influence the level of chargebacks experienced by each dealership, and careful inquiries are required to estimate this liability.

Recording of Parts Prices. Financial reporting of an entity's assets is generally reflected by the original purchase price of these assets. As assets are sold, they are removed from inventory at those historical prices. However, because of the tremendous number (generally several thousand) of parts flowing through a dealership's inventory, the ability to properly match these historical prices with the physical inventory on hand is virtually impossible.

Accordingly, the dealership will generally update its parts pricing computer tape with the most recent pricing on a periodic (usually quarterly or semiannual) basis. Therefore, the physical inventory on hand is valued at the most recent prices.

As a result, a dealership that owns a large amount of old or obsolete parts could have an inventory that is reflected on the financial records at amounts exceeding its fair market value. When dealerships change hands, it is not uncommon to see a reduction in value of 15 to 50 percent in the reported book value of the parts inventory.

Departmental Reporting. Most standard accounting programs provide for departmental detail. Therefore, the valuation professional can assess the performance of the dealership as a whole, as well as departmentally. A dealership's financial performance by department, when viewed in relation to economic and demographic conditions, can provide insight in determining the entity's value.

Dealer Reserve Accounts. In line with the finance and insurance function of the dealership, most financial institutions will require the dealership to maintain reserves to offset potential chargebacks. These reserves are generally reductions of dealership commissions and are often not reflected on the financial records of the company. Although these amounts are generally not material in nature, they are the result of individually negotiated arrangements between the dealer and the financial institutions.

In addition to financial institution reserves, dealerships will often establish reserves to offset future losses. Examples include reserves for losses on used vehicles and demonstration units, and some dealers can get quite creative in this area of accounting. The valuation analyst should make adequate inquiries to properly identify and assess the validity of all reserves being maintained in the company's financial records.

Industry Statistics

The automobile industry is one of the largest worldwide. Industry data are both voluminous and accessible, and the valuation analyst is able to obtain accurate, contemporaneous information from a variety of services. A number of these resources are recorded in the bibliography to this chapter.

The dealership also has a large amount of industry statistics provided directly to it by the manufacturer. Dealership performance data, usually expressed in relation to other dealerships within the geographic zone, may be obtained by the valuation professional directly from the dealer. In addition, the dealer may be a member of a dealer "Twenty

Group," an organization of dealerships (usually similar in franchises and size) designed to share operational information and ideas.

Industry Terminology

The automobile industry, similar to other industries, possesses a unique terminology. The valuation professional will often be confronted with this terminology. The following is a *brief* listing of several terms that are often encountered in the automobile dealership environment:

- **Back end**—another name for fixed operations (parts, service, and body shop) of the dealership.
- **Blue sky**—another name for the goodwill of the dealership.
- **Chargebacks**—the unearned portion of finance income that is repaid to the financial institution when customers prematurely pay their loans.
- **CSI**—customer satisfaction index, a measurement of polled data obtained by the manufacturer to evaluate the customer service performance of the dealership.
- **Demo**—a vehicle, typically driven by sales personnel of the dealership, which is always available for demonstration purposes to dealership customers.
- **DOC**—daily operating control report, summary report, prepared internally for management that details daily and month-to-date sales, gross profit, and expense information by department.
- **Dueling**—a practice of maintaining more than one new vehicle franchise at one common physical facility (e.g., Toyota and Mazda).
- **F&I**—finance and insurance.
- **Factory**—another name for the franchiser or manufacturer (e.g., Ford, Toyota).
- **Fixed operations**—another name for the nonvehicle sales operations (parts, service, and body shop) of the dealership.
- **Floor plan**—financial institution financing of vehicle inventory, with each floor plan note secured by a vehicle.
- **Front end**—another name for the vehicle sales (new and used) operations of the dealership.
- **Holdback**—an amount held by the manufacturer and later remitted to the dealership that is in addition to a new vehicle's purchase price.
- **Rebates**—inventory-related compensation received from the manufacturer.
- **SSI**—service satisfaction index, a measurement of polled data obtained by the manufacturer to evaluate the customer service performance of the service department of the dealership.
- **Water**—a term used to indicate inventory (usually parts and used vehicles) costs carried on the financial statements in excess of true value.

The Valuation Engagement

Document Request Checklist

Although similar to most business valuation engagements, the automobile dealership valuation involves unique issues. Exhibit 20-1 presents a sample data and document request checklist that addresses some of the unique issues.

Key Risk Areas

In every engagement, the valuation analyst is confronted with the need to assess the key risk areas of the subject company. Some of the risk areas unique to automobile dealerships are discussed below.

Environmental Issues. By the nature of the operations of most automobile dealerships, off-balance-sheet liabilities (such as environmental contamination) can be, and often are, significant. Underground tanks, underground lifts, chemical contamination, and leakage are but a few of the environmental issues that affect the dealership.

In dealership transactions involving real estate, Phase I and Phase II (if warranted) environmental impact studies are usually conducted. The costs to replace tanks and lifts, along with the related business interruption, can be significant.

Franchise Agreement Terms. The automobile industry is a franchise industry, and the terms and conditions of the franchise agreements can greatly influence value. Most agreements contain highly restrictive language involving transferability of the franchise, with factory approval being required in most instances. Accordingly, the transferability of the franchise is severely restricted.

Franchise Alignment. The issues of franchise alignment in accordance with the manufacturers' directives have increased in importance. The GM Project 2000 (and similar initiatives by virtually every manufacturer) has impacted dealerships and the vehicle lines maintained. In an attempt to strengthen the dealer distribution network, the manufacturers have recommended desirable alignments of product lines (e.g., Buick, Pontiac, and GMC trucks aligned together, as well as Chevrolet with Oldsmobile or Cadillac).

Manufacturers are realigning these franchises, and many franchises are changing hands. Often, the manufacturer is leading this realignment (e.g., GM has channeling teams throughout the country devoted to this task), and the manufacturer is occasionally subsidizing the process by offering varying levels of financial assistance.

Viability of Location. Another manufacturer initiative, also designed to strengthen the dealer distribution network, involves the viability of the dealership location. As area demographics change, the manufacturer is looking to have its dealerships located in the most desirable areas for sale of its products.

Exhibit 20–1

USA Motor Company, Inc.
Data and Documents Requested for Business Valuation

Financial Statements
*   Annual financial statements, prepared by certified public accountants and dealer operating reports (all pages), for the last seven years.
*   Monthly financial statements for both the current year and the prior year.
*   Federal and state income tax returns for the last seven years.
*   Copies of any forecasts or projections, if available.
*   List of subsidiaries or other businesses in which the subject company has an ownership interest, if applicable, together with their financial statements.

Other Financial Data
*   List of cash accounts and any significant cash investments as of the valuation date.
*   Accounts receivable listing, preferably aged, as of the valuation date.
*   List of items comprising inventory (quantity, description, and cost) and information on inventory accounting policies as of the valuation date.
*   Fixed asset register or depreciation schedule as of the valuation date.
*   List of items comprising significant other asset (including any nonoperating assets) balances as of the valuation date.
*   Accounts payable listing, preferably aged, as of the valuation date.
*   Analyses of significant accrued liabilities as of the valuation date.
*   List of notes payable and other interest-bearing debt as of the valuation date.
*   List of items comprising significant other liability balances as of the valuation date.
*   Copies of sales, capital, or operating budgets, if available.
*   Copies of any business plans, if available.
*   Schedule of officers' and directors' compensation for the last seven years, detailed as to base salary, bonuses, and incentives for each officer.
*   Schedule of key person life insurance and copies of all life insurance policies owned by the dealership.
*   Reports of other professionals:
        Appraisals on specific assets (both personal and/or real property).
        Reports of other consultants, including copies of all valuation reports prepared related to this entity.

Other Operating Data
*   List of stockholders or partners, showing the amount of stock or percentage owned by each person, with dates, and amounts of stock acquisitions; information on prior transactions of the stock or any related party transactions.
*   Organization chart, including personnel profile, manager pay plans, and number of employees by functional groupings, such as new vehicle department, used vehicle department, service department, parts department, and administration.
*   Details of transactions with all related parties.

Legal Documents
*   Articles of incorporation, bylaws, and any amendment to either.
*   All franchise or operating agreements.
*   Copies of significant leases and loans, including notes receivable and notes payable.
*   Copies of stockholder or partnership agreements, including any stock option agreements.
*   Minutes of board of directors meetings for the past several years.
*   Copies of any buy-sell agreements and/or written offers to purchase or sell company stock.
*   Copies of key managers' employment contracts.
*   Copies of any major sale or purchase contracts.
*   Details of any litigation, including pending or threatened lawsuits, contingent or off-balance-sheet liabilities.
*   Details of any employee benefit plans, including pension plans, profit sharing plans, and stock bonus plans.
*   Reports of examinations issued by government agencies such as EPA, OSHA, IRS, and EEOC. Also, a summary of the status of any environmental issues.
*   Attorney's invoices/billing statements during the past 12 months.

Other Company Data
*   Details of all transactions in the dealership's stock during the last seven years.
*   List of any of the following:
        Patents
        Copyrights
        Trademarks
        Similar intangibles
        Customer relationships
        Supplier relationships
*   Details of any contingent liabilities (such as guarantees or warranties) or off-balance-sheet financing (such as letters of credit).
*   Brief summary of the dealership's history from inception, including competitive positions and unique characteristics of the dealership.
*   List of competitors, with location, relative size, and any relevant factors.
*   Resumes or a summary of the background and experience of all key personnel, including experience in the automotive business and number of years with the dealership.
*   Copies of any other value indicators, such as property tax appraisals.
*   A copy of the most recent R.L. Polk registrations.
*   Summary of the dealership's current Project 2000 status, including copies of any written correspondence. Also, a summary of possible plans for realignment.
*   Summary of the dealership's latest CSI information.
*   Marketing literature (catalogs, brochures, advertisements, etc.).
*   List of locations where the dealership operates, with size and recent appraisal.
*   Trade associations to which the dealership belongs or would be eligible for membership.
*   Relevant trade or government publications (especially market forecasts).

The viability of the dealership in a particular location can dramatically influence value. A dealership with a location no longer deemed viable would provide several obstacles to both a potential seller and a purchaser, ultimately detracting from the dealership's value.

Manufacturer Relationship. As indicated previously, the relationship with the manufacturer is extremely important. In addition to the alignment, location, and ownership issues mentioned above, the manufacturer relationship has a major effect on the dealership's ability to be profitable. An example is the CSI and SSI programs of several manufacturers. In many instances, the performance of the dealership in CSI and SSI directly affects their ability to obtain inventory. Vehicle allocations are often tied to CSI and SSI performance, as well as to historical sales performance ("turn and earn" inventory programs relate performance to inventory provided by the manufacturer).

A dealership is also at the whim of the manufacturer and its decisions regarding various programs. For example, the manufacturer's rebate programs and financing terms can greatly influence a dealership's performance and profitability.

Litigation Issues. In recent years, the automobile dealer has become an increasingly larger target for litigation. Dealerships face larger class action lawsuits as well as ever-increasing damage claims filed by their customers. A general evaluation of historical litigation claims, as well as contemporaneous pending and threatened litigation, is a fundamental step in the valuation process.

Economic Issues. Because of its high reliance on consumer spending, the automobile industry is very much at risk with respect to economic trends. On a national level, the automobile industry has been affected by historic events—rising or declining interest rates, the Gulf War, and so forth. Locally, the closing or opening of a major plant, a strike, or similar economic events could greatly influence a dealership's value.

Regulatory Issues. Periodically, certain regulatory issues can affect the value of a dealership. For example, the imposition of the luxury tax and the proposed 1995 tariff against Japan had a significant effect on the value of many dealerships.

Understanding How Dealerships Are Purchased and Sold

Which Assets Are Purchased and Sold Directly?

In most dealership transactions, the value of the following assets are typically negotiated directly between the purchaser and seller:

- Vehicle inventory
- Parts
- Fixed assets
- Blue sky

How Are These Assets Purchased and Sold?

New vehicles are generally purchased at their cost from the manufacturer, with adjustments for holdback and advertising charges, and they are taken subject to the related floor plan (or other financing arrangements). Adjustments to new vehicle inventory are also made for demo units.

The value of the used vehicles is subject to negotiation between the parties. Often the seller is left with the responsibility of liquidating the used vehicles to customers or to wholesalers. Any related financing is also paid off as the vehicles are sold.

Parts are usually valued by taking a physical inventory at the time of sale, with the cost of taking inventory paid equally by both parties (since it is in each of their best interests). However, the price paid for the parts is often negotiated and can range from somewhere between (1) a price of all parts at their current prices (as would be recorded on the dealership's financial statements) and (2) a price equivalent to only those parts that are returnable to the manufacturer (generally nonobsolete parts boxed in their original containers and packaging).

Fixed assets are usually the last tangible assets to be discussed, and their ultimate price is negotiated extensively by the parties. The fixed assets have usually been depreciated by accelerated depreciation methods. Fixed assets often include fully depreciated items, such as parts bins, furniture, and office equipment. Accordingly, the seller almost always believes that the fixed assets are worth more than the book value, while the purchaser looks at the assets as used and worth less than their book value.

Blue sky is another name for the dealership's goodwill. This intangible asset generally consists of the value attributable to a combination of the dealership's:

1. Earnings capacity
2. Reputation
3. Franchises
4. Location
5. Demographics
6. Other factors

To quantify blue sky, the industry generally looks to the normalized pretax, pre-LIFO earnings of the dealership. Obviously, the most recent performance of the dealership is given the greatest consideration, but often the average (usually weighted) of the past two or three years is used. In any event, the ultimate goal is to estimate the most reasonable level of expected earnings of the dealership.

Once the earnings stream is identified, a multiple of these earnings is applied. This multiple is reflective of the other factors listed above. The multiple tends to fall between 1 and 3 times the earnings, with recent trends falling between 1.0 and 1.5 times earnings (higher for more profitable lines, more desirable locations, etc.) in "traditional" sales between knowledgeable dealers.

Thus, a dealership's assets are generally sold between dealers at their adjusted book value, plus blue sky represented by the equivalent of 1.0 to 1.5 times the normalized pretax, pre-LIFO earnings.

What about Stock Purchases and Sales?

Although stock purchases and sales are relatively rare, they occasionally occur. With the lowering of the capital gains tax, as well as the increase in acquisitions by public companies, it is fair to assume that more dealership sales will be transacted through stock deals.

Two major factors influence the prices paid in a stock transaction: (1) the LIFO reserve and (2) the built-in gains income taxes to be "inherited" by the purchaser. To arrive at the adjusted book value of the dealership, the LIFO reserve—in addition to any adjustments to reflect the fair market value of the underlying assets (e.g., an adjustment to reflect the appraised value of real estate owned by the dealership)—is added to the book value. Similarly, any downward adjustments (such as uncollectible receivables, "water" in the inventories, unrecorded reserves for chargebacks and litigation) are also made.

Related income taxes associated with these increases and decreases to the book value are also given strong consideration. Depending on the intentions of the parties, particularly the purchaser, the negotiated adjustment for income taxes ranges between 0 and 40 percent of net adjustments. Often, the difference is split, resulting in a 20 percent adjustment.

The blue sky consideration in a stock transaction is sometimes not incorporated into the stock price paid. Rather, the payment for blue sky can be negotiated separately through noncompete, consulting, or rental agreements. This is done primarily for income tax reasons, since the purchaser desires to maximize the deductibility of the purchased assets, including goodwill. Thus, when the valuation professional is comparing market transactions involving automobile dealerships, careful analysis of all facts of the transaction is critical.

Methods for Valuing Dealerships

Does the Purpose Matter?

Absolutely! The major reasons for valuation listed earlier in the chapter are discussed in relation to the proper methodology below.

Federal Estate and Gift Matters. In most dealer succession matters, estate or gift tax issues are involved. The related standard of value is fair market value, and the valuation guidelines promulgated under Revenue Ruling 59-60 apply.

However, two very interesting court decisions have prevailed for over 20 years, and they provide a strong beacon of guidance in valuing automobile dealerships for estate and gift tax purposes. In *Frank E. Zorniger* v. *Commissioner*,[1] a minority ownership interest in a Chevrolet dealership was valued for gift tax purposes. Although the Internal Revenue Service asserted a higher value, the taxpayer contended that the dealership value was book value. The court held for the taxpayer and found that the franchise agreement was with the dealer, *not* the dealership, and was nontransferable. Therefore, no goodwill was attributable to the dealership.

In *Estate of Bernard Rothgery* v. *Commissioner*,[2] a 50 percent ownership interest in a Chevrolet/Cadillac dealership was valued for estate tax purposes. In this case, the taxpayer established a value on the basis of a multiple of earnings. The Internal Revenue Service asserted that the value was equal to that of its underlying assets, and the court agreed.

According to these two cases, for federal estate and gift purposes, the franchise goodwill is not an asset of the dealership, and the resultant value for the dealership is equivalent to the adjusted net assets of the corporation. This point can be very important when valuing a less than controlling ownership interest or an interest owned by a party other that one possessing the franchise rights with the manufacturer.

Purchases and Sales. In situations involving the purchase and sale of a dealership, it is important to understand how dealerships are bought and sold. In an earlier section of this discussion, the elements of the traditional asset purchase were described. Generally, the dealership is sold for an amount equivalent to the adjusted net assets of the dealership, plus blue sky. Blue sky is equivalent to a multiple (between 1 and 3 times) of normalized, pretax, pre-LIFO earnings.

Another method of valuing a dealership is the excess earnings method. Similar to the adjusted net assets method, the excess earnings method values the goodwill (total intangible assets of the dealership) on the basis of earnings in excess of an industry return on the adjusted net assets of the dealership. Since the dealership employs a significant investment in inventories and capital assets, and since this method somewhat follows the methodology used when dealerships are bought and sold, this method is a useful way to estimate value. However, great care should be given to the specific rates of return assigned to the tangible assets of the dealership, since different dealerships have different asset mixes.

An income approach to valuing a dealership poses a particularly difficult challenge. This is because the dealership earnings can vary so dramatically. Most dealerships have a value of at least their adjusted net book value. A strict capitalization of earnings or a discounting of future earnings/cash flows may not adequately reflect all the elements of value in an automobile dealership. Accordingly, the development of a proper capitalization rate provides an additional challenge to the valuation professional.

[1] *Frank E. Zorniger* v. *Commissioner*, 62 T.C. 435 (1974).
[2] *Estate of Bernard Rothgery* v. *Commissioner*, 475 F.2d 591 (Fed. Circ. Ct. of App., 1973).

As in valuing any business, the choice of an appropriate earnings stream, indicative of the dealership's expected performance, is very important. Earnings of the smaller dealerships tend to approximate cash flows, and the challenge in this volatile industry is to arrive at a conclusion of representative earnings.

Historical performance is extremely important, but the days of the automotive industry being on predictable, five-year economic cycles are long past. Historical performance, coupled with the many and varied economic, industry, and other factors mentioned in this discussion, determines ultimate conclusion of the economic income stream to be capitalized. In addition, this is an industry in which forecasted earnings are often accessible, making the discounted future economic income methods available alternatives.

Market approach methods, including guideline publicly traded companies and market databases, provide some measure of comparability for the valuation analyst. An analysis on publicly traded companies follows later in this discussion.

Although market-derived pricing data are helpful, the availability of comparable sales is extremely limited and difficult to apply. The majority of transactions of automobile dealerships occur between dealers, and very little public information is available. Most information related to these sales is obtained from the dealers themselves, as well as brokers and professionals assisting them.

Limited information for transactions involving dealerships is available from market databases, but the size of the transactions is generally small and the transactions vary widely in their terms and prices.

Divorce and Litigation. Applicable state laws generally define the standard of value, with most valuations using either fair value or fair market value. Asset-based approach and market approach methods are generally used, and the major factor of contention between the parties then becomes the applicability of valuation discounts. Once again, the courts generally determine which discounts are appropriate in the valuation process and whether the premise of value is either liquidation or going concern.

How Does the Emergence of Publicly Traded Companies Influence Value in Automobile Dealerships?

Without question, the emergence of publicly traded companies owning automobile dealerships is the single most significant development in the past few years. In the used vehicle market, CarMax and Auto Nation made early splashes in the industry, followed by United Auto Group and Cross-Continent Auto Retailers in the new vehicle market. Quickly behind them were Lithia Motors, followed by Republic Industries and Sonic Automotive, Inc. The list is continuing to grow.

Hardly a week goes by without news of a large dealer group being acquired by one of the publicly traded companies or news of a publicly traded automobile dealer group being formed. The multiples of earnings paid for these acquisitions have been considerably higher than those traditionally transacted in the industry. This fact has produced an impact on asking prices for most dealerships. However, many dealerships are not being sold, and it is important to view the facts and circumstances currently in the industry to determine the reason.

The rush to go public has been fast and furious, with many groups vying for advantage in the stock market. The public's infatuation with the initial offerings was very high, particularly with the addition of Wayne Huizenga into the market. However, stock prices have become more predictable as the market has become more educated about this industry. The acquisitions of dealer groups have been largely for strategic purposes, with the purchasers seeking to obtain certain geographic locations, market diversity, and franchise diversity. The more actively purchased dealerships are larger dealer groups and larger individual dealerships, with an emphasis on earnings and franchises.

For example, Republic initially purchased large groups and dealerships in its bid to challenge the franchise limitations imposed by both Toyota and Honda. These types of acquisitions are strategic ones and are aimed at certain dealerships and dealer groups.

Do these acquisitions reflect the fair market values of dealerships? In larger dealerships and dealership groups, they certainly should be considered in the ultimate estimation of value. However, in most dealerships with annual sales under $75 million and net income less than $1 million, the applicability of these publicly traded transactions is very limited.

However, the excitement generated by these transactions has, most assuredly, raised the expectation levels of most dealers offering their dealerships for sale. In addition to the publicly traded transactions, another factor influencing the sales prices of dealerships has been the participation by the manufacturer in aligning franchises in desired locations. The manufacturer's influence may result in higher asking prices from selling dealers, but only limited premiums have been observed in prices paid for dealerships with manufacturer involvement.

Even though the economy is solid, skepticism in the industry is fairly high. The ultimate impact of the publicly traded companies is still undecided. These companies are sometimes paying absurdly high prices (blue sky multiples of 3 to 8 times normalized, pretax, pre-LIFO earnings).

Should the prices being paid by the publicly traded companies be considered? Most definitely! Should they be used in the valuation? Only in very unique situations, and even then, with some adjustments.

Common Normalization Adjustments

In the valuation of controlling ownership interests in automobile dealerships, several normalization adjustments are generally applicable. Many of these mirror those adjustments prevalent in valuing most closely held companies, and include the following:

1. Dealer and family member compensation—as with most closely held companies, these can vary greatly from industry standards.
2. Rent—since many dealerships rent their facilities from the dealer (or related parties), the rent expense should be reviewed.
3. LIFO—this method of accounting is generally used for the income tax benefits derived, and it has a financial statement impact on both earnings and the balance sheet.
4. Adjustments for "water" in receivables and inventories.
5. Real estate and fixed asset values.
6. Dealer perks—a thorough inquiry is required to uncover many of these, which can include demo units and other perks for family members; investment vehicles (vintage antiques), motor homes, boats, and other recreational vehicles; club memberships; and a host of personal expenses paid by the dealership.
7. Assets and liabilities not included on the books—dealer reserves, contingent liabilities (chargebacks, litigation), and the like.

With the comparative industry data that are readily available, inquiries can be made about variations in the dealership's performance; and adjustments can be made if appropriate.

Summary

Although many of the traditional approaches to valuing automobile dealerships apply, it is vital that the valuation professional fully understand the intricacies of the industry. An understanding of the industry under "normal" conditions is a difficult task. However, the changes bombarding the automotive business make it especially challenging to accurately value a dealership. Daily events influence value, and the valuation analyst is required to expand existing appraisal knowledge to encompass a vast amount of constantly changing information. Exhibit 20-2 presents a Top 10 list for valuing automobile dealerships.

Bibliography

Periodicals

Automotive Executive, a monthly publication of NADA Services Corporation, a wholly owned subsidiary of NADA, 8400 Westpark Drive, McLean, VA 22102, (703) 821-7150.

Automotive News, a weekly publication of Crain Communications, Inc., 1400 Woodbridge, Detroit, MI 48207-3187, (800) 678-9595.

Black Book, a weekly publication of National Auto Research, Post Office Box 758, Gainesville, FL 30503, (800) 367-3759.

Exhibit 20–2

**Top Ten List
for Valuing Automobile Dealerships**

In our national presentations of valuation topics, we always provide our participants with a Top 10 list that summarizes our discussions. We are pleased to offer the following list to readers of this chapter:

10   Learn the terminology unique to the automobile industry.

9   Carefully research the abundant industry information.

8   Understand the purpose and the standard of value for the engagement.

7   Be aware of publicly traded transactions and consider their applications.

6   Understand the unique dealership accounting practices.

5   Inquire about possible environment and litigation issues.

4   Fully understand the relationship with the respective factories.

3   Inquire about dealership location and viability.

2   Keep up with the current events affecting the automobile industry.

1   Understand how dealerships are bought and sold.

SOURCE: Williams, Taylor & Associates.

Car Dealer Insider, a weekly publication of United Communications Group, 11300 Rockville Pike, Suite 1100, Rockville, MD 20852-3030, (800) 929-4824 ext. 247.

NADA Official Used Car Guide, a weekly guide published by NADA, 8400 Westpark Drive, McLean, VA 22102, (703) 821-7150.

Periodicals (usually monthly or bimonthly) from the applicable state automobile dealership associations.

Standard & Poor's Industry Surveys: Autos and Auto Parts, semiannual publication by Standard & Poor's Corporation, 25 Broadway, New York, NY 20004, (800) 221-5277.

Ward's Dealer Business, a monthly publication of Ward Communications, a division of Intertec Publishing Corporation, 9800 Metcalf, Overland Park, KS 66212-2978, (800) 441-0294.

Publications, Manuals, and Guides

A Dealer Guide to Valuing an Automobile Dealership, by David A. Duryee, an NADA management guide (McLean, VA: National Automobile Dealers Association, 1995).

Auto Dealership Engagement Manual, by Tony L. Argiz, Marc S. Dickler, and Don M. Pallais, an AICPA Integrated Practice System manual (Jersey City, NJ: American Institute of Certified Public Accountants, 1995).

Automobile Dealership Accounting, by Jacob Cohen and Carl Woodward, a continuing professional education course (#735145) (Jersey City, NJ: American Society of Certified Public Accountants, 1996).

Bureau of Economic Analysis, various publications available in print or over the Internet, U.S. Department of Commerce, Washington, DC, (202) 606-9900, www.bea.doc.gov.

DeFilipps' Dealer Tax Watch, a quarterly publication of Willard J. DeFilipps, CPA, P.C., 317 West Prospect Avenue, Mt. Prospect, IL 60056, (847) 577-3977.

DeFilipps' LIFO Lookout, a quarterly publication of Willard J. DeFilipps, CPA, P.C., 317 West Prospect Avenue, Mt. Prospect, IL 60056, (847) 577-3977.

Economic Indicators: The Motor Vehicle's Role in the U.S. Economy, American Automobile Manufacturers Association, 1401 H Street NW, Suite 900, Washington, DC 20005, (202) 326-5500.

Guide to Dealerships, by Don E. Ray, Stephen D. Holton, Marilyn Patterson, and Marilyn Z. Rutledge (Fort Worth, TX: Practitioners Publishing Company, 1996).

The Power Report, published by J. D. Power & Associates, 30401 Agoura Road, Agoura Hills, CA 91301, (818) 889-6330.

Chapter 21

Valuing Radio Broadcasting Companies

Richard M. Wise, FCA, ASA, CBA, FCBV, CFE, and
Drew S. Dorweiler, MBA, ASA, CPA/ABV, CBV, CFE

The Radio Broadcasting Industry

Introduction

Radio broadcasting forms part of the media and entertainment industry, an important and growing sector of the U.S. economy. Companies in the entertainment industry can be classified into two broad categories: (1) those that provide entertainment product or content and (2) those that present or transmit entertainment products. The major radio broadcasting companies in the United States are either "pure play" radio broadcasters or companies for which radio broadcasting represents a significant component of their operations.[1]

Forbes summarized the nature and characteristics of the radio broadcasting industry as follows:

> Radio is one of the least glamorous of the media businesses, but it is the most profitable. The movie industry is plagued by ever-increasing production and marketing costs. Network TV is burdened with high-priced shows and the fees it must pay affiliated stations. The networks are under siege from cable channels and from competition for viewers from the Internet.
>
> But radio has a captive audience. The average person spends 22 hours per week listening to the radio. About 70% of radio listening takes place outside the home and most of that is during commuting time. For advertisers, radio can be extremely effective in pinpointing a market.
>
> Though radio is an old business and technologically mature, its revenues are growing at better than 10% per year, and cash flow is increasing at an even-faster 25% rate. The average operating margin for successful radio companies is about 40%. Compare this with 30% for cable networks and less than 20% for top television networks like NBC.
>
> "Radio is the model for cash flow—the radiomen are going to run the TV business," says Jerry Del Colliano, publisher of *Insight Radio* newsletter.
>
> Radio represents only about 7% of the total advertising pie, compared with 24% for television and 22% for newspapers. But because of its nature and because of recent changes in the law, it is the most profitable segment.
>
> Unlike other media companies that are held captive to escalating production costs, radio's costs are mostly fixed, regardless of market size. Once a company covers the costs of things like a transmitting tower and broadcasting equipment, 85 cents of every dollar flows to the bottom line, subject only to exactions from the tax collector. This is a highly leveraged business. Cash flow margins of 50% are common for successful radio stations; poor ones can lose money.[2]

---

[1] For example, CBS Corporation (CBS), Chancellor Media Corp. (Chancellor Media), Clear Channel Communications, Inc. (Clear Channel), Jacor Communications, Inc. (Jacor), Cox Radio Inc. (Cox), Emmis Broadcasting (Emmis), SFX Broadcasting, Inc. (SFX), and Heftel Broadcasting Corp. (Heftel).

[2] Matthew Schifrin, "Radio Wave," *Forbes*, June 1, 1998, pp. 130–131. Reprinted by permission of Forbes Magazine, © Forbes, Inc., 1999.

Regulatory Environment

Radio stations operate in a regulated environment. The Federal Communications Commission (FCC) performs the following functions:

1. Allocation of spectrum space for AM, FM, and television signals.
2. Assignment of frequency and call letters to stations.
3. Designation of operating power and sign-on and sign-off times.
4. Issuance of construction permits and inspection of technical equipment.
5. Monitoring of transmissions to ensure that the licensee is fulfilling the designated needs and desires of the communities served.
6. Approval of the sale of radio stations and transfer of broadcast licenses.

When a radio station is acquired, and its license transferred from the vendor to the purchaser, the license applicant (purchaser) bears the burden of satisfying the regulator's requirements. These requirements include some or all of the following:

1. The applicant must possess adequate financing, technical resources, managerial skills, and broadcast experience.
2. There must not be an undue concentration of ownership, and/or the level of foreign media ownership must not be raised to an unsatisfactory level.
3. The applicant may be required to provide local news, information, and other programming content, and/or use local broadcasters and station employees (rather than rely on network "feeds").
4. The local market must be of sufficient size and economic strength to support the station's proposed programming.
5. The applicant may be required to utilize an unpopular programming format and/or cover an unprofitable market area.
6. The regulator may stipulate that new technology be implemented to replace older equipment (with potentially significant expense borne by the applicant).
7. The applicant may be required to provide a certain degree of multicultural and/or multilinguistic programming.

In 1992, the FCC relaxed its duopoly rules and permitted companies to own two AM and two FM stations in the same market, up to a maximum of four radio stations for markets having a total of 15 or more viable radio stations. In markets having fewer than 15 stations, ownership was limited to a maximum of three radio stations, with no more than two stations on the same band. Prior to the 1992 deregulation, transaction activity in the United States involving radio stations was negligible; however, activity increased noticeably following deregulation, both in terms of transaction volume and average transaction value.

The Telecommunications Act of 1996 (the 1996 Act) further deregulated the U.S. radio broadcasting industry, providing for ownership of up to eight stations in large markets, and up to five stations in smaller markets, without regard to either the total number of stations or total coverage of the market. Following passage of the 1996 Act, transaction volume soared again, with large station groups being traded or consolidated.

As noted in *Forbes*:

> The Telecommunications Act of 1996 made a tremendous difference. It allowed operators to acquire many stations in the same market—up to 8 stations and up to 35% of total market ad revenues. There was no limit to the number of markets you could enter. The rule changes gave birth to national radio broadcasting companies.[3]

Industry Trends

With no organic growth occurring, and little organic growth expected in the future, the radio broadcasting market is considered mature.

Operating strategies that have been developed in radio broadcasting are:

1. **Targeting large markets.** Large markets typically produce significant advertising revenue. Even small shares of large markets may be profitable, given that large markets have always encountered considerably higher levels of competition. With the recent consolidations, there is an even greater degree of concentration in these markets.

2. **Increasing market share and the ability to control a dominant share of local audience and revenue.** Even though the advertising revenue in smaller markets is significantly less, a dominant or controlling position in the market may nonetheless be profitable.

Networks and Syndication.   Networks are program providers. The radio stations are the vehicles that deliver the programs.

A trend in the radio broadcasting industry (one that precedes deregulation) has been the use of network management contracts.[4] These agreements permit a radio company to manage a nonowned station by paying the owner a predetermined fee. Such arrangements were beneficial to radio broadcasters, because they allowed for the development and marketing of a network brand image, as well as the spreading of fixed operating costs over a number of stations—in effect, circumventing regulations on multiple license ownership. Under the network management

---

[3] Ibid.
[4] Also referred to as "local marketing agreements."

contracts, typically two to four minutes of advertising time per hour of airtime are sold by the local station, and seven to nine minutes of airtime are provided to the network to sell its own advertisements.[5]

Financial constraints have forced most radio stations, including those in major markets, to use network programming for efficiency. Virtually every programming format is available from several suppliers 24 hours a day. Stations typically affiliate with one particular network and carry some or all of its programming. The major players in the radio network industry are ABC, Westwood One, and CBS, each of which offers several programming formats. Network revenues are derived solely from commercial airtime sold by the network.

To receive "network" status, a program or service must meet the following two criteria:

1. Station affiliates must be connected with the network organization (usually via satellite) for live feeds.
2. Station affiliates must broadcast the network's programming on a daily basis, at the same time.

Network radio revenues have been increasing. This growth is primarily attributable to restructuring of major networks, such as Westwood One, which realigned its major programs into specific demographic categories. All other multipoint programming is considered "syndication." Revenue figures for these various programming types are not easily tracked, because they are often part of national-spot buys.

Syndicated radio programming is also important for broadcasters because it is provided free of charge. If such programming attracts a sufficient target audience, the broadcaster benefits. This is because advertisers will pay for airtime during such syndicated programming time slots.

Sports Radio. Sports radio has experienced explosive growth in the 1990s, especially sports talk. By 1995, there were 103 AM sports talk stations and three FM sports talk stations on the air in the United States. In 1990, there were only three all-sports radio stations. The shows are aimed at a male demographic. Some shows feature retired professional athletes. Requirements for a successful sports talk show include knowledgeable hosts, an informal approach to the topic, and an ability to appeal to a broad audience behind the hardcore sports fan.

Sports radio has grown on two fronts:

1. Many major market stations, which already had play-by-play rights, have gone all-sports.
2. A number of stations in markets outside the major league cities are going the sports route with no play-by-play—using lengthy

---

[5] Local radio stations seldom pay anything to the network for their programming (other than providing it with the airtime).

stretches of satellite-delivered sports networks along with locally produced sports talk.[6]

As with sports radio, network syndicators have begun to supply the increasing number of stations switching their format.[7] Most networks and syndicators feature talk shows, play-by-play, and remote game coverage, a format that appeals to smaller market stations. With the growing ranks of sports talk stations, more syndicators are producing and marketing syndicated talk shows.

Revenue from national sports network radio is estimated at 12 to 15 percent of total network dollars.[8]

Digital Radio. Digital radio broadcasting was launched in North America in early 1999. Some broadcasters have already been issued digital radio broadcast licenses. The first receivers were made commercially available in the fall of 1997. The only factor expected to inhibit the implementation of digital radio is the initial cost of the receivers. This new radio technology will provide higher "CD-quality" sound than that received from traditional AM and FM signals. Also, buildings will not obstruct its signal. Radio broadcasters believe digital radio will rejuvenate their industry by providing an entirely new set of ancillary services (because of the ability of a digital broadcast to carry additional simultaneous signals), including traffic and weather information, parking availability, and additional data on songs (e.g., artist identification), as well as commercials.

Digital radio is also expected to benefit broadcasters, who will be able to offer advertisers a "one-stop source." The technology will allow them to provide customized programming and advertising spots targeted at specific local markets, combined with a strong regional (and eventually nationwide) network presence. Although digital radio is fundamentally a new technological medium for broadcasting services to consumers, programming content that meets customers' needs remains the issue.

Digital radio is also expected to take broadcasters into the multimedia world (toward convergence): The consumer will come home, turn on the computer, and from the computer have access to telephone lines, television programs, Internet Web sites, e-mail, and radio programming. *Forbes* notes another convergence-related trend in the radio industry:

---

[6] Top billers in the sports talk format, based upon tabulations reported in Duncan's 1994 *Radio Market Guide*, were WFAN New York at $33.5 million, KNBR at $18.0 million, and WIP (AM) Philadelphia at $7.4 million.

[7] Key sports talk program syndicators include ESPN Radio Network, ABC, CBS, Westwood One, Sports By-Line USA, One on One Sports, The SportsFan Radio Network, American Sports Radio Network, The Team Network, NBA Radio, and Spirit Sports and Event Marketing.

[8] The information is difficult to track, since this industry segment is in a considerable growth mode and statistical sources typically report on network sports in combination with talk radio.

Not to be outflanked again by technology as it was by TV, radio is trying to co-opt the Internet . . . Ultimately, this will allow Web surfers a
chance to listen to, say, football games or music from any station in the
world via their computers. It also could be a source of ad revenue.[9]

From a digital perspective, building brand equity will be even more
critical for radio broadcasters. The challenge will be to convince consumers to choose a particular broadcaster's radio service. For example,
call letters will be meaningless and "frequency" will no longer be relevant; what will remain is brand names. Building both a strong franchise
and strong "brand equity" means that the consumer will choose to listen
to a given radio network for the quality of the programming and for the
perceived values the brand carries.

Many industry participants believe that digital radio will eventually
replace AM stations, and replace analog radio entirely, in 10 to 30 years.

Consolidation.   Since the enactment of the 1996 Act, radio groups have
been making numerous acquisitions, as well as swapping entire groups of
stations. As a consequence, buyers have become very large (and sellers
very rich), as buyer demand and pricing multiples paid for radio stations
have both hit record highs. This is because consolidation leads to (1)
greater operating structure efficiency, (2) increased negotiating ability
with advertisers, and (3) more experienced, sales-oriented management
teams. These result in lower costs and higher advertising revenue.[10] Radio
stations have also become more valuable, as advertisers are beginning to
view this medium as the best way to target specific demographic groups.[11]

Since the 1996 deregulation, the leading participants in the consolidation process have been CBS Radio, Chancellor Media, American
Radio Systems Corp. (American Radio), Jacor, SFX, Westinghouse
Electric Corp. (Westinghouse), Capstar Broadcasting Corporation
(Capstar), and Citadel Broadcasting Co. Although the dramatic volume
of acquisitions in radio broadcasting has attracted considerable notice,
a comparatively less visible trend of individual station purchases, or
station swaps, among radio broadcasters has also occurred, as companies operating in multiple markets seek to further define and
strengthen key strategic markets or regions.

The primary cause of this heightened activity is synergy—more
specifically, economies of scale. For example, although the cost of *creating* programming content for radio broadcasters may be high, the marginal cost of *distributing* this content to each incremental listener is
comparatively low. Hence, radio broadcasters seek to expand their target audience and thereby directly increase profits.

---

[9] Schifrin, "Radio Wave," *Forbes*, June 1, 1998, p. 135. Reprinted by permission of Forbes Magazine,
© Forbes Inc., 1999.

[10] For example, national advertising has increased dramatically for radio, notwithstanding that local advertising still represents more than 80 percent of total ad revenue.

[11] The foregoing trends are summarized in two articles: Eben Shapiro, "A Wave of Buyouts Has Radio
Industry Beaming with Success," *Wall Street Journal*, September 18, 1997, p. A1; and Jill Goldsmith, "Radio
Broadcasters Are Likely to Post Strong Results Amid Consolidations," *Wall Street Journal*, October 17, 1997, p. B6.

Valuation

Value Drivers

Large markets generally yield much higher advertising revenue for radio broadcasters than small markets. In fact, even a small share in a large market can be profitable. However, this consideration is tempered by the fact that large markets tend to attract higher levels of competition. Radio broadcasters face significant competition for advertising dollars from other forms of media, such as television, newspapers, magazines, specialty television, cable channels, and outdoor advertising. Consequently, large-market radio stations are typically worth more than small market radio stations.

A second, related value driver is market concentration and the ability of a broadcaster (or group) to control a dominant share of local audience and revenue. Consolidation trends among radio broadcasters have resulted in the stronger operators controlling greater concentrations of stations in certain markets. Also, some radio companies may seek to control smaller markets, because—even though the advertising revenue may be considerably less—dominant market share in any size market can generate extremely high profits. Broadcasters operating in multiple markets will trade their individual radio stations, or station groups, with each other in order to further define and strengthen key strategic markets or regions.

Radio station pricing multiples often vary according to their perceived "potentials." For example, FM stations typically command higher pricing multiples in urban areas than do AM stations. This is because AM stations do not have as reliable a signal and fewer people listen to these stations. Moreover, AM radio listeners represent an older demographic (over 55 years of age), a less lucrative advertising market.

This trend toward decreased AM station value has been ongoing since the late 1980s. Hence, it is increasingly rare to find new AM stations being established in eastern North American markets. However, because their broadcast signals travel great distances, AM stations tend to be more popular in western North American regions.

Radio advertising revenue is influenced by two components: ratings and rates. Because radio is a "ratings-driven" business, advertising is highly influenced by the number of listeners (i.e., ratings). Radio station ratings, which typically fluctuate on a weekly basis, influence advertising rates charged by the stations. There are also different advertising rates depending on the specific time of day, the time of year, and so on. In seeking to maximize revenues, radio broadcasters attempt to air as many advertisements as possible—up to full airtime capacity. Because advertising expenditures are partly discretionary, corporate spending in this area is influenced by the economic cycle. A widely used statistic, the "power factor," compares the share of listeners with the share of revenue generated by a particular advertisement. To put it briefly, radio broadcasters will initially focus on building audience ratings. This audience level will subsequently drive the advertising rates.

The end result is that purchase price is typically a function of the size of the market and the specific market share a target company may offer an acquirer.

Apart from the standard factors affecting the value of businesses in general, factors influencing the value of a radio company, whether it owns FM stations, AM stations, or networks, include:

1. Degree of risk associated with the historic (and anticipated) level of revenue (i.e., the mix of national, local, network, syndication, and production revenue and extent of network affiliation).
2. Composition of expenditures among the major expense categories, (i.e., programming, technical, sales promotion, general, administrative, depreciation, and debt service).
3. Operating profit margins on historical and projected levels of revenue and operating expenses.
4. Quality, age, condition, and value of the equipment being transferred with the license.
5. Market demographics and the effectiveness of the programming format. The latter can be determined in part by analyzing the market share of the subject station, and comparing it with stations having both similar and dissimilar formats. It is important to look at the change and rate of change in musical and other tastes that have occurred in the overall market, and to consider any adjustments in programming that were made to respond to those changes (a rapid change in format is generally an expensive undertaking for a radio station).
6. Advertising rates that are either too high or too low. One quick test is to compare market share based on number of listeners with market share based on advertising revenue generated. These should be approximately equal for stations with similar formats. Any significant discrepancy could indicate that advertising rates are either high or low in relation to industry averages. Advertising rates are also affected by the "spill factor"—that is, the percentage of the local audience listening to nonlocal stations. Advertisers are sometimes able to buy into nonlocal radio spots to receive local coverage at lower advertising rates.
7. The terms and conditions of the licenses and how they are being used.
8. The degree of difficulty associated with obtaining a new license for the specific, or a similar, market.
9. The size of the company or network.
10. The size of the geographic market served and the potential audience it contains (generally defined by the location and height of the tower, signal strength, regional topography, and amount of interference).
11. The geographic diversification of operations.
12. The rate of growth of the target market, in terms of the number of listeners, advertising rates, and the revenue potential that can be generated from the base.

13. Affiliations with advertising firms.
14. The level of competition in the market served, as well as the presence of other forms of media.
15. The reputation and abilities of key personnel, such as management, sales and marketing staff, and on-air personalities.
16. Diversification of the nature of operations (e.g., AM, FM, television, and other media forms).
17. Transmission frequency.
18. Well-established and recognized call letters for a broadcaster's radio stations (i.e., brand identity).

Valuation Methodology

Radio broadcasting companies are generally valued using one of the following income approach methods:

1. Each radio station property owned by the broadcaster is valued individually, and the resulting values are aggregated in order to estimate total corporate value.
2. The broadcasting company's combined, or consolidated, results are capitalized at an appropriate direct capitalization multiple (or, if the discounted cash flow method is applied, the results are discounted using an appropriate present value discount rate).

These two valuation methods are outlined below.

The advantages of the second method include (1) the ease and convenience of analyzing one set of corporate data, rather than a multitude of financial statements, and (2) the fact that consolidated financial results may allow for a more accurate assessment of the goodwill and/or synergies (including strategic advantages) attaching to the broadcasting company (which may be more difficult to assess when radio stations are valued on an individual basis).

Radio broadcasters appeal to many different types of special purchasers, who are motivated to acquire because of (1) anticipated postacquisition synergies (including economies of scale) from sharing administration, technical development, and marketing through combining acquired properties with radio stations already owned, and/or (2) strategic advantages. Other buyers may be motivated simply by the perceived power or prestige of radio station ownership.

Other factors influencing radio company values include:

• The limited number of licenses available
• Market saturation in certain urban areas
• Long-term prospects for the radio industry

Considering such factors, the pricing multiples paid for radio companies depend on the station's characteristics and on the level of activity in the marketplace at a given time.

Radio broadcasting companies are valued by means of one or more of the following approaches.

Income Approach. Under the income approach, an estimate is made using the following data:

1. A multiple of trailing, or forecasted, EBITDA[12] or other cash flow measure, such as *broadcast cash flow*.[13]
2. A multiple of trailing, or forecasted, revenues.
3. A multiple of one of the following:
    a. The last 12 months' revenue.
    b. The estimated revenue for the current fiscal year.
    c. The projected revenue for the following fiscal years.
4. A multiple of one of the following:
    a. The last 12 months' broadcast cash flow.
    b. The broadcast cash flow for the current fiscal year.
    c. The projected broadcast cash flow for the following fiscal year.
5. A multiple of one of the following:
    a. The last 12 months' operating cash flow (EBITDA).
    b. The estimated operating cash flow (EBITDA) for the current fiscal year.
    c. The projected operating cash flow (EBITDA) for the following fiscal year.
6. Discounted cash flow (DCF) for a period of five years (with the "residual" value estimated as a multiple of the projected cash flow, net of sustaining capital reinvestment, in the terminal year of the projection period). Long-term debt and any working capital deficiency are deducted[14] from the residual value, which is then discounted back to the effective valuation date. Generally, a large percentage of the overall worth of radio stations estimated by applying the DCF method is represented by the residual value.
7. The DCF method based on a five-year stream of unlevered pretax cash flow plus a projected residual value. For purposes of an equity value analysis, preferred stock and total debt are subtracted from, and any excess cash is added to, the aggregate value estimated by applying the DCF method.

The particular present value discount rate applied in valuing radio broadcasting stations is generally based on the weighted average cost of capital (WACC).[15] (See Chapter 1.) Because of the discretionary nature

---

[12] Earnings before interest, taxes, depreciation, and amortization.

[13] In the radio broadcasting industry, operating cash flow is generally the equivalent of EBITDA, whereas broadcast cash flow (BCF) is measured as operating cash flow before the deduction of corporate expenses. BCF may be considered either before or after the deduction of net sustaining capital reinvestment.

[14] Assuming that cash flow is determined on a preinterest basis.

[15] The *Cost of Capital Quarterly 1998 Yearbook,* published by Ibbotson Associates, contains WACC rates attributable to DCF analyses for the "Radio and Television Broadcasting Stations" industry, ranging from 21.30 to 27.03 percent for the "single-stage" DCF model and 13.65 to 17.56 percent for the "three-stage" DCF model, with respective medians of 25.99 and 15.88 percent.

of amortization of the programs purchased, and the related income tax aspects, businesses in the radio broadcast sector have traditionally been valued on the basis of capitalized cash flow rather than some other measure of economic income.

Market Approach.   Under the market approach, an estimate is made using public data of the price that would be paid for the issued shares of the subject, by (1) analyzing the stock prices of guideline publicly traded radio broadcasting companies and (2) adjusting the market-derived pricing multiples to reflect the differences in risk between the publicly traded companies and the subject company.

Guideline Company Selection.   Given the high volume of transactions in the radio broadcasting industry following the adoption of the 1996 Act, as well as the large number of publicly traded radio companies, there are sufficient guideline companies and/or relevant industry transactional data to support the adoption of the guideline company method in most cases.

Because industry transactions are subject to regulatory approval, it is generally not difficult to access relevant documents, including purchase/sale agreements between the transacting parties. Accordingly, when comparable, or guideline, company data are considered, an analysis of market transactions can be performed to assist in developing direct capitalization multiples. Financial and operating data of the guideline radio broadcasting companies should be adjusted by the analyst for valuation purposes to reflect dissimilarities with respect to accounting conventions, minority ownership or controlling ownership interests, and lack of marketability.

In judging whether sufficiently similar radio companies or stations (guideline companies) have been sold in the open market, the analyst should typically ask a host of questions (as would be the case with respect to most other businesses), relating to the available transactional data, such as:

1. Does the implied "multiple of revenues" produce values for the *shares* of the business or for the underlying *operating assets*?
2. How relevant are the market transactions in terms of each of the following factors as they relate to the subject's business: size, diversification of markets and products/services; geographic location; political environment; market share; customer base; employee, customer, and supplier relationships; technological development; growth trends in advertising revenues and profits; capital structure and leverage; liquidity; tangible asset backing; management depth and continuity; profitability; maturity of the business; level of redundant assets; and off-balance-sheet assets and liabilities?
3. To what extent do the notes to the respective financial statements of the acquirees affect the interpretation of the published figures to be used in the valuation ratios?
4. Was the purchaser or vendor compelled to transact?

5. Did any of the transaction prices include a consulting agreement and/or a noncompete agreement with the vendor? If so, what were the terms thereof?
6. What is the time frame of the data used?
7. For how long a period was each acquiree exposed to sale in the marketplace?

Therefore, in reviewing the population of guideline company "candidates," the analyst should give particular consideration to the following factors, which may affect the degree of comparability with the subject:

1. Size (measured by revenue, assets, listener base, or number of stations owned).
2. Degree of diversification into other operational areas (e.g., television and publishing).
3. Regulatory environment (e.g., United States vs. Canada).
4. Demographics of market served (e.g., age of listeners, average income).
5. Degree of competition in the market (e.g., market concentration, market share).
6. Programming and format (e.g., musical genre, sports talk, news, and English, Spanish, or French language broadcasts).

Valuation Pricing Multiples. Guideline company valuation pricing multiples[16] often provide an identifiable basis for ascertaining either the public's perception of a radio broadcasting company's share value or the market's capitalization of a company's selected underlying financial data.[17]

Exhibit 21-1 shows the equity valuation multiples for the radio and television broadcasting industry.

As with businesses in other industry groups, even though no single valuation pricing multiple will necessarily correlate perfectly to a given market-derived multiple, a firm's historical and expected financial performance will influence the purchase price for the target. This is because it provides an indication of the financial benefits the investor should be able to obtain from the investment.

Various market analyses could be performed to assess the respective public market valuations of the guideline companies for purposes of estimating the value of the subject company. These involve the calculation of the market-derived multiples for the guideline companies on the basis of a number of valuation pricing multiples, such as:

---

[16] In valuation pricing multiples, a value or price serves as the numerator and financial, operating, or physical data serve as the denominator.

[17] In the derivation of valuation ratios, a comparative analysis of qualitative and quantitative similarities and differences between guideline companies and the company being valued is made to assess the investment attributes of the guideline companies relative to the subject.

Exhibit 21–1

Valuation Multiples for Radio and Television Broadcasting Stations

	Price/Earnings		Market/Book		Price/Sales		Price/Cash Flow		Price/Operating Income	
	Latest	5-Year Average	Latest	5-Year Average	Latest	5-Year Average	Latest	5-Year Average	Latest	5-Year Average
75th percentile	NMF*	NMF	4.50	4.22	7.37	5.02	NMF	NMF	NMF	65.17
Median	NMF	NMF	1.80	2.68	5.12	3.39	NMF	NMF	26.89	13.72
25th percentile	102.07	22.77	1.34	1.24	3.26	2.11	92.30	20.66	12.58	11.57

SOURCE: *Cost of Capital Quarterly 1998 Yearbook* (Chicago: Ibbotson Associates, 1998). This yearbook includes data through March 1998.

*Not meaningful.

- Market capitalization[18]/revenue
- Market capitalization/EBITDA
- Market capitalization/broadcast cash flow
- RMC[19]/revenue
- RMC/EBITDA
- RMC/broadcast cash flow
- Market price[20]/earnings (before or after taxes)

In applying the valuation pricing multiples, the analyst will ensure that (1) the time periods considered are reasonably congruent and (2) the adjustments to reported financial information and definitions used for the numerator and denominator component of the valuation multiple are consistently applied.

Furthermore, with possibly several valuation pricing multiples selected for application to the subject company and several value indications obtained, the analyst will consider the relative importance of each value indication used in arriving at the valuation conclusion. To the extent that adjustments for dissimilarities with respect to minority ownership interest and ownership control positions and/or lack of marketability[21] have not already been made, allowances are made for these factors, if applicable.

---

[18] Market price (of equity) plus interest-bearing debt. This measures the value of a company's total capital structure, net of redundant assets (if any).

[19] Residual market capitalization (RMC) is market capitalization less cash and cash equivalents. RMC measures a company's overall capitalization on a basis that is prior to the consideration of its cash retention policy.

[20] Total common shares outstanding (giving effect to dilution, if applicable) times share price, less nonoperating assets (if any). This measures the value placed by the market on all outstanding common shares and common share equivalents with respect to a company's primary operations, viewed on a minority (noncontrolling) ownership basis.

[21] An amount or percentage is deducted from an equity interest to reflect lack of marketability—that is, the relative ease and certainty with which an expected value can be obtained for a business, business ownership interest, or security in a typical market, when desired, and the relative promptness with which the business interest or security can be converted into cash or into a replacement asset.

Rule-of-Thumb Method. A rule of thumb for obtaining a value indication is the *price per listener* method. It is not used as a primary valuation method, but it may be used under limited circumstances. For example, this method may be applied when a radio broadcasting group is acquired for noneconomic purposes, such as the nonfinancial benefits of radio station ownership (e.g., perceived power and prestige within a community, similar to ownership of certain sports franchises, in certain cases).

Adjustments. Common adjustments to cash flow or revenue include:

1. Historical and projected results of the subject company (as well as the guideline radio companies used, if appropriate) are adjusted to exclude noneconomic and nonrecurring expenses and revenues.
2. The value of any redundant or nonoperating assets (net of any taxes on withdrawal) is added to the going-concern value of the subject company's operations.
3. Modifications are made to any revenue or expenses attributable to unprofitable or discontinued operations.
4. Any broadcast or advertising contracts that may, in the foreseeable future, expire or possibly be renegotiated are converted to an appropriate forward-looking level.
5. In negotiating a transaction, the impact of taxes on both the seller and the prospective purchaser is considered, primarily in terms of tax advantages that may benefit the purchaser as a result of the manner in which the transaction is structured.

Industry Transactions

Various research departments of the investment banking firms have commented on a number of transactions in the industry since the enactment of the 1996 Act.

Price Trends

Value Line summarizes stock price trends in the radio broadcasting industry as follows:

> TV and Radio have had something of a reversal of [fortunes], of late. For most of the second half of the twentieth century, radio seemed to recede in public consciousness, while the influence of TV grew. Now, the growth of cable-TV, pay-per-view, and the Internet [is] serving to diminish the popularity of free network Television. At the same time, radio is experiencing a resurgence. This is due, at least partly, to longer commuting times. People stuck in traffic in their cars are a captive audience for radio. Also, loosening of standards and the emergence of "shock jocks" seems to be helping radio. *Clear Channel Communications* and

Chancellor Media are major beneficiaries of the renewed interest in radio. *CBS* is also benefiting, due to its large radio group....[22]

Among those companies tracked by *Value Line* as having a material presence in radio broadcasting—namely, CBS, Chancellor Media,[23] Clear Channel,[24] and Jacor[25]—the reported P/E multiples were "not meaningful" (because of reported losses or slim profit margins), and projected annual growth for the ensuing five years ranged from a low of 2 percent to a high of 21 percent. For example, in the acquisition of Jacor by Clear Channel, Jacor had booked a loss of $4.1 million, net of a one-time gain of $11.1 million from asset sales.

Consideration of industry growth trends may prove helpful in analyzing industry market transactions. For example, Morgan Stanley Dean Witter ("Morgan Stanley") noted that Cox was enjoying strong organic growth, with its stock trading at a level which "...appears inexpensive relative to the [overall radio] group, trading at 17 times 1998 projected [after-tax cash flow] versus 21 for the group."[26] Morgan Stanley estimated Cox's five-year annual pre–cash flow growth rate at 20 percent, making it the fastest-growing radio group on a same-station basis in 1996, with a 16 percent same-station revenue gain.[27]

Several months earlier, Cox had been trading at 17.5 times estimated 1997 operating cash flow and 14.8 times estimated 1998 operating cash flow (or at 25 times 1997 estimated after-tax cash flow and 22 times 1998 estimated after-tax cash flow). Cox was described as one the 10 largest radio broadcasting companies in the United States ranked by revenue, stations owned, or audience delivered. At the time, Cox owned or operated 49 radio stations, including stations in two of the Top 10 markets (Los Angeles and Atlanta) as well as in six other high-growth Sunbelt cities.[28]

Although Cox, at the time, was pursuing an organic growth strategy, it had tripled in size following 1996 deregulation, expanding its station portfolio from 16 to 49. In its largest transaction, Cox acquired NewCity Communications Inc. (NewCity) for $253 million in April 1997. NewCity operated 18 stations in seven markets. Merrill Lynch's observations are summarized as follows:

---

[22] Ben Sharav, "Entertainment Industry," *Value Line Investment Survey*, August 28, 1998, p. 1790.

[23] Chancellor Media owns and operates 108 stations in 22 of the 40 largest radio markets in the United States, with a combined weekly listener base of 46 million. The company possesses 79 FM and 29 AM stations, including station groups in 9 of the 10 largest U.S. radio markets.

[24] Clear Channel owns and/or programs 190 radio stations and 18 television stations in 43 markets in the United States. It also owns 29.1 percent of Heftel, the largest Spanish language radio broadcaster in the United States.

[25] Jacor is the third largest radio broadcasting company in the United States in terms of total stations, and is also the third largest provider of syndicated radio programming. Jacor owns and/or operates 169 radio stations in 42 broadcast areas throughout the United States. It was acquired by Clear Channel in October 1998.

[26] Frank Bodenchak, *Morgan Stanley Research Report*, August 7, 1997.

[27] Ibid.

[28] Keith Fawcett and Jessica Reif Cohen, "Cox Radio: Coasting at High Speed," *Comment* (New York: Merrill Lynch & Co., Global Securities Research and Economics Group), November 14, 1997, pp. 177–180.

Purchase price multiples tend to be lower in midsize markets. For Cox's largest acquisition to-date, we estimate purchase-price multiples on 1997E [broadcast cash flow] of 11 [times] for NewCity. These multiples [are] markedly below the entry price for playing in Top 10 markets (e.g., Westinghouse's buy of Infinity at 17 [times] 1997E and Chancellor's buy of Viacom Radio at 17 [times] 1997E) and as such are clearly bigger boosters of near-term shareholder value. By pursuing its midsize market strategy Cox Radio is able to purchase big market share at relatively low cost, while facing less effective intramural competition, compared to companies focused on Top 10 markets.

Radio sector multiples exceed their brethren in broadcast television for several reasons: The radio audience is not eroding, advertising revenue is growing faster, consolidation is easier to execute, the clustering benefits are greater and there are no near-term capital outlays for converting to digital transmission. Cox Radio has seen a recent trading range of 15–18 [times] 1997E [operating cash flow]. Utilizing a multiple of 15 [times] our 1999E [operating cash flow], our price objective is $40 per share, an increase of 23% over current pricing. The [price/after-tax cash flow] multiple is estimated to be 22.5 [times] our 1999E of $1.75.[29]

Market Transactions

Exhibit 21-2 shows the ownership control price premiums paid in the radio broadcasting industry subsequent to the 1996 deregulation. Morgan Stanley commented as follows on the sale of radio assets of American Radio to Westinghouse on the basis of $44 per share:

> The valuation implies acquisition multiples of 18.8 times estimated 1997 radio broadcast cash flow (BCF), 15.8 times estimated 1998 BCF, and 13.7 times estimated 1999 BCF. While these valuations are literally the highest ever paid for a major radio stock purchase, we note that the 35% margin portfolio includes approximately $400 million in stock [non-cash-flow-generating properties] value (over 30 stations with no cash flow). Adjusting for the value of these stocks, Westinghouse's purchase price would amount to 15.9 times estimated 1997 BCF, 13.4 times estimated 1998 BCF, and 11.9 times estimated 1999 BCF.[30]

A press release issued with respect to this transaction on September 19, 1997, noted that American Radio was the fifth largest radio broadcasting company in the United States, having 98 radio stations (including pending transactions) located in 19 predominantly Top 50 markets. These include several major markets where CBS (formerly Westinghouse)[31] had radio and television stations. The press release quotes CBS station group chairman and chief executive officer Mel Karmazin:

---

[29] Ibid., pp. 179–180.

[30] Bodenchak, *Morgan Stanley Research Report*, August 7, 1997.

[31] The name of Westinghouse was changed to CBS Corporation on December 1, 1997. CBS Radio became the nation's largest radio network with its acquisition of Infinity in 1996.

Exhibit 21–2

Ownership Control Price Premiums in Radio Broadcasting

Target Company	Announcement Date	Control Premium*
Citicasters Inc. (Citicasters)	09/96	9.3%
Heftel	08/96	2.2%
Infinity Broadcasting Corp. (Infinity)	12/96	12.7%
Osborn Communications Corp.	02/97	28.2%
American Radio	06/98	12.4%

SOURCE: *Control Premium Study* (Los Angeles: Houlihan Lokey Howard & Zukin, third quarter 1998), pp. 39–40.

*Excess of the total consideration price over the "unaffected" preannouncement price.

The acquisition of American Radio is financially and strategically attractive for CBS. This investment will significantly strengthen CBS's position in the fast growing radio industry. It will enable CBS Radio to expand into top 50 markets and increase its position in its existing major markets. American Radio's stations are located in very attractive radio revenue growth markets where the Company expects to further consolidate its position.[32]

Transactional and Market Data

A sampling of transactions involving "pure play" radio broadcasting companies is presented in Exhibit 21-3.

The acquisition of Chancellor by Evergreen Media Corporation (Evergreen) in September 1997,[33] provides an example of transaction pricing. Chancellor was described by *Value Line* as follows:

[Chancellor Media] is an adept consolidator. The company has been a prime beneficiary of the [1996 Act] . . . Chancellor has an in-house market research division that seeks to locate stations with low market share and determines what potential radio audience in the market is underserved. While [Chancellor] has clusters in all its cities, it could still buy additional stations in most of them, as the Justice Department now allows market shares of up to about 40% in big markets.

Chancellor has formed a national radio network, the AMFM Radio Networks, which will reach 61 million people through Chancellor's stations and stations owned by Capstar. The network will offer two 30-second spots per hour to national advertisers, which will increase its available time for sale by about 10%.[34]

[32] Press release dated September 19, 1997.
[33] The combined entity became Chancellor Media.
[34] *Value Line*, November 28, 1997, p. 1792.

Exhibit 21–3

Transactional Market Data Summarized from
Mergerstat Review and Mergerstat Transaction Roster

Date Announced / Closing Date	Buyer Name / Seller Name / Detailed Description	Seller's Annual Revenues ($million)	Price Offered ($million)	Method of Payment	P/E Offered	Premium Offered	Multiple of Book Value
3/21/96 8/1/96	American Radio *Henry Broadcasting Co.* American Radio agreed to acquire Henry for $111.0 million in cash and stock.	NA*	111.0	NA	Combo	NA	NA
4/15/96 11/22/96	SFX *Multi-Market Radio Inc.*	21.3	62.1	Stock	NEG	4.6%	5.1
5/14/96	Cox *NewCity*	55.6	250.0	NA	NEG	NA	(10.7)
6/3/96 8/5/96	Clear Channel *Heftel* (remaining 79%) Operates Spanish language radio stations.	71.8	183.6	Cash	75.9	4.5%	5.3
6/20/96 12/31/96	Westinghouse *Infinity* The acquisition combines the top two radio companies, giving Westinghouse 83 radio stations with $1 billion in revenues and making it three times the size of its closest competitor, Jacor.	374.4	3,900.0	Stock	70.1	12.3%	11.4
8/5/96	American Radio *EZ* The acquisition creates a portfolio with 96 radio stations in 20 markets, making it one of the largest and most geographically diversified radio groups in the United States.	84.5	428.2	Combo	291.9	47.4%	(3.9)
2/18/97	Evergreen *Hicks, Muse, Tate & Furst Inc. (Chancellor Broadcasting Company)* Along with the acquisition of 10 radio stations from Viacom, Chancellor Media would own 103 radio stations in 21 major markets, including New York City and Los Angeles.	139.2	921.6	Stock	(182.6)	6.3%	NEG
4/16/97	Hicks Muse Tate & Furst Inc. *Patterson Broadcasting Inc.* Hicks Muse's Capstar would acquire Patterson, which operates about 36 middle-market radio stations. Capstar is the nation's largest owner of radio stations.	NA	215.0	Combo	NA	NA	NA
6/23/97 12/12/97	Clear Channel *Paxson Communications Corp.* Clear Channel acquired Paxson's entire radio holdings, consisting of 46 radio stations and 6 radio networks plus 348 outdoor display faces, for $629 million in cash. Paxson originally offered $693 million for the holdings plus Paxson's two minor league teams.	NA	629.0	Cash	NA	NA	NA
8/25/97	Hicks Muse Tate & Furst Inc. *SFX* SFX operates 71 radio stations. Hicks Muse agreed to acquire SFX, paying $75 for each Class A share held by management. SFX would add 71 stations to Hicks Muse's Capstar which would become the nation's third largest radio broadcaster, with 314 stations in 79 markets.	237.3	731.7	Cash	(65.3)	13.6%	NEG
9/8/97	Jacor *Synergy Broadcasting Inc.* Jacor agreed to acquire Synergy for $71.5 mimllion. No other terms were disclosed.	NA	71.5	NA	NA	NA	NA
9/19/97	Westinghouse *American Radio* Westinghouse also agreed to acquire $1 billion of debt.	271.3	1,600.0	Cash	919.0	NA	NEG

SOURCE: *Mergerstat Review* and *Mergerstat Transaction Roster* (Los Angeles: Houlihan Lokey Howard & Zukin, 1998), www.mergerstat.com.

Canadian Radio Broadcasting Industry

Background

Broadcasting is the largest cultural industry in Canada. In 1993–1994, revenue from the broadcasting and cable industry totaled approximately Can $6.7 billion, divided into five main areas:[35]

	Can $
Cable television	2.33 billion
Public broadcasters	1.66 billion
Private television	1.49 billion
Private radio	766 million
Pay and specialty services	471 million

Broadcasters in Canada are supervised and regulated by the Canadian Radio-Television and Telecommunications Commission (CRTC). The Canadian Broadcasting Act requires the broadcasting system to be effectively owned and controlled by Canadians, to operate primarily in the English and French languages, to comprise public, private, and community elements, and to safeguard, enrich, and strengthen the cultural, political, social, and economic fabric of Canada. Among the relevant radio industry sources in Canada reporting statistics for radio stations are the *TRAM Report* (providing data[36] on total radio advertising dollars in the 10 to 12 major markets in Canada) and the Bureau of Broadcast Management statistics.

The radio industry in the United States differs significantly from that in Canada. With about 10,000 commercial radio licenses in the United States, there are approximately twice as many stations per capita than in Canada. The American radio industry is much more deregulated, giving stations almost total control over their format and programming content. Roughly one in every four U.S. AM radio stations is formatted as country, with country being comparatively less popular in Canadian urban markets.

Prior to the April 30, 1998, deregulation of Canadian radio broadcasting, it was comparable in nature to the U.S. radio broadcasting market prior to 1992 deregulation.[37] The radio market potential in Canada is substantially less than what it was in the United States prior to 1992 deregulation. This is because there are approximately 500 radio

---

[35] "Broadcasting in the Information Society," *Strategis*, Industry Canada, March 20, 1997.

[36] These statistics are not itemized by individual radio station.

[37] For example, ownership was limited to one AM and one FM station per market in both regions; local advertising (measured as a percentage of radio station revenue) was similar in the United States and in Canada; radio's share of the local advertising market was nearly identical in both countries; and the industry was highly fragmented in both countries. The United States and Canada had also experienced sluggish growth in national radio advertising.

stations in Canada owned by 147 different companies (compared to 10,000 in the United States). After losing money for most of the 1990s, Canada's fragmented radio industry became marginally profitable during 1996 (although a reported 50 percent of Canadian radio broadcasters are still losing money—largely attributable to poor AM performance).[38]

Currently, there are no "pure plays" among public companies in the Canadian industry; Telemedia Inc. and Standard Broadcasting are the two largest radio operators in Canada.[39] In the United States, however, there are many "pure" radio broadcasting companies. Moreover, although there are 15 radio stations in Montreal and 17 in Toronto, in the United States, a typical market the size of Montreal might feature two to three times more stations.

Radio broadcasters have achieved significant synergies in the United States, benefiting from great cost savings and clout, since they typically use only one advertiser to give them national exposure. In Canada, radio broadcasters will not likely achieve the same degree of synergy. This is because the United States typically has lower-power stations with less signal overlap than Canada, thereby allowing a greater number of radio stations to operate in the United States. However, following the 1998 deregulation in Canada, if a Canadian broadcaster could assemble a certain number of stations, synergies would be achievable.[40]

Another area in which Canadian radio operations differ from those in the United States is in "back end" network administration. Canadian radio networks do not yet consolidate their invoicing procedures. Therefore, radio advertisers typically receive separate invoices from every radio station in a broadcast network, resulting in cost inefficiencies to all parties.

Radio represents only 10 percent of all advertising in Canada, with television being the largest advertising medium (representing 30 percent), newspapers the second largest advertising source, and magazines only 3 to 4 percent of all advertising. The health of radio advertising is a function of television advertising; if television is sold out, advertisers will then use radio and print.

1998 Deregulation

On April 30, 1998, the CRTC handed down a ruling in which for the first time it allowed multiple license ownership. Canadian radio broadcasters may now own two AM stations and two FM stations in major markets,

---

[38] "Lone Station Fights Owner Concentration," *Financial Post*, December 3, 1997.

[39] As measured by hours tuned.

[40] It is not certain as to how this situation will occur in reality, save for WIC Western International Communications Ltd. and Shaw Communications Inc. (Shaw) being expected to combine to become a single radio broadcasting "powerhouse." Moreover, Shaw announced in September 1998 that it would spin off its 23 radio stations and its interests in specialty and pay television channels into a separate, publicly traded entity, tentatively entitled Shaw Media Co. In Canada, there also exists a national advertising conglomerate—Integrated Media Sales (49 percent owned by Telemedia Inc. and 51 percent owned by Standard Broadcasting)—selling national radio advertising slots.

and a total of three stations where the market comprises seven or fewer stations. However, this deregulation was coupled with several significant new obligations, such as playing more music with deemed "Canadian content." The CRTC now requires radio stations to play 35 percent Canadian content, up from previous 30 percent content level. Furthermore, radio stations must play 35 percent Canadian content at all times of the day rather than the previous situation in which they were allowed to play only 25 percent Canadian content during peak hours and then fulfill the remainder of their Canadian content requirement late at night. Moreover, broadcasters were required to hand over more money to Canadian artists (as the "tariff" remitted to the CRTC on station acquisitions was increased from 6 to 10 percent), with such funds being used to promote Canadian talent. Finally, the CRTC would change its rules on issuing new radio station licenses.[41]

Among the numerous benefits anticipated from approval by the CRTC of multiple license ownership are a major consolidation of ownership among radio broadcasting companies, with a concurrent surge in prices paid for radio properties. Radio broadcasting company management should now decide whether corporate strategy following deregulation is (1) to become a consolidator, by acquiring other radio properties, or (2) to place existing properties for sale on the open market.

Moreover, multiple license ownership will likely contribute to improved performance of radio broadcasting companies through factors such as economies of scale (e.g., spreading of costs by combining overhead functions such as sales and administrative departments, operating facilities, and management positions), strategic benefits (e.g., elimination of competition) and complementary programming (e.g., broadening the audience). This latter factor is particularly important in strengthening the clout of radio broadcasting companies in attracting advertisers. However, improved performance will probably occur in Canadian markets only if a radio broadcaster can acquire other stations in the market.

The observed growth in prices paid for U.S. radio broadcasting properties following deregulation in 1992 and 1996 is anticipated to be tempered somewhat in Canada, since there are a limited number of Canadian markets of sufficient size to provide benefits to radio broadcasting companies from multiple license ownership.[42] Furthermore, willing sellers also have to exist and there are currently few sellers in Canada (compared with numerous potential buyers), since most broadcasters are family-owned businesses that wish to continue operating. Many industry participants anticipate that this "seller's market" will cause values of radio properties to climb, partially because of the profit potential to be realized through increased ownership concentration, but also because of increased demand for scarce radio assets.

---

[41] In the past, if there was available capacity on the radio dial, yet local radio stations were encountering financial trouble, the CRTC would not issue any more licenses. However, now it will not use this criterion to deny the issuance of a new license.

[42] Toronto, Montreal, Vancouver, Calgary, Edmonton, Winnipeg, Ottawa, and Halifax.

Another potential regulatory decision anticipated in Canada is a relaxing of foreign ownership restrictions. In general, the rest of the world is heading in this direction and, while not imminent, it is likely that the United States and Canada will ultimately follow the same path. This form of deregulation would further open the door for buyers to enter this market, a move that would again be positive for radio broadcaster valuations.

Conclusion

After years of taking the back seat to other sectors of the entertainment business, the radio broadcasting industry has been changing dramatically as a result of government deregulation, technology advances, and a general increase in commuters' drive times. Radio broadcasting companies have enjoyed increasing profits and have recognized economies of scale resulting in an increase in acquisitions in this industry. The process of valuing radio broadcast businesses has changed in order to reflect this shift in the marketplace.

This chapter described the changing regulatory climate in the United States and Canada. The approaches applied most often in estimating the value of radio broadcast companies are the income approach and the market approach, and these two approaches were explained in detail. Finally, this chapter identified the factors that affect the value of radio broadcast companies and provided sources of data for the analyst to use to evaluate those factors.

Chapter 22

Physician Practice Valuation in an Ever-Changing Health Care Market

Charles A. Wilhoite, CPA/ABV, ASA

Introduction

Since the early 1990s, and particularly in the latter part of the decade, managed care has become the dominant form of health care delivery in most major markets. As a result, the emphasis on health care delivery has shifted, and is expected to continue to shift, to a circumstance in which health care providers—both hospitals and physicians—are required to administer fewer services to an increasing population of patients in order to be successful.

This trend does not suggest that health care providers are withholding needed services from their patients. On the contrary, health care providers are attempting to provide services in a manner that prevents patients from becoming sicker—or their existing ailments from becoming chronic—for the purpose of minimizing the level and severity of future treatments required by patients.

In the traditional "fee for service" delivery system, physicians and hospital providers were compensated for each unit of care or procedure administered. However, in the managed care environment, economic mechanisms and reimbursement fee schedules imposed upon health care providers motivate the providers more *to control and prevent illnesses* than *to treat illnesses*.

Therefore, in conforming to the practice requirements imposed by managed care, health care providers have adopted a fundamental change in practice habits in order to maintain the long-term health of their patients. This change, of course, explains the formation of health maintenance organizations (HMOs), which have come to dominate the coordination and delivery of health services in our country.

In an effort to ensure some level of success in the changing health care market, both HMOs and health care providers have placed increasing emphasis on the formation of integrated delivery systems (IDSs). The goal of an IDS is to create a health care delivery system capable of administering services ranging from the most critical and complex (e.g., inpatient surgery) to the least invasive (e.g., outpatient visits for minor ailments such as sore throats). In essence, the development of an IDS represents an attempt to gain greater control over a patient's passage through the health care delivery system in order to control the cost of that patient to the related system.

In an effort to contend with health insurance reimbursement pressures expected to result from the proliferation of managed care, hospital systems—both for-profit and tax-exempt—throughout the country have embraced the strategy of integration by acquiring physician practices. Both for-profit and tax-exempt hospitals are limited in their practice acquisition efforts by the economic feasibility of the contemplated acquisitions. However, tax-exempt entities must also comply with several significant federal and state regulatory requirements when making acquisitions or else expose themselves to severe penalties and fines, including the potential loss of tax-exempt status.

This chapter focuses on the valuation issues relating to the acquisition of physician practices by tax-exempt hospital systems. Although the chapter focuses on valuation issues in the contemplation of a practice acquisition by a tax-exempt hospital system, many of the issues discussed are generally relevant in any practice valuation. Specifically, this chapter considers:

- Physician practice valuation methodology
- Key valuation issues when performing a physician practice valuation
- The impact of market activity on current practice values

As will be discussed later in this chapter, the actions and financial performances of several significant publicly traded health care organizations during 1998 put downward pressure on the value of physician practices in general. In fact, several health care industry participants were concluding that the value of all physician practices was represented entirely by the hard (i.e., tangible) assets only—implying that no intangible asset value existed in a physician practice.

Although market forces and industry conditions should be considered during the valuation of a physician practice, the blind acceptance of such a generalization clearly ignores local and regional market conditions, market position, reputation, and structural and operating characteristics that differentiate physician practices across the country. Therefore, qualified and experienced financial and legal professionals should analyze the facts and circumstances in each contemplated transaction in order to advance the participants' efforts regarding the successful development of an integrated delivery system.

The recognition and dissemination of a clear understanding of relevant physician practice valuation methodology represent a key step in the process.

Physician Practice Valuation Methodology

Valuation Approaches

Generally, physician practice valuation methods can be categorized into one of three general valuation approaches: (1) the asset-based approach, (2) the income approach, and (3) the market approach. Each approach, as well as each method within an approach, considered relevant for purposes of estimating the fair market value of physician practices, is discussed in the following sections of this chapter.

Asset-Based Approach

Underlying the asset-based approach is the economic principle of substitution. This principle is the premise that an investor will pay no more for an asset (e.g., a business or ownership interest in a business) than the cost to obtain—either through purchase or construction—an asset of equal utility. Although utility can be measured in many ways, generally speaking, the utility measure considered most relevant in purchasing all or part of a physician practice is the economic returns that the investor expects the investment to generate.

With regard to the asset-based valuation of a practice or fractional ownership interest in a practice, a valuation analyst should approach the assignment by viewing the valuation subject as a revenue-producing assemblage of assets—both tangible and intangible. Accordingly, the initial step in an asset-based analysis is to identify each tangible and intangible asset encompassed in the subject health care entity. After it is discretely identified, each tangible and intangible asset is separately valued on the basis of the most relevant method—given the data available. The summation of the estimated values of each tangible and intangible asset represents the overall asset value of the subject practice.

Typically, when an asset-based valuation analysis is performed, the assets are valued according to a fee simple ownership interest. That is, the valuation analyst assumes that, if acquired, the assets of the business will be transferred without any associated current or long-term liabilities.

Typical Physician Practice Assets.   All physician practices maintain some level of practice assets that can be classified into one of three general categories: (1) financial assets, (2) tangible real estate and personal property, and (3) intangible assets.

Financial assets typically include cash, accounts receivable, prepaid expenses, and inventory and supplies (including both office materials and supplies and medical materials and supplies). The tangible real estate and personal property will typically include office furniture and fixtures, medical equipment, medical buildings and land, and leasehold improvements. The potential for the existence of intangible assets in a physician practice, particularly a larger practice, is significant. Generally, the existing intangible assets of a physician practice can be categorized into the following groups:

1.   Technology-related (e.g., proprietary technology, technical know-how, systems and procedures, technical manuals and documentation).
2.   Patient-related (e.g., patient relationships, referral relationships).
3.   Contract-related (e.g., certificates of need, licenses, affiliation agreements, noncompetition agreements with practice partners).
4.   Data processing–related (e.g., computer software, automated databases).
5.   Human capital–related (e.g., a trained and assembled workforce, employment agreements with associate physicians).
6.   Marketing-related (e.g., practice trademarks and trade names).
7.   Location-related (e.g., leasehold interests).
8.   Goodwill-related (e.g., going-concern value).

Although numerous intangible assets within each identified category may exist at a particular practice, generally the most significant intangible assets of a physician practice are represented by patient and referral relationships, a trained and assembled workforce, and going-concern value. The valuation of the identified intangible assets of a physician practice is generally based upon the income approach, typically through a variation of the discounted cash flow analysis which is discussed below. The cost approach is sometimes employed, though practices rarely maintain sufficient cost analysis data regarding internally developed intangible assets. The market approach is less frequently relied upon, because it is generally very difficult to locate market-based data supporting transactions involving specific intangible assets of physician practices.

The following section describes several acceptable methods for the valuation of tangible assets maintained at physician practices.

Valuing Tangible Assets. The theoretical underpinnings of the various asset-based approach methods relate to the following basic economic principles:

- Substitution—affirms that no prudent buyer would pay more for a property than the total cost to "construct" one of equal desirability and utility.
- Supply and demand—shifts in supply and demand cause costs to increase and decrease and cause changes in the need for supply of different types of properties.
- Externalities—gains or losses from external factors may accrue to industrial and commercial properties. External conditions may cause a newly "constructed" property to be worth more or worth less than its cost.

Types of Cost. Within the asset-based approach category, there are several groups of related analytical methods. Each of these groups of methods uses a similar definition of the "type" of cost that is relevant to the analysis. Two types of cost are most common and include subtle but important differences in their definition:

- Reproduction cost—contemplates the construction of an exact replica of the subject health care property.
- Replacement cost—contemplates the cost to re-create the functionality or utility of the subject health care property, but in a form or appearance that may be quite different from the actual property subject to valuation.

Functionality is an engineering concept that means the ability of the subject health care property to perform the task for which it was designed. Utility is an economics concept that means the ability of the subject health care property to provide an equivalent amount of satisfaction.

Even though the replacement property performs the same task as the subject property, the replacement property is often better (in some way) than the subject. As a result, the replacement property may yield more satisfaction than the subject property. In that case, analysts should be careful to adjust for this factor in the obsolescence estimation of their replacement cost analysis.

Several other definitions of cost are encompassed by the asset-based approach. Some analysts consider a measure of cost avoidance as an asset-based approach method. This method quantifies either historical or prospective costs that are avoided (i.e., not incurred) by the property holder as a result of owning the subject health care property. Some analysts consider trended historical costs as an indication of value. In this method, actual historical property development costs are identified and quantified and, then, "trended" to the valuation date by an appropriate inflation-based index factor. All asset-based approach methods typically include an all-inclusive definition of "cost."

It is important to recognize that the cost (whether replacement or reproduction) of a property includes not only hard costs (e.g., materials and labor) and soft costs (e.g., engineering and design labor and overhead), but also the property developer's profit (on both the hard and soft cost investment) and an entrepreneurial incentive (to economically motivate the property development process). Also, the cost of a property should be reduced by all relevant forms of obsolescence—including external obsolescence.

So, even though the asset-based approach presents a distinct and different set of valuation analyses from the income approach, it also entails necessary economic analyses. These economic analyses (which may involve some analysis of income) provide indications both of the appropriate levels of entrepreneurial incentive (if any) and of external obsolescence (if any).

Cost New. The replacement cost of a health care property is the total cost to construct, at current prices, a property having equal utility to the property subject to valuation. However, the replacement property would be created with modern methods and constructed according to current standards, state-of-the-art design and layout, and the highest available quality of workmanship. Accordingly, the replacement property may have greater utility than the subject health care property.

Reproduction cost is the total cost, at current prices, to construct an exact duplicate or replica of the subject health care property. This duplicate would be created using the same materials, standards, design, layout, and quality of workmanship used to create the original property.

Replacement cost new typically establishes the maximum amount that a prudent investor would pay for a fungible property. However, this assertion is true only to the extent that the definition of cost includes consideration of hard costs, soft costs, developer's profit, and entrepreneurial incentive. To the extent that a health care property is less useful than an ideal replacement for itself, the value of the subject property must be adjusted accordingly. The replacement cost new is adjusted for losses in economic value due to:

• Physical deterioration
• Functional obsolescence

- Technological obsolescence (often considered a specific form of functional obsolescence)
- External obsolescence

Income Approach

The income approach to valuation is based upon the premise that the value of a physician practice equals the present value of all estimated future economic income to be derived by the individuals possessing ownership interests in the practice. Ownership interests are understood to represent both equity investments (i.e., various classes of shareholders) and debt investments (e.g., bondholders or other interest-charging lenders).

Discounted Net Cash Flow Method. An example of an income approach method is the discounted net cash flow method. This method requires the following analyses: revenue analysis, expense analysis, investment analysis, capital structure analysis, and residual value analysis. Each of these analyses will be discussed briefly.

Revenue Analysis. Revenue analysis involves a projection of prospective revenues from the provision of health care and related services by the practice. This analysis generally includes consideration of the following microeconomic factors: patients seen, average patient charge, market dynamics, competitive pressures, price elasticity of demand, regulatory changes, demographic analysis, and technological changes.

Expense Analysis. The expense analysis requires consideration of the following aspects: patient and third party payer allowances, fixed versus variable costs, patient-related versus period costs, cash versus noncash costs, direct versus indirect costs, cost absorption principles, cost/efficiency relationships, and cost/volume/profit relationships.

Investment Analysis. The investment analysis requires consideration of the following aspects: required minimum cash balances, days' revenues outstanding in accounts receivable, facilities utilization and related constraints, and capital expenditure budgets.

Capital Structure Analysis. The capital structure analysis requires consideration of the following aspects: current capital structure, optimal capital structure, costs of various capital components, weighted average cost of capital, systematic and nonsystematic risk factors, and marginal costs of capital.

Residual Value Analysis. The residual value analysis results in an estimation of the value of the prospective cash flow generated by the subject practice after the conclusion of a discrete projection period. This residual value can be estimated by various methods—for example, price/earnings multiples, annuity in perpetuity method, or the Gordon dividend capitalization model.

From the results of the above-mentioned analyses, a projection of after-tax, invested capital net cash flow from business operations is made for a reasonable discrete projection period. The cash flow projection is discounted at an appropriate after-tax present value discount rate, resulting in an indication of the present value of each year's cash flow.

The residual value of the subject practice is estimated at the end of the discrete projection period. This residual value is also discounted to the present value. The present value of the discrete net after-tax, invested capital cash flow projection is added to the present value of the residual value.

This summation represents the value of the subject physician practice, based on the discounted net cash flow method.

Internal Revenue Service Position.   Net cash flow is defined by the Internal Revenue Service as cash flow developed on an after-tax basis.[1] The appropriate level of net cash flow is calculated after the subject practice has funded all investments required to sustain profitable earnings growth. In other words, net cash flow is calculated after cash disbursements for capital expenditures (e.g., new plant and equipment) and after investments in net working capital (e.g., investments in accounts receivable and inventory).

The principal components of the net cash flow model for the valuation of medical practices are expressed as follows:

	Gross patient service and medical revenues
Less:	Third party and other contractual allowances
Equals:	Net patient service and medical revenues
Less:	Total operating expenses (including physician compensation)
Equals:	Profit before tax
Less:	Income taxes
Equals:	After-tax profit
Plus:	Tax-affected interest expense
Plus:	Depreciation expense
Less:	Capital expenditures
Less:	Annual increases in (noncash) current assets
Plus:	Annual increases in non-interest-bearing current liabilities
Equals:	Annual net cash flow

[1] *Integrated Delivery Systems and Joint Venture Dissolutions Update* (Washington, DC: Internal Revenue Service, October 1994).

The basic format of our net cash flow projection model is a combination of several traditional income statement accounts, adjusted for changes in several balance sheet accounts that affect net cash flow.

The above model is an after-tax, invested capital cash flow model. That is, there is no provision in the model for either periodic debt service payments or periodic interest expense. Therefore, the conclusion of this particular cash flow model (i.e., the present value of the net cash flow projection) represents the business enterprise value of the practice.

The subject practice's enterprise value (i.e., total invested capital) is the sum of the practice's interest-bearing debt—both current and long-term—plus preferred stock plus common stock. In order to establish the fair market value of the practice's equity, all interest-bearing debt that is expected to be paid must be deducted from the indicated value of the subject practice's capital structure.

Discounted Cash Flow Analysis. Exhibit 22-1 presents a simplified example of a discounted net cash flow analysis. (Typically, a discounted net cash flow analysis is based upon a five-year projection period.)

Projected Practice Performance. The projected performance of the subject practice was based upon empirical research regarding (1) the historical financial and operating performance of the subject practice; (2) the historical performance of the physician services segment of the health care industry—nationally and regionally; (3) the projected performance of the physician services segment of the health care entity— nationally and regionally; (4) the projected performance of service providers for the subject practice and anticipated utilization rates; (5) the historical and expected reimbursement rates of major payer classes; and (6) the analysis of historical and projected demographic statistics for the practice market area.

Present Value Discount Rate. Because we are discounting net cash flows projected on an after-tax, invested capital basis, the appropriate discount rate should represent a combination of risk applicable to both equity investors and debt investors. This rate is typically referred to as the WACC, or weighted average cost of capital (see Chapter 1).

To obtain the WACC, the analyst should estimate (1) the relevant required rate of return on equity, (2) the relevant required rate of return on debt, and (3) the relevant proportions of debt and equity comprising the relevant capital structure of the subject practice.

Return on Equity. The required rate of return on equity is typically developed from empirical market evidence and recognition of the subject practice's investment risk.

Developing a required rate of return on equity begins with estimating a risk-free rate of return that incorporates investors' expectations for the real rate of interest on money and the impact of inflation or loss of purchasing power over time. Because we are interested in concluding a required rate of return for an equity investment, equity risk premiums over the risk-free rate of return must also be researched.

The relevant required rate of return on equity is generally developed from the capital asset pricing model. Under this model, the return on

Exhibit 22–1

Example of Discounted Cash Flow Analysis

	Projected ($millions)			Terminal
	Year 1	Year 2	Year 3	Value
Revenues	$56.50	$62.30	$67.60	
Operating expenses as a percent of revenues	85%	85%	85%	
Pretax income	$ 8.48	$ 9.35	$10.14	
Net income after tax	5.51	6.07	6.59	
Plus: depreciation expense	0.50	0.50	0.50	
Less: capital expenditures	0.60	0.60	0.60	
Less: working capital increase	0.25	0.25	0.25	
Equals: net cash flow	5.16	5.72	6.24	$59.57
Present value factor	0.9285	0.8004	0.6900	0.6507
Present value net cash flow	4.79	4.58	4.31	38.17
Business enterprise value	$52.00			

equity is estimated by adding to the risk-free rate an equity risk premium established by comparison of risk characteristics of the subject practice with guideline publicly traded entities. (With regard to physician practices, guideline publicly traded company information is generally limited to large publicly traded companies that manage physician practices.)

Beta, which represents the relative level of risk for an entity in comparison with general market risk for publicly traded companies, is used to estimate the appropriate risk factor for the subject practice. The appropriate beta factor is then applied to the estimated equity risk premium in order to estimate the relevant equity risk premium for the subject physician practice.

Because no physician practices, in their pure operating form, are publicly traded, financial experts are generally required to make subjective determinations regarding any additional, or reduced, equity premiums warranted for the subject practice, based on factors and characteristics specific to the subject practice.

Given the limited nature of direct comparable information that can be relied upon to estimate the required rate of return on equity for closely held physician practices, analysts often employ a build-up equity method. In this method, analysts start with a risk-free rate and add relevant equity risk premiums to estimate the appropriate required rate of return on an equity investment in the subject practice. The most common source of the equity premium components is Ibbotson Associates *Stocks, Bonds, Bills, and Inflation*.

Exhibit 22-2 presents a sample estimation of a required rate of return on equity based on a build-up method.

Exhibit 22–2

Example of Estimation of Required Rate of Return

Equity Component	Rate (%)
Risk-free rate (20-year Treasury bond)	5.4[a]
Long-horizon equity risk premium	7.8[b]
Small stock equity risk premium	4.7[c]
Company-specific equity risk premium	2.1[d]
Estimated required rate of return on equity	20.0%

[a]Represents the yield on a 20-year U.S. government bond, as quoted in the *Wall Street Journal* and effective November 1998.
[b]Represents the large company stock total returns minus long-term government bond income returns, as presented in Ibbotson Associates *Stocks, Bonds, Bills and Inflation, 1998 Yearbook*.
[c]Represents the small company stock total returns minus the large company stock total returns, as presented in Ibbotson Associates *Stocks, Bonds, Bills and Inflation, 1998 Yearbook*.
[d]Estimated based on consideration of practice-specific factors, including size, physician mix, duration of the practice, and market position.

As indicated, the summation of the risk-free rate of return and the estimated equity risk premiums represents the estimated required rate of return on equity.

Return on Debt. The required return on debt for the subject physician practice is typically represented by the practice's marginal cost of borrowing. Because the discounted cash flow method is performed on an after-tax basis, the relevant borrowing rate is reflected after tax, or as follows: borrowing rate $\times (1 -$ effective income tax rate).

Cost of Capital Weightings. The overall required rate of return, or weighted average cost of capital, for the subject practice can now be estimated from each cost of capital component and the relevant weighting applied on the basis of the capital structure mix.

The relevant capital structure is typically estimated on the basis of a review of the subject practice's historical capital structure and an analysis of the capital structures of the guideline publicly traded health care companies considered to estimate the equity risk premium.

Weighted Average Cost of Capital. Assume that a reasonable weighting of debt and equity components as of the valuation date is 30 percent and 70 percent, respectively. Further, assume that the estimated after-tax required rate of return on equity and debt are 20 percent and 5 percent, respectively.

Applying this capital structure weighting to the subject practice's cost of debt and equity capital produces the weighted cost of capital as presented below.

Required Rate of Return on Capital Components		% of Total Capital Structure		Weighted Cost of Capital
Debt capital at 5%	×	0.30	=	1.50
Equity capital at 20%	×	0.70	=	14.00
Total required rate of return on capital				15.50
Present value discount rate (rounded)				16%

Indicated Value—Discounted Cash Flow Method. As presented in this example, the business enterprise value of the subject physician practice as of the valuation date, under the discounted cash flow method, is $52 million. This value is based on an assumed long-term earnings growth rate of 5 percent, and a discount rate of 16 percent.

The physician practice business enterprise value estimated represents the value of all invested capital—preferred stock, common stock, and interest-bearing debt. In transactions involving larger practices, an analysis of working capital as of the transaction date will be performed. This analysis is performed in order to determine if any deficiency (or excess) in working capital exists relative to that required for the normal continuing operations of the practice. The estimated value of the invested capital of the practice is typically adjusted by any deficiency or excess in working capital noted. For discussion purposes in this chapter, we will assume that existing working capital is at an appropriate level, and no adjustments are required.

In order to arrive at the market value of equity capital, we deducted all interest-bearing debt outstanding at the valuation date. Interest-bearing debt at that date totaled $15 million.

Subtracting the market value of the subject practice's interest-bearing debt from the above-determined business enterprise value of the entity results in the following value of equity:

Total business enterprise value (rounded)	$52 million
Less: Market value of interest-bearing debt capital (rounded)	(15 million)
Equals: Publicly traded equivalent value of equity (rounded)	$37 million

Market Approach

Overview. The third approach to estimating the value of a physician practice is the market approach. The market approach is based on the premise that the value of a physician practice is equal to the price investors are willing to pay for similar assets with comparative economic earnings capacity.

Two methods are typically used in applying the market approach: (1) the guideline publicly traded company method and (2) the guideline merged and acquired company method. The guideline publicly traded company method relies on data from publicly traded health care companies as the source of guidance in the valuation of closely held physician practices. The guideline merged and acquired company method relies on data from completed transactions involving public or private health care companies as the source of valuation guidance for the subject physician practice.

Guideline Publicly Traded Company Method. The first step in the guideline publicly traded company method is to search for similar publicly traded companies by identifying the most appropriate Standard Industrial Classification (SIC) code. Sources typically reviewed for information on publicly traded companies include CD-ROM products such as Standard & Poor's Corporations and Disclosure's Compact D/SEC, which have information for approximately 9,000 and 12,000 public companies, respectively.

The next step is to narrow the list of companies to arrive at a list of guideline companies. The steps to narrow the list of companies typically include reviewing business descriptions, financial data, and pricing information for each of the health care companies.

After a list of guideline publicly traded companies has been compiled, the analyst typically relies on five years of historical financial statement data (and projected data, if available) to calculate various pricing multiples, which are used, after any adjustments, to apply to the subject company's fundamentals.

Pricing multiples that are calculated for the guideline publicly traded health care companies typically include, among others:

1. Equity pricing multiples:
   - Price per share/earnings per share
   - Price per share/cash flow per share
   - Price per share/book value per share
   - Price per share/revenue per share

2. Invested capital pricing multiples:
   - Market value of invested capital (MVIC)/earnings before interest and taxes (EBIT)
   - MVIC/earnings before depreciation, interest, and taxes (EBDIT)
   - MVIC/invested cash flow
   - MVIC/invested net income
   - MVIC/revenues
   - MVIC/tangible book value per share
   - MVIC/physicians

Depending on the circumstances of the valuation, each of the listed multiples may be calculated on the basis of average, weighted average, last 12 months, or projected data.

Invested capital multiples are typically useful when comparing the subject practice to guideline companies that have substantially different capital structures. Applying invested capital pricing multiples to the fundamentals of the subject practice results in the market value of invested capital for the subject practice. To estimate the value of the equity, the market value of the interest-bearing debt for the subject practice must be subtracted from the MVIC.

The next step in the application of the guideline publicly traded company method is to select the appropriate pricing multiples for the subject practice. Adjustments to the pricing multiples for the guideline companies are generally required to reflect differences in expected growth and risk between the subject practice and the publicly traded companies. These include: size of the subject practice (based on assets, revenues, number of physicians, patient base, patient mix, and payer mix); geographic coverage; differences in demographics of areas served; depth of management; profitability; expected growth; variability of earnings; and cash flow.

After estimating the appropriate pricing multiples, the analyst applies the multiples to the fundamentals of the subject physician practice. The earnings data of the subject practice may need to be adjusted to eliminate the effects of any nonrecurring or extraordinary items.

The estimated values from the various pricing multiples are then reconciled into a single value or range of values, to result in an estimated value based on the guideline publicly traded company method.

Guideline Merged and Acquired Company Method. Under the guideline merged and acquired company method, the value of a physician practice is estimated by analyzing completed transactions involving similar physician practices. To search for mergers and acquisitions, the analyst focuses on the appropriate SIC codes, as discussed in the guideline publicly traded company method. Commonly used sources for mergers and acquisitions data include, among others, *Mergerstat Review*, the *Merger and Acquisition Sourcebook,* and SDC OnLine. In addition, various publications summarize completed transactions for specific categories of health care organizations (e.g., hospitals, HMOs, and physician practices). *The Health Care M&A Report*, published by Irving Levin Associates, Inc., is an example.

In addition, with regard to physician practices, *The Goodwill Registry* publishes data for the estimated price paid for intangible assets of physician practices as a percentage of gross revenue. These data, published annually, are sorted by year of the transaction and by physician specialty.

For the guideline merged and acquired company method, the terms of each of the transactions should be reviewed carefully to determine the actual price paid, and whether the transaction involved the sale of equity or assets. If the transaction involved the sale of assets, it is important to determine the exact assets purchased and any liabilities assumed.

After selecting a group of guideline transactions and determining the purchase price, the analyst calculates various multiples of economic income. As in the guideline publicly traded company method, after estimating the appropriate pricing multiples, the analyst then applies the pricing multiples to the normalized fundamentals of the subject physician practice.

A simplified example of the guideline merged and acquired company method is shown in Exhibit 22-3. This example presents pricing multiples resulting from the analysis of 11 acquired[2] multispecialty practices for the valuation of Medical Clinic, Inc. (Medical), which operates as a 100-physician multispecialty practice with five sites in a metropolitan area.

From the information in Exhibit 22-3, the valuation analyst faced with the challenge of appraising Medical should analyze the following factors, among others, for the purpose of making appropriate pricing multiple selections:

- The dates of the guideline transactions relative to the valuation date of Medical.
- Market conditions at the date of the guideline transactions relative to market conditions existing at the valuation date of Medical.
- Size of Medical (based on assets, revenues, and number of physicians) relative to the guideline companies.
- Physician mix (i.e., primary care versus specialty care) of Medical relative to the guideline companies.
- Payer mix (i.e., fee for service, HMO, preferred provider organization, Medicare, Medicaid) of Medical relative to the guideline companies.
- Profitability—measured by consideration of total physician compensation, benefits, and profits—of Medical relative to the guideline companies.
- Historical growth—assets, revenues, physician compensation, and profits—of Medical relative to the guideline companies.
- Diversity of practice (i.e., level of ancillary services) of Medical relative to the guideline companies.
- Location of Medical (i.e., rural versus metropolitan) relative to the guideline companies.
- Market position of Medical relative to the market position of the guideline companies.

Although all the above information may not be readily accessible with regard to the identified acquired companies, an analysis of all pertinent and available information is an important step in the selection of relevant and supportable market-derived pricing multiples.

---

[2] Based on data presented in *The Health Care M&A Report* (New Canaan, CT: Irving Levin Associates, Inc., quarterly).

Exhibit 22–3

Example of Guideline Merged and Acquired Company Method

Acquired Practice	Location	Physicians	Revenues ($)	Price/Physician ($)	Price/Revenues ($)
Riverside Medical Clinic	Riverside, CA	90	50,000,000	355,556	.64
Lexington Clinic	Lexington, Ky	125	51,000,000	512,000	1.25
Arnett Clinic	Lafayette, IN	109	87,438,000	660,528	.82
Diagnostic Clinic	Largo, FL	93	49,000,000	395,699	.75
Glen Ellyn Clinic	Glen Ellyn, IL	89	60,000,000	707,865	1.05
Cardinal Healthcare, PA	Raleigh-Durham, NC	75	34,170,500	573,333	1.26
Summit Medical Group	Summit, NJ	75	47,000,000	736,087	1.17
Lewis-Gale Clinic, Inc.	Roanoke, VA	106	68,200,000	410,377	.64
Clinical Associates	Baltimore, MD	71	35,870,000	245,070,	.49
Meridian Medical Group	Marietta, GA	67	63,950,000	419,597	.44
Berkshire Physicians	Pittsfield, MA	93	43,683,000	317,204	.68

SOURCE: *The Health Care M&A Report* (New Canaan, CT: Irving Levin Associates, Inc., quarterly).
Note this exhibit was compiled from many different issues.

Key Valuation Issues

A thorough understanding of relevant physician practice valuation methodology, as previously discussed, will enable a financial analyst to appropriately address and incorporate the impact of several key valuation considerations specific to physician practice valuations. The most significant of such considerations are listed below:

- Managing expectations
- Identifying and rationalizing value trade-offs
- Handling issues of management/operational control
- Complying with regulatory constraints

Managing Expectations

During the past five years, physician practice acquisitions have occurred at prices implying practice multiples ranging from a low of 11 percent of revenues, or $5,500 per physician, to a high of 300 percent of revenues, or $6.8 million per physician. Clearly, such a wide range of valuation multiples implies an equally wide set of facts and circumstances with regard to the underlying transactions.

As a result of the wide and varying range of physician practice multiples disclosed in publicly available documents, a critical service provided by qualified financial analysts in physician practice acquisition is to manage the expectations of the client—whether the physician seller or the hospital acquirer. Typically, both the physician(s) and the hospital system involved will have read stories or heard anecdotes regarding other, "similar" physician practice transactions and the implied transaction multiples. The success of most transactions should be determined not only by the mere signing of the closing papers, but also by the perceived high probability of long-term financial success with regard to the IDS formed by the transaction. Therefore, success is dependent on an economically sound transaction price.

As a seller, the physician typically will lean, with the support of facts and financial advice, toward market-based physician practice multiples at the higher end of the market-based range. Generally, the hospital acquirer with have well-reasoned justification for multiples at the lower end of the range. The mindset of each participant in a potential transaction can usually be attributed to the rigors of the negotiation process.

The most reliable means through which a valuation analyst can control the expectations of a client is by performing a detailed and rigorous analysis. Prior to releasing any preliminary conclusions of value, the valuation analyst should be in a position, and make it a point, to discuss similarities and differences among the subject physician practice and the guideline merged and acquired practices analyzed for the purpose of developing market-derived pricing multiples.

Similarly, the valuation analyst should discuss key assumptions incorporated into a discounted cash flow analysis, including projected revenue growth and realization rates, operating cost and operating margin expectations, capital expenditure requirements and working capital requirements, capital structure, and the relevant discount rate.

Such critical assumptions are estimable only after the valuation analyst has (1) developed a thorough understanding of the subject physician practice's historical performance through the review of relevant financial and operating statistics, (2) performed necessary industry research—both on a national level and a regional level, and (3) conducted due diligence interviews with relevant financial and operating personnel. Developing and testing key assumptions with the client prior to providing conclusions of value will provide a more narrow and reasonable range within which the preliminary conclusion of value can be expected to fluctuate during any negotiation process.

Because of overzealous client service commitment or compensation arrangements, many valuation analysts strive to attain the highest or lowest price possible (depending on whether their client is the seller or the buyer). Many potential transactions are terminated as a result of initial offers that offend the recipient by virtue of being either too high or too low. Even in those circumstances in which transactions proceed after extremely high or low initial offers, clients whose expectations have not been managed are often less than satisfied with the end result, believing that the price has been inexplicably adjusted by a material amount.

Identifying and Rationalizing Value Trade-Offs

Most closely held physician practices are operated for the benefit of the physician shareholder/owner. In other words, the practice of medicine by the physician shareholder/owner is generally based on two primary motivations: (1) satisfying the internal desire to provide the necessary and valuable service of health care delivery, and (2) satisfying personal financial objectives by generating economic returns commensurate with the value of the services provided.

In responding to the second motivational factor noted above, most physician practitioners in closely held practices realize little benefit from reporting significant practice earnings at the end of a given fiscal operating period. Rather, the maximum benefit realized in most cases results from the withdrawal of substantially all practice earnings in the form of compensation and related economic benefits.

Clearly, a large physician practice that has reported virtually no bottom line profits in the operating periods immediately preceding the contemplated transaction as a result of the physician/owner's historical practice of withdrawing all practice earnings would not appear to represent an investment option promising significant future returns to a potential third party acquirer. Herein lies one of the more significant trade-offs that should be addressed in the acquisition of a large physician practice by a hospital system—the potential sacrifice of future compensation for current purchase price.

Physician compensation and benefits at most closely held physician practices typically range from 30 to 50 percent of gross practice charges.[3] Absent the ability of the physician practice to significantly reduce operating costs in future periods while generating increasing revenues, physician compensation and benefits represent the most significant expense categories available for reduction in order to realize higher future profits.

Through a structured physician compensation plan—generally relating physician compensation and benefits directly to physician production—the expected profitability of a targeted acquisition can be projected. Such a procedure is required in those circumstances in which the targeted practice has reported minimal earnings in the periods preceding the contemplated transaction.

Clearly, any contemplated transaction requires consideration of the impact that a potential future decrease in average physician compensation may exert on both the operating performance and retention rate of the subject practice's physician base. The selling physicians will undoubtedly reflect on past compensation levels, comparing them with projected future compensation levels. The trade-off to be recognized—and presented—relates to the fact that a dollar of reduced physician compensation in the future generally translates into more than a dollar of increased transaction value today.

---

[3] See, generally, *Physician Compensation and Production Survey: 1997 Report Based on 1996 Data* (Englewood, CO: Medical Group Management Association, 1997), p. 56.

For example, if the selling physicians of a $50 million revenue practice agreed to an average reduction in total compensation of 3 percent of revenue, the resulting increase in pretax profits would be $1.5 million, and approximately $900,000 on an after-tax basis (assuming a 40 percent effective income tax rate). Assuming a transaction pricing multiple of 12 times after-tax earnings, the increase in practice value would approximate $10.8 million.

Although the expected remaining practice life of each physician would play a significant role in establishing whether such a trade-off represents an economic benefit, such a trade-off must be analyzed in each practice transaction involving a tax-exempt hospital system in those circumstances where the subject practice historically has reported minimal profits. Existing private benefit and inurement provisions restrict a tax-exempt hospital from paying more than fair market value for physician practices.

Such provisions risk being violated in those circumstances in which (1) the historical earnings of the subject practice are minimal, (2) the transaction does not contemplate the adjustment of physician compensation and benefits in future operating periods to levels that would increase the probability of higher future practice earnings, and (3) the acquiring hospital system pays a price in excess of the fair market value of the target practice's net tangible assets.

The proliferation of managed care, with its attendant precertification and case management requirements, has forced many physicians into the often unfamiliar and unappealing bureaucratic and administrative aspects of practice management. The prospect of selling their practices thus provides an appealing avenue of escape from many administrative burdens.

The potential positive aspects associated with this escape present valuation analysts with the opportunity to carefully address the sensitive topic of the trade-off between potentially lower future physician compensation and higher current practice sales value. Further, the sale of their practices with continued "employee" status—at some level of guaranteed compensation—has provided a financial security unknown to many physicians for over 20 years.

Issues of Management/Operational Control

Although not typically an immediate concern of analysts in performing a valuation, the topic of post-transaction, day-to-day operating control and decision-making authority often becomes a material negotiating point in potential physician practice acquisitions, particularly the acquisition of larger practices. The issue of physician representation on tax-exempt IDS governing boards is regulated by the Internal Revenue Service (IRS).

In the 1997 continuing education text on exempt organizations, *Community Board and Conflicts of Interest Policy*, released by the IRS in September 1996, the IRS increased the limitation on potential physician representation on the board of a tax-exempt IDS from 20 percent to 49 percent. This move was generally recognized within the industry as acceptance by the IRS that many experienced physicians have knowledge and expertise that could reasonably be relied upon to advance the charitable mission of tax-exempt organizations.

As discussed in many of the leading health care industry periodicals and newsletters, one of the primary concerns facing physicians contemplating the sale of their practices is the day-to-day operation and management of their practices after the transaction. In sum, physicians are generally concerned with the amount of operating—primarily decision-making—control that the acquiring hospital will assume after the transaction.

In most cases, a selling physician will have devoted numerous years developing a practice, and will unavoidably continue to view the practice as a personal asset rather than a financial investment. On the other hand, acquiring hospitals should view each acquisition candidate as a financial investment from which a reasonable return should be generated in order to justify the cost of the acquisition.

One could argue that this circumstance is not unique to physician practice acquisitions. In fact, any owner or operator contemplating the sale of a business and expecting to continue as an employee subsequent to the transaction faces some level of internal conflict regarding the loss of control over the post-transaction operations of the business.

Transactional experts generally agree that a component of every negotiated sales price generally represents value attributable to the elements of operating control given up by the owner or operator in the transaction. This generally applies to physician practice acquisitions. However, as most physicians and many hospitals will admit, hospitals generally are not recognized as the most effective managers of physician practices, nor do they have the desire to provide the day-to-day management of physician practices.

The relaxed IRS provisions regarding physician representation on governing boards provide greater negotiating room for physicians concerned with their post-transaction involvement in key decision-making areas affecting their practice of medicine. In order to ensure that governing boards that take advantage of the relaxed provisions and increase their physician membership adopt the necessary steps to prevent inurement problems, the IRS requires the tax-exempt health care organization to adopt a conflict of interest policy. Such a policy includes:

- Disclosure to the rest of the board of a member's financial interest in business activities.

- Standards and procedures for deciding what constitutes a conflict of interest, including provisions for a disinterested person to investigate allegations.

- Procedures for dealing with a conflict of interest when one is identified.

- Procedures, incorporated into the organization's bylaws, for recording conflicts of interest and their disposition.

- An internal audit procedure—independent of the organization's normal business activities—periodically reviewing compensation, contracts, and business deals by board members who do not receive compensation from the organization.

In addition, the new Section 4958 of the Internal Revenue Code enacted by the Taxpayer Bill of Rights 2 strengthens the enforcement powers of the IRS by providing targeted sanctions against responsible individuals when private inurement occurs. (Inurement is discussed in the following section.) These sanctions represent an alternative to the revocation of an organization's tax exemption in cases where violations of inurement provisions are identified.

Under Internal Revenue Code Section 4958(a)(1), a first-tier tax would be imposed on each excess benefit transaction. The tax would be equal to 25 percent of the excess benefit and would be personally paid by the individual who received the excess benefit. Whenever the excess benefit tax is imposed on an individual, an additional 10 percent tax may be imposed on any "organizational manager" in the transaction who knew of the excess benefit.

The conflict of interest policy, previously discussed, and the alternative sanctions provide preventive as well as punitive measures with regard to private inurement violations. Through these measures, physicians are afforded the opportunity to have a greater voice in the operation of IDSs with which they become affiliated. Further, these measures give the IRS a regulated means of permitting physicians to contribute more toward the effective delivery of health care services through an IDS, and an alternative to the revocation of tax-exempt status when violations are identified. Such a severe sanction is generally recognized as having the potential impact of limiting necessary health care services to patients, which is contrary to the tax-exempt requirement of promoting the public good.

Complying with Regulatory Constraints

In valuing a physician practice for the purpose of facilitating its acquisition by a tax-exempt hospital, a valuation analyst needs to understand and consider the impact of several statutory requirements that can affect the price a tax-exempt hospital pays to acquire a practice. On the other hand, proprietary entities—limited only by available capital and their respective boards of directors—may be free to pursue transactions at prices well above those available to a tax-exempt hospital.

Given this fact, valuation analysts should recognize the need to educate transaction participants regarding the limitations placed upon the negotiation process when tax-exempt hospital systems are involved. This generally requires some level of discussion clarifying the difference in transaction price that might exist between an offer from a proprietary entity and an offer from a tax-exempt hospital system.

Valuation analysts should be familiar with regulatory constraints regarding the acquisition of physician practices by tax-exempt hospital systems. These include:

- Private inurement and private benefit restrictions of Internal Revenue Code Section 501(c)(3), Treasury Regulation Section 1.501(c)(3)-1(c)(2). These restrictions forbid the transfer of any portion of the net earnings of a not-for-profit entity to inure to the benefit of any private individual, with violations representing grounds for revocation of a tax-exempt tax status.
- Medicaid/Medicare Fraud and Abuse Statutes, 42 U.S.C.1320a-7(b)b. These statutes prohibit the payment of remuneration in exchange for the referral of Medicare and/or Medicaid business.
- Not-for-profit corporation acts of many states. Under these acts, the attorney general of a state is authorized to regulate transactions involving not-for-profits, including payments by not-for-profits and the distribution of proceeds from not-for-profit transactions.

The end result of these and related regulatory constraints on the acquisition of physician practices by tax-exempt entities is that all transactions should occur at a price representing no more than the fair market value of the assets acquired. Violations of these regulatory constraints that are identified and proved can result in costly fines and penalties, the most severe of which is the revocation of the tax-exempt status of the acquiring hospital.

Clearly, the sellers of a physician practice are motivated to realize the highest sales price achievable. A valuation analyst retained by the selling practice might initially be perceived as "working for the buyer" when informing the management team at the target practice that regulatory constraints may limit the ultimate sales price. However, a thorough understanding of the limitations imposed on physician practice values by regulatory constraints when tax-exempt acquirers are involved, and the knowledgeable dissemination of the information, will benefit all parties to the transaction as operating disruptions relating to costly litigation—possibly resulting in significant fines, the unwinding of the transaction, and the loss of the hospital's tax-exempt status—are avoided.

The Impact of Market Activity
on Current Practice Values

Valuation analysts operate pursuant to both express and implied responsibilities in performing practice valuations. Client demands, IRS rulings, and valuation professional standards require a valuation analyst to examine and review specific industry conditions existing at the valuation date, and to assess the impact that such conditions exert on the value of the subject practice.

Fifty-seven physician medical group transactions occurred during the third quarter of 1998.[4] This total represented a decrease of 19 transactions, or a decline in physician group transaction activity of 25 per-

---

[4] *The Health Care M&A Monthly*, November 15, 1998.

cent, relative to the third quarter one year earlier. In total, the 268 transactions announced during the third quarter of 1998 represented the lowest level of activity in two years for the health care services merger and acquisition market.

The general decline in activity in this market in the third quarter of 1998 suggests a decrease in demand, and/or desirability, on the part of investors regarding the financial attractiveness of participants in the various segments of the health care services industry. Although such a period-to-period decrease may be attributable to an unusually high level of activity in the comparable prior period, due diligence procedures performed by valuation analysts should enable them to ascertain whether such a decline is indicative of a true market trend. A true market trend is one that should be expected to exert a detrimental impact on the value of industry participants currently being valued.

With regard to physician practice transaction activity in the third quarter of 1998, total transactions through the end of the quarter (213) represented an annualized level of 284 transactions for the full year 1998. The annualized 1998 total compares with 291 transactions in 1997, and 218 transactions in 1996, and on the surface would hardly provide sound basis for a conclusion that the physician practice acquisition market was in a free fall as of the fourth quarter of 1998.

However, a current review of the physician practice management (PPM) sector of the health care industry—historically representing the largest acquiring group with regard to the purchase of physician practices during the past five years—does suggest that a general decrease in practice values may be expected.

Since 1994, the physician practice acquisition market has been driven by the acquisition activity of PPMs. Specifically, PPMs such as Coastal Physician Services, FPA Medical Management, PhyMatrix, PhyCor, and, most notably, MedPartners led the fervor in the market for physician practice acquisitions.

Three years during the period from 1994 through mid-November 1998, MedPartners was the industry leader in the physician practice acquisition sector of the health care industry. MedPartners completed some 63 transactions, representing the accumulation of approximately 8,200 physicians during that time frame. However, on November 11, 1998, MedPartners—representing the largest PPM in the country—announced that it was abandoning the PPM business to focus on its Caremark division, which manages pharmacy benefits for about 2,000 employees and a few managed care companies.[5] As stated in a *Wall Street Journal* article discussing MedPartners' plans, the company intended to shed its 238 physician clinics and more than 10,000 affiliated doctors within the next 12 months through sales, a spin-off to shareholders, or some combination of the two.

The MedPartners announcement represented a culmination of several significant events in the PPM sector of the health care industry during 1998, events that were precipitated by significant operating

[5] Anita Sharpe, "MedPartners Is Abandoning Physician-Management Business," *Wall Street Journal*, November 11, 1998, p. A4.

losses and lower than expected earnings for the country's largest PPMs. Only a year earlier, the general market expectation was that PPMs represented one of the keys to successful medical cost control. The general objective of PPMs is to streamline medical costs through the acquisition and integration of physician practices across the country. The resulting larger physician bases and high level of practice integration were expected to enable PPMs to streamline costs and operations and facilitate the negotiation of better contracts with health maintenance organizations.

However, disappointing earnings reported by the nation's largest PPMs in early 1998, reports of practice integration difficulties, and physicians' increasing distaste for working for outsiders—often in a circumstance of significant decreases in personal income—cast a cloud over the benefits initially expected from the PPM operating structure.

As previously mentioned, the MedPartners announcement in mid-November of 1998 represented what many industry experts considered the most significant in a series of blows to the industry. Early in the fourth quarter of 1998, PhyCor, the country's second biggest PPM, announced a shift in focus from buying individual practices and medical groups to managing independent practice associations[6] On July 19, 1998, FPA Medical Management Inc., the nation's third largest PPM, filed for protection in U.S. Bankruptcy Court in Wilmington, Delaware.

In addition, increasing losses and operating difficulties in 1998 for other PPMs such as Complete Management, Inc., Advanced Health Corp., and PhyMatrix Corp., resulted in management at each entity announcing such strategic alternatives as downsizing operations—typically described as a reduction and/or discontinuance of physician practice acquisition and management operations.

Clearly, general operating difficulties experienced by the largest PPMs in the country during 1998, and the resulting general market disfavor regarding the underperforming PPMs, were forcing many PPMs to consider exiting the practice management sector of the market. The exit of several of the largest participants in the PPM sector from the practice management business may result in fewer physician practice acquisitions.

Further, the reduced demand for physician practices would be exacerbated by the objectives of several larger PPMs to sell practices previously acquired. The most likely net economic impact of a decrease in the demand for physician practices combined with an increase in the availability, or supply, of physician practices would be a general decrease in the price paid for physician practices.

According to Joseph Hutts, former president and CEO of PhyCor, the economic impact of market forces in effect during 1998 was already being reflected in the prices paid for physician practices. According to

---

[6] An independent practice association represents an entity formed by physicians (typically in conjunction with a local hospital) to enable effective contracting with managed care purchasers. IPAs contract with HMOs, PPOs, and other managed care purchasers to provide professional medical services to their members. IPAs differ from group practices in that IPA physicians maintain practices independent of the other participating physician members of the IPA.

Hutts, "The cost of acquiring a multispecialty group has dropped as much as 25 percent this year."[7] Industry consultant Daniel Zismer adds, "For PPM companies, values have been cut in half. For hospitals, they've dropped even farther."[8] Zismer continues by stating that it is not uncommon for current transactions to be priced on the hard assets of the practice only, with no payment for goodwill. PhyCor spokesman Shawn Carder reiterated Zismer's position in the November 1998 issue of *Healthcare Practice Management News*, stating that current market conditions caused him to believe that future transactions at PhyCor were likely to be based on an acquisition price equal to or slightly above the book value of the target company.

Clearly, the plight of the leading PPMs creates a circumstance suggesting that physician practices, in general, represent investments of decreasing relative value. However, it is important to note that the acquisition strategy of PPMs historically was closely aligned with the underlying operating strategy of PPMs. That is, practice acquisitions made by PPMs were generally priced on the expectation that economic returns in the form of management fees would be paid to the PPM by the acquired practices. The higher the management fee and the longer the term of the management contract, the higher the acquisition price paid.

As PPMs acquired more and larger practices, the projected management fee income of the acquiring PPMs, and therefore the expected future earnings, increased considerably. This, of course, exerted a positive impact on the price of the related PPMs' publicly traded stock.

As PPMs began reporting lower than expected earnings and sizable losses, it became evident that the management fees established in many transactions—ranging as high as 12 to 18 percent of practice revenues—had been fixed at unrealistic levels. Since the PPM acquisition model historically was based on expected management fee income, an unrealistically high management fee established in a transaction could be interpreted as an overpriced deal.

One could simply conclude that, because market-based physician acquisition multiples during the period spanning 1994 through the fourth quarter of 1998 were largely based on transactions completed by PPMs, the use of these transactional multiples to price other contemplated physician acquisitions during the same time frame would result in overstated practice values. Such a simple conclusion ignores several critical factors. For example:

- Poor integration policies and practices at the related PPMs, not overpriced practice acquisitions, may explain the generally poor 1998 financial performance of several large PPMs.
- The trade-off between current practice price and potentially lower

---

[7] "Practice Prices Tumble: Fall May Help Realign PM Industry," *Healthcare Practice Management News*, September 1998.

[8] Ibid.

future physician compensation, as previously discussed, was inappropriately incorporated into the determination of acquisition prices paid.

- Unexpected external factors such as regional differences and local industry and market circumstances subsequent to acquisition and integration may have lowered returns provided by practices.

In sum, the current circumstance presented by the generally poor financial condition of the PPM sector of the health care industry requires a careful analysis of the key practice factors discussed in the section on guideline merged and acquired companies in this chapter. The market approach represents one avenue to estimate the value of a physician practice.

Circumstances such as those created by the current state of the PPM sector and the resulting impact on current market-based physician acquisition pricing multiples emphasize the need to perform a well-reasoned, well-supported discounted cash flow analysis with regard to the targeted physician practice.

To conclude that the current value of all physician practices is undermined by the state of the PPM sector ignores practice-specific characteristics, operating histories, and market positions that distinguish most practices. Further, to value all physician practices at "book value" ignores the often significant intangible asset values that exist at many larger practices as a result of considerable time and effort expended to develop the related intangible assets. Attributing no value to (1) existing long-term patient and payer relationships, (2) a skillful and experienced trained and assembled workforce, (3) efficiency-promoting policies and procedures manuals, and (4) the organized assemblage and coordination of both tangible and intangible assets into an operating entity ignores completely the functional utility associated with these intangible assets and the time and cost that would be incurred to re-create the assets.

Therefore, a critical review of the facts and circumstances specific to each practice acquisition candidate is an important procedure. Such a review may reveal several dominant practices that are strategically located and strategically positioned in their respective market areas. These practices provide an investment opportunity for a hospital system with the potential for significant economic rewards attributable to the integrated delivery system benefits that could be realized.

Summary and Conclusion

The valuation of physician practices, in light of the ever-changing health care environment, presents significant challenges—particularly in those circumstances where the potential acquirer is a tax-exempt entity. This chapter discussed the valuation approaches typically employed for the purpose of estimating the fair market value of physician practices. This chapter also discussed several key issues that should be addressed during the practice valuation process to facilitate a successful transaction.

The development of a successful integrated delivery health care system is dependent, to a large extent, upon the appropriate estimation of the fair market values of the entities combined to form the network.

Overestimating the values of the entities, and subsequently overpaying to acquire the entities, can lead to the insolvency of the network. Further, acquiring health care entities at prices in excess of their supportable fair market values can lead to serious fines and sanctions imposed by the Internal Revenue Service and the Office of the Inspector General as a result of the violation of private benefit and inurement provisions of Code Section 501(c)(3), Medicare and Medicaid fraud and abuse statutes, and Stark legislation (Health Care Financing Administration legislation [authored by Rep. Fortney (Pete) Stark (D-CA)] that generally prohibits health care providers from receiving economic benefit resulting from the referral of Medicare and Medicaid patients to entities in which they have financial relationships).

Given these facts, the appropriate application of relevant valuation methodology, by qualified valuation analysts, is clearly a vital step in the development of an integrated health care delivery system.

Chapter 23

Valuation of Emerging Growth Companies

James G. Rabe, CFA, ASA, and Tracy Lefteroff

Introduction

The valuation of emerging growth companies is generally more challenging than the valuation of mature companies. This is because the valuation of emerging growth companies is based primarily on expectations of significant growth, which are dependent upon highly uncertain future events. Analysts estimating the value of emerging growth companies should have the ability to successfully gauge the degree of risk associated with factors especially critical to the success of emerging growth companies. Such factors include:

1. The ability of the management team to execute on key deliverables.
2. Unanticipated delays involving key items such as product development and manufacturing.
3. The ability of the company to gain significant market share from existing competition or to market a relatively new concept or product.
4. Unanticipated capital expenditures.

This chapter focuses on the following issues:

1. Typical reasons emerging growth companies may require valuations.
2. The most effective methods for valuing emerging growth companies.
3. The unique capital structure of closely held emerging growth companies.

The classification "emerging growth companies" is generally used in this chapter to refer to companies that are in various early stages of development, from start-up through initial public offering. Emerging growth companies are usually stitched together quite differently from one to the next but have the common thread of high earnings growth expectations.

Reasons for Valuing Emerging Growth Companies

There are a variety of reasons that emerging growth companies may require valuation services. Reasons for estimating an emerging growth company's value include the following: (1) financing events; (2) planning and providing various forms of incentive compensation; (3) gift and estate tax planning; (4) litigation support; and (5) corporate governance, including the management of intangible assets.

Financing Events

The valuation of emerging growth companies is frequently associated with a financing event, such as raising capital to fund continued growth.

The top management of emerging growth companies constantly market their companies to potential investors in order to attract the necessary capital to fund growth. An independent estimate of the company's fair market value is often a valuable tool that assists emerging growth companies in securing additional capital. Investors often rely on the unbiased opinion of an independent valuation report that describes the company and its prospects when considering whether to invest in an emerging growth company.

Incentive Compensation

In order to remain competitive, emerging growth companies should assemble and retain a highly skilled workforce. This process generally requires the additional investment of company resources. However, limited access to capital may prevent emerging growth companies from paying market wages to potential employees. Emerging growth companies often offset lower wages by issuing stock options as a means to attract talented employees.

Because a start-up company typically has low value during the formative stage, stock options are issued at very low strike prices. If a company is able to surpass the projected level of growth, or institute an initial public offering (IPO), the capital appreciation of the stock associated with exercising the stock options significantly offsets below-market wages. Valuing the stock of a start-up company is necessary to estimate the fair market value of the options as of the grant date, providing a supportable basis for comparison in future years.

When a start-up company is preparing for a potential IPO, one of the critical issues reviewed by the Securities and Exchange Commission (SEC) is the determination of whether the grant price of stock options issued prior to the IPO is reasonable—and not a form of compensation to the employees. An independent valuation of a start-up company's stock provides support for the option prices and often plays an important role in discussions on this issue with the SEC.

Gift and Estate Tax Planning

Emerging growth companies often require business valuation services for estate and gift tax planning for the key owners. Obviously, an opportune time for shareholders to gift shares of stock in an emerging growth company is before the company has achieved a substantial amount of growth, rather than after the growth has occurred.

Valuation analysts are frequently retained to estimate the fair market value of a minority ownership interest in the common stock of emerging growth companies for gift tax purposes in the years preceding an initial public offering.

Litigation Support

Valuation analysts are often retained to provide litigation support and dispute resolution services related to emerging growth companies. This is because these companies often become involved in litigation disputes, such as shareholder disputes, intangible asset infringements, contract disputes, intellectual property licensing litigation, and employment agreement and noncompetition agreement violations.

Management of Intangible Assets

For prudent corporate governance purposes, emerging growth companies frequently require valuation services related to intangible assets. Examples of intangible asset valuations include: (1) the valuation of internally developed or to-be-purchased intangible assets for the purpose of a sale or acquisition; (2) assistance regarding arm's-length royalty rates associated with the license of patents, trademarks, or technology; (3) quantification of economic damages related to intellectual property infringement; (4) estimating the value of intangible assets for purchase price allocation purposes; and (5) estimating the value of in-process research and development.

Valuation Approaches

In theory, the generally accepted valuation approaches used to value a closely held business are similar to those used in valuing an emerging growth company. These approaches are the asset-based approach, the market approach, and the income approach.

Within the general approaches are specific methods that are generally more appropriate for the appraisal of emerging growth companies. The application of these valuation methods is presented below.

Asset-Based Approach

The asset-based approach relies on the fundamental accounting principle that assets minus liabilities equals equity. To implement asset-based methods, such as the asset accumulation method, the analyst converts the company's assets and liabilities (which are stated on the balance sheet according to the GAAP historical cost valuation principle) to the appraised value, based on the appropriate standard of value.

The asset-based approach is generally most appropriate when (1) a company's value is heavily dependent on the value of the assets owned by the company, whether tangible or intangible; or (2) there is a plan to liquidate all or some of the company's assets.

Market Approach

The market approach involves identifying either comparable or guideline companies within the industry of the emerging growth company. The comparable or guideline companies may be (1) publicly traded (the guideline publicly traded company method) or (2) acquired within a reasonable period before the valuation date (the guideline merged and acquired company method). Empirical pricing evidence from selected publicly traded companies or transactions are used to provide valuation guidance to the analyst.

Market-derived pricing multiples are extracted from various financial fundamentals (e.g., earnings, cash flow, revenues, book value). The pricing multiples are applied to the subject company's financial fundamentals to estimate an indication of value.

In the market approach, analysts may rely on the guideline publicly traded company method and/or the guideline merged and acquired company method. These methods rely on (1) prices paid for minority ownership interests in the equity of publicly traded companies (the guideline publicly traded company method) or (2) on prices paid for minority or controlling ownership interests in companies that have merged or been acquired (the guideline merged and acquired company method).

The next section of this chapter presents an overview of the guideline publicly traded company method and the guideline merged and acquired company method within the context of the valuation of emerging growth companies.

Guideline Publicly Traded Company Method. The procedures involved in the guideline publicly traded company method include:

1. Identify the guideline companies. Guideline companies are generally selected on the basis of similarity to the subject company. This comparison can include a variety of factors, including product similarity, the position of the company in the industry, markets served, earnings growth prospects, and general risk factors.
2. Determine various historical and projected financial fundamentals for the guideline companies (revenues, earnings, cash flow, etc.), adjusted, if necessary, to reflect accounting policies similar to the subject company or to eliminate nonrecurring or extraordinary items.
3. Calculate pricing multiples paid for various financial fundamentals of the guideline companies. Pricing multiples used in this method may include, among others, price to revenues, price to cash flow, price to earnings, and price to book value. As discussed in the next section of this chapter, the selected pricing multiples can be calculated either on an invested capital or on an equity basis. Pricing multiples should be determined for the relevant historical time periods—the latest 12 months, five-year average, weighted average, projected, or others. For emerging growth companies, which have the expectation of significant future growth, the most appropriate pricing multiples are typically based on latest 12 months and projected financial information, not historical averages.
4. Adjust the pricing multiples for the guideline companies, if necessary, to reflect any differences between the subject company and the guideline companies for factors such as size, diversification, management depth, and anticipated growth.

5. Apply the selected pricing multiples to the adjusted financial fundamentals of the subject company, including, for example, revenues, cash flow, earnings, and book value.
6. Multiply the adjusted financial fundamentals by the appropriate pricing multiple to result in indicated values.
7. Assign weights to the indicated values and determine the overall value estimate, before any appropriate valuation adjustments.

Invested Capital Methodology. Often an invested capital methodology is used for the guideline publicly traded company method when an emerging growth company is valued. This is because many of these emerging growth companies have complex capital structures, including (1) several rounds of convertible preferred stock or (2) combinations of straight preferred stock and common stock warrants.

Under an invested capital analysis, the valuation analyst calculates market-derived pricing multiples on the basis of the market value of invested capital (MVIC), as opposed to reported value measures, such as price/earnings, on a per share basis. MVIC for the guideline publicly traded companies is calculated as follows:

Market value of common equity

+ Market value of preferred equity

+ Market value of interest-bearing debt

= **Market value of invested capital**

The valuation analyst then calculates various pricing multiples, such as (1) MVIC to earnings before interest and taxes (EBIT), and (2) MVIC to earnings before depreciation, interest, and taxes (EBDIT). These pricing multiples are then applied to the subject company's earnings measures. For example, the selected pricing multiple of MVIC to EBIT based on the guideline company multiples is applied to the subject company's EBIT.

The invested capital methodology results in an indication of value of a subject company's aggregate MVIC. Therefore, in order to arrive at the market value of common equity for the subject company, the market value of interest-bearing debt and any preferred equity should be subtracted from the MVIC.

Many mature closely held companies do not have outstanding preferred stock. Therefore, estimating the value of the company's equity after estimating the MVIC only requires the subtraction of the value of the interest-bearing debt from the MVIC. However, since the capital structure of privately held emerging growth companies may include various issues of convertible preferred stock that are held by early stage, risk-taking investors such as venture capital firms, a subsequent section of this chapter addresses valuation issues related to these unique early-stage financing securities.

Direct Equity Methodology. If an invested capital methodology is not used for the guideline publicly traded company method, a direct equity methodology may be implemented. Under the direct equity methodology, the valuation analyst calculates market-derived pricing multiples on the basis of the per share price of each guideline company's common stock, divided by reported value measures, such as earnings, on a per common share basis.

The valuation analyst then calculates various pricing multiples, such as price to earnings per common share or price to cash flow per common share. These pricing multiples are then applied to the subject company's earnings measures. For example, the selected pricing multiple of cash flow per share based on the guideline company multiples is applied to the subject company's cash flow available per common share. The resulting indication of value is the market value of the subject company's common equity.

Valuation of Companies with Negative Historical Earnings.

Many emerging growth companies have not reported positive net income on an historical basis. Also, many of these companies do not project positive profitability in the near future. In addition, many emerging growth companies have reported and project negative EBIT and EBDIT. For these emerging growth companies, the use of the traditional earnings measures under either the invested capital methodology or the direct equity methodology will indicate that the companies are worthless. The use of other measures of economic income for emerging growth companies may result in more meaningful indications of value.

Multiple of Revenues. For emerging growth companies that have reported negative historical earnings and project negative earnings over the next few years, the most common method that is used to estimate value is a pricing multiple of historical or projected revenues. In many industries, pricing multiples of revenue can be selected on the basis of an analysis of the correlation between return on revenues and the multiple paid for revenues for the guideline companies. For industries where there is a relatively high correlation between these two variables, the selected pricing multiple of revenue for the subject company may be based on an analysis of the subject company's current and prospective profitability (positive or negative) compared with the profitability of the guideline companies.

However, some companies that are in the early stages of development have not even reported revenues. In addition, in some instances, development companies report research and development expenses as revenue. When this occurs, it is usually through the formation of a research and development partnership. Such a partnership enters into a contract with the subject development company to conduct research and development. The development company then reports the money from this contract as revenues. In these instances, the analyst will not be able to use the guideline company method. Accordingly, the discounted economic income method is generally used. This method is discussed in a subsequent section of this chapter.

Multiple of Earnings before Research and Development Expense. One factor that has a depressing effect on earnings of some emerging growth companies, such as software development companies, is the relatively high level of spending on research and development. Although research and development is typically expensed, the actual benefit of this spending may not be received until some much later point in the future.

Because of the nature of these companies and the importance of effective and continuous spending on research and development, it may be meaningful to analyze the earnings of these companies before research and development expense. Therefore, an analysis of pretax earnings before interest, depreciation, amortization and research and development (EBDITR) may result in a more meaningful analysis than focusing on earnings measures such as EBDIT.

In many instances, when the subject company has reported negative EBDIT, the only other alternative financial fundamental for analysis is revenues. The analysis of EBDITR gives an additional, and potentially more meaningful, fundamental to analyze.

As an example, Exhibit 23–1 presents the hypothetical financial fundamentals of the subject company, Software Development Co., and of three selected guideline publicly traded companies. Note that, because of the negative EBDIT reported by one guideline company and the subject company, pricing multiples of EBDIT would not result in a meaningful estimate of value for the subject company. However, it is possible to estimate the value of the company from multiples of EBDITR.

Examples of factors to consider in the EBDITR pricing multiple selection process may include the following:

- The relative amount and effective historical use of the company's research and development spending.
- The company's market share and overall size compared with the guideline companies.
- History and expectations regarding the willingness of customers to continue using the company's current product and to participate in upgrades and ancillary products.
- The potential loss of key employees and any key person risk.
- Growth expectations of the market served by the company versus the key markets served by the guideline companies.

Exhibit 23–1

Financial Fundamentals for Software Development Co.

Company	MVIC ($000)	EBDIT ($000)	EBDITR ($000)	MVIC/EBDITR Pricing Multiple
Macrosoft	337,170	23,768	43,360	7.8
Updated Software	108,273	2,390	13,621	7.9
Version Two Software	103,734	(1,490)	10,714	9.7
Software Development Co.	NA*	(4,235)	3,856	NA

* Not available.

- Historical and projected growth of the subject and publicly traded companies.
- A comparison of the subject company's financial position versus the financial positions of the guideline companies.
- The company's return on revenues compared with the guideline companies.
- The subject company's historical volatility of earnings.

After market-derived pricing multiples have been selected and applied to the subject company financial fundamentals, the resulting value is the MVIC for the subject company. Next, the market value of the interest-bearing debt and preferred stock should be subtracted, as described earlier, in order to estimate the value of the company's equity.

Guideline Merged and Acquired Company Method. The guideline merged and acquired company method is also frequently used to estimate the value of emerging growth companies. The procedures employed in the guideline merged and acquired company method are similar to those used in the guideline publicly traded company method. This is true, except that the search criteria involve completed privately negotiated but publicly announced transactions (primarily controlling ownership interests in companies) as opposed to minority ownership positions in guideline publicly traded companies.

However, additional adjustments may be necessary to address discounts for lack of control if the merged and acquired company transactions involve controlling ownership interests and the subject interest being valued is a minority ownership interest.

Income Approach

The income approach is based on the theory that the value of a business is equal to the present value of the expected future cash flows that the business will generate. There are two generic applications of the income approach: (1) the single-period method and (2) the multiple-period method.

The single-period method includes dividing a representative level of recurring economic income (e.g., net income, cash flow) by an appropriate direct capitalization rate.

The multiple-period method consists of estimating economic income for discrete future periods and then discounting these economic benefits using a present value discount rate. The discounted cash flow (DCF) method, a multiple-period method, is typically the most relevant income approach method to use when valuing emerging growth companies.

Discounted Cash Flow Method. The DCF method is particularly applicable to valuing emerging growth companies. This is because, unlike the case of mature companies, the historical financial performance of these companies generally provides little insight into potential future performance.

DCF analysis procedures estimate value on the basis of future return flows over an investment horizon. Using empirical market-derived data, macroeconomic and industry evidence, and the underlying outlook for the subject company, DCF models apply a present value discount rate, known as the required rate of return on investment, to expected future cash flows. This results in a estimation of the net present value of a series of cash flows.

Interim Cash Flows. In the DCF model, it is important that the development of the interim cash flow corresponds with an appropriate present value discount rate. In the valuation of emerging growth companies, interim cash flow is generally defined as net cash flow to equity or net cash flow to invested capital.

Net cash flow to equity is defined as:

Net income after taxes

+   Noncash charges (e.g., depreciation and amortization expense)

−   Capital expenditures

−   Increases (or + decreases) in net working capital

+   Increases (or − decreases) in long-term debt

=   Net cash flow to equity (NCF_e)

Net cash flow to invested capital is defined as:

Net income after taxes

+   Interest × (1− income tax rate)

+   Noncash charges (e.g., depreciation and amortization expense)

−   Capital expenditures

+   Preferred dividends, if any

−   Increases (or + decreases) in net working capital

=   Net cash flow to invested capital (NCF_f)

In the estimation of a present value discount rate to apply to cash flow, it is important that the company's equity cost of capital be used as the discount rate to apply to NCF_e, whereas the company's weighted average cost of capital should be used as the discount rate to apply to NCF_f. A subsequent section of this chapter addresses unique issues related to estimating the present value discount rate for emerging growth companies.

The resulting indication of value from discounting NCF_e by the company's cost of equity capital is the company's equity. The value from discounting NCF_f by the company's weighted average cost of capital is the company's market value of invested capital.

Two-Stage DCF Model. The two-stage DCF model is the model that is most commonly used in the DCF method. The two stages in this model commonly include (1) the financial statement projections for the company for a discrete period such as years 1 through 5 and (2) the terminal value.

The value of the company under the two-stage DCF model is equal to the present value of the cash flow for years 1 through 5, plus the present value of the terminal value. The terminal value is frequently calculated by using the constant growth direct capitalization model, defined as:

$$PV = \frac{NCF\,(1 + g)}{k - g}$$

where:
 PV = Present value
 NCF = Net cash flow in the last projection period
 k = Present value discount rate
 g = Expected long-term growth rate in net cash flow

In some instances, the terminal value may be estimated through the application of a market-derived pricing multiple to a projected earnings fundamental. For example, some analysts apply a price to earnings pricing multiple to projected terminal year earnings for the company.

Three-Stage Model. For emerging growth companies, it may be more appropriate to use a three-stage DCF model instead of a two-stage DCF model. Use of the two-stage DCF model for an emerging growth company incorporates an estimate of growth to perpetuity for calculation of the terminal value, usually after five years of interim cash flow projections. For companies that are entering a high earnings growth phase that is not sustainable into perpetuity, it is difficult after five years of projections to accurately estimate the appropriate long-term growth rate.

For example, assume that a company is expected to report growth in cash flow over the next five years as presented below:

	Year 1	Year 2	Year 3	Year 4	Year 5	Long-Term Growth Rate
Cash flow growth rate	50%	40%	35%	35%	30%	?

The limitations of the two-stage DCF model are apparent in this example, since to estimate the company's terminal value, a growth rate to perpetuity should be estimated after five years of extremely high growth. The two-stage model is sensitive to changes in the estimated residual growth rate in the appraisal of mature companies. However, for emerging growth companies, small changes in the assumptions regarding sustainable long-term growth in cash flow result in extremely large changes in indicated values.

A three-stage model is therefore particularly appropriate for emerging growth companies. This is because these companies generally are expected to report very high rates of growth in the interim periods, followed by declining growth thereafter.

In a three-stage model, the three stages include (1) the financial statement projections for the first stage (say, years 1 through 5), (2) estimated annual growth for the next stage (say, years 6 through 10), and (3) the terminal value. Typically, the subject company management team prepares the financial statement projections for a five-year period. These projections should be thoroughly examined by the analyst. Estimated annual growth for years 6 through 10 may be based on available near-term industry growth estimates. Sources of these industry estimated growth rates vary according to the industry in which the subject company participates.

The value of the company under the three-stage DCF model is equal to the present value of the cash flow for years 1 through 5, plus the present value of the cash flow for years 6 through 10, plus the present value of the terminal value.

Illustrative Example.   Exhibit 23–2 presents a comparison of the indicated value of an emerging growth company under a two-stage model versus a three-stage model. In the two-stage model, the assumed annual cash flow growth rates for years 1 through 5 are presented below:

	Year 1	Year 2	Year 3	Year 4	Year 5
Annual cash flow growth rate	50%	40%	35%	35%	30%

Assuming a 25 percent equity present value discount rate, the indicated equity value for the company based on various assumptions regarding the residual growth rate is presented in Exhibit 23–2. As presented, assuming a 5 percent residual growth rate, the indicated value of the company is $17.61 per share.

Exhibit 23–2 also presents a three-stage DCF model. In this model, an additional stage is added, the estimated annual growth rate in cash flow to equity per share of 15 percent for years 6 through 10, based on industry growth estimates. Again, assuming a 25 percent equity present value discount rate, the indicated value of the company assuming a 5 percent residual growth rate is $21.50 per share.

As presented in Exhibit 23–2, use of the two-stage DCF model significantly understates the value of the company compared with the three-stage model. For example, assuming an expected 5 percent residual long-term growth rate, the two-stage model would have yielded a value conclusion that is 18 percent lower than the indicated value under the three-stage DCF model.

In addition, the three-stage model reduces the variance associated with the estimation of the residual growth rate. As presented in Exhibit 23–2, estimating the residual long-term growth rate at 3 percent instead of 5 percent would have reduced the equity value by 6 percent in the two-stage model, whereas estimating the residual long-term growth rate at 7 percent instead of 5 percent would have increased the equity value by 7 percent. In the three-stage model, estimating the residual

Two-Period DCF Model

	Latest Year	Year 1	Year 2	Year 3	Year 4	Year 5	Terminal Value
Cash flow to equity per share	1.00	1.50	2.10	2.84	3.83	4.98	
Annual growth in cash flow to equity per share		*50%*	*40%*	*35%*	*35%*	*30%*	
Present value discount rate		0.89	0.72	0.57	0.46	0.37	
Number of periods (assumes midyear convention)		*0.50*	*1.50*	*2.50*	*3.50*	*4.50*	*4.50*
Equity discount rate		*25%*					
Present value of interim cash flows		1.34	1.50	1.62	1.75	1.82	
Net present value of interim cash flows		8.04					
Residual growth rate, two-period DCF model		3%	5%	7%			
Cash flow to equity per share, year 6		5.12	5.22	5.32			
Terminal year capitalization rate		4.55	5.00	5.56			
Terminal value		23.29	26.12	29.58			
Present value discount rate		0.37	0.37	0.37			
Present value of terminal value		8.53	9.57	10.84			
Indicated equity value		16.58	17.61	18.88			
% change		*-6%*	*0%*	*7%*			

Three-Period DCF Model

		Year 6	Year 7	Year 8	Year 9	Year 10	
Cash flow to equity per share		5.72	6.58	7.57	8.70	10.01	
Annual growth rate, years 6 – 10	*15%*						
Present value discount rate		0.29	0.23	0.19	0.15	0.12	
Number of periods (assumes midyear convention)		*5.50*	*6.50*	*7.50*	*8.50*	*9.50*	*9.50*
Equity discount rate		*25%*					
Present value of interim cash flows		1.68	1.54	1.42	1.31	1.20	
Net present value of interim cash flows, years 1 – 10		15.19					
Residual growth rate, three-period model		3%	5%	7%			
Cash flow to equity per share, year 11		10.31	10.51	10.71			
Terminal year capitalization rate		4.55	5.00	5.56			
Terminal value		46.85	52.54	59.49			
Present value discount rate		0.12	0.12	0.12			
Present value of terminal value		5.62	6.31	7.14			
Indicated equity value		20.81	21.50	22.33			
% change		*-3%*	*0%*	*4%*			
Understatement of value by use of two-period model		*-20%*	*-18%*	*-15%*			

long-term growth rate at 3 percent instead of 5 percent would have reduced the equity value by only 3 percent, whereas estimating the residual long-term growth rate at 7 percent instead of 5 percent would have increased the equity value by 4 percent.

Developing the Present Value Discount Rate. With the discounted cash flow method, it is necessary to develop a present value discount rate, or a cost of capital, in order to convert the projected income stream to a present value. Estimation of the present value discount rate is a complex task as part of every valuation assignment. However, when the subject company is an emerging growth company, this task becomes even more challenging.

There are several methods for an analyst to use to estimate the cost of capital for the valuation of emerging growth companies when using the discounted cash flow method. Examples of these methods include:

1. An analysis of historical and expected rates of return by venture capital investors.
2. The Gordon growth model.
3. Analyzing historical rates of return earned by investments in similar companies at similar stages of development.
4. The capital asset pricing model (CAPM).

Each of these methods is described below.

Venture Capital Rates of Return.   A starting point for estimating the required rate of return for an investment in an emerging growth company is an analysis of actual venture capital rates of return. Since the venture capital industry invests in closely held emerging growth companies, the actual and expected returns on those investments at any point in time are relevant pieces of information regarding the development of a present value discount rate for an emerging growth company.

Venture Economics, a division of Securities Data Company, conducts an annual study of venture capital rates of return. This study reports actual venture capital rates of return by fund types over various investment horizons (ranging from three months to 20 years). In the latest study, for example, based on an investment horizon of one to five years, the median pooled internal rate of return for all stages of venture capital ranged from 30 to 45 percent.

Obviously, these data are simply a starting point in the estimation of the appropriate present value discount rate for an emerging growth company. This is because required rates of return are forward-looking, and additional factors must be considered to adjust the actual venture capital rates of return to the specific risks associated with an investment in the subject company. However, these data do provide a starting point for the estimation of required rates of return for high-risk investments.

Gordon growth model.   Another method for estimating the appropriate present value discount rate for an emerging growth company is the Gordon growth model presented below:

$$PV = \frac{NCF\,(1+g)}{k-g}$$

where:
PV =   Present value
NCF =   Net cash flow in the last projection period
k =   Present value discount rate
g =   Expected long-term growth rate in net cash flow

Solving for the discount rate, the formula would be presented as follows:

$$\text{Discount rate } (k) = (NCF \div PV) + g$$

In some cases, the net cash flow for minority ownership shareholders can be assumed to be equal to dividends paid, and the present value is the equivalent of the common stock price. Since most emerging growth companies do not pay a dividend, the formula can be reduced to state that the discount rate for non-dividend-paying companies is equal to the expected long-term growth rate in net cash flow. From this assumption, various company and industry growth estimates can be compiled to use as a proxy for projected earnings growth, or the equivalent of an appropriate present value discount rate. However, these shorter-term growth estimates should be adjusted for differences between short-term unsustainable growth and long-term sustainable growth.

Historical Rates of Return for Comparable Investments. A third method that may be used to estimate the required rate of return for an investment in an emerging growth company is to analyze actual historical returns realized by comparative investments. The steps in this method include identifying a list of guideline publicly traded companies and calculating historical annual rates of return realized by investors in the equity of the guideline companies.

Following identification of guideline companies at a similar stage of development as the emerging growth company, the historical annual return on these investments can be calculated. This evidence may provide guidance regarding the appropriate required rate of return for investors in emerging growth companies. Adjustments may be necessary to reflect differences between the perceived risk associated with an investment in the subject company versus the guideline companies.

Capital Asset Pricing Model. The most widely used method for estimating the cost of equity capital for companies is the capital asset pricing model (CAPM). This section provides a brief overview of the CAPM (for a more detailed discussion, see Chapter 1).

An example of the development of an established company's cost of equity capital is presented in Exhibit 23–3.

In this example, the indicated equity discount rate is 18 percent. This method can be used to estimate the discount rate for an emerging growth company, but adjustments are necessary to the size risk premium (based on the emerging growth company's estimated market capitalization), and the company-specific risk premium. With most emerging growth companies, the largest adjustment is to the company-specific risk premium.

The company-specific risk premium is a subjective estimate of the nonsystematic risk facing the company and reflects the unique risk factors associated with an investment in the subject company. Each of these unique risk factors may have either a positive or negative effect on the overall company cost of equity. By examining each of the qualitative factors, the valuation analyst may add or subtract an estimated percentage based on each item's effect on the risk associated with an ownership interest in the company's stock.

Examples of qualitative factors affecting the risk of emerging growth companies include, among others, quality and depth of management, smaller size of the subject company compared with the size of the companies used to calculate the small stock equity risk premium, geographic diversification, product line diversification, customer depen-

Exhibit 23–3

Example of Estimation of the Cost of Equity Capital

Cost of Capital Component	Component Value	Source
Risk-free rate of return	5.4%	20-year U.S. Treasury bond.
General equity risk premium	7.8%	*Stocks, Bonds, Bills and Inflation (SBBI) 1998 Yearbook,* long-horizon expected equity risk premium.
Multiplied by: beta	<u>1.0</u>	Compustat.
	7.8%	
Small size equity risk premium	3.3%	*SBBI 1998 Yearbook,* expected microcapitalization equity size premium.
Company-specific equity risk premium	<u>1.0%</u>	Analyst's qualitative estimate.
Rate of return on equity	17.5%	
Cost of equity capital	<u>**18.0%**</u> **(rounded)**	

dence, supplier dependence, technology risk, competitor risk, volatility of historical financial performance, risk of not achieving projected market share, risk of not achieving projected profitability, lack of historical profitability compared with projected results, key employee risk, license agreements, and supply agreements.

Adjusting the company-specific equity risk premium to reflect any additional risk factors will result in a rate of return based on the CAPM that may be used in a DCF valuation model for the valuation of an emerging growth company. Note that in the example presented in Exhibit 23–3 for an established company, the indicated cost of equity was 18 percent, including a company-specific risk premium of 1 percent. Compared with venture capital actual rates of return ranging from 30 to 45 percent, as presented earlier in this chapter, it is clear that, depending on the unique risks in each situation, the company-specific equity risk premium for emerging growth companies can be substantial.

Early Stage Financing Securities in Emerging Growth Companies

A common feature of all emerging growth companies is that they thirst for capital from various investors to fund early development. This capital typically comes from a variety of sources, including venture capital companies. Valuation analysts are frequently retained to value the common stock of emerging growth companies. In the process, they should estimate the value of early stage financing securities that these companies have issued.

As discussed earlier in this chapter, the steps associated with estimating the value of an emerging growth company's common stock typically include the following:

1. Select and apply the appropriate valuation methods (such as the guideline publicly traded company method or the discounted cash flow method).
2. Estimate the market value of invested capital (defined as the market value of interest-bearing debt, preferred stock, and common stock) of the company, based on the selected methods.
3. Subtract the market value of outstanding interest-bearing debt.
4. Subtract the market value of the outstanding preferred stock.
5. Estimate appropriate adjustments, such as a discount for lack of marketability.

The valuation analyst should consider the rights and privileges of the outstanding convertible preferred stock when estimating the market value of those securities.

This section of the chapter presents a review of the typical features of these venture capital investment securities and a discussion of factors to consider regarding these securities when valuing the common stock of an emerging growth company.

Capital Structure

Convertible preferred stock is the most common investment vehicle used by the venture capital community. In addition, other equity securities, or combinations of straight preferred stock and common stock warrants, may be structured to mirror the economics of convertible preferred stock.

Generally, the unique features of the capital structure of privately held emerging growth companies are the outstanding rounds of convertible preferred stock that are held by entities such as venture capital firms, and outstanding warrants and common stock options.

Illustrative Example

A sample capital structure for a company that has received several rounds of financing from venture capital companies is presented in Exhibit 23–4. In this example, the subject company has no debt but has issued three rounds of convertible preferred securities to two venture capital companies. These preferred rounds are named Series A, B, and C. The company has also issued shares of common stock to founders and

Exhibit 23–4

Sample Capital Structure

	Preferred Stock Series A $1.00	Shares	Preferred Stock Series B $2.00	Shares	Preferred Stock Series C $4.00	Shares	Common Stock Shares
XYZ Venture Capital, LP	$2,000,000	2,000,000	$3,000,000	1,500,000	$2,000,000	500,000	
ABC Venture Capital, LP	—	—	—	—	$4,000,000	1,000,000	
Founders and employees	—	—	—	—	—	—	1,500,000
Options and warrants	—	—	—	—	—	—	3,500,000
Total	$2,000,000	2,000,000	$3,000,000	1,500,000	$6,000,000	1,500,000	5,000,000

employees, and common stock options and warrants.

To value the common stock of this company, it is important to analyze the differences between (1) the rights and privileges of the preferred shares versus (2) the rights and privileges accorded to owners of the common shares. It is a mistake to concentrate only on the mandatory conversion price of the convertible preferred stock when estimating the value of the company's common stock.

Typical Features of Early Stage Financing Securities

Although the preferred stock purchased by venture capitalists is generally convertible into common stock, the preferred stock has substantially different rights, preferences, and privileges from that accorded to an owner of a minority interest in the company's common stock.

Examples of features that may differentiate the preferred from the common include the following:

- **Liquidation preferences.** Preferred stock shareholders will generally require preference over common shareholders on the value of their principal investment, in the event of a liquidation or sale of the company.
- **Redemption rights.** Holders of convertible preferred securities with redemption rights receive the right to "put" the preferred shares, generally at cost.
- **Voting rights.** In many instances, the convertible preferred securi-

ties give the holder the ability to control one or more seats on the company's board of directors and the ability to block certain corporate actions.
- **Conversion rights.** The convertible preferred is usually automatically convertible into common stock in the event of an initial public offering, generally at a stated minimum initial public offering price.
- **Dividend rights.** Many early stage financing securities have features such as cumulative dividends, and the accrued but unpaid preferred dividends must be paid before dividends are paid to any other stock of the company. This feature has the potential of increasing the rate of return on these securities above the return associated with an investment in the common stock.
- **Antidilution rights.** Antidilution rights enable holders of the securities to minimize the impact of dilution related to subsequent rounds of financing.

The rights and privileges attributed to the convertible preferred stock give venture capital investors the ability to participate in the management of the company and some upside potential. At the same time, the downside risk of their investments is limited to some extent.

Valuation Considerations

In the early stages of a company's development, owing primarily to the liquidation and redemption privileges, most of the company's total value may be assigned to the preferred securities. The residual value attributable to the company's common stock may be minimal.

As the company's revenue and profitability increase and the total value of the company grows, the relative value of the liquidation and redemption privileges is reduced, and the value associated with the convertibility feature of the preferred shares increases.

In the example presented above, (1) if the total market value of invested capital indicated by the selected valuation methods is $12 million, and (2) if the combined liquidation preference of the Series A, B, and C preferred shares is $11 million, then (3) the indicated value of all 5 million of the common shares is $1 million—before adjusting for the lack of liquidity. That indicated value is substantially less than the conversion price of the convertible preferred securities.

This value differential exists because of the valuable rights and privileges associated with the convertible preferred shares.

Discount for Lack of Marketability

The typical methods used to estimate the value of a closely held emerging growth company, such as the guideline company methods and the discounted cash flow method, result in value indications on a fully marketable basis. However, the common stock of closely held emerging growth companies is not fully marketable. Therefore, in many instances an adjustment is required to address the difference in marketability between an interest in a closely held company and a fully marketable security.

There have been two general types of empirical studies designed to quantify the discounts for lack of marketability associated with minority ownership interests in closely held companies:

• Discounts on sales of restricted shares of publicly traded companies
• Discounts on private transactions prior to public offerings

Restricted stock is identical in all respects to the freely traded stock of a public company except that it is restricted from trading on the open market for a certain period. The difference between the price at which restricted stock transactions take place compared with open market transactions in the same stock on the same date provides evidence on the price spread between a readily marketable security and one that is identical but subject to certain restrictions on its marketability (see Chapter 5).

Since restrictions on the transfer of restricted stock eventually lapse, more relevant studies to estimate the discount for lack of marketability associated with minority ownership interests in emerging growth companies should be considered. Willamette Management Associates and Robert W. Baird & Company have performed studies that compare the prices of private transactions to the prices of subsequent public offerings in the stock of the same companies (see Chapter 4).

These studies cover hundreds of transactions during a span of over 20 years. Average differentials between private transaction prices and public market prices varied under different market conditions, ranging from about 40 to 63 percent, after the "outliers" were eliminated.

The discount for lack of marketability may be magnified when valuing emerging growth companies such as start-up companies. A start-up company is characterized by opportunities for significant growth far into the future that result in additional risk. There is also a limited pool of potential investors willing to invest in these companies. The inability to dispose of ownership interests at exactly the moment investors change their attitude about the prospects of the subject company may justify a discount for lack of marketability that is higher than the typical discount for the average closely held business. It is within the judgment of the valuation analyst to estimate the discount that is appropriate according to the specific circumstances of the subject interest being valued.

Conclusion

Estimating the value of emerging growth companies is a more challenging task than estimating the value of mature, slower-growth companies. This is because there is generally less of an historical track record of success for emerging growth companies. In addition, it is difficult to accurately assess the myriad of risks associated with an investment in an emerging growth company.

This chapter focused on the typical reasons that emerging growth companies may require valuations, the valuation approaches that prove most effective for valuing emerging growth companies, and the valuation considerations involving the unique capital structure of closely held emerging growth companies.

Chapter 24

Special Considerations in the Valuation of Closely Held Government Technology Service Firms

Thomas J. Millon Jr., CFA, ASA, and Michael Mendelevitz

Introduction

The office of Minority Enterprise Development (MED) program was created to help companies owned and operated by socially and economically disadvantaged businesspeople to (1) gain access to the resources necessary to develop their business and (2) improve their ability to compete in the mainstream of the American economy. The most well-known element of the MED program is the 8(a) program, named from Section 8(a) of the Small Business Act.

Under the 8(a) program, the Small Business Administration (SBA) enters into prime contracts with federal departments and agencies and subcontracts the performance of the work to disadvantaged small businesses that are certified participants in the program. During the government's 1996 fiscal year, total contract and modification dollars awarded to the 6,115 firms participating in the 8(a) program were approximately $6 billion.

Among the major areas of contract activity, firms under the Standard Industrial Classification (SIC) Code 7379, Computer Related Services, Not Elsewhere Classified, ranked number two with respect to the dollar amount of contracts. Firms in this category provide a wide variety of computer-related support services that enhance their clients' abilities to become more efficient and to improve upon operating policies.

Closely held information technology firms participating in the 8(a) program may be subject to a professional business valuation for a variety of reasons. These reasons may include:

- Attracting new investors
- Planning and providing various forms of incentive compensation
- Gift and estate tax planning
- Litigation and other controversy purposes
- Transaction pricing purposes
- Preparing for the formation of an employee stock ownership plan (ESOP)

Many business valuation analysts may be unfamiliar with the 8(a) program and, therefore, may not understand how a closely held firm's participation in this program affects the valuation process. Independent of the purpose of the assignment, there are several special considerations that should be kept in mind during the course of any valuation analysis. This chapter will discuss a number of these special considerations.

Since some of these considerations stem from the attributes of the 8(a) program, we will describe the essential features of the program. After a brief overview of the marketplace for information technology services, we shall discuss several of the special considerations that come to bear in conducting a business valuation of an 8(a) information technology company. These special issues include:

- The impact of the firm's participation in the 8(a) program
- Key person valuation discounts
- The mix of government versus commercial business
- Matters involving the valuation of controlling ownership interest blocks

The 8(a) Program

The 8(a) program is a business development program that provides its participants with access to a variety of business development services, including the opportunity to receive federal contracts on a sole source or limited competition basis. Under the 8(a) program, the SBA enters into prime contracts with federal departments and agencies and subcontracts the performance of the work to disadvantaged small businesses that are certified participants in the program.

In order for a business to qualify for the 8(a) program, at least 51 percent of each class of voting stock (or other form of equity) in the firm, as well as 51 percent of the aggregate number of all outstanding shares of stock, must be unconditionally owned by an individual(s) who is (are) a citizen of the United States and who is (are) certified by the SBA to be socially and economically disadvantaged. The management and daily operations of the firm must also be controlled by the disadvantaged majority owner(s).

For 8(a) certification purposes, in order for the disadvantaged individual to exert effective control of the firm, he or she must possess some degree of managerial or technical experience and competency directly related to the primary industry in which the firm is seeking 8(a) certification. For those industries requiring professional licenses or certifications, the SBA has the right to determine whether the firm or its employees hold the requisite license(s).

At least one socially and economically disadvantaged full-time manager must hold the position of president or chief executive officer. This requirement also precludes any outside employment or pursuit of any other business interest that may conflict with the management of the 8(a) firm or that may hinder the firm in achieving the objectives of its business development plan.

Individuals who are not socially and economically disadvantaged may also be involved in the management of the firm, and they may also be stockholders, partners, officers, or directors. However, these nondisadvantaged managers, or their spouses or any other household members, may not be in a position to render effective control of the 8(a) firm.

With prior SBA approval, an 8(a) firm may continue participation in the program after a change of ownership. Prior SBA approval is not required when the change in ownership represents less than a 10 percent interest in the firm or results from the death or incapacity, due to serious or long-term illness or injury, of a disadvantaged principal. However, the firm must notify the SBA as soon as possible of such a change in ownership.

To evaluate whether a firm has the potential for success, the SBA evaluates (1) the technical and managerial experience and competency of the individuals upon whom eligibility is based, (2) the financial capacity of the applicant firm, and (3) the firm's historical performance on previous federal and private sector contracts in the primary industry in which the firm is seeking 8(a) certification.

In assessing the degree of diminished credit and capital opportunities of a socially disadvantaged individual, the SBA considers factors relating both to the firm and to the owner as an individual. An individual whose personal net worth exceeds $250,000 is not considered economically disadvantaged for purposes of evaluating eligibility for the 8(a) program. When the SBA calculates the personal net worth of the individual claiming disadvantaged status for purposes of the program, it excludes that individual's ownership interest in the applicant 8(a) firm as well as the equity in his or her primary personal residence. However, any portion of such equity in that primary residence attributable to excessive withdrawals from the applicant or participating 8(a) firm is not excluded.

The applicant must also demonstrate that it has been in business in the primary industry classification in which it seeks 8(a) certification for two full years prior to the date of its 8(a) application by submitting income tax returns showing revenues for each of the two previous years. Waivers to this two-year requirement may be granted if the individual upon whom eligibility is to be based has demonstrated substantial business management experience and technical expertise, and if the firm has adequate resources to carry out the business plan and fulfill the contract.

Program participation is divided into two stages: the developmental stage and the transitional stage. For firms approved for 8(a) participation after November 15, 1998, the developmental stage is four years and the transitional stage is five years.

The developmental stage is designed to help newly certified 8(a) businesses overcome their economic disadvantage. Development assistance includes (1) sole source and competitive 8(a) contract support, (2) transfer of technology or surplus property owned by the United States to program participants by grant, and (3) training sessions to enhance participants' skills in business principles.

The transitional stage is designed to help participants overcome the remaining elements of economic disadvantage and to prepare participants for leaving the 8(a) program. Assistance includes (1) sole source and competitive 8(a) contract support, (2) transfer of technology or surplus property owned by the United States to program participants by grant, (3) training sessions to enhance participants' skills in business principles, (4) assistance from procuring agencies in forming joint ventures, and (5) training and technical assistance in business planning to help ensure the firm's successful transition from the 8(a) program to the competitive market.

The SBA's 8(a) program has recently undergone increasing political scrutiny. In September 1998, the SBA announced details of its new program to certify firms as small disadvantaged businesses. This revised certification process is an important part of the Clinton administration's initiative to "mend not end" affirmative action programs. The new certification process will categorize a small business as disadvantaged only if the SBA review finds the firm is owned and controlled by someone who is socially and economically disadvantaged. The new certification process is intended to effectively expand the number of white female entrepreneurs who would be eligible to qualify for the contracting preferences. The proposed changes also included certain latitudes for teaming up with larger firms and for bidding on larger contracts.

Information Technology Business Services

At nearly $200 billion in size, the worldwide information technology services market is growing at 15 to 20 percent per year. The opportunities presented by this fast-growing market are many and varied.

The marketplace for professional information technology services is fragmented and very competitive. There are a substantial number of organizations, varying widely with respect to their sheer magnitude (as measured in any number of ways, including the size of technical staff), customer diversification, and access to financial resources. Such companies may be either publicly owned or privately held. Some information technology providers may be divisions of much larger organizations, including large manufacturing companies and large accounting firms.

Different business strategies characterize firms in the information technology services industry. Firms can specialize in particular vertical markets, establishing themselves as experts in an industry or a function. Examples of vertical markets include telecommunications and financial services. Specific products and services include order processing, billing, collections, and customer information systems. Alternate strategies involve developing a more general expertise and the use of local relationships.

Some information technology firms are more project-oriented, in that they design and develop a project at the beginning, and then also implement it, rather than merely implementing solutions developed by the client's staff, or even some other consulting firm.

Firms that provide high-performance, technology-based solutions and services have experienced significant expansion during the last decade. This growth has been driven in part by the increasing trend by both government and commercial organizations to focus on their core competencies and to outsource their noncore functions, such as information technology (infotech or IT). This trend toward concentration on core competencies is taking place within both the private and public sectors.

The Private Sector

Within the private sector, the dynamic business environment, as exemplified by more intense competition, deregulation, innovation, and rapid technological advancements, has compelled many firms to modify some of their essential business processes. Within this changing environment, the improvement of a business's infotech system greatly enhances its ability to realize greater productivity and to manage its operations more efficiently. These process improvements may take place in any number of functional areas, such as product development, service delivery, manufacturing, sales, and human resources.

However, this increased popularity in business reengineering projects presents a company with significant challenges. The design, development, and implementation of a significantly updated infotech solution requires a number of highly skilled individuals, the supply of which remains short of current demand.

The shortage of skilled and trained professionals makes it more difficult for medium and large firms alike to expand their in-house IT departments, especially during an era when sizable additions to corporate fixed costs are discouraged. As a result of these and other factors, many large firms choose to engage outside specialists to develop and implement their IT projects, particularly on a fixed price, fixed time frame basis, in order to minimize the overall financial and operational risks associated with such large-scale technology projects. Outsourcing of IT projects allows growing companies to control variable costs while permitting the organization to focus on its core capabilities. Outsourcing represents a particularly cost-effective solution for labor-intensive IT projects.

The Public Sector

The U.S. government is the largest single buyer of information technology services. One independent market research firm, Federal Sources, Inc., estimates that the federal government spending on information technology approached $28 billion during the 1997 fiscal year, which is 1.4 percent higher than spending in 1996. IT spending by civilian agencies in 1997 is estimated at $17 billion, while Department of Defense spending is expected to amount to $11 billion. Federal Sources, Inc. also estimates that total U.S. government spending on IT services will increase at an annual average rate of 6 to 8 percent over the next few years.

Recently, the federal government has shifted from the awarding of very task-specific contracts to the awarding of very general IDIQ (indefinite delivery/indefinite quantity) information technology contracts. These contracts provide the contractor with the right to market its products and services directly, rather than with a commitment from the issuing department to buy a fixed quantity of products and services. Although this setup has facilitated the federal government's purchases of goods and services, it has also contributed to additional competitive pressures among IT service providers.

In addition to increased reliance on IDIQs, there is a growing use of other General Services Administration (GSA) schedules, blanket purchase agreements, and governmentwide contracts, which tend to concentrate government buying into larger and larger companies. This constitutes a "bigger is better" sentiment. The impact of this sentiment on the 8(a) contractor is for federal government agencies to switch their emphasis to very large contracts—a shift that may reduce not only the potential number of qualified bidders, but also the 8(a)'s opportunity to serve as the prime contractor.

Even though overall government spending has remained fairly level over the past few years, the government marketplace for IT services continues to be very large. This portends well for outside or private service providers. The federal government employs fewer people, performs fewer oversight functions, and therefore relies more on the private sector for increasing levels of support. As federal procurement rules change, the government seeks to establish long-term, successful contracts with reliable industry partners.

The Department of Defense continues to dominate the awarding of federal contracts to 8(a) companies that provide information technology services. According to INPUT, an independent market research firm, the Navy and the Army combined spent over $1.2 billion for IT services rendered by companies in the 8(a) program.

The federal government possesses its own in-house capabilities, which, in effect, compete against private sector service providers in that government employees may perform many of the services that would otherwise be provided by outside contractors.

Special Considerations

Participation in the SBA's 8(a) program brings some obvious benefits to the certified firm. At the same time, there are commensurate risks to factor into the valuation process.

Some view the 8(a) program as a marketing tool, one that provides a way to ease the procurement process for prospective information technology customers. However, 8(a) status alone does not guarantee the procurement of federal contracts. At the very least, accreditation within the 8(a) program provides the small company with a launching pad to develop the bidding and proposal skills needed to successfully participate in the federal government contract procurement process. Therefore, 8(a) firms may be poised to grow faster while incurring less marketing expenses than their non-8(a) peers.

Ultimately, firms want to be regarded as mainstream enterprises, regardless of whether they were at one time 8(a) companies. As part of due diligence, the valuation analyst should assess the degree to which the 8(a) company is creating a solid platform that will support its long-term business development efforts after graduation from the program. The long-term initiatives could include the development of innovative or niche technologies, establishing a superior reputation in the marketplace for quality service, and so forth.

Section 8(a) companies also make attractive partnering candidates for larger government contractors. Although the 8(a) program certainly affords its participants opportunities to obtain sole source contracts in order to expand their businesses, reports indicate that the increased popularity of GSA supply schedules among government infotech buyers has tended to decrease the number of sole source awards to 8(a) firms. Many large contracts have a portion set aside for an 8(a) firm.

In order to win the contract, the prime contractor has to have a cadre of qualified firms that are technically qualified to perform the services. This highly competitive contest to be considered a "preferred 8(a) subcontractor" to a major prime contractor increases the competitive nature of the 8(a). These "prime/sub" relationships affect the 8(a)'s value, in that they represent a significant intangible asset of the corporation.

Upon graduating from the 8(a) program, the firm will need to expend more marketing effort to make up for the guidance and assistance provided within the program. A more focused marketing strategy will need to be formulated and implemented by what will probably entail a larger dedicated staff. As the 8(a) firm edges toward the day on which it graduates from the 8(a) program, resources will be devoted to the development of new business opportunities within its areas of expertise. As this happens, the maturing 8(a) firm is essentially entering a turnaround phase.

Generally speaking, a business enterprise entering a turnaround situation finds itself struggling along in its traditional line of business, earning less than a normal rate of return on its assets. At some point that struggling firm's ownership or management realizes that continued support of its status quo business strategy does not represent a viable long-run strategy. If only the firm's ownership group holds this opinion, management changes may be required

In the case of an 8(a) participant, the program's statutory nine-year term limit imposes a turnaround, or new direction, upon the firm. Since a turnaround company is headed in a new strategic and operational direction, the financial projections of the firm play a prominent role in any valuation exercise. Valuation analysts should spend considerable effort to review the assumptions underlying the financial projections prepared by the management of the soon to be graduating 8(a) company. A complicating factor is the "long tail" of 8(a) contracts, which can stretch for many years after graduation. This will affect the value of the company years after it has graduated.

One obviously crucial aspect of the financial projections is the revenue projections, which are influenced by the status of the firm's contract backlog. As graduation from the program approaches, 8(a) contracts represent a shrinking portion of projected revenue. In other words, revenue growth or maintenance can be supported only by projecting new revenue from non-8(a) business sources. These new sources operate in a more competitive environment, which introduces additional elements of risk to the 8(a) firm, as compared with the more protective environment of the 8(a) program.

The valuation analyst should be qualified to assess these relative risks. The valuation analyst should carefully scrutinize and validate the source of new business projections as part of the due diligence exercise. At the same time, the projected margins should be carefully analyzed with reference to historical margins. The sole source and limited competition contracts obtained through the 8(a) program more often carry a different profit rate than do competitively bid contracts. Accordingly, projected profit margins should also be carefully evaluated.

In many turnaround situations, stock options serve as a common management incentive. Their existence may require the involvement of a valuation analyst on a more continual basis, since the value of those options should be periodically updated.

As mentioned above, the discounted net cash flow method plays a prominent role in estimating the equity value or invested capital value of the turnaround company. Therefore, valuation analysts should thoroughly and consistently review management projections to minimize the possibility that financial projections have not been developed for the purpose of inflating the value of management's stock options.

In connection with the use of market approach guideline company methods, the analyst may choose to place less weight on versions of the market approach that rely upon historical subject company data covering periods when the company was participating in the 8(a) program. As the company transitions out of the program, the firm's overall level of revenue, earnings, and cash flow may change as it ventures into a "new" market.

Besides confining the search for guideline companies to those in the same SIC code, it may still be applicable to look for guideline companies that operate outside the subject company's industry but that are in turnaround situations.

Key Person Valuation Discount

When a valuation analyst is charged with estimating the value of an information technology firm participating in the 8(a) program, it may be appropriate to consider the impact on value of the possible loss of the disadvantaged person. Since the disadvantaged person's ownership and management underlie the firm's participation in the program, the loss of this key individual may impair the value of the subject firm or its securities to a greater degree than it would for a more traditional company.

The valuation discount that reflects the potential loss of a key individual depends on several factors. Typically, one of the most important factors is the extent to which the disadvantaged person performs actual duties, takes on responsibilities, and makes other tangible contributions to the firm. As discussed above, one of the requirements of a firm's participation in the 8(a) program is that the disadvantaged person play a significant role in the company's management.

These contributions may take the form of both day-to-day management duties as well as more strategic and judgmental responsibilities. They may also take the form of establishing and maintaining longstanding client relationships and general industry know-how and in maintaining the earlier discussed prime/subcontractor relationships.

Another important factor the analyst should consider is the ability of the 8(a) firm's other officers, directors, and management to assume the position and responsibilities that would be hypothetically vacated upon the departure of the key "disadvantaged" individual. Ideally, a strong and stable organization will provide this capability. In the case of an 8(a) firm, however, the likely succession plan must involve disadvantaged managers who would most likely take over the reigns of the corporation, thereby allowing the firm to maintain its 8(a) status.

Other factors to consider include the compensation necessary to replace the disadvantaged party, the anticipated reaction of clients and competitors upon learning of the loss, and the amount of any proceeds from life insurance policies to which the company is the designated beneficiary.

A discount for the loss of a key individual can be incorporated into the valuation conclusion by several methods. The analyst may adjust normalized earnings or price to earnings pricing multiples to reflect a potential loss, or reduce estimated projected cash flows that are subject to discounting. However, it is most common to deduct a percentage discount from the overall conclusion of the value of the 8(a) firm. Because of these factors, the key person discount may be slightly higher than in conventional companies.

Commercial versus Government

From an investment perspective, publicly traded information technology firms that principally service commercial customers are distinguished from those that primarily serve units of government. There are significant differences between these two sectors, including their respective marketing dynamics, contract structures, and client relationships.

Generally speaking, publicly traded predominantly commercial information technology firms (those generating most of their revenues from commercial rather than government sources) earn higher profit margins, have higher returns on capital, higher market valuations, and higher risk than government firms.

As mentioned above, the 8(a) program provides the participating firm with assistance in procuring federal government contracts. Program participation, however, does not preclude the 8(a) firm from seeking and securing non-8(a) work. Therefore, the valuation analyst should investigate the subject's client list to evaluate the source of contract work. If the 8(a) firm generates a significant amount of revenue from commercial contracts, the analyst may view the firm as two separate entities, with one line of business providing services to the government and the other serving private sector clients.

There are several ways to approach the valuation of a closely held business engaged in two or more separate and distinct lines of business. One approach is to treat the company as a number of separate entities, each of which requires a separate valuation analysis. This approach, which requires an adequate segregation of historical financial data among the distinct business lines, involves the use of assorted valuation data (e.g., market-derived pricing multiples, discount rates, and projected data) that are uniquely applicable to each separate business unit.

Absent the ability to carry out separate valuation analyses, the assorted valuation data can be developed by combining valuation data from respective industry groups via a weighting mechanism in accordance with the business mix of the subject company. These weights typically are based on top-level data, such as sales revenue or gross margin dollars.

A third alternative for multiple business unit firms is to seek valuation data from similarly positioned conglomerates in the marketplace. This procedure is more tractable within the information technology industry, in that many guideline publicly traded companies are engaged in both commercial and government source business. Therefore, it is theoretically possible to compare the industry lines of the subject company to the same lines of the guideline company conglomerates.

Controlling Ownership Interest Situations

Usually, partial interests in a closely held corporation are worth less than their proportionate share of the value of the total enterprise. Conventional wisdom within the valuation profession holds that indications of value derived by guideline publicly traded company methods represent the minority, or noncontrolling, ownership interest level of value. On the other hand, value indications generated by guideline merged and acquired company methods conclude values on a controlling ownership interest level of value.

The bridge between these two different "levels of value" is the ownership control price premium, and its conceptual and mathematical corollary, the minority ownership interest discount. In the simplest sense, applying an ownership control premium to the results of a guideline publicly traded company method converts its minority ownership interest basis results to a controlling ownership interest basis. In the opposite direction, adjusting the results of a guideline merged and acquired company method by a minority ownership interest discount converts the unadjusted controlling ownership interest value to a minority ownership interest basis.

Up until recently, the market-derived pricing multiples of publicly traded information technology firms have, on average, approached the pricing multiples of merged and acquired companies within the same industry group. This phenomenon placed the valuation practitioner in somewhat of a dilemma, in that the value of the firm derived from publicly traded company data and minority ownership interest pricing multiples was approximately the same as the value of the firm derived from merged and acquired company data and controlling ownership interest pricing multiples.

Over the past few years, mergers and acquisitions of information technology companies have influenced the stock prices of publicly traded firms within the industry. Stock prices of these public firms were materially affected by investors' expectations of possible future mergers in the industry. Despite this observed phenomenon, merged and acquired companies in the information technology industry were still merged or acquired at prices involving ownership control premiums. Those merged and acquired companies that were publicly traded prior to their merger or acquisition, however, generally had been priced at multiples that were less than the median pricing multiples of their publicly traded peer group. Thus, the ownership control price premiums involved in these merger transactions elevated the multiples toward the average publicly traded company levels.

The question then arises as to whether the valuation analyst should consider and apply ownership control price premiums to publicly traded company evidence in estimating the controlling ownership interest value of an 8(a) information technology firm. The obvious response is: It depends. Just as in considering the key person valuation discount, the analyst should understand the potential loss of a key individual when valuing a controlling ownership interest.

If the valuation analyst concludes that the subject 8(a) company and the guideline publicly traded companies are extremely homogeneous, then the mean or median of the guideline companies' value multiples, or market-derived pricing multiples, may represent the most appropriate pricing multiples to apply to the subject company. If the selected pricing multiples appropriate to the subject company are below the central tendency multiples of the guideline company group, then an ownership control price premium may be appropriate. On the other hand, in those cases where the analyst believes the subject firm deserves a pricing multiple at or above the typical multiples in the publicly traded marketplace, an ownership control price premium may not be justified.

The lesson here is that 8(a) companies that are performing in a manner consistent with guideline publicly traded companies may not deserve an ownership control premium, in that no merger partner would consider acquiring that company for a price in excess of what the stock market indicates.

Summary and Conclusion

The analysis of a closely held 8(a) government technology services firm presents special considerations to the valuation analyst. The strategic issues regarding when an 8(a) company's value can be realized, and what the effect of these limits mean for the 8(a)'s "true" value, are directly influenced by the special considerations discussed in this chapter. The relative importance and implications of these factors on the value of the 8(a) government technology services firm will obviously vary from case to case.

Index

E

Earnings before depreciation, interest, and taxes (EBDIT), 257, 262, 472

Earnings before interest and taxes (EBIT), 284, 472

Earnings before interest, depreciation, amortization, and research and development (EBDITR), 473–475

Earnings before interest, taxes, depreciation, and amortization (EBITDA), 71, 425

Economic dependencies, 36–37

Economic damages, 273–294
   estimation of, 277–285
     before and after approach, 277
     yardstick approach, 277–278
   ex ante damages, 286–288
   ex post damages, 286–289
   ex post information, use of, 274, 287–289
   income tax effect, 278–282
   lost profits, 282–285
   mitigation of, 276

Economic income, 5, 19–20

Economic obsolescence. *See obsolescence.*

Economist, The, 36, 45

Ehrhardt, Michael, 68

8(a) Program, 490–493, 495–498

Emerging growth companies, 467–487
   lack of marketability discounts, 485–486
   valuation methodology, 470–482

Emory, John D. Jr., 297n, 301n

Employee Retirement Income Security Act (ERISA), 224–226, 229–230

Employee stock ownership plans (ESOPs), 219–245, 362–363
   adequate consideration for, 225, 230
   distribution requirements, 223–224
   dividends, 222–223, 227, 238–241, 243
   in S corporations, 224
   leveraged transactions, 226–230
   post-transaction ESOP debt, 235
   put option, 224, 231, 233–234
   repurchase obligation, 224, 228, 231, 234
   Section 1042 (*see Internal Revenue Code*)
   statutory requirements, 220
   types of, 220–221

Entrepreneurial profit, 268, 444

Equity cost of capital. *See cost of capital*

Equity risk premium, 10–13, 50, 55–80, 447–448
   arithmetic vs. geometric averages, 12, 61–62, 67–68, 77
   company-specific risk premium, 10–11, 13, 15, 481–482
   estimation of, 12
     bottom-up approaches, 64–66
     realized return approach, 57–59
     top-down approaches, 66–67
   for foreign investments, 33–34, 47–48
   minority ownership vs. controlling ownership returns, 62–63
   observation period, 59–61
   size effect, 68–79
   size premium, 10–11, 13, 15, 78–79, 481

ERISA. *See Employee Retirement Income Security Act*

ESOPs. *See employee stock ownership plans*

Estate of Artemus D. Davis v. *Commissioner*, 83, 137, 143

Estate of Bernard Rothgery v. *Commissioner*, 409

Estate of Bonner v. *United States*, 211n

Estate of Christie v. *Commissioner*, 143

Estate of Dorothy B. Foote v. *Commissioner*, 143

Estate of Friedberg v. *Commissioner*, 143

Estate of Kopperman v. *Commissioner*, 143

Estate of Mario E. Bosca v. *Commissioner*, 143

Estate of Mary Frances Smith Bright v. *United States*, 158

Estate of Mueller v. *Commissioner*, 124n

Estate of Myrtle M. Sawade, 140n, 143

Estate of Samuel I. Newhouse, 124, 212

Estate of Van Horne v. *Commissioner*, 150

Estate of Wright v. *Commissioner*, 143

Estate planning, 207–217, 469

Estate tax, 150–151, 157–158, 208, 408–409

Estate Tax Regulations, 140

Oppressed shareholder cases,
296–297, 299–301, 304–305
Oppressed shareholder statutes,
296, 305
Orchard v. *Covelli*, 297n
Ownership control, 162–163, 262, 296
in automobile dealerships, 411–412
premium for, 231–233, 236,
313–314, 323,
in dissenting shareholder cases,
302, 304
with government technology service
firms, 499–500
with radio broadcasting
companies, 431–432
in sports teams, 381
Ozanian, Michael K., 370n, 374n

P

Paone, Louis A., 303n
Partial interests. *See minority
ownership interests*
Partnership Profiles, Inc., 168
Partnership Profiles, 168
Partnership Spectrum, 168
Pass-through entities, 120, 157
Patel, Ajay, 65n
Patell, James M., 286n
Performance stock, 240
Perlman v. *Permonite Mfg. Co.*, 304n
Phillips, John R., 286
Phipps v. *Commissioner*, 141n, 143
Physician practice
management (PPM), 461–464
Physician practices, 439–465
compensation issues, 456–457
inurement provisions, 459–460
regulatory constraints, 459–460
valuation methodology, 441–454
Pittock, William F., 99
Polaroid case. *See Martin* v.
NationsBank
Polaroid Corporation v. *Eastman
Kodak Company*, 281
Political risk analysis, 27–28, 34,
44–45, 51–52
Political Risk Services, 44–45, 48,
51–52
Portfolio approach, 42
Poterba, James, 62n
Pratt, Shannon P., 18n, 98, 99, 123n,
125n, 142n, 262n, 301, 302n, 305n
Preferred stock, 221, 241, 484–485
call protection, 239

fixed dollar convertible
preferred, 240, 483
floor put convertible
preferred, 239, 242
high-yield convertible
preferred, 239
standard convertible
preferred, 238–239, 244
Premise of value. *See value, premise of*
Premium for control. *See
ownership control, premium for*
Present value discount rate, 5, 18,
19–20, 26, 330–332
comparable country
analysis, 39
development of, 42–44,
51–51, 64
example of, 49–53
for ad valorem taxation
purposes, 261
for emerging growth
companies, 476–482
for foreign investments, 30, 40–41
for minority ownership vs.
controlling ownership interests,
62–63
for physician practices, 447
for radio broadcasting
companies, 425
for S corporations, 128, 135–136
for sports teams, 385
vs. direct capitalization rate, 5–6
with blockage discounts, 146
PricewaterhouseCoopers LLP (PwC),
69–74
Pricing analysis, 327–333
Pricing multiples. *See pricing analysis*
Principles of Corporate Finance, 67
Private Equity Week, 101
Private Placement Letter, 101
Private placements, 360–361
Property taxation. *See ad
valorem taxation*
Publicly traded equivalent value, 233
Purchase accounting, 176

Q

QED Research, Inc., 186
Quantitative Profiles, 64
Queenan, J., 339n
The Quest for Value, 68

R

Radio broadcasting, 415–437
  in Canada, 434–437
  transactions, 431–433
  valuation methodology, 424–429
  value drivers, 422–424
Radiology Association, Inc., 307n
Rapid-American v. *Harris*, 304n, 314
Rappaport, Alfred, 67n
Rate of return. *See required rate of
  return* and *risk-free rate of return*
Ratio analysis, 326
Real estate, 167–170, 179, 190, 196,
  388–389
Registration rights, 115–116
Reilly, Frank K., 32n
Reilly, Robert F., 99, 123n, 125n, 142n,
  262n, 301, 302n
Replacement cost, 264–267, 270,
  443–444
Reproduction cost, 263–267, 443–444
Required rate of return, 5, 8, 260–261
  for foreign investments, 39
  for physician practices, 447–448
  for small stocks, 79
Research and development. *See
  in-process R&D*
Residual market capitalization
  (RMC), 428
Restricted stocks, 83–85, 97–116,
  141–142 (*see also discounts,
  marketability, lack of, restricted
  stock studies*)
Revenue Reconciliation Act
  of 1993, 387
Revenue Ruling 59-60, 123, 132, 231,
  302n, 305n, 408
Revenue Ruling 77-287, 105–107, 141
Revenue Ruling 83-30, 150–151
Revenue Ruling 93-12, 151, 158
Rigel Corp. v. *Cutchall*, 304n
Rising, Jeffrey M., 63n
Risk, 4
  horizon risk (*see maturity risk*)
  interest rate risk (*see maturity risk*)
  maturity risk, 10
  systematic, 10
  unsystematic, 10–11, 15, 481
Risk-free rate of return, 10, 12, 49,
  57, 69
Rizzi, Joseph, 31
Robert Morris Associates (RMA), 9, 19
Robert W. Baird & Co., 82, 85–87, 486

Robert W. Baird & Co. study. *See
  discounts, marketability, lack of,
  pre-IPO studies*
Robinson, E., 379n
Robinson v. *Commissioner*, 143
Romaine, R. Craig, 286n
Ronald v. *4-C's Elec. Packaging,
  Inc.*, 304n
Rosenberg, Michael R., 38n
Rosenblatt v. *Getty Oil Co.*, 306n
Rules of thumb, 332–333,
  358–359, 429
Rushton v. *Commissioner*, 143, 151

S

S corporations, 119–138
  definition of, 120–122
  income tax rates, 133
  with ESOPs, 224
Safe Deposit & Trust Co. of Baltimore
  v. *Commissioner*, 141n
Sandomir, Richard, 392n
Schechter v. *Watkins*, 306n
Schifrin, Matthew, 416n, 421n
Schweihs, Robert P., 99, 123n, 125n,
  142n, 262n, 301, 302n
Schwert, G.W., 58n
SDC OnLine, 452
*The Search for Value: Measuring the
  Company's Cost of Capital*, 68
SEC Rule 144, 100–101, 105, 110–111
Securities Act of 1933, 100
Securities and Exchange Commission
  (SEC), 83, 103, 165, 168, 176,
  319, 469
Securities Data Company, 480
Securities Data Publishing, 101–102
Sensitivity table, 48–49
Shapiro, Alan C., 27n
Shapiro, Eben, 421n
Sharav, Ben, 430n
Sharpe, Anita, 461n
Shaw v. *U.S.*, 282
Shell Oil Co., Matter of, 301n
Shumway, Tyler, 78
Siegel, Jeremy, 59n, 68
Silber, William L., 85, 99
Simpson, William E., 122n
Size effect. *See equity risk
  premiums*
Size premium. *See equity risk
  premiums*
Small Business Act, 490

United States Baseball League
  (USBL), 381
United States v. *Bess*, 208n
United States v. *Tabor Court Realty
  Corporation*, 340

V

Valuation date, 251–252, 304–305, 324
*Valuation: Measuring and Managing
  the Value of Companies*, 68
Value in use, 266–267, 269
Value
  premise of, 233, 249, 251, 308
  standard of, 6, 23, 123–125, 133,
      249, 324
    acquisition value, 327
    fair market value, 6, 123–125, 140
      in ad valorem taxation cases,
          249–251
      in dissenting shareholder
          cases, 302
      in ESOP cases, 230–231
      in estate tax cases, 158, 208,
          211–212
    fair value, 295–308, 312–314
    investment value, 6, 123, 125, 314
    market value, 314, 327 (*see also fair
        market value*)
Value Line, 26, 65–66, 429–430, 432
Valuing ESOP Shares, 230
Van Vleet, Daniel R., 302n
Venture capital, 480, 482
Venture Economics, 480
*Vision Hardware Group, Inc.,
  Application of*, 307n
Vogel, Harold L., 372, 375n
Vogel, Thomas T. Jr., 47n
Voting rights, 224, 243

W

Wall Street Journal, 26, 29, 41, 461
Walter, Ingo, 43n
Walter S. Chessman Realty Co. v.
  Moore, 304n
Weighted average cost of
  capital (WACC), 4, 26, 33–34,
      48–53, 330, 332
  capital structure used in, 9
  definition of, 8–9
  for emerging growth
      companies, 476

  for in-process R&D valuations,
      178, 188
  for physician practices, 447, 449–450
  for radio broadcasting
      companies, 425
  for sports teams, 385
  in ad valorem taxation cases,
      260, 268
  in damages estimation, 283
Weil, Roman L., 286n
Weinberger v. *UOP, Inc.*, 304n, 305n,
      306, 307n, 314–315
Welch, Ivo, 67n
Welch v. *Helvering*, 209n
*Wiedy's Furniture Clearance Center,
  Matter of*, 300n
Willamette Management Associates,
      82–84, 86–96, 486
Willamette Management Associates
  study. *See
  discounts, marketability, lack of,
  pre-IPO studies*
Williams, Taylor & Associates, 413
Wilson, J.W., 58n
Wolfsen, Mark A., 286n
Women's National Basketball
  Association (WNBA), 380
Wood, Robert W., 281n
Working capital, 178–179, 189, 196
Working capital analysis, 450
World Trade, 44
Wrobel, Peter D., 122n

Y

Yardstick approach. *See
  economic damages,
  estimation of*
Yield differentials, 29–30, 34, 52

Z

Zack's, 16
Zismer, Daniel, 463